Lift Up Your Voice Like a Trumpet

lift up your voice like a trumpet

White Clergy and the Civil Rights and Antiwar Movements, 1954–1973

Michael B. Friedland

The University of North Carolina Press

Chapel Hill and London

© 1998 The University of North Carolina Press

All rights reserved

This book was set in Electra by Keystone Typesetting, Inc.

Book design by April Leidig-Higgins

Manufactured in the United States of America

The paper in this book meets the guidelines for permanence and
durability of the Committee on Production Guidelines for Book
Longevity of the Council on Library Resources.

Library of Congress Cataloging-in-Publication Data

Friedland, Michael B.

Lift up your voice like a trumpet : white clergy and the civil rights and
antiwar movements, 1954–1973 / by Michael B. Friedland.

p. cm. Based on the author's thesis (doctoral)—Boston College, 1993.

Includes bibliographical references and index.

ISBN 0-8078-2338-4 (cloth : alk. paper).

ISBN 0-8078-4646-5 (pbk. : alk. paper)

1. Clergy—United States—Political activity—History—20th century.

2. Civil rights workers—United States—History—20th century.

3. Vietnamese Conflict, 1961–1975—Protest movements—United States
—History. 4. Whites—United States—Politics and government. I. Title.

BL65.P7F73   1998   97-18418

261.7′0973′09045—dc21   CIP

A portion of this work has appeared in substantially different form as
"Giving a Shout for Freedom: The Reverend Malcolm Boyd, the Right
Reverend Paul Moore, Jr., and the Civil Rights and Antiwar Movements
of the 1960s and 1970s," in *Nobody Gets Off the Bus: The Viet Nam
Generation Big Book*, a special issue of *Viet Nam Generation*,
vol. 5, nos. 1–4 (April 1994): 94– 107.

02 01 00 99 98 5 4 3 2 1

To Julie, Benjamin, and Rachel

acknowledgments

*Of making many books there is no end,
and much study is a weariness of the flesh.*

ECCLESIASTES 12:12

The writing of doctoral dissertations—of which this was one—has a tendency to be a lonely and grueling experience, not only for the scholar but also for the family members and friends who have to put up with long absences as the author faces self-imposed exile in libraries and at computer keyboards. My experience was mitigated to a large extent by the encouragement, advice, and tolerance of many people during both the original writing process and the later revisions. My parents, Stephen and Anne Friedland, my sisters Alison and Jane, brother-in-law Mark Yovella, and father-in-law David Ballard have been and continue to be exceptionally supportive and understanding about my academic career. For similar reasons I am also indebted to a number of friends and colleagues whose insights have meant a great deal to me, especially Carol M. Petillo, Thomas O'Connor, Francis Murphy, Jane Haspel, J. Randall Baldini, Nan Woodruff, Kathi Kern, James Fisher, David M. Esposito, Charles Eagles, Robert Norrell, John Dittmer, Mary Beth Ross, and Pam and Danny Lassitter. The advice and sense of humor of two friends and fellow church historians, Gardiner H. "Tuck" Shattuck, and Jill Gill, both models of collegiality and support, continues to be a source of inspiration. The staff at the University of North Carolina Press, especially Lewis Bateman and Katherine Malin, have been very helpful, instructive, and patient in marshaling the manuscript through the stages of publication, and their faith in this project has kept mine from flagging.

Several of the individuals discussed in the book generously made time for lengthy interviews. Paul Moore Jr. graciously invited me to his home one afternoon to discuss his involvement in the civil rights and antiwar movements; Robert Hughes, William Sloane Coffin Jr., and Robert McAfee Brown answered long and convoluted questions over the telephone, as did Malcolm Boyd, who gave up two hours of an afternoon to discuss his career just one week after an earthquake rocked his Santa Monica parish. Frequent conversations and correspondence with John B. Morris were especially helpful in understanding his work with the Episcopal Society for Cultural and Racial Unity, as was his generous sharing of numerous documents and newsletters. The staffs at several archives—including the Department of Special Collections of Mugar Memorial Library at Boston University; the American Jewish Archives in Waltham, Massachusetts; and the Presbyterian Church (U.S.A.) Office of History in Philadelphia, Pennsylvania—were courteous and prompt in helping track down important documents in their varied manuscript collections.

Special thanks are due two invaluable friends, Roy and Kim Robson. Their good humor, faith, support, and advice has proven to be a bulwark of encouragement and a source of much pleasure through graduate school and beyond—much more, perhaps, than they ever can understand.

Finally, a word of appreciation for the three most important people in my life. The greatest debt—one I can never repay, although I look forward to a lifetime of trying—is to my wife Julie, who has been a tower of strength throughout the entire project, putting up with stacks of books and papers and a tired and often distracted husband with an amazing combination of empathy and optimism. This work could never have been completed without her, and if anything of note shines forth from these pages, much credit is due to her inspiring influence. Special thanks are due our son Benjamin. He came into our lives on a fine spring morning when the dissertation was only half done, but his easygoing temperament made the work flow that much more quickly. More importantly, his wonderful smile, frequently bestowed on a father who spent more time staring at a computer screen than at his adorable face, served to remind me of the truly important things in life. Since that time several years ago he has found somewhat more persistent and effective ways of distracting his father, but the end result—my delight in his presence—has remained the same. And now, with the manuscript having moved well beyond dissertation committees and taking up a new life in the world of university presses, we have been blessed with a daughter, Rachel. Being the author of a monograph, especially with all the support I have received over the years, was an enjoyable enough task, but being a parent is far more gratifying. It is to my beautiful wife and two wonderful children that this work is gratefully dedicated.

Lift Up Your Voice Like a Trumpet

Cry aloud, spare not, lift up your voice like a trumpet; declare
to my people their transgression, to the house of Jacob their sins.

Yet they seek me daily, and delight to know my ways, as if
they were a nation that did righteousness and did not
forsake the ordinance of their God . . .

ISAIAH 58:1—2

Thus says the Lord: Do justice and righteousness . . .

JEREMIAH 22:3

On the afternoon of April 9, 1865, Union cavalry entered Selma, Alabama, destroyed the town's foundries, and marched on to Montgomery, forcing its citizens to surrender. One hundred years later, a combined force of 3,200 black and white nonviolent marchers led by the Student Nonviolent Coordinating Committee (SNCC) and the Southern Christian Leadership Conference (SCLC) followed the same route to demand voting rights for blacks. The atmosphere of the second march could not have been more distinct from that of its predecessor. "It was like a Fourth of July picnic and a pilgrimage, a protest and an exultation," wrote *Washington Post* reporter Paul Good. "It was like nothing Selma had ever seen before or dreamed of."[1]

Or the rest of the nation, for that matter. It was a pilgrimage, and if its goals fell short of a strictly spiritual journey, the presence of hundreds of white Jewish, Protestant, and Catholic clergy and nuns belied that fact. Feeling the need to witness to and show repentance over the sins of racial discrimination, their participation in the march was the most dramatic sign up to that time of the comparatively recent church involvement in the civil rights movement.

Calls for the white churches to act more decisively in the racial struggle had been mounting since the Supreme Court ordered school desegregation in 1954. For the most part, the initial impetus for clerical action on behalf of civil rights in the years immediately following the *Brown v. Board of Education* decision came from a handful of southern white clergy, yet the pressures placed on them by parishioners hostile to racial equality quickly led to a silencing of all but the bravest of them. When the civil rights movement turned to tactics such as sit-ins and freedom rides in the early 1960s, groups of sympathetic, nonsouthern, white clergymen took part with effective results: as several were nationally known, their arrests and trials focused widespread attention on the demonstrations and their goals.

Yet the shift from moral suasion to direct action also posed a problem to the

3

northerners' work in the South. Although subjected to harassment and violence at the hands of segregationists during their brief sojourns in the southland, their professional positions were seldom threatened, and there were instances where their activism enhanced their status at home. It was not uncommon for northern clerics to become increasingly vexed at racial discrimination the farther they went from home, with the result that they tended to pass judgment not only on segregationists but also on southern moderates, whose challenges to the status quo, they felt, were not strong enough.

A further impediment to the effectiveness of outside white clerics among southern whites (but a considerable enhancement to their standing in northern liberal circles) was their close identification with the Reverend Dr. Martin Luther King Jr. and other black leaders of the civil rights movement. Moved by both the problems faced by African Americans in the South and their reliance on religion for strength, many northerners viewed them as embodying virtues that the more affluent, complacent society around them had lost. Caught up in the Cold War rhetoric of the era, the mainstream churches' proclamations tended to be a celebratory paean to the "American way of life," with a special emphasis on the role religion played in society. It was not hard for many Americans to perceive the United States as "God's country," leading the forces of light against totalitarianism. The fact that the Soviet Union and the People's Republic of China were officially atheist made this task all the easier. The dark side of this national self-righteousness, of course, was that any criticism of U.S. domestic or foreign policy was politically and ideologically suspect—either a sign of naïveté or, worse, subversion.

Realizing this, King couched his early criticism of the nation's tolerance of racial injustice in terms of sorrow and of promises unfulfilled, an approach designed to appeal to the liberals' belief in a society that was basically sound and whose flaws could be corrected without a drastic overhauling of the existing political, social, and economic order. Moreover, he targeted his speeches and writings to those liberal clergymen who, like himself, had studied philosophers and theologians such as John Locke, Friedrich Nietzsche, Georg Hegel, Paul Tillich, Reinhold Niebuhr, and John C. Bennett, and made a point of stressing his intellectual debt to their writings.[2] As Keith Miller has shown, King's theological and oratorical background did not develop solely from university and seminary education; rather, the civil rights leader was also influenced by published sermons and the black folk pulpit. Nevertheless, Miller argues, by "appropriating the language of well-established white preachers," King "created and maintained a self who grappled with urgent public issues and was also a scholar, a philosopher, and a theologian."[3] In this way, he did not merely gain the respect of his white liberal colleagues in the pulpits. By taking up the mantle of the Social Gospel, which had a long and honored history within American Protestantism, he became for many the nation's leading religious proponent of racial justice. To them, King represented and led the religious wing of the civil rights movement, one that showed the immediacy and relevancy of Old Testament prophecy and Christian gospel alike, as well as called attention to the traditionally weak response of the white churches to racism. "The church is too little and too late," an Episcopal bishop told a black clergyman during the demonstrations in Selma. "But you are going to renew us."[4] King and his fellow black ministers in SCLC were able to put such sentiments to good use during civil rights demonstrations in cities such as Albany, St. Augustine, and Selma. It became common practice for them to call on clergymen of all denominations to join the marches when additional publicity was needed to put pressure on Congress and the White House to support the movement's goals.

However, it would be a mistake to suggest that white liberal clergy merely reacted to the work done by black civil rights groups. Andrew Young of SCLC recalled that whenever his organization had trouble deciding on a course of action, King would ask his colleagues to "[s]ee what John Bennett thinks."[5] Another spur toward the rediscovery of an activist theological tradition was the liberal theology taught at the major American seminaries, especially Union Theological Seminary, Episcopal Theological Seminary, and Yale Divinity School. Writing in the late 1960s, sociologist Jeffrey Hadden argued that such schools had long been centers for "progressive political thought" and noted that churches seeking clergy from such prestigious institutions were "system- atically hiring men who are politically more liberal than . . . the congrega- tion." This suffusion of liberally educated ministers, priests, and rabbis oc- curred at roughly the same time as the nation's reawakening to the racial injustices suffered by black Americans. By the 1960s, many clergy viewed their ministry as an opportunity to challenge their parishioners to create a better so- ciety.[6] The participation of white churches in the civil rights movement be- came more organized and institutionalized with the fight for the Civil Rights Act of 1964; the creation that same year of the Delta Ministry by the National Council of Churches of Christ in the U.S.A. (NCC), an interdenominational and ecumenical organization; and the Voting Rights Act of 1965.

Ironically, as white clergy took an increasingly visible part in civil rights demonstrations, the escalation of American involvement in Vietnam changed the focus of the protest movement, though it did not necessarily follow that those clerics active in the civil rights movement were equally committed to criticizing the Vietnam War. Some of the most visible antiwar protesters in the pulpit had not been nearly so active in championing civil rights, but others who had first marched in the streets on behalf of racial justice found themselves lending their voices and their prestige to the burgeoning antiwar movement, in which they were some of the most committed and articulate participants. Distinct from both students and leftist antiwar groups, religious figures provided a rallying point for more moderate critics of the war, in a way that they could not in the civil rights movement, led as it was by black activists. Clergy who had been involved in the civil rights movement brought to their antiwar activities not only their theological beliefs about human dignity and justice but their newfound organizational and tactical tools as well, from mailing lists of liberal clerics to expertise in mounting peace conferences, demonstrations, and educational campaigns consciously patterned after events designed to combat domestic racism.

Neither the conservative clergy nor the majority of the laity admired such activism, and they reminded those who persisted in it that religious bodies in the United States are, first and foremost, voluntary associations in which the clergy have only a nominal amount of leverage that they can bring to bear on their parishioners. While traditional Judeo-Christian teaching emphasizes concern for the poor and oppressed, not all are in agreement as to how this concern should manifest itself. In 1967, theologian Harvey Cox identified three general categories of clergy: the pietists, who believed that their duty was to proclaim the word of God and focus their congregation's attention on the afterlife and not involve themselves in protests they considered secular and political; the theologically and politically conservative clergy, who believed that religion, like politics, had a duty to uphold the status quo; and the "new breed," whose liberal outlook often paved the way for their personal involvement in demonstrations.[7]

The motivation that led some pastors to take sides on such highly charged issues while others refused to involve themselves must also be understood in light of the various constraints and tensions between themselves and the laity they served. The likelihood of a clergyman becoming involved in social activism depended on several factors, including his own conception of his duties; how the laity perceived his role; the issue in question; support (or lack of it) from a religious hierarchy, if one existed; and his position on the hierarchical ladder within the denomination. Unlike other professionals who have sharply delineated roles and whose decisions are seldom determined by their clients, the clergy at the parish level live among and socialize with those they serve more than they do with peers. Such ministers, priests, and rabbis have a variety of responsibilities—including those of spiritual leader, administrator, counselor, and civic leader—and all provide close ties with a congregation that already has its own expectations.[8]

Such a multifaceted role often caused problems. If a clergyman felt that his duties included giving advice on certain social or political issues, the laity might not agree, and tell him to attend only to his spiritual functions. "If their advocacy from their pulpits (in which they are, in the last analysis, the paid guest speakers) becomes sufficiently obnoxious to their listeners to cause a substantial decline in attendance and gross receipts," explained a conservative Georgian parishioner in the 1960s, "the clergyman mustn't be too surprised when the church fathers arrange for his transfer to more favorable climes."[9] For many laypeople, the church or synagogue was viewed as a sanctuary from the pressures of the outside world, and the duty of the presiding cleric was to comfort his flock, not disturb it by bringing up potentially divisive social problems.[10] Critics of clerical activism insisted that the clergy's function "should be restricted to influencing the moral tone of their members" by giving them "some broad, general moral guidance, and then [leaving them] free to apply their Christianity as they see fit in their daily personal and civic lives."[11]

While racial prejudices existed on both sides of the pulpit, research suggests not only that those in the pews were often considerably more conservative and prejudiced than those who faced them from the altars but also that those who regularly attended services tended to be more prejudiced and intolerant than more sporadic churchgoers.[12] One is tempted to recall Samuel Butler's description of parishioners in an English church: "good, sensible fellows" who "would have been equally horrified at hearing the Christian religion doubted, and at seeing it practiced."[13]

In the face of lay hostility to social activism, it was natural for clergymen to turn to their denominational hierarchy for support. Yet whatever the strength or weakness of any particular hierarchical structure, no church was completely immune to pressure from the laity. As bureaucratic organizations, religious bodies have always been concerned equally with institutional self-preservation and with their mission in the world, and generally have avoided antagonizing those who tithed or filled the collection plate. Such conflicting desires often put the individual minister in an awkward position, unable to know how far to go on any given issue, unsure of how much support he would be given by ecclesiastical leaders. Not surprisingly, those who were able to devote much of their energies to social activism tended to come from positions where they were not subject to pressure from the laity and had more freedom (and job security): bishops or other members of the denominational hierarchy, administrators, seminarians or the faculty of divinity schools, and campus chaplains.[14]

Arriving at the same time as the civil rights and antiwar movements was a new spirit of interfaith cooperation, demonstrated markedly by the Second Vatican Council and various proposals for Protestant denominational unions in the early 1960s. In light of the limited number of ecclesiastical allies that activist clergy could muster on their behalf, it is no surprise that many of these individuals welcomed the burgeoning ecumenical movement. As Trappist monk Thomas Merton reflected toward the end of the decade, Protestants would seek out like-minded Catholics, and vice versa. Among such people, he wrote, one found "new grounds of sympathy; people with a new look and a whole new background," which proved stimulating and provoked involvement with each other. To those wary of such developments, warned Rabbi Abraham Joshua Heschel of the Jewish Theological Seminary in New York, himself an activist in the civil rights and antiwar movements, there was "another ecumenical movement, worldwide in influence: nihilism. We must choose between interfaith and inter-nihilism."[15]

Clergymen involved in ecumenical or interfaith ventures found the religious and tolerant nature of the early civil rights movement particularly appealing.[16] The civil rights marches, wrote one scholar, "brought people together from . . . widely differing church traditions, not only Christian but also Jews and humanists," and in so doing "pointed the way to cooperation in faith and action . . . which sometimes far transcended the achievements arrived at hitherto by the ecumenical movement."[17] Joining with others to establish personal and organizational contacts in order to protest racism in the early 1960s, several religious leaders, Heschel and Merton among them, were able to maintain this interfaith cooperation to challenge the growing American involvement in Vietnam for the rest of the decade, joined by such ecumenists as John Bennett, professor of theology and later president of Union Theological Seminary, who had helped create the World Council of Churches in 1948; Baptist minister Will D. Campbell; Reverends Daniel and Philip Berrigan, the former a Jesuit and the latter a Josephite; Malcolm Boyd, a priest-playwright in the Episcopal Church; William Sloane Coffin Jr., Presbyterian chaplain of Yale University; Robert McAfee Brown, Presbyterian minister and professor of religion at Union and later Stanford University; the Reverend Eugene Carson Blake, Stated Clerk of the Presbyterian Church in the United States of America; and Bishop Paul Moore Jr. of the Episcopal Church.

One must keep in mind that such figures were able to devote much of their careers to the causes they cherished precisely because they were either employed by universities or served as high-ranking members of religious organizations, and hence were considerably freer from the constraints placed on individual ministers, priests, and rabbis. It would be false to portray this predominantly northern group as representative of the white religious community that became involved in social protest. Their ability to don the prophet's mantle and warn the nation of its moral lapses was not open to all, and attention must be paid to southern white clergy who lived in the midst of the society they were attempting to change and often suffered as a result of their convictions—men such as Robert Hughes, Methodist minister and president of the Alabama Council on Human Relations; Dunbar Ogden Jr., Presbyterian minister in Little Rock, Arkansas; Rabbi Charles Mantinband of Hattiesburg, Mississippi; Rabbi Jacob Rothschild of Atlanta, Georgia; Robert McNeill, Presbyterian minister of a church in Columbus, Georgia; Edwin King, Methodist chaplain of Tougaloo College, a black institution in Mississippi; and John B. Morris, Episcopal priest and executive director of the Episcopal Society for Cultural and Racial Unity (ESCRU).

By studying the role of the white southern clergy in some detail, we can understand the second edge of the church: the conserving edge. Not all clergymen were called to be prophets, and many did not wish to shake society to its foundations. Clearly there were those whose conservatism was often a cloak for inaction, but there were others who emphasized the reconciliatory aspect of their vocation as much as, if not more than, their prophetic one. If there were many ministers, priests, and rabbis who refused to raise their voices to criticize the flagrant racial abuses in the South, some of them, it must be understood, felt that in order to genuinely serve as reconcilers, they had to work quietly, at the local level, in order to achieve their goals.

Substantial scholarly work on white clerical activism in this era came out of the 1950s and 1960s, but much of it was sociological in nature, and until recently such information had little counterpart in historical scholarship.[18] Most monographs that discuss religious activism in the 1950s and 1960s understandably concentrate on the black clergy in the civil rights movement, particularly the leaders of SCLC. Other studies, especially Ronald Flower's *Religion in Strange Times: The 1960s and 1970s*, concentrate on black civil rights leaders such as Martin Luther King Jr. and Ralph Abernathy and then segue into an exploration of fundamentalist evangelism among whites in the 1970s, as if the liberal religious activism of white clergy in the 1960s deserved no more than a footnote. Stephen Carter addresses religious activism in the civil rights and antiwar movements in more depth in *The Culture of Disbelief: How American Law and Politics Trivialize Religious Devotion*, but his emphasis is not to delve into that issue so much as to point out how uncomfortable contemporary Americans are with explicit references to religion made by conservative politicians. Although he contrasts this discomfort with the liberals' embrace of King's religious rhetoric on behalf of causes they supported, he does not address the conservative distrust and hostility toward this use of theological doctrine.[19]

Happily, historians recently have been correcting such omissions in the historical record. Charles DeBenedetti and Charles Chatfield treated the white clergy's opposition to the war in Southeast Asia in great detail in *An American Ordeal: The Antiwar Movement of the Vietnam Era*. Two more recent works, James F. Findlay Jr.'s *Church People in the Struggle: The National Council of Churches and the Black Freedom Movement, 1950–1970* and Mitchell Hall's *Because of Their Faith: CALCAV and Religious Opposition to the Vietnam War*, are excellent treatments of organized white clerical opposition to racial segregation and the war; Stephen Longenecker's *Selma's Peacemaker: Ralph Smeltzer and Civil Rights Mediation* and Charles W. Eagles's *Outside Agitator: Jon Daniels and the Civil Rights Movement in Alabama* are two outstanding biographies on the efforts of a Church of the Brethren minister and an Episcopal seminarian, respectively, to combat racial segregation in Alabama in the mid-1960s. Ongoing research by other scholars—including Gardiner H. Shattuck Jr.'s work-in-progress on the Episcopal Church's stand against racism in the 1960s, tentatively titled *Dwelling Together in Unity: Episcopalians and the Dilemma of Race*, and Jill Gill's dissertation, " 'Peace Is Not the Absence of War But the Presence of Justice': The National Council of Churches' Reaction and Response to the Vietnam War 1965–1972"—promises to further our knowledge of the intersection of religious belief and social activism.

The present work attempts to add to such scholarship by focusing on the work of several white clergymen within the broader context of religious social activism as it developed through different stages in both the civil rights and antiwar movements. While some may criticize this approach as "history from the top down," it does provide a sense of narrative cohesion to what is admittedly a broad topic; furthermore, by tracing these individuals' careers—beginning in the 1950s with their growing disenchantment with the conservative religious atmosphere of that decade, through the resurgence of liberalism and activism in the 1960s—this study adds to an understanding not only of the role of the clergy in contemporary society but of the gulf between the ideals that most Americans profess and the behavior that they exemplify.

Clerical activism was not a new phenomenon in American history. Predicated on various theological and philosophical precepts that had evolved during the nineteenth century, it had been altered by the two world wars and the Cold War. The Social Gospel, dating from the turn of the century, held that the

Christian essence of social justice was love toward both God and humanity. Institutions, as well as individuals, stood under God's judgment, and as the Old Testament prophets had been concerned with moral uplift in their times, so should modern churches work to eradicate the ills in the world by involving themselves in political and social issues. Striving to create a fellowship of humanity under God, the social gospelers believed that if institutions followed Christian ethics, righteousness and justice would appear on earth.[20]

Despite the efforts of such ecumenical organizations as the Federal Council of Churches of Christ in America to implement the goals of the Social Gospel, the idealistic foundations of such a doctrine were rudely shaken by the First World War and the Great Depression. Relations within society were not quite so simple as the social gospelers believed, argued Reinhold Niebuhr, professor of theology at Union Theological Seminary in New York City, in his seminal *Moral Man and Immoral Society*. In this 1932 work, he disabused religious liberals of their hopes that society could be reformed through good-will, moral suasion, and education, for while all were helpful on an individual level, groups did not have the capacity to transcend their "unrestricted egoism." The perfect society, Niebuhr argued, could never be created in history, and individuals who believed that education would destroy ignorance were guilty of "sentimentality and romanticism"; power, he insisted, not ignorance, was the real factor in group relations. Humanity had to content itself with the more modest goal of reforming existing structures.[21] Niebuhr himself continued to work with several radical Christian action groups in their efforts to aid tenant farmers in the South, educate seminarians, and campaign for Socialist Party candidate Norman Thomas in the 1932 presidential elections. While he did not singlehandedly destroy the Social Gospel, Niebuhr helped pave the way for a critical reassessment of Christianity as simply a religion of ethics.[22]

Having alienated religious liberals and practitioners of the Social Gospel, in the early 1940s he directed his fire at pacifists, joining with theologian John Bennett and several other prominent clergymen to found the journal *Christianity and Crisis*. "When men or nations must choose between two great evils, the choice of the lesser evil becomes their duty," the first editorial read. "We hold that the halting of totalitarian aggression is prerequisite to world peace and order."[23] Pacifism, according to Niebuhr, was "unable to distinguish between the peace of capitulation to tyranny and the peace of the Kingdom of God." Such "modern liberal perfectionism," he wrote, made democratic nations "weak and irresolute before a resolute and terrible foe."[24]

By the end of 1941, the United States was engaged in fighting totalitarian and racist regimes, and in so doing, Americans began to reexamine their own patterns of racial discrimination. At war's end, the Federal Council of Churches issued a statement renouncing "the pattern of segregation as unnecessary and undesirable and a violation of the Gospel of love and human brotherhood" and asked its constituent churches to work for a "non-segregated church and a non-segregated society."[25] Unfortunately, the council failed to act on its own suggestion. During the meeting where the resolution was passed, council leaders arranged to have their vice president, Benjamin E. Mays, president of Atlanta's Morehouse College and one of the nation's leading black theologians, sit with the audience rather than share the stage with themselves. Members of the Southern Baptist Convention, the Presbyterian Church, U.S., and Southern Methodists insisted that the declaration was an unwarranted interference in the activities of local churches, and instead passed resolutions calling for equal opportunity within the system of segregation.[26] Clergy and congregations at all levels reflected their culture more than the beliefs they professed, and it was left to smaller organizations such as the Committee on Interracial Cooperation (founded in 1919), the Fellowship of Southern Churchmen, and the Catholic Interracial Council (both founded in 1934) to challenge, with little success, the complacency, conservatism, and embedded racism of the established churches.[27]

The Cold War and its concomitant fears of domestic subversion in the late 1940s and 1950s further dampened the reform spirit. Charges of Communism were freely leveled at anyone who proposed changing the status quo, for whatever reason. Segregationists charged that Gunnar Myrdal's *An American Dilemma* (which detailed how Americans seldom lived up to the creeds of equality they espoused, especially with regard to race) was written by a "notorious Swedish Communist" and a "Red psychologist" when he was in fact an anticommunist economist. Religious figures were not immune to such pressures, which conspired to either limit the social activism of all but the most committed of liberal clergymen or redirect their energies toward defending themselves against charges of leftist sympathies.[28] Methodist Bishop G. Bromley Oxnam became the object of such vehement attacks for his wartime leadership of the Council of American-Soviet Friendship and his espousal of liberal causes (one critic claimed that he was "serving God on Sunday and the Communist front for the balance of the week") that he demanded and received a hearing by the House Committee on Un-American Activities in 1953, in which he effectively discredited all questionable evidence against him.[29]

The following year, another liberal, Bishop Bernard J. Sheil of Chicago, director of the Catholic Youth Council, also spoke out against red-baiting at a CIO–United Automobile Workers convention. It was time to "cry out against the phony anti-Communism that . . . flouts our traditions, and democratic procedures and sense of fair play," he urged, singling out Wisconsin's Senator Joseph McCarthy for his questionable investigating tactics.[30] Partly as a result of this speech, Sheil was forced to resign as director of the CYC.[31]

Other clerics, most notably Francis Cardinal Spellman, Archbishop of New York, went on the attack against perceived Communist infiltration. His support of McCarthy angered liberals but won him the respect of conservative Catholics and Protestants alike. "Anguished cries and protests against 'Mc-Carthyism' will not deter America from trying to root Communists out of the government," Spellman warned, and made a point of joining the senator at a postcommunion breakfast in New York City, afterwards shaking his hand for the photographers at a policemen's rally in McCarthy's honor.[32]

Spellman's frequent linkage of Catholicism with true anticommunism often angered Protestants, but nothing so infuriated them as an attack by one of their own. In July 1953, the *American Mercury* published an article by J. B. Matthews, a Methodist minister and former Communist, entitled "Reds and Our Churches," in which the author charged that the "largest single group supporting the Communist apparatus in the United States today is composed of Protestant clergymen," and went on to accuse "at least 7,000 Protestant clergymen" of being "party members, fellow travelers, espionage agents, party line adherents and unwitting dupes."[33] Predictably, moderate clergymen of all faiths rose up in protest, as did other sectors of the community. The National Conference of Christians and Jews published a strong condemnation of the article, warning that the destruction of trust in any religious leaders by "whole-sale condemnation is to weaken the greatest bulwark against atheistic materialism and Communism." President Dwight Eisenhower concurred, adding in his public response that the churches were "citadels of faith" in freedom and human dignity, and "our matchless armor in the worldwide struggle against the forces of godless tyranny and oppression."[34]

Such thoughts were reflected by the National Council of Churches of Christ (NCC), founded in 1950. Unlike its predecessor, the Federal Council of Churches, its mission was not to champion the Social Gospel but to emphasize evangelism, religious education, and, in the face of Cold War realities, support for the United States and other champions of "Christian freedom" and liberty against totalitarian and materialist philosophies.[35] When the NCC passed a resolution in 1952 criticizing racism, its tone was timid. Admitting that the church lagged behind secular institutions in integration, it renounced segregation and recommended that its member churches do likewise, recognizing that "historical and social factors make it more difficult for some churches than for others to realize the Christian ideal of non-segregation."[36] There was room for all convictions under this resolution, and by upholding integration as an ideal rather than a tangible goal, the NCC undercut its own message. Similarly vague and inoffensive resolutions followed, leading one observer to complain that "[i]n the area of prophecy, the glibness of the NCC has already taken its toll." Each pronouncement began with a "lifeless theological generalization," after which it wound up with "a bold proposal for solving the problems of the year before last." Such "hierarchical wisdom," he continued, could "lead one to the despairing cry, 'How could so many mean so little by so much?' "[37]

Bennett took the NCC for task for being too concerned with internal cohesion to challenge society's complacency. Such criticism rankled the Reverend Eugene Carson Blake, the council's president. Broad-shouldered and square-jawed, the powerfully built, six-foot-tall Blake still resembled at age forty-eight the football player he had been at Princeton University in the late 1920s. Born into a devout Presbyterian family in St. Louis, Blake traveled to northwestern India (now Pakistan) after he graduated to teach philosophy and theology at Forman Christian College, then married and continued his theological studies at the University of Edinburgh, New College, and at Princeton Theological Seminary. After his ordination in 1932, he worked in parishes in New York and California, greatly increasing the size of his congregations through his powerful preaching style. He attended the opening session of the World Council of Churches in Amsterdam in 1948 and returned to the United States a committed supporter of ecumenical and interfaith dialogue. Three years later he was named Stated Clerk of the Presbyterian Church in the U.S.A. That office had been created to coordinate meetings and committees, but Blake turned it into a position through which he could actively lead his church in the postwar years.[38]

This impressive background did not qualify Blake as the standard-bearer for religious liberalism, however, nor did it give any indication of his future activism in the civil rights movement. While dangers did exist from compromise, he acknowledged, he argued that Bennett did not "sufficiently recognize the danger of the equally abhorrent and typical sins of the prophet which are those of pride and arrogance." In Blake's view, the NCC had to heed "not only the voices of the prophets among us" but also the "voices of wise men . . . who do not always agree with the prophets." Hope lay in the "creative combination . . . of a larger cross section of Christian faith and conviction than has been anywhere available to the American Churches heretofore." Such a balanced approach, retorted Dr. Henry P. Van Dusen, president of Union Theological Seminary, did not take into account the fact that the prophet "strives for goods which are not primarily for his own interest but for the good of his society," while the conservative was "characteristically motivated . . . by desire to safeguard his own security and privilege." Furthermore, said Van Dusen, Blake overlooked the historic role of the prophets in the advance of the church. Human institutions were always characterized by lethargy, and progress was "almost always due to insistent, tireless, courageous (and often unreasonable, tiresome, and annoying) pressure from the prophets." It would be a great mistake, the seminary president concluded, to "suppose that advance can be achieved by some simple and comfortable median way."[39]

However, it was precisely the middle-of-the-road approach, not the call for prophecy, that symbolized the churches' role in society in the early 1950s. Unease over the Cold War, McCarthyism, and racism did not propel religious leaders into social activism; rather, many clergy felt that their mission was evangelism. This era, wrote one sociologist, was a time of peril and promise— peril because of the fears of nuclear annihilation, Communist ideology, and subversion, but promise because with the return to financial stability after the Depression and the war, the work of the churches in spreading the Gospel could begin anew.[40]

The new beginning, however, saw the churches become firmly entrenched in the secular society, often reflecting and mimicking its values of conformity, patriotism, financial success, and the need for psychological comfort. Anthropologist Margaret Mead observed the existence of a "vague positive attitude toward a religious system characterized by a kindly God who stands for all good things but who, after all, will not punish you for what are mostly mild infractions of his will."[41] This was not the time for a clerical campaign against social evils, for in a time of international tensions, people turned to religion for comfort and solace, and it was not coincidental that the Reverend Norman Vincent Peale's books on positive thinking became bestsellers in the 1950s.[42] Others believed that their religious beliefs were the crucial difference between them and their atheist foes, as clumsily described in Eisenhower's comment that "Our government makes no sense unless it is founded on a deeply felt religious faith—and I don't care what it is."[43] Evangelism became the order of the day. And of all those who proclaimed the need for personal salvation, none was more famous than William Franklin Graham.[44]

Born in North Carolina in November 1918, Billy Graham (as he was more commonly known) attended Florida Bible Institute in Tampa, where he became a Southern Baptist. After his marriage and graduation from Wheaton College in Chicago, he became the pastor of a small church that sponsored a religious radio show. Polishing his considerable oratorical skills on the air, Graham was convinced that his career lay in evangelism, and he embarked on a national religious tour with the Youth for Christ in 1947. Still a relative unknown, he was asked to be the main speaker at a Los Angeles revival in the fall of 1949, and on the night of September 25, in the midst of what had been a series of mundane tent meetings, Graham captured a national audience. Capitalizing on the news of the recent detonation of the first Soviet atomic bomb, he told his audience that no one knew when the first bombs in a war would fall, but "we do know this, that right now the grace of God can still save a poor lost sinner." The audience enthusiastically responded to his call to accept Jesus as its savior, for he had hit a nerve. People were "afraid of war, afraid of atomic bombs, fearful as they go to bed at night," and "trembling because they feel that we are on the verge of a third world war, a war which could sweep civilization back into the Middle Ages."[45]

His success was astounding. Newspaper magnate William Randolph Hearst instructed his reporters to "Puff Graham," and the revival was extended from three weeks to two months. Graham continued to hammer home the threat of imminent destruction throughout the next decade.[46] Personal conversion rates were high during these crusades, as he liked to call them, and doubtless his listeners felt that even if they had no control over whether war would break out, at least they would have some say where their souls ended up after the bombs fell.[47]

In time, Graham would drop the apocalyptic tone, but his calls for individual salvation and personal piety disturbed the more intellectual theologians such as Niebuhr, who charged that Graham had clothed the gospel in "petty moralizing" which offered "impossible answers to the dilemmas of this generation."[48] His crusades did not always offer petty answers to America's dilemmas; while his contention that the hydrogen bomb would not be dangerous if people accepted Christ as their savior was theologically weak, his insistence on holding racially integrated crusades in the early 1950s, even in southern cities, did call attention to the inclusiveness of the gospel message. Graham's methods would eventually be eclipsed by those in the civil rights movement, but his belief that the church had fallen behind the rest of American society in following its ideals of equality and social justice, coupled with his willingness to act on his views, were viewed with justifiable pride by his admirers.[49]

If some of Graham's theology might not have withstood a more stringent examination, it was far superior—and more biblically rooted—than much of what passed for religion in the 1950s. Even taking into consideration the inaccuracy of polling data, statistics clearly pointed to a surge in church membership, church and synagogue construction, and a greater respect for the profession of the clergy than at any other time in the century. The reasons for this revival were varied and complex. Third-generation Americans, desiring a sense of belonging, adopted not the languages and customs to which their grandparents adhered and their assimilated parents shunned, but identification with a religious group, "the old family religion."[50]

Other Americans turned to the faith they once dismissed as sentimentality, often in hope that it would reassure them that, as one editor put it, "despite everything that has happened in this dismaying century, the world is good, life is good, [and] the human story makes sense." Still others, mindful of the threat of materialistic Communism, wanted to prove that they cherished the religious values their enemies so clearly derided.[51] This revival, however, was considerably different from those of the past. It was an "utterly new thing," wrote theologian and church historian Martin E. Marty, "a revival that goes not against the grain of the nation but with it; a revival that draws its strength from its safe residence in the mores of the nation." As such, he noted, it was marked not so much by religious belief but by an "interest in religion" that denoted self-advantage and mere curiosity rather than concern with God and others.[52]

As the churches and synagogues catered to such sentiment, critics faulted them for not providing sufficient spiritual and moral guidance in the face of racism and war and for turning religion into a vague belief system that automatically supported the "American way of life" at the expense of its mission. The flight of affluent white parishioners from the cities to the suburbs, others argued, led to the creation of social and racially homogeneous communities whose church members were unable or unwilling to communicate with different ethnic groups.[53] The voice of the church, complained one critic, "when it has been heard at all, has been weak, tardy, equivocal, and irrelevant"; religion, instead of following its own values, "now merely gives its blessing to the majority-held values of the community around it."[54] Americans were "living on the residue of an age of faith," Margaret Mead had written in 1945, "drawing our spiritual energy from sources . . . diluted almost beyond recognition." It remained to be seen, she wrote, whether "the sheer spiritual challenge" of creating a society in which different racial groups could be given dignity "may give new impetus to religion in America."[55] What was uncertain was whether the nation's churches and synagogues were ready to meet such a challenge. Once the highest court in the land declared school segregation unconstitutional, the religious community was confronted with issues that it could no longer ignore.

one

Prophets are not without honor except in their
own country and in their own house.

MATTHEW 13:57

Prophets Without Honor

The Travails of the Southern Clergy,
1954–1960

After the Supreme Court ordered the desegregation of public schools in *Brown v. Board of Education* in May 1954, a reporter asked white residents of Savannah how they felt about the overturning of the fifty-eight-year-old "separate but equal" ruling from *Plessy v. Ferguson.* "It's a good thing," said one. "We can now practice the true Christian principles of brotherhood."[1] Though the admission that one needed a secular court ruling before one could act on one's religious beliefs might seem surprising, similar opinions were voiced by many religious organizations and denominational hierarchies that proclaimed themselves solidly behind the court. The governing boards of the National Council of Churches of Christ in the U.S.A. (NCC) and the World Council of Churches, various conferences and assemblies of several Protestant denominations, including the southern Presbyterian Church in the U.S. and the Southern Baptist Convention, passed resolutions praising the decision, as did the Synagogue Council of America and various councils of Catholic bishops.[2]

Given such widespread support, it was not surprising that editors of religious journals were confident that the devout citizens of the Bible Belt would listen to their spiritual leaders, see the error of segregation, and open their schools to all children. The editors of the *Christian Century*, the nation's most widely read Protestant weekly, commended the justices' decision against setting a specific timetable for desegregation, saying it would give "responsible elements" time to "put the race-baiters firmly in their place"; besides, they claimed, the "silent public opinion of the south has already marked off segregation as a doomed and dying social arrangement." The editors of the Jesuit journal *America* were similarly hopeful that desegregation would be carried out peacefully.[3] Individual clergy were not as certain that segregation would die a quick and unmourned death, but they were nonetheless optimistic that the prognosis was terminal. The South would see "very vicious efforts to avoid" the ruling, warned the Reverend Louis Twomey, a Jesuit professor at Loyola University in New Orleans, but he was "convinced that despite some years of unrest and bitter opposition, the movement toward racial integration is well on its way. Within ten years . . . the South will have so changed for the better . . . in this regard that we will not be able to recognize the 'old' South."[4]

White conservatives were determined not to see this come to pass. Despite the flurry of resolutions, they were not about to give up their support of segregation, and challenged the resolutions on the grounds that the churches had no business judging the actions of the government.[5] Religious bodies had acquiesced in the separation of the races for decades, and to have segregation suddenly denounced as un-Christian perplexed many. A Methodist layperson explained that "being a Christian is accepting the Lord Jesus Christ as my personal Savior . . . and just because I don't want my granddaughter to go to school with a Negro boy, I don't see what it has got to do with my being a Christian or not."[6] Adding to the bewilderment and the sense of hypocrisy was the continued existence of segregated, church-related private schools and colleges such as the Lovett School in Atlanta, Loyola University of the South in New Orleans, and the University of the South in Sewanee, Tennessee.[7]

Official ecclesiastical boundaries were hardly free from the taint of segregation; most had been organized after the Civil War when blacks were systematically excluded from white congregations. The Methodist Church had formally established segregated jurisdictions under the 1939 Plan of Union, which reunited the southern and northern branches after the schism of 1844. In 1955, Southern Methodists threatened to secede if the Central (Negro) Jurisdiction was merged with the five white geographic jurisdictions (a feat that was finally accomplished in 1968).[8] In 1953, the Episcopal Diocese of South Carolina had invited black parishes to apply for admission to the Episcopal General Convention. After the *Brown* decision, however, an influential white layperson introduced a resolution at the 1956 Convention claiming that "there is nothing morally wrong in voluntary recognition of racial differences." Despite the opposition of the Reverend John B. Morris, the twenty-seven-year-old priest of St. Barnabas's Episcopal Church in Dillon, South Carolina, the invitation was rescinded.[9]

Some believed the resolutions in praise of *Brown* had been issued only because of the publicity that followed the decision and were confident that they did not have to accept statements passed at national gatherings miles from home. "They were just a little bit exalted," explained one Southern Baptist, describing why his denominational leaders had gone against cherished local values. "When they got back with the home folks a lot of 'em wondered how they did it."[10] A study made by the NCC's Department of Racial and Cultural Relations indicated that the strongest influences on local church policy were local pressures, not denominational resolutions, and admitted that when the "controlling elements" in the church shared society's values, "there is little hope that the church will pioneer in changing patterns of race relations."[11]

Other clergy were openly hostile to the resolutions. The Reverend W. A. Criswell of the First Baptist Church in Dallas, the largest Baptist church in the world, denounced the "bunch of infidels" who "sit up there in their dirty shirts and make all their fine speeches."[12] Those who supported the racial status quo with scripture quickly became popular in a region that prided itself on religious piety and biblical literalism. Some resurrected the old defense of slavery by arguing that Noah's curse on Ham condemned the black race to perpetual servitude. Others quoted portions of Acts 17, which told of God's determining the "bounds of their habitations," a passage that quickly became one of the key pieces of evidence to show that "God was the original segregationist."[13] One Episcopal priest argued that the social structure under attack from liberals was "more in accord with the will of God" than a "society of forced integration," for in the South, "where the kingdom of God is taken seriously," a "very workable social order" had developed under segregation.[14]

Defense of the southern way of life led to a resurgence of the Ku Klux Klan, whose chapters had their own chaplains, or "Kludds," some of whom were ordained ministers. One Klansman noted that churches often welcomed them: "We come in singing . . . and leave a nice, big donation for the plate."[15] Those who found the blue-collar Klan too violent for their tastes joined Citizens' Councils, which emphasized using economic pressure against anyone even suspected of favoring integration. Boycotts, cancellation of bank loans, and other means of economic coercion were effective in silencing dissent, and those who were driven into bankruptcy or forced to move served as good examples to others who might be tempted to question the racial orthodoxy of the South.[16]

The "responsible elements" favored by the *Christian Century* failed to materialize in force, although the notion that clergymen might fill that role proved to be enough of a concern for Robert Patterson, executive secretary of the Citizens' Councils of America, to urge the laity to "bring pressure on ministers to support segregation and change the position of . . . church organizations which have endorsed mixing of races."[17] This pressure was often financial, for such groups repeatedly urged that "weak-kneed preachers" be "whipped into line" by withholding contributions: "Money talks and they all listen."[18] As a result, few were willing to risk their careers by calling for desegregation. Even those who supported it in principle and had support from their local ministerial councils shied away from openly calling for its implementation.[19] A Methodist minister in Louisiana doubted that it would make much difference whether or not clergymen spoke out. Did anyone really believe that citizens would "reverently bow their heads in obedience if a pastor tells them what their attitudes and actions . . . should be?" he asked. "Our society just doesn't accord that kind of power to ministers."[20] Other clerics insisted that they preferred to work quietly, out of the limelight. "I keep hearing about white people who say they've been working behind the scenes," a black lawyer remarked at the end of the decade. "Yes sir. It must be getting mighty crowded back there, behind the scenes."[21]

Those who spoke publicly in favor of desegregation risked opprobrium, their jobs, and sometimes their personal safety. Although the Reverend Duncan Gray Jr., an Episcopal priest from Cleveland, Mississippi, did not lose his job when he asked parishioners to adhere to the *Brown* decision, in Mansfield, Texas, an Episcopal priest had to be rescued from a mob by a sheriff for doing the same thing. When John Morris and several other white Protestant ministers published a tract calling for racial moderation entitled *South Carolina Speaks*, Governor George Timmermann denounced them, and vigilantes bombed one's house. Two others had to leave their parishes.[22]

Those who looked to Billy Graham, the nation's most prominent minister, to provide strong and consistent moral direction found themselves quickly disappointed, for Graham's discussions of desegregation suffered from a lack of conviction. Although he called for a nationwide "baptism of Christian love, tolerance, and understanding," his equivocations robbed whatever moral weight his declarations might have carried. He insisted that black leaders (always unnamed) had told him that blacks "really do not want to intermingle with the whites, but that they rebel at laws and ropes that bar them. As someone has said, 'Take the dare out of it, and 90% of the problem is solved.'"[23] Despite such views, Timmerman announced that Graham's plans to hold an integrated revival meeting at South Carolina's state house violated the separation of church and state and forced him to move the rally elsewhere. "As a widely known evangelist and native Southerner," the governor explained, "his endorsement of racial mixing has done much harm."[24]

If the popular and financially independent Graham sometimes felt constrained by southern mores, priests, ministers, and rabbis who were relatively unknown and more dependent on their congregations were even more limited in what they could say. Most contented themselves with making equivocal pronouncements on the need for charity, forgiveness, and patience, without specifically relating these to racial issues. The connection between controversy and dwindling contributions was not lost on institutions other than the church, and southern universities, loath to alienate wealthy alumni, sought out conventional speakers for important events. When the administration of the University of Mississippi discovered that Alvin Kershaw, an Episcopal priest from Ohio and their guest speaker for Religious Emphasis Week in 1956, was also a member of the National Association for the Advancement of Colored People (NAACP), a minor crisis faced university officials, including the Reverend Will Davis Campbell, the university's director of religious life, who had suggested Kershaw for the program.

A somewhat stoop-shouldered man with a prominent forehead and a receding hairline, Campbell was born in 1924 to a poor farming couple from the small town of Liberty, Mississippi. At sixteen, he was ordained a minister by the local Baptist pastor, and later attended Louisiana College, leaving after a year to become a medic in the United States Army in 1942.[25] While stationed in the South Pacific, he read Howard Fast's *Freedom Road*, a novel about a black family in the South during Reconstruction. "I certainly did not think of myself as a bigot," Campbell recalled. "I just found no occasion to violate the behavioral norm of my Mississippi upbringing." Yet reading the book completely changed the way Campbell viewed the South.[26]

After the war, Campbell attended Yale Divinity School, graduating with a bachelor of divinity degree in 1952.[27] While he was at Yale, the Supreme Court began hearing the school desegregation cases, and Campbell and his southern friends lamented that "this issue would be settled before we got back

South," as they would be denied the opportunity to witness to their beliefs. "Unfortunately," he added, "we were slightly off the mark."[28] He became pastor of a Baptist church in Taylor, Louisiana, whose middle-class congregation was proud to have "one of the three Yale preachers in the whole state."[29] Eager to be considered a conscientious pastor, he threw himself into his duties, trying to fit the expectations of what a Yale-educated minister should be, even wearing a tweed cap and smoking a pipe. After he visited the homes of striking mill workers and walked with them on the picket lines, his parishioners called for his resignation. In August 1954, he accepted the position of director of religious life at the University of Mississippi, thinking he would have more freedom in the world of academia.[30]

His responsibilities included planning the university's Religious Emphasis Week. Dubbed "Be Good to God Week" by fraternities, it was considered important enough to warrant the selection of a nationally known guest speaker to conduct programs on religious issues. Campbell, who had already made the administration uneasy by visiting Providence Farm, a nearby interracial cooperative community, invited Kershaw, who had recently won $32,000 on a television quiz show for his knowledge of contemporary drama. After Kershaw announced that he would give a sizable portion of the prize money to the NAACP, state representatives, University Chancellor J. D. Williams, and the local chapter of the American Legion, which screened the speaker lists, asked Campbell to rescind the invitation one week before the program was to begin. A majority of students, however, supported Kershaw's right to speak on "Religion and Modern Drama" as planned.[31] To answer charges that Kershaw was a member of "un-American" organizations blacklisted by the Federal Bureau of Investigation, state officials investigated him and announced that Kershaw was not only an "outstanding Episcopal minister" but free of radical taint; his patriotism was beyond reproach, because he was a graduate of the University of the South in Sewanee, Tennessee, and had attended the University of Louisville in Kentucky—in effect, "most of his life was spent in the South."[32]

When Kershaw wrote a letter to the student newspaper describing his support for the NAACP's goals and his belief that all people "need to be accepted and respected as of equal worth as children of God," however, student opinion turned against him.[33] Williams rescinded the invitation, and, although it was a popular move on campus, it caused several other scheduled clergy to withdraw from the Religious Emphasis Week program, including the Reverend Joseph Fichter, a liberal Jesuit professor of sociology at Loyola University in New Orleans, himself active in civil rights, and Rabbi Milton Grafman of Temple Emanu-el in Birmingham.[34] Local ministers refused to take their place, not out of any sympathy with Kershaw's views, but, in their words, because the excitement created by the dispute made it "difficult to maintain an atmosphere in which real religious values could be given proper attention."[35]

Russell Barrett, a professor at the university, believed there was little doubt that the majority of faculty members agreed with the chancellor's action, but a minority, including himself and history professor James Silver, supported Campbell and the principles of academic freedom. When the Baptist minister announced that he would go to the campus chapel each day during the hour scheduled for speakers and meditate, sympathetic faculty, students, and townspeople joined him while a spotlight shone on two empty chairs on the stage. "Perhaps we have relied too long upon our own power," Campbell wrote. "This call to prayer is not a display of superficial piety. It is rather the recognition that we have gone as far as we can go and perhaps it is as such [an] admission that God chooses to enter human history."[36] At week's end, the chancellor announced that Religious Emphasis Week had been permanently abolished.[37]

Campbell's remaining time at the university was filled with increasing controversy. When Carl Rowan and Richard Kleeman, reporters for the *Minneapolis Tribune*, traveled to Mississippi to cover the southern reaction to the desegregation controversy, Silver asked them to stay with him, but when he found out that Rowan was black, he extended the invitation only to Kleeman, recalling that he did not dare invite Rowan. Instead, Campbell and his wife opened their home to him, recalled Silver, "as befitted their uncomplicated Christian logic." The state's Sovereignty Commission complained to university officials, but as the Campbells owned their home rather than rented one from the university, officials could take no disciplinary action against him.[38]

Shortly afterward Campbell was harassed by two students who had observed him playing ping-pong with a black minister in the campus YMCA building. When Williams asked him about his indiscretion, Campbell tried to lighten the tension by explaining that they had used separate but equal paddles, a white ball, and had been separated by a net. Williams was not amused. A few nights later, at a reception for new students given by Campbell and his staff, someone placed human feces in the punch. Discouraged with the lack of administrative support, Campbell resigned in 1956 and moved his family to Nashville, Tennessee, where he had accepted a position as the director of the Southern Project of the NCC's Department of Racial and Cultural Relations.[39] "The Council hired me and turned me loose," he said later. "They didn't know what to tell me to do, so we got along fine. . . . I was a kind of troubleshooter, a mediator."[40] Working with little publicity, Campbell trav-

PROPHETS WITHOUT HONOR

eled through the South, meeting with ministers and trying to convince them to work for peaceful school desegregation in their communities.[41]

Clergy in the border states had already demonstrated a willingness to act as peacemakers in such situations. After white supremacists urged students in Baltimore and Washington, D.C., to resist integration, various ministerial associations and individual clergymen spoke out against them, going to local high schools to calm and convince students to return to class. School integration then proceeded with little incident.[42] When black teenagers enrolled in a high school in Sturgis, Kentucky, in September 1956, C. Sumpter Logan and Theodore A. Braun, two ministers from the nearby town of Henderson, tried to convince white ministers to seek solutions to the crisis with several black ministers. When the whites refused, they met with the black clergy themselves, earning the enmity of Sturgis's poor whites, who made up the majority of the protesters outside the schools. The other townspeople were absent, the ministers reported, "either giving silent assent from afar or, more common, not wanting to get involved in the mob scene."[43] When Henderson was faced with school integration, members of the town's ministerial association attended a Citizens' Council meeting, and when Logan, the association's president, called for acceptance of the Supreme Court's decision, he was nearly drowned out by boos.[44] Afterward, when the Citizens' Council organized a school boycott, the ministerial association took to the radio and visited school assemblies to ask townspeople to keep their children in school.[45] Within two weeks, the boycott ended, due in large part to the efforts of the handful of white ministers. One white supremacist paid them an unintended tribute when he grudgingly admitted, "[i]f it hadn't been for the ministerial association, we'd have emptied the schools on the third day."[46]

Will Campbell was able to capitalize on their success by circulating copies of Braun's and Sumpter's articles in the *Christian Century* among white clergy in Nashville, one of the Southern Project's "target cities" (a euphemism for "let's all get shot together," Campbell wrote), during a time of similar tension. While the city's clergy had been relatively silent on the matter, noted Campbell, "[t]he imminence of desegregation has stirred some into a form of activity." The successful integration of Catholic parochial schools in Nashville served as an incentive to others to see that the public schools followed suit, and the local ministerial association issued a letter calling upon citizens of all faiths to work peacefully and successfully toward school integration. The city also benefited from the presence of several "denominational headquarters with clergymen who don't have to answer to local congregations," he added, "and who, for other reasons, are a bit more liberal" in interfaith relations.[47]

Officials in Clinton, Tennessee, found themselves confronted with a Citizens' Council–led school boycott that fall, and as school attendance decreased, segregation rallies continued to grow.[48] With the potential for violence always present, the NCC sent Campbell to meet with local white ministers and ask them to help calm the town. He found them to be "cordial" but "helpless," especially the Reverend Paul W. Turner of the First Baptist Church, the largest church in town. Convinced that the Clinton ministers were captives of the status quo, Campbell left, after what he considered to be a fruitless journey.[49] Whether he succeeded in convincing Turner to act or whether the Clinton minister had already made up his mind will never be known. After Turner escorted six black children to the local high school, a group of nine men and women knocked him down and began beating him until the police arrested them. Bruised, with deep cuts around his eyes and nose, he nevertheless insisted on accompanying town officials to Knoxville, where they met with the district attorney and asked him to take immediate steps to stop the violence.[50]

Standing in his pulpit five days later, Turner told an audience of almost 1,000 that Americans should stand for law and order, "knowing that wherever anarchy prevails, no one has any freedom." If need be, he said, he was prepared to escort children to school the next day. He was heartily congratulated by many individuals after the service, which had been filmed for Edward R. Murrow's *See It Now* television program. In a pastoral message in the church bulletin, Turner admonished all people to conquer prejudices, asked them to pray for guidance and constructive ideas, and called for equal rights for all people. The next year, the Clinton Junior Chamber of Commerce awarded him their distinguished service award for 1956.[51]

While the bravery of individual southerners did not go unnoticed in the middle of the decade, it was the efforts of black clergy and citizens in Montgomery, Alabama, to combat segregated seating on the city's buses that captured the nation's attention. The story of the Montgomery bus boycott has been covered in depth elsewhere, and its intricacies do not need to be retold here.[52] Suffice it to say that from its inception, the bus boycott, which catapulted the Reverend Martin Luther King Jr. to national prominence, was managed and led by black leaders and proved successful because of the courage, enthusiasm, and patience of the black citizens of Montgomery. However, a handful of white moderates also braved segregationist threats and bombs to support the protest and attempt to open channels of communication between the black leaders of the Montgomery Improvement Association (MIA) and the city council.

The boycott's success during the first week of December 1955 had a galvanizing effect on Montgomery's blacks, but the Alabama Council of Human Relations (ACHR), the city's only interracial organization, feared that the longer it lasted, the more difficult it would be to get both sides to the negotiating table. Dedicated to the idea of biracial communication, the ACHR, an affiliate of the Southern Regional Council (SRC), gave sympathetic white clergy the opportunity to involve themselves in the boycott. The SRC had been established in Atlanta in 1944 to work for social justice through interracial dialogue, publications, and policy analysis rather than direct-action protests and political challenges. Funded by nonsouthern foundations yet staffed by southerners, the SRC developed several state councils on human relations in early 1954, hoping that they would smooth the way for the peaceful implementation of the *Brown* decision. By 1956, unfounded charges that the SRC was a haven for Communists had become so damaging (and burdensome) that executive director George Mitchell was forced to cut back on the organization's support of the state councils and focus instead on regional initiatives out of Atlanta.[53]

Two white clerics led the ACHR. The Reverend Thomas P. Thrasher of the Church of the Ascension, the largest Episcopal church in the city, served as council president; Methodist minister Robert E. Hughes served as executive director. Both decided to help arrange a meeting between the city commissioners, the bus company, and members of the MIA.[54]

The twenty-seven-year-old Hughes had joined the council in January 1953, soon after completing his seminary studies at Emory University in Atlanta. He had planned to go abroad as a missionary, but the Methodist Board of Missions wanted him to have pastoral experience before going overseas and had sent him to Rockford, Alabama, in 1952 after his graduation. He joined the Alabama Council the following year, and shortly afterward became its director, with the blessing of the mission board, which believed that a year's work in Alabama in that capacity would serve as good preparation for his future work in Southern Rhodesia.[55] When the Supreme Court declared school segregation unconstitutional, Hughes and a Baptist minister, fearing that angry citizens would lead a demonstration, went to the town courthouse to calm the expected mob, but none existed, for local sentiment against the *Brown* decision was muted rather than violent. When Hughes tried to convince the local white ministerial association to meet with black ministers to discuss the desegregation ruling, his proposal died, as he recalled, because his colleagues were "scared to support it." He made a point of preaching about racial justice, but only occasionally did he debate segregationists who used the Bible as justification for their views, believing it to be a "useless exercise" because "scripture was being used as a crutch by some prejudiced patrons [and] logic would be of little use."[56]

Much more important than abstract debates, in his opinion, were concrete examples of interracial cooperation. He and Thrasher managed to arrange a meeting between the city commissioners and the leaders of the MIA in City Hall on December 8, 1955. Despite their hopes that both sides would be reasonable and unemotional in their discussions, nothing was achieved at either this or future meetings; instead, conservative white clergy tried to browbeat King, the Reverend Ralph Abernathy, and other black members of the MIA with theological arguments in a futile attempt to get them to call off the boycott.[57]

While the ACHR continued to offer its services as a mediator, Hughes helped drive boycotters around the city. While segregationists harassed him, more of their abuse was showered on Robert Sylvester Graetz Jr., white pastor of the predominantly black Trinity Lutheran Church. The boyish-looking minister had supported the boycott since its inception and had joined the MIA executive committee, much to the delight of his congregation and the consternation of local whites. Born in Clarksburg, West Virginia, in 1928, Graetz attended Capitol University in Columbus, Ohio, in the late 1940s, where he organized a race relations club and joined the NAACP. After spending two years in a Los Angeles parish, where he and his wife helped black families move into previously all-white neighborhoods, Graetz, like Hughes, planned to become an overseas missionary. Instead, he was sent to Montgomery, where he and his family quickly became friends with liberal whites, including Robert and Dorothy Hughes and Virginia and Clifford Durr, the latter well-known for their longstanding work on behalf of civil rights.[58]

Graetz attended the first mass meeting sponsored by the MIA and, impressed with the moral justification for the boycott, asked his colleagues in the white ministerial association to support the MIA's reasonable demands. None did. Graetz also helped drive blacks around the city on the first day of the boycott and was detained by police officers who insisted he was running an unlicensed taxi and refused to believe his claim that he was driving friends. He received a lecture from the sheriff on the proper duties of a minister, and after his release resumed his carpool duties. He told reporters from the *Montgomery Advertiser* that despite what segregationists were saying, his views were not Communist-inspired; he considered himself a conservative "Eisenhower Democrat." Although the article was favorable, his family began receiving vituperative telephone calls at all hours, and segregationists vandalized his car. Worse yet were the bomb threats and the actual explosions that rocked the Graetz home several times, leading the family to take shelter at the Hughes home.[59]

The symbolic importance of a white minister risking his own safety by supporting a black-led movement was not lost on the media. The black magazine *Jet* published a photograph of him, and Graetz was the subject of stories in the *New York Times* and religious journals. His church log listed several appointments with journalists and photographers from newspapers and magazines across the country. The most moving thing about his work, he told Harold E. Fey, editor of the *Christian Century*, was that many blacks had thanked him for proving that a white person could really be a Christian, as they had begun to doubt that such a thing was possible.[60] For his part, Hughes considered Graetz a "real saint," yet noted the crucial distinction between the Lutheran pastor and other white clergymen sympathetic to the boycott's aims. "You have to understand that Bob was . . . very publicly identified" with the boycott, as his parishioners wanted him to be, because it was "reflecting their interest in all of this" in a way that contrasted markedly with clergymen who presided over white congregations.[61] It was well known that the president of the Montgomery Council on Human Relations, a white Methodist minister, had been driven out of town for being "too soft" on the race question.[62]

Nonetheless, the publicity accorded Graetz and the leaders of the boycott helped garner much-needed money for MIA legal fees and operating costs, as donations came from church groups, both black and white, from around the world.[63] The Reverend Eugene Carson Blake, president of the NCC, commended Montgomery's black ministers and told them that "the wider fellowship of the churches . . . support you and all others who are struggling with these grave problems."[64] "I know of very few white Southern ministers who aren't troubled and don't have admiration for King," Will Campbell told a reporter. The Reverend William Finlator of Raleigh, North Carolina, a fellow Baptist, concurred: "King has been working on the guilt conscience of the South. If he can bring us to contrition, that is our hope."[65]

In late 1956, the Supreme Court declared segregation on Montgomery's buses unconstitutional, but peace did not come with victory. After rifle fire injured several riders on buses during evening runs, the city suspended nighttime bus transportation on several routes. In January 1957, a wave of bombings swept the city; in one night, the Graetz and Abernathy homes and three black Baptist churches were destroyed. For the first time since the boycott began, the white members of the Montgomery Ministerial Association lent their collective voice to a condemnation of the bombing. *Time* magazine described the scene in sensational terms: "No one was injured, but Graetz and his family might well have been slaughtered as they ran from the house in panic." Nothing was further from the truth, Graetz responded. "We can take the bombs and the nasty phone calls and letters; we can take the insults and stares," he explained. "But please, we don't want people to think we've started to get panicky and to run away. We have not moved, and we do not intend to." A year later, however, Graetz received an official call to become pastor of a church in Columbus, Ohio (there is no indication in his memoirs that the order was motivated in any way by his civil rights activities). The Graetzes decided that they could not refuse the request of their denominational officials, and moved in August 1958.[66]

He was not the only white minister connected with the boycott to leave the city. Thomas Thrasher, once so popular with his parishioners, had angered them by his liberal stand on racial issues and refused to stop speaking about them from the pulpit. When he rebuked them for hiring a guard to prevent blacks from attending services, they asked the Episcopal bishop of Alabama, Charles C. J. Carpenter, to have him removed. The bishop transferred him to the chaplaincy of the University of North Carolina.[67]

Hughes's forced departure from Alabama took a little longer. He refused to curtail his civil rights activities, and the Klan had burned a cross on his family's lawn in retaliation (leading his young daughter to announce upon its discovery the next morning that Jesus had visited them). His family continued to receive threats, aggravating the young minister's already troublesome ulcer. His older brother Preston, a fellow Methodist minister and member of the Alabama Council on Human Relations, had also been harassed for his liberal views on racial equality, with the result that his parishioners forced his transfer to North Carolina. When Harrison Salisbury, a reporter for the New York Times, arrived in Birmingham to cover the city's worsening race relations in early 1960, he sought out Hughes and other clergy for their views, including Rabbi Milton Grafman, who had installed floodlights outside his temple after two attempts had been made by segregationists to dynamite Birmingham's synagogues in the past year. A seasoned reporter who had covered Moscow during the Second World War, Salisbury knew not to mention names in his stories where the safety of others was concerned, but he did not suspect tapped telephones in his hotel room. After the Birmingham city council filed libel suits against Salisbury and the New York Times (which were eventually dismissed five years later), police authorities reconstructed a list of all telephone numbers dialed from his hotel room and subpoenaed several individuals, including Grafman. All were browbeaten by a grand jury for talking to the northern reporter, but only Hughes faced prosecution.[68]

PROPHETS WITHOUT HONOR

As director of the ACHR, Hughes possessed lists of members and contributors whose liberal stand on racial issues made them targets of the state's white supremacists. Called before a grand jury in September 1960 on the pretense of investigating the Salisbury affair, the court ordered Hughes to divulge all membership rolls, lists of contributions, and correspondence pertaining to the council. He refused, and a circuit judge ordered him jailed for contempt. The large law firms in the area refused to take the case, and two Birmingham attorneys, James Shores and Charles Morgan, agreed to represent him, assisted by Will Campbell and the Reverend Albert Foley, a Jesuit priest who served on the ACHR. All feared that white prisoners would attack Hughes if they discovered the reason for his incarceration, and Morgan arranged to have him separated from the other prisoners at night. As it turned out, when Morgan arrived at the jail, bringing Hughes a bottle of milk for his ulcer, he was pleasantly surprised to find that prison officials had become quite courteous to the minister, concerned as they were about his health. Hughes, meanwhile, had begun giving Bible lessons to prisoners and had started teaching one of them to read.[69]

While Hughes remained in prison, Foley was "running around the north meeting with Jewish groups to try to get a Protestant minister out of jail in Alabama," Hughes recalled, adding that the Birmingham chapter of the Anti-Defamation League and other Jewish groups in the North, as opposed to local rabbis, were "especially helpful [and] sympathetic with what we were trying to do."[70] After a few days, the court dropped all charges and released Hughes, who learned that the North Alabama Methodist Conference had revoked his ministerial credentials. Bishop Bachman G. Hodge insisted that the decision had nothing to do with the grand jury incident, explaining that conference rules clearly outlined such procedures for ministers who had not accepted pastorates within a set period. Many people, including Hughes, believed that Hodge had given in to pressure from segregationist Methodist lay organizations.[71] In "these convulsive last days of racism, church leaders may be increasingly persecuted by extremists who realize that a vital Christianity is their worst enemy," remarked the Reverend John Morris, who by this time had left his parish in South Carolina to move to Atlanta, adding that "Robert Hughes has set an example for committed Christians throughout the South in all churches."[72]

In light of the unfavorable publicity surrounding his decision, Hodge restored Hughes's credentials after he accepted an immediate transfer to the Southern Rhodesia Conference in Africa. At the time, that country's racist government was rocked by plans to secede from the British Commonwealth as well as by stirrings of black nationalism. Police had stepped up their arrests of any person suspected of having loyalties to either the commonwealth or the idea of black majority rule. Hughes and another Methodist, Bishop Ralph Dodge, began meeting with former political prisoners and black clergymen who were fighting for an end to racial discrimination, circulating copies of Martin Luther King Jr.'s sermons and letters and other writings the government deemed subversive. Both were put under surveillance, but the wiretap placed on Hughes's telephone was so poorly connected that he could hear conversations from the police station across the street. In July 1964, immigration officials notified them that they had one week to leave the country. Fifty-eight ministers held an illegal interracial march through the streets of the capital to protest their expulsion. Hughes and his family moved to Zambia, where he joined the staff of the Mindola Ecumenical Center. Several years later, he returned to the United States to work for the community relations office in the Department of Justice in Seattle.[73]

Despite the efforts of a handful of ministers, the vast majority of white clergy either remained opposed to the nascent civil rights movement or refused to take a public stand. The very success of the bus boycott had convinced segregationists that they could not yield to pressures for integration. And for those white liberals who still clung to the hope that an end to racial discrimination would arrive sometime in the near future, the upsurge in violence directed against those who violated southern racial customs quickly disabused them of such notions, especially when it occurred in nominally progressive cities such as Little Rock, Arkansas. Several graduate schools in the state capitol as well as buses and other facilities had been desegregated without incident by 1956, and various church organizations—including the state council of the Disciples of Christ, the Women's Society of Christian Service of the Little Rock Methodist Conference, and the interracial ministerial alliance—supported school desegregation in principle. When the Reverend Colbert S. Cartwright, the white minister of the Pulaski Heights Christian Church and president of the Arkansas Council on Human Relations, and Daisy Bates, president of the Arkansas NAACP, successfully brought lawsuits resulting in a federal court order admitting fifteen black children to Central High on Tuesday, September 3, 1957, however, the moderate voices all but disappeared.[74]

Always mindful of his standing with the electorate, Governor Orville Faubus proclaimed a state of emergency and ordered the Arkansas National Guard to Central High, ostensibly to maintain law and order and protect the peace, safety, and security of local citizens. By the time classes began, 250

National Guardsmen surrounded Central High School, along with 300 on-lookers. The Reverend Wesley Pruden and other white Baptist ministers commended the governor's support for segregation; other clergy from prominent, well-to-do Protestant churches sent Faubus a strongly worded letter protesting his failure to comply with federal law. The strongest condemnation of the governor on the basis of religious grounds came not from clergymen, but from the local Council of Church Women, which lamented the un-Christian nature of segregation, and called for prayers of repentance and reconciliation.[75]

Fearing for the safety of the black students, Daisy Bates and other NAACP officials telephoned the Reverend Dunbar Ogden Jr., a white Presbyterian minister and president of the Greater Little Rock Interracial Ministerial Alliance, who had moved to the city three years before. A descendant of a wealthy southern family, Ogden's ancestors included a Mississippi slaveholder and an uncle who had fought many of the Reconstruction measures after the Civil War. He in turn asked several black and white ministers to escort the children to school the next day. Few were willing to entertain the idea, and faced with such lack of support, Ogden agreed to meet the students himself the next morning. Relieved that she would have at least some ministerial support, Bates notified the parents of the children that they would be accompanied by clergy on their way to school the next day. A crowd surrounded the high school as the children arrived at Central High that morning, where they were met by Ogden; his twenty-one-year-old son John, an employee of the Arkansas Highway Commission; two black Methodist ministers, Z. Z. Driver and Harry Bass; and Will Campbell. After being pushed and shoved by the mob, the ministers made it to the front of the high school, where an officer of the National Guard refused to admit the children.[76]

Ogden's parishioners reacted mildly to his actions, as many felt that he really did not want to walk with the children but was compelled to do so as president of the Ministerial Alliance. When he continued to call upon the clergy of the state to support desegregation, his parishioners became more outspoken in their criticism, some comparing him to Judas for betraying his race.[77] For the next two weeks, tension remained high. "Integration should take place at Central, as the courts have ordered," Ogden insisted to a reporter for the *New York Times*. "It must not stop or be postponed."[78] When Faubus announced the withdrawal of the National Guard from around the school, in effect granting control to the mobs, segregationists claimed victory, vowing that Arkansas would lead the way in crushing integration.[79] "The vocal element of the community" was now led by people such as Pruden, who had never "been a molder of public thought in our city before," lamented Elizabeth Huckaby, vice principal for girls at Central High, and were now "in charge, supported by the silence of the many who were normally our community leaders."[80]

When Campbell and Cartwright visited Bates, they found her frustrated and angry at the turn of events, especially over the silence of ministers whom she knew to be privately in favor of integration. When they asked to pray with her, she told them if they wanted to help, they should pray with the black students, as they would be facing the mobs. Little Rock's ministers were not quite as silent as she had supposed. From pulpits across the city that Sunday came the message to parishioners to peacefully accept the integration program, maintain calm, and stay away from Central High. Unfortunately, few heeded this advice. When school started the next day, a handful of police officers and state troopers were met by an angry, hysterical mob of segregationists, and the black students had to be escorted out of the school by a side door and into waiting cars. The nation was shocked by the violence and hysteria. President Eisenhower federalized the Arkansas National Guard, sending it and the 327th Airborne Battle Group to Little Rock. Locals passed by the soldiers warily, many grumbling that the South was being occupied yet again. For the next few days, the soldiers' time was occupied by dispersing crowds, arresting troublemakers, and, most importantly, protecting the black students as they went to school.[81]

Local clergymen on both sides of the issue were disturbed by the outcome. A Missionary Baptist congregation in North Little Rock sent Eisenhower a telegram protesting the "unholy invasion of [their] customs, rights, and privileges," adding, "if you had been spending as much time on your knees in prayer as . . . on the golf course you never would have sent troops into Arkansas." The Capitol Citizens' Council passed a resolution asking why those ministers who were so concerned with integrating the schools had failed to integrate their churches, adding that if they did so it would "greatly clarify a confused situation, and help people to know what church to attend and support." If such ministers had "courage to match their convictions and a willingness to suffer for their principles," the resolution continued, children "would not be asked to accept a situation which the adults are unwilling to tolerate."[82]

On Sunday, September 29, the Right Reverend Robert R. Brown, Episcopal Bishop of Arkansas, issued a pastoral letter to be read from all Episcopal pulpits in the state in which he said the violence at the school shamed the church; he castigated its failure to "exert an adequate Christian leadership." Several priests refused to read the letter. When Brown contacted Eisenhower to see if there was anything that Little Rock's clergy could do to ease the situation, the president responded with gratitude, noting that the ministers, as the "spiritual and moral leaders of the community," had a responsibility to remind their congregants to disregard agitators and support the law and the federal government, especially as "the very concepts of freedom" were "under relentless attack by an atheistic ideology."[83] A few days later, Brown presided over a meeting of forty local clergymen, including Monsignor James O'Connell, Rabbi Sanders of Temple B'nai Israel, and Bishop Paul Martin of the Methodist Church in Arkansas and Louisiana, which resulted in a call for a day of prayer and repentance on October 12, when they would read special prayers for the preservation of law and order and the "casting out of rancor and prejudice in favor of understanding and compassion." Religious and political leaders, as well as editorial staffs of newsmagazines across the country reacted to the news of the services with general approval. "Action is always ecumenicity's best vehicle," emphasized the editors of the Christian Century.[84]

The Catholic and Episcopal churches, as well as the majority of the middle-class Methodist, Baptist, and Presbyterian congregations participated in the prayer services. Segregationist clergy had held their own services the night before, where they condemned Eisenhower's actions. Compared to their strong and clear statements, the vague prayers of guidance recited by the ministers in the well-to-do churches left something to be desired; a reporter for the New York Times described their prayers as merely "neutral."[85] As the services came to an end, so did the participation of most of the city's moderate ministers. Perhaps they felt that they had done all they could and that any further participation would involve them in disputes they considered to be too political. Even had they continued to speak out, it is unclear what effect they would have had. "Religious values are dominant in the lives of only a minority of men," wrote Thomas Pettigrew, a Harvard sociologist. No matter how well ministers used their influence, they could not remove the pressures placed on their parishioners by other institutions and values, and while the Little Rock ministers might have worked harder to calm the situation, they "could not . . . have prevented the 'march of Faubus.'"[86]

Those few who continued to support integration were ostracized, however, and none more than Dunbar Ogden, who was vilified and harassed by segregationists. His well-to-do parishioners withheld their financial contributions, not because he was in favor of integration, so their explanations went, but because he was neglecting his parish duties. People he considered friends either were silent or urged him to find a position elsewhere, reminding him of falling attendance and financial contributions. Eventually he resigned, and the family moved to Charleston, West Virginia, where he became the assistant minister of a Presbyterian church. His son, who had walked with him to provide protection against the mobs at Central High, remained in Little Rock, but segregationists forced him out of his job. Despairing over the lack of support from fellow whites, he left town for California and, while staying overnight in a Tennessee motel, killed himself with a shotgun.[87]

It was becoming clear to southern moderates that if the events at Little Rock taught any lessons, it was the need to speak out against those resisting the Supreme Court. From the fall of 1957 to the end of 1959, several so-called manifestos were published by various groups of Protestant and Jewish clergy calling for freedom of speech, obedience to the law, the preservation of public schools, communication between the races, and prayer. While their implied purpose was to avoid the situation that had befallen Little Rock, most were weighted heavily in favor of discussions of law and order and mentioned desegregation sparingly. Significantly, these pronouncements often emanated from cities such as Atlanta, Houston, and Dallas, whose inhabitants tended to be more moderate on the race question, and where the clergy of major faiths worked in closer contact than did their counterparts in more rural locales. In all cases, the signatories made it clear that they spoke as individuals, not as representatives of any faiths or organizations.

Segregationists drew their own lessons, the primary one being not to risk federal intervention by using the state militia to prevent school desegregation. As school closings in the South became widespread after 1957, the Prince Edward County Educational Corporation in Virginia decided to follow suit and open free private schools for white children, funded by private donations, and housed in church buildings. Senator Harry F. Byrd enthusiastically supported the proposal, and local Baptist, Methodist, Episcopal, and Presbyterian churches offered the free use of their basements and parish halls. In June 1959, the county implemented the plan. It took five years before court challenges succeeded in reopening the public schools, during which time white students had received a minimal education almost completely devoid of extracurricular activities. Black children had received no schooling at all.[88]

The use of church buildings to evade the court decision angered and dismayed prominent Protestant clergy, including Reinhold Niebuhr, Benjamin Mays, and Eugene Carson Blake, who strongly denounced it in the *Presbyterian Outlook*, the national magazine of the Presbyterian Church, U.S.A.[89] "Enforced segregation not only defies the basic law of the land, but, more importantly, contradicts that very Gospel which we are called to preach," read a statement signed and circulated by forty-eight Protestant and Catholic clergymen of Fairfax County, Virginia.[90] The strongest protest, however, came from Rabbi Emmet Frank of Temple Beth-El in Alexandria. During a Yom Kippur sermon, he told his congregation that he had chosen that holy day to "root out the evil in our midst in the form of bigots and hate peddlers who, for a headline, a misplaced vote, would attack minority after minority," for Jews especially should not remain silent in the face of injustice. Byrd and his "invertebrate crew" had "done more harm to the stability of our country than McCarthyism."[91]

Reaction to the sermon was swift. A states' rights group of business and civic leaders demanded that the local Jewish community repudiate the rabbi's "slanderous statements and innuendoes," hinting darkly that if they did not, it would "cause irreparable damage to the hitherto friendly relations between Jews and Christians." When Frank was about to address the Unitarian Church in Arlington, a bomb scare emptied the church moments before the sermon was to begin. Some Jews unsuccessfully demanded that their congregations draft an apology to the senator; others wrote to Byrd and explained that Frank did not speak for them.[92] While a handful of Protestant clergymen publicly insisted that Frank's comments had not threatened interfaith relations, southern Jews were badly unnerved. They were a vulnerable minority, making up little more than half of 1 percent of the entire regional population save for Florida, and they had never forgotten the lynching of Leo Frank in 1915 or the fact that the current president of the NAACP, Arthur Spingarn, was Jewish.[93] Suspicion was rife among Klan members and others that Jews were behind integration, and many southern Jews wanted to put as much distance as possible between themselves and anyone who insisted on racial equality. "If white Christians are fearful, the Jew is panic-stricken," wrote Rabbi Jacob M. Rothschild of Atlanta. "He prefers to take on the protective coloration of his environment, to hide his head in the cotton patch in the dual hope that he won't be noticed and the problem will go away."[94] Harry Golden, a Jewish newspaper editor in North Carolina, believed that Jews feared that Gentiles needed a scapegoat, and if they lost the one they had in blacks, "they might very well look around for another."[95]

Reticence on the part of southern Jews to identify themselves with the civil rights movement varied from city to city. The New Orleans Jewish community was very quiet on the subject of integration, in part because discrimination against Jews was still prevalent in the city's clubs and civic associations, and Jewish citizens feared that if they spoke up against racial discrimination, they would replace blacks as the objects of hatred for lower class whites in outlying towns where anti-Semitism was already considerable. Jews in Atlanta and Dallas were more united, had a fairly good relationship with neighboring Christians, and were more outspoken. Some Jewish businessmen, fearing economic reprisals and/or genuinely supporting their platform, joined the Citizens' Councils.[96] Many southern Jews resented the tendency of national Jewish organizations to speak out against segregation. When the Anti-Defamation League (ADL) of B'nai B'rith publicly supported the NAACP efforts to speed up school integration in the spring of 1958, the editors of Virginia's *Richmond News Leader* rhetorically asked southern Jews what was causing widespread anti-Semitism in a region that had no tradition of it. Perhaps the ADL wanted to identify all Jews with integration, they suggested, thereby stirring up anti-Semitism and giving it a reason to "combat it by declaring, 'Look how much anti-Semitism there is.'" What possible service could "some of the South's many esteemed and influential Jews" find in a "Jewish organization that foments hostility to Jews?"[97]

Many southern Jews asked themselves the same question. "The participation of our 'defense' organization" regarding segregation, wrote Rabbi William Malev of Houston, Texas, "is not an advantage but a liability." Another southern rabbi believed that "Northern Jews should not press Southern Jews to take a stand at present, until the danger of threat to synagogues and Jewish life and limb is passed."[98] The fears were well-grounded. In 1958, a series of bombings rocked temples and Jewish community centers in Miami, Nashville, and Jacksonville. In each case the rabbis connected with the institutions had been warned prior to the attacks to stop discussing integration. Extremists in Atlanta bombed the temple of Rabbi Jacob Rothschild, a strong supporter of civil rights since his arrival from Pittsburgh in 1946. Segregationists did not approve of the integrated meetings at his temple or his socializing with blacks. A group calling itself the "Confederate Underground" claimed credit for the destruction. Catholic and Protestant clergymen decried the violence, as did President Eisenhower, who also complained that the vandals had given the Confederacy a bad name.[99] "It would be the acme of irony," wrote Ralph McGill, editor of the *Atlanta Constitution*, if southern governors deplored the bombing, for it was "not possible to preach lawlessness and restrict it." Rabbi Perry Nussbaum of Beth Israel Congregation in Jackson, Mississippi, sent his sympathies to Rothschild, adding that he doubted that his own congregation would escape a similar fate. Another Mississippi rabbi, Charles Mantinband, of Congregation B'nai Israel in Hattiesburg, agreed, adding that local whites had said that they "will do a better job, when they are ready for Mississippi."[100]

Like Rothschild, Nussbaum and Mantinband were not natives of the South; the former was from Canada, and the latter was born in New York and, although raised in Virginia, attended school in the North. A member of the Southern Regional Council and the Mississippi Council on Human Relations, Mantinband spoke his mind on matters of race, and invited black families to his home; when one fearful Jewish neighbor asked about a particular family, Mantinband replied that they were "some of his Christian friends."[101] When he went on vacation, the local Citizens' Council advised his congregation to rid itself of the "mischief-making rabbi" or else, it warned, "we cannot be responsible for the consequences." The parishioners refused.[102] Nussbaum was more discreet in his dealings with controversial subjects and worked with his parishioners, trying to convince them of the need to support desegregation.[103]

The violence directed at Jewish clergy and institutions "should have shattered the illusions that the Jewish community can be 'neutral' or 'safe,'" wrote two rabbis in 1959, but it did not. Most rabbis insisted that Protestant and Catholic clergymen lead the way in improving race relations before Jews joined them.[104] Christians had created the problems, explained a New Orleans rabbi, and until they took a positive stand, integration would never happen.[105] Fewer realized that extremists did not limit their attacks to any one group in the community, and warned others to take heed. "The attack upon the Negro," wrote Rabbi William Silverman of Nashville, "is the undeniable portent of the attack upon the Jew, and ultimately the Catholic Church, civil liberties, democracy, and Christianity itself."[106]

Had the octogenarian Joseph Francis Rummel, Roman Catholic Archbishop of New Orleans, read Silverman's article, he probably would have agreed with much of it, especially in light of the successful efforts of local segregationists to block his plans to integrate the city's parochial schools. His ban on segregated pews from the city's Catholic churches in 1949 caused grumbling, but there was no outright defiance of his authority until 1955, when he announced that Catholic schools in the Archdiocese of New Orleans would be integrated "not before September 1956." Local Catholics took this to mean that desegregation would occur at that time or shortly afterward, and a vocal and virulent opposition grew. Segregationists burned a cross on his lawn; Catholics among them formed the New Orleans Association of Catholic Laymen under the leadership of businessman Emile Wagner Jr. to pressure Rummel into abandoning his plans.[107] If integration came, wrote one worried parent, "[I would have had to] remove my children from school and deprive them of a Catholic education. . . . I cannot see my daughters intermingling with negro children, especially the negro boys, who are far advance [sic] in their knowledge of sex because of their degraded home life."[108]

Most clerics in New Orleans privately supported the status quo, and several priests were outspoken advocates of segregation, including the Reverends

Joseph Pyzikiewicz in Carrollton, and Martin Burke, a professor of philosophy at Loyola University. Fortunately for Rummel, Burke's racist appeals were challenged on his own territory by the Reverends Louis Twomey and Joseph H. Fichter, described by a sympathetic journalist as "the terrible Loyola twosome whose names stuck in the throats of the Loyola alumni." Although both priests had the archbishop's support, Rummel's failing health and the strong backlash against his plans for parochial school integration (and his unwillingness to mount a protracted fight) meant that the two led an often lonely battle, exacerbated by the fact that the southern province of the Society of Jesus continued to maintain segregated schools.[109] Twomey, who taught labor studies, had been criticizing segregation in New Orleans since he arrived at the university in 1947, always being careful to remind listeners that he was no "Yankee intruder," but "a Southerner, born and raised in the South and proud of most of our Southern traditions. . . . my great-grandfather and five great uncles [were] killed fighting for the South during the Civil War."[110]

Twomey's family history mattered little to white supremacists. He received so much mail from local segregationists and, from farther afield, pro-integrationists, that he created a "Fan/Pan" file to organize it. The letters made for painful reading on their own merits and illustrated in stark terms the laity's unwillingness to follow church mandates even in an institution as hierarchical as the Catholic church. After Twomey delivered a commencement address at Xavier University in June 1955, in which he argued that unjust treatment of blacks would spur the rapid growth of anti-American, Communist ideology, a self-acknowledged Catholic accused Twomey himself of putting such ideas into the head of "the negro," claiming that such "political claptrap" would make blacks "ripe for Communism." Emile Wagner, a Loyola graduate, seconded such views in a letter to the president of Georgetown University. If segregation were a moral wrong, he asked, why had the church not taken a dogmatic position on it before? Wagner had canvassed clerical opinion throughout New Orleans, both Catholic and Protestant, and discovered that "a fairly extensive" number "are convinced that the question of integration has no moral significance."[111]

After Twomey called for racial toleration and integration at an education conference in Baton Rouge, he received many letters of both praise and vilification. "I haven't noticed any Southern rabbis who have shown your kind of courage in speaking out—and we Jews should be the first to do so—for obvious reasons," wrote a New York businessman. A correspondent from Hong Kong commended him for his "criticism of segregation in the US southern states interpreting Christ's teaching on brotherly love among mankind." The positive letters were far fewer than the negative ones he received. A Texan complained that "*any person*—man, woman, preacher or whomever advocates desegregation is lower down than a snake, a skunk and a rat. . . . You are simply criticizing God for making the negro but most of us think He knew what He was doing." A traveling salesman criticized Twomey of talking "of segregation, instead of God" and assured him that in his travels throughout the country, he had discovered that "negros are *not* as good as the white people I know." While Twomey jocularly wrote to a colleague, "I am in a real battle, and I love it," he was dismayed by the tone of the letters. "I never thought that human beings could put into writing what I have received."[112]

Joseph Fichter had also arrived at Loyola in 1947, and his sociological research and numerous publications gave him a profile even higher than Twomey's. Like his counterpart, Fichter had spoken out against segregation from the outset and had also been a consistent critic of police brutality against the city's black citizens. Fichter brought black speakers to campus, worked with the Catholic Commission on Human Rights (CHR), and served as the chaplain for an integrated intercollegiate student association, which became the Southeastern Regional Interracial Commission. (One of the association's members was Aaron Henry, who became the leader of the Mississippi Freedom Democratic Party in 1964.)[113] By the late 1940s, the university's board of directors was increasingly concerned that Fichter was "moving entirely too fast in view of conditions here in the city."[114] Like Twomey, Fichter received his share of hate mail. More was to come after the events of October 1955.

That month, Rummel sent a black priest named Reverend Gerald Lewis to celebrate mass in Jesuit Bend, a small town fifteen miles south of New Orleans. The congregation prided itself on its racial exclusiveness, and when the Reverend Lewis arrived to officiate, several members barred him from the mission. The parish then voted to oppose further assignments of any black priests to any missions within its jurisdiction.[115] Rummel responded by suspending services at the mission and reducing others within the parish. In a pastoral letter, he condemned their action, claiming that it violated "the obligations of reverence and devotion which Catholics owe to every priest of God." Every human, regardless of race or color, "is created in the image and likeness of God." The suspensions would remain in effect until the offenders expressed their "willingness to accept . . . whatever priest or priests we find it possible to send them."[116] "Who decides that a priest may say Mass—the Church or a committee of laymen?" demanded the archdiocesan unit of the Catholic Committee of the South.[117] The *Osservatore Romano* applauded the archbishop's stand, stating that racism denied the universality of Roman Catholicism.[118]

Twomey and Fichter urged Rummel to excommunicate the individuals for their interference in a worship service. The threat of such punishment had effectively ended similar disruptions of church services and classes in Lafayette Parish; when Bishop Jules Jeanmard learned that segregated catechism classes had been held in his jurisdiction and that a catechism teacher opposed to such practices had been assaulted by members of the parish, he ordered that the text of a pastoral letter and decree of excommunication be read from the pulpit of Our Lady of Lourdes Catholic Church, where the violence had taken place. Rummel refused to follow suit, requesting only that the guilty parties pray and reflect on what they had done. Twomey and Fichter renewed their appeals after a white usher ordered blacks at gunpoint to sit at the back of a Catholic church, and again after a black Catholic student was attacked after attending Sunday service at a white suburban parish, but Rummel refused to act. While Fichter later wrote that he "greatly revered" Rummel for his pronouncements on racial equality and an end to segregation, "he was ineffectual as a social activist. . . . because of an excess of prudence and a failure of nerve."[119]

Rummel's failure to act emboldened the segregationists, who continued to pressure him to abandon his plans to integrate the Catholic schools. In July 1956, he announced that unspecified difficulties had caused him to postpone integration until at least the autumn of 1957, when it was expected that integration of the public schools would begin. Flushed with victory, the lay association wrote to Pope Pius XII, questioning Rummel's authority to define a matter of morals, and requested that he order Rummel to cease both his plans for integration and his harassment of the association's members. An official from the Vatican, speaking for the pope, refused the request and rebuked the association.[120] Such a reprimand carried little weight and was more than made up for by praise from sympathizers. Senator James Eastland of Mississippi told his constituents that southerners owed the people of southeastern Louisiana "a great debt of gratitude for resisting integration moves by the Roman Catholic church."[121] Hate mail to Twomey and Fichter continued. "In so much as you are not satisfied with segregation in the South," one woman wrote Fichter, "I suggest that you go up north where you can eat & sleep with the negroes if you like." Another warned that it was people like herself who filled the churches, paid for the parochial schools, and supported him and other liberal priests—and who could withdraw such financial support and put them out of work if they saw fit.[122]

After continued disturbances in local parishes, including the beating of two black youths who sat in the front pew of a white Catholic church in March 1959, Rummel notified the attackers and the members of the lay association that he would excommunicate them unless they ceased their agitation for segregation within the churches. Wagner obediently disbanded the Association of Catholic Laymen, but that was the only result of Rummel's threat. The handful of frustrated liberal Catholics in Louisiana watched as the public schools were desegregated in 1960 in advance of the parochial schools. That fall, the Reverends Lloyd Andrew Foreman and Jerome Drolet, a Methodist minister and a Catholic priest, respectively, escorted several black children to an integrated school, braving a screaming mob of women, and their example served to break a proposed boycott.[123] Mathew Ahmann, executive director of the new National Catholic Conference for Interracial Justice, while pleased with the progress made by Protestant churches (particularly the black churches) in the field of civil rights, regretted that "Catholic activity in the interracial movement in the South has in recent years all but come to a halt."[124]

Finally, in March 1962, Rummel ordered the integration of New Orleans parochial schools. Militant segregationists picketed his residence and called for him to rescind or delay his order, but the aging archbishop refused. When several spoke at a Citizens' Council rally, Rummel warned them to stop their activities; instead, Leander Perez, the president of the Plaquemines Parish Council, told his supporters to withhold contributions to the church until Rummel backed down. With the Vatican's approval, Rummel excommunicated Perez and his two allies. All three insisted that they would remain Catholics and expressed dismay at the evidence of Communist ideology within the ranks of the church hierarchy, illustrated by the push for integration. By the fall of 1962, desegregation of the city's parochial schools had been accomplished peacefully.[125]

While liberal religious journals and their readers applauded Rummel's decision, Fichter felt that the archbishop should have imposed excommunication in the earlier cases involving interference with church services and beatings, and worried that Rummel had punished Perez and his colleagues for what they had said, thus raising questions about freedom of speech within the church. Other prelates, such as Bishop Jeanmard and Archbishop Joseph Ritter of St. Louis, used the threat of excommunication effectively, the latter doing so at the first sign of lay challenges to his authority when he ordered the integration of parochial schools in 1947, far in advance of the public schools. Rummel, by comparison, had allowed secular officials to make the first move toward school integration and had excommunicated opponents only when the integration of public schools was underway. The church hierarchy had considerable ecclesiastical authority in predominantly Catholic New Orleans. Rummel's age and infirmity doubtless had as much to do with his unwillingness to do battle (he resigned in October 1962, a month after parochial schools began to be integrated, and died three years later at the age of 86), as did the hostility of many Catholic priests toward integration.[126] But it was a clear indication that religious bodies—even one considered to be authoritarian—would lag behind the rest of society in putting creeds into practice.

Although they were members of the nation's majority faith, Protestant ministers had even less influence because of the congregational polity of most denominations. Despite a southern rabbi's claim that he and his colleagues should not be expected to do much until after Protestant ministers had acted positively on race relations, because they "could change the situation overnight," such expectations as to what Protestant clergy were capable of doing were wildly inflated.[127] By the end of the decade, tensions in the South had developed to such an extent that it became dangerous for a minister to even discuss the race issue, let alone attempt to integrate his church. In most instances, suggestions by church boards to cease all talk of controversial issues were enough to make most clergy shy away from any mention of desegregation; when that failed, threats of physical harm often succeeded in dampening a cleric's enthusiasm for social activism. In one case, however, criticism of a minister for a rather mild interview he gave to a national newsmagazine led not to a retreat on his part but to renewed courage to follow his convictions.

A handsome, gray-haired man in his early forties and a graduate of Union Theological Seminary in Richmond, Virginia, Robert Blakely McNeill had first broached the subject of race relations as chair of the Christian Relations Committee at the 1950 Alabama synod of the Presbyterian Church, U.S. There he presented a report that criticized racial discrimination, admitted the inevitability of desegregation, and warned that blacks would no longer accept the paternalistic attitudes of whites. The report outraged conservative clergymen and elders, but after a heated debate it passed by a vote of forty-five to twenty-two. Moving with his wife and family to Columbus, Georgia, in 1952, McNeill became pastor of the First Presbyterian Church, where he departed from tradition and appointed a white minister to serve at one of the black churches in town, earning him the enmity of the local Klan.[128] He believed in "creative contact," in which representatives of both races would work together on city councils, school boards, medical societies, ministerial associations, and grand juries. Whites could no longer pretend to understand the desires and needs of blacks, he argued, and once this was realized, white ministers could help bring about change, though their power should not be exaggerated. "Ours is hack work; we are the plodders," he wrote in an article for *Look* magazine. But the church, he insisted, even with all its human failings, still embodied the "true meaning of the redemptive society." Passage of just laws was important, but only the church could alter people from within and, accordingly, would "always be as strong as it is self-critical." The church, for McNeill, was the "conscience of society," and there he chose to remain.[129]

A handful of segregationists, including church elders, hoped otherwise. The article had unleashed a storm, and it had little to do with what he had written. He had met with the enemy, a northern reporter who had traveled to the South to convince ministers to write articles debunking the notion that southern preachers were solidly behind the Klan. McNeill's opponents called on the Southwest Georgia Presbytery to investigate their pastor, which it did and found no grounds for dismissal. Threats continued, but they only made him more committed to working for social justice.[130] Impressed with his courage, the editors of *Look* decided to do a follow-up story on him. McNeill asked his parishioners to reserve their judgment until after they had read the article. Steve Lesher, the author, wrote a concluding draft in which he commented that Columbus had "looked at its own bare conscience, and common sense has reared its level head."[131]

The draft proved to be too optimistic. In June 1959, the presbytery notified McNeill that it had decided to let him go. The following Sunday, after Mc-Neill had concluded his sermon, a representative told the congregation that the time had come when "what has been the voice of the pulpit, should also become the voice of the people of the church as a witnessing whole."[132] Some choir members burst into tears. "If we kick a Christian man and his family out like this," one asked, "then what hope have we?"[133] In his last sermon, delivered that night, McNeill described the differences between what he called an "Organization Church" and a "Proclaiming Church." The former, he said, substituted a "manager for a minister, promoter for pastor, reporter for preacher," and measured its success in terms of numbers of parishioners and contributions. "The caliber of its gospel depends upon the satisfaction of its clientele," and thus became subordinate to the institution. Was this the kind of church they wanted?[134]

Three days later, he suffered a massive heart attack. Some opponents said that it was a "fake attack" designed to get sympathy; others said that the Lord had "finally taken care of him." Concerned friends set up a reception table outside his hospital room to screen visitors after a segregationist had harangued his wife at his bedside. After four days, he regained consciousness. Offers of employment came from throughout the country, and after he recovered, he and his family moved to Charleston, West Virginia, where he became assistant pastor of Bream Memorial Presbyterian Church. The regular minister was none other than Dunbar Ogden of Little Rock; a third exile, the Reverend John Payne, former chaplain at the University of Tennessee, also worked in the church after he was forced out of his parish for opposing the work of the House Un-American Activities Committee.[135] Nestled in the Kanawha River valley, surrounded by the Appalachian Mountains, the three nicknamed the region "the Ecclesiastical Siberia of the church," but all agreed that it was "a lovely place in which to be exiled." According to McNeill, there was no "abolitionist temperament" in the congregation; the parishioners "just don't like to see people pushed around or forced to conform to conventional standards."[136] Neither he nor Ogden ever involved themselves in the struggle for civil rights in such a dramatic fashion again; after their tribulations in Columbus and Little Rock, they took a well-earned rest from controversy.[137]

What made a handful of southern clergy speak out against racial discrimination when the majority of voices in the pulpit remained relatively silent, leaving the initiative to the segregationists? Clearly the larger group, as defenders of the status quo, reflected the majority viewpoint, whereas the liberal clergy were trying to alter tradition. Most of the conservative clergy and their parishioners believed that God had ordained racial segregation. As they believed segregation to be a Christian doctrine, it necessarily followed that those who sought to undermine it were atheists, and they concluded that as all atheists were Communists, all integrationists took their orders from Moscow, and were thus seeking to impose a foreign ideology on the South.[138] For his part, Will Campbell believed that racism had become part of the segregationist's "religious heritage" and a "heresy" with which Protestantism had not yet learned to cope.[139]

Unlike their conservative brethren, the ministers who called for moderation did not do so with a united voice. Few were fundamentalists, and hence did not rely on the Bible for solid scriptural arguments in favor of desegregation. Instead, they often tried to persuade listeners of the validity of their argument without directly mentioning integration, focusing instead on the need for peace, law, and order. As practitioners of either the Social Gospel or neoorthodoxy—both of which stress change at the corporate, institutional level rather than at the individual level—such clergy did indeed bring an "outside" doctrine to the discussion of southern mores, for neither had many adherents in a region whose clergy more often emphasized personal piety.

In their study of Little Rock ministers, sociologists Ernest Campbell and Thomas Pettigrew classified the moderate or liberal ministers into three groups to explain their reaction to the city's school desegregation crisis: innovators, influentials, and inactives. Innovators tended to be young, new to the community, and thus more willing to risk a position in which they had not spent much time. Several of the clergymen under discussion fit this description.[140] Hughes, Graetz, Campbell, and McNeill were all recent graduates of seminaries and had been employed only a short time; Ogden had been in Little Rock for only three years before the school desegregation crisis; and Rabbis Nussbaum, Mantinband, and Rothschild were all recent transplants from the North. Most were affiliated with local ministerial associations from which they could get some measure of support; Graetz was responsible to a black congregation, certainly an atypical situation for a white southern minister.

The innovators, as described by Campbell and Pettigrew, were clearly in the minority. The larger groups of nonsegregationist clergy were the inactives and the influentials. The former had spent more time in their churches, were considerably older, and, while integrationists at heart, feared to jeopardize their well-earned positions. Many favored desegregation, but their desire to maintain the peace of their congregations and community (and their own standing in each) outweighed their desire for racial justice.[141] In the end, the influentials and inactives agreed to days of repentance and the passage of resolutions and manifestos, because they "relieved the influential ministers' compulsions to act, answered national pressures on them to act, and symbolized their desire to put the whole experience behind them and get on with the noncontroversial aspects of church work."[142] The fault lay not with the ministers alone, noted a professor of religion at Andover-Newton Theological School. A church with stable membership had lay leaders who challenged the authority of the minister, "whom they expect to outlast even as they predate his arrival." Such leaders sought to "circumscribe the minister's freedom to be controversial," but those ministers who became too caught up in church administration, the budget, and social customs reflected a Christianity that had "lost the capacity for transcendence."[143]

McNeill, Ogden, and the others, in attempting to resist the constraints placed on them, partially succeeded in making their views known, although their efforts to communicate their beliefs and educate their parishioners were often blunted by their opponents and by their short tenure. They were not prophets out of the Old Testament, nor did they see themselves as such. Instead, they considered their ministries as ones of reconciliation, often tending to emphasize admittedly vague concepts of fellowship and humility as well as respect for law and order—a phrase that would have somewhat different connotations several years later. Still, "as timorous as we might have sounded to non-Southerners," McNeill wrote in the early 1960s, "we held the fort until reinforcements finally arrived."[144]

And the reinforcements did arrive, however belatedly, to lend support to a civil rights movement that was in the process of redefining itself. While school desegregation remained important, the focus in the 1960s shifted to direct-action protests in which people of all races and religious persuasions took part. The struggles over public schools had been fairly localized, but the massive street marches in southern towns, freedom rides, and other demonstrations depended on large numbers for their visibility and success. Such factors opened the way for northern priests, ministers, and rabbis not directly affected by southern segregation to involve themselves in the struggle for racial justice. Church boards and denominations would continue to pass resolutions and debate the wording of official pronouncements into the next decade and beyond, but many northern clerics believed that the time for speeches was past. It was now time for action.

two

But an angel of the Lord said to Philip,
"Rise and go toward the south . . ."

ACTS 8:26

Going South

Northern Clergy and Direct-Action Protests,
1960–1962

When asked in 1964 what mistakes he may have made in leading the civil rights movement, Martin Luther King Jr. replied that his "most pervasive" one was believing that "white ministers of the South, once their Christian consciences were challenged, would rise to our aid." Instead, he reported, when he appealed to them, "most folded their hands—and some even took stands *against* us."[1] As the goals of the civil rights movement broadened to demand an end to racial discrimination in all facets of American life—using techniques such as sit-ins, freedom rides, and marches—fewer southern clergy were willing to risk their jobs and their careers by participating in demonstrations that their congregations perceived to be as menacing as school integration.

Protesters from outside the region, including clergymen, made up the difference. Many northern clergy who went south sincerely believed they were doing what their southern colleagues wished to do but could not—and were often told that was true, but only in private.[2] Not only did their presence in the streets underscore the moral nature of the civil rights movement, but it made for a good story in the media, and thus gained increased coverage. King and other members of SCLC knew that the media were more likely to cover whites, and so they repeatedly issued calls for white clergy to take part in protests in several cities, especially when the demonstrations appeared to be flagging. By casting their lot wholeheartedly with civil rights activists, some of the northern clergy antagonized white southerners, who increasingly saw themselves as being besieged by the rest of the country, thus stiffening their resolve and resistance. Other northern clergy were unfamiliar with the history of white southern challenges to segregation, which resulted in a tendency to pass judgment on the complacency and complicity of all whites who were not joining in the demonstrations.

National awareness of direct action began in February 1960, when four black college students who had been refused service at a Woolworth lunch counter in Greensboro, North Carolina, remained seated until the store closed. As sit-ins spread, student activists formed the Student Nonviolent Coordinating Committee (SNCC) to organize the demonstrations, and sympathizers in the rest of the country picketed chains whose stores refused to serve blacks in the South. Sitting-in was a dangerous task, for segregationists harassed and beat the peaceful protesters, often with the support of police officials, who broke up such scenes by arresting the sit-in participants for breach of the peace. Will Campbell traveled throughout the South on behalf of the NCC, observing such demonstrations to take notes in case he was called as a witness for trials, but this passive role made him feel both uneasy and guilty, especially when he witnessed segregationists beating students with brass knuckles and burning them with lit cigarettes.[3]

Church groups and clergymen in the North as well as the more cosmopolitan centers of the South praised the self-composure and goals of those taking part in the sit-ins.[4] In fact, wrote one historian, it was not the students' neat appearance alone, nor their close ties to the black church, but the "support of a large number of religious bodies within the white community" that helped make the sit-ins respectable for liberal whites, who were themselves looking for opportunities for "social activism and involvement."[5] The General Assembly of the United Presbyterian Church and the NCC endorsed the protests, as did the National Council of the Episcopal Church, over the strong objections of Bishop Charles Carpenter of the Episcopal Diocese of Alabama. Thirty Protestant, Catholic, and Jewish clergymen in the Ministerial Association of Chapel Hill, North Carolina, passed a resolution in March 1960 praising the student participants in a local sit-in for their nonviolence.[6]

At a conference in February 1960, the board of directors of the Episcopal Society for Cultural and Racial Unity (ESCRU), founded in December 1959 in Raleigh, North Carolina, also pledged its support to those who demonstrated peacefully against segregated public facilities. Such public protests disturbed some delegates at the conference who wanted ESCRU to merely discuss strategy, reflecting, perhaps, the longstanding conservatism of the denomination that has been described as "the Republican party at prayer."[7] However, those who wished it to become "an uncompromising action arm," in the words of John Morris, the executive secretary of the new organization, carried the day. The entire Christian life was determined by tension between the perfect and the possible, he explained, and there was a time for militancy and a time for discretion. If he was to err, said Morris, it would be "on the side of militancy, as a fool for Christ's sake" in an attempt to bring about change.[8] Recognizing that the Episcopal Church was guilty of perpetuating racial discrimination within its own churches, ESCRU asked its members to protest against segregated church organizations and functions.[9] The churches "will not escape involvement," warned Morris. If religious bodies refused integration, it was very probable that "churchmen will find themselves picketing their own institutions. . . . Students at lunch counters and churchmen trying to set their house in order need only look to Jesus for both an example of direct assault on sin as well as for the strength to persevere."[10]

The churches' failure to integrate themselves while their denominational boards were supporting such aims in the secular realm did not escape the notice of segregationists. When the Reverend Merrill Proudfoot, a white Presbyterian minister from Knoxville, Tennessee, asked the assistant manager of a department store to desegregate his eating facilities on moral grounds, the man replied that other equally devout ministers did not agree with such views. Besides, he added, when the "major churches in town each have a number of Negro members, then it will be time for you to talk to Rich's about desegregating our lunch counter."[11] Aware of such discrepancies, black students began "kneel-ins" in which they attempted to worship alongside whites in their segregated churches. Beginning in the border states and continuing throughout the South, the "kneel-ins" attracted much attention among clergy and the religious press. While ushers in some churches turned blacks away, dismissing them as "outside agitators" with no serious desire to worship, some ministers recognized in these protests a presence that confronted "the Christian conscience with a concrete flesh-and-blood test on the crucial moral issue of racism and segregation."[12] Religious organizations such as ESCRU and NCC praised the demonstrators for their Christian witness, but segregationists did not hesitate to threaten them with arrest.[13]

The venom directed against white clergymen who welcomed blacks into their churches or supported sit-ins was considerable. When the interracial ministerial alliance of Knoxville, Tennessee, called for the desegregation of lunch counters, unsigned handbills began appearing throughout the city, warning readers that the "Communistic Ministerial Association," an "organization of sixty-two White Trash and African Idiots" was calling for race-mixing. If a minister advocated such ideas, he was a "rotten Communist and . . . unfit to stand in the pulpit. Will you run him off or let him run you off? Remember the Church is yours and does not belong to him."[14] Accordingly, few southern white ministers involved themselves in such affairs, leaving the protests to black students, a handful of white allies, and black ministers such as Birmingham's Fred Shuttlesworth. At the same time, opportunities for involvement of northern clergy were developing, as civil rights leaders understood that when sit-ins were conducted at the local level, national press coverage was not always forthcoming. It would take large-scale demonstrations such as the freedom rides and marches to secure widespread attention and the desired federal intervention.

The freedom rides were the brainchild of the Congress of Racial Equality (CORE), whose national director, James Farmer, understood that his organization needed to stage an event that would gain widespread publicity with minimal participants and funding, both of which were in short supply for CORE. Expanding on the theme begun in the Journey of Reconciliation in 1947, in which an interracial team of pacifists tried to integrate bus stations in the Upper South, a small integrated group of activists traveled throughout the Deep South on Greyhound and Trailways buses in May 1961, testing Supreme Court decisions that declared segregated terminal facilities for interstate travel to be unconstitutional. At Anniston, Alabama, mobs set fire to one bus, attacking the travelers with bottles and rocks until they could make it to safety; other white segregationists wielding lead pipes beat the passengers who made it to Montgomery.[15] Faced with the threat of continued bloodshed and negative international publicity, President John Kennedy sent federal marshals to protect the riders when Alabama Governor John C. Patterson refused to have his state police forces "escort invaders all over Alabama to permit them to flagrantly violate our laws and customs."[16]

Once the White House had intervened, northern liberals believed that CORE had made its point and urged it to call off the freedom rides and pursue desegregation in the courts during what Attorney General Robert Kennedy termed a "cooling-off period."[17] Black civil rights leaders angrily insisted that a cooling-off period had been in effect since the Civil War and that blacks were tired of listening to whites advising them to be patient.[18] But not all whites agreed with Kennedy, and among their ranks were clergymen who continued to take part in freedom rides throughout the summer of 1961. Even before the first freedom riders had left Washington, D.C., on May 4, two Roman Catholic priests of the Society of St. Joseph, an order created in 1871 to work with freed blacks, had received word of the trip and planned to help CORE members desegregate lunch counter facilities at the bus terminal in Jackson, Mississippi. One was the Reverend Richard Wagner, a twenty-nine-year-old chaplain at Xavier University in New Orleans, a black Catholic college, and a teacher at the all-black St. Augustine's High School. The other was the Reverend Philip Berrigan, eight years his senior and also a teacher at St. Augustine's.[19]

"I have the impression that I first met Phil Berrigan on the back of a Wheaties box when I was twelve," recalled James Forest, a Catholic pacifist and antiwar protester, years later. A tall, athletic man with a crew cut, Berrigan did look like the all-American type. He had seen action in the Second World War as an enthusiastic second lieutenant in a field artillery battalion in France. It was while training in boot camps in the South that he first came into contact with racial segregation, which repulsed him. He returned to Holy Cross College in Worcester, Massachusetts, to continue his education after the war and entered the Society of St. Joseph, becoming an ordained priest in 1955 and moving to New Orleans shortly afterward.[20] The tense racial situation among the city's Catholics disturbed him. Segregation, he wrote, not only denied human solidarity and destroyed national reputation, but also denied the church's doctrine of the unity of all believers.[21] Given the volatile nature of the racial crisis in the South, preaching the common humanity of blacks and whites was not an easy task. During a sermon in which he reminded his listeners about the biblical injunction to love one's neighbor, irate parishioners repeatedly interrupted him, complaining that they hadn't "come here to listen to this junk" but to hear Mass. Berrigan refused to end the sermon, and almost fifty people left the service.[22]

When Berrigan and Wagner received word of the freedom ride, they traveled to Atlanta, where the Very Reverend George F. O'Dea of Baltimore, Superior General of the Society of St. Joseph contacted them and ordered them to return to New Orleans immediately. Although O'Dea's terse explanation to reporters was "I did it, but I have no comment," there was some reason to believe that Bishop Richard Gerow of Jackson had warned him that if they continued on their journey, he would see to it that all Josephite Fathers would be thrown out of Mississippi.[23] An angry Berrigan criticized his superior's attitude as one of "glibly" repeating the lofty religious messages but failing in the "desperately important encounter with those who need us, in the hard and hot work of the vineyard where hope is extended."[24]

Protestant and Jewish clergy unencumbered by such strict obedience to a religious order were more successful in taking part in the freedom rides. After seeing newspaper photographs of the violence in Anniston, the Reverend William Sloane Coffin Jr., Presbyterian chaplain at Yale University, and John Maguire, professor of religion at Wesleyan University in Middletown, Connecticut, decided to hold their own freedom ride. Several black and white ministers expressed their support for the idea but refused to go, out of fear of losing their influence with their college administrations; only two other white professors and three black students agreed to join them. After receiving enthusiastic support from a crowd of Yale students and faculty at a rally on the New Haven Green to protest the beating of the freedom riders in Montgomery, the group flew to Atlanta, where they would begin their journey.[25]

Little in Coffin's background suggested the radical nature his life was taking on. Born in 1924 into a wealthy and prestigious New York family (his uncle Henry Sloane Coffin was president of Union Theological Seminary), Coffin attended Phillips Academy in Andover, Massachusetts. He joined the army when the United States entered the Second World War, and during his training in Georgia he witnessed segregation for the first time. A visit to the concentration camp at Dachau after the war further confirmed his disgust of prejudice. After graduating from Yale University in 1949, he attended Union Theological Seminary for one year, worked for the Central Intelligence Agency during the Korean War (from 1950 to 1953), then continued his theological studies at Yale Divinity School, graduating in 1956. Ordained a Presbyterian minister that same year, he returned to Yale, this time as chaplain, in 1958.[26] Described as "an athletic-looking, collegiate fellow who rides a motorcycle around the campus," Coffin had a reputation for sharp wit. When his future father-in-law, pianist Arthur Rubinstein, told him, "I'm not sure I want a Billy Graham in the family," Coffin responded by saying that he did not want a Liberace in his. Others found him too young and brash. "We expect him eventually to mellow," one Yale professor icily told a reporter.[27] Such a prospect seemed unlikely. Impressed with the nonviolence of the Montgomery bus boycott, he had invited Martin Luther King Jr. to address Yale students in 1959. He spent the next summer in Africa working with the precursor of the Peace Corps, Crossroads Africa, and had learned firsthand that American claims of democracy and freedom versus Communism tyranny sounded hollow to people familiar with the racial crises in Little Rock and Montgomery.[28]

But it was Coffin's journey to Montgomery on a Greyhound bus that first catapulted him into the national spotlight, and not all the coverage was favorable. The conservative editors of *Time*, who had criticized the original freedom riders for "provoking trouble" and then finding "the trouble they wanted" when they arrived in Alabama, took a dim view of both the journey and the man. Described as a person who "has never lacked for privilege of his own," he was portrayed as a young upstart seeking publicity, which is exactly how Harvard graduate Robert Kennedy saw it. "Those people at Yale are sore at Harvard for taking over the country," joked the attorney general, trying to downplay the chaplain's involvement, "and now they're trying to get back at us." Privately, Kennedy was incensed at Coffin's decision to embark on a dangerous journey the same day he had requested civil rights activists to suspend the freedom rides.[29]

After holding a press conference in Atlanta, where Coffin responded to questions about his Yale affiliation by telling reporters that he was exercising his academic freedom, the travelers left for Montgomery. A crowd of surly whites met them at the station, kept away from the freedom riders by National Guardsmen, whose bayonets did not prevent the mob from showering Coffin and the others with rocks and bottles until the Reverends Ralph Abernathy and Wyatt T. Walker of SCLC arrived to pick them up and drive them to the safety of the Abernathy home, where the group met with King and other SCLC officers to work out their strategy for integrating the Montgomery bus terminal.[30] The following day, Coffin and his companions purchased tickets at the terminal, and then sat down with Abernathy and Walker to order coffee at the lunch counter. A hostile crowd cheered as the sheriff arrested the clergymen and theology students as they were about to pay their bill. "Now everyone is happy," commented Major General Henry V. Graham, state adjutant general. "This is what they wanted and we have accommodated them. They've been arrested quietly, like they wanted to be, and now I'm happy too."[31] While unpleasant, the stay in jail was relatively quiet and safe. The white travelers were placed apart from potentially violent white prisoners, while their black companions shared a cell with black inmates. Students and faculty at Yale and Wesleyan raised bail for the five prisoners, who were released the next day.[32]

Appearing "tired and unshaven," Coffin told reporters that they had all been detained for more than twenty-eight hours, "a precedent which is blatantly illegal and a travesty of justice." Noting that he was a member of the advisory council for the new Peace Corps, he warned reporters that "any men or women who will go to Tanganyika, the Philippines, and Colombia this fall will bear the burden of Montgomery, Alabama."[33] One month later, a Jackson judge sentenced every member of Coffin's group to one month in jail, a verdict that was appealed and eventually overturned in 1965.[34]

Coffin's usefulness to the movement was unquestionable. The freedom rides depended not only on the participation of people from outside the community, but publicity as well. In a racist society, the attention given to the journey and arrest of one white individual, especially a prominent man of the cloth, insured that Americans would at least take notice of the injustices suffered by blacks under segregation. This pattern would continue for the rest of the decade, for the travails, beatings, and deaths of white participants would always receive more attention than that given to black civil rights workers. If the role of pastor was to witness to evil, then Coffin had more than matched word with deed by being arrested, even if the brevity and conditions of his jail term were very dissimilar to those endured by lesser-known white activists, let alone blacks. As a result of his actions, Coffin received some "very supportive mail" from white southern clergy who thanked him for "doing for us what we couldn't do for ourselves." He had helped provide them with an issue that could be talked about, he recalled, "and so there was a group that understood what we were doing and that it was helpful to their cause as white moderates."[35]

Still, Coffin made little effort to understand the plight of the whites whose challenges to segregation were less dramatic, but no less sincere, than his own. When he returned to Montgomery to stand trial, Clifford and Virginia Durr, the city's most eminent white champions of civil rights, invited Coffin to their home for drinks. According to Mrs. Durr, Coffin said that he could not come unless she invited all the other defendants, some of whom were black. Because of the city's tense atmosphere, the couple felt they simply could not host an interracial party. While Coffin was "very sweet about it," she said, his refusal angered her. "Cliff and I had been on the front line for about ten years, and this man was making us feel that we were just sorry Southern segregationists because we refused to have the black defendants to our house for a drink." Such attitudes were common among northern liberals, she continued, "but they always got on the airplane to go back home, where they were perfectly safe."[36] The nature of the freedom rides, however, put a premium not on working within a southern community for an extended time but on short trips, publicity, and arrests of as many people as possible. The dramatic nature of this form of protest led other white clergymen to follow Coffin's lead and supplement their sermons on racial harmony with visible action.

Scholarly-looking Robert McAfee Brown decided to accompany an interracial group of rabbis and Protestant ministers on a freedom ride from South Carolina to Tallahassee, Florida, in June 1961. Like Coffin, he was a Presbyterian minister affiliated with a prestigious institution, Union Theological Seminary, where he had been professor of systematic theology since 1953. Born in Carthage, Illinois, in 1920, Brown received a bachelor's degree from Amherst College in 1943, the year before he married and was ordained a minister in the United Presbyterian Church in the U.S.A. The plight of European Jews during the Second World War disabused him of his previously held pacifist beliefs, especially when he met Polish refugee students at the Jewish Theological Seminary near Union, where he was studying for his divinity degree under the tutelage of Niebuhr and Bennett. Discussions with them made it clear that pacifism was not an effective challenge to the evil of Nazism. He gave up his seminary exemption to join the Chaplain Corps in the United States Navy, and after the war went to Columbia University, where he received his doctoral degree in 1951. While teaching religion at Macalester College in St. Paul, Minnesota, Brown worked on the staff of Democrat Eugene McCarthy, a Catholic, during his 1952 campaign for Congress. There he came into contact with Catholics at the beginning stages of the Protestant-Catholic dialogue in the United States and began collaborating with other ecumenists, most notably the Reverend Gustave Weigel, S.J.[37]

Brown soon came to realize that the study of theology did not exist apart from the secular world, especially after attending a church service in East Berlin in May 1960, where he was amazed at the courage of the parishioners who dared to attend church in a state that frowned upon such activities. Whatever else theologians were, he noted, they were people of the world and did not cease being people when they became theologians.[38] Years later, he recalled that the faculty at Union often talked about the nation's racial problems, but after a while, he said, discussions became arid and "you find that you feel you're beginning to be a little bit of a charlatan, if you can commend that other people go and get arrested and maybe beat up, but you're not willing to run that risk yourself." When CORE asked Brown to take part in a freedom ride in June 1961, he readily assented. Training in nonviolence prior to the trip helped them cope with the insults and abuse from segregationists. Most of the journey was relatively uneventful, but trouble arose when the group tried to use the "whites only" facilities; nobody cared when they integrated the "colored" restrooms or waiting areas.[39] He later described how he had the less-than-heroic task of desegregating restrooms, finding himself spending "four days and nights urinating to the greater glory of God."[40]

When the group sat down to order coffee at Tallahassee's airport terminal, a threatening mob quickly surrounded them, but police averted violence by arresting the freedom riders for "unlawful assembly with incitement to riot." The group spent several days in jail, visited frequently by black ministers and laypeople. The only threats to their safety came from white inmates who singled out a rabbi but left him alone when the other clergy surrounded him for protection. A few days later, the local court released them on bail. Brown had no illusions that journeys like his would change the hearts of the segregationists outright; their real purpose, in his mind, was to encourage white southern liberals who might be able to capitalize on any weakening of segregationist resolve in their communities.[41]

The freedom rides continued sporadically through the summer, tepidly supported by the National Council of Churches, which refused to endorse them by name, mentioning only the "non-violent movement."[42] Such half-hearted advocacy did not sit well with ESCRU, which organized a prayer pilgrimage in which twenty-eight black and white Episcopal priests from across the country would meet in New Orleans on September 11 and travel north in time to attend the General Convention of the Protestant Episcopal Church in Detroit one week later.[43] The purpose of the trip, according to John Morris, himself a participant, was to preach "a sermon in action . . . to set the household of faith in order so that prejudice may be eliminated."[44] The participants did not see themselves as "ecclesiastical freedom riders, trying to shame recalcitrant church institutions" through adverse publicity, wrote the Reverend Merrill Orne Young of New York, although they would "certainly rejoice if any concrete change for the better were to come about in any of the places we visited."[45]

Among the travelers was the Reverend Malcolm Boyd, a priest who had already received national coverage for his views on the church's mission in the world. Born in 1923, Boyd grew up in a prosperous New York family, later moving west with his mother when his parents divorced. He attended the University of Arizona, working at a local radio station, which led to a job with the National Broadcasting Company, where he became the first president of the Television Producers Association of Hollywood. Unhappy with his vocation, he entered the Church Divinity School of the Pacific in 1951, studied at Oxford in England, worked in the industrial missions of the Anglican Church, and returned to the United States to be ordained in 1955. Two years later, he became rector of a lower-middle-class parish in Indianapolis, where he remained until 1959, when the parish was closed because of the migration of white members to the suburbs.[46]

His multifaceted career made him something of a celebrity on the lecture circuit, and in 1959 the administration of Louisiana State University asked him to be guest speaker. Boyd used that forum to deliver a sharp rebuke to the churches for their conformity and hesitancy in fighting racism.[47] Speaking engagements in the South quickly dried up after that, and those that had been scheduled beforehand were abruptly canceled. "[W]e received word of difficulties you met while at Louisiana State University," wrote the chaplain of Mississippi Southern College, explaining why "it would be an injustice to you and to the great cause of our program to have you appear as our principal speaker for the year 1960." Should the "climate of our society change in the coming years," he added, "we will be not only proud but happy to present you as a main speaker of our Religious Emphasis Week." How society was to be changed if freedom of speech was abrogated was left unclear.[48]

After leaving Indianapolis, Boyd became college chaplain at Colorado State University, where he was quickly dubbed the "espresso priest" for his practice of holding drama, poetry, and Bible readings at a university coffeehouse, where he discussed the roles of the individual and rebel in society. Rumors quickly spread that he was hearing confessions in taverns and conducting communion using beer and potato chips. Although Boyd denied such stories, he insisted that for the modern minister, "confession is not heard so much in confessional booths and in rigid form. It is over the oatmeal or martini that people, without form, express themselves."[49] Bishop Joseph S. Minnis of the Episcopal Diocese of Colorado took a dim view of such "beatnik" activities. Complaining that playing bongo drums "with doleful countenances or enraptured twisting of the body have no place in the worship of the Church," he argued that no sacrament should be given to anyone who had been drinking alcohol or was under the influence of any other drugs, for "we are created in God's image and that dignity is a precious attainment. . . . You can't think of yourself as a beloved son of God, and at the same time go around with matted hair, a dirty body, and black underwear."[50]

Boyd sharply disagreed, asking, "Must one wear white underwear and smell pretty to be a good Christian?"[51] Feeling that he could neither disobey Minnis nor curtail his preaching style, he resigned. "Although my ministry is not specifically to beatniks," he wrote in his letter of resignation, "I believe that Christ loves the beatnik just as much as the more socially respectable front-pew member of a church congregation." He upbraided Minnis for his use of the word "beatnik," calling it an ugly stereotype, and reminded him that the church would deny its "reason for being" if it adhered to labels, be they "'negro,' 'Jew,' 'wop,' 'dago' . . . or 'beatnik.'" After all, he wrote, Christ, "in His earthly life . . . identified Himself with the publicans and the frequently socially outcast more than with the pharisees and the self-labeled 'nice' or 'best' people."[52] He could have added "homosexual" to the list of those barred, for he himself was gay at a time when homosexuality was not publicly discussed. Years later, he wrote that his life was "split down the middle. When I preached to a congregation about being honest, I could not be honest. I had to disguise my true feelings."[53] Not surprisingly, Boyd became a champion of dissent and the rights of other minorities who were forced to adopt the practices of the dominant culture in order to survive; indeed, the theme of masks, of disguises, permeated much of his writings, including several plays on race that he wrote in the 1960s.

The clash between Boyd and Minnis became feature stories in the *New York Times* and the *Christian Century*, prompting a flood of telegrams and letters.[54] People of vastly different religious persuasions sent Boyd sympathetic messages. A self-described fundamentalist woman in Colorado thanked him for bringing religion back to "Young College Folks," for "God knows how many Atheistic Professors there are tearing every thing that is good and fine into shreds and dragging it in the dust before your children today," adding that she didn't care where he saved souls. Another complimented him on his stand against making Christianity a religion for "gentlemen and suburbanites," adding that the apostles "must certainly have smelled of fish." Fewer correspondents opposed him, one of them a temperance supporter who disliked the fact that he had set foot in a tavern. She criticized Boyd for resisting Minnis's counsel, complaining, "not submitting yourself to your Spiritual Pastor and teachers, you are trying to bring Corruption into our Church. . . . Our kind bishop is only trying to guide and save you. He knows what's right."[55]

Offered several jobs by sympathetic ministers and bishops, Boyd chose to serve as chaplain at Wayne State University in Detroit, Michigan, arriving there when the call came for priests to take part in the Prayer Pilgrimage. When he asked the Right Reverend Robert DeWitt, Episcopal Bishop of Michigan for his advice, DeWitt advised him to act on his own judgment, but he brought up several important points for Boyd to ponder. As students saw the civil rights movement as one of the most significant moral issues of the time, wrote DeWitt, Boyd's involvement would have a "positive impact" on his work as chaplain. However, he added, had not Robert Kennedy advised Americans not to take part in further freedom rides and similar ventures? DeWitt told Boyd that he also had to weigh the "risk and realities" involved in such a decision. His responsibility, in DeWitt's view, was to his new duties at Wayne, which would be "difficult to discharge from prison!" Because Boyd had not been at Wayne for long, he had had "no opportunity to build up any spiritual 'equity' there, DeWitt continued, pointing out that "letters from prison, like Paul's and Bonhoeffer's, had great meaning for those who knew Paul and Dietrich." Nonetheless, he offered to support Boyd regardless of his decision.[56]

Boyd decided to take part in the journey from New Orleans to Jackson, Mississippi, where fifteen were arrested when they tried to integrate the bus terminal there. The publicity surrounding the Prayer Pilgrimage made the priests special targets for the authorities, who arrested all the participants except the Reverend Layton Zimmer, chaplain of Swarthmore College, and Boyd, who were not in clerical garb. After their release, they continued their journey to the University of the South in Sewanee, Tennessee, founded by the Episcopal Church, where they were denied service at the university's Claremont Restaurant because they were an interracial group. The priests began a sit-in, and an angry crowd, many of whose members had been drinking, gathered around the restaurant and later burned a cross on its lawn. Police arrested the interracial group, but the school's regents, upset over the negative publicity and fearful that the clergy would make good their threats to hold a hunger strike in protest, agreed to pass a resolution desegregating the restaurant the following month. Satisfied with the outcome, all the priests left Sewanee, save for two, who chose to remain in jail during the Protestant Episcopal General Convention, to remind their brethren in Detroit of the continuing racial discrimination.[57]

Throughout their journey, the priests discussed the problem of segregation with local priests and laypeople. At the convention, they spoke of their "admiration for the clergy of the South . . . who are ministering faithfully under an almost unbearable tension between what the Gospel says and what their people will hear," reminding their audience that the North was not free of complicity in segregation, especially residential segregation in places such as Detroit. Clergy could expect little of God's mercy, they warned, "if out of willful blindness, indifference, or fear of inconvenient consequences Churchmen in the North tolerate in comfort the evil which is crucifying brave Churchmen in the South."[58] A Dearborn newspaper tried to deflect such criticism by publishing statistics showing that their city had the highest percentage of Christians per square mile in the state, leading Boyd to ask why the churches had lost sight of important matters and "become something like the John Birch Society."[59]

The conclusion of the pilgrimage proved anticlimactic. A Mississippi court dismissed charges of disturbing the peace "out of respect for the Episcopal Church" the following April, but when nine of the priests returned to Jackson to intercede for other nonclerical freedom riders in jail, requesting that charges against them be dropped as well, the judge responded by announcing that the priests would be tried as originally scheduled. After a jury found one priest not guilty, charges against the others were dropped, to the relief of most of the priests, who were nonetheless troubled by the impression that they had received special treatment due to their profession. ESCRU continued to stage sit-ins throughout the region, targeting the University of the South after the

regents admitted that they had only planned to study a proposal on desegregation, not implement it. In a sad and ironic footnote, after another interracial
group held a sit-in at the restaurant in April 1962, they were followed by a
white kitchen employee in his car. As he sped up to overtake them, he lost
control and crashed. As he lay dying on the roadside, the Reverend Robert
Chapman, one of the black priests, gave him last rites.[60]

Parishioners' reactions to their priests' taking part in the Prayer Pilgrimage
were sharply divided. In some cases, half the congregation (usually well-to-do,
young, and recent members) approved, on the grounds that the priests were
putting their creed into action. Most opposition came from the vestry, of
whom only one-quarter agreed with the priests' actions and who complained
that they had not sought the vestry's approval for the trip, were interested only
in the publicity, and did not care that church integration could mean a
decline in property values. Such statistics suggest that members of the vestry
were conservative pillars of the community, a helpful situation when it came
to fundraising and church suppers, but not one that boded well for a clergyman who wanted to involve himself and his congregation in more controversial issues.[61]

While able to publicize the racist policies of institutions affiliated with the
Episcopal Church, ESCRU was seldom able to change them. Officials and
supporters of the organization discovered that they had little support from
the church hierarchy when they led campaigns to protest discrimination at
schools affiliated with the denomination. After the Lovett School in Atlanta
turned down the application of Martin Luther King III, a decision supported
by the Episcopal Diocese of Atlanta, Rev. John Morris led pickets outside the
school throughout 1963, losing his license to officiate at Episcopal services on
the grounds that he had "abused the hospitality of the Diocese" of Atlanta.
The church had other means of combating criticism too. When Ralph Mc-
Gill, editor of the *Atlanta Constitution*, criticized the church's handling of the
Lovett affair in an interview with the *Diocese*, the monthly diocesan publication, Canon Milton Wood had 13,000 copies of the issue destroyed and others
reprinted with portions of the interview deleted. The Right Reverend Randolph Claiborne Jr., bishop of Atlanta, refused to criticize Wood.[62] Malcolm
Boyd, who left Wayne State University to become ESCRU's field secretary in
1963, failed to enlist the support of Bishop Daniel Corrigan, director of the
National Council of the Episcopal Church, in a drive to add more black
members to the predominantly white board of trustees of St. Paul's College
in Lawrenceville, Virginia. Corrigan declined, insisting that Boyd had conducted his investigation in a slipshod and subjective manner.[63] "Idealistically,
I have to keep telling myself that the church will step out in front" to lead the

way in civil rights, Morris told a reporter, "but realistically I don't believe any longer that it will."[64]

Although Episcopal priests were less than successful in challenging their own institutions, Protestant and Jewish clergy had helped begin making the issues of discrimination visible to a broader public. Their willingness to risk injury and imprisonment indicated a desire to make their religion relevant by addressing racial problems facing society. Unfortunately, most media coverage continued to revolve around the plight of such clergy while they were in the South; criticism of racial discrimination elsewhere, as noted by the Episcopal priests in Detroit, was largely underreported. Northerners, therefore, could be lulled into a false sense of security that racial discrimination in the South was of far greater concern, largely because it was so obvious and visible a problem south of the Mason-Dixon Line.

Certain southerners realized the power of such coverage. Beginning in the fall of 1961, SNCC members had embarked on a black voter registration drive and a series of boycotts designed to desegregate public facilities in Albany, Georgia. Police Chief Laurie Pritchett had studied the methods of nonviolent protest and ordered his men to refrain from violent attacks in public, thus removing a significant source of publicity for the movement. The arrival of King, Abernathy, and other SCLC leaders to join forces with SNCC workers at the end of the year created interest but little success, for as demonstrations continued into the summer of 1962 with no tangible gains, fewer blacks were willing to go to jail. National interest in the protests waned, and with no overt violence, the Kennedy administration felt there was no need to involve itself in what it viewed as a local matter; Robert Kennedy even sent Pritchett a telegram congratulating him on keeping the peace. When forty-six white ministers and four black clergymen went to the White House to present petitions with 5,000 signatures calling on President Kennedy to use his influence to bring about negotiations between Albany's city commissioners and the civil rights workers, he had an assistant meet with the black ministers as the remaining clergy stood outside the gate in silent prayer. He took no action on the petition.[65]

In order to gain support and publicity, King issued a national appeal to clergymen asking them to join the Albany Movement. An interracial group composed of Protestant ministers, rabbis, Catholic laypersons, and four Protestant churchwomen answered the call. On August 28, they marched to the city hall, where Pritchett met them and prayed with them before ordering them to move on, telling them that they should return home and fight sin and violence in their own cities. The seventy-five demonstrators, whose ranks included the Reverend L. W. Halverson, a Lutheran from Chicago, and Rabbi Richard Israel of Yale University's Hillel Foundation, refused and were arrested as onlookers cheered.[66]

The prisoners had no doubt as to the righteousness of their actions, which allowed them "to bear witness to a belief in morality and justice," as one said. "We didn't come here to be holier than thou," Halverson told reporters. "We have a serious problem of our own up North. But we were answering the call of a group of Christians for help." Few journalists took notice of the event, coming as it did at the end of months of demonstrations that were clearly, and quickly, winding down. Those who did could not resist tweaking the group for what was admittedly a short-term gesture, for most returned home the next day after paying bond, and the remainder were released before a week had passed. When several ministers began a fast, reporters from *Time* suggested that it was motivated more by "glancing at the prison fare of cornbread, beans, greens, and fatback" than by any spiritual concerns. The editor of the *Albany Herald* criticized the protesters, quoting Matthew 6:5 in his editorial: "And when you pray, you must not be as the hypocrites, for they love to stand and pray in the synagogues and on the street corners, that they may be praised by men."[67]

The majority of local white ministers wanted nothing to do with the visitors, and the Albany Ministerial Association rebuffed their request for a conference. Of the few who had shown any interest in the year-long demonstrations, only the Reverend Brooks Ramsey of First Baptist Church had tried to establish a dialogue between the races. In spite (or perhaps because) of such activities, an usher at his church had three black students arrested when they tried to enter the all-white First Baptist to attend a service. When Ramsey, who had not known of the affair, later discovered that they had been sentenced to a $200 fine or sixty days in jail, he told his congregation, "This is Christ's church and I can't build any walls around it that Christ did not build, and Christ did not build any racial walls." Following his comments, church deacons passed a resolution, not to support the admission of blacks to the church but to state that their pastor had the right to "exercise a free pulpit according to his own sincere Christian convictions" even if church members disagreed with him—which, given the times, was an unusually progressive step.[68]

Despite the brevity of the white outsiders' visit, as well as its lack of any palpable gains (including favorable publicity), SCLC's explicit invitation to northern clergy represented a significant shift in tactics. Before, black ministers had emphasized working with their white counterparts in the communities they were trying to desegregate, and had been unsuccessful in convincing most of them of the morality of their cause. By securing the assistance of outside clergy, they were able to work with a select group of individuals who had the freedom of action that southern pastors lacked. Northern clerics were less likely to be fired from their positions for taking part in a civil rights demonstration, as long as it was in the South, and were therefore in a far better position to join forces with King and SCLC. Direct-action techniques such as freedom rides and marches had shifted the emphasis from school integration to dramatic, high-visibility demonstrations that had the potential to reap needed publicity and funds for civil rights organizations. Footage of whites in clerical collars or yarmulkes made interesting copy, but it also conveyed the message that the movement was as much a moral and ethical issue as it was a political, social, and economic matter and, as such, affected all Americans. A disturbing corollary for some, however, was the possibility that those who demonstrated might be considered to have cornered the market on moral purity.

Few wrestled with this problem as intensely as Will Campbell, and fewer still did so in a public setting. As a native southerner working for one of the most liberal religious organizations in the country, the National Council of Churches, he was troubled not only by the negative depictions of white southerners but also by the increasing identification of black civil rights workers as "an instrument in the hand of God" (to quote the editors of the *Christian Century*) and by the tendency of sympathetic northerners to compare demonstrators with Old Testament prophets. To Campbell, this implied a too-close connection between temporal society and the will of God. Blacks and whites alike were governed by self-interest, and no matter how idealistic the ends were, human corruption and failure always managed to find their way into social organizations, even SNCC and SCLC. Besides, Campbell noted, civil rights demonstrations were not based solely on the Gandhian philosophy of satyagraha, or "truth force"; they also involved economic pressures such as boycotts of stores and public facilities that failed to serve black customers on an equal footing with whites.[69]

Campbell was arguing against a concept of absolutes—absolute right on one side of the equation (those for civil rights) against those who lacked moral virtue (those opposed)—and for a more balanced appraisal of the sinfulness of humanity. This approach was firmly grounded in the theological doctrine of original sin, but it made a poor rationale for social change, because it condemned any tactic that involved pressure. His emerging belief that one did not have to do anything to be a Christian, that one could simply "be" a Christian and the rest would take care of itself, may have been effective on an individual basis in his later ministry to Klan members and white supremacists, some of whom turned away from violence, but it never satisfactorily explained how broad social changes would come about.[70]

The insistence on a shared sinfulness, moreover, sometimes blinded Campbell to the fact that some individuals had more pronounced moral failings than others. He agonized over how both sides lacked an understanding of "the depth and complexity of human sin," including citizens of Albany who had cheered the arrest of the northern protesters and were "[j]ust good church-goers, good people" unwilling to see how their racial pride jeopardized their claim to faith.[71] These views, appearing in the *Christian Century*, quickly earned Campbell the criticism of those who felt that his sympathetic portrayal indicated approval of what the authorities were doing in Albany.[72] He pointed out that sympathy was not agreement, but NCC officials were unconvinced and asked him to submit all future articles and speeches to their New York offices in advance. He refused. No one in Mississippi had requested that of him, he wrote, "and I would not do it for what was supposed to be the most liberal and free religious organization in the nation." Campbell, who had been shunned by family and their friends for his support of civil rights, was now finding himself under attack from liberals.[73]

Campbell was correct to insist that "[t]he "racist is the greatest challenge the church faces today in both the North and South," and argued that this meant that the church should "love and redeem [the racist with] the same love that it is commanded to shower upon the innocent victim of his frustration and hostility," as they were both God's children.[74] While the concept of loving one's enemies was very much in keeping with biblical injunctions, it was unclear how to carry out the redemption. Martin Luther King Jr. had originally hoped that moral suasion would convince whites of the justice of the cause for which he fought, but he soon came to see that coercive economic strategies such as boycotts were also necessary to bring about substantive change.

By the autumn of 1962, it was evident that even stronger measures were necessary to combat racial discrimination. Nowhere was this more apparent than at the University of Mississippi in Oxford, where Governor Ross Barnett and segregationist mobs attempted to prevent the enrollment of James Meredith, a black Korean War veteran, which had been ordered by a federal district court judge.[75] Few clergymen had been willing to challenge segregation in Mississippi, let alone the edicts of a governor at the height of his popularity, and those who were known to be racial moderates were ridiculed and threatened.

In one case, a segregationist editor had composed a telegram attacking the Citizens' Councils for their bigotry and irreligiousness, signed the Reverend Edward Harrison's name to it, and had it read on a local television station. The ensuing controversy forced the moderate rector of St. Andrew's Episcopal Church in Jackson not only to resign but to leave the state. He later expressed his disappointment in a letter to James Silver, history professor at the University of Mississippi, noting that people who never paid dues to the Citizens' Councils gave "all the support the CC could hope for by their silence." Rabbi Charles Mantinband agreed, writing to Silver that there was "a conspiracy of silence in respectable middle-class society. Sensitive souls, with vision and the courage of the Hebrew prophets, are drowned out."[76]

Mantinband himself did not retreat into silence. Resisting the pressure from segregationists and fearful Jews in his own congregation, he continued to work with the Southern Regional Council and the Mississippi Council on Human Relations, and protested Barnett's actions.[77] A handful of clergymen from Oxford did likewise, foremost among them the thirty-six-year-old Duncan Gray Jr., the Episcopal rector of St. Peter's Church and son of the Episcopal Bishop of Mississippi. Gray had long been supportive of school desegregation, traveling to Tougaloo College in Jackson to meet with Aaron Henry, the black leader of the Clarksdale branch of the NAACP. Along with seven other white clerics, including the Reverend Wofford K. Smith, the university's Episcopal chaplain, Gray had issued a statement in September 1962 calling on their congregations to "act in a manner consistent with the Christian teaching" and to "exert whatever leadership and influence possible to maintain peace and order among us." Gray went on the university's radio station later in the month to urge students to accept Meredith.[78] On September 26, the eight churchmen, "convinced of the Christian call to obey the laws of the land," sent Barnett a telegram warning him of the "anarchy thrust upon us and our people through continued defiance of federal court orders." They received no reply.[79] Unfortunately, according to Russell Barrett, a professor of government at the university, the ministers were "a small collection of voices" whose message was ignored by other ministers and local newspapers alike.[80]

By the evening of September 30, thousands of angry students and outside agitators, many of them armed, had arrived on the campus and cheered retired Major General Edwin Walker when he climbed atop a Confederate monument and congratulated them on their defiance of the federal government. Duncan Gray also climbed up and asked the students to disperse, calling instead for peace and reconciliation. Walker replied that Gray made him ashamed to be an Episcopalian, and those nearest the statue hauled the priest off the monument, pushing him and Wofford Smith through the mob, where they were struck repeatedly until the campus police rescued them. More violence ensued later that night, when the mob set fire to cars and threw Molotov cocktails and bricks at the vastly outnumbered federal marshals, who responded with tear gas. Sporadic firing began, and by the end of the night, two civilians had been killed. The arrival of federal troops early the next morning quelled the riot, and Meredith was enrolled.[81]

The seven clergymen declared the following Sunday a day of repentance. "You and I didn't go out there and fire the guns," Gray told his restive and sullen congregation. "Yet you and I, along with every other Mississippian, are responsible in one degree or another for what happened. For we are responsible for the moral and political climate in our state which made such a tragedy possible."[82] Once again, the segregationists ignored them, which was relatively easy given that few local newspapers gave them any coverage. Those magazines that might have carried news of the sermons, such as the bulletin of the NCC, had lost subscriptions in the South as a result of sympathetic coverage of the civil rights movement and enthusiastic support of integrated churches. "The U.N., integration, the National Council of Churches, civil liberties in general—there is a tendency to lump them all together under the heading of Communism," Gray told a reporter.[83] Others were able to give a more realistic appraisal of the connection between racial discrimination and Communism, including Ross Barnett's second cousin, who blamed him for making her work as a missionary in Nigeria all but impossible. "You send us out here to preach that Christ died for all men," she complained, and then "make a travesty of our message by refusing to associate with some of them because of the color of their skin. . . . Communists do not need to work against the preaching of the Gospel here; you are doing it quite adequately." (Her mother told reporters that "Antonina doesn't understand that Ross is doing the best he can.")[84]

Few people in Mississippi saw the connection as perceptively as did Antonina, and many insisted that integration was a Communist plot. Mantinband was eventually forced to leave his congregation in 1963 for his support of Meredith's enrollment, as were several Protestant clergymen. Other clergy, suspicious of the efforts of such activists, elected Rabbi Benjamin Schultz, a transplant from New York City, to the presidency of the regional ministerial association in 1964 on the basis of his support for states' rights, anti-Communism, and the removal of subversive intellectuals from college campuses.[85]

The riot at Ole Miss helped awaken the nation to the realization of how far segregationists would go to preserve their way of life. It also illustrated a need for continued, organized involvement for racial justice. For the Kennedy administration, it would take the form of civil rights legislation; for the churches, a greater level of organization across denominational boundaries. By the end of 1962, Protestants, Jews, and Catholics at the highest denominational levels were ready to work together to address social concerns in the spirit of ecumenism that had blossomed at the Second Vatican Council earlier in the year. Of these concerns, few loomed as large as the fight for civil rights. Realizing this, the social action departments of the National Catholic Welfare Conference, the Synagogue Council of America, and the NCC made plans to invite almost 700 delegates from over 70 religious groups to attend the opening session of the National Conference on Religion and Race in Chicago in January 1963.[86]

three

Thus says the Lord to you: "Do not fear or
be dismayed at this great multitude; for
the battle is not yours but God's."

2 CHRONICLES 20:15

The Call to Battle

The Churches and Synagogues Enter the
Civil Rights Struggle, 1963

Until 1963, most of the clergy's involvement in the civil rights movement had been the work of individuals or small groups who had responded to calls for support from major civil rights organizations; the churches, as organizations, had largely been content to issue proclamations and resolutions. The televised violence inflicted on civil rights workers in Birmingham would awaken liberal clergy nationwide to the fact that such declarations, however well-meaning, were largely ineffectual. Organization and action on the part of the clergy were needed to combat discrimination on three fronts: in the southern communities where SNCC and SCLC were sponsoring demonstrations; in Washington, D.C., to push for stronger federal civil rights legislation; and in the communities of the North and Midwest, where white liberal clergy urged their representatives and senators to support such legislation. Such tasks demanded coordination, and new religious organizations were formed specifically to provide the organizational skills and funding needed to fight the battle in all three areas, while at the time furthering the cause of interfaith cooperation. These activities did not preclude the need for personal witness, and individuals such as Brown, Boyd, and Coffin continued their work in this area; others, including the Reverend Eugene Carson Blake, Stated Clerk of the United Presbyterian Church in the U.S.A., and Rabbi Abraham Joshua Heschel, the fifty-six-year-old professor of Jewish Ethics and Mysticism at the Jewish Theological Seminary in New York City, would take their first steps into the world of social activism in 1963.

Although a slight man only five feet six inches tall, Heschel possessed a commanding presence. His strong bass voice and his full beard, turning whiter as the years progressed, gave him the appearance of an Old Testament prophet, or even of an anthropomorphized God, according to several of his colleagues in the civil rights and antiwar movements.[1] The analogies were fitting, for Heschel had spent his life writing about the relationship between God and humanity. According to rabbinic theology, the divine or holy presence in the world has always been affected by human deeds, which, if good, hasten the redemption of the presence and of the world itself. Heschel's definition of Jewish religion was "the awareness of God's interest in man, the awareness of a covenant, of a responsibility that lies on Him as well as on us." In his view, God needed humanity "for the attainment of His ends," and religion was "a way of serving these ends."[2] Yet belief without action was incomplete, he wrote, for more was needed than inward piety: the Lord "asks for the heart because He needs the lives," because it is through them "that the world will be redeemed."[3]

Few people were better suited to putting into words the sense of anguish over discrimination and persecution than Heschel, whose life and work represented a link between eastern European Jewry decimated by the Holocaust and the activist American clergy of the 1960s. He "felt within himself the world's pain," one of his colleagues explained, "which most of us can conceive only in the mind."[4] Born in Warsaw, Heschel was descended from several generations of prominent Hasidic rabbis. The wisdom he found among the works of the Hasidic masters was to have a lasting influence on his life, particularly the conflict between a loving God and the persistence of evil in the world, which he never fully resolved in his writings or his approach to life. He left Poland in 1927 to study at the liberal rabbinical seminary at the University of Berlin and the Hildesheimer Seminar, the Orthodox seminary. He accepted much modern philosophy, but never forgot the fervent piety of the Hasidic community and tried to bridge the two in his work. Heschel received his doctoral degree in 1933, and later began teaching at the Central Organization for Jewish Adult Education in Frankfurt am Main, where he began denouncing the Nazis. In 1938, he was among the thousands of Polish Jews deported by the Nazis and placed in a detention camp on the German-Polish border. After relatives brought him back to Warsaw, he left for England in July 1939 and from there traveled to Cincinnati to teach at Hebrew Union College.[5]

Six weeks after he left, Germany invaded Poland. Twenty-six years later, in an address given at Union Theological Seminary on the occasion of his acceptance of a visiting professorship there (the first Jewish theologian to be so honored), he described himself as "a member of a congregation whose founder was Abraham, and the name of my rabbi is Moses. . . . My destination was New York, it would have been Auschwitz or Treblinka. I am a brand plucked from the fire, in which my people were burned to death."[6] Although grateful for the opportunity to teach at Hebrew Union College, Heschel was not happy there. He learned before the war was over that the Nazis had murdered his family; adding to his loneliness was the fact that he was not yet fluent in English. Moreover, the college was so enamored of Reform sentiments that its cafeteria served non-Kosher food, a situation he abhorred. In 1945, Heschel accepted a position at the Jewish Theological Seminary in New York City as Professor of Jewish Ethics and Mysticism and became an American citizen.[7]

For the next decade and a half, Heschel concentrated on his academic responsibilities and his writing, particularly *Man Is Not Alone: A Philosophy of Religion* and *God in Search of Man: A Philosophy of Judaism*, both of which received critical acclaim for their probing insights into the process and meaning of revelation, ethics, and the sense of God's mystery and glory; Reinhold Niebuhr considered him "a commanding and authoritative voice not only in the Jewish community but in the religious life of America."[8] In the vastly expanded version of his dissertation, published as *The Prophets* in 1962, Heschel discussed at length the "intellectual relevance" of such individuals. Immersing himself in their writings, he described himself as "being exposed to a ceaseless shattering of indifference." One could no longer remain prudent or impartial, for the prophets "remind us of the moral state of a people: Few are guilty, but all are responsible." Such reflection gave way to a desire for action, and he, like Amos and Isaiah before him, was ready to speak out against injustice.[9]

His forum was the Edgewater Beach Hotel in Chicago on January 14, 1963, where he delivered the keynote address to the National Conference on Religion and Race, an assembly of 657 clerical and lay representatives from 67 Protestant, Catholic, Jewish (mainly Reform), and Greek Orthodox organizations and denominations. It was precisely because the churches and synagogues as institutions had not adequately confronted the problem of racial discrimination that the social action departments of various organizations felt compelled to sponsor the conference. Planned in part to commemorate the centenary of the Emancipation Proclamation, its primary purpose was to call together the first joint assembly of major religious groups to discuss the racial crisis from a moral and religious standpoint. In addition to Heschel, speakers included Benjamin Mays, president of Morehouse College in Atlanta; Roman Catholic Archbishop Albert Meyer of Chicago; Rabbi Julius Mark, president of the Synagogue Council of America; and the Reverend Martin Luther King Jr.[10]

Heschel's address set the tone for the entire assembly. "At the first conference on religion and race, the main participants were Pharaoh and Moses," he began. "The outcome of that summit meeting has not come to an end." Pharaoh was still not ready to capitulate, and although the exodus had begun, it was far from completion; in fact, said Heschel, "it was easier for the children of Israel to cross the Red Sea than for a Negro to cross certain university campuses." The spirit of religion called for the uniting of what lay apart, he urged, for regarding people according to skin color was "more than an error," it was "an eye disease, a cancer of the soul." And more insidious than that evil was indifference to evil, for it was "more universal, more contagious, more dangerous."[11]

The rest of the speeches sounded similar themes of a common humanity under God and the responsibility of the churches to follow their creeds of universal love and fellowship by working for an end to racial discrimination both within their own houses of worship and in the larger society. One of the more eloquent calls to arms was given by King, who reminded his audience that the church had been "content to mouth pious irrelevancies and sanctimonious trivialities," remaining "silent behind the anesthetizing security of stained-glass windows." If it continued to do so in the face of growing racial tensions, it would become "little more than an irrelevant social club" with only a tenuous tie to religion. The conference's concluding "Appeal to the Conscience of the American People" echoed such sentiments, noted the participants' sorrow over their churches' late entry into the struggle for civil rights, and called for all Americans to eradicate racial prejudice and work for minority voting rights and equal protection under the law. All were fully aware that their efforts to create a favorable moral climate for racial justice had just begun.[12]

Of the formal speeches, the only one that raised eyebrows was Will Campbell's, who reiterated his familiar refrain that it was probably too late for the institutional churches to act; the only service they could provide was of a reconciling nature after racial disputes had been solved, if then. The greatest contribution religious communities could make was to "preach and proclaim and live their own particular" religious beliefs, and if people could not say "this is what it means to be a Jew, this is what it means to be a Christian, this is how we behave because of what we believe," then all well-intentioned efforts would fail, including the conference.[13]

Editorial reaction to the gathering was mixed. The Reverend John LaFarge, S.J., senior editor of *America*, praised it as a historic first effort to convene members of three major faiths in a single ecumenical gathering on behalf of a social issue; the editors of the *Commonweal*, the *Christian Century*, and members of the Central Conference of American Rabbis viewed the conference in much the same light. The editors of *Time*, fond of mocking those clergy who involved themselves in direct-action protests, now criticized the churches for not doing enough. Religious institutions, the editors claimed, had "never summoned enough resolution, originality or unity to help the country significantly in dealing with racial discrimination," and their participation in the National Conference had shown that they were "still unable to offer much wisdom." Ignoring most of the speeches, the *Time* editors focused on Campbell's criticism and the admonition of Episcopal lay theologian William Stringfellow, a white attorney from Harlem, who told the assembly that the only practical and decent thing it could do at this late hour was weep.[14]

Stringfellow had more acerbic things to say, which went unreported by *Time*. After Heschel's address, he stood and accused the assembly of being "too little, too late, and too lily-white"—on the surface a valid charge, for only three of the speakers were black. What he either failed to mention or did not know was that black religious groups and denominations had been invited to send delegates but did not. Other participants—including Jean Russell, a white civil rights activist from Tennessee; Rabbi Irwin Blank; and Anna Arnold Hedgeman, a black churchwoman who had been involved in civil rights at the political and denominational levels—agreed with his indictment that white liberals had arrived on the scene belatedly without a real understanding of the problems faced by blacks and were thus unable to remedy the situation.[15] Equally telling was the conversation Russell had with a black taxi driver en route to the Edgewater Beach Hotel. When asked about the nature of the convention, she explained that it was a religious conference on race relations. The cab driver laughed. "Well, honey," he told her, "you be sure and let us know downtown what you all decide."[16]

Such skepticism was understandable. Nine years before, religious denominations had responded to *Brown v. Board of Education* with a flurry of resolutions and promises to work for an integrated society and eradicate discrimination within their own households of faith. Well-meaning as they were, little else had been attempted either by the denominations or by religious organizations such as the NCC. It had been left up to individual ministers, rabbis, and priests, or small organizations like ESCRU to bear lonely witness against racial injustice.

The Chicago conference, however, was not simply one more forum to preach against racial discrimination. Claims that the churches were too late to do anything were certainly too extreme. While it may have been naive to expect the same institutions that had given religious sanction to slavery and segregation to be at the cutting edge of the civil rights movement, at least the conference participants understood that repentance was the first step toward reconciliation. Every speaker acknowledged that the churches had lagged behind other sectors of society in breaking down barriers between people, but the fact that they were late did not absolve them of the responsibility to shoulder some of the burden. None of the delegates considered the work complete when the conference ended. Before the sponsoring committees left Chicago, they established the groundwork for a network of similar conferences throughout the nation, which would assist local religious leaders in their attempts to solve the specific racial issues facing their own communities, such as equal access to public accommodations and open housing. A steering committee chose ten cities, including Chicago, Oakland, Detroit, New Orleans, and Atlanta, for these regional conferences on religion and race and moved the headquarters for the National Conference from Chicago to New York City.[17]

These grassroots movements wasted little time in getting down to business. Participants attended workshops to learn how churches and synagogues could lobby for civil rights legislation. While the southern conferences on religion and race concentrated on desegregating public accommodations, their northern and midwestern counterparts spent much of their time fighting for fair housing laws. In April 1963, 800 Protestant, Jewish, Catholic, and Greek Orthodox clergymen and lay leaders held a conference on religion and race in Rhode Island to demand such legislation from its state assembly. In Washington, D.C., forty-one Protestant, Catholic, and Jewish leaders under the leadership of Archbishop Patrick O'Boyle, head of the District's Roman Catholic archdiocese, formed the Interreligious Committee on Race Relations, which participated in civil rights rallies and successfully petitioned the district commissioners to pass antidiscrimination ordinances; members also resolved that their churches would neither accept contracts from construction companies that had discriminatory hiring practices nor build in segregated areas. The Episcopal Diocese of the District of Columbia withdrew its request for construction of a church in Belair, Maryland, on the grounds that the community was notoriously restricted. The Des Moines and Chicago conferences on religion and race issued similar declarations later in the year.[18] Few clerics failed to take note of the ecumenical significance of the gatherings. "Look what the race problem is doing for us," Roman Catholic Auxiliary Bishop Leonard Cowley of St. Paul said with regard to the city's conference on religion and race. "It's the first time we've sat down together. It took the race problem to get our committee together."[19]

Despite this promising beginning, religious organizations never contributed sufficient funds to the National Conference to enable it to carry on a sustained battle against racism. In two years its budget was pared down from $50,000 to $13,000, and it was forced to close its New York headquarters in late April 1964. Its remaining funds were sent out to the fifty or so local conferences on religion and race, which continued their lobbying efforts and programs to educate white parishioners and civil servants on the immorality of racial discrimination. Other ventures not affiliated with the National Conference continued the fight, however. Episcopal priests helped create the Urban Training Center for Christian Missions in Chicago to work in the inner cities; Protestant, Catholic, and Jewish clergy were instrumental in preventing a county council in Maryland from rescinding ordinances providing for equal accommodations in public places. Interfaith councils in Miami, Omaha, Seattle, Portland, and St. Paul took part in local civil rights marches and called upon state legislatures to support federal civil rights legislation and eliminate poll taxes and bans on interracial marriage. In July of 1963, seven Roman Catholic nuns, the Sisters of St. Francis, and a priest joined students who were picketing the Illinois Club for Catholic Women at Loyola University in Chicago for its refusal to include black women as members. Shortly after the demonstrations began, the club reversed itself and opened admission to Catholic women of all races, but the mother superior received so many letters criticizing the nuns' participation that she asked them not to accept an award from the Chicago commission on human relations for fear of bringing further attention to their stand.[20]

Important as such efforts were, the specific gains remained mixed at best. While some clergy proved themselves effective lobbyists, much of their involvement remained at the level of counseling and community education, hardly surprising in light of the commonly held view of the pastor as counselor. (The growing network of contacts between ministerial associations and clergy of different faiths throughout the Midwest, however, would ultimately prove helpful in the passage of the Civil Rights Act of 1964.) Perhaps most importantly, these ecumenical efforts showed that growing numbers of white clergymen, nuns, and laypersons, saw civil rights as a moral issue. While few were vilified to the same extent as their colleagues in the South (for example, the black population in the midwestern states was comparatively small, and therefore advocating the desegregation of public facilities there did not generate much hostility), northern clergy and laypeople met harassment for their challenges to residential segregation, which was one of the most divisive racial issues outside the South.

Despite these local efforts throughout the country, most Americans remained focused on the South during the spring and summer of 1963. Prejudice and discrimination prevailed throughout the country, but they were more readily visible there. It was also easier to call for changes in a distant part of the country; as one observer put it, "a widely held rule of thumb is that the farther away the ministers are from their home churches, the more liberal they are on all issues."[21] Still, there was good reason why many Americans found the moral issues surrounding the southern civil rights movement especially compelling. In the spring of 1963, when they could turn on their televisions and see police dogs and fire hoses turned on nonviolent black marchers, seldom had the evils of racism seemed so clearly defined.

Southern blacks had always been physically and emotionally victimized by the treatment they received under the system of segregation, of course, but few whites paid much attention or were fully aware of the brutality until they witnessed it openly on television. Civil rights leaders were determined to bring the inherent violence of segregation to as wide an audience as possible. Focusing on Birmingham, Alabama, the SCLC began a campaign to desegregate public facilities and places of employment and to provoke city leaders, particularly Commissioner of Public Safety Eugene "Bull" Connor, to a confrontation that would result in federal intervention.[22]

Most of the city's moderate white clergy counseled against both the violence perpetrated by white segregationists and the pressures put upon white authorities by black activists. Dismayed by Governor George Wallace's announcement in January 1963 that he would personally stand in the schoolhouse door to prevent the integration of the University of Alabama, ten Jewish, Catholic, Protestant, and Greek Orthodox clergy from Birmingham issued "An Appeal for Law and Order and Common Sense," hoping to dissuade Alabamans from trying to subvert the Supreme Court decision. "In these times of tremendous tensions, and change in cherished patterns of life in our beloved southland," the appeal began, "it is essential that men who occupy places of responsibility and leadership shall speak concerning their honest convictions." Admitting that they did not have answers to all the questions, and professing sympathy for southerners who resented the court order, they nevertheless declared that "defiance is neither the right answer nor the solution. . . . inflammatory and rebellious statements can lead only to violence, discord, confusion and disgrace for our beloved state." Challenges to desegregation should be brought peacefully to the courts.[23]

These sentiments might have been notable had they been voiced in the wake of the *Brown* decision, but coming in 1963, they were unremarkable and ineffectual. When the SCLC began its campaign of nonviolent direct action on April 3, such voices of moderation became more muted as the white community tried to create the appearance of a united front.[24] Eight of the clergymen who had signed the appeal now turned their criticism on the civil rights workers, in an open letter published in the April 13 edition of the *Birmingham News*. Without mentioning either Martin Luther King Jr. or his organization by name, Bishops Charles C. J. Carpenter, Paul Hardin, Nolan Harmon, and Joseph Durick, Rabbi Milton Grafman, and the Reverends Earl Stallings, Edward Ramage, and J. T. Beale questioned the wisdom of demonstrations "directed and led in part by outsiders." They recognized "the natural impatience" of groups who felt that their hopes were only slowly being realized but insisted that their actions were "unwise and untimely." Open negotiations between whites and members of "our own Negro community" would achieve the desired ends, not boycotts and street marches. These actions, they argued, incited "hatred and violence, however technically peaceful they may be," and would not resolve the problems.[25]

In response, five white pastors from the Alabama Council on Human Relations risked social opprobrium by joining four black ministers in issuing a public statement sympathetic to the demonstrations. The leader of the council, thirty-three-year-old Joseph W. Ellwanger, was the white pastor of the all-black St. Paul's Lutheran Church and had been the only white minister who participated in the demonstrations, marching alongside members of his congregation. Expressing concern over their city's racial turmoil, the ministers reaffirmed both the constitutional right of peaceful assembly and protest and supported the "rightness of the aims" of all who sought equal employment opportunities and equal access to all public facilities, arguing that these aims were rooted "in the historic Christian teaching of the oneness of humanity in Christ." The group concluded by calling for negotiations. Given the traditionally violent nature of race relations in Birmingham, it took considerable courage for these ministers to speak out as they did, but their suggestions were dismissed by Birmingham whites and ignored by most of the national media.[26]

During these exchanges, King was in the city jail for disobeying a court injunction against street demonstrations, and he refused to ignore the challenges put forth in the *News*. Noting that he seldom answered criticism of his work, he explained why he was not an outsider, gave the reasons for the campaign, and then criticized those who prided themselves on their racial moderation. It was not the Klan or the Citizens' Councils that were the "great stumbling block in the stride toward freedom," he wrote, but the moderates more devoted to order than to justice, especially the leaders of the white southern churches, who stood out for their silence and timidity. But all was not lost, he counseled, for there were some "noble souls from the ranks of organized religion" who had rejected conformity and marched with blacks, been jailed, lost their jobs, but "had the faith that right defeated is stronger than evil triumphant"; these few were "the spiritual salt that has preserved the true meaning of the gospel in these troubled times."[27]

For all its future fame, the original audience for King's "Letter from a Birmingham Jail" was relatively small. Smuggled out of his cell by his lawyers, it was first printed in pamphlet form by the American Friends Service Committee. The *New York Post* and *Christianity and Crisis* published excerpts, but it was not until the *Christian Century* printed it in its entirety in June of 1963 that King's "Letter" found its larger audience. "In all my years . . . I have never been more moved by a single issue. What a shaking experience!" one minister wrote to the editors. "If the canon of the Holy Scriptures were not closed, I would nominate [it] either as a continuation of the Acts of the Apostles or as an addition to the Epistles in the best tradition of the Pauline prison letters."[28]

Not all readers were as taken with the letter. After Bishop Carpenter finished reading it, he resignedly told George Murray, bishop coadjutor of the Episcopal Diocese of Alabama, "This is what you get when you try to do something. You get it from both sides." According to Taylor Branch, who in 1987 interviewed both Murray and Carpenter's son, King's response made the Alabama bishop, a "sophisticated critic of segregation," feel "abused and misunderstood for his efforts to act as a progressive force in race relations. The clash of emotion turned him . . . into a more strident Confederate."[29] Given Carpenter's well-documented stand against the sit-ins and marches and his willingness to transfer priests who were supporters of civil rights, one may well question whether the bishop was not already firmly in the Confederate camp, let alone a critic of segregation, well before the spring of 1963.

Despite its eloquence, the "Letter from a Birmingham Jail" did nothing to spur on the lagging spring campaign in Birmingham. What proved to be of vastly more help was the collapse of "Bull" Connor's restraint and his orders to use police dogs and fire hoses against marchers. For a week, scenes of police brutality would be repeated not only on the streets of Birmingham but on television screens across the nation. White sympathizers, disgusted by what they saw, packed their bags and left to join the demonstrators in Alabama. Walter Fauntroy, an SCLC minister in Washington, D.C., organized a group of nineteen Conservative rabbis to fly to Birmingham. According to one, nobody was entirely sure what they were doing. All had been taught about the equality of human beings, but the only blacks they had known in their middle-class suburbs were domestic help, and hence an "abstraction." A welcoming delegation of black civil rights leaders met them at the airport, as did a hostile group of Birmingham rabbis and Jewish civic leaders who urged them to return home, fearful that their presence would renew anti-Semitic attacks on synagogues and Jewish community centers.[30]

The reception in the black community was overwhelmingly positive. Congregations applauded the bearded rabbis in their yarmulkes and prayer shawls as they entered Baptist churches; the visiting rabbis, in turn, came to see blacks as real, not a sociological abstraction. Meetings with the city's Jewish leaders were considerably stormier. The Birmingham Jews spoke of bomb threats and death, and insisted that the rabbis would go home as heroes and leave them to face the wrath of segregationists.[31] "We will concede that the visit of the rabbis created a reservoir of good will among the Negroes," wrote a Jewish physician to the northerners' rabbinical assembly. "We regret to advise you that it did not create a reservoir of good will among the whites, and we fear that it will be a long time before that ill will and hostility will be dissipated."[32] However, the northern rabbis had desired to make a prophetic witness, not to soothe consciences, and they not only received an education in race relations but confirmed their belief that "the rabbi is a symbol of what ought to be important"; as one of them explained, when a rabbi "succeeds in resolving his own ambivalence on an issue of crucial importance, the 'ought' implicit in his communal existence becomes that much clearer."[33] Their southern brethren, even those who sympathized with their ideals, considered the northern rabbis to be first and foremost publicity-seekers—a charge that, with variations, would be echoed in every southern community faced with the arrival of northern clergymen determined to support the civil rights movement.

By May, King, the Reverend Fred Shuttlesworth, and other SCLC officials won concessions from city merchants, who agreed to desegregate lunch counters and hire blacks for clerical and sales work. It was a major victory for the movement, coming on the heels of the failure in Albany, but the brutality inflicted on Birmingham's blacks led James Baldwin, Lena Horne, and other black intellectuals and entertainers (but, curiously, no civil rights leaders) to discuss the administration's stand on civil rights with Robert Kennedy. Disappointed at his failure to comprehend their concerns, they then turned to officials of the NCC, J. Oscar Lee of the Department of Cultural and Racial Relations, and Jon Regier, director of the Division of Home Missions, and asked them to involve the council in the civil rights struggle.[34]

In some ways the selection of Lee and Regier was a strange choice. Since its creation in 1950, NCC had emphasized education and moral suasion, rather than direct action, to further the goals of racial equality. Even the Southern Project was designed to study racial conflict in the field and report its observations to the general board. A convergence of events in May 1963 provided those council members interested in social action with the opportunity to rechannel their energies in a direction they found more meaningful and relevant. The sight of nonviolent black youths careening into trees and buildings under the weight of hundreds of pounds of water had helped lead executive councils of the NCC to draft a proposal for a new organization committed to activism. The United Presbyterian Church had already established a Presbyterian Commission on Religion and Race at the end of May, giving it a mandate to work within the denomination and with commissions of other faiths to sponsor civil rights initiatives within the churches. Stated Clerk Eugene Carson Blake strongly supported the new organization and helped convince the NCC to create its own Commission on Religion and Race the following month.[35] In its founding resolution, the NCC admitted that the council had to reconsider its gradualism: "The world watches to see how we will act—whether with courage or with fumbling expediency"; at this time, it said, the church was "called upon to put aside every lesser engagement, to confess her sins of omission and . . . move forward to witness." Now was the time for action, even if it jeopardized the institutional security of the church. The general board authorized the commission to "make commitments, call for actions, [and] take risks" on behalf of the NCC, and to work with similar agencies established by Catholics, Orthodox, and Jews.[36]

To guarantee the commission's freedom of action, the board made it responsible only to itself, bypassing normal bureaucratic channels as well as the Department of Cultural and Racial Relations, and several denominations pledged substantial funding for the commission's direct use. Two months later Will Campbell resigned from his position as director of the Southern Project, later citing as reasons a lack of freedom to express himself and the NCC's tendency to blame southerners for what was, after all, a national problem. As he perceived it, the council's conviction that it alone was doing God's work was a position no better than that of the segregationists. Historian James Findlay has argued convincingly that the creation of the new commission meant that the general board was moving beyond existing civil rights departments, and "[c]learly, too, the Southern Project was to be supplemented, or even supplanted." In fact, the council ended the project within the year. Campbell's resignation at this time was perhaps not a coincidence, and his criticisms of the National Council probably not the sole reason for his departure; a shrewd man, he may have seen which way the prevailing winds were blowing.[37] Rather than turning away from the racial crisis, however, Campbell soon embarked on an itinerant gospel ministry for which he was particularly well suited.

From the outset, the NCC Commission on Religion and Race was a small organization (at its largest it would only have thirty members) but generally effective. Pressures from conservative laypersons within the NCC could not affect it, and it had been given an enthusiastic and independent mandate by the general board, which appointed Blake, Mrs. J. Fount Tillman of Tennessee, and Bishop B. Julian Smith of the Christian Methodist Church (Negro) as vice chairpersons (Blake shortly became chair). Anna Arnold Hedgeman accepted the position of coordinator of special events. The position of executive secretary was given to the Reverend Robert W. Spike, the forty-year-old general secretary for the board of homeland ministries of the United Church of Christ and a veteran of inner-city parish work in New York City.[38] He had long believed the church needed to expand beyond its four walls and grapple with the problems facing the larger society, writing that if the church chose "an antiseptic gospel of the good life and gentility of spirit," it would become little more than a "decoration."[39] It was Blake, however, who quickly became the organization's most visible member. After the commission's first meeting at the Interchurch Center on New York City's Riverside Drive, he convened a press conference to announce his participation in a joint CORE–Americans for Democratic Action integration march on July 4 in Maryland. He would be acting as representative of the Commission on Religion and Race, he told reporters, but as the highest ranking executive in the United Presbyterian Church, he urged all Maryland Presbyterians to join the protest.[40]

Independence Day in Baltimore turned out to be a mild, sunny day, perfect for family picnics and outings to local amusement parks. No doubt James Price, one of the owners of the Gwynn Oaks Amusement Park near Baltimore, expected a sizable turnout and a decent amount of business. What he received instead was four busloads of people from forty interracial church, political, labor, and peace organizations intent on desegregating the park. Prominent among them was a group of twelve clergymen, including Blake; Dr. Furman L. Templeton, the black chairperson of the National Presbyterian

Interracial Council; Bishop Daniel Corrigan of the Episcopal Church; Monsignor Austin J. Healy and other priests of the Catholic Archdiocese of Baltimore; and Rabbi Morris Lieberman of the Baltimore Hebrew Congregation. According to Blake's biographer, both he and Templeton were as concerned about what they would do if they succeeded in desegregating the park as they were about being arrested, for neither cared for amusement park rides. Police standing at the entrance made no effort to stop them until they reached the ticket booth inside the gate, where Price and his assistants read them the state trespass law before asking them to leave.[41]

The clergymen refused, and were escorted to patrol wagons to be driven to a nearby police station and booked on violating the trespass law. "Almost all the churches have made the right statements about discrimination," Blake told reporters, "but we can no longer let the burden of winning freedom for the Negro or any other oppressed people be the burden only of the oppressed people themselves," adding that Americans had to stop thinking of God as a "white divinity." When reporters asked Lieberman why he had participated in the protest, he replied that it was a meaningful way to celebrate the holiday. For the next three hours, hundreds of protesters tried to enter the park, and when stopped by authorities insisted that the state trespass laws be read aloud to them. Two hundred eighty-three people were arrested that afternoon, including William Sloane Coffin, who had not been in the original group of clergymen. He had tried to go to the assistance of his wife, who had been arrested inside the park, and had been taken into custody as well. Except for five black ministers from Baltimore, all the clergy were released on bail, returning to their homes that night.[42]

The crowds who had come to the park for recreation were strongly against the protesters and cheered each time they were put into patrol wagons. Some made a special point of mocking the clergy, derisively shouting that the assembly looked like a revival meeting. When Price was asked what he thought of the ministers' involvement, he told reporters that it was "unfortunate" and analogous to "my shooting crap and when the police come I begin to pray and say I was arrested for praying."[43] What were grounds for ridicule by segregationists made for good copy in the press, however. Photographs of the imposing, six-foot Blake dressed in his clerical collar and dark suit being placed in the patrol wagon were displayed on the front pages of national newspapers, and the story of this first interfaith direct-action protest, in which so many prestigious clergymen had taken part, was given favorable treatment in several religious journals. In recognition of Blake's role in the demonstration, as well as his efforts to promote the work of the National Conference on Religion and

Race, the Catholic Interracial Council of Chicago presented him with its annual John F. Kennedy Award, given to those who furthered the cause of interracial justice and goodwill.[44]

The negative publicity convinced Price and his associates to reconsider their policies, and on August 28, when the nation's attention was centered on the March in Washington, the amusement park was quietly integrated without disturbance.[45] The fact that the demonstration succeeded was "not really relevant," Blake told the congregation at Riverside Presbyterian Church in New York City later in the summer. The proper question was, when was it right, if ever, to break the law? Such action was not to be undertaken lightly, for it risked anarchy, but when property rights took precedence over human dignity, a higher law needed to be followed. "Let us be entirely clear," he told his audience, "that law is not God," citing the example of Peter and the apostles who, after being repeatedly jailed for preaching that Christ had risen from the dead, replied to the authorities that "We must obey God rather than men." The willingness of someone so prominent in denominational and interfaith circles to be arrested in a civil rights demonstration led Dr. Harvey Cox, professor of religion at Harvard Divinity School, to dub Blake "a hero of the New Breed" of socially activist clergy, a small but influential class of ministers, priests, and rabbis concerned not only with theological dogma but with involving churches and synagogues in the plight of the poor, downtrodden, and racially oppressed. As Blake himself later wrote, the church had to "identify itself much more radically with the interests of the poor, the 'losers,' the outcasts and the alienated," for the "mark of the presence of the awaited Messiah is still related to the poor having the Gospel preached to them and the captives being released."[46]

The commission's first venture into the South was not nearly so successful as the protest in Maryland. After several representatives went to Jackson, Mississippi, for the funeral of slain civil rights leader Medgar Evers in June, officials of the state's NAACP branch asked the commission to send others to Clarksdale, Mississippi, where it had begun a campaign of sit-ins and marches to desegregate public facilities and win voting rights. Two groups of white ministers went there in July in hopes of meeting with black and white leaders and beginning mediation efforts. The black leaders told the white visitors that the most effective thing they could do would be to join them in the streets; the local white clergy refused to meet with them, and the authorities served them with an injunction forbidding their participation in the demonstrations, which they obeyed. The end result was that the commission's efforts pleased no one. Even a white cleric who favored integration was indignant because it appeared that the visit of the northern ministers was designed to "show up" their southern colleagues. As one critic wrote, "no clear theology of involvement in the current struggle has been propounded or adopted."[47] While the Commission on Religion and Race would never again suffer complaints that it was insufficiently committed to activism, charges that its goals lacked clarity—especially with regard to reconciliation between the races in the South — would hound the organization for the remainder of its often stormy four years of existence.

Although the commission failed to provide leadership in a place to which it had been invited, it had a far greater impact on an event in which no white organizations were originally asked to participate. The March on Washington for Jobs and Freedom had been conceived as a black-organized, black-led demonstration to call for stronger federal civil rights legislation. The intervention of liberal white clergymen and labor leaders lent support, but their concerns about alienating the administration led them to pressure some of the more militant black leaders to tone down their rhetoric. Unwittingly or not, white involvement substantially altered the mood of the march from protest against injustice to support of civil rights legislation, but the presence of white clergymen of all three faiths, and the resulting ecumenical spirit, illustrated that the fight for human rights was not the domain of one group, but of all. Perhaps the sight of so many white religious leaders also made the demonstration seem that much safer, and its goals that much more palatable, to the white community.

The success of the Birmingham campaign concerned President Kennedy, who feared that a series of similar campaigns throughout the South would enervate his administration both domestically and overseas, where the Soviet Union and emerging African nations had made great propaganda out of the police brutality in Alabama. For these reasons, as well as a growing conviction that the executive branch had to provide leadership in the crisis, Kennedy not only underscored the moral imperatives in helping black people achieve first-class citizenship in a television address in June, but met with religious leaders to sound them out on church support for civil rights proposals he was submitting to Congress. The proposals included provisions to cut federal aid to institutions practicing discrimination, to end segregation in public facilities, and to empower the attorney general to work for desegregation of public schools on his own initiative rather than wait for the aggrieved parties to bring suit against the school boards or local authorities. No mention was made of fair employment practices or voting rights.[48]

Weak though the proposals were, civil rights leaders grudgingly rallied around them. Veteran civil rights and labor activist A. Philip Randolph, Martin Luther King Jr. of the SCLC, Roy Wilkins of the NAACP, James Farmer of CORE, SNCC's John Lewis, and Whitney Young of the Urban League met with Kennedy on June 22 to discuss plans for a march on Washington to call attention to the need for stronger civil rights legislation. The "Big Six" spent the next two months planning the event under the guidance of Randolph, who had conceived of but did not carry out a similar march in 1941 to force President Franklin Roosevelt to end discrimination in the wartime defense industries. Not wanting to be shut out of the demonstration, Blake, Spike, and other officials from the NCC and the Leadership Conference on Civil Rights, a lobbying organization for civil rights legislation formed in 1949, conferred with the "Big Six" and added the Commission on Religion and Race to the March on Washington Committee. Believing an ecumenical witness to be more powerful than a show of support from the Protestant churches alone, Blake and Spike brought Mathew Ahmann, executive director of the National Catholic Conference for Interracial Justice, and Rabbi Joachim Prinz, president of the American Jewish Congress, into the fold.[49]

It remained an unequal partnership, however. Hedgeman recalled the time when black civil rights leaders left a meeting with their white counterparts to give interviews to visiting television crews, leaving the whites with nothing to do. Another time, when speeches were being scheduled, a black leader suggested that one white person speak for all three faiths, an idea Hedgeman considered unfair because no one seriously entertained the notion, given the clash of egos among the six black activists, that one of them represent all six organizations. "The civil rights leaders were not always as considerate of these allies as they should have been," she wrote afterwards. "There was a new undercurrent among Negroes generally that this was to be *their* protest to the nation and the world, and that allies were, after a fashion, appendages rather than equal participants."[50]

Despite such treatment, the Commission on Religion and Race threw itself into the task of contacting state councils of churches and asking them to take part in the march. Blake joined Rabbi Irwin Blank, chair of the social action department of the Synagogue Council of America, and the Reverend John F. Cronin, associate director of the social action department of the National Catholic Welfare Conference, to underscore the ecumenical nature of the religious support for civil rights legislation. On July 25, they presented a joint interfaith statement to the Senate Committee on Labor and Public Welfare, emphasizing that the "religious conscience of America condemns racism as blasphemy against God" because it denies "the worth which God has given to all persons." Their "moral principles" as religious leaders, said the trio, made them particularly aware of the need for such legislation.[51]

As interest in the march grew, so did the emphasis on the need for white participation. "What if vacation plans had not included a trip to Washington?" asked the editors of the *Christian Century*. "Plans can be changed!" To facilitate this, they reprinted a list of suggestions for those who would be traveling to the capital, advising readers to bring bag lunches and drinking water, follow the instructions of the trained marshals, and "pray that the spirit of Christ moves in and through the march." The last suggestion was no idle bit of religious sentiment. Supporters of the march understood that a large demonstration might invite violence at the hands of extremists in hopes of discrediting its goals. To this end, on Sunday, August 25, the organizers issued a public appeal for discipline and order, reminding participants that the march would be "unified in purposes and behavior" and that the "eyes and the judgment of the world" would be on Washington, D.C.[52]

Such declarations hid the fact that serious disputes had arisen over the content of John Lewis's planned speech. The chair of SNCC, Lewis had vowed that civil rights activists would march throughout the South pursuing their own "scorched earth" policy of burning "Jim Crow to the ground— nonviolently." Archbishop Patrick O'Boyle strongly disagreed with Lewis's contention that SNCC could not support Kennedy's civil rights bill because it was "too little, and too late" and refused to deliver the invocation unless Lewis softened his rhetoric. The night before the march, O'Boyle met with Lewis, James Forman of SNCC, labor leader Walter Reuther, and Burke Marshall, assistant attorney general for the Justice Department's Civil Rights Division in an emergency session, but they reached no agreement. The debate spilled over into the next afternoon, August 28, after the March on Washington had already begun. As organizers told the musicians on the steps of the Lincoln Memorial to extend their performances, the same individuals—this time joined by King, Abernathy, and Randolph as mediators—and Blake met in the guardhouse under the statue of the sixteenth president and continued the argument. Blake demanded that Lewis omit phrases like "the masses" and "serious revolution," as suspect phrases from a foreign ideology, until Randolph pointed out that he himself had been using such phrases for years. Under pressure from Blake and persuaded by King, Lewis agreed to delete the "scorched earth" reference and modified his criticism of the civil rights bill. Hurriedly revising the draft on a manual typewriter, Forman had the speech ready in time for O'Boyle to acquiesce in the changes.[53]

Forman later wrote that SNCC people were comfortable with the modification being made because they had already given the press copies of the original draft; what they did not know was that Marshall had told reporters that O'Boyle would not speak if changes were not made. The admission made it appear that the black militants had caved in to the demands of the white clergy. Years afterwards, it became clear to Forman why Blake wanted the change, for it was "not just quibbling over words, but a matter of substance." At some undetermined point, Forman wrote, the clergy and labor leaders "had been told that this was a march to support the administration's Civil Rights Bill," and people throughout the nation, thinking they were participating in a protest march, never realized that "the sellout leadership of the March on Washington," including the religious hierarchy, was "playing patsy with the Kennedy administration." Other young militants in SNCC, both black and white, were certain that their leaders had sold out to pressure from the older, more established black leadership and their white guests. Others not so young, such as the radical journalist I. F. Stone, concurred, writing that the "price of having so many respectables on the bandwagon was to mute Negro militancy . . . in [a] picnic atmosphere." Malcolm X derided the "Farce on Washington" and the whites and "'integration'-mad Negroes" who muted the angry tide of black resentment.[54]

Most of the 200,000 to 300,000 black and white participants in the March on Washington probably did not entertain such thoughts. According to Russell Baker of the *New York Times*, the "vast army of quiet, middle-class Americans . . . had come in the spirit of a church outing," and although the event was not billed as a religious convocation, the presence of 10,000 representatives from church and religious groups, led by 200 religious leaders, gave it the appearance of one.[55] Some carried signs reading "We March Together— Catholics, Jews, Protestants—For Dignity and Brotherhood of All Men Under God, Now!" A delegation of Reform Jews carried signs in Hebrew and English, including one inscribed with a passage from Leviticus, "Proclaim liberty throughout the land, and unto all the inhabitants thereof." Thirty-four clergymen and heads of religious denominations and organizations were visible on the platform at the Lincoln Memorial, including an aging Reverend John LaFarge, S.J., founder of the Catholic Interracial Councils in the 1930s, senior editor of *America*, and the only white clergyman who had publicly supported Randolph's proposed march twenty-two years before.[56]

Adding to the moral fervor was the religious nature of many of the speeches given at the Lincoln Memorial; even Wilkins's touched on biblical themes. Blake, his six-foot frame dwarfing the podium that overlooked the Reflecting Pool, announced that he wished he could speak for all Protestant, Anglican, and Orthodox Christians making up the membership rolls of the NCC, as he

THE CALL TO BATTLE

spoke on behalf of "justice and freedom." Yet that was "precisely the point": if all the clergy and laity of the NCC's constituent churches, the Catholic Church, and all the synagogues were ready to march with blacks for jobs and freedom, the fight against racial discrimination "would be already won." None of the white clergy came to the march in an "arrogant spirit of moral or spiritual superiority to 'set the nation straight' or to judge or to denounce the American people," he concluded. "Rather we come—late, late we come—in the reconciling and repentant spirit . . . that we may be found on God's side." It was not merely sympathy for black Americans that motivated Jews to work on behalf of civil rights, Rabbi Joachim Prinz told the crowd, but "a sense of complete identification and solidarity born of our own painful historic experience." When he had been a rabbi in Berlin during the late 1930s, the most important thing he had learned was that "bigotry and hatred are not the most urgent problems. The most urgent, the most disgraceful, the most shameful, and the most tragic problem is silence. . . . America must not remain silent."[57]

Despite the eloquence and the earnest entreaties of the white religious leaders, they could not disguise the fact that they had indeed been latecomers to the civil rights struggle, and that not all white clergymen shared their opinion of the March on Washington. This was made painfully apparent to those who had tried to enlist the support of the capital city's clergy for the march. Although several Episcopal parishes followed the request of the church's presiding bishop and provided lodging for visitors, other Protestant congregations refused to cooperate or officially endorse the march. When the editor of a Catholic journal telephoned the city's Catholic priests for their opinions on the march, many were "curiously friendly, confused, and uninformed," and had no plans to participate, one excusing himself on the grounds that his obesity made it unwise for him to march. Because of the fear of violence, nuns were forbidden to take part in the day's events. Several local radio stations spread stories that not all clergy were who they appeared to be, describing a run on clerical collars, black cloth, and crucifixes in New York City costume shops and clerical supply stores. Such rumors of ecclesiastical impostors were fanned by Republican Representative William H. Ayres of Ohio, who asked the FBI to conduct an investigation into these allegations after notifying reporters that fake ministers had been in his office. When asked how he could tell, Ayres told the reporters that he was the son of a Methodist minister and so could tell a preacher when he saw one. As no crime had been committed, however, the FBI refused to honor his request.[58]

Strange though it was, Ayres's accusation made sense, in a perverse sort of way. If one considered civil rights legislation to be a purely political issue and as much a part of the legislative bailiwick as pork-barrel legislation and congressional pay raises, the insistence that it was different because it was a moral problem sounded a discordant note. Rather than consider the possibility that moral questions, not to mention religious beliefs, might actually impinge on the nature of civil rights legislation, it was easier to dismiss those who looked at the matter in that light as impostors. The fact that similar allegations of rented clerical collars and purloined nuns' habits proved popular throughout the South whenever clergy and religious figures took part in a civil rights demonstration was a telling point, for it illustrated the inability of some residents of the Bible Belt to concede that equally devout Christians had a different understanding of the nature of the gospel and their mission in the world. This is not to suggest that every clergyman who participated in the March on Washington did so out of purely altruistic reasons. William Stringfellow related how one "high-ranking ecclesiastical" bluntly told him shortly afterward that it had finally dawned on churchpeople that society was in the midst of a serious revolution, the outcome of which was no longer in doubt, and they wanted to be on the winning side. Even if that was a minority viewpoint, the "burst of direct involvement in the demonstrations by some of the churches" only proved to Stringfellow that "they are again followers of public policy, neither leaders in social change nor prophets in the land."[59]

Whatever one's views of white clerical participation, the fact remained that it was "supportive rather than dominant," as Harold Fey, editor of the *Christian Century*, related. The day belonged to the black civil rights leaders, especially King, whose address at the end of the day became one of the most inspiring speeches in American history. As wave upon wave of cheers and applause reached the speakers' platform at the conclusion of his speech, King and the other leaders departed for the White House, where they met with the president. Served tea, coffee, and sandwiches by Filipino mess boys, the meeting was a mix of exuberance and ego-boosting. Blake explained to Kennedy and assembled reporters and photographers that the purpose of including white church groups was to "produce an integrated march," adding that he hoped that there would never again be a need for an all-black demonstration. Continuing his remarks, he described King as "clearly the religious leader of this demonstration." Randolph tried to soothe feelings by quickly referring to Wilkins as "the acknowledged leader of the civil rights movement in America," and it was left to Prinz to extricate them from an embarrassing situation by naming as "the hero of the day" the people who had traveled to Washington for the march.[60]

Sensitive egos notwithstanding, the planners of the March on Washington had every reason to be proud of the nonviolent nature of the demonstration. Hundreds of thousands of people of all races had shown that peaceful integration was possible, if only for an afternoon. Millions more who watched the event on television were impressed by the orderliness of the affair. Other, larger marches would take place in the nation's capital, many protesting the Vietnam War, but there would never again be one filled with so much hope that the nation would be able to overcome its legacy of racism. But more work needed to be done, especially by the religious community, in order for this to occur. Columnist James Reston noted this the next day, writing that the first test of the March's success "will come in the churches and synagogues of the country this weekend." It was useless to wait for Congress to take the lead, "for if there is no effective moral reaction out in the country, there will be no effective political reaction there." The campaign for equal rights had to return to "first principles," for as "moral principles preceded and inspired political principles in this country . . . there will have to be a moral revulsion to the humiliation of the Negro before there can be significant political relief."[61]

Only days after the march, church groups in the Midwest subjected their senators and representatives in Washington to a deluge of mail supporting Kennedy's civil rights legislation; the Wall Street Journal reported that "Almost half the mail of some Midwest lawmakers reveals church influence."[62] While the flood of mail remained strong throughout the autumn, it would not peak until after the new year, when both the House and the Senate were about to vote on the bill. The NCC Commission on Religion and Race assisted such efforts. Not only did some members remain in Washington after August 28 to lobby for the bill before the legislature, but the commission's leadership established networks in the Midwest to assist both clergy and laity in making their voices heard in the Capitol. Staff member James Hamilton had already begun working with the Leadership Conference on Civil Rights and served as one of its observers in the House when the bill was being debated in the summer and fall of 1963. At the same time, Robert Spike and other commission members sponsored a workshop in Lincoln, Nebraska, in which 200 people listened to theologians and members of Congress explain the moral necessity for passing the bill. Similar meetings were held throughout the Midwest, an important base of congressional support due to its large number of Republicans uncommitted to civil rights, the influence that could be brought to bear on them by churchpeople, and, significantly, a lack of racial tension, owing to the comparatively small size of the minority population.[63]

The churches had hardly begun to gear up for the fight for the bill when the man responsible for introducing the legislation into Congress was cut down by an assassin in Dallas. It was left to his successor, Lyndon B. Johnson, to help engineer its passage. For his strenuous efforts on behalf of the civil rights program, Johnson would be viewed as a hero by liberals across the country. In time, many of the same liberals who were so glowing in their praise of Johnson for his domestic legislation would castigate him for his increasing involvement in the Vietnam quagmire. But that was in the future. The most pressing concern at that moment was to further the cause of civil rights, both by direct action and by influencing the legislature to pass the civil rights bill into law. Liberal white clergy would be firmly behind both ventures.

four

The Spirit of the Lord God is upon me, because the Lord has anointed me; he has sent me to bring good news to the oppressed, the broken-hearted, to proclaim liberty to the captives, and release to the prisoners; to proclaim the year of the Lord's favor . . .

ISAIAH 61:1–4

Bringing Good News to the Oppressed

Clerical Organization in the North and South, 1964

Standing before the Metropolitan Conference on Religion and Race in New York City on February 25, 1964, Abraham Joshua Heschel again delivered a pointed address to assembled churchpeople. Like any good speaker, he knew the value of a well-turned phrase, and was not against recycling one if it fit his purpose. Speaking of the civil rights bill and its passage fifteen days before in the House, he observed that "it was easier for the children of Israel to cross the Red Sea than for the Civil Rights legislation to pass the floor of the United States Senate." Recalling Moses' plea to the Lord to find someone else to lead the Israelites out of bondage because he was slow of tongue, Heschel commented, "How marvelous it would be if some of our Senators who are preparing for a filibuster would share this quality of Moses!"

Other parallels existed between the Exodus and the plight of black Americans, Heschel continued. When the Israelites reached safety, it was a moment of "supreme spiritual exultation." Yet after several days without water, their joy had turned to exhaustion and bitterness. The March on Washington had shown blacks that millions of whites shared their desire for civil rights, but day-to-day concerns remained after the glow of the March had faded. Although Americans were "ready to applaud dramatic struggles once a year in Washington," he cautioned, or "for the sake of lofty principles, spend a day or two in jail somewhere in Alabama," to many the demands for sanitary housing, for good schools, for employment seemed "so devoid of magnificence." But the teaching of Judaism, he reminded his audience, was "the theology of the common deed." The challenge came not from demonstrations, "but in how we manage the commonplace." Unless whites acted on the prophetic qualities of the Judeo-Christian heritage, the gains of the past year would be lost.[1]

Despite such warnings, most Americans continued to focus on problems in the South, specifically Mississippi, during 1964, even though blacks took to the streets of northern and midwestern cities to protest police brutality, substandard housing conditions, discriminatory hiring practices, and school segregation. The first of these riots occurred in the spring, when civil rights groups in Cleveland, Ohio, staged a campaign of school boycotts, picketing, and lie-ins at building sites to protest the school board's hurried construction of schools in black neighborhoods to maintain de facto segregation and forestall bussing. Over 200 Protestant ministers and almost a dozen rabbis formed the Emergency Committee of Clergy for Civil Rights (ECCCR), thus representing 40 percent of the city's white Protestant and Jewish clergy.[2]

One of the committee members was the Reverend Bruce Klunder, a white Presbyterian who had been active in civil rights as a student at Oregon State University, where he helped raise money for the Montgomery Bus Boycott, and at Yale Divinity School, where he picketed the local Woolworth and other stores whose southern affiliates had been the site of sit-ins. Upon his arrival in Cleveland in 1962 he helped found a local chapter of CORE. The Christian faith was not "the oneness of jolly good fellowship," Klunder believed; rather, it was built on suffering for others. A Christian did not "deny or ignore pain, suffering and death" but emerged "victorious, from the pain of our dying to what we once were." The words proved prophetic. On April 7, he joined demonstrators on a construction site who were lying down in front of bulldozers to keep them from being used. The driver did not see the minister lying in the mud and drove over him, killing him instantly. "Bruce Klunder did not seek to be a martyr," Eugene Carson Blake told the grieving crowd of family members, friends, and civil rights workers at a memorial service two days later. "He did not expect to die . . . but he was one of those ministers of the church who had joined up, responding to the call of Jesus Christ, refusing in the national crisis to stand safe and eloquent behind the pulpit." Although the death of a white ally had been an accident, it shook the black community not only in Cleveland but across the nation, and the black newsmagazine *Ebony* carried a lengthy feature story about the Presbyterian minister two months later.[3]

Despite the tragedy, the city refused to halt construction of the schools. The Emergency Committee called for the resignation of the school board members, and the local newspapers, which had looked upon picketing ministers with disdain, published the names of ECCCR members, with the result that a dozen ministers lost their jobs and at least six others left the ministry. After continued protests turned into a riot that left twenty people injured, the core group of liberal clergy that had made up the ECCCR never regained its unity of purpose. Two years later, when more serious riots swept the city, the same clergy, affiliated with the Cleveland Council of Churches, made promises to improve the lot of the black citizens in the city, but by 1968, few of them had been realized. Throughout the summer of 1964, riots spread throughout Jersey City, Harlem, Rochester, and other cities in the Northeast. Few whites were aware of the depths of black frustration in the inner cities, and most of the assistance their churches gave in the aftermath consisted of food, clothing, and temporary shelter. Although veteran organizer Saul Alinsky later claimed that the churches "were the big dominant force in civil rights," at least with regard to Rochester, they had involved themselves only after humanitarian organizations and black churches established educational and job-training programs in hopes of preventing future unrest.[4]

Clerical participation on behalf of open housing was another matter entirely. Regional conferences of religion and race and other religious bodies had taken part in working for fair housing legislation since 1963, despite the scorn showered upon them by real estate agencies and developers, who derided their interest as being purely political. While civil rights and church groups in Chicago successfully defeated a referendum that would have forbidden the state legislature from enacting any fair housing laws, their counterparts in California failed to prevent a similar act from being repealed that November. Their defeat was especially frustrating because the overwhelming majority of clergy of all faiths had thrown themselves into the fight, sponsoring petition drives and speaking against the repeal from their pulpits. The editors of the *Christian Century* called the fair housing issue one of the most important facing the American people, for while it was a local matter, the duty of the churches was to uphold the right of all people to live where they wished, regardless of race, religion, or national origin. Robert McAfee Brown agreed, arguing that the clarity of the ethical positions meant that any minister, rabbi, or priest who "equivocates on the issue . . . has surrendered his claim to moral leadership in the community where he works . . . and can no longer expect to be taken seriously on other issues."[5]

What made the outcome especially galling was that although clerical opposition to repeal ran four to one, the referendum in favor of repeal passed by a margin of two to one. Most of the clergy had argued their case on moral and religious grounds, on the basis of a common humanity under God, yet their parishioners were looking at the referendum as an economic and political matter involving property rights, in which God and the Bible, let alone the pastor, had little input. In the wake of defeat, some ministers whose commitment to liberal activism had been lukewarm at best quickly beat a hasty retreat and renounced their former moral arguments. One pastor wrote in his church bulletin that "the issue was far more complex than the simple choice between good and evil, a choice made so evident in ecclesiastical propaganda," and blamed the liberal ministers for reactivating "an old anticlerical spirit which has been dormant for some time."[6]

Other clergy suffered not only from the embarrassment of realizing that their moral arguments carried little if any weight in their congregations but also from shortfalls in church contributions and attempts to remove them from their pulpits. The Episcopal Diocese of New York lost hundreds of thousands of dollars in pledges due to its support of civil rights, which included Bishop Horace W. Donegan's decision to hire a black priest to serve in the Cathedral of St. John the Divine. In one unusual case, after James Francis Aloysius Cardinal McIntyre, the elderly archbishop of the Archdiocese of Los Angeles, ordered his priests to refrain from giving sermons on civil rights and the fair housing referendum, a young clergyman, the Reverend William DuBay, wrote to Pope Paul VI, requesting him to remove McIntyre for "gross malfeasance in office" and his failure to exercise any moral leadership among California's Catholics. The Vatican refused to consider the request, and the archbishop retaliated by relieving DuBay of his administrative duties until he renewed his vows of obedience. Two years later, McIntyre suspended DuBay indefinitely for proposing a "priests' union" to radically democratize church polity.[7]

Aside from such bursts of attention surrounding the clergy's opposition to repeal of fair housing legislation, news coverage continued to emphasize the efforts of white clergy who worked for civil rights in the South. Economic and housing discrimination in northern and midwestern cities, while pervasive, could not provide the stark contrast between good and evil via the media of photography and television; the sight of nonviolent black protesters being attacked by police dogs provoked a far more visceral reaction among television viewers. Northerners repeatedly insisted that the problems of the inner cities were complex, and the white churches and synagogues, with few exceptions, did little to remedy them. Part of this may have been the reluctance of the white middle-class parishioners to reflect on their own complicity in such developments, for they had eagerly left the cities to build their white enclaves in the suburbs.[8]

Accordingly, for both moral and tactical reasons, black civil rights leaders continued to make direct requests for white participation in demonstrations. When William Sloane Coffin learned of SCLC's efforts to desegregate public facilities in St. Augustine, Florida, he decided to lend his assistance. The peripatetic chaplain joined other New Englanders—including Mary Peabody, the wife of the Right Reverend Malcolm Peabody, Episcopal bishop of Massachusetts, and mother of the state's governor; Dr. Lawrence Burholder of the Harvard Divinity School; and the wives of several Episcopal clergymen—in their trip to St. Augustine on Easter Sunday.[9] A black colleague had called him shortly before he left New Haven and told him that he had "one major responsibility and that's to get Mrs. Peabody into jail," as Coffin remembered it, "because if she gets jailed, that obviously is going to make quite a stir."[10]

Upon hearing of the trip, the Right Reverend Hamilton West, Episcopal bishop of Florida, telephoned Bishop Peabody and failed to convince him of the need to ask his wife to abandon her plans, and St. Augustinians prepared themselves for the expected attempts to integrate their churches. Most local clergy had steered clear of any involvement in the civil rights struggle. The Most Reverend Joseph P. Hurley, Catholic archbishop of St. Augustine, refused to discuss the matter with his priests, and the lack of a citywide ministerial alliance isolated those moderate Protestant ministers who otherwise might have succeeded in working together as a group. Still others were faced with conservative vestries or congregations whose members made no effort to hide their sympathies with the local Citizens' Council. When the interracial group walked up the steps of Trinity Episcopal Church that Monday, vestry members met them at the door and informed them that the usual morning service had been canceled and, unmoved by the northerners' arguments, proceeded to lock the doors of the church. Failing to integrate the church, Mrs. Peabody and several black women spent the rest of their three-day visit trying to desegregate restaurants, for which they were promptly arrested.[11] Coffin telephoned reporters to tell them what was taking place. The sheriff arrived, he recalled, "and to my amazement, and, I must say, malicious delight, I saw that he had a police dog in the car with him, and I thought, oh, boy, that's going to make a great picture, wait 'til the *Boston Globe* carries this one." When Mrs. Peabody and her companions emerged from the restaurant, the sheriff put them in the back seat with the dog. The journalists got their photographs, and his job done, Coffin had himself arrested and went to jail.[12]

By this time, however, his activism was old news, and most of the media coverage centered around the arrest of "Grandmother Peabody." After spending one night in jail, she and the other New Englanders posted bond and returned home. With them went many of the northern students who had joined the demonstrations, for the Easter break had come to an end, along with most of the nation's interest. The city's civic leaders and clergy insisted that St. Augustine had had peaceful and healthy relations between the races before the arrival of the outsiders, and when a handful of white clergymen insisted that they would open the doors of their churches to persons of all races, locals dismissed the statements as empty rhetoric. Desegregation efforts continued into the late spring, but with dwindling funds and lack of interest, SCLC officials fell back on a plan they had used in Albany and Birmingham when those campaigns appeared to be failing: they contacted northern clergymen and asked them to lend their moral presence to the protest. A delegation of rabbis traveled to St. Augustine in mid-June to participate in integrated marches through white neighborhoods, in front of restaurants, and down the city's thoroughfares. Rabbis Eugene Borowitz, Balfour Brickner, Israel Dresner, Michael Robinson, and several others from New York and New Jersey, joined SCLC's Fred Shuttlesworth in a prayer vigil outside a motel. After they refused to leave, state troopers arrested them; two others were arrested when they and three black youths tried to integrate a restaurant.[13]

Their incarceration allowed them time to reflect on their purpose in coming to St. Augustine. While they realized their symbolic importance to the black community as the spiritual heirs of the Exodus, the rabbis also remembered the "millions of faceless people who had stood quietly, watching the smoke rise from Hitler's crematoria" and dwelled on the evils of silence and inaction. But they also confessed that their presence reflected their need to salve their own consciences as well as help the black community, and in a joint statement they were honest enough to admit that their participation did more for the former than the latter.[14] Still, their convictions did not always translate into action; when the rabbis protested the sheriff's demand that Shuttlesworth be separated from them and put in a cell with blacks, he threatened them with cattle prods. "In a moment, we became not only nonviolent, but even non-resistant," one admitted, and some of the rabbis detected a "bitter and knowing smile on Shuttlesworth's face as our resistance collapsed so easily."[15]

Unlike their colleagues who had met staunch opposition from Birmingham's Jewish community the previous year, the sixteen rabbis received little attention from their fellow Jews in St. Augustine, who perhaps wanted to keep as much distance between themselves and the northerners as possible. The rabbis remained in jail overnight and, after posting bond, returned north; charges against them were later dropped. Had they decided to remain in St. Augustine for a longer period, it is unlikely that their presence would have made much difference. The SCLC campaign there was poorly planned and badly executed, and King, desperate to extricate himself from the situation, agreed to end demonstrations in late June after the city established a biracial committee. Even though the involvement of the rabbis had not affected the outcome of the campaign, they regarded it as not only a high point in their lives but a turning point as well.[16] Several would take part in later civil rights demonstrations; Brickner, Robinson, and Dresner would also devote their energies to the antiwar movement.

Part of the problem facing SCLC in St. Augustine was that the campaign had begun to seem superfluous after the Senate passed the Civil Rights Act on June 19. The fact that the bill made it through the Senate in the first place was due in no small part to the efforts of concerned clergy and laity. The "Midwest strategy" of the Commission on Religion and Race continued to be executed into the spring of 1964 as that region's churchpeople, ministers, priests, nuns, and small number of rabbis flooded first their representatives and then senators with letters and telegrams and, in some cases, paid personal visits to Capitol Hill to urge support for the bill.[17]

President Johnson welcomed such efforts, telling a group of 150 Southern Baptist ministers in the Rose Garden that the leaders of state and local government "are in your congregations, and . . . sit there on your boards," that "[t]heir attitudes are confirmed or changed by the sermons you preach and by the lessons you write and by the examples you set," and pressed on them the necessity of the legislation.[18] In a similar meeting later that month with religious leaders of all faiths, he urged them to "reawaken the conscience of your beloved land." If the assembled clergymen "were not momentarily dazzled by the President's flattery," theologian Kyle Haselden wrote, "they must have sensed in his remarks a touch either of mockery or naivete," for his implication that the racial crisis came from outside the religious community but that its solution lay within its grasp did not make sense. Far from being apart from racial discrimination, Haselden went on, the churches had given it biblical sanction as soon as the first slaves were brought over from Africa.[19]

Remorse was not enough; true repentance had to carry within it a modicum of healing, and so clergymen and religious figures witnessed to and lobbied in

Congress on behalf of the civil rights bill. "There was an agreement among religious groups that this was a priority issue," recalled James Hamilton of the Leadership Conference on Civil Rights, "and other things had to be laid aside." Robert Spike, executive secretary of the Commission on Religion and Race, agreed. "What is most at stake on Capitol Hill," he wrote, "is the integrity of the white majority in this nation."[20]

Evident, too, was the growing ecumenical spirit among those clergymen who had made the civil rights movement an issue of near-paramount importance. Nowhere else was this more visible than at Georgetown University, where on April 28 a crowd of over 6,000 Protestants, Catholics, and Jews attended an interfaith rally to emphasize the need for such legislation on the basis of morality and religious ideals. Loudspeakers were set up outside the hall for the benefit of those who could not get in. "What our Congress considers in terms of public policy, we uphold in terms of human dignity," Archbishop Patrick O'Boyle said in his invocation. "We are diverse in religious heritage, but together we proclaim that all men are equal under God." Similar themes were mentioned in the addresses given by Bishop Julian Smith, vice chairperson of the Commission on Religion and Race; Rabbi Uri Miller, president of the Synagogue Council of America; Archbishop Lawrence J. Sheehan of the Catholic archdiocese of Baltimore; and Eugene Carson Blake, who praised the assembly for illustrating that never before had the churches and synagogues "been so fully united intellectually on any moral issue confronting the American people."[21]

Interfaith unity was also demonstrated at the Lincoln Memorial, where Catholic, Protestant, and Jewish seminarians from across the nation held an uninterrupted vigil from April 19 until the civil rights bill was passed in late June, and at the Lutheran Church of the Reformation, which invited Protestant and Orthodox clergy to lead daily services that included prayers for passage of the legislation. At Spike's request, no benedictions were offered until that event occurred. By June, it appeared that the vigils would soon be coming to a close. On the 10th, the Senate, for the first time in history, voted cloture to end a filibuster. Nine days later, the bill passed by a vote of seventy-three to twenty-seven, and on July 2, with appropriate fanfare, Johnson signed the Civil Rights Act of 1964, witnessed by King, Roy Wilkins, and other black leaders.[22]

The first foray by religious groups into purely political lobbying in Washington had proved exceptionally successful. Both at the time and later, Vice President Hubert Humphrey insisted that "[w]ithout the clergy, we could never have passed the bill." Historian James Findlay's study of letters sent from midwestern church groups to their representatives and senators, who made up the swing vote, as well as of the group's lobbying efforts on Capitol Hill, gives credence to his suggestion that "a combination of such forces had strongly influenced the outcome" of the vote, although he approvingly quotes Clarence Mitchell, Washington lobbyist for the NAACP, who insisted that everyone's support was vital, be they religious figures or union leaders.[23]

Such a balanced appraisal was accurate, but the fact that southern senators singled out the religious community for criticism because of its support of the Civil Rights Act is indicative of the churches' perceived influence. Senator Richard B. Russell of Georgia noted that while thousands of ministers "did not permit themselves to have their vestments dragged in the mire of publicity seeking and political turmoil," others, "having failed completely in their efforts to establish good will and brotherhood from the pulpit, turned from the pulpit to the powers of the Federal Government to coerce the people into accepting their views under threat of dire punishment." Such a "philosophy of coercion by the men of the cloth . . . is the same doctrine that dictated the acts of Torquemada in the infamous days of the Spanish Inquisition."[24]

On the same day Russell was deriding the efforts of the clergy in Washington, his senatorial colleague John Stennis of Mississippi criticized the NCC for its support for a new civil rights drive in his home state. Quoting from Louisiana's *Shreveport Journal* of March 27, 1964, he noted that the religious organization had announced the creation of a "task force" that would be sent to the Mississippi Delta on a permanent basis to combat poverty and racial injustice. Its tentative annual budget would be $250,000, with the NCC paying 60 percent and the World Council of Churches contributing the remainder. "Officials of the National Council of Churches are entering into this project with the frank acknowledgement that they expect to become involved—on the Negroes' side—in clashes between white and Negro residents of Mississippi," he read. The piece concluded with a pointed warning to its readers: "If your church is a member of the NCC, part of every church donation you make will be used to finance this racial strife. Is this what you want?" Stennis described himself as "appalled" when he saw a recent television show in which clergymen were discussing why they had "enlisted in the army of zealots going to Mississippi this summer . . . like it was some foreign country and we were in the midst of all-out war."[25] What the senator was describing was the Mississippi Summer Project, a voter registration and education campaign coordinated by civil rights groups working together under the Council of Federated Organizations (COFO).

The project had its roots in the "Mississippi Freedom Vote" of the previous fall. Developed by Robert Moses of SNCC, white activist Allard Lowenstein, and members of COFO, this campaign illustrated black citizens' will to exercise their voting rights. Aaron Henry, president of the state branch of the

NAACP, and the Reverend Edwin King, the white Methodist chaplain of the predominantly black Tougaloo College in Jackson, were chosen as candidates for governor and lieutenant governor. A native Mississippian, the twenty-eight-year-old King had been involved in the civil rights struggle for over a year, often at great risk. In January 1963, just before he arrived in Mississippi, twenty-eight Methodist ministers had published a statement titled "Born of Conviction," which reaffirmed freedom of the pulpit, the church's policy forbidding discrimination on the basis of color or creed, and the need to support the *Brown* decision. White supremacists, furious that this action challenged their sought-after image of united resistance to integration, succeeded in immediately driving ten of the ministers out of the state through threats and intimidation. Methodist Bishop Marvin Franklin of Jackson, although acknowledging that his congregations had no right to dismiss their ministers, acquiesced, and replaced those who had left with more pliable pastors. By 1964, more than half the signatories had left Mississippi; five years later, only seven of the twenty-eight remained. Fifty-three other ministers also left the state to protest their persecution.[26]

Ed King was all too familiar with such tactics. After arriving at Tougaloo in February 1963 to serve as chaplain, he and his wife had begun working with the campus NAACP Youth Council to plan sit-ins, boycotts, and other direct-action protests in Jackson. Failing to convince the city's white ministers to either issue a public declaration against racial discrimination or allow blacks into their churches, King joined Tougaloo students in a series of sit-ins, during which they were assaulted by white gangs. Despite being the victim of a near-fatal car accident caused by the son of a Citizens' Council member, he continued to support the students' efforts to desegregate Jackson businesses, public facilities, and churches.[27] Oftentimes he accompanied students to the whites-only churches, which were "prepared for our visit," recalled one, "with armed policemen, paddy wagons, and dogs—which would have been used in case we refused to leave after 'ushers' had read us the prepared resolutions."[28] Because of such actions, the (white) Mississippi Conference of Methodists voted against admitting King to membership, thus excluding him from all benefits and pastorates served by that conference. The decision proved to be two-edged, for if King was not able to to depend on the white conference for support, neither could it exact punishment for his activism. On the recommendation of Bishop Charles Golden, one of the few black bishops in the Methodist Church, the Central (Negro) Jurisdiction of the church welcomed King into its fold. His fight against racial discrimination continued, and when northern Methodist clergy, including Bishop James K. Mathews of Boston, visited Jackson to assist in these efforts, King acted as unofficial sponsor.[29]

More than 80,000 blacks had voted in the "Mississippi Freedom Vote" election in November 1963, and SNCC and COFO decided to embark on a summer voter registration campaign that would bring the black community a measure of political power. While the original intent was to have a program organized and run by blacks alone, the realization that northern clergymen and students had also been active in the symbolic election campaign and had plans to continue their own voter registration drives led to a coordination of all efforts under COFO. In late March, representatives of the NCC, teachers, and sociologists met in Manhattan to discuss the establishment of "freedom schools" in Mississippi to give black children and adults the decent education denied them in the state's impoverished segregated schools. The NCC underwrote several training camps in nonviolence, which were the first stop for participants in the Mississippi Summer Project. The first contingent of students (there would be 800 in all) and ministers arrived at Western College for Women in Oxford, Ohio, on June 13, where they met Moses and other civil rights veterans who warned them of the dangers they faced and the necessity to learn the nonviolent self-defense tactics taught at the workshops. Other groups went to Tougaloo College, where they met with King and listened as he warned them about the factors that made Mississippi "a police state." All the students were impressed with the Tougaloo chaplain's quiet determination to continue the sit-ins begun the previous year.[30]

A total of 235 clergymen and laypersons took part in the summer project, counseling, delivering supplies, and, less often, sharing the students' task of helping to register black voters. Members of this ecumenical ministry came from all over the nation: the Reverend James Groppi, a Catholic priest from Milwaukee who worked with his city's NAACP Youth Council; Rabbis Arthur J. Lelyveld of Cleveland and Michael Robinson of New York; and the Right Reverend Paul Moore Jr., suffragan (assistant) bishop of the Episcopal Church, who left his diocese in Washington, D.C., to lend his support. Such diversity led one reporter to compare the volunteers to the ethnically mixed battalions of Hollywood war movies. All worked through the coordinated efforts of the Ministers Project in Hattiesburg led, wrote Moore, by "a deceptively easy-going" Reverend Robert Beach, a Presbyterian who deployed the "creaky denominational executives, . . . respectable suburban middle-aged pastors, [and] Rabbis . . . with careful skill" as they visited local white clergymen and counseled volunteers when necessary.[31]

Once described as "a hero of the radical-chic, New York–oriented types" in a 1978 polemic that contrasted liberal and conservative Episcopalians in the controversy over the ordination of women, Paul Moore was in fact no stranger to social justice programs. Far from being a "trendy" ecclesiastic, he had been involved in community work on behalf of race relations and the plight of the poor and homeless since the late 1940s, long before those causes became popular.[32] Born into a wealthy New Jersey family, Moore had had a sheltered youth up to and including his education at Yale University. After the bombing of Pearl Harbor, however, he entered the Marine Corps, rose to the rank of captain, and was wounded at Gaudalcanal. He entered General Theological Seminary in New York City in 1945, and, with two faculty members, set up an inner-city ministry in one of the most dilapidated sections of Jersey City. Described by fellow seminarians as the "G.T.S. social conscience crowd," the three held counseling sessions, intervened in housing disputes, went to court with their parishioners, and picketed against substandard public housing. In 1957, Moore left his parish to become dean of the Cathedral Church of Indianapolis, where he used his leverage to bring about successful negotiations between blacks and city officials for open housing. While there, he worked with other like-minded Episcopal clergy, including Malcolm Boyd, discussing common social concerns with them over weekly breakfasts.[33]

By 1963, Moore had been named suffragan bishop of the Episcopal Diocese of Washington, D.C., where he picketed for home rule for the nation's capital and had driven around with Martin Luther King Jr. giving civil rights speeches from a sound truck. He had considered participating in the marches in St. Augustine in March, but black leaders had told him that more people were needed in Mississippi. He was still weighing his decision one Sunday morning, wondering if he should risk his life, but the text of the sermon from Luke 5:4, in which Jesus told the apostles to go into the deep to fish, convinced him to go to the Deep South. ("I'm not a fundamentalist," he recalled years later, "but once in a while a piece of scripture just hits you, and you really do believe that somehow the Holy Spirit is telling you something.") On July 27, Moore headed to Mississippi.[34]

He had seen his share of courage on Guadalcanal and in the inner city, but was nevertheless greatly impressed with the heroism and bravery of the student volunteers and their counterparts in Mississippi's black communities. Even more moving was the interfaith cooperation among the clergy. Writing of the ministers' dormitory in Hattiesburg, he noted that "the Holy Spirit inhabited this improbable tabernacle, and the ecumenical movement thrived there beyond the hopes of the most optimistic." It was important for the churches to be in Mississippi, he continued, for the clergy's presence helped keep some of the local vigilantes in check, as well as contributed a moderating influence and "in some cases needed man-power." But what made clerical participation especially important was symbolized when Methodists, Catholics, Disciples of Christ, and members of other denominations congregated around the makeshift altar, an ironing board, to celebrate the Eucharist one Sunday morning. "[W]e were there to celebrate with him, the glory of his kingdom as it appeared around us in courage, in patience, in love, in fire, in Faith," he wrote. "We were there just to be there, just to say 'This is the Church, these purposes are of God.' "[35]

Despite the symbolic and real importance of the presence of the ministers, priests, and rabbis, their tenure lasted only a couple of weeks. Welcomed into the black communities, where they lived, worked, and made friends, they struggled with the differences in outlook and background that came with a clash of cultures. Scorned by local whites, the northerners' attempts to reconcile them to the cause of equal rights met with little success. When they visited local churches to discuss race relations with white pastors, they were refused entrance and were sometimes literally thrown out of the building. Black churches and COFO headquarters became the places of worship—and their source of much-needed inspiration.[36]

Hanging over everything was the climate of fear: fear of arrest, beatings, and violent death at the hands of white supremacists. There were no local authorities to whom the northerners could turn for help, for the police regarded them as outside agitators and often refused to give them protection. One layperson from the Disciples of Christ recalled how the sight of police cars unnerved her for weeks after she had left Mississippi; a minister remembered having to dive into a ditch as a truck barreled down the road toward him and his companions. Reverend Beach was repeatedly threatened and once assaulted. The Heffners, a white family in McComb, had invited northern clergymen to their home for dinner, with the result that their neighbors shunned them, their pets were poisoned, and the husband lost his business. When the Heffners learned that Moore was in town, they invited him to their house for a dinner party. Because no neighbors would visit, they invited FBI agents to join them. As night fell, cars filled with Klan members began circling the house, and the agents, who had code-named Moore the "Big Fisherman" for use on tapped telephones, drove him back to his lodgings. Eventually, the Heffners were forced to move out of town.[37]

The Klan and its allies were unable to drive the northerners out of the state or to silence local black activists, but the latter's perseverance came at a great cost. As black churches were often the focal point of civil rights organization, they became a common target for white supremacists armed with bombs and gasoline, who destroyed several churches during the summer. Clergymen from nine churches and synagogues in Mississippi—including Rabbi Perry Nussbaum from Jackson's Temple Beth-Israel; the Right Reverend Richard Gerow, Roman Catholic archbishop of Natchez-Jackson; and William P.

Davis, the white president of the state's Baptist seminary for blacks—formed the Committee of Concern to raise funds to rebuild the churches. By year's end, they had received $50,000, and college students from Ohio, Pennsylvania, and California had helped rebuild six churches as part of the "Beauty for Ashes" project.[38]

The seriousness of the danger facing those who challenged segregation was made all too apparent when civil rights workers James Chaney, Andrew Goodman, and Michael Schwerner were declared missing on June 21. Despite their disappearance, voter registration continued. On July 10, Arthur Lelyveld, a fifty-one-year-old rabbi long active in the peace movement, accompanied an interracial group of civil rights workers in Hattiesburg, where two white men armed with iron pipes attacked them. The students remembered the lessons learned in the workshops and protected themselves by crouching; Lelyveld had either not attended the sessions or had forgotten what was taught, and as he remained standing, unprotected, he was hit repeatedly in the head. The students helped the rabbi, weak from loss of blood, to the city hospital, and two days later Lelyveld left the state. A grand jury hearing in early August resulted in a suspended sentence for his attackers. By this time, federal agents had found the bodies of Chaney, Goodman, and Schwerner, who had been murdered and buried in an earthen dam. At the request of Goodman's parents, who were close friends, Lelyveld gave the eulogy at their son's funeral service at the Ethical Culture Society in New York City. Over 1,000 people attended the service; more than 500 stood outside the building in prayer. The murdered students, Lelyveld told the mourners, had become "the eternal evocation of all the host of beautiful young men and women who are carrying forward the struggle for which they gave their lives."[39]

By the time of the funeral, the summer project was drawing to a close. The last act took place not in the South, but at the Democratic National Convention in Atlantic City, where the Credentials Committee was holding hearings to decide whether to seat the delegates of the newly created Mississippi Freedom Democratic Party (MFDP) in place of the state's white delegates. Edwin King, one of the MFDP delegates, bitterly assailed Mississippi racists during his testimony, but the chair of the Democratic National Party asked him to confine himself to the legal issues before them and not expound on "the general subject of life in Mississippi."[40] In the end, the committee refused to seat the MFDP delegates, and leading Democrats, particularly Hubert Humphrey and Walter Mondale, hammered out a compromise whereby the white Mississippians would retain their seats if they swore loyalty to the Johnson ticket and promised to integrate future delegations; two MFDP delegates, Ed King and Aaron Henry, would be "at large" rather than represent the state. Neither the Democratic "regulars" from Mississippi nor the MFDP embraced the compromise, although Martin Luther King Jr., other black civil rights leaders, and a large number of liberal Democrats urged the MFDP to accept it. Robert Moses, Fannie Lou Hamer, and others who had spent years registering voters, believed that the liberals had sold out, and although Ed King continued to work with the MFDP, running in elections in 1966, it was at the Atlantic City convention that distrust of liberals in particular and whites in general began to grow at an accelerated pace within SNCC.[41]

Ironically, from the perspective of the mainline white churches, the spring and summer of 1964 underscored the benefits that could be achieved through widespread ecumenical cooperation in the political and social realm. Clergy of all faiths had been able to lend their considerable support to the passage of the Civil Rights Act, and members within their ranks had proven themselves able to work in the field alongside civil rights organizations in one of the nation's most staunchly segregationist states. While ecumenism in its deepest sense involved the reunification of a divided Christendom, wrote Robert McAfee Brown, "the concern to draw together, which ecumenism represents," extended beyond the churches to embrace all people. Brown himself understood this firsthand. Returning to Tallahassee, Florida, in August 1964 to appeal his 1961 sentence for trying to integrate the airport terminal, he was promptly jailed. Religious leaders of all faiths, including Martin Luther King Jr., sent him telegrams of support, and local Jewish, Protestant, and Catholic clergy visited him. After being released three days later, he had coffee with black clergymen in the now-integrated terminal, which was, for Brown, "as close to a sacramental experience as I ever expect to have away from the communion table."[42]

Not only was ecumenism flourishing on the front lines, but, in the minds of supporters of clerical activism, so was the prospect of a newfound relevancy for the churches. Ministers were no longer only saying the right things about race relations but were actually involving themselves in the cause of civil rights, some seeing in their criticism of society's complacency a return of prophetic witness. The Social Gospel had returned with a vengeance. If the Niebuhrian emphasis on the sinfulness and corruptibility of all human endeavor seemed outdated or irrelevant to such ministers, so did the emphasis on the individualistic religion and piety of the kind practiced by Billy Graham. Their model was Martin Luther King Jr., whose understanding of human frailties did not keep him from leading a moral crusade in the streets. Granted, clerical supporters of the status quo still greatly outnumbered the "new breed" of clergy, and there were still plenty of pietists in the country who believed that the church should not be involved in secular affairs. But for the activist clergy, the summer of 1964 was a heady time indeed, and the days when a only a handful of ministers dared speak out against racism in sermons, let alone take part in some form of witness, seemed an increasingly distant memory.

But more than one summer of activity was needed to help solve the plight of poor blacks in Mississippi, a fact readily understood by civil rights organizations as well as the NCC's Commission on Religion and Race, which had already decided in early 1964 that a small team of white ministers would remain in the state after September to establish the Delta Ministry. Executives from both the NCC and the commission and administrative officials from the Church of the Brethren, including the Reverend Ralph Smeltzer, decided to establish this ministry as an independent long-term relief and reconciliation effort. Paul Moore was named chair of the Protestant interdenominational ministry, but the real motivating force behind the new organization was its director, Reverend Arthur Thomas, a Methodist pastor who had been active in civil rights in Mississippi for several months. Funded by the NCC with extensive support from the World Council of Churches, the Delta Ministry's goals included direct relief services, community development, and a ministry of reconciliation between the black and white communities of Mississippi.[43]

Such work was desperately needed in a state whose black population had the highest illiteracy rate in the nation, an infant mortality rate twice as high as the white population's, chronic health problems, and no access to adequate medical care. Many homes in black communities in the Delta had no running water and no indoor toilets. Thomas's staff numbered four: Reverend Warren McKenna, an Episcopalian; Reverend Larry Walker, a Baptist; Reverend Wilmina Rowlands, a Presbyterian, former missionary to China, and one of the few ordained female ministers in the nation; and Thelma Barnes, the only black staff member as well as the only native Mississippian, who served as secretary and receptionist. Operating out of offices in Hattiesburg, Greenville, and McComb, the small ministry had a number of successes in the realm of community development and relief services. It supported black textile workers in their successful strike against segregated working conditions in Greenville mills, established a tent city in the spring of 1965 for black tenant farmers who had been driven off their land either for striking against the white landowners or as a result of increasing mechanization on the cotton plantations, circumvented the state's logjam of government food supplies to needy black families, and continued to conduct freedom schools, workshops, and voter registration drives with other civil rights organizations.[44]

From the beginning, most of the white population regarded the Delta

Ministry's work with suspicion and outright hostility. In January 1966, several hundred poor blacks, some from the ministry's tent city, staged a "live-in" at Greenville Air Force Base, to protest wretched living conditions in their own communities, and vowed to stay until the federal government offered them financial assistance. Thomas and his staff publicly disagreed with the tactic, and at a press conference in Washington, Moore refused to condone the "live-in," although he noted that it was important to consider the deep sense of frustration that had led to it. Authorities from the air base quickly evicted the protesters, but rumors spread just as quickly that the event had been planned by the Delta Ministry and the NCC. Local whites, including clergy, charged that the ministry had come to stir up trouble; they were joined even by some who had previously supported the ministry, such as Hodding Carter III, editor of the *Delta-Democrat Times* in Greenville. Their most frequently voiced (and damaging) charge was that the ministry was failing to live up to its goal of fostering reconciliation between the races—a version of the charge of worsening race relations, which had always been leveled at civil rights workers. Conservative southern churches stepped up their campaign of withholding funds from the NCC, this time to protest what they considered to be a radical reform program.[45]

Denominational hierarchies within the state, sensing the popular mood, reacted accordingly. In December 1964, Coadjutor Bishop John A. Allin of the Episcopal Church in Mississippi marshalled through the executive council of the Episcopal Church a resolution declaring that if church funds were to be used for civil rights projects in the South, participating Episcopal priests had to receive permission from bishops to work in their states. Once the resolution passed, Allin used it to stop visiting priests from conducting civil rights work in Mississippi, a situation that lasted only until February 1965, when the council rescinded the decision.[46] The Catholic Church had a similar policy requiring visiting priests to receive permission from the diocese before working within its boundaries, and whenever Roman Catholic priests arrived in Mississippi with the intention of working with the Delta Ministry, they were sent home on the grounds that the Catholic Church did not want to "endanger our relations with the Methodists here."[47] The Methodist bishop of Mississippi, the Reverend Edward J. Pendergrass, repeatedly flew from Jackson to New York in unsuccessful attempts to convince his church's National Board of Missions to cancel its proposed contribution to the Delta Ministry on the grounds that it was neither providing reconciliation nor truly ecumenical, as it "does not involve church people in Mississippi."[48]

Pendergrass's statement was true to a point, but this was not because of any design on the part of the Delta Ministry staff. James Findlay has described in detail how local white clergymen refused to have anything to do with the ministry's staff or, at times, invited them to church services only to hector them during the sermon. Staff members made sure that when poor whites showed up at food and clothing distribution sites, they too received whatever the ministry had to offer. One of the fundamental differences between the local white churches and the Delta Ministry was how each group defined reconciliation. To white Mississippians, reconciliation meant a reversion to the race relations before the civil rights era; the Delta Ministry staff saw it in quite a different light. As Moore described it, the ministry was pursuing reconciliation by helping impoverished blacks gain self-confidence and power, for "true reconciliation between unequal and alienated groups is not possible without justice."[49] By following the biblical injunction to help the poor, the Delta Ministry was challenging both the racial and the economic status quo in Mississippi. In time, middle-class blacks affiliated with the NAACP began questioning the ministry's work with the poor, leading to a rapprochement of sorts with middle-class whites. One native white minister even praised the NAACP in a speech at a Rotary Club, deriding the Delta Ministry as being, by comparison, "way out."[50]

Despite its pariah status, the Delta Ministry managed to promote a small measure of economic self-sufficiency, by developing local industries for poor blacks; politically, it was able to maintain some of the momentum of the civil rights movement after COFO ended in 1965, and it continued to support the MFDP throughout the 1960s. The staff's insistence on black empowerment helped it weather the advent of the "Black Power" movement, which weakened other civil rights organizations by frightening off white supporters. By the late 1960s, most of the ministry's staff, now larger than the original four members, was black.[51] The Delta Ministry's work among the poor and oppressed, especially voter registration and political education, was commendable, and theologian Harvey Cox concluded that "we need a dozen more ventures like [it]."[52] Unfortunately this was not to be. Curtailment of federal poverty programs by both the Johnson and Nixon administrations, financial disarray of the ministry itself, and severe cutbacks in funding from the NCC (which helped lead to the resignations of both Thomas and Moore), led the council to dissolve all administrative ties to the ministry in 1972. Although funds were still channeled through the Protestant interfaith organization, the ministry finally disbanded two years later.[53]

A ministry of reconciliation was very much on the mind of one former NCC staff member in the mid-1960s, but its emphasis would be very different from that of the Delta Ministry. In 1963, with financial assistance from the Field Foundation, Will Campbell had left the NCC to create a successor to the then-defunct Fellowship of Southern Churchmen. The Committee of Southern Churchmen, with Campbell as director, was composed of probably no more than a hundred men and women at its peak, but with no membership rolls, all numbers were estimates at best. Reflecting Campbell's growing disenchantment with institutions, it purposely had little organization. Located on a twenty-acre farm near Mt. Juliet, Tennessee, twenty-five miles from Nashville, the loose-knit assembly was, as Campbell later wrote, composed of Christians of various denominations who held that the gospel "has to do with poor folks, black folks, drug folks, military deserter folks, Ku Klux Klan folks, and others of God's children." Members often contributed articles free of charge to the committee's journal *Katallagete*, whose editor was James Holloway, professor of religion at Berea College.[54] The journal's name came from the Greek word for reconciliation, and it was this emphasis on the reconciling nature of Christ's life and death that was the motivating force behind the new organization. Southerners, by creating their own racial distinctions between people, had ignored the unity of all people under God, and had "led the Church to become like the nations, instead of being a light to the nations."[55]

Reveling in his freedom from institutional constraints, Campbell embarked on a personal ministry in his pick-up truck, bringing to the homes of poor whites and blacks a sympathetic ear as well as his customary supplies of chewing tobacco, walking sticks, bourbon, and his ever-present guitar. Wearing horn-rimmed glasses, dressed in Western-cut suits, and always adorned with a broad-brimmed hat, he resembled a bizarre cross between an Amish farmer and a country singer, an image probably created deliberately by the shrewd Baptist preacher. What remained important to Campbell, however, was his message; his appearance merely made him more approachable to other southerners. He insisted that Christianity was not a matter of doing but of being, because Christ had already reconciled humanity through his death and resurrection. Rather than try to convert people to a cause, he argued, one should preach the message of reconciliation, for once people realized and accepted the fact that God had already forgiven them, they would be radically transformed. "God is not the church, or politics, or civil rights, or liberalism," he once said. "God is no cause, no movement. And all this leaves you is to proclaim what has been done for you."[56]

Campbell's ministry to the poor earned him the respect and plaudits of fellow southerners. Nonetheless, despite the radicalism Campbell and his supporters claimed for their ministry of reconciliation, its theological underpinnings were not much different from what Billy Graham had been calling for since the early 1950s—an acceptance of the teachings of Christ would change people from within. The difference was that Graham's audience had been and continued to be the powerful, including presidents, while Campbell was preaching to the marginalized people of the South. Both were calling for individual redemption as the basis for social redemption. The problem with this system, as Graham's critics had been pointing out for over a decade, was that the great mass of white southerners *were* Christians—devout Christians, often with a literal belief in the Bible. And yet, at best, many were unwilling or unable to see what their religious beliefs had to do with segregation and racial discrimination; at the worst, the white southern churchgoers had deliberately used the Bible to sanction the racial status quo.

It was not enough to strive for individual conversion, they argued, as noble a cause as it was, if meaningful change was to come about any time soon. As Martin Luther King Jr. and other civil rights leaders had consistently warned, gradualism invariably played into the hands of the segregationists. Reforms had come about through pressure, through nonviolent direct action, through publicity. Such tactics had triumphed throughout the South since 1955, although not without cost. The same would be true of events in Alabama in 1965.

five

But let judgment run down as waters, and
righteousness as a mighty stream.

Amos 5:24

Flood Tide

Bearing Witness in Alabama, 1965

If it had not exactly become de rigueur for clergy to take part in public demonstrations by 1965, the sight of men in clerical collars marching alongside civil rights activists had certainly become more commonplace. American religious bodies had thrown their support behind the civil rights movement, and it was hard to ignore the impact the "new breed" had had via the March on Washington, voter registration efforts in Mississippi, and their contribution to the passage of the Civil Rights Act of 1964. Hostile laypeople continued to question their motives, but there was every reason to expect that for the rest of the decade the white churches would continue to expend their energy and funds in the struggle to end racial discrimination.[1]

The high-water mark of the white clergy's support for the civil rights movement arrived in the spring of 1965, with the highly visible presence of hundreds of priests, nuns, rabbis, and ministers in the SCLC-led Selma-to-Montgomery March, and continued with the passage of the Voting Rights Act that summer. Many had arrived in Selma in March 1965 after seeing dramatic and horrific footage of white law enforcement officials savagely attacking non-violent black marchers on the evening news, but few white sympathizers knew what had led to the idea of the march in the first place. On the night of February 18, 1965, a mob led by police and state troopers attacked a group of black marchers and reporters in Marion, Alabama. An officer fatally shot Jimmie Lee Jackson, a black youth trying to protect his mother from a state trooper, and civil rights leaders made plans to have a memorial march to bring attention to the violence routinely inflicted on blacks.[2]

The presence of hundreds of clergy, not to mention that of Martin Luther King Jr. and other high-level SCLC officers, underscored the failure of attempts by Selma's white clergy to improve race relations in their community. Like many southern ministers, priests, and rabbis, most in Selma were willing to tolerate what they considered to be a traditional way of life; only a few felt compelled to risk their livelihood by suggesting the need for change. In September 1963, three officials from the NCC, two of them ministers, had traveled to Selma to investigate the prospects for a ministry of reconciliation between the races. They succeeded only in alienating the city's white civic and religious leaders, including the moderate Reverend John Newton of the First Presbyterian Church, whom they urged to "join the Negroes vigorously in the name of Christ"; they acted, Newton later complained, as if they "had authority on integration." The NCC team believed that Selma's white moderates were retreating in the face of conservative opposition to the demands made by leaders of the SNCC voter registration drive, which had begun in Selma that autumn. "[M]any white members of the Selma community disagreed with the position of the leaders of the town," they wrote, "but felt themselves absolutely helpless to do anything concrete about it."[3]

The commission staff found only one kindred spirit, thirty-seven-year-old Father Maurice Ouellet, a Catholic priest of the Society of St. Edmund, an order founded to work with black Catholics, and pastor in charge of the St. Elizabeth Mission, a black hospital. He was the only clergyman who publicly supported the civil rights movement, allowing its leaders to use the mission for meetings. Not only had local white citizens threatened him, but Mayor Chris Heinz had also asked him to leave Selma, and other authorities requested that Archbishop Thomas J. Toolen of the Archdiocese of Mobile-Birmingham have him transferred. Although Toolen refused, he did ask Ouellet to curtail his "secular" activities. Meanwhile, as the voting rights campaign continued, Selma's Protestant churches adopted closed-door policies, refusing in most cases to seat black worshipers. The investigating team gloomily concluded that the only hope for change would have to come from the federal government, and that it would be unwise for the NCC to send a team of ministers to

Selma on a permanent basis, fearing, perhaps correctly, that they would be blamed for instigating further civil rights protests.[4]

Another white clergyman from outside the region, the Reverend Ralph E. Smeltzer, had also begun his own ministry of reconciliation that autumn. A Church of the Brethren minister from Illinois, he had traveled to Selma to work as a mediator between black leaders and white officials in Selma, trying to bring about peaceful change without large demonstrations that would inevitably polarize the community. Having worked among interned Japanese-Americans and Austrians during and after the Second World War, Smeltzer was particularly well-suited to such a low-key approach, yet in his one and a half years of service in Selma he met with almost constant rebuffs from the city's white Protestant clergy. Nonetheless, his voluminous notebooks, in which he recorded his conversations with Selma's citizenry, tell much about the struggle of conscience among white clergy there.[5]

Smeltzer's own self-described "mediation-reconciliation ministry" involved traveling back and forth between the Brethren headquarters in Elgin, Illinois, and Selma, meeting with black and white leaders in an attempt to get them to talk with each other and thus, in time, make his ministry unnecessary. Knowing the low regard with which many conservative southerners viewed the liberal NCC, Smeltzer went to great lengths to keep his work as free from association with that organization as possible. His concerns were well-founded. Recently, segregationists had severely beaten two white Lutheran and Presbyterian ministers, mistaking them for northern clergy involved in civil rights work, when they were actually carrying out routine mission work.[6] There were moderate whites in Selma, but they had no cohesion. "I need to talk to the moderates occasionally," he wrote in his notebook. "Just listen and gain their trust and confidence," and, most importantly, develop a "good strong church-related base."[7]

Despite efforts to establish his impartiality, Smeltzer failed to convince Selma's political leadership to enter into negotiations with local black leaders. Church of the Brethren officials had sent letters on his behalf to Mayor Heinz and Sheriff James Clark, but the former replied that while he appreciated the concerns of the Brethren, "we are of the opinion that we are able to handle our own affairs, without outside assistance." Privately, two white ministers told Smeltzer that far from objecting to its growing intransigent image in the national press, the city government actually liked it, and wanted to live up to it. While black leaders such as the Reverends Frederick Reese and Claude C. Brown were more supportive of his ministry, Smeltzer found it difficult to work with the two of them together, as they were always vying for personal power and prestige.[8]

His desire to get a "good strong church-related base" went largely un-fulfilled. Several priests, rabbis, and ministers refused to discuss civil rights, and the largest Methodist church in the city, he found, was a bastion of "segregationists and Wallace supporters," whose ranks included the pastor, George Kerlin, and a leading layperson who was a former president of the local Citizens' Council.[9] The Reverend Frank T. Mathews, rector of St. Paul's Episcopal Church, struck Smeltzer as an "able, congenial, back-slapper," and although respected in the white community, he had no desire to get involved in the tense racial situation. Opposed to "outside people" coming in and "whipping people up," Mathews believed that blacks were not willing to present their grievances in an orderly manner. It was "terrible" that white politicians refused to talk to any black leaders, but that was the "way it is." Before the outside agitation, Mathews explained, there was no racial tension in Selma anyway; "in fact," Smeltzer noted, "he said Selma really has no racial problem."[10]

Of all the white clergy, Newton was the most promising contact for Smelt-zer's ministry. The Presbyterian minister had been trying to convince his fellow clergymen to publicly take a moderate stand, to counter the city government's refusal to negotiate with black leaders. When he proposed that the ministerial alliance at least adopt a resolution for freedom of speech regardless of racial position, Kerlin used his prestige to defeat it, explaining that it would only stir up problems and serve no useful purpose. Even Mathews, whom Newton characterized as a "fine guy," had surprised him when the priest wrote a strong letter in the local paper condemning civil rights demonstrations as a violation of property rights. A frustrated Newton confided to Smeltzer that Selma's black citizens should keep the pressure on the city administration by demonstrating, for if they did not, the community "would go on another hundred years without concessions." Smeltzer was very impressed, consider-ing Newton a "great soul, [and a] tower of a personality." Still, such accolades did not alter the fact that "Newton sort of feels he stands alone," as Smeltzer noted in his journal.[11]

The only other cleric to receive similar praise from him was Father Ouellet. Like Newton, he was a relative newcomer to Selma, having arrived there in 1961, which suggests that neither individual was faced with the decision of risking a ministry that had taken years to establish. What separated the two was that Ouellet had no family dependent on him, and not only could he not be fired by his congregation, he had support from his bishop. Despite accusations that he had been seen dancing and singing with black women (presumably because he had attended civil rights rallies in black churches), the headstrong Catholic priest continued to work with the community's black leaders, believing that they were sufficiently organized and needed no assistance from out-side civil rights groups. When he tried to organize a meeting of white ministers and priests to discuss the racial crisis in the city, Ouellet met with the same hesitation on the part of white clergy as Newton had. At first the response seemed encouraging, as twenty-eight out of thirty showed up. But when Ouel-let suggested that the assembled clergy consider three avenues of action—a strong statement of support for the demonstrators, a statement of tolerance and mild support for justice, or nothing—the group chose the last. Most remained silent, and several walked out.[12]

Ouellet responded by writing a letter to the local paper criticizing them for their timidity, and while that brought him the private support of a handful of white moderates, it did nothing to endear him to his Protestant colleagues. Such a public stand was dangerous in Alabama, but Ouellet felt that he had a moral responsibility to speak out.[13] Believing that silence was the worst sin of all, he displayed a framed motto in his study to remind him that "The hottest places in hell are reserved for those who in time of great moral crisis maintain their neutrality."[14] Ouellet was not oblivious to the dangers that faced him for his outspokenness, however, and knew that he could be killed at any time. He was prepared to die, he told Smeltzer, but the pressures were taking their toll. He was exhausted, burdened by civil rights work to such an extent that he had allowed parish responsibilities to fall to other priests. Ouellet felt that he was alone in the religious community in his support for civil rights; when Smeltzer told him about a "fellow spirit" in the person of Newton, Ouellet admitted that he knew nothing about him.[15]

Had the Catholic priest wanted to develop a working relationship with the Presbyterian minister, it was unlikely that the latter would have welcomed such a move. Ouellet was a marked man in the community, and Newton presumably would not have wanted to jeopardize his standing among whites by striking up a public acquaintance with him. Furthermore, the ecumenical spirit so evident elsewhere in the country had not reached Selma. Whites crit-icized Ouellet for attending civil rights rallies at Protestant churches, speaking from their pulpits, and singing Protestant hymns.[16] One local judge referred to the priests at the St. Elizabeth Mission as "the Popes," and singled out Ouellet as a race-mixer, "un-American, [and] Roman poison."[17] Nor was anti-Catholicism limited to whites; several black Protestant ministers did not want to work with the only white individual who had risked his life to speak out on behalf of equal rights. One insisted that Ouellet's only concern was for the Roman Catholic Church "first and last," and his real interest was proselytiza-tion among Protestants, his civil rights efforts merely a pretext to increase black converts.[18]

Smeltzer's hopes for a biracial ministerial committee that would lessen racial tensions in Selma remained unfulfilled. The majority of ministers remained fearful, uncommitted, or disinterested. The only time they raised their voices in protest was when Sheriff Clark offered the services of his police officers to prevent black teenagers from entering "white" churches during Easter services, as they believed he had overstepped his authority by interfering in church affairs. In a letter sent to every white church in the city, Clark noted that he had received information that there would be an attempt made on Easter Sunday "to intergrate [sic] white churches in the community by kneel-ins, sit-ins, lie-ins and other methods." He went on to say that if it was "within the policy of your congregation to remain segregated, the sheriff's office and posse stands ready to protect your rights and property." It was only necessary for "each church governing body" to advise his office in writing if it wanted such services, and whether the police were to answer a call "from anyone whether in authority or not." Any such notification would be held in confidence. Clark's sources were accurate. SNCC workers had planned to "kneel-in" at various churches, including First Baptist, but black leaders dissuaded them from doing so, in order not to divert attention from the voting rights drive.[19]

Newton dismissed the letter as a publicity gimmick that reflected city politics, and was confident that most pastors would not even bother to reply. His own committee of deacons and elders voted that they would not even acknowledge the letter. Indeed, few clergymen wanted Clark's posse to be riding up and down the streets on Easter Sunday. Nonetheless, he believed that it was time for the white clergy to take a stand, even if only to call for moderation on all sides. The church had to take its position in regard to Christ, not society, he told Smeltzer; secular groups could do what they saw fit, but the church had to be the church; perhaps it was not too late for Selma's clergy. Such hopes were quickly dashed when Newton tried to arrange a meeting of ministers to discuss the deteriorating situation, only to be told that almost everyone planned to be out of town on the day of the meeting. Only a handful showed up, and the attempt failed. When rioting broke out between Clark's posse and local blacks in June 1964, Newton confessed that his position was becoming more tenuous and less productive, and gloomily told Smeltzer that there was no chance of even integrating the ministerial association, let alone convincing it to provide leadership. He was running into a stone wall, and was considering whether he should remain in Selma.[20]

With the voter registration drive at a standstill, Martin Luther King Jr. announced at the end of 1964 that he was going to go to Selma. The editors of the *Selma Times-Journal* tried without success to downplay the affair, telling readers that the visit of the "controversial darkie" was "scarcely an event of significance, nor of any great consequence," and stated their doubts that "our responsible citizens—white or colored—will be much concerned with him one way or the other."[21] When King announced in mid-January that he would remain in Selma to assist with the voter registration drive, the white community was thrown into an uproar. Opponents impugned his motives, charging that his stay was a manipulative gesture designed to create violence and thus gain financial contributions from the North; even some of his supporters questioned his timing, if not his motives. Robert Spike, head of the NCC's Commission on Religion and Race, believed that King's timing was premature, and complained that he had jumped the gun without making any prior contacts with the NCC, which was then involved in northern cities and unable to raise the necessary financial support for King on such short notice. The civil rights groups, not the NCC, had the right to set the timetable, Spike admitted, but added that white allies "still have the choice as to when we go in."[22]

The decision to mount a concerted, massive, publicity-generating campaign was exactly what Smeltzer had spent over a year trying to prevent. His ministry of reconciliation and mediation depended not only on his own ability to work quietly behind the scenes but also on finding a solution from within Selma's community. Furthermore, the campaign changed the nature of power relationships affecting the city, for indigenous civil rights leaders, persons with whom Smeltzer had been working since October 1963, were now relegated to the background as the focus centered on the confrontation between King and Selma's white authorities: the volatile Sheriff Clark; Wilson Baker, the new Director of Public Safety; and the new mayor, Joseph Smitherman.

The failure of Smeltzer's ministry was not a reflection on him, nor was it an indictment of Selma's black leaders. The consistent refusal of city authorities to seriously consider the demands of black citizens regarding voting rights or other grievances meant that pressures for change would have to come from outside the community—specifically, from the federal government. But the Johnson administration would not intervene unless there was a reason to do so, and King, Abernathy, Young, and other SCLC staff members hoped to provide the president with that reason. Charges that they hoped to provoke violence were met with the rejoinder that the violence already existed within the system of segregation and racial discrimination; all they were doing was bringing the violence out in the open where it could then be dealt with. As

Andrew Young later explained, "Sheriff Clark has been beating black heads in the back of the jail for years, and we're only saying to him that if he still wants to beat heads he'll have to do it on Main Street, at noon, in front of CBS, NBC, and ABC television cameras."[23]

The altered conditions spurred Selma's white ministers to finally hold meetings to discuss what role they should play in the new scenario. Not surprisingly, they offered no strong leadership. Like many in the white community, they resented SCLC's intervention and rallied behind the city administration, drafting a resolution in support of Smitherman and Baker, pointedly omitting Clark. It was the hope of the white moderates and Baker himself that if he could restrain the sheriff from using violence, national interest in the civil rights activities in Selma would dwindle, and King would suffer the same setback as he had at the hands of Police Chief Pritchett in Albany. At a meeting of the Dallas County Ministers Union, Baker told the assembled white clergy that the best thing they could do would be to advise their parishioners to let the demonstrators alone and leave the work to law enforcement officials.[24]

The new city administration refused to bow to pressure to establish a biracial committee, and local whites took their cue from Smitherman and called for unity in the face of demonstrations led by "professional civil rights agitators." "Not since drunken units of Wilson's Raiders burned, plundered and sacked this city on the night of April 2, 1865 has Selma faced a more tragic confrontation to the dignity and harmony of it's [sic] community life than that caused by the unwarranted actions of irresponsible Negro groups," ran a local newspaper editorial.[25] Reverend Mathews wrote in his church bulletin that the "[u]ndignified displays of rebellious violence against local laws" were not representative of the "responsible thinking" characteristic of Selma's citizenry. Calm would return when "troublesome immigrants have packed their bags and gathered their photographers and reporters and have left to wreak havoc in some other unsuspecting community."[26]

The repeated emphasis on the news media was telling. Newspapers with national circulation prominently featured photographs of Sheriff Clark and his police officers beating black demonstrators on the city's streets, and the resulting negative publicity threatened to hurt Selma's economy, especially after officials from the Hammermill Paper Company announced they were reconsidering their plans to build a plant in Selma because they believed their open hiring policies would not be respected by Selma authorities. Some segregationists, in collusion with the police, decided that it was time to focus their ministrations on northern journalists as well as civil rights workers. Television viewers saw examples of this when Clark punched the Reverend C. T.

Vivian, an SCLC staff member, in the face on the courthouse steps and then had his deputies push the television crew away with billy clubs.[27]

It was in this atmosphere of violence that Jimmie Lee Jackson was killed. While few local whites seemed to care about his death, the Reverend Joseph Ellwanger of St. Paul's Lutheran Church in Birmingham was deeply upset by the brutality. On March 6, he led a group of seventy whites, mainly ministers and university professors, to a rally on the steps of Selma's courthouse to support the voter registration drive and show that not all whites were in favor of segregation and police harassment of blacks. The Concerned White Citizens of Alabama, as they called themselves, listened as he called for the registration of black voters throughout the state. A larger crowd of hostile whites surrounded them, striking up a chorus of "Dixie," whereupon the moderates responded with "America" and black civil rights workers across the street chimed in with "We Shall Overcome." When the musical interlude was over, the segregationists moved in. Only the quick arrival of Baker and his lieutenant prevented the shoving from escalating into greater violence. Shaken, Ellwanger and his followers left the courthouse and returned to the Reformed Presbyterian Church, where the Reverend Claude Brown and SNCC members met them with rousing applause.[28]

SNCC and SCLC workers in Selma and Marion also had plans to lead a demonstration, this one to protest Jackson's death. On Sunday, March 7, 525 marchers, led by John Lewis of SNCC and Hosea Williams, one of King's aides, assembled in Selma to begin the journey. Leaving Brown's Chapel, an African Methodist Episcopal church in downtown Selma, they arrived at the Edmund Pettus Bridge that led toward Montgomery. On the other side of the bridge, standing three deep and blocking the entire highway, were 200 state troopers wearing gas masks and armed with clubs, bullwhips, and tear-gas canisters. Major John Cloud gave the marchers three minutes to disperse. One minute later he ordered the troopers to advance.[29]

Settling down to watch the ABC Sunday night movie *Judgment at Nuremberg* that night, television viewers were startled when the movie was interrupted by footage of the march in Selma. Millions of Americans saw the state troopers give a yell as they charged the black marchers in a wedge formation, clubbing and whipping them, and then firing tear gas as the screaming and blinded marchers retreated. Immediately following the carnage, mounted troopers pursued the fleeing blacks as they ran for the safety of their neighborhoods, continuing to beat them with clubs and rubber tubing wrapped with barbed wire. Those marchers who could walk took the wounded to Good Samaritan Hospital to be cared for by the Edmundite Fathers. "We carried young children into the parsonage screaming in agony from the tear gas and billy clubs," the Reverend John B. Morris, executive director of ESCRU wrote shortly afterward. "A few volunteer doctors did what they could, but it was plain that hospitalization was required for many."[30]

As shock, horror, and outrage over the atrocities gave way to action, thousands of Americans gave vent to their anger by taking part in demonstrations of their own. Thousands marched in the streets of Washington, D.C., Chicago, Detroit, and dozens of other cities, demanding federal protection for civil rights workers; others began making plans to travel to Selma to take part in the march when it resumed. Some simply dropped what they were doing and went to the nearest airport to catch the next flight to Birmingham and from there proceed to Selma, sometimes without a change of clothing or a pair of walking shoes. The Reverend Charles Carroll of St. Philip's Episcopal Church in San Jose, California, decided to purchase an airline ticket at the San Francisco airport without having any idea how to get to Selma; he simply felt that he had to show his support for the marchers. As a student in Germany in the 1930s, he remembered all too well the Nazi persecution of the Jews. After Martin Luther King Jr. (who was in Atlanta at the time) heard about the carnage, he decided to follow the suggestion of ESCRU's John Morris and do what he had done before in Albany, Birmingham, and St. Augustine. He called on the nation's clergy to defy Governor Wallace's ban on further marches by joining him in a "Ministers' March to Montgomery" on Tuesday, March 9.[31] In this way, Morris believed, the nation, "representatively through its clergy, could bear some of the burden Selma residents had suffered that day."[32]

The response was much greater than it had been for earlier requests. The violence at the bridge had disturbed Americans far more than had any other civil rights demonstration, including the brutality in Birmingham. After spending two days in his hotel room making telephone calls to clergy across the country, Morris and SCLC officials reported that over 500 ministers, rabbis, and, for the first time, Catholic priests, had agreed to take part in a SCLC-sponsored march. Episcopal and Methodist bishops, monsignors, NCC officials, and parish priests, ministers, rabbis, seminarians, and theologians from all parts of the nation arrived in Selma, either at SCLC's request or, like Carroll, having decided independently to make their way to Alabama. Many of them had nearly jammed the switchboard at the NCC's Commission on Religion and Race headquarters in New York City calling for information. In turn, the commission issued an appeal of its own, asking clergy from around the nation to respond to King's call.[33]

Robert McAfee Brown was discussing racism in his Christian ethics class at Stanford University when he decided to fly to Selma, explaining later that it seemed "hypocritical" to simply talk about it and that he felt he could educate his students more by going to Alabama. Rabbi Israel Dresner, who had marched in St. Augustine the year before, left his congregation at Temple Sharey Shalom in Springfield, New Jersey, to travel to Selma. Malcolm Boyd also made his way there. He had been asked to leave Wayne State University as a result of his outspokenness not only on racial matters but on the humanity of Jesus as well, insisting on television that Christ, being human, possessed a penis like any other man. Bishop Paul Moore had arranged with other Episcopal prelates to make Boyd a salaried "chaplain-at-large," or a "secular priest," which enabled him to work on behalf of causes such as civil rights without being tied down by daily parish duties or the conservative sensibilities of any one congregation. By the fall of 1964, Moore formally invited him to the Episcopal Diocese of Washington, D.C. As a canonical resident in the diocese, Boyd would serve as assistant to the Reverend Quinland Gordon, the church's black Episcopal priest, but his responsibilities would also include working as as national field representative for ESCRU. Boyd wasted no time in taking advantage of his newfound freedom. Joining up with William Jacobs, managing editor of the Catholic weekly *Ave Maria*, he spent the rest of 1964 traveling throughout Mississippi to research the role of black and white churches in the struggle for civil rights; the two men later received an award from the National Catholic Press Association for their articles.[34]

For others, the Selma-to-Montgomery march would be their first southern civil rights demonstration. After seeing the carnage on the evening news, the Reverend James Reeb, a Unitarian minister from Boston, told a colleague that it was time for people who really believed in freedom to make a direct witness for it, and left his wife Marie and four young children and the black community of Roxbury, where he worked as a secretary and field worker for a low-income housing project sponsored by the American Friends Service Committee, to go to Alabama. Jonathan Myrick Daniels, a twenty-six-year-old white seminarian at the Episcopal Theological School in Cambridge, Massachusetts, also made the journey south. A native of Keene, New Hampshire, Daniels had attended the Virginia Military Institute after graduation from high school; he was continuing his education at Harvard University when his father died, and in his grief he found himself turning increasingly to the Episcopal Church for solace. By 1962 he had decided to become a priest and had enrolled in the Episcopal Theological School. During evening prayers in the chapel in March 1965, he had an epiphany, realized that he had to put others before himself, exalt the poor, feed the hungry, and knew then that he had to go to Selma.[35]

"It was a very exhilarating experience," Robert McAfee Brown remembered, even for those who, like himself, stayed only a short while and left before the marches began. When he went to the airport to board the plane, "about fifteen clergy in their collars" disembarked, ready to take the place of Brown and the others who were leaving. These rotating visits "involved many people who had never done anything like this before in their lives, and . . . there was exhilaration in the fact that for once folks in the churches and synagogues seemed to be doing more than just talking or bemoaning the state of the world and so forth."[36]

Not everyone shared Brown's enthusiasm. "There was a time when a person could drop in at the parish rectory to discuss a problem with his clergyman," complained a Chicago woman in a letter that was reprinted in several of the city's papers. "Now, one must first telephone the rectory to find out if the clergyman is down in Alabama picketing. Why don't the clergy stick to the pulpit?" The editors of *Time* praised some of the ministers for traveling to Selma because "their consciences and their sense of Christian duty demanded no less" but faulted others who were there "simply to win merit badges," quoting one minister who seemed to treat the entire situation as a game: when he stepped off the plane in Montgomery, he turned to a friend and said, "Fix bayonets! Charge!" The conservative Catholic journal *Ave Maria* asked religious leaders whether the "appropriate moral response of clergymen is always the same as the appropriate moral response for civil rights leaders."[37]

The only white clergy to welcome the northern ministers to Selma were the Edmundite fathers; Ouellet volunteered the use of the maternity ward and other wings of the Good Samaritan Hospital for lodgings. Several of the city's ministers and rabbis refused to meet with their northern brethren, and while the Reverend Mathews received an integrated group of fellow Episcopal priests in his study, the meeting soured when he insisted that there was nothing wrong with blacks and whites worshipping separately. Despite his affirmation of segregation, the visit did not please his vestry, who persuaded Mathews to take a vacation from Selma later in the week. Any contact with the northern ministers was deemed suspect, for most of Selma's white population viewed the visitors as "outside agitators," an appellation that disturbed some of the out-of-towners not at all. "Why not?" said one minister. "An agitator is the part of the washing machine that gets the dirt out."[38]

By Tuesday, March 9, more than 400 clergy had arrived in Selma to take part in the ministers' march. With Ralph Abernathy and Martin Luther King leading the way, black and white clergymen, SNCC workers, SCLC staff members, and local black townspeople headed toward the Edmund Pettus

Bridge. Wallace had ordered state troopers to block their passage again, but it was not the threat of troopers that stopped the march. A federal judge had requested a postponement of the march until hearings could begin on the legality of Wallace's injunction. King, not wanting to alienate federal authorities and not yet having received assurances from President Johnson that federal troops would guard the route from Selma to Montgomery, agreed, and ordered the marchers to turn around. Back at Brown's Chapel, many of the white clergy became instant civil rights strategists and urged that the march continue. Rabbi Dresner argued that they had to choose between God's law and man's law; others insisted that waiting any longer would cost public support. But King and his aides, who were far more familiar with the human cost of demonstrations, saw no purpose in a second bloodbath, and they asked the northern clergy to remain in Selma while they waited for the court to lift the injunction.[39]

James Reeb was all set to travel back to Boston when fellow Unitarians convinced him to stay in Alabama in case they were needed for another march later in the week. The group joined the dozens of other marchers crowded into a black-owned restaurant for dinner. Afterwards, Reeb and his companions, Reverends Orloff Miller and Clark Olsen, left the restaurant to go back to SCLC headquarters, but they walked in the wrong direction. It proved to be a fatal mistake, for as they passed by a restaurant patronized by white segregationists, four white men ran at them with clubs and iron pipes. Miller crouched in a self-defensive position, hands over his head, Olsen was grazed by a club, but Reeb absorbed the full impact of the blow aimed at him, which struck him on the head. The two others assisted their stricken colleague to his feet, and, realizing that his speech was garbled and his vision impaired, brought him to the SCLC office, where he complained of a terrible headache. An ambulance took Reeb to Burwell Infirmary, one of the few black hospitals in the vicinity, but physicians there realized that he needed to be attended to at the better-equipped hospital in Birmingham.[40]

By this time, Reeb had lapsed into a coma, and a series of ambulance breakdowns and delays in getting a police escort resulted in a four-hour delay before he reached the hospital in Birmingham. Physicians there realized that Reeb's massive skull fracture was fatal and that it was only a matter of time before he died. News of his condition quickly reached Selma, and groups of ministers, civil rights workers, and local blacks milled around in Brown's Chapel and the streets outside, waiting to hear further reports. The story of the assault had also reached Washington, D.C., and Senators Robert and Edward Kennedy sent Mrs. Reeb a personal letter of sorrow, while President Johnson sent her yellow roses and his presidential jet to take her to Birmingham.[41]

Despite the brutal attack on Reeb, or perhaps because of it, more clergymen descended on Selma to join the protests around the courthouse. They were joined for the first time by large numbers of nuns from the archdioceses of St. Louis, Missouri, and Washington, D.C. Ouellet provided them with lodging at the St. Elizabeth Mission, driving several groups from the airport himself. While the nuns' ecclesiastical superiors, Joseph Cardinal Ritter and Archbishop Patrick O'Boyle, had given them permission to go to Selma, Archbishop Toolen had not, and he charged that the nuns (and the out-of-state Catholic priests) were violating the custom whereby visiting parish clergy and religious workers sought permission of the resident archbishop to work in his archdiocese. Ignoring his complaints, the nuns from St. Louis and Washington, D.C., named Martin Luther King Jr. their de facto archbishop for the remainder of their visit.[42] Dressed in their traditional black and brown habits, they were even more conspicuous than the priests and rabbis—and the target of a great deal of anger from Selma's white citizens. "What are you doing to the white race?" shouted one man to Sister Mary Peter of Chicago as she walked down the city's main street to join a demonstration. "Educating it," came the reply.[43]

Demonstrations and convocations continued beyond Selma. The NCC's Commission on Religion and Race convened a meeting at the Lutheran Church of the Reformation in Washington, D.C., calling for a voting rights bill and federal protection of the marchers in Alabama; the audience listened as bishops and priests who had been in Selma three days before for the aborted march described the role that the white clergy had to play in the struggle for civil rights.[44] Some feared that it was already too late for the white churches, insisting that King and other black clergy were God's instruments for change. "The tragedy of the Christian church in its white manifestation is not that God has judged us," one minister said, "but that the Master has shaken the red dust of Alabama from His feet and passed on into the Negro church, where His spirit lives, and His name is glorified." After the meeting, several groups of clergymen went to the offices of their senators and representatives to urge support for a voting rights bill.[45]

Paul Moore cochaired rallies in Lafayette Park with SCLC's Walter Fauntroy, where protesters heard the Episcopal bishop and civil rights activists speak. "I remember one day I was supposed to give a speech," Moore said, and had worked out a "rational, Anglican" argument for federal action. Just before him, though, Fannie Lou Hamer, a powerful speaker and one of the black founders of the Mississippi Freedom Democratic Party in 1964, got up and "really belted it out, with a strong southern voice," he remembered, and there he was, ready to give a closely reasoned sermon. He strongly denounced

Johnson's "unbelievable lack of action" and suggested that another march on Washington might be necessary to spur the president's involvement. Afterwards, he donated money for the establishment of a kitchen to be set up to feed the protesters in the park, and then joined demonstrators picketing the White House.[46]

Johnson agreed to meet with two groups of clerical representatives the following day to discuss his civil rights strategy. The first meeting was less than cordial. Moore demanded to know what was taking the president so long to draft a voting rights bill and send it to Congress. Johnson replied that he had to be extremely careful about the language of the bill to insure its safe passage and then proceeded to remind the ministers of all he had done on behalf of civil rights. The conversation drifted to more general topics. Moore remembered Johnson's eagerness to discuss the Bible with ministers; he had his assistant Bill Moyers, himself a Baptist minister, retrieve a Bible so he could read his favorite passage from Isaiah 1:18, "Come now, let us reason together." By the time the ministers left, many were deriding the meeting as a "snow job."[47]

The second group, led by the Reverends Joseph Ellwanger, Eugene Carson Blake, and other NCC representatives, was less contentious, and the ministers had a lengthy talk concerning the need for federal intervention in Selma. But Johnson's comments elicited little praise from other clergy who heard about them later. Others were not only angry at him but angry about the racial makeup of the delegations, for out of sixteen clergymen, only two had been black. "We didn't come 1,500 miles to be jeered at," complained a black minister from Minneapolis. "I think you have been pleased with the prestige of being appointed to a committee to talk to the President. . . . Whose fight is this anyway?"[48]

The minister's concern that more attention was being focused on white clerical participation than on black was well-founded, as shown by the reaction to Reeb's death that weekend. Across the nation people paid tributes to the murdered white minister at rallies in support of voting rights. Twenty-five thousand attended a memorial service in Boston. Johnson left an official function to telephone Marie Reeb and offer his condolences. Francis Cardinal Spellman of the Catholic Archdiocese of New York sent a $10,000 check to Bishop James Crowley, chief administrator of Selma's Good Samaritan Hospital, in memory of Reeb, and the Unitarian Universalist Association, SCLC, and American Friends Service Committee (AFSC) established funds for his widow and children. Johnson also pointedly mentioned the death of "a man of God" in his address before Congress on the evening of March 15, two days before his voting rights bill reached the Senate.[49]

In their grief over Reeb's death, few whites remembered or were even aware that the march had originally been conceived as a memorial tribute to a slain black man. What had happened the previous year regarding the deaths of Chaney, Schwerner, and Goodman was happening again: the deaths of blacks elicited little response, but when whites were murdered, the nation took notice. "There is a sense of national outrage and shame over Reeb's death, but how many people know the name of the young Negro laborer who died two weeks earlier?" asked David Riley in the *New Republic*. "This young Negro was killed not by crazed ruffians, as Mr. Reeb was, but by a law officer of one of the 50 states of our aroused country. And we can't recall his name."[50]

SNCC workers were outraged over the fact that many whites had discovered the Selma movement only after Reeb's murder. "Now, I'm not saying we shouldn't pay tribute to Rev. Reeb," said Stokely Carmichael, one of the organization's young firebrands. "What I'm saying is that if we're going to pay tribute to one, we should also pay tribute to the other. And I think we have to analyze why [Johnson] sent flowers to Mrs. Reeb, and not to Mrs. Jackson."[51] King also used this example years later to explain why militant blacks were turning away from nonviolence, writing that Johnson's failure to extend the same recognition of Jackson's sacrifice "only reinforced the impression that to white America the life of a Negro is insignificant and meaningless."[52] Still, it must be pointed out, as David Garrow has done so cogently in his study of the Selma protests, that Reeb's death, unlike Jackson's, took place at a time when national attention was riveted on Selma, and this may have been a contributing factor in the different ways Americans reacted to the murders.[53]

Representative George Andrews of Alabama admitted that he was "deeply, deeply grieved that a fine Christian man of God should end his virile ministry in such a sordid way," but he singled out King as being "solely responsible for the trouble we are having today. . . . If he were to leave the State of Alabama today, . . . there would be no further trouble." Representative Williams of Mississippi was less charitable, insisting that "one of these invading ministers, who went to Alabama with a martyr complex for the purpose of finding trouble, found the trouble he was looking for."[54]

The majority of Selma's blacks were less angry over the differing reactions to Reeb's and Jackson's deaths and grieved alongside the white visitors over the death of yet another person in the struggle for civil rights. Local whites were less remorseful. The people of Selma were all very sorry about Reeb's death, one explained, but then asked, "those visiting preachers who now stand in the street defying authority, are they completely blameless in the death of Rev. Reeb?" They had defied a federal court injunction and state and city edicts against marching; could they, "in their prayers to God [and] in their hearts feel that they had no relation to the influenced passions of the hoodlums who that night killed Rev. Reeb?"[55] Similar sentiments boded well for those accused of the minister's murder, all of whom were acquitted by an all-white jury after a ninety-minute deliberation.[56]

Smeltzer also found local whites unwilling to admit any complicity. He asked Reverend Newton, who had drafted a telegram from the city to Mrs. Reeb expressing sorrow over her husband's death, whether one of the white ministers of Selma would be willing to participate in a memorial service for Reeb. Newton told him that he knew of no one but himself who would cooperate. The city was filled with too much hatred, he said, and no one appreciated the visits of the northern ministers; besides, they disliked the idea of making a martyr out of Reeb. Too many local clergy were already saying "What would you expect?" and "He asked for it," Newton warned Smeltzer.[57] Ironically, Newton, one of the city's few moderates, was deluged with angry letters from across the country after Reeb's death; a February interview for the *Los Angeles Times* may have given him some name recognition once the crisis in Selma had begun.[58] One midwestern pastor consigned him to the "nether regions" for having failed to make Christians out of Selma's whites; a Miami resident wrote that "Rev. Reeb's blood touches you. Shame, shame on you Rev. Newton"; and a Presbyterian in Georgia assured him that "if your church is still in existence today, it is a mockery and has already been destroyed by its own members and their apathy."[59]

Civil rights activists held a memorial service in Brown's Chapel on Monday, March 15. It was a stirring ceremony, if not so much for the speeches as for the sight of so many religious leaders assembled for the interfaith ceremony, flown to Selma on an airplane chartered by the NCC. Among the notables were Archbishop Iakovos, head of the Greek Orthodox Archdiocese of North and South America, the Right Reverend John Hines, presiding bishop of the Episcopal Church, the Reverend Dana McLean Greeley, president of the Unitarian Universalist Association, Rabbi Eugene Lippmann of Washington, D.C., and Bishop-Elect James P. Shannon of the Catholic Archdiocese of St. Paul. All took their places at the front of the church with King and Abernathy. A congregation of almost 500, many of them white nuns and clergy, crossed arms and swayed as they sang "We Shall Overcome," followed by a rabbi's intonation of the Kaddish, the Hebrew prayer for the dead. At the end of the ceremony, the assembled crowd moved slowly toward the courthouse, walking three abreast, in a federal court-sanctioned march in honor of the slain minister.[60]

Coretta Scott King later described the ceremony as "perhaps the greatest and most inspiring ecumenical service ever held," and while such a claim might be overstated, few failed to recognize the ecumenical cast of the memorial service. *Life* magazine devoted its cover to a photograph of Iakovos and King and the others on the steps of the courthouse; Reinhold Niebuhr commended the church for finally marshaling all its resources on behalf of the civil rights struggle. For those who had been in Selma during the previous week, however, the ecumenical spirit had been in abundance in the lesser things as well: the participation of nuns, priests, and rabbis in a vigil held on a cordoned off section of Sylvan Street; the dubbing of the living quarters in Good Samaritan Hospital "Ecumenical Hall," the small prayer sessions and daily conversations held by those of different faiths.[61] "Men who differed in every conceivable respect—faith and race and culture—found themselves bewildered by a sudden unity whose implications went far beyond the unpredictable days they were enduring together," wrote a Jesuit priest, seemingly oblivious in his choice of language to the large numbers of nuns present. "But they knew beyond any doubt that they would never again be the same men who had lived Before Selma."[62]

The fact remained, however, that the clergy and religious figures had come to Selma to join the march to Montgomery, and with tension rising and nothing to do until the federal court had ruled on the governor's injunction against the march, tempers of both clergy and law officers flared. Even after the judge ruled in favor of the demonstrators, time was needed to make preparations for the march, slated for Sunday, March 21. In the meantime, SNCC sent more than 300 people, most of them white and many of them clergymen, to march through Selma to arouse the conscience of the white community, and probably to give the northerners something to do. Unfamiliar with the city, they shortly found themselves marching into well-to-do white neighborhoods, where they were met by crowds of hostile whites. Wilson Baker arrived to accost one of the clergymen, a Catholic priest from Chicago. "Do you know where you are? Do you know where you're going?" he asked the rattled priest, who admitted he did not. Baker grabbed him by the shoulders and escorted him across the street, announcing that he was going to put them all into protective custody in a community center. "They want people killed," muttered Baker. "They really want people killed." As the white priests and others were led away, they broke into a chorus of "We Shall Overcome," a rendition one reporter found "rather unmelodious." "This has ceased to be a Negro movement. It's become a misfit white movement," Baker remarked. "At least we had good music when the Negroes were demonstrating."[63]

On March 19, King, acting on behalf of SCLC, sent out a second telegram to clergymen and religious groups across the nation asking them to join the civil rights workers in a march that would begin in Selma in the early afternoon of March 21 and end at the state capitol later in the week. "The President and Federal Judiciary have spoken affirmatively of the cause for which we struggle," it began. "All citizens must now make their personal witness. The freedoms of suffrage and assembly are fundamental to all our traditions."[64] A copy of the telegram reached Rabbi Abraham Joshua Heschel at his home on Friday afternoon, and he and his family hurriedly made arrangements before the sun set and the Sabbath began. At dusk the following day, they kissed him goodbye as he left for the airport, wondering if they would see him again.[65]

Upon hearing of the march, Bishop Carpenter of the Diocese of Alabama urged his fellow Episcopalians from outside the state not to participate, and asked those already in Alabama to go home. "This 'march' is a foolish business and a sad waste of time," reflecting a "childish instinct to parade at great cost to our state," he complained.[66] Presiding Bishop Hines had neglected to consult with Carpenter when he arrived in Alabama on March 8, which had further angered the Alabama bishop, who also objected to his church's "spending the money we send up there for the spread of the kingdom of God" to finance such trips. His objections were duly noted and promptly overruled by the Executive Council of the Episcopal Church in New York City.[67]

On March 20, President Johnson called up 4,000 National Guard and regular troops to protect the civil rights marchers as they walked from Selma to Montgomery. Everything was now in place, and King and his lieutenants anxiously waited for the next day. As they did so, SNCC workers completed their list of 300 people who could take part in the entire march; the federal judge had ruled that an eighteen-mile stretch of Route 80 through Lowndes County could accommodate only that number because it was a narrow two-lane road. The rest of the participants could begin the march and then meet up with the others outside of Montgomery.[68]

Sunday, March 21, dawned bright and cool, a perfect day for the march. The day began with a morning worship service at Brown's Chapel, which, as had been the custom for the past two weeks, was ecumenical. Heschel, dubbed "Father Abraham" by civil rights workers, read the Old Testament lesson, Protestant and Catholic clergy participated in other parts of the service, King preached a moving sermon, and it concluded with the singing of "We Shall Overcome." By midday, more than 3,000 people were milling around the chapel, waiting for the march to begin. A delegation from Hawaii, carrying a banner proclaiming that integration worked in their state, placed a lei around King's neck. After making a few opening statements, he and Abernathy led the march across the Edmund Pettus Bridge, accompanied by Cager Lee, Jimmie Lee Jackson's grandfather, and Heschel, his white hair and beard glistening in the sunlight. John Lewis, James Forman, and other SNCC officers walked closely behind. Thousands of civil rights workers, clergymen, nuns, men and women in suits and dresses, local blacks in overalls, labor leaders, and others followed them out of town.[69]

Hostile whites lined the route, and a loudspeaker played "Bye Bye Blackbird." Some waved signs reading "Too Bad, Reeb," "Open Season on Niggers," and "Rent Your Priest Suit Here," a reminder that many local whites dismissed the possibility that a real minister could genuinely feel that his Christian conscience demanded involvement in such a protest. Many white citizens continually prefaced their comments about northern ministers and priests with the words "so-called," reported Newton, and were certain that there was some leftist taint to such persons. The epithets hurled at the nuns were unprintable.[70]

Helicopters circled overhead as the marchers crossed the Alabama River and headed toward Montgomery on Route 80, flanked by National Guard and Army Reserve units sitting in jeeps, monitoring their progress on radios. By the end of the first day, after five hours of marching, the majority of the walkers returned to Selma or made their way to Montgomery by bus or car as the 300 camped out for the night. Clergy, theology professors, and nuns eagerly threw themselves into the chores assigned them at the campsites, standing watch at night and digging out delivery trucks mired in the spring mud, many of them driven by self-described "fish-and-loaves" committees composed of seminary professors and students.[71]

By March 24, the 300 marchers had cleared the eighteen miles, and their numbers were again augmented by those who rejoined them to complete the march. By evening, 5,000 people were trying to keep dry amidst the mud on the grounds of St. Jude Hospital in Montgomery County, where Archbishop Toolen had given them permission to camp out. Mrs. Viola Liuzzo and other volunteers at the first aid station ministered to those who were exhausted and suffered from blisters, and then joined them the next morning as they entered Montgomery. Those who had marched the entire fifty miles wore bright orange vests to distinguish them from the 30,000 people crowding into the area in front of the state capitol to listen to King and others demand that the right to vote be upheld.[72]

It had been an exhausting and exhilarating march, but few doubted that much work still needed to be done; the sight of the Confederate and Alabama state flags flying atop the state capitol building in Montgomery, with the American flag nowhere to be seen, was a stark reminder. If any more proof was needed, the brutal murder of Mrs. Liuzzo by members of the Ku Klux Klan as she drove civil rights workers back to Selma that night convinced the overly optimistic few that the struggle was far from over. Still, clergymen and nuns from across the nation could take pride in the fact that they had, as they saw it, done their part to revitalize the church. Editorials in newsmagazines and religious journals all commented on the new breed of social activism found in the streets of Selma, the strengthened ecumenical spirit, and the demise of the stereotype of the rectory-bound parson who ventured forth on Sunday afternoons to take tea with elderly spinsters.[73]

Nonetheless, there were plenty of critics who felt otherwise, believing that the northern clergy were mere publicity seekers, as Clayton Sullivan, a white Southern Baptist minister, put it, "twenty-four hour prophets from New Jersey and New York who flew down South . . . with martinis in their hands and roundtrip tickets in their pockets," who wanted to "return home as moral 'heroes.' "[74] Others complained that they had violated the separation of church and state by trying to act as a court or legislature on matters of public policy, in the process alienating their congregations by ceasing to act as examples of a higher calling. "Many clergymen seem to have lost the halo of God's light and to have been plunged into the darkness of life itself," wrote David Lawrence, editor of the conservative *U.S. News and World Report*. A young Baptist minister in Lynchburg, Virginia, told his parishioners at the Thomas Road Baptist Church that the church did not have a mandate to involve itself in marches and demonstrations. Preaching the "pure saving gospel of Jesus Christ," he said, was a full-time occupation that gave those who did it properly no time to do anything else, "including fighting communism, or participating in civil rights reforms." Ministers "are not called to be politicians but to be soul winners," he warned. The young preacher's name was Jerry Falwell.[75] By the 1980s, his views had changed considerably: he had founded the Moral Majority, a fundamentalist lobbying group that fought pitched political battles against legalized abortion and for a return to school prayer.

Passage of the voting rights bill remained a priority for liberal clergy and religious organizations, and hundreds of clergy and churchpeople renewed their lobbying efforts on Capitol Hill. In the National Cathedral, the Catholic Interracial Council, ESCRU, and several other religious groups joined Representative Frank Horton of New York in sponsoring four of Malcolm Boyd's plays on race, performed in the immense Gothic structure. After the performances, Boyd himself delivered a sermon on the need for the legislation. "The freedom revolution has given American life a redemptive awareness of the very transitory quality of false peace," he warned. "This is a revolution posing for every man the question of his own freedom. A light has been cast into a locked room of horrors; there is terror inside it but also the key to reconciliation and peace."[76]

The National Cathedral was a far cry from what Boyd was used to. As ESCRU's national field representative, he had spent the previous fall traveling throughout Mississippi; the spring of 1965 found him in the Deep South again, sometimes in the company of integrated groups of ministers, at at other times traveling with black folk singers, performing his plays in front of black citizens in Jackson, Natchez, and McComb. What he remembered most, he later wrote, were the persons in the audience, "many of whom had never been inside a theatre."[77] By July, he was back in Selma. The city was still reeling from the events of the past few months, and out-of-state white clergy were especially unwelcome. Reverend Newton cautioned such ministers to remain at home, for such northern clergy were "thoroughly despised by the white townsfolk" and were unable to follow through on their "professed desires to be reconciling agents."[78]

If Boyd was perturbed by the hostility he faced from whites, he did not let it stop him from performing his plays in Brown's Chapel. At the conclusion of one performance he met Jonathan Daniels, an Episcopal seminarian and fellow member of ESCRU who had arranged for a sabbatical from the Episcopal Theological School in Cambridge, Massachusetts, so that he could remain in Alabama and help with voter registration. The intense young seminarian made a deep impression on Boyd as they talked and drank beer well into the evening. A deeply devout man, Daniels had studied the works of theologian Dietrich Bonhoeffer and, like him, had come to see the importance of renewing one's faith through repentance, discipline, and confession.[79] The church "ought never to conclude that because its proper end is Heaven, [it] may dally at its work until the End is in sight," the seminarian wrote that April. Throughout the trials and doubts, "we are called to be saints. That is the mission of the Church everywhere. And in this Selma, Alabama, is like all the world: it needs the life and witness of militant saints."[80]

Daniels and fellow seminarian Judith Upham stayed with a black family living in a housing development on the outskirts of the city, but pressure from the city housing director forced them to find lodgings elsewhere. They ended up moving in with the Wests, a black family in East Selma, who had taken them in when they arrived prior to the Selma-to-Montgomery march.[81] While their nine-year-old daughter felt comfortable enough with him to sit on his knee, he wrote later, there was a "hesitancy in her eyes" when she looked at the white visitors, and when her father asked her if she loved John, she said no. "A part of me died inside," he admitted, but a few days later, when she "pulled me down to her, cupped my face with her tiny hands and kissed me," he realized that "something very important and incredibly beautiful had happened," something on the order of a sacrament.[82] He had finally been accepted into the family by the youngest member, no mean feat in itself. The older children had already taken to him, laughing at his northern accent, going with him to the store where he bought them candy, and holding hands with him during the street demonstrations.[83]

This close identification with a black family did not bode well for Daniels's relations with local whites, nor did his efforts to integrate St. Paul's Episcopal Church. Members of the congregation accosted both Daniels and Upham on the street, demanding to know if they were the "scum" who had been bringing blacks to church; others in town called them "white niggers" and spat on them. Angered at the interference with his church policies, Reverend Mathews refused to publicly welcome the mixed group of worshipers, but he agreed to meet privately with Daniels and John Morris to discuss the situation. When nothing was resolved, Mathews suggested that they make the acquaintance of Ralph Smeltzer, who was winding up his ministry of reconciliation and mediation. Smeltzer's superiors believed that he was becoming too involved to be objective, and he himself was feeling the need to devote his time to other projects. The NCC agreed to send a Methodist seminarian, David Smith, to continue his work. To some extent, such efforts were no longer needed, for the emotional shock of the events in March had not only prodded groups of white ministers, including Newton and Mathews, to begin meeting with the Reverend Claude Brown and other black clergy but had convinced Mayor Smitherman and his aides of the necessity of beginning tentative discussions with black civic leaders.[84]

Smith continued the mediating efforts with little success. He could no longer count on Ouellet's help, for Archbishop Toolen had ordered Ouellet to leave the diocese by July 1, and had refused to reconsider even after Selma's black citizens sent him over 2,000 letters of protest. When the superior-general of the Fathers of St. Edmund asked Toolen the reason for his decision, the archbishop curtly replied that he did not owe him a reason, that he simply wanted the priest to leave.[85] Ouellet was perplexed and defiant as he made his preparations to move to New England. "I felt that as a priest my obligation was to help my people in every way I could, not just to sit in church but to be actively concerned about their welfare," he told New York Times reporter John Cogley. For years the archbishop had been, if not supportive, at least tolerant of Ouellet's work with the voter registration drive, but now he had told Ouellet that although he was a good priest, he was "too wild on this racial question," he related. "But I never disobeyed one of his orders. I never demonstrated. I felt, though, like a man who had been allowed to walk out to the middle of a stream and then was forbidden to swim in either direction."[86]

After Ouellet's departure, Smith turned to others for help. He and Daniels met separately with a group of Selma's white women to discuss ways of reducing the tension in the city, but although the meetings went well, the women refused to meet again after hearing unfavorable comments from other whites. Frustrated, Smith would leave Selma by the end of the summer. But there were some occasions for celebration, and when President Johnson signed the Voting Rights Act into law on August 6, providing for federal examiners to register voters who had been turned away by state officials, Selma's blacks went to register at the city courthouse in droves. Daniels and the Reverend Richard Morrisroe, a twenty-five-year-old white Catholic priest from Chicago, volunteered to help with the registration efforts by going to nearby Fort Deposit with black SNCC workers, including Ruby Sales and Joyce Bailey. Police arrested them as soon as they entered town on August 14, and placed them in jail in nearby Hayneville. They remained there for six days, until the police released them on their own recognizance, which immediately struck Bailey and Sales as suspicious, for authorities usually ordered blacks to pay exorbitant bail before they could be released.[87]

As the two women and two men walked out into the hot, dusty, and empty main street in Hayneville, Daniels and Morrisroe decided to buy some soda before calling SNCC headquarters to have someone pick them up. They crossed the street to a grocery store, where Thomas Coleman, a special deputy, was standing with a shotgun. He said later that he had heard that civil rights workers were demonstrating and had come to investigate. When the integrated group approached the front of the store, he shouted racial epithets and leveled his shotgun at them. Daniels grabbed Sales, who was standing in front of him, and pushed her to the ground as Coleman fired. The blast struck Daniels directly in the chest, throwing him twelve feet back, and killing him instantly. A second shot caught Morrisroe in the back, critically wounding him. Bailey and Sales managed to run around the corner and hide. Afterwards, Coleman walked to a telephone and called police to tell his version of the story. An hour later medical help arrived for Morrisroe, who was still lying in the street in a pool of blood.[88]

Coleman remained in custody for a few hours and was released on his own recognizance. Lowndes County Prosecutor Carlton Perdue left no doubts as to where his sympathies lay when he told witnesses that he had been in his office when it happened, "working like a damned dog—which is what they ought to have been doing—minding their own business like I was—and they'd be living and happy today."[89] ESCRU officials announced that memorial services would be held for Daniels in five Alabama counties, including Dallas, where he had worked, and Lowndes, where he had been killed.[90] Reverend Mathews refused to allow a memorial service to be held at St. Paul's Episcopal Church, but he did invite the Reverend John Coburn, Dean of the Episcopal Theological School in Cambridge, to be a guest speaker at a regularly scheduled Saturday service. When Coburn arrived at the church, Mathews greeted him cordially and then informed him that the vestry had rescinded the invitation. Coburn stayed anyway and attended the service the next morning. Some parishioners moved away from him; others asked, "Dean, why can't you leave us alone?" "Because Jonathan's death won't leave us alone," he replied.[91]

Reactions to Daniels's death were often profound. Boyd read about it in a newspaper on a plane from Los Angeles; he remembered breaking down and sobbing on the airplane. Later, he traveled to Keene, New Hampshire, for the funeral service in Daniels's hometown, along with John Morris and Stokely Carmichael. For years afterwards, Boyd would refer to Daniels as a saint. Trappist monks at the Abbey of Gethsemani in Kentucky erected an outdoor chapel in memory of the slain student; twenty-six years after his death, the General Convention of the Episcopal Church approved the addition of Daniels to the church's calendar of saints and martyrs. Throughout the outpouring of grief, the only minister to visit his murderer was Will Campbell, who was himself devastated by Daniels's death. The Baptist preacher had had an epiphany of sorts after learning of the murder, in which he realized that if his ministry of reconciliation was to mean anything, it had to include not only poor blacks and whites, but extreme racists as well, and that included Coleman. From there it was only a short step to bringing his ministry to the Ku Klux Klan, and Campbell became something of a fixture in the homes of Klan members, preaching the news of reconciliation and forgiveness.[92]

Coleman's acquittal later in the year outraged much of the nation. As historian Charles Eagles has illustrated, the defense strategy "involved providing the jury with a legally acceptable justification for Coleman's actions" by making "Daniels the offender and Coleman the defender," by insisting, without evidence, that the seminarian was armed; furthermore, the defense "appealed to the jury's meaner instincts" by portraying Daniels as a dangerous outsider, whose style of dress and choice of reading material offended segregationist sensibilities. The jury deliberated for ninety minutes before returning a verdict of not guilty. Newspaper editors and clergymen around the nation, including the South, were convinced that a travesty of justice had occurred. John Morris had attended the entire trial, and was stunned by the outcome.

An "almost total conspiracy of the civil and religious leadership of Lowndes County" had exonerated "one of their own," he noted, adding that "the most depressing part of this charade was the manner in which the church was trotted out in the person of local clergy, both on the stand and in the audience, to bless and announce absolution over the whole ritual of absolution."[93]

The Daniels case was a sorry end to what had been a remarkable year for clerical activism, yet the sacrifices made in the struggle for the right to vote were not made in vain. Blacks continued to be registered at the polls, and by the next decade the racial patterns in southern politics had been entirely transformed. As with the Civil Rights Act of 1964, clerical support had played a significant role in the passage of the Voting Rights Act of 1965. David J. Garrow has suggested that one reason for the success of the Voting Rights Act was the fact that the victims of brutality in Selma included women, children, and clergy. The repeated references in congressional speeches to the deaths of the Reverend Reeb and Mrs. Liuzzo, a wife and mother, not to mention the religious nature of the protest, created an "implicit theme that children, women, and members of the clergy were especially undeserving victims of such unjust treatment." While the Voting Rights Act was not a conscious memorial to the Reverend James Reeb, his death, as well as that of Mrs. Liuzzo, and the visible participation of the clergy in the protests all played significant factors in its passage.[94]

The larger question of the role of the church in the world was voiced frequently after Selma. Would the clergy "accept the less dramatic but more difficult risks of challenging racial and other injustices in their own communities?" asked Newsweek reporters. "Or will the spirit of Selma dissolve in the teacups of a thousand rectories and parish houses across the nation?"[95] As Americans found out, there was no putting the genie of clerical activism back into the bottle after the summer of 1965, even if, as Robert Spike warned, the churches were "very susceptible to faddism," and concentrated efforts were needed to keep effective action from dissolving into "a study-social-problems-in-limbo kind of orientation."[96] Continued concerns over the secular realm brought different responsibilities for the "new breed" of clergy and, in the minds of some, demanded a new theology, one that was not as tied down to traditional religious rituals and dogma. Harvey Cox's book The Secular City celebrated the coming-of-age of the new city, in which the shift from rural to urban society had brought humanity from the tribal stage through the age of towns to the thriving metropolis. Through each evolution more religious rituals and institutions could be discarded as meaningless and outdated, for

God was not found in antiquated dogma, he wrote, but in social activism, even in the realm of politics.[97]

Many liberal clergy welcomed the intellectual and theological support given social activism, and in the aftermath of Selma, few protest marches or demonstrations took place without their participation, including those in support of Cesar Chavez and striking migrant workers in California in their attempt to create a full-fledged, accredited union. And while no one seriously believed that the civil rights movement had done all it could to eradicate racism and its legacy in this country, some clergy and religious organizations, believing that the death throes of Jim Crow were imminent, began to look beyond the nation's borders and challenge U.S. support for the republic of South Africa and its system of apartheid.[98] As ESCRU's John Morris pointed out, "we have never operated in the Civil Rights Movement on the assumption that one problem must be settled before another is raised. All issues, ultimately, are dealt with concurrently."[99]

Paradoxically, the outpouring of clerical support for civil rights crested at the same time the movement was about to undergo a sharp transformation. There would be other interfaith marches after Selma, but never again on such a scale, with such hope, clarity of purpose, and resolve. Once Martin Luther King Jr. and others in the SCLC turned their attention to the more subtle de facto segregation in northern cities, the goals of the civil rights movement shifted from public accommodation and voting rights to open housing, fair employment, and other more complex problems. Solutions to these problems necessarily required intensive economic transformations and a fundamental shift in relations between classes as well as ethnic groups, and this proved to be too much for some of those who had supported the movement's goals when they were targeted at the South.

It would not be simply differences over opinions and strategies that would rend the liberal, religious, and interracial alliances built on behalf of civil rights, however. White clergy would still be found in the ranks of those struggling for racial justice for the rest of the decade, from cosmopolitan areas such as Atlanta to the most isolated places in the Mississippi Delta. It would be another delta region, the Mekong, thousands of miles away, and the escalating war there that would preoccupy and divide the American public until the early 1970s—as it would the nascent, ecumenical coalition of activist clergy.

six

*For the Lord your God is he that goeth with you, to
fight for you against your enemies, to save you.*

DEUTERONOMY 20:4

Going Against the Grain

Clergy and the Antiwar Movement,
1963–1965

Nineteen hundred sixty-five was a watershed year, in some ways almost as tragic as 1968, that pivotal year when assassinations, student unrest, and apparent reversals in Vietnam so badly unnerved the American people. What made 1965 significant was the hope in liberal circles of strong, decisive federal action on behalf of civil rights; what made the year tragic were the events of July and August, which gave the lie to such dreams. As journalist Nicholas Lemann wrote, "[j]ust at that moment . . . the 1960s turned as if on a hinge." Johnson's escalation of the war in Vietnam in July, followed a month later by the riots in Watts and the resulting concern and confusion over the poverty and despair in the nation's ghettos "destroyed the mood of liberal comity that was supposed to be the foundation on which the solution to the [civil rights] crisis would be built."[1]

In the aftermath of the Watts riots in August 1965, white liberals, including those in the churches, began to voice concerns that blacks were pushing too hard for further reforms, and financial contributions to civil rights organizations began to decline. When white mobs attacked civil rights marchers in Chicago the following July, in some cases specifically targeting white clergy and nuns who had joined the demonstrations against residential segregation, officials of the Catholic Archdiocese of Chicago convinced SCLC not to continue with the marches into the white suburbs. Liberal northerners had decried such moderation and gradualism when it had come from denominational officials south of the Mason-Dixon Line, insisting that those who supported such views had succumbed to pressure from segregationists, but when Archbishop John Cody of Chicago used essentially the same arguments to persuade King to end the demonstrations, the same people praised him for trying to avert violence. Those religious leaders who persisted in calling for open housing and fair employment practices, such as Bishop Moore of Washington, D.C., found themselves facing a sharp drop in contributions from local churches as a result of the "white backlash" against the civil rights movement.[2]

As for Vietnam, most Americans viewed the conflict there as little more than a sideshow until Johnson sent 50,000 additional troops there in July 1965; until 1967, the majority of Americans continued to support their commander-in-chief's decision to shore up the Republic of [South] Vietnam with a massive infusion of American soldiers, money, and materiel.[3] Before 1967, only a relative handful of Americans were willing to criticize the escalation of the war; of these, few were clergymen. Activists in the pulpits continued to look upon the fight against racial discrimination and inequality as the most pressing challenge facing the country. Doctrinaire pacifist groups such as the Catholic Worker and the War Resisters League had protested Johnson's decision to send Marines to South Vietnam in March 1965, but their demonstrations were small and ineffective.[4]

This is not to imply that ministers, rabbis, priests, and members of religious orders were unconcerned with peace in a global perspective. The onset of the arms race between the United States and the Soviet Union in the late 1940s and early 1950s had caused many theologians to question the wisdom and morality of nuclear war and whether the doctrine of just war still had any validity. It was unclear whether the tenets of just war—especially the call for limited war and the immunity of noncombatants from indiscriminate attack— could be applied when discussing the use of thermonuclear weapons. Due in large part to Cold War fears of domestic subversion, the calls for peace and disarmament were left largely to the historic peace churches: the Society of Friends, the Brethren, and Mennonites.[5] The majority of Americans in the mainstream churches were caught up in the religious defense of the "American way of life" prevalent at the time, but the arms race, the reliance of the Kennedy administration on civil defense, and the Cuban Missile Crisis of 1962 prompted others to speak out against the use of nuclear weapons, including several religious figures who would become staunch opponents of the Vietnam War by the middle of the 1960s.

Concern over the likelihood of nuclear Armageddon led several Protestant clergymen to help form chapters of the National Committee for a Sane Nuclear Policy (SANE) in the late 1950s. Among them was Daniel Harrington, minister of New York City's Community Church.[6] In the early 1950s, recalled John C. Bennett, professor of social ethics and dean of Union Theological Seminary, "it was easy to overlook the moral problem of nuclear war because there was confidence that the possession of the weapons would prevent war."[7] By the 1960s, however, Bennett believed that deterrence would no longer work, for if the arms race continued unabated, it was possible that war would begin due to a technical accident, a miscalculation, or the enlargement of a limited war to include nuclear weapons.[8] Fears of an escalating limited war fought on amoral precepts soon led Bennett to become one of the earliest clerical critics of the war in Vietnam.

After a Buddhist monk set himself on fire in June 1963 on a Saigon street to protest the repressive policies of Ngo Dinh Diem, the president of South Vietnam and America's ally, Bennett joined twelve other American clergymen, including Harrington, Reinhold Niebuhr, Rabbi Julius Mark, and Episcopal Bishop James Pike to form the Ministers' Vietnam Committee. The group published full-page advertisements in the *Washington Post* and the *New York Times* criticizing not only United States military aid to a government that denied its citizens essential freedoms but also the use of chemical defoliants on crops and the establishment of "strategic hamlets" designed to separate the peasants from the Vietcong, southern insurgents supplied by the North Vietnamese under Ho Chi Minh who desired to reunify Vietnam under a nationalist and Communist government. It was not worth the loss of American lives and money, they wrote, to support such a regime, a regime that was "universally regarded as unjust, undemocratic and unstable."[9] When Diem's troops carried out a widespread attack on Buddhists that August, the Ministers' Vietnam Committee reissued their advertisement, adding, "17,358 American clergymen of all faiths have joined this protest. Will you?"[10] Doubts were growing among some members of the Ministers' Vietnam Committee as to the wisdom of American intervention. As Harrington told historian Charles DeBenedetti almost twenty years later, the photos of the burning monk "caused me to feel that we simply were not being told the truth about what was happening there, and about what would come out of our sending so-called 'advisors' to South Vietnam."[11]

Bennett agreed, publicly questioning why Americans were becoming militarily involved in what he described as a civil war, not a war of Communist aggression, and wondered whether there was any military solution to be had. "A movement away from our past policy of maintaining a holding operation," he prophetically warned, "could easily lead to hopeless involvement in a conflict in which our power would not be relevant."[12] Until the mid-1960s, however, only a few clergy were willing to protest the war, even after President Johnson had asked for and received assurance from Congress in the Tonkin Gulf Resolution of August 1964 that he could prosecute the war as he wished without a formal declaration of hostilities. Late that year, the Washington Ministers' Association and the Council of Churches of Greater Washington circulated a petition calling upon Johnson to initiate a cease-fire in Vietnam and begin peace negotiations. Out of the 750 clergymen and theologians in the capital, only 105 agreed to sign. One who did not, Francis P. Sayre, Episcopal Dean of the Washington Cathedral, explained, "[a]s a minister I don't feel competent to know as well as the President's technical advisers about what should be done."[13]

This was one of the earliest utterances of what would become a common refrain throughout the Vietnam debacle: ministers were uncertain about the war but felt, like most Americans, that the experts in the White House, State Department, and Pentagon were privy to confidential diplomatic information and intelligence reports, were far better informed on foreign policy, and therefore knew better than anyone else what they were doing. Editor Kyle Haselden of the *Christian Century* denounced Sayre as "timid," reminding him of the commandment "Thou shalt not kill." "One need not be a pacifist to conclude that not killing is better than killing and a negotiated settlement better than bloody coercion. . . . we cannot beat our way out of the blunder we stumbled into in south-east Asia."[14]

Using the fifth commandment was "not only unfair but dreadfully oversimple," retorted Sayre. No one doubted that the use of napalm bombs on civilians or enemy troops was terrible, and, he insisted, "silence in the face of such practices would be moral cowardice." Yet, he suggested, that did not address the question of American military and diplomatic policy in Vietnam. In his view, the assertion that the United States had blundered into Vietnam could not be proven without a "comprehensive review and appraisal of the economic, political and military complexities of the situation" through a study of "technical and often privileged information" which "the average minister simply does not have." Moreover, he continued, proposing a cease-fire on the grounds of a commandment raised more questions than it answered, for was it even possible to negotiate with Communists? How would other nations such as Thailand, Japan, and India view American commitments if the United States abandoned South Vietnam? Such an action would embolden the Communists, and thus "pacific concession" would "breed conflict more barbarous and widespread than at the start." The answers to such questions were never simple, he acknowledged, but they had to be determined, and such a task was "what makes statesmen wary—and so it should editors and clergymen. And that's not timidity!"[15]

Such sentiments disgusted Norman Thomas, who had himself been a Presbyterian minister until 1931, when he left the ministry to work for the Socialist Party. "Once more in the Vietnam crisis we seem to be observing the Christian churches in their familiar role of opposing all wars except the one they are in," he wrote. Why did the churches have to accept "cruel guerrilla war in Vietnam, fought by American conscripts alongside unwilling Vietnamese" in an alleged war for liberty? "I have lived to see something of an awakening in the church on civil rights," he continued. Had the clergy a new message as well for "a nation, to a world, already on the brink of World War III? Has the Christian church no answer to communist progress but the bombs of which we have enough to destroy the world?"[16]

Other activist clergymen, who had no prior involvement in the peace movement (antinuclear or otherwise) but had instead concentrated their efforts in the civil rights movement, became concerned over the sharp escalation of the war after July 1965. "I figured if [National Security Advisor] Mac Bundy, [Secretary of Defense Robert] McNamara, even the president [were for the war,] it must be because they were doing it for the right thing," remembered Paul Moore, reflecting on his views in the early 1960s. After arriving in Washington, D.C., in the middle of the decade and making the acquaintance of more radical clergy opposed to the war, his perspective on the war began to change. At a dinner with Bundy and other friends, Moore asked him what the military policy was in Vietnam and received, he remembered, a "very ambiguous" response. Having fought as a Marine in the Second World War, Moore explained later, "the one thing you're taught above all else is never get into a military operation unless you're quite clear what your mission is." The combination of such factors, coupled with his reading about the conflict, led the bishop to become "more and more against the war."[17]

Robert McAfee Brown and William Sloane Coffin came to the same conclusion by following newspaper coverage and talking to their students at Stanford and Yale, who helped convince them of what they considered to be the unjust nature of the war. Both also believed that race played a significant factor in the destruction leveled against the Vietnamese, in the same sense that American segregationists treated blacks with brutality because they were nonwhites. In their view, sanctity of human life, the worth of the human person, and moral strictures against injustice and suffering had the same applicability in Haiphong, Danang, and Hanoi as they did in Birmingham and Selma.[18] Furthermore, by the end of 1965, it was clear that if the war continued, it would drain funds away from the Johnson administration's war on poverty programs, which were designed to remedy the plight of poor Americans, blacks as well as whites.

Nonetheless, not every religious figure who had taken part in civil rights demonstrations felt the same need to protest the Vietnam War. Some of the white clergymen most prominent in the civil rights movement refused to become part of the antiwar movement until later in the decade. For example, Eugene Carson Blake, troubled by the American bombing campaign begun in the spring of 1965, met with Secretary of State Dean Rusk, McNamara, and Undersecretary of State George Ball in August of that year and was relieved to learn that the use of force would be limited, as they had received indications that the fighting would soon be over. Reassured, Blake wrote to Johnson promising that he would "continue to refrain from joining the public, church, and university criticism which on the whole has seemed to be to be irresponsible."[19] John Morris, executive director of ESCRU, flatly opposed any suggestions that his organization should engage on debates on the war, emphasizing that ESCRU had "taken no position on the Vietnam War issue, nor should we in my estimation"; unlike Blake, he stuck to this position throughout the 1960s.[20]

The reasons clergymen became active in either movement, or in both, varied from individual to individual. Studies indicate that far fewer clergymen participated in antiwar demonstrations than in civil rights marches; perhaps only 5 percent of the nation's clergy were actively opposed to the war. (Approximately 5 percent were active supporters of the war; the rest did not air their views publicly.)[21] Nonetheless, it is possible to suggest reasons why more white clergy participated actively in the civil rights movement than in the antiwar movement, as well as why the radicalism of some of those in the antiwar movement surpassed anything done by their fellow clerics in the fight for racial justice.

Throughout the 1950s and the first half of the 1960s, the struggle for civil rights had been waged in the name of fellowship, justice, and love, of bringing people together in legal, moral, and ethical terms. The issue was clear-cut—

equality or discrimination. None of this was foreign to the basic tenets of Judaism or Christianity; indeed, even SNCC, the most secular of the civil rights organizations (as contrasted to the religious pacifist origins of CORE and the ministerial presence in SCLC), had explicitly sounded a religious tone when calling for "a social order of justice permeated by love" in its founding statement of purpose.[22] Ministers, priests, and rabbis found it hard to ignore Martin Luther King Jr.'s skillful use of prophetic imagery from the Old Testament; even those moderates who were unwilling to support civil rights marches could condemn racial bigotry. Those who used the Bible to support segregation and racial inequality were generally looked upon as a fringe group, a minority. By appealing to Americans to live up to their creeds of equality and democracy, civil rights activists tried to invoke the most favorable images that Americans had of themselves, even if the reality was found wanting. As the issues were moral ones, it made sense that those most suited to making moral pronouncements—the clergy—would play a part in the public discussion (even though the churches had tacitly or overtly supported slavery and segregation throughout the nation's history).

Liberal white clergy who not only spoke out but took part in protests did so out of a sincere moral outrage over bigotry and discrimination. While the more honest admitted that these problems were not confined to any one part of the country, they agreed that the problems were most onerous and obvious in the South. Sitting-in at a southern lunch counter would bring with it penalties or a jail sentence and a fine, or both, but those who chose to appeal the sentence could oftentimes look to the Justice Department, or other branches of the federal government, for redress. Civil rights organizations, especially SCLC, were therefore careful to maintain good relations with the executive branch and federal justices.

The antiwar movement, by comparison, was faced with many different problems. The issues surrounding the Vietnam War were far less clear-cut. One could be against the war and still not agree on tactics or goals. Was the aim to seek a ceiling on the number of American troops sent to Vietnam, a partial or full bombing halt, or a complete withdrawal of all American forces at the earliest possible date? Calls for peace could be, and were, couched in moral terms—but how to achieve that peace was another matter. Before the advent of the credibility gap that developed between the people and the government under the Johnson administration, many Americans were confident that their political leaders, having more knowledge of world affairs and military matters than the general public, were more competent to manage such affairs. Besides, most Americans viewed the war as a political rather than moral issue, and to hear clergy speaking out against the war seemed to blur the distinction between church and state (this did not, however, prevent Lyndon Johnson from turning to Francis Cardinal Spellman, archbishop of the Catholic Archdiocese of New York, and Billy Graham for moral support for the war).

Those who chose to protest the war often found their patriotism questioned. Charges of Communist sympathies had been leveled at civil rights demonstrators throughout the 1950s, but such accusations had more resonance when hurled at antiwar protesters, who, after all, were criticizing the United States for fighting Communism abroad. Individuals who went further and assisted draft evaders and burned draft cards and conscription records did not have allies in the government; rather, they found themselves prosecuted by the Justice Department and thus had the entire weight of the federal government against them, not to mention the social opprobrium of being considered traitors by a hostile public.

The antiwar movement also played out on a different stage from that of the civil rights movement. Washington, D.C., and universities became the focal point of protests, as befitted a struggle concerning foreign policy, war, and the draft. Instead of protests at lunch counters and bus stations, students and clergy picketed draft boards. The grassroots conflicts over integration in the churches of Selma, Columbus, or Little Rock had no domestic counterpart in a war fought thousands of miles away in the jungles and grasslands of Vietnam. There were no stirring marches through southern towns—although visits by American clergy to Southeast Asia during the war possessed a drama all their own. Despite the careful orchestration of such journeys by the host governments, the American guests were able to glean insights not only into the war but into a country of which very few of them had ever taken note, and which had been on the periphery of American interests until only recently.

To many who were active in both movements, however, the differences were minor, and the solution to the nation's racial problems inextricably bound up with the war. Besides sapping the funds for antipoverty programs, critics charged, the war in Vietnam was a racist war on two levels: it perpetuated racism at home by making the poorest, least educated segment of the population, black males, bear the burden of fighting while giving white college students draft deferments. Even more disturbing to many antiwar protesters was the use of carpet bombing, napalm, chemical defoliants, and antipersonnel weapons to such destructive effect, seemingly out of all proportion to the goals for which the war was being fought, one of which was to bring the North Vietnamese to the negotiating table. Civil rights activists had hoped to bring the violence inherent in the southern system of segregation out in the open, to expose it to a horrified nation as part of its eradication; in the same manner, antiwar activists wanted to make the nation aware of what its leaders were doing in Vietnam. As the bombing increased and the casualties mounted, some drew uncomfortable parallels between the United States and Nazi Germany, and charges of genocide and war crimes flourished. As the Johnson administration remained committed to escalating the war, antiwar protesters escalated their level of dissent, not wanting to share any culpability in the destruction, not wanting to appear to be part of any war machine. Keeping this in mind, it is not too difficult to understand the activist trajectory of some clergy, who had looked to the federal government for support for civil rights demonstrators and legislation in the early 1960s but within five years were burning draft cards, blocking entrances to draft offices, and, for some, embracing the militancy of the Black Panthers and the Weathermen.[23]

There was one salient difference between the religious nature of the civil rights and antiwar movements, however. While black ministers led the former, their entrance into the antiwar movement came considerably later than that of their white counterparts. This was not because individuals such as Martin Luther King Jr. and Ralph Abernathy agreed with the Johnson administration's policies in Vietnam; rather, they did not want to risk alienating the president's support for civil rights. White clergymen did not have the same constraints, and so individuals such as Coffin, Brown, Moore, and Heschel assumed the clerical leadership roles in challenging the American government, serving as the most articulate members of the religious wing of the antiwar movement. Having been schooled in social protest by King, the pupils were now ready, if not to replace their teacher, then at least to emerge from behind his shadow. And the lessons learned in the struggle over civil rights would stand them in good stead as leaders of one of the branches of the antiwar movement.

Two of the most important lessons they had mastered were tactics and organization. Using the civil rights movement as a blueprint, committed clergy began sponsoring church resolutions at national conventions, calling for a negotiated settlement to the war as well as publishing petitions in major newspapers. In terms of organization, the antiwar clergy had at their disposal not only church bureaucracies but also mailing lists generated for the civil rights movement's fundraising and publicity efforts.[24] After the protest by the Ministers' Vietnam Committee in June of 1963, the next instance of unified clerical opposition to the war came in early 1965, when the Fellowship of Reconciliation established an ad hoc committee calling itself the Clergymen's Emergency Committee for Vietnam. On April 4, this six-member body placed a full-page advertisement in the *New York Times* headlined "2,500 Ministers, Priests and Rabbis Say: MR. PRESIDENT, In the Name of God, STOP IT!" The statement called on Johnson to halt the bombing and "call a conference of all the nations involved, including China, not alone to conclude peace but to launch at once a major and cooperative effort to heal and rebuild that wounded land." Submitted to over 30,000 clergy of all faiths for their approval, the letter was signed by 2,500 individuals in time for their names to be printed in the advertisement; in the end, more than 3,000 clergy signed it.[25]

"It is not a light thing for an American to say that he is dismayed by his country's actions," the statement read. "We do not say it lightly, but soberly and in deep distress." The Johnson administration's conduct in Vietnam was called "unworthy either of the high standards of our common religious faith, or of the lofty aspirations on which this country was founded." The United States, "so proudly self-described as 'under God,' is not content even with 'eye for an eye' retaliation, but returns evil for evil on a multiplying scale." As ministers and religious figures who had "committed their lives to the attempt to explain and interpret the will of God," agreed the signatories, they had no option but to constantly remind Americans that "these methods are not God's methods, but will bring the judgment of God upon our nation."[26] The strident tone of the advertisement made even the editors of the *Christian Century* uneasy, and although they praised the message, they questioned whether the committee was "too cocksure about 'who speaks in the name of God.'" Others dismissed the statement altogether. "You can count that day lost that doesn't produce a statement by one or more clergymen insistent that the U.S. get out of Vietnam immediately, regardless of the consequences," sarcastically noted Monsignor George Higgins of Washington, D.C.[27]

Early antiwar protest was not limited to advertisements, however. Since the beginning of 1965, Philip Berrigan had been protesting the war by taking part in sidewalk vigils in Times Square and helping form the Emergency Citizens' Group Concerned About Vietnam in March, but nothing angered his superiors at the Josephite seminary in Newburgh, New York, where he taught, as much as his speech to the Newburgh Community Affairs Council in April. "Do you honestly expect that we could so abuse our black citizens . . . so resist their moral and democratic rights, so mistreat . . . and murder them without all this showing itself in our foreign policy?" he asked. "Is it possible for us to be vicious, brutal, immoral and violent at home and be fair, judicious, beneficent, and idealistic abroad?" The local newspaper accused Berrigan of alienating "those good and loyal Americans who dearly want to help the Negro, but who are reluctant to put themselves beside individuals actively serving communist objectives." A barrage of protests to the seminary resulted in Berrigan's transfer to an inner-city parish in Baltimore two weeks later.[28]

Philip was not the only member of his family involved in social activism. His older brother Daniel was a Jesuit who had attended seminary in Poughkeepsie, New York, before being ordained in 1952 at the age of thirty-one. A year later, he traveled to France to study with the Catholic worker-priests, who worked in industry and lived among their fellow laborers, and also served as an auxiliary chaplain for the American military in West Germany, defending, as he noted later, the altruistic nature of United States foreign aid.[29]

After returning to the United States in the fall of 1954, he taught at Brooklyn Preparatory School before moving to Syracuse, New York, to teach theology at Le Moyne College. Considered aloof and smug by some of his students, he was nonetheless an accomplished speaker and poet, winning the Lamont Prize in 1957 for his first book of poetry, *Time without Number*, and went on to write a number of well-received if fairly conventional devotional works in the late 1950s and early 1960s.[30] There was little in Berrigan's manner to suggest the radicalism that would be manifested in his life later in the decade. James Forest, a member of the pacifist Catholic Worker movement, recalled that when he met him in 1962, he was discussing papal encyclicals and was well-fed, well-dressed, and "so much the earnest liberal."[31]

There was another Catholic writer and religious figure who saw something beneath Daniel's complacent exterior, however. Thomas Merton had left the tumultuous world of New York City to become a Trappist monk in 1941 at the age of twenty-six, when he entered the Abbey of Our Lady of Gethsemani in northern Kentucky. His embrace of Christian mysticism and his new life as Brother Louis of the Order of the Cistercians of the Strict Observance strongly tinged his autobiography, *The Seven-Storey Mountain*, which became a best-seller, and for the remainder of his days Merton was confronted with the tensions of being an accomplished writer and poet and desiring monastic solitude. Encouraged by his superiors to write works of religious devotion, Merton generated letters and essays that focused increasingly on Christian ethics in the nuclear age. In 1961, his article "The Root of War," which appeared in the *Catholic Worker*, strongly criticized both the United States and the Soviet Union for the arms race. Similar articles led his abbot to forbid him to publish any more articles on peace issues, but he allowed Merton to receive visitors who were themselves concerned with such matters, including Daniel Berrigan, who had written to compliment him on "The Root of War." A correspondence blossomed, followed by Merton's invitations to Berrigan to travel to the abbey to teach the novices. For his part, the monk viewed Berrigan as a reinvigorating individual in the Catholic church, and the Jesuit began to look upon Merton as a father figure.[32]

By the early 1960s, Daniel Berrigan, influenced by his brother Philip, had begun speaking out on behalf of civil rights, focusing his writing on social concerns, and picketing the Syracuse Niagara-Mohawk power plant near Le

GOING AGAINST THE GRAIN

Moyne for the company's discriminatory hiring practices. When the 1963 civil rights campaign in Birmingham began, Daniel was convinced that he should participate, but not only did his Jesuit superiors refuse to give him permission but, upset with his outspokenness against racial discrimination, suggested that he take a sabbatical leave from Le Moyne and travel throughout Europe and Africa for the 1963–64 academic year.[33] Berrigan attended the All Christian Peace Conference in Prague and met with Catholic priests elsewhere who were involved in movements for liturgical reform, nonviolence, and peace. In Paris, he met with the Reverend John Heidbrink, director of interfaith activities of the pacifist organization the Fellowship of Reconciliation (FOR), Catholic lay-theologian James Douglass, and James Forest, whose impression of the leaner, more informally dressed, and more accessible Berrigan contrasted markedly with his desultory opinion of him only a couple of years before.[34]

The four individuals decided to form the Catholic Peace Fellowship, an organization loosely affiliated with FOR and created to complement the work being done by the Catholic Worker movement. When Berrigan returned to the United States to become assistant editor of the journal *Jesuit Missions* in New York City, he found a changed atmosphere. American religious bodies, Catholic as well as Protestant, had thrown their support behind the civil rights movement, and when Berrigan asked to travel to Selma, his superiors did not refuse.[35]

In the end, it was not his concern for civil rights that would propel him into the forefront of social protest but his response to the escalation of the war in Vietnam. The same would be true of his brother Philip and, to a lesser extent, Merton.[36] For them, civil rights had been something of a detour from their overarching concern for world peace and against the continuing arms race. Merton had joined FOR in 1962 and consented to have his name used as a sponsor for its new affiliate, the Catholic Peace Fellowship. In the fall of 1964, he invited a handful of clergymen and pacifists to the Abbey of Gethsemani for a retreat to discuss peace. Among the guests were the Berrigans, Forest, veteran pacifist Abraham Johannes Muste of FOR, Catholic priest Robert Cunnane, and Methodist minister Elbert Jean of the Committee of Southern Churchmen.[37]

The theme was the spiritual roots of protest, to reflect on the "common grounds for religious dissent" at a time when total war appeared to be inevitable and most governments sought only military solutions to what were at bottom social and economic problems. Their protest was not based on sectarian concerns but was grounded in acting and speaking ecumenically "for the manifestation of the justice and truth of God in the world."[38] Their rationale for protest became Jeremiah's attempt to avoid his prophetic role decreed by God: "If I say, 'I will not mention him, or speak any more in his name,' there is in my heart as it were a burning fire shut up in my bones, and I am weary with holding it in, and I cannot" (Jeremiah 20:9).[39] The metaphor of fire turned out to be apt, for, in a matter of years, it ceased to be merely a figure of speech for the Berrigans and the other members of the "Catholic Left" and became instead a weapon with which to protest the Vietnam War.

More prominent religious figures were also concerned about peace and were determined to lend their prestige to the antiwar movement, hoping to make it more palatable to middle America by depicting the war as a mistake rather than an indicator of a major flaw in the national character. Martin Luther King Jr., John Bennett, Episcopal Bishop Daniel Corrigan, Methodist Bishop Charles F. Golden, and all six members of FOR's Clergymen's Emergency Committee decided in April 1965 that they should speak out. Calling themselves the Interreligious Committee on Vietnam, they asked "religiously concerned men and women" from all over the nation who were "appalled by the human tragedy and suffering involved" in the Vietnam conflict to attend a silent vigil at the Pentagon on May 11 and 12, the purposes of which were to protest escalation and urge Johnson to make good his pledges of "unconditional discussions" with the North Vietnamese and economic development for their shattered nation.[40]

Despite its significance in terms of its ecumenical nature and size—almost 1,000 Protestant, Catholic, and Jewish clergy and laypersons took part in it— the vigil had little impact. A lengthy meeting between the committee's leaders and Pentagon officials, including Secretary of Defense Robert McNamara, resolved nothing. Later in the month, over 500 religious figures traveled to the capital to lobby for a negotiated peace, but senators and representatives were able to safely ignore their entreaties. Unlike the lobbying for the Civil Rights Act of 1964 (or the ongoing pressures for the then-pending voting rights bill), the clergy clearly did not have the backing of their parishioners. Gallup polls showed that 60 percent of Americans supported Johnson's Vietnam policies, seeing in them, as he himself did, the application of lessons learned from Munich: there could be no appeasement of aggressors, only containment. By the end of May, Johnson received from Congress more funds to enlarge the American effort in South Vietnam and authorized American forces to go on the offensive, seeking out and fighting enemy forces. Such a task required more men, which in turn required an intensification of the draft.[41]

This decision disturbed not only young men of draft age, but also those who had been against American involvement since the Buddhist crisis of 1963. The persistent Bennett, a "fighter far more by conviction than by temperament," as Coffin described him, joined Niebuhr, Robert Brown, Robert W. Spike, Harvey Cox, and other members of the editorial board of *Christianity and Crisis* to continue their questioning of American policy. "Much of what we are doing in Vietnam has the opposite effect of what is intended," they wrote. Americans were running the risk of destroying all chances for peace in Asia, and were "likely to drive the North Vietnamese into the hands of the Chinese." Despite the fact that Americans did not have the intricate details of the political and military situation possessed by the government, they argued, they were "still entitled to challenge what seem to be the presuppositions that underlie the present policy."[42]

The oft-repeated analogy of Munich was erroneous, the editorial staff explained, because Communism, unlike Nazism, could be resisted "when nations can find constructive [political] and social alternatives." The United States' task in Asia should therefore be to help develop political and economic alternatives to Communism in independent nations, even if it meant sitting down with all parties in Vietnam, including the National Liberation Front (NLF), to begin negotiations. "[A]lthough we do not claim that these political judgements are the only ones compatible with Christian faith and ethic, we are guided by our faith and ethic [to seek the] prevention of general war and the holding down of violence at all stages," they concluded. "We should not expect too much, but we hope for some transcending of the absolute hostility on both sides."[43]

Unlike radical pacifists in such organizations as the Committee for Non-Violent Action, or even the traditional religious pacifists within FOR, the editorial staff of *Christianity and Crisis* could not be dismissed out of hand as starry-eyed or naive. The criticism of the Munich analogy was especially telling because the journal had been born out of divisions between Christian liberalism and Christian realism in the 1930s precisely over the question of how to deal with Hitler. Neoorthodox theologians such as Niebuhr and Bennett, convinced that the pacifism and isolationism of Christian liberals posed a threat to the United States almost as much as the rise of the Third Reich, had founded *Christianity and Crisis* in 1941 to urge support of Great Britain abroad and military preparedness at home.

Yet while their arguments could not be dismissed as utopian, they could be—and were—dismissed as misguided by Johnson, McNamara, Secretary of State Dean Rusk, Bundy, and others in the administration who, as "can-do" people, believed in the exercise of power and the rightness of their cause. Doubts and discussions of morality were for lesser men, they thought, according to David Halberstam's lengthy study of those individuals responsible for

American involvement in the morass of Vietnam. The "best and the brightest" were not evil people; they were liberals, "committed to the good things in life, to decency and humane values. . . . urbane, modern, if they were for a war, it would be a good war."[44] They would be cordial to those clergymen who visited them in their offices to discuss the moral and ethical aspects of the war, because that was the job of the clergy, to be concerned with ethics. But they themselves would not be swayed. Nor, perhaps, would clergymen be able to effect such a change even if they tried. Religious figures "cannot accomplish in a few crucial months what Isaiah, Buddha, Jesus, St. Francis, Tolstoy and Gandhi could not do in 2500 years," wrote journalist I. F. Stone. "If all hope of stopping a wider conflict disappears, they will perform a moral duty by resistance and abstention. But though this will ease their consciences, it will not affect the course of events."[45]

Much of the power that the government had at its disposal was the marshaling of statistics with which to back up their argument, figures unavailable to the rest of the citizenry. When members of the Committee for Non-Violent Action met with McNamara and asked him about the number of American troops needed to successfully fight a guerrilla war, he gave the "standard bureaucratic answer. . . . 'I can't discuss that with you. We know things that you don't.' "[46] The perennial disadvantage of not having information to challenge the government's claims of how the war was progressing was partially offset by clerical visits to Vietnam throughout the war. The first took place in July 1965 when the Clergymen's Emergency Committee sent a team of fourteen religious leaders to South Vietnam to meet with students, soldiers, teachers, government officials from both sides of the conflict, NLF deserters and supporters, and clergymen of all faiths.[47] Rabbi Jacob Weinstein, president of the Central Conference of American Rabbis, noted that while Americans tried to gain the trust and support of the Vietnamese peasants by building medical clinics, irrigation systems, and roads after clearing the area of Vietcong, the value of such work was "largely lost on the people, coming as it does in the wake of so much death and destruction."[48]

The most important exchange of information, in the opinion of Weinstein and Alfred Hassler, executive secretary of FOR, was between the visiting westerners and the leaders of the Unified Buddhist Church, including Thich Nhat Hanh, a leader of the peace movement in Vietnam. During their visit, Thich Nhat Hanh told them of a "third solution" to the political struggle in South Vietnam. The peasants, he explained, needed a combination of patriotism and peace. The Americans and the NLF provided neither, but if given the choice of Communism or war, the Vietnamese would choose the former. The South Vietnamese regime was seen as a puppet government, the monk told them, and the United States had to let the Vietnamese find a solution to their own problems. He outlined his solution in the following steps: the establishment of a temporary interim government representative of the religious and political groups in South Vietnam, which in turn would work with either the International Control Commission (a body composed of Canadians, Indians, and Poles set up in 1954 to monitor the Geneva Accords that had divided Vietnam) or the United Nations to create a constituent assembly; a cease-fire between the United States and the NLF and North Vietnamese during the formation of the government; eventual withdrawal of U.S. troops; and normalized trade and diplomatic relations between the two Vietnams.[49]

Hassler and the others were deeply moved by the monk's earnestness and sincerity. Thich Nhat Hanh was pleased with the interest fellow clergymen had in the plight of the Vietnamese. He had already tried to enlist the aid of Martin Luther King Jr. the month before in a letter asking him to join the protests against the war. After explaining the rationale behind the "self-burning" of monks (he insisted that they were not suicides but a means of "moving the hearts of the oppressors" and making the world aware of his nation's suffering), he went on to remind King of the link between the sufferings of American blacks and the Vietnamese people. "I am sure that since you have been engaged in one of the hardest struggles for equality and human rights, you are among those who understand fully, and who share with all their heart, [their] indescribable suffering."[50]

Whether the monk's appeal directly influenced the Baptist minister to speak out against the war is unclear. King had already privately expressed doubts about it, and in August 1965 he publicly called for negotiations between the United States, Hanoi, and the National Liberation Front, offering his services as a mediator. Journalists, editors, and politicians were quick to chastise him for involving himself in foreign affairs, and after Bayard Rustin, Roy Wilkins, and other colleagues begged him not to jeopardize Johnson's support of civil rights, King quickly retreated, rescinding his offer. Hassler and his colleagues, meanwhile, extended an open invitation to the Buddhist monks to come to the United States and give lectures on the "third solution," but it was not easy for critics of the South Vietnamese government to get permission to leave the country. It would be a year before Thich Nhat Hanh was able to travel, and by that time much would have happened in the American peace movement.[51]

Upon their return home, the fourteen Americans published a second newspaper advertisement, "We Have Seen the Anguish in Vietnam," in which they admitted finding "a deeply complicated situation in which we could not judge either side to be wholly right or wholly wrong." This did not stop them from criticizing the way in which "major powers have used and are using the villages of Vietnam as a testing ground for ideological positions such as 'wars of national liberation,' or 'containment of communism' by military force." Immediate withdrawal of American troops was not the answer, nor was escalation. The only hope was for the United Nations to convene a conference of all the belligerents as well as the People's Republic of China. The real problems in Vietnam, said the ad, were "what they always have been" throughout history: "injustice, poverty, disease, national pride, the abuse of power, and . . . hatred and war," and "to . . . focus our attack on these evils rather than to fight within the family of man is to stand with the God of history."[52]

The second advertisement was markedly more subdued than its predecessor and not nearly as condemnatory of the United States. The journey to Vietnam had proved to be enlightening in many respects, but it gave no clear answers to those who had so readily faulted the Johnson administration a scant four months before. Rather than bringing the judgment of God down on the United States, the statement lamented the ills facing all peoples, and as the wording became more generalized, more of the cutting edge was lost. Perhaps the signatories had discovered from the South Vietnamese that the North Vietnamese were not the pillars of virtue some in the United States were making them out to be. The only certainty was that there would be no easy solution to the Vietnam debacle.

Not only did the Johnson administration remain unmoved by such petitions, but the president was able to count on his friend Billy Graham to use his powerful reputation to counter such criticism. Graham's routine access to the White House had been curtailed by Kennedy's victory in 1960, but with Johnson in office, Graham was again called to the White House for advice. Both men "bragged on each other," recalled Johnson. "I told him he was the greatest religious leader in the world and he said I was the greatest political leader." If Graham got the satisfaction of being in the inner circle once again, Johnson knew he could count on the evangelist's support.[53] And support him he did, thundering against monolithic Communism whenever the opportunity arose. Communists planned for "ultimate triumph," he wrote, warning that the Communist flame "becomes evermore dangerous—and in some areas of the world it is out of control!" Graham also reported that "[a] President of the United States" had told him he was "sick and tired of hearing preachers give advice on international affairs when they do not have all the facts straight." It was one thing, he wrote, for a clergyman to "give his own personal views . . . as a citizen, but it becomes a different matter when the church speaks as the church on every social and political issue that comes along."[54] He was more explicit in his speeches. "I have no sympathy for those clergymen who [urge] the U.S. to get out of Vietnam," he told the Denver Press Club. "Communism has to be stopped somewhere, whether it is in Hawaii or on the West Coast. The President believes it should be stopped in Vietnam."[55]

Others questioned the belief in monolithic Communism, believing the solution to peace in Southeast Asia might lie with Beijing and a more realistic foreign policy with regard to China. "If Americans could bring themselves to live in the same world with Mao," Coffin reasoned, "couldn't they bring themselves to live in the same world with Ho Chi Minh?" Working with Allard Lowenstein, attorney and student organizer, he formed Americans for the Reappraisal of Far Eastern Policy (ARFEP), which soon had chapters in several colleges and universities. And there ARFEP remained, on the campuses, despite the efforts of Coffin and Lowenstein to make it a grassroots movement; its influence was minimal if not nonexistent.[56]

Existing peace organizations fared somewhat better. James Forest and Thomas Cornell of the Catholic Peace Fellowship went on speaking tours to colleges and universities, discussing the draft, which was quickly becoming a major source of concern to those eligible to be conscripted. Groups like theirs and the Jewish Peace Fellowship, also affiliated with FOR, were increasingly seen as conduits of information on how to achieve conscientious objector (CO) status from local draft boards. By the middle of the decade, Catholic Peace Fellowship offices in New York City were receiving fifty letters a week requesting help from men of draft age who opposed the war in Vietnam.[57]

While individuals from the historic peace churches had little problem receiving classification as CO's, those from the mainline Protestant, Jewish, and Catholic denominations had greater difficulty in convincing draft boards of the sincerity of their convictions. The Selective Service did not recognize the validity of "selective conscientious objection," or objection to one particular war, and while members of all three faiths had a difficult time challenging their draft boards, Catholics and Jews faced particular handicaps. Antiwar Catholics did not believe that the Vietnam War satisfied any of the criteria of the Catholic doctrine of the just war: it was not defensive, civilians were being harmed, and American retaliation went far beyond the limits of acceptable and necessary response. Yet as Catholics they could not prove themselves to be CO's because their church did not oppose war in any and all forms. Young Jewish males who claimed CO status reported that they were repeatedly singled out by draft board officials who doubted that Judaism could be a pacific faith and asked them what they would have done had they been old enough to fight against the Nazis during the Second World War. Any admission that they would have fought in that war effectively ended their chances of being granted CO status.[58]

Those who refused to accept the legitimacy of conscription and thus fight in a war they believed to be immoral and unnecessary had very few alternatives from which to choose. They could go to jail for five years, flee the country, or challenge the draft itself. Pacifists in the 1940s had burned draft cards in protest against the selective service laws; others had simply mailed their cards back to the draft boards. On July 29, 1965, as 400 antiwar protesters picketed the U.S. Army Induction Center on Whitehall Street in New York City, a member of the Catholic Worker movement set fire to his draft card. His action received much press coverage, and before a month had passed, South Carolina's Representative L. Mendel Rivers and Senator Strom Thurmond had introduced identical pieces of legislation making the willful destruction of draft cards a federal offense. President Johnson signed the bill into law on August 30.[59]

The first open defiance of the law came in the middle of October during the "International Days of Protest." A variety of peace, pacifist, and left-wing organizations—including the Catholic Worker, the Committee for Non-Violent Action (CNVA), Catholic Peace Fellowship, the Committee for a Sane Nuclear Policy (SANE), the War Resisters League, the Student Non-violent Coordinating Committee (SNCC), the American Friends Service Committee (AFSC), and Students for a Democratic Society (SDS)—had come together under the umbrella organization of the National Coordinating Committee to End the War in Vietnam to sponsor antiwar parades in New York City, Chicago, and Berkeley in coordination with similar demonstrations in other countries. On October 15, the day before the march, a much smaller demonstration took place at the induction center on Whitehall Street in New York. In the midst of speeches denouncing the war, David Miller, a twenty-two-year-old pacifist and former student at Le Moyne College who had been influenced by Daniel Berrigan's teachings, stood up in front of the crowd and announced that he was going to burn his draft card as a sign of protest. This action captured the interest of the media, and antiwar protesters decided to repeat the symbolic act a few weeks later.[60]

Both the march and the draft card burning were denounced as acts of Communists, beatniks, and traitors; J. Edgar Hoover, director of the Federal Bureau of Investigation, argued that "Anti-Vietnam [sic] demonstrators" were "for the most part composed of halfway citizens who are neither morally, mentally nor emotionally mature." More thoughtful individuals, such as James Reston of the New York Times, claimed that the protests were "not promoting peace but postponing it." Attorney General Nicholas deB. Katzenbach and President Johnson also questioned the loyalty of the demonstrators.[61]

Determined to uphold the right of dissent, representatives of an ad hoc committee of almost 100 Catholic, Protestant, and Jewish clergymen from New York City held a press conference at the United Nations Church Center on October 25 to protest the charges of Communism directed at antiwar demonstrators. Among the speakers were Rabbi Abraham Joshua Heschel and the twenty-nine-year-old Reverend Richard Neuhaus of the Lutheran Church of St. John the Evangelist in New York City, whose involvement in the civil rights movement included establishing a "freedom school" at his church earlier in the year for black and Puerto Rican students who had been placed in substandard schools.[62]

Pleased with the interest shown in the conference, the representatives decided to organize themselves as Clergy Concerned About Vietnam (CCAV), under the ecumenical leadership of Neuhaus, Heschel, and Daniel Berrigan. According to the two Christian clergymen, neither had originally considered the press conference to be a prelude to the creation of a new antiwar organization. When Heschel announced at the October 25 news conference that the ad hoc committee would continue its efforts as a formal entity, he caught both of them by surprise.[63] Berrigan recalled how, at the end of the conference, Heschel laid a firm hand on their shoulders and asked, "Are we then finished, do we go home content, and the war goes on?" "We should have known," Berrigan wrote years later, as "the question was quintessential Heschel."[64]

Heschel probably spoke for others besides himself when he admitted that for many years he believed that the federal government, possessing information that the average person did not have, was competent to manage the war. Continued escalation had completely changed his outlook. "I had previously thought that we were waging war reluctantly, with sadness at killing so many people," he explained. "I realize that we are doing it now with pride in our military efficiency."[65] Leaving the decision-making to the people in Washington was an abandonment not only of practical responsibility but of moral values themselves. "Do they have the wisdom?" he asked. "Can I turn over my soul and conscience to them?"[66]

Others were even more despondent over the course the war was taking. On November 2, Norman Morrison, a thirty-two-year-old Quaker, decided to take his life in protest against the war in the same manner as Buddhist monks had done. Sitting in front of the Pentagon, he doused himself with kerosene and struck a match, instantly engulfing himself in flames. A long-time pacifist,

Morrison had withheld money from his income taxes to protest defense spending and had become increasingly determined to find a way to protest the war that would capture the attention of the American people. He had not been the first person in America to die this way, however; Alice Herz, an eighty-two-year-old survivor of concentration camps, had set herself on fire on a Detroit street in March to protest the arms race and Johnson's escalation of the war.[67] But it was Roger LaPorte's death on November 9 that had the largest repercussions on the religious antiwar movement.

LaPorte's death had its origins in a draft card-burning ceremony presided over by A. J. Muste and Dorothy Day, founder of the Catholic Worker movement. The protesters stood in Manhattan's Union Square, dressed neatly in suits and ties, and solemnly lit their draft cards in front of 1,500 applauding sympathizers to protest the war, the "draconian" law providing for five years in prison for destruction of a draft card, and the stifling of dissent.[68] As the cards burned, hecklers chanted "Drop dead, Red" and "Give Us Joy, Bomb Hanoi"; others carried signs reading "Burn Yourself Instead of Your Card." When one of them ascended to the platform, at Muste's invitation, to explain why he thought that the affair was Communist-inspired, the hecklers booed him as well. After the antiwar protesters sang "We Shall Overcome" and dispersed, hostile gangs roamed the streets, beating up several of the demonstrators who were still wearing their "Practice Nonviolence" buttons.[69]

LaPorte, a twenty-one-year-old member of the Catholic Worker movement, had been extremely disturbed by the hostility. On the morning of November 9, he sat in front of the Dag Hammarskjöld Library at the United Nations, poured gasoline over himself, and lit a match. Unlike Morrison, he did not die right away, and was able to tell paramedics who tried to save him, "I am a Catholic Worker. I'm against war, all wars. I did this as a religious action." With burns covering ninety-five percent of his body, he lingered in Bellevue Hospital for thirty hours before dying.[70]

When members of the Catholic Worker movement heard of the news, they were "deeply shocked, perplexed, and grieved," James Forest told a reporter. "He never told us what he had planned. If he had we would have discouraged him."[71] Others were convinced that LaPorte burned himself "in an effort to absorb part of the violence that he had felt at the demonstration on November 6th."[72] Coming one week after Morrison's death by fire, LaPorte's suicide confused and distressed many. Merton questioned whether burning draft cards was hurting the peace movement by stirring up hostility, writing to Forest that the suicides were an indication that "there is something radically wrong somewhere, something that is un-Christian. . . . the whole thing gives off a very different smell from the Gandhian movement . . . and the non-violence of Martin Luther King."[73]

In his eulogy at LaPorte's funeral, however, Daniel Berrigan refused to consider his death a suicide, saying instead that he had given his life "so that others might live."[74] On November 16, Berrigan's superiors sent him to Mexico.[75] His colleagues in the peace movement immediately concluded that Cardinal Spellman had used his authority to pressure the Reverend James P. Cotter, S.J., director of *Jesuit Missions,* and the Very Reverend John McGinty, Jesuit Provincial of New York, to order him to stop his peace activities and exile him. Spellman had been the most outspoken critic of the Geneva Accords that had divided South and North Vietnam in 1954, claiming that the agreements meant "[t]aps for the newly betrayed millions of Indochinese who must now learn the awful facts of slavery from their eager Communist masters," masters whose ideology had to be destroyed lest we "risk bartering our liberties for lunacies, betraying the sacred trust of our forefathers, becoming serfs and slaves to Red rulers' Godless goons."[76] The archbishop, moreover, had ardently supported Diem, a Catholic, before his ouster and assassination in November 1963.[77]

"We view with sorrow and shock the removal of our brother, Daniel Berrigan, as cochairman of Clergy Concerned About Vietnam," wrote Neuhaus and Heschel in a joint statement on November 21. Not only did they "find it difficult to appreciate a form of religious authority that is exercised in a manner offensive to our common Jewish and Christian understanding of human dignity," but they were "saddened also because an injury has been done to the ecumenical character of the conference's leadership." The *National Catholic Reporter* claimed that Berrigan had been "silenced" as a result of "intervention by the New York chancery office." Berrigan himself viewed his reassignment as a disciplinary measure for his work in the peace movement, telling Paul Montgomery of the *New York Times* that "definite and very heavy pressures" from the Archdiocese of New York had been brought to bear on his Jesuit superiors.[78]

Not so, claimed Reverend Cotter, director of the magazine of which Berrigan was associate editor, saying he had sent Berrigan on a "routine assignment" to Latin America. There were "no calls or directives from the New York chancery. . . . It was my decision; I made it, and I stand by it."[79] Few believed such assertions. Berrigan had been given only three days' notice to fly down to Mexico to begin a three-month reporting tour of South America; besides, it was increasingly apparent that the Catholic hierarchy did not approve of priests taking antiwar stands. At the same time Berrigan was sent abroad,

McGinty had also ordered two other Jesuits, the Reverends Francis M. Keating and Daniel V. Kilfoyle, to cease their activities in Clergy Concerned About Vietnam. Kilfoyle decided to attend one last meeting to tell his colleagues the news himself. Heschel was again deeply moved and distressed at the further diminution of Catholics within the movement, and when the Jesuit had finished speaking, he embraced him.[80]

If his superiors had wanted Berrigan's trip to dampen his social activism, they could not have picked a worse place to send him. Traveling through Mexico and South America, the Jesuit came into contact with Catholic priests far more radicalized than himself. He met with worker-priests in São Paulo whose impoverished life rekindled the hope and the joy he had felt in Paris when he lived with worker-priests there. In Peru, he experienced the pain of hearing a wealthy bishop's Lenten letter read to a parish in the slums of Lima, a missive telling the starving and poverty-stricken people of the glories of heaven and the pains of hell, extolling them to fast and pray, and accept their station in life. As Berrigan noted, they were already conditioned to fast, and while the Church remained wealthy, no prelate would convince them of the usefulness of prayer. The poverty reminded Berrigan of the conditions in which the Vietnamese peasants lived, and his concerns over the war in Southeast Asia followed him throughout South America, as did his desire to "turn others toward peace," which did not disappear simply because he had been forced to leave New York. The war was "destined to become much more decisive for me and for a few others than the civil rights struggle had been," he continued. "Most of us were not with this former struggle with anything like the same intensity."[81]

Berrigan's supporters picketed Spellman's New York chancery calling for Berrigan's reinstatement, and on December 12 the Institute for Freedom in the Church published a half-page advertisement in the *New York Times*. Criticizing the decision to send Berrigan away as a mistake, the piece went on to commend him for his activities in both the civil rights and peace movements. The first was "now crowded with priests and nuns. There is a Catholic consensus. Catholics concerned with interracial justice are not alone. Father Berrigan is not essential to their work." On the subject of pacifism, however, his was an often solitary voice among Catholics. Even though not all agreed that his actions were wise, his removal suggested that a priest could talk about Vietnam "only if he supports the American actions there" or "counsel civil disobedience to those whose conscience leads them to support civil rights, but . . . not counsel the same thing to those who find all war or a specific war contrary to Christian morality." If the Catholic hierarchy's response was to silence dissenters, such a decision "denies what the Church has achieved" under Vatican II.[82]

One thousand Catholics signed the statement, including the editorial board of the *Commonweal*, students from Le Moyne College, the Reverends Robert Cunnane and William DuBay, James Forest and Thomas Cornell of the Catholic Peace Fellowship, faculty members at various Jesuit institutions of higher learning, and the Catholic Worker staff, with the exception of Dorothy Day, who disagreed with the statement as a violation of the Catholic tradition of obedience.[83] Merton wrote to Berrigan, teasing him about his newfound notoriety, but warned him against "big symbolic confrontations," although the need for such might come about at a later date. Above all, advised Merton, he should move quietly and not hurry, for he had a long road ahead of him and "in any case nobody is going to stop the Vietnam war for a long time, it seems to me."[84]

The newspaper advertisement, picketing, and publicity surrounding Berrigan's transfer resulted in his recall the following March. In a press conference at the Biltmore Hotel in New York City, Reverend Cotter announced that Berrigan's journalistic assignment was over and that he could resume his peace activities.[85] There was clearly a need for such work. By the end of 1965, there were over 180,000 American forces in South Vietnam, and although Johnson announced a temporary bombing halt in December, no end of the war was in sight.

seven

*They have treated the word of my people carelessly,
saying "Peace, peace," when there is no peace.*

JEREMIAH 8:11

A Voice for Moderation

Clergy and the Antiwar Movement, 1966–1967

Berrigan's absence did not mean the demise of Clergy Concerned About Vietnam, although his presence was missed. At a study conference at Christ Church (Methodist) in New York City, an empty chair was placed on stage symbolizing his absence. But there was more to the organization than gestures. On January 11, 1966, John Bennett invited several nationally prominent clergymen to his New York City apartment to formally establish the National Emergency Committee of Clergy Concerned About Vietnam. The original members included the host, Heschel, Neuhaus, the Reverend Harold Bosley of Christ Church (Methodist), David Hunter, deputy general secretary of the NCC, and Rabbis Maurice Eisendrath and Balfour Brickner, the president and the director of Interfaith Activities of the Union of American Hebrew Congregations. Toward the end of the month, they were joined by Robert McAfee Brown and William Sloane Coffin, the latter becoming the acting executive secretary.[1]

While several of these individuals had been arrested and jailed for their activities in the civil rights movement, none were considered radicals. Their distress over the attempts to stifle dissent, coupled with their growing concern over the war, had been the catalysts for their coming together to form a permanent organization. Their goals were moderate: a continuation of the bombing halt and the beginning of negotiations for an end to the war. They did not call for immediate withdrawal, nor did they advocate civil disobedience. Significantly, none of the members of the committee were clergymen at the parish level; they were editors of religious journals, denominational heads, college chaplains, professors of theology, and leaders of national religious groups, giving them a level of freedom that rank-and-file clergy did not enjoy.[2]

Missing from the committee were members of the Catholic hierarchy. Richard Cardinal Cushing of the Archdiocese of Boston had at first agreed to allow his name to be used but withdrew the offer, explaining to Coffin through a monsignor that he stood behind the president. Heschel understood the pressures Catholics were under, for there were those in the Jewish community who had begged him not to involve himself in the antiwar movement for fear that if Johnson believed that Jews were not solidly behind him, he would not give his wholehearted support to Israel. Some Orthodox rabbis even criticized him for forging closer ties with Christians due to his support of ecumenism and his work in the civil rights and antiwar movements. Nevertheless, several of Heschel's students at the Jewish Theological Seminary, as well those from Union Theological Seminary, were more than willing to help Coffin and Heschel make telephone calls from the NCC headquarters on Riverside Drive, trying to establish a network of antiwar clergy in each state, the greatest number coming from the Upper South, the Midwest, and the Northeast.[3]

At a New York press conference in mid-January 1966, Coffin publicly announced the formation of the National Emergency Committee of Clergy Concerned About Vietnam. "The moment is crucial, for it may well be that morally speaking the United States ship of state is today comparable to the *Titanic* just before it hit the iceberg," he warned his audience. "If we decide on all-out escalation of the war in Vietnam, then to all intents and purposes of the human soul, we may be sunk." He concluded with an appeal to fellow clergy to support negotiation and protest escalation.[4] Shortly thereafter he reiterated the group's desire to appeal to middle-class Americans. "Do not let the hawks monopolize patriotism," he wrote in a letter sent out to the new chapters on February 2, the day the bombing of North Vietnam resumed. "As a committee we cannot now call for withholding of income tax or other acts of civil disobedience." If such activities took place, he wrote, the job of the committee would be not to support or denounce them but "rather point again to the situation that produced them."[5]

The moderate tone of the new organization was also underscored in a press release. While the executive committee believed that the renewed bombing of North Vietnam after a thirty-seven day halt "overshadowed all recent efforts for peace" and pronounced themselves "shocked at the intransigence of Hanoi [and] unpersuaded that our own Government has exhausted every possibility for peace," they praised Johnson for seeking assistance from the United Nations to end the war, saying that the effort "reflects a willingness to accept the judgment of others and a recognition that the war and its solution are not our responsibility alone but that of the entire world."[6] This careful balance of praise and blame of the Johnson administration, coupled with anger directed at North Vietnam, would not be long-lived, but its existence at this relatively early stage illustrates the lengths to which the executive committee was going to reach the broadest possible base of support.

It was not easy to ignore the criticism coming from the religious establishment, however. Bennett continued to use his position as cochair of the editorial board of *Christianity and Crisis* to challenge the propriety of the war in Vietnam. The journal had not adopted the "assumptions of Christian pacifism," he wrote, insisting that the editors still recognized the need for military power and the "moral obligation to use power at times to check power." However, he continued, "we believe that the circumstances under which military power is being used in Vietnam are sufficiently different from those under which it was used to defeat Hitler."[7]

Others believed that the limited American response to Vietnam was an indication that the conflict satisfied the qualifications of a just war, and berated the editorial staff for what they considered to be a virtual abandonment of Christian realism. "Even Reinhold Niebuhr signs petitions and editorials as if Reinhold Niebuhr had never existed," grumbled Paul Ramsey, professor of religious thought at Princeton University.[8] Even Niebuhr's old friend Hubert Humphrey had disagreements with the aging theologian on the merits of the war. Especially annoying to Niebuhr was Humphrey's use of his own arguments to defend the administration's Vietnam policies in a speech delivered at a twenty-fifth anniversary dinner for *Christianity and Crisis*—"[a]ll to the end," Niebuhr wrote, "of claiming my anti-Nazi stance of the thirties for the present war" by a man who was trying to outdo "the Machiavelli in the White House." The issue in Vietnam, Niebuhr believed, was not containment of Communism but a nationalist war, a situation in which the United States had no business being involved. The completely mistaken foreign policy greatly upset Niebuhr, who admitted that for the first time, "I fear I am ashamed of our beloved nation."[9]

Some antiwar clergymen completely failed to convince the moderates of the rightness of their convictions. When Daniel Berrigan returned to the United States in March, he spent his first week going to New York and Washington for teach-ins, and fulfilling speaking engagements on the radio and at college campuses. Much of what he had to say was impressive, but the Jesuit priest's oftentimes broad arguments did nothing to dispel the image of activist priests as fuzzy-headed moralists. When a student at the College of St. Elizabeth asked him to be "realistic" about the Communist threat in Vietnam, Berrigan's response was that "communism as an issue in the Vietnam war is a myth. Nobody . . . buys our vision of the war." The more serious issue, countered Berrigan, was what the war was doing to Americans, as it was a distraction, "a turning aside from one another in the direction of hatred."[10] If Berrigan was trying to make a point about larger, deeper issues about humanity, he failed; if he was sincere in his belief that Communism was not an issue, he was seriously misguided, for even those who viewed the war as primarily a civil one realized that Marxist ideology did play some role in Hanoi's decisions.

Political intricacies aside, the easygoing, casually dressed Jesuit was a popular figure among antiwar activists in the United States, no doubt because he gave of himself unstintingly in the peace movement. On March 29, he joined Richard Neuhaus in leading a group of sixty priests, nuns, rabbis, ministers, and laypersons in a peace march through New York City. Carrying white banners reading "Peace," "Pax," and "Shalom," they spent two hours visiting several synagogues and churches, including St. Patrick's Cathedral, where the group's ten-minute prayer service was the first interfaith venture in the building's history. The small group then made its way down Fifth Avenue to hold a short prayer vigil at the United Nations Church Center.[11]

Not all antiwar initiatives came from CCAV or its members, of course. On March 15–17, 1966, almost 500 clergy and laity attended the National Inter-Religious Conference on Peace in Washington, D.C., which had been funded by the NCC, the Synagogue Council of America, the National Catholic Welfare Conference, and other religious bodies. The peace conference was consciously modeled after the 1963 National Conference on Religion and Race, whose success in the field of civil rights had inspired those in the peace movement to try to form a similar body to address problems of war and religion. As the Reverend Homer Jack, director of the Department of Social Responsibility of the Unitarian Universalist Association and one of the members of the conference's secretariat, later wrote, the escalating war in Vietnam "made many churchmen who participated in Selma-like demonstrations for greater civil rights transfer their experience more quickly into actions for peace."[12]

The list of participants at the conference read like a who's who of clergymen who had been active in the civil rights movement. Among the cochairs were Rabbi Maurice Eisendrath, Dr. Dana McLean Greeley, Archbishop Iakovos, and Bishop John Wesley Lord; sponsors and members of the executive committee and secretariat included Bishop Daniel Corrigan, Eugene Carson Blake, and Rabbis Arthur Gilbert, Michael Robinson, and Balfour Brickner. Mathew Ahmann, one of the leading spirits behind the National Conference on Religion and Race, was one of the participants, as were John and Anne Bennett, Rabbi Arthur Lelyveld, the Reverend John B. Sheerin, and Ralph Smeltzer. A spirit of ecumenism pervaded this working conference. Addresses were limited; two keynote speeches were given, by Rabbi Jacob Weinstein of the Central Conference of American Rabbis and Bennett, and the closing address was by Bishop John Wright of Pittsburgh, a Catholic prelate. Vice President Humphrey made a speech, and President Johnson and U Thant, Secretary-General of the United Nations, sent letters expressing their hopes that religious people of all faiths would cooperate and work together to reduce tensions worldwide.[13] "As you seek to advance such wisdom," Johnson wrote, "no one watches you with deeper interest—or higher hopes— than your President."[14]

Johnson's good wishes were not insincere—but he had not embraced dissenters, either. The National Conference was not specifically directed toward discussion on Vietnam alone; rather, its purpose was to discuss the nature of peace and religion at a global level—to find guidelines for behavior in religious belief and moral principles as they pertained to questions of war and peace; to study existing religious peace initiatives and organizations in the United States, the United Nations, and overseas; and to discuss current problems and issues from a religious viewpoint. It was thus not incongruous for Humphrey to give a short speech filled with platitudes about his desire for peace and to offer an open door to all who wanted to come and discuss that subject with him.[15]

Only the last session dealt specifically with Vietnam, although mention of that conflict crept into all the speeches given by the clergy. Not everyone shared the same views, however. Bennett advised his audience to question the use of terms such as "honor" by government spokespersons when discussing Vietnam, for it was difficult, he said, to "distinguish between its use to refer to national face-saving and its use to refer to a genuine moral obligation." Both he and Weinstein argued that Communism was not the worst fate that could ever befall a country, although unending civil war, right-wing tyrannies, or years of neglected economic and social problems might be. Wright disagreed, taking issue with Bennett's description of American "obsession" with Communism. Fear of that ideology in the "religious and even democratic world" was not obsession, he countered, but realism of a sort that was needed to "keep us from having the gentleness of the dove while lacking that wisdom of the serpent which the Divine Teacher linked to His counsel concerning the conduct of 'doves.' "[16]

Nonetheless, given the latitude of topics and the disagreements over how to define the Communist challenge, the conference's final declaration was marked by a frank resolve to try to find ways to end the war in Vietnam. Recognizing that the "matter is complex and intense and solutions are not easy," the participants called for an immediate bombing halt; a cease-fire of indefinite duration to begin on Good Friday, 1966; the use of the United Nations and other channels to find a peaceful solution to the war; a negotiated rather than military settlement, with members of the NLF included as representatives; and economic and financial aid to rebuild Vietnam and other areas of Southeast Asia. It also requested that all religious and interreligious groups continue to intensify their work for peace.[17]

The steering committee of Clergy Concerned About Vietnam—composed of Heschel, Bennett, Coffin, Neuhaus, and David Hunter of NCC—needed no urging. With no end of the war in sight, they announced that their organization would continue to exist for the duration of the war, as Heschel had wanted. Richard Fernandez, an ordained minister of the United Church of Christ, was elected executive director on May 1, and quickly set about expanding office space in the NCC building at Riverside Drive. Clergy and Laymen Concerned About Vietnam (CALCAV), as it was called after May 1966, remained a moderate organization, however, and kept its distance from the more radical organizations.[18] "We came into being specifically to provide a religious comment on the war that would not be allied to the traditional peace movement," Heschel wrote, and there were no plans for the organization to continue after the war was ended.[19] Still, frustration was growing within the ranks of the moderates. Robert McAfee Brown faulted the Johnson administration for its refusal to take dissenters seriously but admitted that he would refrain from embracing radicalism and would work through the system, hoping for the "emergence of a serious rival" to Johnson in the 1968 presidential elections, "unlikely as this may be."[20]

The subject of Brown's anger, meanwhile, continued the war against Vietnam. As the bombing failed to achieve the desired results, Johnson ordered more bombing over a wider area; sorties numbered 148,000 in 1966, almost three times the number flown the year before. By the summer of 1966, the targets had shifted from military bases and supply routes in the southern part of North Vietnam to industrial areas, fuel storage facilities, and transportation sites in the northern half of the country, with raids all the time inching closer to Hanoi and Haiphong. All the while, the Johnson administration vehemently denied that civilians in villages and cities were being targeted. Coupled with the escalation in bombing came an increase in the number of American ground forces. By the end of 1966, 400,000 American troops would be in South Vietnam.[21]

The summer of 1966 thus saw an increasing sense of urgency among religious antiwar protesters. Thich Nhat Hanh's arrival in the United States in May did nothing to dispel the pervading gloom, for his accounts of the destruction and poverty wrought by the war only confirmed the fears of those who opposed the war on moral and religious grounds. The Buddhist monk had already signed a third newspaper advertisement paid for by FOR and the International Committee of Conscience on Vietnam in January, a statement calling upon the leaders of the United States and the two Vietnams to end the bombing and political assassinations and asking the leaders of the People's Republic of China to refrain from statements that "harden already bitter attitudes on both sides." It called on all sides to negotiate an end to the war on the basis of the 1954 Geneva Accords. Over 10,000 religious leaders of all faiths from over forty countries signed the statement, including Alfred Hassler, Daniel and Philip Berrigan, Heschel, King, Rabbi Jacob Weinstein, and the Reverend W. Harold Row, executive secretary of the General Brotherhood Board of the Church of the Brethren. Thich Nhat Hanh was not identified by name but only as "A Vietnamese Buddhist—a leading monk in South Vietnam, whose name is withheld for prudence."[22]

Thich Nhat Hanh's original purpose for coming to the United States was to present a lecture on Vietnamese Buddhism at Cornell University, but upon the request of the faculty, FOR sponsored a three-week tour for him to travel around the country talking about what the war was doing to his homeland. Explaining that the tension between the South Vietnamese government and the Buddhists was not due to a power struggle but to the desire of the latter for an independent civilian government, he called on Vietnamese Catholics to join with Buddhists in the creation of a stable government. The conflict, he said, was an internal matter in which the United States had little business being involved. Only by destroying the entire country could Americans win a military victory, but if the United States "were to make it unmistakably clear that it is actually seeking peace and is committed to leaving when peace has been secured, the Viet Cong would lose much of its appeal." What little goodwill there was toward Americans was quickly evaporating, he reported, because most Vietnamese suspected that the United States was interested in Vietnam only as a forward base against the Chinese.[23]

When Thomas Merton heard that a fellow monk was coming to the United States to talk about peace, he invited him to the Abbey of Gethsemani to speak with the Trappist community. "It seems to me the Vietnam Buddhists are about the only ones who are making much sense," he wrote, "though that is not an opinion shared by all in this monastery."[24] Merton's meeting with Thich Nhat Hanh so moved him that he wrote a touching piece about him for the August issue of the popular religious magazine *Jubilee*. The Buddhist monk, Merton explained, was "more my brother than many who are nearer to me by race and nationality, because he and I see things exactly the same way." Both despised the war for "the needless destruction, the fantastic and callous ravaging of human life, the rape of the culture and spirit of an exhausted people." It was Merton's hope that the bonds between peace activists in Vietnam and the United States be taken seriously, for they represented a new spirit of fellowship that was uniting young people in something "that is more concrete than an ideal and more alive than a program."[25]

When word reached FOR officials that South Vietnamese officials might jail Thich Nhat Hanh or even have him assassinated, they convinced him to extend his trip by a few months, but he did not cease his activities in the United States.[26] When Neuhaus, Heschel, and Daniel Berrigan led 150 people in a two-day fast over the Independence Day weekend as "a call for repentance," they held a meeting in the Community Church of New York City to honor Thich Nhat Hanh.[27] "Is it not true that Communists are fellow human beings first, antagonists second?" asked Heschel in his address to the group. The United States, he said, had been "enticed by her own might," adding that there was "nothing so vile as the arrogance of the military mind." Compounding the problem was the tendency for the government to "behave as if there were a division of qualities: infallibility of judgment in the possession of the State and Pentagon; ignorance, sentimentality everywhere else."[28]

Still the war dragged on, and even its moderate opponents began to question whether the war was an isolated mistake or symptomatic of a greater problem in the national psyche. The unwillingness of Johnson and his advisers to negotiate unless North Vietnam ceased its aggression, their refusal to consider the NLF as a political entity, and, most importantly, the increasing destructiveness of the bombing raids indicated to some that the Johnson administration would rather prosecute the war than negotiate, despite its claims to the contrary. "The escalation of the war in Vietnam makes it difficult to be an American," wrote Bennett regretfully.[29]

Some saw in the carnage evidence of genocidal tendencies similar to those of the Nazis. White House policies revealed "no sign of swerving from a final solution to the Vietnam problem," wrote the editors of *Commonweal* in the middle of 1966.[30] I. F. Stone agreed with the analogy. Describing the burned and bombed peasant villages, napalmed children, and begging orphans in the streets of Vietnam's cities, he argued that "the world's conscience must be mobilized. This is the horror we must not let any phony olive branches elsewhere hide from view." The United States was committing grave crimes in Vietnam, and Americans had to condemn them, "lest a later generation ask of us, as they ask of the Germans, who spoke up?"[31]

While cautioning those in the peace movement that both sides in the war were guilty of terrorism and murder, pacifist Gordon Zahn also saw reminders of the past and compared the small number of Catholic clergy critical of the war in Vietnam with the few German Catholic priests who had spoken out against Hitler. "Our spiritual leaders," he wrote, "have far less to justify their silence: no Gestapo is likely to be pounding on their doors or dragging their priests off to concentration camps. At least not yet."[32] Writing a year later, theologian Harvey Cox looked back to an earlier war for a point of comparison, noting how the world was outraged by the bombing of Guernica in the Spanish Civil War and how so many were indifferent to the bombing in Vietnam. While the protests of a few would not change national policy, it might "keep alive in us that fragile capacity to feel another's pain without which even the most sublime moral philosophy becomes irrelevant."[33]

Adding to such concerns was mounting evidence that Vietnam was not the only nation being bombed; Cambodian officials were complaining that their citizens were being killed in border towns in American bombing raids. Authorities in the United States admitted that although they had reason to believe that the NLF had supply routes leading from that country to South Vietnam, no American planes had struck targets in Cambodia. A group calling itself Americans Want to Know sent a fact-finding mission to Cambodia to investigate charges that the war was spreading. The team included Floyd McKissick, the new national director of CORE; Donald Duncan, a former sergeant in the United States Special Forces who had become a vocal critic of the war; author Kay Boyle; and Rabbi Israel Dresner of Temple Sharey Shalom in Springfield, New Jersey. After holding a news conference in Washington, the group left the country at the end of July to spend a week in Cambodia touring the border, having been promised full cooperation from Prince Norodum Sihanouk, who had broken off relations with the United States over the war.[34]

The team failed to discover any evidence of Vietcong military activity on the Cambodian side of the border, nor did they find any of the 28,000 Chinese guerrillas that the Saigon government reported were hiding in Sihanoukville.

They did, however, see many examples of American bombing attacks, including several corpses in the Cambodian village of Amlong Trach, over 800 yards from the border. During their visit, American planes attacked the village of Thlok Trach, killing three Cambodians and injuring several others. Sihanouk demanded an apology from the United States and refused to meet with special envoys to begin talks on resuming official diplomatic relations. The investigating team managed to compile enough evidence to show that the United States had indeed bombed Cambodian villages, which American officials acknowledged at the same time they insisted that their maps showed the towns as being located in South Vietnam.[35]

Increasing numbers of clergy and religious organizations called for a negotiated end to the war. Still praising the Johnson administration for its stated interest in negotiations, the NCC, following the earlier lead of the Synagogue Council of America, urged a bombing halt, and asked that the matter be settled by the United Nations, along with representatives from the NLF. Rabbi Weinstein and the executive board of the Central Conference of American Rabbis urged rabbis to speak out against the war if their consciences compelled them to do so, arguing that every cleric should be able to exercise freedom of the pulpit. Rabbi Eisendrath, Dr. Greeley, Archbishop Iakovos, Methodist Bishop Lord, Roman Catholic Bishop Wright, and Bishop William Crittendon of the Episcopal Diocese of Erie, Pennsylvania, issued a joint statement in support of U Thant's proposals for a negotiated settlement. Even Eugene Carson Blake, who had promised Johnson the year before that he would not add his voice to the "irresponsible" antiwar protests, called for deescalation and peace negotiations, telling reporters following his election as general secretary of the World Council of Churches that "the more successful the U.S. policy seeking victory in Vietnam, the greater the disaster will be in the long run."[36]

Of all the religious groups that opposed the war in Vietnam, Johnson was puzzled most by the opposition of Jews. Stories circulated that the president had privately remarked that Jewish citizens should be behind him, because they were known to be compassionate, politically informed, anti-Communist, and interested in seeing the United States fulfill its commitments to Israel. When Malcolm A. Tarlov, national commander of the Jewish War Veterans, went to meet with Johnson, he reported that the president had compared South Vietnam and Israel as small nations surrounded by enemies, a view echoed by Zalman Shazar, president of Israel, who pointed out during a visit

to the United States in 1966 how appreciative his government was over Johnson's "leadership . . . in the preservation of the independence of small nations."[37] The linkage between Jewish support for the war in Vietnam and
American aid to Israel, while not explicit, upset many Jewish secular leaders,
so much so that Arthur J. Goldberg, United States representative to the United
Nations, met with them to assure them that there was no need for alarm. He
failed to convince his guests, one of whom announced at the end that there
was agreement on only one issue: "That the talks would be off the record and
that there would be no statements."[38]

Many members of the Jewish religious community were also disturbed by
Johnson's supposed attempt to single them out. "When [the President] seems
to suggest that American policy toward Israel depends on Jewish good behavior, that is, on support for his policies, he is going too far," said one
anonymous rabbi. Heschel told a reporter that while he admired Johnson's
position on civil rights, he could not hide his anguish over the war in Southeast Asia. "If Abraham had no hesitation about challenging the judgment of
God over Sodom and Gomorrah," he asked, "should not an American have
the right to challenge the judgment of our President when horrified by the
war in Vietnam?" Dr. Herbert Goldstein, rabbi emeritus of New York's West
Side Institutional Synagogue and Chancellor of the Rabbi Herzog World
Academy in Jerusalem, took issue with such criticism. Johnson was "really
endeavoring to save the world from Communism's encroachment," he argued. "If the United States succeeds, the world will be safe; if not, the whole
world is sitting on a keg of fire."[39]

Disagreement over the war also existed among Catholics. "The great majority of American Catholics seem to have no particular moral convictions with
regard to the war in Vietnam," complained the Reverend John B. Sheerin,
editor of *Catholic World*. "Is it not strange that so many of our clergy who have
no hesitation about making positive moral judgments week after week in
confession have no opinions on the great moral problem of our generation?"
The war could not be considered a just war, argued Sheerin, for the morality
of American involvement in Vietnam was "very doubtful." All Americans, he
urged, "should reaffirm their demands for negotiations and for cessation of
this seemingly interminable slaughter."[40]

Although Pope Paul VI had made specific references to the conflict in
Southeast Asia in his 1966 encyclical *Christi Matri*, calling on "all those
responsible [to] bring about the necessary conditions for the laying down of
arms," the assembly of American Roman Catholic Bishops supported the president. While supporting the search for alternatives to war, the bishops never-

theless argued that "our presence in Vietnam is justified," because of the right of self-defense, for "what a nation can do to defend itself, it may do to help another in its struggle against aggression."[41] Cardinal John Cody, Archbishop of the Catholic Diocese of Chicago, took part in a ceremony at that city's Navy Pier, blessing with holy water tanks that were then loaded on ships bound for Vietnam. Sixty Catholic seminarians picketed the pier and his residence, carrying signs reading "Stop Blessing Death" and "End the War," with the result that religious superiors ordered them to undertake psychological tests. Many left the seminary instead, and only four out of the sixty became priests.[42]

Of all the members of the Catholic hierarchy, Francis Cardinal Spellman, the Military Vicar of the Armed Forces for the Roman Catholic Church, sounded the loudest clarion call to arms. Declaring "my country, right or wrong," Spellman enthusiastically supported the Johnson administration both at home and abroad. During his Christmas visit to the troops in South Vietnam, he proclaimed that the conflict was a "war for civilization" and later sent out as Christmas cards photographs of himself standing next to American bombers.[43] Describing his visit as an "unforgettable and inspiring experience" upon his return home, the Cardinal said that the American soldiers were in South Vietnam "helping to defend the freedom and independence of the Vietnamese people and, incidentally, our own people, against Communist aggression."[44]

The president could not have agreed more. Drawing parallels between the Vietnam War and the Second World War, Johnson left no doubt in anyone's mind that the "nervous Nellies" calling for peace were latter-day Neville Chamberlains bent on appeasement. He was unwilling to consider any negotiations except those that called for the North Vietnamese to cease their infiltration of the south, and after North Vietnam hedged on several conditions, the White House decided to resume bombing. McNamara and Henry Cabot Lodge, American ambassador to South Vietnam, advised Johnson against this, but the president, convinced that the diplomatic ventures were "a dry creek" and further discussions useless, gave the order in early December 1966 to bomb rail yards near Hanoi, which resulted in heavy casualties. When reports in the foreign press described the damage to residential areas, the Johnson administration denied them, later explaining that it must have been caused by North Vietnamese antiaircraft fire.[45]

Traveling through North Vietnam during the bombings, journalist Harrison Salisbury of the New York Times reported extensive destruction not only of residential areas of Hanoi but also of rural villages with no military significance. Whether it was intentional or not, he wrote, "one can see that United

States planes are dropping an enormous weight of explosives on purely civilian targets."[46] Such accounts helped widen what was already being called a "credibility gap," for official reports on military strikes were being contradicted by professional journalists and others. During an air raid, Salisbury shared a shelter with Barbara Deming, one of the editors of *Liberation*; Diane Nash Bevel, one of the founders of SNCC; and two other antiwar activists who had been invited to Hanoi by the Vietnamese Women's Union to see the carnage firsthand.[47]

The North Vietnamese had long realized the publicity value of having antiwar activists visit their nation and had suggested that A. J. Muste bring a group of them to Hanoi in early 1967. Over time the original group of twelve, which had included Daniel Berrigan, was cut down to the three oldest members, reflecting the veneration the Vietnamese had for the elderly: Muste; sixty-seven-year-old Richard Ambrose Reeves, an Anglican Bishop who had been deported from South Africa in 1960 for criticizing apartheid; and Abraham Feinberg, the sixty-seven-year-old American rabbi emeritus of Holy Blossom Temple in Toronto. An outspoken critic of the Cold War, which had earned him the nickname "the red rabbi," Feinberg had first made a name for himself as a radio singer in New York City. Rediscovering his religious roots during the Nazi persecution of the Jews, Feinberg had left a promising career in music to enter the rabbinate.[48]

During their ten-day visit, the North Vietnamese took the three clergymen to see the devastation wrought by American bombs in the rural areas south of Hanoi, where they examined undetonated antipersonnel bombs, and to a kindergarten in the village of Phu-Xa, where they saw the deep trench that had been dug in the middle of the floor for protection from air raids. The schoolchildren sang to the "three uncles," after which their guests, visibly moved, handed out candy. The three clerics also saw the damage done to Hanoi itself, and if further proof was needed that the Americans were bombing the capital, they were forced to take shelter four times during their visit as airplanes flew overhead, dropping their bombs on areas near Hanoi.[49]

The high point of their visit took place when they met with Ho Chi Minh. Relying on an interpreter for part of the discussions, he summed up his main points in English, inviting President Johnson to come to North Vietnam as his guest to talk about peace, but "not with a gun at his hip."[50] When the three apprised the U.S. press of the statement, however, it was dismissed as symbolic rather than substantive, and Johnson never replied to Muste's letter urging him to usher in a new climate through negotiations and an end to the bombing. Feinberg was able to get an audience with staff members of the U.S.

Embassy in London, State Department officials, and U.N. Ambassador Goldberg, but nothing came of his reports.[51]

Given the administration's unwillingness to listen to religious critics of the war, CALCAV decided to mount more effective protests. By the beginning of 1967, the organization's membership included some of the most prominent churchpeople in the country, including the Reverend John McKenzie of Notre Dame University, Methodist Bishop Lord, Harvey Cox of Harvard Divinity School, and the Reverend Peter Riga of St. Mary's College. Capitalizing on such support, CALCAV held an "Education-Action Mobilization" in Washington, D.C., inviting ministers, priests, and rabbis to come to the capital and participate in workshops, meet with government officials, and take part in an interfaith vigil for peace. Prior to the mobilization, the executive committee met in New York City to work on a position paper for the organization to distribute. Brown flew in from California, arriving at eight in the morning, and for forty-eight consecutive hours he labored on the paper, adding revisions as the others read it, and finally went to bed the day before they were all due in Washington.[52]

"There comes a time when silence is betrayal," the statement began. "That time has come for us in relation to Vietnam. Our allegiance to our nation is held under a higher allegiance to the God who is sovereign over all nations. . . . Each day we find allegiance to our nation's policy more difficult to reconcile with allegiance to our God." The exercise of religious faith and the privileges of a democracy, it argued, obliged the clergy to make their opinions known and their voices heard. High civilian casualties, the use of napalm and defoliants and torture, coupled with Johnson's denial of the damage done to cities and nonmilitary regions, made the war immoral, and the only way to peace was a bombing halt and a negotiated peace with no victor.[53]

The Washington Mobilization broke no records for massive demonstrations, but what it lacked in numbers it made up for in commitment. Over 2,000 clerics, seminarians, nuns, churchwomen, and laypeople from across the country gathered in the basement and halls of the New York Avenue Presbyterian Church on January 30, cluttering the floor with bedrolls and sleeping bags. The next day, the participants marched silently in front of the White House. No slogans, no banners, no placards surfaced among the demonstrators, for the organizers had made it clear that the protest was to be one of discipline and moderation, befitting both an act of penance and the desire of CALCAV's members to reach out to the middle class. Defrocked Presbyterian minister Carl McIntire and 100 followers from the staunchly conservative American Council of Christian Churches had no such scruples, and they staged a counterdemonstration across the street, carrying signs reading "Fight to Win in Vietnam" and "Unleash Chiang."[54] Coffin made his way to the small group to discuss the issues with them, and found that few had any idea what the mobilization meant. "[O]nly among religious folk could a man of such limited intellect raise so large a following and so much money," he reflected.[55]

After the vigil, the marchers divided up into groups to meet with their senators and representatives. Not everyone was glad to see them; Republican Senator Everett Dirksen of Illinois told them to "Hush up," while others welcomed them into their offices to talk about the war. Over 150 people visited Senator William Fulbright of Arkansas to commend him on his stand against the conflict, much to his delight. On the whole, the visits were discouraging, for most of the participants in the mobilization received the "general impression that most of the congressmen feel powerless to determine the direction in which the nation will go," having "abdicated that responsibility" when they passed the Gulf of Tonkin resolution in 1964.[56]

More encouraging was the church service at the New York Avenue Presbyterian Church that evening, where the congregation heard addresses by Coffin, Rabbi Weinstein, Bishop Paul Moore, and the Reverend John F. Cronin, assistant director of the U.S. Catholic Conference's Social Action Department. Speakers at a second service the following afternoon included Senators Wayne Morse of Oregon and Ernest Gruening of Alaska, who condemned the war as immoral, and Senator Eugene McCarthy of Minnesota, who received a standing ovation when he told his audience, "We must be prepared to pass a harsh moral judgment on our nation's commitment."[57] What made this gathering important, McCarthy reflected later, was that it was made up of "the more or less regular clergy of almost every denomination. They could hardly be described as 'alleged churchmen' or peaceniks or pacifists. Many had come from very conservative churches or synagogues, and they came from all over the country."[58]

In his own eloquent and moving address that day, Rabbi Heschel reflected the fears of many that the nation's conscience would not be roused from lethargy until it was too late. Recounting an experience he had at the age of seven when he was studying the sacrifice of Isaac, he told the hushed crowd how his heart "began to beat even faster," and as he read of Abraham lifting the knife, his heart "froze within." When the angel finally appeared to stop Abraham from sacrificing his son, Heschel broke into tears. When his rabbi asked him why he was crying, the young Heschel replied, "But rabbi, supposing the angel had come a second too late?" The rabbi comforted him and told him that angels could not come late. "An angel cannot be late," Heschel warned his audience, "but man, made of flesh and blood, may be."[59] Robert McAfee Brown spoke next, maintaining that God was not necessarily in the churches or synagogues, but "in the efforts of humble citizens" who cried out "on behalf of those who suffer nakedness and want." If Americans did not seek a new direction, he continued, sounding every inch an Old Testament prophet, they could be sure that God would judge the nation severely and hold it accountable. If the nation repented, however, and sought to undo the damage that had been done, God would be with the nation to "chasten and sustain us."[60]

Like the March on Washington, the vigils for the Civil Rights Act, and the rallies in support of the Voting Rights Act, the Washington Mobilization was markedly ecumenical in scope and purpose, though little was made of this by the participants. Although speakers had lamented the late arrival of the churches onto the civil rights scene from the steps of the Lincoln Memorial that brilliant day in August 1963, there had seemed to be a glimmer of pride that the clergy was nonetheless involved in what was turning out to be a major showcase for the ecumenical movement. There were no similar grounds for self-congratulation in Washington in early 1967. The reason the clergy and laypersons were there was too painful. What ecumenical spirit there was existed as a salve to soothe those who felt isolated in their opposition to the war. "Roman Catholics, Jews and numerous varieties of Protestants sang, prayed and worshiped together in penitence, in shared suffering and in a common commitment to peace," wrote Kyle Haselden. "Unity on this occasion was no designed formality; it was a vital experience." Coffin felt the same way, recalling the number of small peace rallies he had attended where counterdemonstrators vastly outnumbered the antiwar protesters. In Washington, "we were deeply moved just to be jammed one against another in the pews, an experience of solidarity. . . . Now instead of feeling alone and isolated, we were all together in the church."[61]

But not quite all. Not one Catholic bishop attended the Washington Mobilization. CALCAV's executive committee sent telegrams to each one, inviting them to take part or at least to make public their approval. Only eleven responded, and while they made clear their desire for peace, none of them showed up. In an open letter, Brown asked them the reasons for their silence. "Is it the Vietnam issue that disturbs you, or is it the ecumenical aspect that disturbs you?" If the latter, he noted, the bishops should know that "one of the individuals most frequently appealed to" had been Pope Paul VI. Jews and Protestants had "tried to take our lead from him, and we were sad that his own fellow bishops would not do likewise." Religious communities, Brown explained, could not "afford the luxury" of speaking out independently and occasionally on the issue of Vietnam,voicing his fear that such "unilateral actions will increasingly become frivolous if not immoral in the face of the immensity of the task that confronts us."[62]

Even some Catholic priests who did attend the mobilization disagreed with some of the suggestions made by the speakers. The Reverend John F. Cronin, assistant director of the U.S. Catholic Conference's Social Action Department, complained that it was "easy to don the mantle of the prophet and to thunder: 'Let justice be done even if the heavens fall.'" It was "infinitely more difficult to give responsible prophetic counsel in complex situations where no clear solution is in sight." Calling for a negotiated end to the war with terms that would allow the South Vietnamese to choose their own form of government would be "within the realm of morality and prophecy," said Cronin, but the insistence that a bombing halt would lead to negotiations was a "political judgment, not a moral decision."[63] Brown took issue with this view, explaining that too many clergy feared to make specific decisions for fear of being proven wrong but insisting that clergy had to take that risk. If the religious establishment was to err, he argued, let it be "on the side of overinvolvement rather than underinvolvement. . . . Let it be too radical rather than too conservative. Let it spend itself now for a bleeding and bent world, rather than conserving itself for a future it may never have."[64]

A dialogue with those who made political decisions was exactly what Brown and his colleagues had scheduled for the afternoon of February 1. As clergymen, nuns, seminarians, and laypersons packed their bedrolls and left the New York Avenue Presbyterian Church, Brown joined Heschel, Bennett, Coffin, Weinstein, Neuhaus, the Reverend William Spurrier, chaplain of Wesleyan University, and Michael Novak, a Catholic layperson and one of Brown's fellow professors in the Stanford religious studies program, and headed to the Pentagon to meet with the Secretary of Defense. A second group of seven clergymen met with presidential adviser Walt Rostow. As the first group sat down, McNamara told them that clergy had every right to be concerned about matters such as war, adding that he wished they had been as concerned with civil rights. ("Glancing around the table, I recognized it was the wrong remark to make to that particular group of men," Coffin recalled.) Speaking for the group, Coffin was outlining the points made in Brown's position paper when an overwrought Heschel lost his composure and began to speak out against the war in anguish and despair. A somewhat startled McNamara assured them that he understood their views and was doing everything he could to restrain those in the Pentagon who wanted to escalate the war. The group left the meeting impressed and saddened by McNamara's decency and sincerity, agreeing that it was a dangerous state of affairs when a person of such character could oversee such a destructive war. The other delegation received the same explanations from Rostow, who told them that the Johnson administration was actually practicing restraint and trying to ignore the military's demand for more forces.[65]

The least dramatic events of the Washington Mobilization, but some of the most important, were the workshops held the second day, in which participants developed proposals for carrying the antiwar message to their own congregations and communities. Before the mobilization was over, CALCAV members, led by a group of clergy and laypersons from St. Louis, called for Christians and Jews throughout the nation to join them in a three-day "Fast for the Rebirth of Compassion," which would begin on February 8, to coincide with Ash Wednesday and the beginning of the Buddhist New Year. The fast was described as an act of penance for the war. One million people took part, subsisting only on fruit juices and water or rice and tea, and while the event would not change the nation's foreign policy, wrote Brown, it showed that at least that many Christians and Jews were "concerned enough to make this kind of token identification with the poor and hungry of Vietnam."[66]

Other peace ventures soon followed. In early March, CALCAV sponsored an ecumenical study conference on "Vietnam and the Religious Conscience," a function attended for the first time by a member of the Roman Catholic hierarchy. Archbishop Paul Hallinan of Atlanta decried the carnage in Southeast Asia, telling the assembled religious leaders that "[o]ur conscience and our voice must be raised against the savagery and terror of war." Calling upon clergy of all faiths to unite behind the demands for de-escalation and a negotiated peace, he reminded them of the high point of clerical involvement in the civil rights struggle not long before: "We need a second Selma to convince our people that justice, freedom, human compassion as well as peace are at stake."[67]

By the spring of 1967, other Catholic bishops were speaking out. The only member of the Roman Catholic hierarchy to have marched in Selma, Auxiliary Bishop James P. Shannon of Minneapolis–St. Paul, along with ten Catholic college presidents, drafted an open letter to their coreligionists criticizing the discrepancy between "the moral principles enunciated by the Church and the uncritical support of this war by so many Catholics," especially in light of the high number of civilian casualties. Shortly after this, Shannon became the first Catholic bishop to become a member of CALCAV, joining Daniel and

Philip Berrigan and a handful of other Catholics in the organization.[68] But their numbers remained small, due in large part to the fact that the majority of Catholic bishops mistrusted CALCAV's aims, believing it to be too left of center on the political spectrum. Bishop James A. McNulty of Buffalo, on the other hand, ordered a diocesan priest to resign from the Buffalo chapter of CALCAV, of which he was cochair, and cease his activities in the organization on the (erroneous) grounds that it was "Republican-party supported and financed . . . as a rebuke to the Johnson administration for its stand about Vietnam."[69]

It was not Shannon's involvement in CALCAV that drew the largest headlines, however, but that of another participant in the Selma march. Martin Luther King Jr. had continued to criticize the war both in private and from his pulpit at the Ebenezer Baptist Church in Atlanta, but it was not until February 1967, in a speech in Los Angeles, that he publicly criticized the atrocities, the repression and criticism of dissent, and the funding drained from the War on Poverty as a result of the war. In turn, CALCAV invited him to speak at an antiwar assembly at New York City's Riverside Church on April 4. Sharing the speaker's platform with him were Bennett, Heschel, and historian Henry Steele Commager, but it was King's address that captured the attention of the thousands in the audience and the rest of the nation.[70]

Breaking what he called "the betrayal of my own silences," King commended the assembled religious leaders for moving beyond uncritical patriotism to challenge the war on the basis of their spiritual beliefs. He condemned the war in Southeast Asia for drawing people, skills, and funding away from the War on Poverty, and the Johnson administration for its hypocrisy in decrying the destruction in the northern ghettos by frustrated black youths while inflicting great violence on Vietnam. The United States had to declare a unilateral cease-fire in hopes of producing negotiations; in the meantime, churches and synagogues had to continue to assist those who decided to oppose the war and become conscientious objectors. Clergy of draft age should voluntarily give up their ministerial exemption and join them. But the "popular crusade against the war in Vietnam" could not end there. The conflict in Southeast Asia, he believed, was evidence of a "far deeper malady within the American spirit." If the assembled clergy ignored this, they would be "organizing clergy-and-laymen-concerned committees for the next generation" to address the problems inherent in U.S. support for repressive regimes in South America, Asia, and South Africa until American society and policy underwent a profound change.[71]

King received a standing ovation from CALCAV members, who asked him to become one of the cochairs on their executive committee, praise from the editors of the *Christian Century* and *Christianity and Crisis*, and almost universal condemnation from the media, black civil rights leaders, the FBI, and the Johnson administration. Most of his critics described his foray into foreign policy as a mistake, insisting that he had left his work in the civil rights movement to meddle in affairs in which he had no competence; others worried that he was burning his bridges with the president, a stalwart supporter of civil rights. The editors of the *Washington Post* noted solemnly that King had done a "grave injury to those who are his natural allies" in the struggle to end racial discrimination. "Many who have listened to him with respect will never again accord him the same confidence. He has diminished his usefulness to his cause, to his country, and to his people." The editors of the *New York Times*, arguing that it was possible to "disagree with many aspects of United States policy in Vietnam without whitewashing Hanoi," warned, "There are no simple or easy answers to the war in Vietnam or to racial injustice in this country. Linking these hard, complex problems will not lead to solutions but to deeper confusions."[72]

Many were particularly incensed at the comparisons King had made between the military tactics used by the Joint Chiefs of Staff and the Nazis. Malcolm Tarlov of the Jewish War Veterans said it was "utterly incredible that Dr. King's denunciation of our Government should manifest itself in such an ugly parallel," and said his organization considered King's "extremist tirade to reveal an ignorance of the facts, pandering to Ho Chi Minh, and an insult to the intelligence of all Americans. . . . His speech could have been written in North Vietnam."[73] Raphael Gould, director of development for FOR, on the other hand, believed that King's speech was a correct "assessment of America's position in the world, politically, spiritually and morally," but he was sufficiently concerned about criticism from Jewish citizens to ask Rabbi Isidor Hoffman, honorary chair of the Jewish Peace Fellowship to write to Tarlov and explain the moral anguish and "painful guilt" Americans bore that made such a speech necessary.[74]

Four days later, King joined antiwar activist Benjamin Spock and Monsignor Charles Owen Rice as they led 400,000 people in a march from Central Park to the United Nations Plaza as part of the demonstrations organized by the Spring Mobilization Committee to End the War in Vietnam. In addition to King, the speakers included Daniel Berrigan and Dorothy Day. Several blocks north, students in Central Park burned almost 200 draft cards in a massive show of resistance to the federal government and its prosecution of the war.[75] Seventy-five thousand took part in a similar march in San Francisco, where Coretta Scott King and Robert McAfee Brown addressed the assembled crowd at Kezar Stadium. Brown warned that the government would not listen to the antiwar movement until it was clear that opponents of the war spoke for thousands of Americans, not a mere handful of dissenters. "And if that sounds hopelessly square," he added, "I remind you of one elementary fact of political life—squares have votes."[76]

CALCAV voted not to endorse the protests, fearing that the radical nature of some participants would alienate the middle-class constituency it was trying to attract, although the executive committee encouraged members of the organization to take part as individuals if they so desired. Richard Fernandez, CALCAV's executive secretary, was more interested in developing antiwar sentiment at the grassroots level, and to this end he worked with members of SNCC, SCLC, and SANE to develop the Vietnam Summer project. Inspired by the Mississippi Summer Project of three years earlier, volunteers organized local chapters of CALCAV, gave lectures at school auditoriums, developed curricula dealing with political dissent and the history of Southeast Asia for use in high schools, and built a political base to challenge Johnson in the presidential elections of 1968.[77]

Other clergymen not affiliated with any peace group chose to speak out as individuals. Eugene Carson Blake, general secretary of the World Council of Churches, sharply criticized Johnson's Vietnam policy. The American course of action had become tragic, he said, and the nation, "caught in a dilemma that makes any decision increasingly difficult . . . seems to be stumbling on towards final disaster." The Joint Chiefs had the capacity to destroy Vietnam, but, he asked, "when the swamps of the Mekong delta are filled up with dead Vietnamese and when the flower of our youth lies dead with them, what victory will we have won?"[78]

Still others rallied around new peace organizations developed by leading figures in what radical pacifists dismissed as the "liberal-labor coalition." Arthur Schlesinger Jr., John Kenneth Galbraith, and Joseph Rauh of Americans for Democratic Action founded Negotiations Now in May 1967, an organization that called for a bombing halt but insisted on a multilateral cease-fire and no immediate withdrawal of American forces. Its strong anti-Communist stand was welcomed by the Catholic hierarchy, and several prelates quickly became national sponsors by endorsing its platform. Monsignor Rice, however, was dropped as a sponsor because of his participation in the Spring Mobilization demonstration in April, and Bishop Fulton J. Sheen of Rochester, New York, who advocated immediate withdrawal of all American troops, was never asked to join.[79] The influx of Catholic bishops, even into such a moderate group as Negotiation Now, reflected the increasingly ecumenical nature of the religious antiwar movement. The significance of this trend, as well as the need to present alternatives to calls for escalation or immediate withdrawal, served as the basis for the 1967 book *Vietnam: Crisis of Conscience*.

According to Brown, he and Novak had been discussing the possibility of a book on their way back to Stanford, and as they "already had a running start on boxing the ecumenical compass," he recalled, they "realized that such a venture would be more significant with a Jewish collaborator." The next morning, Brown telephoned Heschel, who readily agreed to join them.[80] What had prompted the idea was their visit to Washington the previous winter and their impression that a fair number of government officials seemed to want a negotiated peace but were not at all certain that the public would back them if they called for one. It was the book's major purpose to persuade the public of the wisdom of such a policy.[81]

While Novak's contribution was a cogent discussion of the historical roots of American involvement in Vietnam, Heschel's and Brown's chapters were masterful and eloquent exercises in moral persuasion, designed to further the interfaith nature of the antiwar movement—hardly a surprising development given their longstanding interest in ecumenism. The problem of Vietnam, they noted, arose not only from American pride and unwillingness to change course but from "the dilemma of either losing face or losing our soul." When individuals were ill, wrote Heschel, "in danger or in misery, all religious duties recede, all rituals are suspended, except one: to save life and relieve pain. Vietnam is a personal problem." Priests, ministers, and rabbis had to awaken to the moral necessity of denouncing the the carnage. Heschel had a stern admonition to those who did not: "To speak about God and remain silent on Vietnam is blasphemous."[82]

Not only did members of the religious community need to urge individuals to speak out, and protect them when they dissented, wrote Brown, but they also had *"a responsibility to speak and act corporately"* (emphasis in original). Groups of Jews and Christians, not merely individuals, had to speak up, for only then would the Johnson administration be unable to discount the voices of protest. "If ever there was an 'ecumenical' issue," he argued, "it is Vietnam." If the churches and synagogues did nothing to challenge the war, he predicted, the question that would haunt the religious community would inevitably be "where was your voice?" The failure of the German churches to speak out against Nazism in the 1930s and 1940s was widely remembered; history asked the same question about the struggle for civil rights and noted "the failure of the churches and synagogues to act until the eleventh hour." The churches' and synagogues' response to the Vietnam War would soon be scrutinized, he warned. Religious bodies could keep silent or raise a "great chorus of concern" in order to *mobilize enough support for specific next steps so that our policymakers will be forced to move in new directions.*"[83]

Vietnam: Crisis of Conscience sold 50,000 copies its first year, and although it proved popular among moderates opposed to the war, it failed to sway supporters of the Johnson administration.[84] The Reverend John J. O'Connor, a Catholic chaplain in the United States Navy, took issue with many of the points set forth in the book, considering it "highly misleading" for its portrayal of the president and his advisers as acting in "bad faith" and the government of Saigon as "completely corrupt." The authors' method, wrote O'Connor, was to "replace reasoned argument and documented evidence with rhetorical questions and clichés"; its tone, he complained, was "judgmental to the point of being morally apodictic." O'Connor contended that the Americans were winning the trust of the people of South Vietnam, not forfeiting it. However, while the chaplain believed that the president and his advisers were doing everything they could to limit civilian casualties and create a climate for negotiation, he refused to impugn the loyalty of those who dissented. He had read *Vietnam: A Crisis of Conscience* as the work of individuals he considered to be "sincere and reputable . . . who have proved themselves in the market-place of modern ecumenism, who are dedicated to truly noble causes and unselfish public service," a rare tribute to the opposition in an era that saw an increasing lack of civility between antiwar activists and those who supported the government's actions.[85]

For all the kind things said about ecumenism, there was a brief period in the spring of 1967 when it appeared as though the ecumenical movement itself was too frail a reed to withstand storms blowing in another corner of the globe. On the morning of June 5, Israeli forces launched an attack against Egyptian, Jordanian, and Syrian troops that had been massing near their borders, and in six days managed to seize control of Jerusalem, the West Bank of the Jordan River, and the Gaza Strip. American Jews who had been indignant at the silence with which the plight of Israel had been met in the Christian communities during the tense weeks leading up to the war found themselves and their opinions questioned after the victory. Many of these Jewish spokespersons were also opposed to the war in Vietnam, and it was not long before antiwar activists, including the clergy, were asking "[h]ow could the Vietnam dove be the Israel hawk?"[86]

Daniel Berrigan remembered that his friendship with Heschel became strained as the rabbi refused to speak out against the June War in the same manner as he criticized the conflict in Vietnam. Rabbi Balfour Brickner, another antiwar activist and leader in the ecumenical movement, warned

Christians that "[u]nderstanding the very existence of the Jew precedes any interfaith conversations we might wish to have about . . . conscience, morality, or worship." Rabbi Weinstein, president of the Central Conference of American Rabbis, shrugged off any comparisons, telling fellow rabbis that they had to "beware of package deals." "We must not," he advised, "be embarrassed by the charge that we are doves on Vietnam and hawks on Israel, that we believe in universal truth and international co-operation until our tribal interests are touched." Differences between South Vietnam and Israel abounded, he continued, and could perhaps be symbolized by asking whether the government of South Vietnam or Israel could be "better entrusted with the encouragement of the democratic process in their respective spheres of influence!"[87]

For all the complaints about Christian silence in the face of threats to Israel, and there were many, several of the same ministers and priests who had become involved in the antiwar movement nevertheless understood the different circumstances surrounding each conflict, and they were quick to speak up even before the war had started. Several ministers and priests, including Bennett, King, Niebuhr, Brown, and Sheerin—none of them pacifists like Berrigan—signed a joint statement on May 29 calling for all Americans to support Israel's integrity and freedom.[88] In the West, wrote King in a separate article, it was no longer popular to "proclaim openly a hatred of the Jews," and he noted that the anti-Semite "must seek new forms and forums for his poison. How he must revel in the new masquerade! He does not hate the Jews, he is just 'anti-Zionist!' "[89] "The Israel-Arab crisis resulted in a crisis in Jewish-Christian relations," admitted Rabbi Marc Tannenbaum of the American Jewish Congress. "But it is a crisis that is also a great opportunity."[90] There is no doubt that the war in the Middle East jeopardized the ecumenical spirit between members of the two religious groups, agreed Richard John Neuhaus, but the "alliances to end the war in Vietnam" remained unbroken."[91]

Johnson and his advisers must have looked wistfully upon the swift and decisive Israeli military victory. But what was possible in the deserts of the Middle East could not be replicated in the jungles of Southeast Asia, against an enemy far better organized and with a much clearer set of goals. The Pentagon had to make do with a limited bombing campaign against an enemy who could rarely be seen. Fissures were growing among members of Johnson's cabinet, between those who had come to believe that the bombing was achieving little and the Joint Chiefs, who argued that a more intensive bombing campaign would completely destroy North Vietnamese supply routes and strongholds. Although he refused to give the generals carte blanche, Johnson extended the approved list of targets. By the end of the year, a total of 864,000 tons of bombs would be dropped on North Vietnam, and McNamara, increasingly at odds with the President's policy, would prepare his resignation. At the same time, Johnson was trying to underscore South Vietnam's alleged strengthening of democratic institutions by sending governors, members of Congress, and other influential Americans to observe the September 1967 elections there. "Brought to Vietnam and toured around," recalled a journalist, "they saw what their official guides wanted them to see—and their confusion was reflected in the malapropism of one of them, a Texas clergyman who kept referring to the country as 'South Vietcong.'"[92]

Fissures, shifts, and confusion were also appearing in the religious antiwar movement. CALCAV had always gone to great lengths to stress the differences between itself and the more radical peace organizations. Brown had repeatedly warned supporters against calling for immediate withdrawal of American troops, stressing the need to avoid radical pronouncements of the kind made by the "far, far left, among certain pacifist groups, among the beatnik and hippy [sic] crowd," because such pronouncements would be ignored by the government and especially the middle-class. It was from this class, he argued, that "the voters are found, and it is from here that must come the kind of pressure that can make a difference."[93] Yet, by the the middle of 1967 the Johnson administration had proven itself unwilling to honor its pledges to discuss peace at any place and at any time, all the while growing increasingly defensive and intolerant of dissent. The ministers, priests, and rabbis who identified themselves with and appealed to moderates would themselves in turn become more militant. These individuals, pillars of the moderate Clergy and Laymen Concerned About Vietnam, would shortly be advocating actions on behalf of civil disobedience that only one year before had seemed the height of radicalism.

eight

I am for peace; but when I speak, they are for war.

PSALM 120:7

The Escalation of Dissent

The Antiwar Movement, 1967–1968

For most Americans, the summer of 1967 would be remembered less as "Vietnam Summer" than as the "long hot summer" during which riots in the black sections of several northern cities resulted in dozens of deaths and millions of dollars in property damage. White Americans, and their religious leaders, were caught off guard by the intensity of the violence, despite having received a foretaste of it in similar riots in the same cities years before. Again, the reactions of the white religious institutions in Detroit, Cleveland, Newark, and elsewhere were the same: promises to improve education and housing, which were rarely realized; and donations of food, clothing, and temporary shelter, which did little to alleviate the long-standing conditions of poverty and despair that had sparked the riots in the first place.[1]

Another indication that the civil rights movement had embarked on a new direction was the advent of "black power," a phrase first coined during the Meredith March through Mississippi in 1966. Depending on the speaker, the term meant anything from pride in one's African heritage to black nationalism and separatism from whites in all venues, including (and especially) in the struggle for civil rights. Advocates of black power demanded black control of the movement, expunging sympathetic whites from administrative and staff positions in formerly interracial organizations such as SNCC and CORE, thus alienating many former supporters in the white community.[2] Even Malcolm Boyd, who had long stressed the need to look beyond color to the humanity of all people, found himself accosted by black nationalists who demanded to know what had led him to involve himself in the affairs of black people instead of staying among whites and trying to educate them, but he insisted on remaining in the movement. Other white clergymen such as the Reverend James E. Groppi, a Catholic priest who had marched in St. Augustine and Selma, continued his work with Milwaukee's NAACP Youth Council, unperturbed by the new emphasis on black separatism.[3]

Nonetheless, the shift away from integration and interracial alliances could not but hurt many longtime civil rights supporters who happened to be white. Black activists needed their autonomy, explained Paul Moore years later, not without a trace of sadness, "because it's true, the leadership of many civil rights groups at that point was in the hands of liberal whites as well as blacks." But after the rise of "black power" in 1966, he recounted, "we white folk were asked, sometimes not very politely, to get out of the movement."[4]

Black power manifested itself within the ranks of religious organizations as well. After Eugene Carson Blake and Robert Spike resigned from the NCC's Commission on Religion and Race in 1966 to pursue other interests, Dr. Benjamin Payton, a black staff member of the Protestant Council of the City of New York, was elected as Spike's successor. While other black clergy greeted his appointment with approval, established civil rights leaders such as Whitney Young, Roy Wilkins, and Bayard Rustin considered his ideas too radical, especially his insistence that funds be used to support separate racial programs. Their inability to work smoothly together led to decreased funding for the commission and Payton's resignation in the summer of 1967. Shortly afterward, the General Board announced that the commission would no longer have the independent mandate it had been granted in 1963, and, after drastic budget cuts, the revamped organization was placed under the direction of the Department of Social Justice.[5]

A new organization calling itself the National Committee of Negro Churchmen drafted a resolution in support of black power, arguing that blacks had to wield power as a group in the same way as other ethnic groups in the nation in order to ensure racial justice. Separatist tendencies were clearly evident in the fall of 1967, when for the first time at a NCC assembly separate white and black caucuses were formed to discuss black power. Black organizations such as

Black Presbyterians United and the Episcopal Union of Black Clergy and Laity contributed to the disintegration of existing interracial bodies such as the Presbyterian Interracial Council in the late 1960s and the Episcopal Society for Cultural and Racial Unity in 1970. The growing body of work on "black theology" also indicated that blacks had little to learn from the white churches whose visions of a white Jesus permeated their power structure. Even those black clergy with moderate views began to voice concerns over whether integration with white churches would displace black ministers from positions of authority.[6]

Perhaps the clearest indication that the alliance between the white churches and the civil rights movement had changed occurred when James Forman interrupted a service at Riverside Church in New York City in May 1969 to present the "Black Manifesto," which included the demand that "racist white Christian churches and Jewish synagogues" pay $500 million in reparations for the historical wrongs done to black Americans, with the money to be used by the Black Economic Development Conference for the establishment of black-controlled educational and media programs. While several Protestant denominations increased their contributions to minority programs under their jurisdiction, most of them rejected the Black Manifesto itself, as did the Catholic Church and several Jewish religious organizations.[7]

Black power had helped speed the demise of what the Episcopal layperson Malcolm Peabody termed "the grand coalition of conscience" forged between King and SCLC on one hand and white liberals, especially clergy, on the other. The success of this coalition, wrote Peabody, was due in part to the effectiveness of organizing "public opinion within the church in the North to bring pressure on the South," but the breaking of the ties between whites and blacks had destroyed this consensus, as had the urban unrest that summer. The final straw in the coalition's destruction, he argued, was the Vietnam War, which "shoved the issue of race to the back pages, by making it impossible to get funds to work on the growing problem, and by diverting the energy of the national political leadership."[8] Both the black power movement and the northern riots had considerably altered the role white clergy could play in civil rights at roughly the same time the war escalated; as Moore put it, "a lot of us drifted out of the [civil rights] movement . . . and right at that point, into the antiwar movement."[9]

But not all did. "I stand without apology by my position that ESCRU should not see itself as a part of the peace movement," John Morris replied to Peabody, saying he did not believe there was "the intrinsic connection between peace and civil rights which some espouse." Although Morris considered himself a dove, he thought that "part of the rush into the peace field [was] escapism from unfinished business."[10] Nonetheless, after a bitter dispute with Peabody over whether the organization should remain in the South and continue its work of church renewal or move its headquarters to the North and work with black power advocates outside the Episcopal Church, Morris, the founder and executive director of ESCRU since its inception, resigned in 1967.[11]

It was perhaps a fitting time for individuals such as Coffin and Brown to reflect on their trajectory of social activism, from civil rights to the antiwar movement. While CALCAV, as an organization, was not yet ready to embrace illegal actions, they, and others, had grown sufficiently frustrated with their inability to influence the government through vigils, petition drives, and moral suasion that they began to consider civil disobedience. In February 1967, Coffin called upon the clergy to take part in such actions. "I do not think any man ever has the right to break the law," he said, "but I do think that upon occasion every man has the duty to do so." The Vietnam War was "just such an occasion," he said, and the war was so immoral that massive civil disobedience was necessary. He also proposed that seminarians and younger clergy opposed to the war give up their draft exemption status, "in order to make it count on moral grounds," and become conscientious objectors; clergy too old for the draft should publicly support them and thus also be subject to the penalties for violating the Military Selective Service Act of 1967, which provided fines up to $10,000, five years in jail, or both for those who evaded the draft and those who counseled them to do so.[12]

Brown, who had also begun calling for similar acts of involvement on the part of the clergy, explained at greater length in a commencement address in June why he felt it was crucial that the religious community speak out against the war. The Bible had a rich tradition of dissent against civil authorities, he argued. "Yahweh did *not* say on Sinai, 'You shall have no other gods before me, except your own national security as Jews,'" nor had Peter told the Sanhedrin that "On the whole, we prefer to obey God rather than men, but if you're really insistent we'll make an exception this time." Loyalty to God had to come before loyalty to any other authority, including the state, and if the latter's decrees conflicted with the former, religious people had to champion not only the right but the practice of dissent. Four months before, at the close of the Washington Mobilization, he believed that the "voice of the perturbed middle" would have an effect on policymakers. "But now," he admitted, "I fear that whispers or even agonized speeches may be too little and too late."[13]

Why had Brown and Coffin been so hesitant to embrace civil disobedience in the case of Vietnam but so willing to travel south to take part in freedom rides and sit-ins, particularly when the issues at stake in Vietnam were, in Brown's words, "even more momentous than those at stake in the civil rights struggle"?[14] Brown believed that the the term "civil disobedience" was incorrect when used to discuss the civil rights movement, for while individuals had broken state laws, they had done so in the name of federal statutes. The situation regarding the war was not so "tidy," though, and he believed that the "extremity of the present situation means that if we are to obey God rather than men, we must now live with something less than spick-and-span tidiness."[15] He had little reason to think that civil disobedience would change things, but he believed that the issues were "so clear and so crucial" that individuals no longer had the time to leisurely weigh all their options; they had to move quickly, as he had, through the process of simply signing statements to embracing civil disobedience. It was the last step, he wrote, that was crucial, "the one in which I part company with most of my friends in the liberal groups where I politic . . . and with most of my friends in the church where I worship." His one regret was that he had not come to that decision sooner, but having made it, he would help young men oppose the draft until he was arrested, for he was unwilling to see them "pay with their lives for the initially bumbling but now deliberate folly of our national leaders."[16]

Secular and religious figures alike were voicing similar ideas. Arthur Waskow and Marcus Raskin of the Institute for Policy Studies in Washington drafted "A Call to Resist Illegitimate Authority," which challenged the legality of the Vietnam War, and urged Americans to support draft resisters. When it was released on October 2, over 200 clergymen, scientists, artists, and writers signed it, including Brown, Coffin, Philip Berrigan, Thomas Merton, Martin Niemoeller, Michael Novak, Episcopal Bishop James A. Pike of California, and Dr. Benjamin Spock. Three weeks later, CALCAV made public its own paper, the "Statement on Conscience and Conscription," written largely by Coffin and Neuhaus and signed by Heschel, Brickner, Daniel Berrigan, Brown, Sheerin, Harvey Cox, Martin Marty, and David Hunter. Stating that mere vocal support for the right of dissent was inadequate, it called upon the signatories to challenge the right of the government not only to continue the war but to claim to be able to define the limits of conscience; those who refused to participate in one particular war should be granted conscientious objector status in the same manner as those pacifists who refused to fight in all wars.[17]

By this time, Coffin had already seen action on the civil disobedience front. A small group calling itself the New England Resistance had organized a turn-in of draft cards in the Boston area, receiving the enthusiastic cooperation of the Reverend Jack Mendelsohn, the Unitarian pastor of the Arlington Street

Church, who offered the use of his church for the event. Coffin, the Reverend George Williams, professor of divinity at Harvard University, and the Reverend Robert Cunnane were some of the featured speakers at the service on October 16. Young men who wanted to turn in their draft cards, accompanied by families and friends, filled the church. Coffin praised them for following their consciences, adding that Christians and Jews had a responsibility to offer their houses of worship as sanctuaries to conscientious objectors. He had no doubt that the authorities would not hesitate to go into a church or synagogue and arrest draft resisters (which is what happened the few times this was tried); rather, the proposal was "less a means to shield a man, more a means to . . . make a church really be a church." Addressing himself to the young men carrying their draft cards, Coffin reminded them that it was fitting that their action was taking place within two weeks of the 450th anniversary of the Reformation, as a new reformation, one of conscience, was exactly what was needed in the United States. "What in our technological age shall it profit a man that he be able to fly through the air like a bird and swim through the sea like a fish," he asked, "if he be not able to walk the earth like a man?"[18]

As the last speaker finished his sermon, the men stood up to turn in their draft cards. Reverend Williams invited them to burn their cards instead, and while 60 did so, the remaining 200 cards were handed to Coffin and the others. It was a moving conclusion to a dramatic service, portions of which were shown on the NBC evening news. "If men like this are beginning to say things like this," noted commentator John Chancellor, "I guess we had all better start paying attention."[19] Four days later, Coffin was in Washington, D.C., with Spock, Raskin, Waskow, and other members of the draft resistance to make speeches condemning the war and questioning the right of the government to decide which person's claims to conscientious objection were valid.[20] It was not easy to stand up against the government and the public's support of the war, Coffin admitted, but he and his colleagues could not remain silent. They could not advocate that young men become conscientious objectors "only to desert them in their hour of conscience. So we are resolved, as they are resolved, to speak out clearly and to pay up personally."[21] At the conclusion of the speeches, Coffin, Spock, and Raskin, accompanied by members of the Resistance, entered the building, left the briefcase containing the collected draft cards with an ill-at-ease deputy assistant attorney general, John McDonough, and walked out.[22]

Shortly afterwards, FBI agents began showing up on the Yale campus, asking questions about the chaplain and his associates. Students at the Divinity School responded by posting a message on their bulletin board reading

"Dear FBI: 'Let your foot be seldom in your neighbor's house, lest he become weary of you and despise you.' Proverbs 25:17." After the dean of students accused the agents of trespassing and interfering with the process of education, they withdrew. While the students supported Coffin, the alumni were displeased with his radicalism and made their objections known in letters and complaints to the president of Yale, Kingman Brewster.[23] During his Parents' Weekend address, Brewster noted that while he objected to Coffin's "strident" advice and "unworthy" tactics, he admitted that because of his "personal verve and social action, religious life . . . reaches more people at Yale than on any other campus I know about."[24] While no doubt many parents, as well as alumni, would have liked to have seen the chaplain removed from his position, the respect for academic freedom was strong enough to preclude such a decision being made by the university administration.

Coffin did not return to Yale immediately after the confrontation at the Justice Department. The weekend of October 21–22 had been selected for yet another antiwar demonstration in Washington, D.C. To placate both the moderates and the radicals, two separate events had been scheduled: a massive rally for the former in front of the Lincoln Memorial, in which an estimated 100,000 heard Coffin, Spock, and others speak, followed by a march across the Arlington Memorial Bridge; for those interested in committing civil disobedience, David Dellinger, Abbie Hoffman, Jerry Rubin, and other members of the National Mobilization Committee to End the War in Vietnam proposed a march on the Pentagon to block the entrances, fill the hallways, and shut the building down. The rally itself went smoothly, the march on the Pentagon less so. Lines of soldiers with rifles at the ready stood between the protesters and the Pentagon, but there was little violence until midnight, when the troops and federal marshals began arresting people who remained near the Pentagon once the permit for the use of the mall expired.[25] Years later, McNamara reflected on the march, some of which he had witnessed from the building's roof. "I could not help but think that had the protesters been more disciplined—Gandhi-like—they could have achieved their objective of shutting us down," he told a reporter. "All they would have had to do was lie on the pavement around the building. We would have found it impossible to remove enough of them fast enough to keep the Pentagon open."[26]

One of those arrested was Daniel Berrigan, who had joined the faculty of Cornell University only a few months before to teach courses in New Testament theology and drama. Charged with a misdemeanor for refusing to move on when ordered, he refused to pay the fine, and found himself sharing a cell with other protesters. He went on a hunger strike for five days, then posted bail and left the prison on October 27, the same day his brother Philip was arrested for pouring blood on draft files kept in the United States Customs House in Baltimore.[27]

The dramatic gesture came at the end of a series of more traditional protests, which Philip Berrigan had found to be increasingly futile and, to his mind, irrelevant. After his transfer to Baltimore in the spring of 1965, he sought out the company of other Catholic priests and seminarians to discuss methods of protesting the war. He began attending the Baltimore chapter of CALCAV, but, dismayed with what he considered a tendency to talk rather than act, he formed the Baltimore Interfaith Peace Mission in the fall of 1966, and the predominantly clerical group demonstrated their opposition to the war by picketing the homes of the Secretaries of State and Defense, demanding a bombing halt and the beginning of negotiations under the auspices of the United Nations. McNamara refused to see them, but Rusk telephoned Berrigan the next day and arranged a meeting.[28]

It went poorly. According to Berrigan, Rusk refused to look him in the eye, and his comment "I leave all morality up to you clergymen" further angered the priest.[29] Two sympathetic studies of Philip Berrigan imply that this rebuke propelled him into more radical, direct-action protests at a Virginia army base later in the year, but historian Charles DeBenedetti has documented that Berrigan and fellow peace activist Sanford Gottlieb were trying to work with the State Department into the middle of January 1967, thus suggesting that direct-action protests and working with government officials to achieve the same ends were not mutually exclusive activities.[30] Both Berrigan and Gottlieb offered to visit Hanoi "on an absolutely private and confidential basis" to establish contact between the North Vietnamese and American governments. State Department adviser Chester Cooper later explained that although such offers were usually made by "very, very good people," it was "awfully hard to rely on them for any serious objective accounts of what was going on or really very difficult to use them as confidential channels. . . . Their discretion was suspect; their judgment was suspect; their emotional biases were suspect."[31]

After failing to provoke arrests and gain publicity by trespassing on the army base at Fort Myers, Virginia, with twelve demonstrators, eight of them Catholic and Protestant priests (the military police simply dropped them off at Arlington National Cemetery, where their cars had been towed), Berrigan, Thomas Lewis, the Reverend James Mengel of the United Church of Christ, and Catholic layperson David Eberhardt began to consider different tactics, eventually settling on the decision to deface the draft files in Baltimore. They entered the Customs House under the pretense of wanting to look at their own draft records, poured a mixture of their own blood mixed with that of animals over the documents as the receptionists protested, shouted, and, in one case, threw one of the proffered Bibles at Eberhardt, hitting him in the head. When they finished, the four sat down and waited to be arrested.[32]

This time there was plenty of publicity, for the group had notified the press that there would be an unspecified event at the Customs House on the afternoon of October 27, and reporters were there with cameras at the ready. The four had even drafted a statement that they handed to journalists in sealed envelopes earlier in the day. Their sacrificial act was designed to remind others that it was at draft boards where the "pitiful waste of American and Vietnamese blood ten thousand miles away" began. The four said they wished for no "labels of martyrdom or messianism" but insisted, after denouncing the war as immoral, that they would "submit to apprehension and the consequences" of their action.[33]

A noble statement in the grand manner of Gandhian civil disobedience, it was also ironic. Philip Berrigan's later displays of arrogance would lead some friends and many contemporaries to question whether the Josephite did indeed have a martyr or messianic complex, and his later attempts to go underground and avoid imprisonment for later actions would cast serious doubt on the validity of both his and his brother Daniel's claims to be authentic practitioners of civil disobedience and nonviolence. As John Bennett noted, true civil disobedience did not invite anarchy, for to "disobey a particular law and take the consequences, allowing that law to run its course in exacting punishment, is not to engage in an act against public order."[34]

After their arrests, Eberhardt and Mengel were released on their own recognizance; Berrigan and Lewis served seven days in jail, going on a hunger fast in protest. A trial date was set for April 1. Not surprisingly, the Baltimore archdiocese was highly critical of the blood-pouring, but aside from a few news items about a radical Catholic priest working in the draft resistance, the event received little coverage outside Maryland. Had it received more, it probably would have been negative. Gallup polls taken in November 1967 indicated that only 18 percent of the American public favored withdrawal of American troops from Vietnam, while 55 percent favored increasing attacks on North Vietnam.[35]

What did spark the interest of the media, however, were the federal indictments of Coffin, Spock, Raskin, Michael Ferber, and Mitchell Goodman. A grand jury in Boston had indicted them on January 5, 1968 for conspiracy to "counsel, aid, and abet" violations of the Selective Service law and to hinder the administration of the draft by their actions the previous October. By all accounts the indictments were handled shoddily. To ensure maximum publicity, the Justice Department released the information first to the press, and then to the five men indicted. Spock learned of the news when he saw the newspaper headlines while riding the subway. While all those charged realized that they ran the risk of prosecution, the idea of a conspiracy seemed farfetched, as they hardly knew each other. Leonard Boudin, one of their lawyers, recalled that the first thing he did when he met with them was to introduce them to each other. Arriving in court on January 29, they pled not guilty and were released on bond. The trial date was set for May 20, and the defendants began to prepare a defense that would not only challenge the legality of the draft but of the war itself.[36]

Speculation as to the reasons for the conspiracy charge abound, but the most probable explanation was a letter that General Lewis Hershey, Director of the Selective Service, wrote to over 4,000 draft boards on October 26, 1967, requesting that persons up to thirty-five years of age who had been deferred by their draft boards and then participated in illegal protests such as draft card burning or blocking induction centers be reclassified 1-A. This threat to the right of dissent provoked an outcry from liberal secular figures as well as religious leaders, but it was applauded on the right by Representative Edward Hebert of Louisiana, who advised his colleagues, "Let's forget the First Amendment! When is the Justice Department going to get hep and do something to eliminate this rat-infested area?" In the end, Hershey's proposal was shelved, but to appease the conservatives the Justice Department decided to prosecute the five individuals.[37]

Robert McAfee Brown rallied to the defense of his colleague Coffin, calling for clergymen of all faiths to join with him in a service at Glide Memorial Church in San Francisco on the evening of the group's arraignment. Threat of prosecution would not dissuade other antiwar clergy from continuing to help men avoid the draft, he told his audience, and at an ecumenical service that night, he and other clergy received draft cards from conscientious objectors and forwarded them to the Selective Service. Another member of CALCAV was dealing with federal authorities that month, but instead of planning trial dates, Daniel Berrigan and Howard Zinn, a professor of history at Boston University, were discussing their upcoming trip to Hanoi with State Department officials. The North Vietnamese Peace Committee had offered to release three prisoners of war to a designated representative of the American peace movement in honor of Tet, or lunar new year, and both readily agreed to make the journey. As travel to North Vietnam was officially forbidden, one official offered to validate their passports, but they refused, claiming that the government had no right to approve where they could or could not travel. After numerous delays, they arrived in Hanoi on February 9.[38]

The two Americans spent their first several days with the same members of

THE ESCALATION OF DISSENT

the peace committee who had escorted Muste, Feinberg, and Reeves the year before, and, like their predecessors, were taken around the city to see the destruction and learn about the war from the North Vietnamese perspective. Berrigan was very impressed with the earnestness of the Vietnamese, especially the head of Hanoi's journalist union, who assured them that capital punishment had not been practiced since 1954 and that at that time not even former collaborators with the French were executed. This and other information Berrigan described as "balanced" and downplayed the idea that they were mere propaganda. Berrigan and Zinn were less enthusiastic about the American officials in Laos, who insisted that the captured fliers be flown back to the United States on a military carrier, not a commercial flight as originally planned and as the North Vietnamese had requested. Their hopes that the trip would be seen as an independent peace project, and the first of several prisoner releases, were crushed. Even more galling to them was that the prisoners had originally agreed to follow their captors' requests while in Hanoi, but changed their minds once they arrived in Laos.[39]

Berrigan never forgot the betrayal he felt as a result of the trip: betrayal not only by the American government, but even on the part of one of the pilots long after the fact. "They made a promise as the condition of their release— which I thought was a very minimal condition—that they would have nothing to do with the future bombing of North Vietnam, once they got back to their country," he told a biographer in the late 1970s. "I read years later that [one of them] was teaching at an Air Force base in Florida—teaching those who were going into bombing during the war. So he broke his promise. But one would have expected that."[40] One might also have expected a little more charity toward someone who, facing the prospect of a long imprisonment, would have promised anything to gain release, but Berrigan's dislike of the war impeded such sentiments.

Adding to his disappointment at the time was the fact that the trip proved to be far less of a news event than Muste's had been the year before. Not only had Berrigan and Zinn brought no messages from Ho Chi Minh, but the attention of the American media was directed elsewhere in Vietnam. On the morning of January 30, North Vietnamese and Vietcong forces launched a massive attack on Saigon and other South Vietnamese cities. During the initial stages of the Tet Offensive, guerrilla forces managed to get into the grounds of the American Embassy in Saigon and engage American troops in a firefight, which ended several hours later when the attackers were killed. More than half the provincial capitals, cities, airports, and the headquarters of the South Vietnamese general staff were attacked. Although taken by surprise, American and South Vietnamese forces struck back, and within several days man-

aged to inflict heavy casualties and drive the surviving NLF and North Vietnamese soldiers back into the countryside. It took three weeks of relentless
bombardment to force the North Vietnamese out of Hue, which had once
been an important cultural and religious center. Once the battle was over,
American troops found mass graves containing the bodies of 2,800 South
Vietnamese executed by the North Vietnamese and Vietcong, grim testimony
to the ruthlessness of the enemy which some in the American peace movement were inclined to romanticize.[41]

General William Westmoreland, commander of the United States forces in
Vietnam, declared that the enemy had been defeated. Tactically, he was
correct, for enemy forces had not only had been routed after suffering massive casualties, but they had failed in their mission to rouse the South Vietnamese to join them. Psychologically, however, the Tet Offensive was a re-
sounding victory for Hanoi, as it flatly contradicted the contentions of the
White House, the Joint Chiefs, and the State Department that a weakened
and broken enemy was almost ready to come to the negotiating table on
American terms.[42]

Television audiences witnessing the carnage began to wonder whether anything the Johnson administration was saying about the war was true.[43] The
violence on both sides lent credence to the longstanding claims of those in the
peace movement who insisted that the war had escalated beyond the realms of
military necessity and human comprehension. When an American officer
remarked after the destruction of Ben Tre that it was necessary to "destroy the
town in order to save it" from the Vietcong, the editors of the *Christian
Century* lamented, "This is the genius of our war effort—to destroy Vietnam in
order to save it. This is the logic of men maddened by murder. We have all
been made murderers."[44]

CALCAV had sounded the same charge in January 1968, with the release of *In
the Name of America*, a compilation of published articles on the American
conduct of the war juxtaposed with selections from the Hague and Geneva
Conventions, the "Nuremberg Principles," and Department of Army field
manuals concerning the international rules governing warfare and treatment
of civilians. The report was not intended as a legal brief, wrote Robert McAfee
Brown, Rabbi Arthur Lelyveld, president of the American Jewish Congress,
and the Reverend John Sheerin in their introduction, but as a basis for showing how "our nation must be judged guilty of having broken almost every
established agreement for standards of decency in time of war." Responding to

anticipated objections, the authors explained that rather than detailing the war crimes of the Vietcong, whose atrocities were already well-documented in the American and foreign press, they had decided to inform the American public of the less readily accepted accounts of crimes perpetrated by their fellow citizens. Besides, they argued, the fact that the Vietcong committed crimes did not absolve American soldiers of doing the same.[45]

Although the moral problems of the treatment and/or killing of prisoners and civilians were a main source of concern to the authors and signers of the document (who included Bennett, Heschel, King, Paul Moore, Harvey Cox, Edwin Dahlberg, and the Reverend Robert Drinan, Dean of the Boston College Law School), they were also worried about what the destruction of moral restraints would do to Americans at home. What would happen to the soul not only of the soldiers who were ordered to burn villages and crops, but the soul of America itself? Coming after the "long, hot summer" of 1967, when sections of American cities burned in the midst of riots, the concerns were especially acute. If Americans did not take international law seriously when it did not work to our military advantage, they asked, "how can we be surprised if members of minority groups do not take domestic law seriously when it works to their civilian disadvantage?" In the final analysis, they wrote, "[e]thics cannot be determined by geography."[46]

CALCAV distributed a copy of the book to every senator in Washington, D.C. By the middle of the year more than 30,000 copies of the book had been sold, although there is little evidence to suggest that it succeeded in rousing a population that preferred not know about such things. In order to further underscore their conviction that the war was eroding moral values, CALCAV sponsored a second Washington Mobilization in early February 1968. In many respects, it was like the first. Twenty-five hundred participants sat or stood in the New York Avenue Presbyterian Church on the morning of February 5, listening to speeches and meditations by Coffin, who chaired the assembly, and Bennett, Drinan, Rabbi Maurice Eisendrath, and Malcolm Boyd. Like his colleagues, Boyd had become increasingly concerned about the course of the war and had become more active in the antiwar movement as a result. He had taken part in several teach-ins against the war and had once been hit in the head with a baseball thrown from the rear of a crowded auditorium as he addressed students at the University of Oregon. In September 1967, he had traveled with forty other Americans opposed to the war to Bratislava, Czechoslovakia, to attend a meeting with North Vietnamese and NLF representatives.[47]

A portion of the second mobilization was given over to workshops dealing with the specific issues of the upcoming presidential election; another dealt with the draft, and Coffin was the natural choice for speaker. Carl McIntire and his followers again made an appearance, this time to interrupt the speeches, and Coffin invited him to share the platform and his opinion. The audience applauded when he discussed the need for conscience to be enlightened by the word of God, but they greeted his admonition to "Let every soul be subject to the higher powers" with silence. Coffin reminded him of the imprisonment of the church fathers, asking him to explain "why St. Paul was in and out of the pokey with a regularity similar to Secretary McNamara's shuttling back and forth to Vietnam."[48] The exchange convinced neither the ordained nor the defrocked Presbyterian minister, and McIntire remained convinced that CALCAV was "the advance guard of Ho Chi Minh."[49]

The most moving part of the mobilization was a prayer vigil at the Tomb of the Unknown Soldier in Arlington National Cemetery on February 6. CALCAV had wanted to use the cemetery's amphitheater to hold a memorial service for those killed in the war, but the Army refused permission. So on a cold winter day, 2,500 people stood on the steps at the tomb to take part in the silent vigil, bowing their heads as Martin Luther King Jr. intoned, "In this period of absolute silence, let us pray." As silence reigned on the steps below the tomb, the participants could hear the sounds of the changing of the guard, rifles clattering and heels clicking. The silence lasted several minutes until Heschel's baritone voice carried above the crowd the words of Christ crucified, "Eloi, Eloi, lama sabachthani?" ("My God, my God, why hast thou forsaken me?"). "Let us go in peace," said Bishop James P. Shannon, concluding the service, and the thousands of people quietly left the cemetery, each carrying a small American flag. In the distance, apart from the crowd, two men carried a Torah and a crucifix.[50]

By March, it appeared that the prospects for peace were improving. Senator Eugene McCarthy's strong showing against Johnson in the New Hampshire Democratic primary helped pave the way for a vigorous challenge to the incumbent from within his own party, as Robert F. Kennedy entered the race shortly afterwards. At the end of the month Johnson announced both a bombing halt and his decision not to run for reelection.[51] Several members of CALCAV's executive committee were guardedly optimistic. The president's decision created "the real possibility that we can move to a different policy," commented Bennett. "I think that he has seen that he himself has become a divisive factor." Heschel simply said, "[It] represents a victory for America. Period." Others were less sure about Johnson's announcement; Coffin believed the bombing halt might be a prelude to further escalation.[52]

Martin Luther King Jr. was in Washington the night of Johnson's speech, and when he heard the news that the president would not run for reelection, he was both amazed and reinvigorated. Perhaps this was an indication that the nation was turning around. If so, the country sorely needed such a sign, as did King himself. In the midst of planning a Poor People's March that would bring thousands of unemployed people to Washington, D.C., in a massive campaign of civil disobedience, he had become involved in a sanitation workers' strike in Memphis, Tennessee.[53] Despite the pressures on him, he still had speaking engagements to fulfill. A week before Johnson's address, King had been the guest speaker at the sixty-eighth annual convention of the Rabbinical Assembly in New York City. Heschel gave the opening remarks. "Where does moral religious leadership in America come from today?" he began. "Where in America today do we hear a voice like the voice of the prophets of Israel? Martin Luther King is a sign that God has not forsaken the United States of America. God has sent him to us. His presence is the hope of America."[54]

As the applause died down, King stood up and thanked the rabbis for their invitation and the chance to be with people of goodwill, admitting that while he had heard "We Shall Overcome" "probably more than I have heard any other song over the last few years," that night was the first time he had ever heard it sung in Hebrew. He then turned his attention to Heschel, saying that it was wonderful to "be here on the occasion of the sixtieth birthday of a man that I consider one of the truly great men of our day and age . . . one of the persons who is relevant at all times, standing with prophetic insight to guide us through these difficult days." Recalling Heschel's participation in Selma and his address at the National Conference on Religion and Race, King credited him with inspiring "clergymen of all the religious faiths of our country." After hearing Heschel's words, he said, "many went out and decided to do something that they had not done before." "So I am happy to be with him," he concluded, "and I want to say Happy Birthday, and I hope I can be here to celebrate your one hundredth birthday."[55]

Returning to the South later that month, King quickly resumed work on his projects. Two family friends, a white Quaker couple, had been urging King to go on a retreat before the Poor People's March, and had recommended the Abbey of Gethsemani. Thomas Merton was enthusiastic about the proposal, and a tentative date was set for early April.[56] King never made it to the retreat. On the evening of April 4, he was shot and killed on the balcony of the Lorraine Motel in Memphis, Tennessee. Riots flared up in cities across the nation as blacks took out their frustrations and anger by looting and burning. Washington, D.C., received the brunt of the violence, as smoke from over 700 fires obscured the Capitol. "These have been terrible days for everyone, and

God alone knows what is to come," wrote Merton. "I feel that we have really crossed a definitive line into a more apocalyptic kind of time. . . . We will need a lot of faith and a new vision and courage to move in these new and more bitter realities."[57]

Roman Catholic Archbishop Terence Cooke was at a reception at the Greek Orthodox headquarters in New York City when word of King's death arrived. Kneeling with Archbishop Iakavos before the Byzantine altar, they said the Lord's Prayer and prayed for King and the nation. Rabbi Arthur Lelyveld, Episcopal Bishop Horace Donegan of New York, Presiding Bishop John Hines of the Episcopal Church, and Dr. Edwin Espy, general secretary of the NCC were among hundreds who expressed grief at the news. In what must have been the understatement of the week, Reverend James Groppi of Milwaukee announced, "This is not going to be conducive to peaceful racial relations." From one of his revival meetings in Australia, Billy Graham was uncharacteristically harsh. The murder showed that "tens of thousands of Americans are mentally deranged," he said. "It indicates the sickness of the American society and is going to further inflame passion and hates."[58]

Three days later, on Palm Sunday, New Yorkers took part in a memorial march through Manhattan. Bishop Donegan told the congregation in the Cathedral of St. John the Divine that "God permits His friends to receive no worse treatment than that which was meted out to His Son, but true crosses are never light, and a bullet serves as well as ropes and nails." Eugene Carson Blake and Ambassador John Hayes attended a memorial service in St. Peter's Protestant Cathedral in Geneva; at St. Peter's Cathedral in Rome Pope Paul VI likened the death of King to Christ's passion. Before giving his blessing to the crowds in the square below, he told them that the cause of peace still suffered throughout the world, from Vietnam to the Middle East, from Nigeria to the United States, "where the killing of a defenseless Christian prophet of racial integration . . . reveals a deep and almost implacable conflict of souls and interests. But the olive branch is still green."[59] Among the dignitaries at King's funeral in Atlanta on April 9 were several prominent clergymen, including Archbishop Cooke, Bishop Donegan, Archbishop Iakovos, Archbishop John Dearden of Detroit, and Archbishop Lawrence Sheehan of Baltimore. Participating in the service were Heschel, who read the Old Testament lesson, and Roman Catholic Bishop John Wright, who gave a tribute.[60]

Shortly before his death, King had joined the other members of the executive committee of CALCAV in calling for a national fast during Holy Week, April 8–12, to repent for the suffering caused by the Vietnam War. With King's death, Bennett, Daniel Berrigan, Brown, Heschel, Coffin, Eisendrath, Dana McLean Greeley, Richard John Neuhaus, Richard Fernandez, Sheerin, and Brickner announced that the focus of the fast would no longer be peace in Vietnam alone, but "the cleansing of our national domestic life. The sign and consequence of our nation's defilement is the brutal slaying of that American who, more than any other, symbolized all that is hopeful in man's struggle to retain his humanity."[61]

Still the war dragged on, as did the resistance. On April 1, Philip Berrigan and his colleagues from the draft board raid stood trial and were found guilty, to no one's surprise. Sentencing was scheduled for May 27.[62] Coffin, still awaiting his trial, continued to advocate civil disobedience. Addressing a crowd of 2,000 people at Riverside Church in New York City, he claimed that the nation had "exhausted its spiritual substance." The church remained "the bland leading the bland," he said afterwards, and called upon the "posh churches in this town, including Riverside, to support a ten percent tax on income earmarked for the United Nations" as a "first step toward an international income tax and a start to raise money for the internationalization of power."[63]

The fact that formal peace talks had begun in Paris on May 13 did not change the Justice Department's stand on prosecuting Coffin, Spock, Raskin, Ferber, and Goodman, popularly known as the Boston Five, nor did it change the defendants' minds about wanting to challenge the war on moral and constitutional grounds. When the trial began on May 20, however, it quickly became apparent that the judge had no intention of allowing his courtroom to be used as a forum to discuss the right of conscientious objection, the legality of the draft, or the war. Instead, the trial was consumed with defining the terms of a conspiracy rather than addressing any of the broad questions for which the defendants had been prepared.[64]

With the exception of Raskin, the jury found the four men guilty of conspiracy as charged on June 9. The judge shortly thereafter sentenced them to two years in the penitentiary and assigned fines of $5,000 each for Coffin, Spock, and Goodman; Ferber was fined $1,000, leading him to quip that he had been given the special student rate. All announced they would appeal.[65] At a press conference, Coffin summed up the defendants' feelings: "The trial of the Boston Five was . . . unworthy of the best of America. . . . [The government] skirted the uncomfortable, it ducked the difficult," and instead of addressing the issues of the war, "availed itself of the sweeping provisions and paranoid logic of an outdated conspiracy law."[66] Coffin received word of the outcome of the appeal in July 1969, when a reporter interrupted his tennis game to tell him that Spock and Ferber had been acquitted and that there was to be a new trial for Goodman and himself. "This is good news for Spock, Ferber and free speech," Coffin told him. "For Goodman and me it's medium good news, I guess. I'm sure only of this: that of all the courts I've been in I prefer the one I'm in right now." In the middle of 1970 the Justice Department announced that they were dropping the charges.[67]

Long before a verdict was announced, the members of the Boston Five were widely regarded as heroes for their actions, which helped spur similar acts of resistance. In Philadelphia, the Reverend David Gracie, an Episcopal priest, announced his support for conscientious objectors in a rally outside Independence Hall, although his remarks fell short of advocating draft card burnings. When Bishop Robert DeWitt of the Episcopal Diocese of Pennsylvania announced that not only would he not dismiss Gracie but was proud of the priest's support of dissent, a lay group calling itself the Committee for the Preservation of Episcopal Principles demanded that they both be dismissed. "It would be irresponsible for us to abandon our work which ministers to those who dissent," retorted DeWitt. "We will not abandon one of our clergy who, in our name, carries out that ministry." It would be a "faint-hearted Bishop," he added, "who would even consider resigning from a diocese which is currently struggling, as it should, with the problems which rack our world."[68]

Philip Berrigan, however, did not think much of such actions. As for the members of the Boston Five, he saw them as "being people who sort of reacted to the government, instead of initiating action," Daniel recalled. "Phil didn't find that very exciting."[69] There was little that either of the Berrigans found exciting that winter that was not of their own planning. Philip and Thomas Lewis had decided to embark on another draft board raid before being sentenced on May 27 for the previous one, and they had tried to enlist the help of others for this venture, which they deemed "serious," a favorite word they used to distinguish their own work from that of others in the draft resistance. Both Berrigans had resigned from CALCAV, considering its emphasis on mobilizations and massive demonstrations as "another liberal bag." Philip also tendered his resignation from the Catholic Peace Fellowship in a long, self-righteous letter to James Forest. The work of both organizations, he wrote, was "safe, unimaginative, staffish, and devoid of risk or suffering." He and his brother, he said, had ideas that were "more at grips with this awful war," and they could not be blamed if they had "little time for those who want to run ads in the New York Times."[70] Similarly arrogant expressions alienated several friends, one of whom told a journalist writing a piece on them that they "look down on anyone who hasn't risked as much as they have. They'll barely break bread with you if you haven't burned your draft card. Talk about ghettos! That ghetto of martyrs is the most exclusive club of all."[71]

It was indeed becoming exclusive. The judgmental nature of the leaders in the Catholic Left inspired not cooperation but a clash of egos. Philip had little use for Eberhardt and Mengel once they began worrying about how their prison terms would affect their families, and he began espousing celibacy as an integral component of a revolutionary lifestyle. He and Lewis found the types of people they wanted in the persons of George Mische, a peace organizer; David Darst, a Christian Brother and schoolteacher in the inner city of St. Louis; Mary Moylan, a Baltimore nurse; John Hogan, a member of the Mary-knoll order who had been recalled from Guatemala because of his outspoken admiration of guerrillas there; and Thomas and Marjorie Melville. The latter had been Maryknoll missionaries who, like Hogan, openly sympathized with the guerrillas, but when their superiors discovered that they had secretly married while in Guatemala, they expelled them from both the order and the country. The group decided to target the draft files at Catonsville, a small, middle-class suburb west of Baltimore, and they set the date at the middle of May, shortly before Lewis and Berrigan were to be sentenced for the previous draft board raid. After repeated invitations to join them, Daniel agreed.[72]

And so it was that the nine Catholics entered the office of Local Board 33 in Catonsville, Maryland, seized almost 400 draft files after restraining one of the receptionists, and carried the papers outside to the parking lot, where they set them on fire with homemade napalm. As reporters swarmed around, taking notes and photographs, the group held hands and recited the Lord's Prayer, waiting for the FBI agents to arrive and arrest them. All were released on bail except Philip Berrigan and Thomas Lewis, who served time in jail.[73]

Philip Berrigan had no doubt that their action would be criticized by people misunderstanding what they had done, and so he drafted an open letter in *Christianity and Crisis*. To those who complained that the nine "disregarded legitimate dissent at the expense of law and order," he replied that they had all had experience with such dissent and had seen it "first ridiculed, then resisted, then absorbed. To become in effect, an exercise in naïveté." For Americans to ask others "to restrict their dissent to legal channels is asking them to joust with a windmill," he argued. "More than that, it is to ask them for silent complicity with unimaginable injustice."[74] Attorney William Kunstler, impressed with Daniel Berrigan after meeting him in Manhattan, agreed to represent the Catonsville Nine at their upcoming trial in October.[75] Others who were even more taken with what the Berrigans and their friends had done followed suit.

For the rest of the decade and into the fall of 1972, groups such as the Milwaukee Fourteen, Brothers and Sisters, U.N. Four, Flower City Conspiracy, East Coast Conspiracy to Save Lives, and the Planetary Peoples' Liberation Front undertook similar action at draft board offices.[76]

Few were more impressed with the actions of the Catonsville Nine than the participants themselves. At the dedication of a new Catholic Worker house in New York City, Daniel Berrigan compared the burning of draft files with the acts of the Christian martyrs and with Christ overturning the tables of the money changers. While David Miller and Thomas Cornell could not attend the ceremony, as they were both serving time in jail for burning draft cards, their wives went in their places, and one wonders what must have gone through their minds when Daniel Berrigan casually dismissed draft card burnings as old news and "establishment." There was a tendency, not uncommon among protesters in the 1960s, to believe that they had been the first to embark on a radical new course of action unlike anything else that had come before, and the Berrigans relished the fact that they had achieved a certain notoriety for moving beyond burning draft cards to destroying draft files. It was fairly common knowledge in the resistance, however, that the defilement of draft records had first occurred in February 1966, when Michigan native Barry Bondhus celebrated Washington's Birthday by dumping a bucket of his own and his family's feces into the files of his local draft board to protest conscription, an event that pundits later described as the movement that started the movement.[77] Of course, there had been even earlier incidents of dissenters burning documents. When Daniel Berrigan described to an interviewer that the Catonsville action was "a new day of creation," explaining that nothing like that had happened before, Howard Zinn, who was also being interviewed, pointed out that William Lloyd Garrison had burned a copy of the Constitution to protest slavery over 100 years before. "Well," Berrigan responded, "I don't want to become complicated about it."[78]

As might be expected, the burning of draft files by priests elicited a variety of responses from their fellow clerics, ranging from the Reverend Andrew Greeley's angry charge that they were prolonging the war by giving hope to the enemy to Jesuit Edward Duff's praising them for destroying the myth of monolithic American Catholicism eager to support the political status quo.[79] Robert McAfee Brown questioned whether the Berrigans were "*signs* pointing to some truths we would otherwise forget (and might indeed prefer to ignore) even when they have not always served as *models* whom people have directly imitated." At the least, wrote Brown, the burning of draft files certainly helped to point out the "grotesque moral priorities that have been erected in our country: we give medals to men who drop napalm on civilians in Southeast

Asia, but imprison men who drop napalm on pieces of paper in southeast United States." Perhaps if the rest of America had been protesting the war with more vigor years earlier, there would have been no need for the action the Berrigans took. The implicit problem, however, was whether they had raised the stakes so high that no other Americans would follow.[80]

Pacifist Gordon Zahn commended the brothers and their colleagues for following their consciences, although he argued that their analysis of the situation did not have to be accepted as valid by all. Those who continued to march and circulate petitions should not be considered moral cowards, he wrote, but perhaps reaffirmed that something could still be accomplished through the system that the Berrigans had abandoned. The issue that Zahn raised was that while people who were already supporters of the Berrigans and opposed to the war approved of the burning of draft files, it had a negative effect on those who were uncommitted. The same Milwaukee neighbors who had supported and encouraged Zahn when he was a conscientious objector during the Second World War, when the issues between good and evil seemed so clear-cut, strongly disapproved of the Catonsville action. Even more troubling, he added, was that the raids contributed "to the new mood of radical dissent which takes it for granted that one is free to disregard and disobey any law with which he does not agree." Classic civil disobedience called for the identification of a specific law or practice deemed offensive; instead, radicals were choosing a "highly indiscriminate and individualized rejection of all authority which is then justified in the name of a vaguely defined and romanticized revolutionary ideal" and ran the risk of "creating as much civil disruption as possible."[81]

Daniel Berrigan responded heatedly to such arguments, claiming that many of his critics, especially Catholics, had ignored the circumstances of the war in their response. "[They] judge us in a vacuum of their own making," he complained, arguing that only "those who are aware of the war and have re-acted in some real way are worthy to stand in judgment on us."[82] Not surprisingly, Berrigan left it up to himself and his brother to define what constituted reacting "in some real way" to the war. There was one person from whom Daniel Berrigan wanted approval for his actions, but it was not forthcoming.

"The napalming of draft records by the [Catonsville] nine," wrote Thomas Merton, "is a special and significant case because it seems to indicate a borderline situation: as if the Peace Movement too . . . may be escalating beyond peaceful protest," which in his view meant that it might also be "escalating into self-contradiction." While he did not think that the Berrigans and their compatriots had yet done this, their act was provocative and bordered on violence. The extreme and troubled times, he wrote, explained the "evident desperation" of the Berrigans and their colleagues, but he felt their action "frightened more than it has edified." Besides, he argued, "The country is in a very edgy psychological state"; such actions as burning draft files might appear to an adversary as an "apparently arbitrary attack on law and order, dictated by emotion or caprice—or fanaticism of some sort."[83]

Berrigan was disappointed but not surprised by Merton's reaction. "He was stirred, fearful, didn't know where such acts might lead," the Jesuit later wrote. "He trusted us, but his trust was tested hard."[84] While it is impossible to know whether Merton would have eventually accepted something as radical as the Catonsville raid, evidence suggests that he might have. Although he himself shied away from controversy, as his letters to colleagues indicate, he had shown himself capable of change. In 1965, he had faulted Forest and Cornell for burning draft cards, but by November 1966 he wrote that they were "utterly right before God" to do such things.[85] What Merton needed, Berrigan reflected, was "more time to make up his mind."[86]

But that was the one commodity of which the Trappist monk had precious little. By the summer of 1968, the solitude he had so desired in his hermitage was disappearing, as more and more people made unannounced visits to meet with the famous Trappist poet and essayist. When the new abbot allowed him to travel, Merton took advantage of this newfound freedom to visit Alaska in September and make preparations for a trip to Asia the following month.[87] Philip Berrigan invited Merton to attend the upcoming trial, but he declined. "I am going to India in October and am busy raising money for it now," he wrote. "I wish you all luck. Hope you enjoy your new Trappist vocation," he added, alluding to the probability that the brothers would be convicted and imprisoned in a setting not unlike the living conditions of his monastery. "But don't get too much of it. Enough is enough."[88]

The trial proved to be everything that the Boston Five debacle was not. Judge Roszel Thomsen gave the Catonsville Nine a great degree of latitude in their testimony, possibly to keep outbreaks of speechmaking to a minimum, and while the jury deliberated, he and the defendants spoke for over forty minutes about what they had done, the war in Vietnam, domestic crises, and their personal philosophy. Afterwards, he gave them permission to join hands and recite the Lord's Prayer. As expected, all were found guilty of destruction of federal property and violation of the Selective Service Act. Hogan, Darst, Moylan, and Marjorie Melville were eventually sentenced to two years in prison; Daniel Berrigan, Thomas Melville, and George Mische received three years, and Philip Berrigan and Thomas Lewis were sentenced to three and a half years to run concurrently with their earlier sentences of six years for their previous raid.[89]

Released on bond, Daniel Berrigan and the others began setting in motion the appeals process. To his disappointment, an appeals court upheld the convictions, and the Supreme Court declined to review the cases. He had not heard from Merton in months, nor had he visited the Abbey of Gethsemani since the Catonsville action; now that the trial was over, Merton was overseas.[90] December found the monk in Bangkok, attending a meeting of Asian abbots and looking for a possible site for a new hermitage for Trappists. "I have not found any place of hermitage that is any better than the hermitage I have, or had, at Gethsemani," he wrote his friend John Howard Griffin, "which is after all places, a great place." He would never see it again. Two days later, on December 10, he was accidentally electrocuted by a fan with faulty wiring. It was twenty-seven years to the day since he first entered the gates of the Abbey of Gethsemani. In a further irony he no doubt would have relished, his body was flown home on an army transport plane.[91]

With regard to Merton's literary talents and spiritual insights, his death was a serious loss to the religious community of all faiths. In relation to the peace movement, however, Merton's passing, while tragic, did not have as serious an impact as, say, the death of King. The monk had been at the height of his powers in the peace movement in the early and mid-1960s, when he and his compatriots were attempting to grapple with the spiritual crises of the nuclear age and early involvement in the Vietnam War, but as protest turned to resistance, Merton's inherent conservatism led him to take a path different from his friends', and his advice was requested and followed less frequently. At the same time, he had less to give, because he was trying to come to terms with his life in the hermitage. Ironically, as he concentrated on solitude and his study of mysticism, including Zen and Buddhism, his presence became something of an attraction to admirers who sought him out. He began to go for walks in the woods in the afternoon to avoid uninvited guests and would watch for cars before he returned to his hermitage. As his close friend Griffin surmised, had Merton lived and returned to Kentucky, he probably would have become more silent.[92]

For his part, Daniel Berrigan was to long regret not having visited Merton after the Catonsville raid to explain to his friend and mentor his reasons for taking part in it. When he heard of the monk's death in Bangkok, the griefstricken Jesuit wandered around the streets of New York City, trying to come to terms with his loss. But he still had to come to terms with his own fate as well, and he and Philip began discussing the possibility of going underground as "fugitives from injustice" rather than turning themselves over to authorities as they were supposed to in April 1970. This action, coupled with their draft board raids, would give the brothers a claim to preeminence among radical

Catholics in the antiwar movement. But it would also further alienate many of their colleagues, and their indiscretions, in the end, would help destroy the Catholic Left.[93] Radical Catholic clergy would not be the only ones to suffer during the opening years of the new decade, however. The election of Richard Nixon and the implementation of his plans to win peace with honor would put the entire peace movement on defensive and tenuous ground.

nine

Peace, peace, to the far and the near,
says the Lord; And I will heal them.

ISAIAH 57:19

The Costly Peace

The Antiwar Movement, 1968–1973

Despite the Berrigans' claims of the group's ineffectiveness, Clergy and Lay-men Concerned About Vietnam continued its educational and lobbying efforts into the summer of 1968. By July its mailing list exceeded 20,000 people, and the organization had begun to broaden its scope by calling for amnesty for draft resisters.[1] A joint statement issued by CALCAV and signed by Episcopal and Methodist bishops requested the government to grant clemency to the approximately 700 young men imprisoned for resistance and the estimated 5,000 who had gone abroad rather than fight in Vietnam. "It is more for our country's sake, than for their sake, that we plead," they wrote. "Political imprisonments are a shame to any land, but a grievous scandal to those who affirm the promise of American democracy."[2] In late October, a delegation of eleven CALCAV members, including Novak, Neuhaus, and Cox, traveled to France and Sweden to meet with young men who had fled there and help set up liaison teams between them and clergy from the United States. Not all clergy involved in such endeavors were affiliated with CALCAV. Will Campbell, director of the Committee of Southern Churchmen, opened his home in Tennessee to deserters on their way to Canada, at times visiting them there once they were settled in. While understandably reticent about discussing such things at the time, Campbell did not hesitate to speak out against the war itself, often tying the brutality abroad to the violence at home.[3]

Helping ameliorate the symptoms of war was one thing, but trying to find a cure for the disease itself was another. Those who had counted on the 1968 presidential elections to provide a strong candidate for peace were sadly disappointed as the once-promising field of contenders had dwindled to Humphrey, Nixon, and third-party candidate George Wallace. Malcolm Boyd, now visiting chaplain at Yale for a year, summed up his frustrations in his column for the *Yale Daily News*.[4] A supporter of McCarthy, Boyd was going to vote for Humphrey not because of any fondness for the man or for what the priest perceived as his outdated liberalism, but because his domestic view had a place for black Americans and political dissent, his foreign policy was a "shade better" than his peers, because "Spiro Agnew is not his running mate," and because "Nixon has avoided speaking clearly on virtually all issues and is simply too dangerous a public relations fabrication to be entrusted with the U.S. presidency."[5]

The executive committee of CALCAV was also concerned about the upcoming election. The positions of the candidates indicated quite clearly that "the Vietnam war will not be terminated, by any necessary logic, because of a new administration," warned director Richard Fernandez in early November. CALCAV would therefore continue its activities and "persevere until the day when the United States government is finally deflected from its abortive and immoral venture in Vietnam."[6] Despite Fernandez's concerns, other moderates felt that there were grounds for hope in Nixon's presidency if for no other reason than that his slim victory marked the departure of the administration that had so greatly escalated the war. Some of this optimism was reflected at CALCAV's third Washington Mobilization in early February 1969, held at the Metropolitan African Methodist Episcopal Church, but it was also alloyed with a radicalism that had not been seen at the two earlier mobilizations. Still, there were reminders of gatherings past: Presbyterian Carl McIntire and his supporters returned to harass the protesters, and the overall atmosphere of the gathering, like the first others, retained, in the words of one observer, the "earnestness, the religiosity, the desire to influence the real world, which much of the [peace] Movement has lost along the way."[7]

Only 1,000 persons attended the three-day affair, less than half the number of participants in previous years. The 1969 paper presented at the mobilization concerned itself with foreign policy issues beyond Vietnam, implying that the war would be coming to a close in the near future. Its strident calls to end aid to those governments that were simply anti-Communist but not democratic and to pay reparations to black Americans for past discrimination were, in the words of historian Mitchell Hall, "irritating assertions that probably hampered its potential effectiveness within the churches." Even the workshops, traditionally given over to discussions of the antiwar movement and amnesty for draft resisters, now included such topics as housing cooperatives, apartheid in South Africa, and the formation of a third political party. Richard John Neuhaus, hardly a militant, reflected this shift in tone when he announced in a sermon that the Vietnamese were "God's instruments for bringing the American empire to its knees."[8]

Still, there were indications that perhaps the Nixon administration might be more willing to listen to the voices of opposition than had been Johnson and his advisers. On February 5, National Security Advisor Henry Kissinger met with Brown, Neuhaus, Coffin, Coretta Scott King, Heschel, Fernandez, and Gerhard Elston, secretary of the National Council of Churches.[9] The meeting started off awkwardly. Fernandez remembered Heschel, who looked "like Moses [and] in a place like this, always talked as if he was reading off a tablet," asking the national security advisor whether he thought that if the United States kept bombing Vietnam it would be "more and more like Nazi Germany?" Kissinger, like Heschel a refugee from Nazi Germany, was stunned.[10] Regaining his composure, Kissinger listened to their comments and answered their questions about the status of the Paris peace talks, amnesty for resisters, and nuclear disarmament, then posed a question of his own. "How would *you* get the boys out of Vietnam?" he asked. "Mr. Kissinger," replied Coffin, "our job is to proclaim that 'justice must roll down like waters, and righteousness like a mighty stream.' Your job . . . is to work out the details of the irrigation system."[11] At meeting's end, Kissinger assured them that the new administration would do everything in its power to bring the war to a quick end. Nothing had been resolved (Coffin later described the meeting as "terrible"), but it was encouraging if only because it was the first time since 1967 that a high-ranking official had met with representatives from the peace group.[12]

The administration had better luck with another clergyman, Billy Graham, a longtime friend of the Nixons. The first Sunday after his inauguration, the president invited Graham to lead the first of what would become regular Sunday services at the White House. Despite the Baptist preacher's insistence that there was no "political connotation" to the worship, that Nixon "wanted to set an example for the whole country," it was soon apparent to almost everyone else that the administration was inviting only conservative clergymen who supported Nixon and had large constituencies.[13] Liberals were harshly critical of Graham's support for Nixon and his willingness to ignore Nixon's play for the religious vote. I. F. Stone denounced Graham as the president's "smoother Rasputin."[14] A frail Reinhold Niebuhr penned a savage piece in which he compared Graham and his colleagues at the prayer services with Biblical prophets who had told the kings of Israel only what they had wanted to hear and had often come to a bad end. Unleashing his scorn of Graham, which had barely subsided since the early 1950s, Niebuhr described him as a "domesticated and tailored leftover" of frontier evangelism and likened him to Amaziah, the minister of the king who did not listen to the warnings of Amos, the shepherd-prophet. It was "wonderful what a simple White House invitation will do to dull the critical faculties," he wrote, and pondered what Martin Luther King Jr. would have thought about the prayer services.[15] For his efforts, the aging theologian received stacks of hate mail from Graham's supporters, which "rather pleased him," according to his wife.[16]

CALCAV lost faith in Nixon's ability to win a quick peace, despite his assurances that a negotiated settlement would provide for a strong, independent South Vietnam even after the withdrawal of American troops. As Kissinger negotiated with the North Vietnamese, the president initiated massive bombing attacks against enemy supply routes and depots in neutral Cambodia.[17] While the bombing was not yet public news, CALCAV placed an advertisement in the New York Times reminding the public that one year had elapsed since Johnson had curtailed the bombing of North Vietnam and announced he would seek a peaceful settlement of the conflict. "You thought the corner had been turned," it read. "You were wrong. A year later our country is on the same bloodied and blundering course in Vietnam," largely because of Nixon's continued support of the "corrupt Thieu-Ky regime." Free elections were needed to give South Vietnam new leaders who could gain the popular support of the South Vietnamese.[18] The traditional Easter peace marches through the streets of New York City, Chicago, San Francisco, and Atlanta reminded the White House that there were still those who were going to continue to protest the war until peace was declared.[19] Four men of draft age set up thirteen-foot crosses in front of the White House on Easter Sunday, and symbolically hung from them with the explanation that "as long as this war continues, it is always Good Friday."[20]

Much of the criticism for prolonging the war was directed at the unwillingness of the government of South Vietnam to make the necessary political reforms that would lead to a coalition government acceptable to Hanoi. The corruption and venality of officials under President Nguyen Van Thieu were well-documented, as was the suppression of dissent; opposition newspapers had been closed down, political candidates arrested, and Buddhists imprisoned or placed under house arrest. To see such practices firsthand, as well as investigate allegations of torture, the FOR sent a study team to South Vietnam in the summer of 1969 to gather evidence on prison conditions. Nine individuals—including Methodist Bishop James Armstrong of the Dakotas; Anne M. Bennett, wife of John Bennett and a member of the U.S. Inter-Religious Committee on Peace; Robert Drinan, S.J.; and Rabbi Seymour Siegel, professor of theology at the Jewish Theological Seminary of New York—spent late May and early June in Saigon conducting interviews with prison wardens, Buddhists, students, and journalists, as well as Thieu and American Ambassador Ellsworth Bunker.[21]

Their findings were grim. Thousands of people had been arrested and denied a fair hearing and counsel and sometimes even a trial, by military tribunals, and were languishing in filthy, overcrowded prisons where torture was common. The police, military, or special security forces were given wide discretion over whom they could arrest, following the lead of the government itself, which used the phrases "communism," "neutralism," and "coalition" to describe any opponents of the government. Student peace groups, the Buddhist "third force," and opposition newspapers had all felt the tactics of suppression.[22] Acknowledging that South Vietnam did not have a constitution and that some mitigating circumstances were understandable in a poor nation at war, the team nevertheless felt compelled to send a telegram to Nixon asking him to reconsider his support for Thieu, noting that "[t]here must be no illusion that this climate of religious and political suppression is compatible with either a representative or a stable government."[23]

Although Nixon had no plans to reconsider his support for the South Vietnamese leader, he was about to change the nature of it. On June 5, he met with Thieu at the island of Midway to announce his plans for "Vietnamization," a policy whereby American troops would be withdrawn from South Vietnam in order to allow the Army of the Republic of Vietnam to shoulder more of the fighting. The United States would continue to supply Thieu with weapons and would insist on his participation in a South Vietnamese coalition government at the end of the war. This strategy effectively curtailed any hopes for an outright American victory on the battlefield; for Thieu, this meant that he would have to build up his defense forces and attempt to win a war at the same time.[24]

Despite the phased withdrawal, the North Vietnamese were not impressed with Nixon's policies and continued to insist that American troops leave unconditionally and that a coalition government be established without Thieu. As the Paris talks dragged on, various groups within the peace movement began planning the next wave of antiwar demonstrations for the fall. After

Nixon received what he considered to be a peremptory note from Ho Chi Minh, demanding that the United States cease its intervention in the affairs of a sovereign state, he began to devise strategy for Operation Duck Hook, which called for a massive four-day bombardment of North Vietnam's cities and the mining of its ports and harbors if Hanoi did not make concessions by November 1. The President instructed Kissinger to tell Soviet Foreign Minister Andrei Gromyko that his country should bring pressure to bear on Hanoi to negotiate, especially as "the train had left the station and was heading down the track," one of Nixon's favorite phrases.[25]

But trains can be derailed, and the Vietnam Moratorium of October 15 did exactly that. Conceived by Sam Brown and David Hawk as the first in a series of strikes and work stoppages that would increase by one day a month as long as the war continued, the protest involved not a major demonstration in the nation's capital but instead grassroots protests in separate communities across the United States. Such moderate tactics hit a resonant chord among Americans dissatisfied both with the war and with radical antiwar protesters, and the day was marked by peaceful demonstrations in New York, Boston, Philadelphia, Ann Arbor, and smaller towns nationwide. One hundred thousand people gathered on the Boston Common to hear speeches and see a skywriter create a giant peace-sign overhead; Senator Eugene McCarthy addressed 250,000 in Bryant Park in New York City, whose mayor, John Lindsay, ordered the flags to be flown at half-mast. Still, there were some disturbances. The Students for a Democratic Society (SDS) chapter of the State University of New York at Buffalo ransacked the campus offices of the Air Force ROTC. The Reverend Kenneth Sherman, a Lutheran pastor who had resigned his office as chaplain to devote himself to building a local chapter of CALCAV, broke his ties with SDS, denounced the campus radicals, and called for the peace movement to develop more appropriate alliances with liberals and encourage "doves" to run for office.[26]

Many of the day's events were religious in nature. Bill Moyers and Roswell Gilpatrick held a memorial service in Wall Street for the war's victims, and seminarians and faculty members from Union Theological Seminary and Woodstock College held a prayer service in Grand Central Station. Thousands of people attended an evening service in St. Patrick's Cathedral, holding lighted candles while they sang "America the Beautiful" and then prayed for peace. Americans at home were not the only ones interested in the demonstrations. "If you do not get to go to that big peace demonstration [on] October 15th I hope you do protest against the war or sing for peace—I would," wrote

Staff Sergeant Joseph Morrissey, stationed in Vietnam, to his brother Paul, a Catholic priest in Brooklyn. "I just can't believe half of the shit I've seen over here so far."[27]

Radio Hanoi broadcast a letter to the United States praising the "large sectors of the U.S. people, encouraged and supported by many peace- and justice-loving American personages" for their efforts to end the war and immediately bring American soldiers home, adding "[m]ay your fall offensive succeed splendidly." An angry Nixon denounced this "blatant intervention in our domestic affairs" and later complained that the peace demonstrations "had probably destroyed the credibility of my ultimatum to Hanoi . . . [and] destroyed whatever small probability may have still existed of ending the war in 1969."[28]

One month later, over 500,000 antiwar protesters traveled to the nation's capital to take part in the two-day National Mobilization, the largest demonstration in American history. On the afternoon of November 13, in an event not planned by the New Mobilization Committee to End the War in Vietnam, almost 200 people, including several clergymen, were arrested while trying to celebrate an "Ecumenical Mass for Peace" on the steps of the Pentagon. Sponsored by the Catholic Peace Fellowship, the Episcopal Peace Fellowship, and the Church of St. Stephen and the Incarnation in Washington, D.C., the ranks of clergy included two Episcopal bishops, the Right Reverends Edward Crowther and Daniel Corrigan; three Episcopal priests, Nathaniel Pierce, Ian Mitchell, and Malcolm Boyd; and a Catholic priest, the Reverend John White. The service had just begun when R. Kenley Webster, deputy general counsel of the Army, arrived to tell the worshipers that they would be arrested unless they stopped the service. When no one complied, the police moved in, accompanied by the cheers of onlookers who had been taunting the clergy. Before he left for the U.S. Magistrates Court, Pierce walked up to Webster and shook his hand, saying, "That was great. I almost kissed you. It was great press."[29]

The single most impressive event of the National Mobilization was the March Against Death. On the evening of November 13, in near-freezing temperatures and a cold rain, marchers began walking from the Virginia side of the Potomac across the Arlington Memorial Bridge, led by drummers beating a slow, mournful cadence. Each marcher carried a placard bearing the name of either a loved one killed in the war or a destroyed Vietnamese town and, during the night, a lighted candle. Mrs. Judy Droz, carrying the name of her husband, who had been killed seven months before, led the way as the chairpersons of the march, Benjamin Spock and Coffin, and 45,000 marchers passed the Lincoln Memorial and the White House, where each person called out the name on his or her placard, and then proceeded to the

Capitol to place the placard in one of forty coffins. The march took two days to complete.[30]

Not everyone appreciated what was, for some, the most moving aspect of the march. "I'm with that lady who promised to sue the moratorium if they read her son's name again," Captain Corbin Cherry, a chaplain from Connecticut who had lost a foot in Vietnam, told a reporter. "Thousands and thousands of parents who lost children don't appreciate their sons' names being read."[31]

The White House resembled a fortress besieged during the entire mobilization. It was ringed with buses, arc lights were turned outward, and a bright mercury vapor lamp illuminated the sidewalk in front of the north facade. On the roofs of nearby buildings, one could make out armed guards and sharpshooters. "Now you guys will see how it feels to be prisoners in the White House," former Johnson aide Jack Valenti told Nixon staffers sympathetically. The president announced that he was going to remain in the White House watching football games on television, a callous gesture that did nothing to endear him to the moderates in the march, the radicals having long since disavowed him and the political system that had put him there.[32]

CALCAV was given permission to hold an antiwar service at the National Cathedral on the evening of November 14 on condition that neither Coffin nor Daniel Berrigan, due to their criminal records, give a sermon, although the former was allowed to conduct portions of the service, entitled "Liturgy for Peace." The responsibility for the sermon devolved on Eugene Carson Blake, who had flown in from Geneva, and he spoke at length to the standing-room only crowd in the 3,000-seat cathedral. Thousands more heard him through loudspeakers outside.[33] Folk singer Pete Seeger led them all in "We Shall Overcome" at the close of the service, and when he had finished, as Coffin recalled, "no one moved. . . . The silence was awesome."[34]

Coffin was less enthusiastic about the huge rally on the grounds surrounding the Washington Monument, as he had begun to question the usefulness of such demonstrations. His spirits sagged as the speakers, each with a particular political agenda, droned on. Symptomatic of the divergent trends within the peace movement, Sidney Lens's 1,500-word "Call to the Fall Offensive to End the War," called upon the United States, the "bastion of counter-revolution," to stop supporting "fascist and semifascist governments" around the world, and then demanded "aid for the poor and hungry, the Black and Brown communities, the sick, the cancer victims of air pollution, [and] the accident victims of automobiles" in order to "free us all to live, to love, and to run our own lives."[35]

As the speeches continued, members of the Weathermen, a revolutionary group that had broken away from SDS, heckled speakers, waved NLF flags, and tried to rush the platform, but were prevented from doing so only by marshals blocking their way. The "peace movement was no longer peaceful," Coffin realized. Even though most people within the movement were still adherents of nonviolence, a minority were not, and he worried that they were alienating others whose support was needed. As he put it, "Even more than Nixon, they were isolating themselves from the American public." While violence committed by the Weathermen later in the day was minimal, it underscored the factionalism that was becoming rampant in the peace movement.[36]

Nixon, meanwhile, had managed to put the antiwar movement on the defensive even before the Mobilization. On November 3, he asked the "great silent majority of my fellow Americans" to support him in his quest for an end to the war that would help "win the peace." The more divided the nation was at home, he said, the more unlikely it was that the enemy would take the negotiations at Paris seriously. "Let us be united for peace," he concluded. "Let us also be united against defeat. . . . North Vietnam cannot defeat or humiliate the United States. Only Americans can do that." Telegrams deluged the White House supporting his policy and it appeared that he had succeeded, if only briefly, in drawing "the battle lines between us and them— of the folks versus the elitists," as his speechwriter William Safire recalled.[37]

Moderates in the antiwar movement decried the administration's policy of continuing the air war, believing that the entire Vietnamization program was designed mainly to placate Americans with merely token troop withdrawals. "[T]hose who regard it as an awkward war may be satisfied by the avoidance of American casualties," warned John Bennett, "but those who regard it as an immoral war . . . will continue to protest and protest."[38] Despite his hopes, most Americans refused to see the war as immoral, only as a mistake that needed to be fixed. As increasing numbers of American soldiers were withdrawn from Vietnam by the end of the year, the numbers of protests dwindled. The antiwar movement had seemingly been deprived of an enemy, explained one peace activist, because the president had managed to "identify himself with the cause of peace."[39] American Jews, concerned that Nixon might withdraw support for Israel, which was now in an even more tenuous position after the June War, began to curtail their criticism of his Vietnam policies. Although Rabbi Balfour Brickner continued his work in CALCAV, trying to rally opposition to the war, the American Jewish community remained largely quiescent. A handful of rabbis did continue to speak out against the war, but even the preeminent voice for peace in the Jewish religious community,

Rabbi Heschel, had become less active. Weakened by a heart attack in 1969, he was directing much of his depleted energy into the fight for the right of Soviet Jews to emigrate.[40]

Other developments led to fewer demonstrations. The triumphs in October and November represented the pinnacle of success in terms of numbers and organization, and there was little that people could do to top them. The original idea of adding one day a month to further moratoria and rallies seemed impractical and was discarded; as one organizer asked, "What could we do for eight days in May?" With no unifying event to rally around, the various factions continued to splinter and go their separate ways.[41] The Fellowship of Reconciliation and CALCAV tried to bring the protest back to the center by sponsoring a Lenten-Passover Fast in the spring of 1970, during which time small groups marched in front of the White House each day. As an act of witness, it was touching, but, like most of the antiwar activities, it failed to move those who had the power to end the war.[42]

Faced with the lack of interest in moderate tactics, some clergy embarked on strange tactics. During the NCC's triennial assembly in Detroit at the end of 1969, a group of clergymen and laity, including Malcolm Boyd and the Reverend Stephen Rose, a Presbyterian clergyman, formed a group called "Jonathan's Wake" (named after eighteenth-century Calvinist theologian Jonathan Edwards) to stage "happenings." As the assembly debated the role of the NCC in the larger world—including the status of minorities within its highest offices, and environmental and industrial issues—Jonathan's Wake called for the "disestablishment" of substantial portions of church wealth, and then took up residence in the hallways outside the meeting rooms, declaring one hall to be a "liberated area" where critics of the NCC could speak and preach. At one point, fifty members of the group carried a flag-draped coffin into a meeting and began conducting a "wake" for organized religion. Dancing in the aisles and wearing flowers, the members then performed a service of "exorcism" to get rid of "the demons of exploitation, suppression, and war" they felt were present among the more solemn members of the NCC. While Bishop James Matthews likened the protest to a "camp meeting," describing it as a "healthy way of freeing us up," most delegates looked on without amusement.[43]

Such antics pointed to a deeper problem concerning the direction of the church in the modern world. By the end of the decade, significant numbers of clergy were leaving the churches for a variety of reasons, many of them dealing with what they considered to be the increasing irrelevance of the institution in the face of social upheaval.[44] A study by the Board for Homeland Ministries of the United Church of Christ indicated that most of those who had left the parish ministry did so because they felt that they could not wait while "the local church makes its tortuous and glacially slow moves towards the future." Some had gone into social work, which they found to be much more fulfilling than their ministerial duties. One respondent explained that the concerns of God's world were infinitely more serious than any crises facing the institutional church: the question of feeding starving children was "much more urgent than how many turkeys to order for the 'fellowship dinner,'" the matter of continued killing in Vietnam was "of more consequence than whether one can pick up a tenor for the choir," and the issue of creating reconciliation between the races at home was "more important than whether we need wall-to-wall carpeting in the chancel."[45]

Others went into politics instead. The congressional elections of 1970 saw a substantial number of clerics who believed that the only way they could have a significant impact on ending the war was to work through the political process. A great deal of media coverage was expended on these candidates, but when election time arrived, only a few of them won. The Reverend Robert Drinan, S.J., was elected state representative from Massachusetts, and he served faithfully in the House of Representatives until 1981, when Pope John Paul II ordered him to leave politics. Drinan obeyed him, but insisted that in his years in Congress he had done more priestly work as a representative than he had done in the rest of his career (he did not elaborate on whether his casting a vote in favor of Nixon's impeachment in 1974 as a member of the House Judiciary Committee fell into this category).[46]

A smaller number of clergymen, not wanting to abandon the ministry, yet feeling that the institutional church did not offer them the sense of community they and some of their parishioners desired, formed "underground churches" to conduct services in homes and pray, sing, and celebrate unencumbered by strict liturgical rules. Malcolm Boyd, a frequent participant in such services, was also one of the more outspoken critics of the institutional church, and his acerbic comments often annoyed more traditional church-people.[47] "Several days ago I heard over the NY NBC station the radio program in which you [and several other ministers] discussed the church. It was a very bad program. You . . . were not persuasive to anyone," complained Eugene Carson Blake. He admitted that after reading some of Boyd's meditations he felt that he understood him a little more but cautioned him against trying "to be an 'enfant terrible' on the Radio—it doesn't do you or the cause justice."[48] Undaunted, Boyd continued to support the idea of nontraditional religious practices, including his conducting of a series of nightclub performances where he would read meditations from his book *Are You Running with Me, Jesus?*[49]

Another enthusiast of the underground church, Daniel Berrigan, decided in April 1970 to become an underground priest in deed as well as thought. He and Philip had decided not to turn themselves in to authorities on April 9 as they had been ordered. They would resist the "automatic claim on our persons announced by the U.S. Department of Justice," Daniel wrote to his Jesuit superiors. Such a claim was "manifestly unjust, compounded of hypocrisy and the repression of human and civil rights." The only option left to them was to call themselves "fugitives from injustice" and become "exiles in our own land." Their message at Catonsville had gone unheeded, their antiwar work ignored, and the courts, in which they had pleaded their case, had become "the instruments of the warmakers." As Christians, he wrote, they chose not to submit to such authority and to put their consciences in Jesus Christ's charge alone.[50]

Philip Berrigan did not last long in the underground. The FBI found him two weeks later, hiding in a closet in the rectory of St. Gregory's Church in New York City, and authorities sent him to the federal penitentiary in Lewisburg, Pennsylvania. Not only was he separated from his colleagues in the antiwar movement but also from Sister Elizabeth McAlister, whom he had met in 1966. Both had pledged themselves to each other in May 1969 in a secret service they considered tantamount to marriage, although his personal relationship did not prevent him from publicly criticizing those priests and nuns in the Catholic Left who had openly left their orders and married.[51] Celibacy was "crucial in the priesthood as an aid for revolutionary life style," he told an interviewer the same month he and McAlister were "married," and insisted that both he and Daniel "believe this very strongly."[52]

On April 17, Daniel returned to Cornell University to attend a festival in honor of the Catonsville Nine and, at the end of the ceremony, eluded waiting FBI agents by hiding in a costume of one of the twelve apostles. From that point on he surfaced periodically to give lectures, television interviews, and sermons and to visit friends, enjoying every moment of what he termed "guerilla theater."[53] Not everyone was so caught up in his escapades. The Reverend Joseph Wenderoth and other members of the Catholic Left were planning a raid on a draft board in Wilmington, Delaware, when Berrigan decided to visit them unannounced, unintentionally bringing the FBI and federal marshals in his wake. The raid had to be canceled. The Jesuit's penchant for suddenly showing up to make an appearance "was just interfering," Wenderoth later complained. "I felt that we were getting into cat-and-mouse games. . . . People were just doing things for the sake of doing them, it seemed, rather than sitting down and really thinking about what they could and could not do."[54]

Philosophically, the Berrigans' thumbing of noses at the federal authorities, coupled with their refusal to submit to the consequences of their actions, represented an abandonment of two major tenets of civil disobedience as practiced by Gandhi and King: accepting the penalties of violating a law in order to illustrate its unjust character, and refusing to humiliate one's oppressor. However, Daniel Berrigan believed that the circumstances surrounding his sentencing were different from those faced by the black civil rights leader. Where King could appeal to a federal court for redress, he argued, the Berrigans had no such recourse. There was no other higher court; the International War Crimes Tribunal, the United Nations, and the World Court, he wrote, were "straw men," for the United States had ignored them. Addressing those antiwar demonstrators who were willing to go to jail, Berrigan wrote, "we must seek our analogies elsewhere than in the civil rights movement if we would seem to be politically serious."[55]

The brothers' decision not to turn themselves in won them the plaudits of many figures in the antiwar movement, including Cox, Coffin, and Robert McAfee Brown, all of whom agreed that extralegal means were necessary to draw attention to the cause of peace in Vietnam. During the admittedly raucous trial of the Chicago Eight, in which individuals were charged with conspiracy to riot at the 1968 Democratic National Convention, the judge ordered defendant Bobby Seale, a member of the Black Panthers, bound and gagged.[56] Coffin later insisted in 1994 that "fifty years from now the Berrigans will be folk heroes. I can hear the guitars strumming now."[57] Coffin's enthusiasm was ill-founded; in the fall of 1971, only months after the Berrigans had been implicated in an alleged conspiracy to kidnap a government official and blow up heating tunnels in Washington, D.C., a *Newsweek* poll indicated that 62 percent of Americans surveyed had no idea who the Berrigans were; 69 percent answered negatively the question, "Do you think Catholics who raid draft boards to protest the war in Vietnam are acting as responsible Christians?"[58]

Nonetheless, Daniel's successful evasion of federal authorities gave the struggling antiwar movement some much-needed cheer, a precious commodity in the dark days of April 1970. While Nixon had announced that 150,000 more troops would be withdrawn by the end of the year, he did not want to give Hanoi the impression that he was giving up in Vietnam. When Prince Sihanouk of Cambodia was overthrown by a pro-American faction led by Prime Minister Lon Nol, Nixon saw the opportunity to send American troops there, under the pretense of buttressing the new government, to destroy North Vietnamese supply routes and depots, thus buying time for South Vietnam to continue shoring up its defense forces.[59] When the president announced his decision on April 30, it touched off a wave of campus demonstrations across the country.[60] Nixon excoriated the demonstrators as "bums"; Vice President Agnew compared them to Nazi storm troopers or members of the Klan and suggested that the public "act accordingly" in their dealings with them.[61] Governor James Rhodes of Ohio called out the National Guard to keep order at Kent State University, where on May 4 troops fired into a crowd of demonstrating students, wounding several and killing four. Nixon released a statement the following day in which he reminded Americans that "when dissent turns to violence, it invites tragedy." Agnew called the deaths predictable and went on to lash out at the "elitists" who used the Bill of Rights to protect "psychotic and criminal elements in our society."[62]

The deaths of the students outraged members of the antiwar movement, and protests at colleges continued. Conservative supporters of Nixon struck back both verbally and physically. On May 8, 200 construction workers in New York City attacked a group of students calling for an immediate withdrawal of American forces from Vietnam before going on a rampage in the Wall Street area, hauling a Red Cross flag down from the gates of Trinity Episcopal Church and attempting unsuccessfully to tear down the flag of the Episcopal Church as well ("I suppose they thought it was the Vietcong flag," said the angry rector).[63]

The volatile situation unnerved Nixon, who spent the entire night of May 8 on the telephone, calling old friends and receiving assurances from Reverends Billy Graham and Norman Vincent Peale that he was doing the right thing.[64] Graham rallied support for his longtime friend, later sponsoring an Honor America Day on the steps of the Lincoln Memorial on July 4. Convinced that citizens needed to express reverence, not ridicule, for national institutions, Graham exhorted Americans to "Honor the nation! . . . And as you move to do it, never give in. Never give in! Never! Never! Never! Never!"[65] Will Campbell and James Holloway of the Committee of Southern Churchmen were dismayed to see Graham turning into a "court prophet." Addressing themselves to their "Baptist brother," they expressed regret at his decision not to challenge the White House. "We believe that the connection between your power and influence and what you say . . . must be broken," they wrote. "[T]he only way you, or any of us, can *minister* to the troops and inhabitants of Vietnam is *to prophesy* to the Pentagon and White House" in the style of the prophet Micah. For "you, our brother, have been and will be the prophet summoned to those halls. We shall not."[66]

Other religious figures were not silent in the aftermath of the violence at Kent State. The Episcopal, Catholic, and Jewish Peace Fellowships, FOR, and CALCAV sent a telegram to Nixon urging him to "act against this spirit of senseless violence." Heschel and Neuhaus went to the funeral of Jeffrey Glenn Miller, one of the students killed on May 4, as representatives of CALCAV, and spoke out against the killing at home and in Vietnam.[67] John and Anne Bennett had planned a farewell party for colleagues at Union in honor of his retirement as president, and although it was held, they did not attend. Both had gone to Washington, D.C., to protest the Kent State killings and the invasion of Cambodia and had been arrested. Later in the month, CALCAV and several denominations held a convocation at the New York Avenue Presbyterian Church in the nation's capital to commemorate the dead of Kent State, Vietnam, and Cambodia. One thousand people attended, and listened to speeches in support of congressional doves, who discussed cutting funds for the war and repealing the Gulf of Tonkin resolution.[68]

On the afternoon of May 14, Richard Cardinal Cushing of the Archdiocese of Boston joined with Episcopal Bishop John M. Burgess of the Diocese of Massachusetts, Bishop James Mathews of the Boston Area of the United Methodist Church, Rabbi Murray Rothman, president of the Massachusetts Board of Rabbis, and several other clergymen in an interfaith witness for national repentance and renewal in Boston, issuing a joint statement deploring the Kent State killings and denouncing the invasion of Cambodia. "The extension of the Vietnam War into Cambodia shocks and angers us," it began. "Inherent in the decision is haste and deception and a cruel heedlessness to the nature and temper of our times." In order to forestall a prolongation of the war, they urged Christians and Jews to pray for the victims, maintain peace vigils, and write to Senators Edward Kennedy and Edward Brooke to insist that no federal funds be appropriated to pay for military operations in Cambodia.[69]

In an open letter, Robert McAfee Brown singled out Agnew and his invective for causing the upsurge in violence at home. Letters, speeches, and peaceful marches of protest, had been met with Nixon's announcement that he would watch football games rather than listen to them and by Agnew's characterization of peace activists as rotten apples that should be thrown out of the barrel. Such ill-considered responses, wrote Brown, "made students despair of being heard without speaking more bluntly and acting more determinedly"; even Agnew, deep in his heart, had to realize that his vitriolic rhetoric, especially as vice president, "helped cause those bullets to fly." As for Agnew's oft-repeated charges that clergy should stick to denouncing evil rather than discussing contemporary issues, Brown insisted that such was a false dichotomy. God was the the father of all humanity, he wrote, not just white Americans; those who criticized using napalm in Vietnam were not "secret agents of the ghost of Uncle Ho" but individuals who deplored "burning the flesh of innocent villagers who are created" in the image of God.[70]

On May 9, in a two-hour ceremony marked for its grandeur, Episcopal Bishop Paul Moore Jr. was installed as bishop coadjutor of the Episcopal Diocese of New York in the yet unfinished Cathedral Church of St. John the Divine. But the mood of the 2,000 in attendance was somber, as was that of the three bishops at the altar: Moore, Horace Donegan, and J. Stuart Wetmore, the latter two bishop and suffragan bishop, respectively, of the Diocese of New York. During the offertory, Donegan asked for a minute of silence for the students killed at Kent State and "for those who have given their lives in Cambodia. Let us pray that unity and peace and understanding will be restored to our beloved country." Wetmore read a statement that had been drafted by all three bishops, calling on the churches to exert whatever influence they had to convince the federal government of the right of dissent and to halt the invasion. "At this moment," Moore sadly noted, "young people all over the land are converging with cries of rage and grief. . . . Young people in uniform have killed other young people who could well be their brothers or their sisters. . . . We older people do not fully understand what is happening around us. I am sure our President does not fully understand."[71]

Another blow to the antiwar movement came three months later. When Daniel Berrigan decided to visit Block Island, Rhode Island, against the advice of all his friends, he effectively ended his status as a "fugitive from injustice." Once he was on the island, with nowhere to go, it was only a matter of time before he was caught. On August 11, a group of FBI agents incongruously disguised as birdwatchers despite a howling storm, met up with the Jesuit priest on the beach, who welcomed them and submitted to arrest. Photographs of a smiling Berrigan in handcuffs flanked by dour agents prompted commentaries on which of the men were truly free and which were bound.[72]

The saga of the Berrigan brothers did not end once they were behind bars. On November 27, 1970, J. Edgar Hoover, director of the FBI, announced before the Senate Appropriations Committee that his agency had uncovered a plot by a Catholic Left group called the East Coast Conspiracy to Save Lives to blow up heating tunnels in the capital and kidnap a highly placed official in the White House. Hoover named the Berrigans as the leaders of the group. Many Americans were as shocked by the charges as they were by the way in which they were presented. No indictments had yet been made, and the accused had no recourse to defend themselves. It appeared that the director had jeopardized one of the Justice Department's ongoing cases merely to garner publicity and receive desired funding.[73]

Indictments were handed down in January 1971, naming several members of the group, including Philip, as conspirators; Daniel was named as an "unindicted co-conspirator." A paid informer, Boyd Douglas, had volunteered to pass letters between Philip Berrigan and Liz McAlister. Some of the letters dealt with a variety of plans, such as the heating tunnel project and kidnapping a government official, but Berrigan had quickly dismissed them as impractical and immoral.[74] The trial at Harrisburg, Pennsylvania, which began in February 1972, became a cause célèbre, and a painful one at that. Not only had McAlister's letters served to lay the groundwork for conspiracy charges, but they mentioned the location of upcoming draft board raids as well as Daniel Berrigan's hideout. Most damaging of all was the revelation of the romance between Philip Berrigan and McAlister, a fact that shocked and embittered many of their supporters and led to their dismissal from their respective orders. The trial of the Harrisburg Seven continued into March, ending during Holy Week, when the jury returned with a ten-to-two vote for acquittal. Most of the jurors found parts of the conspiracy story too extraordinary to be real. The judge declared a hung jury, and ordered freed those defendants who were not serving time for other crimes. The victory was mixed, for while the group had been cleared, the frustrations and bitterness resulting from the private correspondence, as well as the high number of arrests in the summer of 1971, effectively destroyed the Catholic Left.[75]

While not undergoing quite so great a crisis, other sectors of the religious antiwar movement were also experiencing shifts and strains. CALCAV tried to persuade the Dow Chemical Company and Honeywell to stop manufacturing napalm and antipersonnel weapons. Tactics included the publication of advertisements questioning the necessity of such weapons, picketing, and, most ambitious of all, the purchase of stock, which led to dramatic, if inconclusive, confrontations at shareholders' meetings when members of the antiwar organization demanded that the companies sever ties with the Department of Defense. The campaign for corporate responsibility was only part of an increasingly multifaceted agenda, for CALCAV had decided to branch out and tackle issues not directly related to ending the war, such as sexism, racism, and world poverty. Reflecting this change was the decision to drop the words "About Vietnam" from the organization's name, made at a national conference in Ann Arbor in August. Yet the war continued, and when Coffin, Neuhaus, Brickner, Brown, and other members of CALCAV called for a Washington Mobilization in February 1971, the turnout was small. The organization did support antiwar rallies in April sponsored by the National Peace Action Coalition and other similar secular bodies, which not only illustrated the paucity of purely religious protest but led to a growing concern among some of CALCAV's founders that the dissipation of energies into other projects had taken away the focus on the right of dissent.[76]

One of them, Robert McAfee Brown, came to view his counseling of draft resisters as not a strong enough statement of protest, and he joined his sons and his wife, as well as other Stanford faculty and students, in blocking every draft board in the Bay Area in one coordinated act of massive civil disobedience that lasted for three days during Holy Week in 1971. The police refused to arrest them, Brown surmised, because they were "respectable" faculty members, ministers, and students.[77] A few days later, on Good Friday, he and his son joined others blocking the entrance to the draft board in Berkeley, telling the assembled crowd of police and onlookers that he chose to preach his Good Friday sermon "not in a church but on a pavement, not with words but with a deed." Oftentimes the power of nonviolent love appeared to fail against the power of the state, as it appeared to have done during the first Good Friday, he continued. The arrival of Easter "turned the apparent defeat into victory, and showed that love can defeat fear and hate, that freedom is not finally held in bondage," he concluded, warning that as long as good people were being drafted to fight "evil wars," dissenters would continue to protest and block draft boards. This time they were arrested and spent three days in jail.[78]

But 1971 seemed like one long Good Friday. No advances were made on the diplomatic front, and the war dragged on. Grisly details of atrocities committed in the midst of it were made public in testimony at the Winter Soldiers Investigation and the trial of Lieutenant William Calley for the murder of 300 civilians at the hands of his platoon in My Lai in March 1968, but even three years later, after Calley was found guilty, many Americans preferred not to examine too closely what was going on in Southeast Asia. In June of 1971, it was still possible for Senator Sam Ervin of North Carolina to tell 2,000 cheering chaplains at the Military Chaplains Association meeting in Washington, D.C., "if you get into a war, you should get in to win."[79] Few Americans wanted to draw the parallels that Richard Fernandez saw in the outcome of the trial: "If it was illegal for Lt. Calley to kill civilians at a distance of 30 feet," he reasoned, "it is just as illegal for pilots to kill, injure, and refugee [sic] thousands of civilians at 30,000 feet!"[80] The publication of the *Pentagon Papers* in the *New York Times* on June 13 precipitated yet another crisis for the Nixon administration, as Americans could read how the Kennedy and Johnson administrations had deceived the public and dragged the nation ever more deeply into the morass of Vietnam.[81]

To counteract growing domestic frustration with the war, Kissinger embarked on a renewed diplomatic offensive to convince the North Vietnamese to accept Thieu as part of a peace offer that included gradual withdrawal of American forces and a return of prisoners of war. The North Vietnamese refused to consider Thieu and suggested that the United States withdraw support from him prior to the September elections in South Vietnam. The Nixon administration refused to do this, much to the chagrin of the North Vietnamese and Americans in the peace movement, who increasingly saw Thieu as a stumbling block in the way of peace.[82] Hopes for a neutralist "third force" coalition government in the south made up of neither the NLF nor Thieu's henchmen had never disappeared from the purview of the moderate wing of the antiwar movement. In the summer of 1971, a group of American students and religious leaders met with South Vietnamese students and neutralists in Saigon. The chairperson for the assembled visitors was Paul Moore, who felt uncomfortable about demonstrating in a foreign country with which his own was at war. Yet when they met with Vietnamese students who had had their fingernails pulled out and their backs scarred by the police for their antiwar activity, he agreed to attend a rally at the student union, and from there march to the American Embassy. "These same kids, who had already been tortured, were ready to go out and risk their very lives," he remembered. "Who were we to risk a little protocol?"[83]

After the rally—during which one of the American antiwar activists had succeeded in setting fire to a large papier-mâché dove hanging from the ceiling when he lifted a torch up and proclaimed, "for peace!"—Moore was asked to lead the way to the embassy. Vietnamese soldiers in full battle dress stopped them in a narrow side street and fired tear gas at them. "I ran out of there . . . as fast as I could," Moore recalled, not realizing at first that he was being followed by demonstrators who thought he was leading them on an alternate route; "So I was weaving in and out of the alleys of Saigon, trying to get away from all of these people and get to the hotel for safety, and they keep going right on." After passing another group of soldiers, who flashed them the peace sign, they finally made it back to the assembly hall, where the demonstration broke up.[84] When he returned home, Moore glowingly described the sentiments of those "thoughtful people" who wanted a neutral government to bring peace to South Vietnam.[85] His reception at home was not as friendly; among the criticism was a lengthy letter from his former Marine battalion commander during the Second World War, who questioned the former Marine's willingness to meet with representatives of an underground peace movement. Years later, Moore maintained that he was criticized far more for going to Saigon than for any of his civil rights work.[86]

Other religious leaders also wanted to see a neutral coalition government in South Vietnam. In January 1972, 600 clergy and laity met in Kansas City under the auspices of Clergy and Laymen Concerned to hold an "Ecumenical Witness for Peace," in which they criticized Vietnamization as "immoral" and requested that Congress cease funding for the war. Such pleas were to no avail. The ground war had intensified when the North Vietnamese mounted a large-scale invasion of the south, driving the South Vietnamese government forces back toward Saigon. By this time American personnel numbered only 95,000, with less than 10,000 in the combat forces, and as Nixon was not about to reintroduce American troops into Vietnam, he ordered a massive bombing campaign against North Vietnam, including Hanoi and Haiphong, and mined the Haiphong harbor. During June 1972 alone, more than 100,000 tons of bombs were dropped.[87]

This intensification of the war reinvigorated some sectors of the peace movement, including the religious community. Bennett, Brown, Novak, and Cox wrote an editorial in *Christianity and Crisis* denouncing the renewed air war, implying that the administration did not care whether Asians died as long as American casualties were limited. "[F]or an increasing number of Americans the enemies are not overseas," they wrote. "They are now in Washington." The National Federation of Roman Catholic Priests decried the immoral nature of the "automated air war" and the "antiseptic" yet evil "electronic battlefield." Clergy and Laymen Concerned called upon members to take part in a demonstration in Washington, and over 500 people arrived on Capitol Hill on May 16 to urge their senators and representatives to cut funding for the war. One hundred twenty people, mainly priests, ministers, and rabbis, held a sit-in at the Capitol Rotunda, singing hymns and holding prayer sessions for three hours until police arrested them and put them in jail for one night. (Spock remembered that the singing was "particularly wonderful" because clergy not only had spent years "leading the singing in their churches" but also "knew all the verses to the hymns.") Coffin, who had helped direct the services, continued to lead the hymn-singing in prison, a particular favorite being "A Mighty Fortress Is Our God."[88]

It was to be a busy season for the Yale chaplain, and an exhausting one. He had admitted to Malcolm Boyd in 1970 that he sometimes felt "professionally a bit at loose ends" and that he sometimes felt as if he had been at Yale long enough. "Perhaps if I didn't have two small children I would be tempted to do full time work with Clergy and Laymen," adding, "But I love this place and could hardly bear the thought of not being a chaplain."[89] Two years later, he subsequently wrote, his mood regarding the antiwar movement had altered considerably. "I was fed up with the war, already the longest in our history, and I was tired of fighting Nixon."[90]

Still, when the North Vietnam Peace Committee offered to release three prisoners of war in the fall of 1972, he agreed to go to Hanoi and meet them. He met with David Dellinger, Cora Weiss, Jane Fonda, Tom Hayden, Ramsey

Clark, and Daniel Berrigan, who had been released from prison in February, at the United Nations Church Center to discuss the conditions of the trip. Berrigan insisted that his brother Philip should go with them as a symbolic gesture of a prisoner receiving other prisoners. If the federal government refused to release him for the purposes of the trip, he argued, then the trip should be canceled. "Dan knew how to go for guilt!" recalled Coffin, but his idea was quickly vetoed by the others, who thought linking the two situations would be a mistake. At that, Berrigan left.[91]

Coffin, Dellinger, Weiss, and several others made the trip to Hanoi shortly thereafter, and after the three American pilots were turned over to them, the antiwar activists toured Hanoi and neighboring villages, took the obligatory tour of the War Crimes Museum, and met with government officials. The Yale chaplain found the experience interesting, but the destruction of lives and homes further depressed him, and he experienced some of the same resentment that Daniel Berrigan and Howard Zinn had felt when the three pilots changed into full dress uniforms at the end of the trip prior to meeting their superiors at Kennedy Airport.[92]

By the time they returned to the United States, the antiwar movement had grown quiet, concentrating on building support for Democratic presidential candidate Senator George McGovern in an attempt to bring peace through the electoral process. Even Heschel, aging and ill, took pen in hand to write a letter to the New York Times urging support of the Democratic candidate:

> If the prophets Isaiah and Amos were to appear in our midst, would they accept the corruption in high places? . . . Would they not be standing amidst those who protest against the violence of the war in Vietnam, the decay of our cities, the hypocrisy and falsehood that surround our present Administration, even at the highest level?
>
> . . . George McGovern's call for a revival of our national values echoes the demands of Israel's ancient prophets.
>
> By word and by deed, Senator McGovern is committed to the idea that "setting the moral tone of this nation is the most serious responsibility of the President." Regrettably, the same cannot be said of Mr. Nixon.[93]

The majority of Americans felt otherwise, and reelected Nixon in a landslide victory.

It was to be one of the last public utterances by the venerable rabbi. Heschel had never completely recovered from his heart attack in 1969, and the strains of a busy life were continuing to make themselves felt. Nonetheless, when Philip Berrigan was due to be released from prison on December 20, he asked to travel with Daniel to be there to welcome him as he left the penitentiary in

Danbury. The two men, the tall, crew-cut Philip, and the shorter, bearded rabbi stood facing each other, greeting each other after the long separation. On the way back to New York City, Heschel invited them to his house to have tea with him several days later.[94]

Exhaustion and frustration were taking their toll. Holocaust survivor, theologian, and novelist Elie Wiesel, a colleague of Heschel's who had worked with him on behalf of Soviet Jewry, recalled a telephone call he received from Heschel that December asking him to visit him at the Jewish Theological Seminary. Concerned, Wiesel left the conference he was attending, and when he arrived in Heschel's study, he recounted, the rabbi "did not speak. He cried, he fell on my shoulder. He did not say a word, he simply cried."[95] "While I am absorbed in the writing of a book, I forget myself, engulfed in the overwhelming presence of God," a student heard Heschel sigh on December 22. "But as soon as I step out of this room, I can hardly bear the burdens of the world around me. Oh, what a tragic world it is. . . ."[96]

The next day, Abraham Joshua Heschel died at his apartment on Riverside Drive. He was only sixty-five years old. Five hundred mourners attended the Conservative service for him at Park West Memorial Chapel in New York, after which his body was brought to the Beth David Cemetery on Long Island.[97] He had touched many lives with both his ecumenical witness and his work in the civil rights and the antiwar movements; moreover, he was a profound theologian, that rare combination of a person of deep intellect and unswerving devotion to action. Philosophically, he had contributed much to the scholarship of Judaism, but his contributions to interfaith dialogue were equally substantial. Shortly after his death, the Jesuit journal *America* devoted its entire March 10, 1973, issue to a tribute and discussion of the rabbi's life and works. "No Christian who ever entered into conversation with Professor Heschel came away without having been spiritually enriched and strengthened," wrote the editors.[98] To encounter the rabbi, they wrote, was to encounter "the living tradition of Judaism in all its energy, holiness, and compassion."[99] Heschel's influence reached not only the Jesuit community in the United States, but into the Vatican itself. "Even before we have moved in search of God," Pope Paul VI told an audience on January 31, 1973, "God has come in search of us," a quotation from a French translation of Heschel's *God in Search of Man.*[100]

The rabbi's influence in the civil rights movement, and especially the antiwar movement, was also significant. Heschel helped serve as the linchpin to the moderate religious wings of both, counting among his close friends Martin Luther King Jr., Coffin, Brown, and Daniel Berrigan, all of whom, like himself, had devoted much of their lives to the struggle for civil rights and an end to the war in Vietnam. Daniel Berrigan, despite their differences on Israel, had high praise for his rabbinical friend and paid tribute to his Jewish colleague in eloquent words that Heschel the writer would have appreciated. Speaking of the "unique affection" he had for Heschel, who was a father figure to him, Berrigan wrote, "[his] image endures, far deeper than a patriarchal beard, an Old World graciousness." He was, in Berrigan's words, "an ancestor of the spirit."[101]

Heschel had lived long enough to see the last and single most destructive phase of the war begin. Increasingly frustrated with his inability to bring Hanoi to the negotiating table ready to make concessions, Nixon ordered the Joint Chiefs of Staff to conduct a massive bombing attack against North Vietnam, targeting Hanoi's industrial centers, transportation networks, and residential areas. Despite Kissinger's preelection claims in October that "peace was at hand," it appeared that peace was as far away as ever.[102]

On December 18, bombs began raining down upon the urban centers of North Vietnam, continuing for twelve days. Thirty-six thousand tons of bombs were dropped during the "Christmas bombings," destroying much of Hanoi and Haiphong, and killing at least 2,200 people, according to the *New York Times*, whose editors denounced the bombing as a reversion to "Stone Age barbarism." (According to official North Vietnamese figures, approximately 1,600 people were killed; antiwar activists visiting Hanoi during the bombing urged the mayor to claim 10,000 casualties, but he refused to lie.) Forty-one religious leaders from the Catholic, Mennonite, and Methodist churches criticized Nixon in a joint pastoral letter, called for the cessation of all bombing and an end to congressional funding of the war, and asked other denominations to take part in a religious convocation to protest the war on January 3–4, 1973.[103]

Philip Berrigan, Coffin, and Ramsey Clark were some of the speakers at the National Religious Convocation and Congressional Visitation for Peace in Washington, D.C. Thirty-five hundred people visited their representatives and senators calling for an end to the war, attended services in various churches, and prayed for peace. There were those who would argue that calling on Congress to stop funding the war would weaken Nixon's position at the negotiating table, Coffin reminded his audience. "That is exactly what we have in mind. For if peace was at hand, the President should never have allowed it to slip through our fingers."[104]

Nixon, meanwhile, had notified Hanoi that if representatives were willing to resume negotiations, he would stop the bombing, and the North Vietnamese accepted the proposal. After further negotiations, Kissinger and the North Vietnamese signed the Paris Agreement on January 27. The accords "barely met Nixon's minimal terms for 'peace with honor,'" wrote historian George Herring. While it provided for the withdrawal of American troops and the return of prisoners of war and left the Thieu government untouched, the North Vietnamese forces were allowed to remain in the south. Both sides knew, as did Thieu, who had been browbeaten by Kissinger and Nixon to accept the treaty, that the political situation in Vietnam was as untenable as ever and that it was only a matter of time before the question of which government would remain in existence was answered.[105]

For the American peace movement, however, the agreement to withdraw American troops meant that the goal they had so long sought would now be achieved. The Vietnamese would be able to settle their affairs themselves. For most Americans, clergy included, the 1970s would be a time of coming to terms with the upheavals that the nation had undergone in the past decade.

epilogue

For everything there is a season, and a time for every matter under heaven . . . a time to kill, and a time to heal . . . a time for war, and a time for peace.

ECCLESIASTES 3:1–8

The fall of Saigon in April 1975 marked the end of the Vietnam War, but not the end of American peace activists' interest in that ravaged country. Pacifist groups sponsored a "War Is Over" festival in Central Park in May to honor the North Vietnamese triumph, leading critics to question the propriety of pacifists celebrating a military victory. When it became apparent that the victors in Vietnam were not the noble revolutionaries of leftist imaginations but practitioners of a brutal realpolitik who crushed dissent by imprisoning and torturing political prisoners and closing Buddhist pagodas, some of the most prominent antiwar activists began to reexamine their support of the North Vietnamese. Neuhaus, James Forest, and Thich Nhat Hanh drafted an "Appeal to the Government of Vietnam," asking officials in Hanoi and Ho Chi Minh City (formerly Saigon) to answer the charges. When radicals in the peace movement charged the three with being agents of the Central Intelligence Agency, because they were raising such uncomfortable questions, Alfred Hassler, former executive secretary of FOR, came to their defense—if the claims of government repression were true, he asked, what good was the much vaunted Vietnamese revolution accomplishing? Daniel and Philip Berrigan asked themselves the same question after getting a noncommittal response to a letter they had sent to Hanoi asking for information on the torture of American prisoners of war. The peace movement's admiration of the North Vietnamese had developed into idolatry, they wrote, causing some activists to be blinded to the faults of the new regime.[1]

Others were bothered about the increasingly radical stance taken by members of what had been moderate antiwar organizations. When a member of Clergy and Laity Concerned delivered a "strident, leftist cliché," as Neuhaus described it, during a memorial service for Heschel in 1974, he realized that it had become "appallingly clear to me that in no way did I believe what this organization was about anymore."[2] He was far from alone. The 1970s marked a time of self-reflection and retrenchment for many of the ministers, priests, and rabbis most involved in the civil rights and antiwar movements. Many of them continued to fight for social justice and human rights both in the United States and around the world in the ensuing decades, but they did so under a vastly different set of circumstances.

The subdued mood of the early 1970s brought with it a shift away from direct action and civil disobedience; instead of confrontation, the growing emphasis was on change through the electoral process. An obvious example of this was the support McGovern garnered from civil rights and antiwar activists during his 1972 campaign. That same year, black delegates met in Gary, Indiana, for the National Black Political Convention, whose agenda called for black Americans to form their own congressional representation and support the newly formed Congressional Black Caucus. While disregarding what they termed white politics, the delegates nonetheless called for blacks to build their own power structure within the electoral system.[3]

At the same time, it was unclear whether the churches would have been able to maintain the same level of social protest that they had demonstrated in the 1960s. Some of the clergy had simply grown frustrated and exhausted after years of protesting with little to show for their efforts. Some left the church to pursue careers in the burgeoning field of social work. "There is little doubt that most of these men who have opted out of the pastoral ministry are men who have allowed the radical changes of this world, and the radical difference of this age, to penetrate their conscious life," explained a report prepared for the Board of Homeland Ministries of the United Church of Christ.[4]

If anything, the laity were more opposed to clerical activism in the early 1970s than they had been during the height of the civil rights and antiwar movements. In a 1973 poll, clergymen and laypeople were asked how the churches' stand on "race, poverty, or peace" should be determined. Forty-six percent of the clergy felt that a general conference or convention should decide such things at the highest denominational level; only 14 percent of the laity agreed. Only 18 percent of the clergy believed that the choice was up to each individual alone, compared to 56 percent of the laypeople. In another survey, Episcopal laypersons ranked public affairs as twenty-fourth in a list of twenty-five priorities for church programs. Despite such attitudes, when Bishop John Hines of the Episcopal Church presided over the General Convention Special Program in the early 1970s, hundreds of thousands of dollars were given to the Black Economic Development Committee (as a result of the Black Manifesto), and to striking farm workers, liberation movements in the Third World, and the American Indian Movement. Not only did conservative Episcopalians wonder what their church was funding, but the Internal Revenue Service warned church leaders that the denomination could lose its tax-exempt status if it continued giving money to political causes such as strikes.[5]

Given the constricted economy of the 1970s, as well as a tightening job market for the clergy, it was not surprising that church bureaucracies began to listen more intently to the opinions of the laity, many of whom felt that the activist clergy of the 1960s had abandoned their spiritual and counseling duties in favor of a presence on the picket line. The rapid growth of conservative, evangelical churches in the mid-1970s echoed this desire to return to a more spiritual religion. Martin Luther King Jr. had been fond of saying that if the churches were concerned only with the hereafter and not with the gospel imperatives dealing with the here and now, institutional religious bodies would become nothing more than "country clubs with stained-glass windows." Yet if the churches spent most of their time and budgets on secular and social problems, letting the world set the agenda, and not on issues concerning souls and personal morality, what would keep them from becoming social service agencies with altars?[6]

Activist clergymen had also begun to grapple with the tension between pressing secular forces and personal spiritual matters. Convinced that too many religious figures in the antiwar movement were moving away from their spiritual roots to embrace secular attitudes, Neuhaus helped draft what was called the Hartford Statement in January 1975, which asked liberal religious bodies such as the NCC to reemphasize the spiritual and supernatural quality of their convictions. Coffin was one of the eighteen church leaders who signed the document. They assured their readers that they were not abandoning social activism in the future, nor were they repudiating what they had done in the past. "There are historical times when evil is so clearly defined that all Christians are called to come to witness," they wrote. "The 1960s was one of those times. But we are concerned with reexamining some of the excesses and mistakes of the movement." Harvey Cox and other theologians, meanwhile, drafted a separate document a year later, calling on the churches to become even more involved in social activism, especially on behalf of the oppressed people of the world.[7] What was encouraging, commented one minister, was that there was "more social sensitivity on the part of the churches than there's ever been," but it was "less visible, more in the areas of social services than political or social action." Yet the issues were vague for progressive clergymen. As he put it, "In the 1960s, if we weren't making sense out of Christianity . . . we went to Selma for reassurance. And then, wham, here we are in the 70s with no clear function whatever."[8]

Still others doubted whether the churches could successfully undertake social reform; as inherently conservative institutions, could they reform and challenge other conservative institutions in American society? The concern here was not whether they should continue to involve themselves in social protest but whether they could do so effectively. Malcolm Boyd and Daniel Berrigan believed that the institutional church was too narrowly focused and favored the approach of the "underground church," small eucharistic gatherings designed to foster community across ecumenical lines and provide believers with a radical involvement of the church in contemporary problems.[9] Baptist preacher Will Campbell dismissed the idea of institutional religion out of hand, complaining that "[e]very time a group of believers has moved from a catacomb or a brush arbor into a steepled sanctuary, they've lost something they once knew about Jesus." The result, he said, was that "all over this nation, these magnificent church steeples [were] casting their grand shadows over people living in almost prehistoric hunger and misery."[10]

Yet not all activists were so ready to give up on organized religion. Paul Moore agreed that the churches had a tendency to be too institutionally involved but argued, "if we didn't have our institutional churches, in a place like, say, New York, scattered around town, in Harlem and the Bronx and elsewhere, we wouldn't be there. And they act as sort of anchors for the church as a whole." A stewardship of money, or talent, or power did exist among the established churches, and for a denomination not to use it, he said, "seems to be a shame." He himself had used different tactics depending on his position, and while picketing had been effective, he said, so had "the two-martini lunch—if you're a bishop, with a cathedral, you get to see the mayor for lunch." In the end, he added, a decent hearing sometime "depends on who you are."[11]

It also depended on where you were, noted the Reverend Duncan M. Gray Jr. of Oxford, Mississippi. Churches had a major role to play in combating social ills, he wrote, but prospects for "growth, understanding, and a measure of reconciliation" came from contacts with other regular churchgoers, a group "who will never be marching in the streets, but who are, in the final analysis, the real key to the ultimate resolution of our problems."[12] As might be expected, Eugene Carson Blake, one of the leading figures on denominational boards and church organizations in the postwar era, also supported institutional religion. In March 1971, fourteen years before his death at the age of seventy-eight from complications arising from diabetes, he told an audience that "[h]aving spent my adult life in the service of organized Christianity, I nevertheless do not want to appear over-defensive of it. But . . . there is a great deal of nonsense spoken against organized religion." Without organization, he said, a religious person "has very limited influence of any kind even upon his contemporaries, let alone upon succeeding generations." In his view, a single person's influence was limited by "simple arithmetic," but he argued that "even a simple organization, such as Jesus used, 12 apostles and 12 disciples being sent out to heal and preach, multiplied his influence by geometric rather than arithmetic progression."[13]

One segment of the church not only took such lessons to heart, but borrowed heavily from the examples of King and the civil rights movement in swaying public opinion through the tactics of demonstrations and religious and moral appeals to the federal government—but did so in ways that were very disturbing to liberals. When the Supreme Court legalized abortion in Roe v. Wade in 1973, conservative and evangelical churches rallied in protest against what they considered to be an immoral decision. The Reverend Jerry Falwell, who had told his parishioners in 1965 that the church had no business involving itself in demonstrations, began holding rallies as leader of the Moral Majority, a conservative religious lobbying group dedicated to overturning Roe v. Wade, bringing back school prayer, and damning homosexuality. (After he had become famous as a confidante of President Ronald Reagan, his 1965 sermon "Ministers and Marches," in which he so strenuously abjured ministerial activism, came back to haunt him with a vengeance, and he half-jokingly told a biographer that he wished he could buy up every copy of the sermon and destroy them.)[14] Spurred by the growth of conservative fundamentalist and evangelical churches in the 1970s, Falwell's brand of politics included calls for increased defense spending in light of renewed tensions between the United States and the Soviet Union. He also urged Americans to support the racist South African government under P. W. Botha by reinvesting and buying South African gold and dismissed black activist Archbishop Desmond Tutu as "a phony, period, as far as representing the black people of South Africa." One fundamentalist minister in California admitted that when he was growing up, all he heard was that churches "should stay out of politics. Now it seems almost a sin *not* to get involved."[15]

While the New Christian Right under the leadership of Falwell, Pat Robertson, and others began to wane by the end of the 1980s, it reemerged under the leadership of the younger, more politically adept Ralph Reed. As the leader of the Christian Coalition, he called for a "new Christian agenda" that would include "a change in public attitudes through moral persuasion" rather than replacing "the social engineering of the left with the social engineering of the right by forcing compliance with the moral principles that motivate us so deeply."[16] Still, Reed's rhetoric, moderated in 1996 in time for the presidential election, was still gauged to the conservative, white lower-to-middle class that felt threatened by affirmative action, welfare, and the growing tolerance for homosexuality. Instead of racial epithets, however, members of the Christian Coalition were known to use "code words" such as "problem causers" and "underclass" to refer to blacks in their rejection of affirmative action and welfare. Still, not every evangelical was taken with the Christian Coalition. "Everyone has a right to be included in the mainstream," insisted M. Gasby Greely, vice president of communications for the National Urban League and a self-described progressive evangelical. "To me, that's justice, that's biblical, and that's Christian."[17]

Racism as a factor in American society persisted in whatever guise, be it cultural, social, or economic, but the civil rights movement had helped to raise the level of interracial tolerance. Predominantly white churches remained committed to the goal of eradicating racial prejudice in the 1970s and 1980s, but on the whole, most of the efforts came in the form of pastoral letters and resolutions passed at the higher denominational levels. Part of this was due to the formation of several black church organizations in the early 1970s. Modeled after their secular counterparts, these new clerical groups were committed to helping blacks consolidate the gains of the civil rights movement and further racial equality in employment within the larger denomination itself. They included the American Baptist Black Caucus, the National Black Catholic Clergy Caucus, the National Black Sisters' Conference, the National Office for Black Catholics, the National Black Evangelical Association, and the Union of Black Episcopalians.[18] While these groups often operated as special-interest groups, there were occasions when they served as a reminder to the churches of the continued need for toleration, as the Bishops' African American Catholics Committee did in the aftermath of the racially divisive O. J. Simpson trial and the controversial all-black Million Man March sponsored by the Nation of Islam in the fall of 1995. "Very seldom do people see God in the faces of one another," Bishop Curtis Guillory, chair of the committee, noted in a report that urged parishes to prepare for the 1996 Lenten season with ecumenical dialogue that addressed "issues relating to racial reconciliation, and public repentance for the divisions in the church and the sin of racism."[19]

More dramatic evidence of the changing nature of race relations in the churches came in the late spring of 1995, when the 15.6 million-member, predominantly white Southern Baptist Convention, the nation's largest Protestant denomination, formally apologized for its complicity in racism at its annual meeting in Atlanta. Southern Baptist delegates denounced racial prejudice "in all its forms, as deplorable sin," and lamented and repudiated "historic acts of evil such as slavery from which we continue to reap a bitter harvest"; they also apologized to black Americans for the persistence of racism in their own lifetimes and promised to "eradicate racism in all its forms from Southern Baptist life and ministry." The Reverend Gary Frost, the convention's first black vice president, accepted the apology on "behalf of my black brothers and sisters" and offered "our forgiveness in the name of Jesus Christ," adding that "the genuineness of your repentance will be demonstrated in your attitude and your action." In his closing address, an aging and ill Billy Graham received a standing ovation when he urged his fellow Southern Baptists to "pull down the barriers which divide."[20]

The convention's decision received mixed responses from black Baptists. "Even though it's late, I'm still delighted that it's come," Reverend Emmanuel McCall of Atlanta told a reporter. "There is a real sincere effort to say, 'We were wrong.'"[21] Others were less certain. "The civil rights struggle is still going on," insisted the Reverend E. Edward Jones, president of the National Baptist Convention, the country's second-largest black Baptist denomination, "and we need more than an apology." It was well known that the Southern Baptist Convention was losing white members and wanted to add new members from the black middle class in the urban South, and Jones said he "sensed a scheme" in their apology.[22] Some black pastors who "want gifts of buildings, finances, and other favors probably will now find the Southern Baptist Convention attractive," charged the Reverend Dr. Randolph Meade Walker of the New Philadelphia Baptist Church in Memphis. It was "ludicrous" for blacks to "abandon their own conventions . . . to run after those who historically oppressed and ostracized them. What sense does it make to turn your back on your own institution to make somebody else's stronger? . . . Black Baptists should not give away their birthright."[23]

Similar sentiments (although less charged) were voiced when United Methodists announced plans to merge their 8.6 million-member congregation with the three largest black Methodist congregations. "The time is right now for us to openly confess to sins of our past and to realize these brothers and sisters belong in one church," Bishop Melvin Talbert told the General Convention in the spring of 1996. The Commission on Pan-Methodist Union was charged with submitting a plan of union with the African Methodist Episcopal (AME) Church, the African Methodist Episcopal Zion Church, and the Christian Methodist Episcopal Church, to take effect by 2002. Several bishops of the AME Church and the AME Zion Church approved in theory of the idea of

Christian unity, although Bishop Thomas Hoyt Jr. of the Christian Methodist Episcopal Church said he was "very skeptical" about the proposal. If the color barrier in the churches were truly to be broken, he said, predominantly white churches needed to show a willingness to share power in the church hierarchy.[24]

In some cases, church mergers at the parish level have taken place because of shifting demographics. In New Orleans, for example, the white congregation of Central Baptist Church had become so small by the early 1990s that it ran the risk of not being able to afford the upkeep of the church. At the same time, a thriving black ministry called Faith in Action, part of the Southern Baptist Convention, was moving between rented churches to hotel rooms each Sunday for worship services. In 1993, both churches formally united in Central Baptist Church, renamed First United Baptist Church, with two copastors, the Reverend Robert Kirby, white, and the Reverend Dr. Marshall Truehill, black. The churches not only merged their leadership but their music and distinct styles of worship. Ironically, Central Baptist Church had enforced a whites-only policy as recently as 1982.[25]

The churches' concern for civil rights was not limited to black Americans. As the feminist and gay liberation movements emerged out of the secular civil rights movement, so did debates and discussion over the role of women and homosexuals in the churches. After a self-imposed exile from national church circles in Michigan in the early 1970s, Malcolm Boyd created a storm of controversy in 1976 when he announced publicly that he was a homosexual.[26] "I don't want anything more to do with masks," he told the *Chicago Sun-Times*. "I'm tired now with all the preoccupation with public relations packaging. I'm tired of politicians and churchmen who are liars and hypocrites."[27] The poet, writer, and activist was "treated like a leper," according to Boyd's colleague, the Reverend Fred Fenton of St. Augustine-by-the-Sea in Santa Monica, California, and there were numerous calls for his removal from the priesthood.[28] Understandably upset at the treatment accorded him, Boyd withdrew from public life and left his California home, returning in 1981 to join the staff of St. Augustine as parish priest, where he continues to write, conduct an AIDS ministry and workshops, and write a bimonthly advice column for *Modern Maturity*.[29] An important focus of his life has remained constant: to make the church more inclusive. "I would like a change in the environment so that a great many gay and lesbian priests could come out of their closets and find acceptance," he recently told a reporter.[30] Despite the

Episcopal Church's refusal to take a stand on same-sex marriages, by 1994 Boyd had performed over two dozen of them since the mid-1980s.[31]

Paul Moore was caught up in similar issues. In the 1970s, he supported the ordination of female Episcopal priests, against the wishes of conservatives in the church, who were led by Presiding Bishop John Allin, the former bishop of Mississippi who had opposed the Delta Ministry that Moore had chaired. In 1977, he ordained Ellen M. Barrett, a lesbian, which further angered the conservatives, some of whom began discussing the possibility of a schism within the denomination.[32] One of the most important facets of his work in New York City was what he had done in the late 1940s as a parish priest in New Jersey: helping the city's destitute and homeless and assailing those whom he felt were not doing enough. "The churches . . . feel very comfortable doing social service," he explained. "They really feel good about having people sleep in the basement." The problem lay in the fact that they "use up all their energy doing that and not getting *furious* at the city, the mayor, the governor, for not providing housing." Too much energy, he complained, went into the symptoms instead of the causes. The clergy, he added, were still "a long way from using what power we have in the church to shove the government around."[33] Putting some of that power into practice, he used his position to go head-to-head with John Cardinal O'Connor, the Roman Catholic Archbishop of New York, over equal rights for homosexuals. "My ideas are based on theology and not on knee-jerk liberalism," Moore insisted, "although the two sometimes coincide." On Easter Sunday 1989, he preached his last major sermon before taking a leave of absence that June, after which he officially retired in October of that year.[34]

Some of Moore's former colleagues in the civil rights and antiwar movements embarked on campaigns for human rights worldwide, whose overtones, and sometimes outright claims, demonstrated a lack of trust of the U.S. government that dated from the Vietnam era. The 1970s and 1980s found Robert McAfee Brown and his wife Sydney Thomason Brown in South America and South Africa, meeting with the poor and the radical Catholics who championed their cause at the risk of their own lives. The couple became firm believers in the "liberation theology" propounded by Latin American theologians, which held that God moved through history, sometimes through specific historic events such as revolutions, to free people from oppression.[35] The "promise of God's involvement in establishing justice on earth is predicated on human involvement . . . ," Brown wrote in 1989. "There is no possibility of sitting back and watching the Almighty move into high gear."[36] It was not enough for the churches and the synagogues—or the laity—to spawn endless statements and resolutions on the "empowerment of the powerless" and the "preferential option for the poor"; clergy and laity alike had to reach out to the poor in their own communities and form action groups to battle sexism, unemployment, labor issues, and assistance for those persons on the margins of society.[37]

The intensity with which these individuals assailed the Reagan administration—and supported the governments that it opposed—far surpassed that with which they had criticized Johnson and Nixon and praised the North Vietnamese. Liberals in the pulpit supported sanctuary movements for illegal immigrants fleeing U.S.-backed regimes in Guatemala and El Salvador and demanded improved relations with Nicaragua. As one scholar has noted, much of this was couched in a double standard of hostility toward repressive right-wing governments supported by the United States and acceptance and, at times, "great warmth . . . and understanding of authoritarian systems on the left," especially when its leaders claimed to be fighting wars of national liberation or struggling against Western hegemony.[38] When Brown visited Nairobi in 1975, he told the assembled members of the World Council of Churches that he was ashamed of the wrongs his country was doing in underdeveloped nations, evils that included commercial exploitation, and so he would give his speech in Spanish "to avoid the language of 'imperialism,'" apparently forgetting Spain's long history of colonization and exploitation.[39]

Brown's erstwhile colleague in Clergy and Laity Concerned and fellow freedom rider William Sloane Coffin Jr. was also a staunch critic of U.S. foreign policy. Leaving Yale in 1977 to become minister of New York City's Riverside Church, he continued his civil rights efforts by working with an ecumenical housing program in Brooklyn sponsored by Catholic and Protestant churches. Within his own church, which in the early 1980s was 35 percent black, Coffin insisted on rigorous adherence to affirmative action, hiring black and white assistant ministers of both sexes. At the same time, he began to speak out against the arms race, eventually becoming president of the National Committee for a Sane Nuclear Policy in the late 1980s.[40] Even more than Brown, Coffin demonstrated a "moral equivalence thesis," which likened Soviet repression of its citizens to American repression abroad, and once went so far as to compare the Pentagon to the Reverend Jim Jones, the cult leader who orchestrated the mass suicide of his followers in Guyana in 1978.[41]

When President Jimmy Carter imposed sanctions on Iran after militant students seized the United States Embassy in Teheran in November 1979, Coffin denounced both the president's decision and his support for the deposed Shah, comparing the sanctions against Iran to Lyndon Johnson's bombing campaign against North Vietnam. His analogy was faulty, as he later admitted, explaining that he meant to show that the Iranians would resist American entreaties as stubbornly as the Vietnamese had the bombing, but at the time it earned him the scorn and contempt of many Americans, including his parishioners. Members of Iran's Revolutionary Guard, however, were sufficiently impressed with his critique of American foreign policy to invite him and three other clergymen to officiate at Christmas services for the hostages.[42]

For other activists, the end of the Vietnam War had allowed them to pick up where they left off before that conflict escalated so dramatically in 1965. "Indochina, in a sense, had deflected the antiwar movement from its primary objective—terminating the nuclear arms race—for about a decade," wrote radical Sidney Lens, and he was not alone in resuming his work on behalf of nuclear disarmament.[43] Daniel Berrigan continued to protest the development of nuclear weapons as he had done since the early 1960s, taking part in demonstrations at the White House, the Pentagon, and arms manufacturers in 1976, for which he was arrested. After teaching at Yale and New Rochelle, he decided to resume dramatic protests similar to those he and his brother Philip had undertaken in the late 1960s.[44] In September 1980 the two brothers joined several other Catholic radicals in walking into a restricted area of the General Electric Space Division in King of Prussia, Pennsylvania, denting the nose cones of intercontinental ballistic missiles with hammers and, in what had become a Berrigan trademark, splashing blood on nearby documents before they were arrested. All were given sentences ranging from three to ten years, which were duly appealed.[45]

Unlike their earlier activities, the actions of the so-called Ploughshares Eight failed to excite much interest among most Americans, even those in religious circles, and only a very small number of radicals emulated their work by pouring blood on the steps of nuclear research facilities and bases.[46] "The liberal Protestant pulpits that once welcomed me (the Catholic pulpits were never so venturesome) have closed their access," wrote Daniel somewhat resignedly. "One is told that such activities as we intransigently sponsor are needlessly provocative, [and] will bring down the skies, presumably on innocents or bystanders." Perhaps the practice of blood-pouring, which had never caught on among peace activists anyway, was now seen as a quaint, if vaguely troubling, relic of the Vietnam era, a realization Berrigan himself may have acknowledged when he noted in 1987 that the scenario had become "familiar" and "predictable."[47] Nonetheless, Berrigan continued his own brand of protest into the 1990s, pouring blood on the steps of the Riverside Research Institute near Times Square in protest of its work on strategic weapons. He admitted to a reporter that sometimes "it seems so fruitless," but said he believed that results were not important. "If you want to profess your faith, you have to seek consonance with Christ and let the chips fall."[48]

Berrigan had planned to go back to teaching, but had had little success in finding a position. An offer to teach a course at High Point University in North Carolina had been canceled by the university president when the Gulf War broke out, as the administration did not want to have such a radical teaching on campus after President George Bush had committed large numbers of American troops to defend Saudi Arabia against Iraqi aggression in the winter of 1990–91.[49]

For someone who professed not to care what others thought, Berrigan was upset that no one from the New York Times had asked him his views on the war. Others, not waiting for a reporter to arrive, readily spoke out. Coffin bluntly declared that the conflict was solely about oil, and all of Bush's claims that the armed forces of the United States and United Nations were stopping the spread of a despotic regime were simply subterfuge to safeguard the West's supply of petroleum. "Were oranges Saudi Arabia's chief export, not a single American would have been sent there," he wrote. "Were Kuwait famous for its figs and dates, we'd hear nothing louder than tongue-clicking."[50]

As he was wont to do, Coffin acted on his beliefs, offering Riverside Church as a sanctuary to soldiers who felt that the war was immoral. Unable to apply for conscientious objector status until they reached Saudi Arabia, four men from a Marines reserve unit due to be sent to the Persian Gulf entered the church that December to surrender themselves to authorities for being absent without leave. That night, Robert McAfee Brown, speaking on behalf of the First Presbyterian Church in Palo Alto, and other Bay Area ministers announced that they were also going to open their churches for sanctuary, having received inquiries from more than 200 individuals in the military. When the Senate Armed Services Committee began hearings on the Gulf crisis, the National Interreligious News Service Board for Conscientious Objectors in Washington, D.C., received over 100 calls from persons wanting information.[51]

The NCC also felt that the decision to commit ground forces to the Middle East was a mistake and sent church leaders on a "peace pilgrimage" to the Gulf region, where officials in Baghdad assured them that they did not want the war that was being forced on them by a reckless American foreign policy. Armed with such information, the peace pilgrims returned to the United States and helped the NCC's General Board draw up a statement claiming in apocalyptic tones that a war between the two countries in that part of the world would "unleash weapons of mass destruction" resulting in "tens and hundreds of thousands of casualties."[52] While more muted, the U.S. Catholic Conference's international policy committee also expressed opposition to the war, as did the Right Reverend Edmund L. Browning, presiding bishop of the Episcopal Church.[53]

Yet not all those who had stood shoulder to shoulder against American intervention in Vietnam were on the same side of the issue this time. Dismissing the allegations that the Middle East faced a nuclear holocaust as "hysteria," Richard Neuhaus defended Bush's description of the conflict as a just war, arguing that it was being waged to stop aggression, it was undertaken by legitimate authority, and the goals and means were proportional to the cause. The Lutheran pastor was not alone. John Cardinal O'Connor of New York also implied in a homily delivered on the eve of the United Nations counterattack that other nations had an obligation "not to abandon a nation that is attacked."[54]

Had the war not ended several weeks later in a decisive victory for the forces of the United States and the United Nations, it is likely that the same issues that had traumatized American society during the Vietnam War would have been resurrected for new debate. Still, this is not to suggest that peace activists or religious organizations had turned pacifist nor that they were unwilling to see American forces committed in any but the most optimistic of circumstances. During the Bosnian crisis of the 1990s, when Muslims, Croatians, and Serbs engaged in a bloody struggle over control of former Yugoslavia, clergy who had been opposed, or at least reserved, about sending American troops to the Middle East supported the use of force to quell the "ethnic cleansing" then going on throughout the region. In a radio interview, Coffin explained that such force, especially if American troops went as part of a United Nations peacekeeping force, was just, because of the massacres, rape, and torture of civilians. It was one thing for Americans and others to disbelieve the rumors of what the Nazis were doing to the Jews of Europe during the Second World War, but such moral isolation could not exist in the latter half of the twentieth century. Stories of massacres were also publicized by Jewish and Muslim organizations in the United States, including the Union of American Hebrew Congregations, whose vice president, Rabbi Eric Yoffie, admitted to sharing the skepticism of others when the atrocity stories were first aired by the media. "But as they became more graphic," he said, "it had an enormous impact on the Jewish community. It is bad enough, and close enough and comparable enough [to the Holocaust] that the Jewish community felt a profound obligation to respond morally, whatever the strategic issues."[55]

In a letter to Secretary of State Warren Christopher, Roman Catholic Archbishop John R. Roach, representing the official view of U.S. Catholic bishops as chair of the U.S. Catholic Conference's international policy committee, urged the commitment of U.S. forces to "defend largely helpless people in Bosnia against aggression and barbarism." The Reverend Herbert W. Chilstrom, head bishop of the Evangelical Lutheran Church, and Bishop Browning of the Episcopal Church agreed. While the NCC passed a resolution calling for a United Nations peacekeeping force, it refused to condone the lifting of the U.S. arms embargo, although officials admitted that if the peacekeeping force failed, "we cannot in good conscience block besieged populations from access to means of self-defense."[56]

Most of those who called upon the administration of President Bill Clinton to send troops to Bosnia did so with the understanding that they would be operating in tandem with the United Nations. Although the forces sent to the Persian Gulf were also under the auspices of that organization, it was clear that many clergy and clerical organizations found the plight of civilians in Bosnia more worthy of concern than the ownership of the vast oil fields in the Gulf, as the former seemed to represent a clear moral issue. It was also apparent that even twenty years after Vietnam, there would be few clergy or religious organizations willing to give unquestionable support to policymakers in Washington. In March 1995, at a conference at the National Cathedral held to commemorate the fiftieth anniversary of the bombing of Hiroshima and the creation of the United Nations, liberal clergy called upon the American public to increase their efforts on behalf of nuclear disarmament and to resist the Republican calls to limit the country's support for the United Nations. "Religious people particularly are called on to moderate national sovereignty and to increase global loyalty and so help the United Nations," Coffin told the assembled dignitaries.[57]

To underscore their appeals, a group of religious leaders and peace activists began a three-week fast the following month to publicize the need to extend the Nuclear Non-Proliferation Treaty, due to expire in May 1995. Among those fasting outside the United Nations headquarters were Coffin, Brown, and Bishop Thomas Gumbleton, former Roman Catholic auxiliary bishop of Detroit; Dr. Helen Caldicott, former head of the Physicians for Social Responsibility; and Miuko Matsubare of Hibakusha, the Japanese organization of survivors of the atomic bomb dropped on Hiroshima. While fasting at the Isaiah Wall at the United Nations, Coffin and Brown learned of John C. Bennett's death on April 27. Ninety-two when he died, the former president of Union Theological Seminary had remained active and interested in religious and political debates until the end. In a letter to the *New York Times*, Coffin and Brown noted that Bennett "has left us the legacy of disturbed but focused consciences. We loved him. He was our mentor."[58]

The Reverend Larry Rasmussen of Union Theological Seminary rightly noted that an era had ended with Bennett, "the dean of Christian ecumenical ethicists for the long stretch after World War II through the civil rights movement, Vietnam, and beyond." In his lifetime, Bennett had helped lead the ecumenical movement in the United States, beginning in 1937 when he and Henry Pitney Van Dusen led the U.S. delegation to the Oxford Conference on Life and Work, which helped lead to the formation of the World Council of Churches eleven years later.[59] He had seen a portion of the American religious establishment move away from the complacency of the immediate postwar era and rise to the challenges posed to American society by the civil rights movement and the Vietnam War. As a whole, the churches and synagogues of the nation, as institutions, did not meet the challenge, caught up as they were in their own institutional well-being, and, in some cases, serving as bastions of racism and intolerance. The effectiveness and decisiveness of the influence of white clergy on the civil rights and antiwar movements is another matter, for it is unlikely that either movement would have achieved the impact it did without clerical participation.

In the case of the former, the efforts of priests, ministers, and rabbis to confront and combat racial discrimination proved significant to the passage of two important pieces of civil rights legislation. Well-organized groups of clergymen, with grassroots support from churches outside the South, helped convince Congress to pass the Civil Rights Act of 1964, while the presence of hundreds of clergymen and nuns in Selma, and the death of the Reverend James Reeb, highlighted the moral nature of voter registration in Alabama and helped lead to passage of the Voting Rights Act of 1965. On a much smaller scale, the courage and willingness of a few southern ministers to challenge the racial status quo in the face of white intransigence gave at least some members of their congregations pause to reflect on the meaning of the scriptures in relation to their treatment of their black neighbors. Little was accomplished through civility or reconciliation; "to have smart-ass liberal clergy come down and beat up on white southerners, some of whom were doing their best," was not conducive to building good relations with fellow whites, recalled Moore. "And I think a lot of us were very self-righteous and arrogant, pretentious, and patronizing. On the other hand, I don't think that the voter registration movement could have gotten off the ground without help from the North. And I'm glad that it came through the churches."[60]

The effectiveness of the clergy in the antiwar movement is more difficult to discern, for it is impossible, given the varied nature of the groups opposed to the Vietnam War, to attribute to any one organization success or shifts in public sentiment. The reluctance of organized religious bodies, especially the mainstream churches, to protest the war angered those strongly opposed to the conflict, but a moderate organization such as CALCAV was, in the view of historian Mitchell Hall, able to "communicate with a moderate, middle-class constituency that would not listen to the radical Left." Such a legitimizing influence helped gain the support of doves in Congress, who in turn looked to CALCAV's "visible constituency for antiwar legislators to draw upon when confronting prowar forces in the halls of government."[61] If neither CALCAV nor the other antiwar groups could claim credit for ending the war, argued the late Charles DeBenedetti, their perseverance and the continuous tensions resulting from the polarization of American society at least "made it stoppable."[62]

Looking at the issues from a purely moral standpoint, however, effectiveness was immaterial. Thomas Merton once cautioned a dejected member of the Catholic Peace Fellowship who felt that his work was meeting with a wall of public indifference not to depend on any hope of results. When one took on a certain kind of work, advised Merton, it was best to understand from the outset that the work "will be apparently worthless and even achieve no result at all." But once that was understood, one could "start more and more to concentrate not on the results but on the value, the rightness, the truth of the work itself."[63] In the end, it was not the degree of success, or lack of it, that made the clerical activists noteworthy; nor was it their numbers, which were small; nor their influence, which was limited. What made these individuals important in both religious and historical terms was their very act of witness, their willingness and determination to back up their religious convictions with action.

notes

Abbreviations

CC	*Christianity and Crisis*
CCAR	Central Conference of American Rabbis
CCY	*Christian Century*
ESCRU	Episcopal Society for Cultural and Racial Unity
JPF	Jewish Peace Fellowship
MBP	Malcolm Boyd Papers
NCC	National Council of Churches of Christ in the U.S.A.
NYT	*New York Times*
RES	Ralph E. Smeltzer Manuscript Notes and Correspondence

Introduction

1. *Battles and Leaders*, 4: 760; *Washington Post*, March 22, 1965, 1.

2. For example, see M. L. King Jr., *Stride toward Freedom*, 96–124.

3. K. D. Miller, *Voice of Deliverance*, 7.

4. Quoted in Fager, *Selma, 1965*, 132.

5. Leon Howell, "Ethical Engagement," CCY 112 (May 24, 1995): 556.

6. Hadden, *Gathering Storm*, 85, 206–7.

7. Cox, " 'New Breed,' " 137.

8. Quinley, *Prophetic Clergy*, 167–69; Nelsen, Yokley, and Madron, "Ministerial Roles," 75–386.

9. John Bodo, "The Pastor and Social Conflict," in Lee and Marty, *Religion and Social Conflict*, 25.

10. Glock, Ringer, and Babbie, *To Comfort and to Challenge*, 204–8.

11. Callahan, "The Quest for Social Relevance," 165.

12. Stark and Glock, *American Piety*, 69–76; Allport, *Nature of Prejudice*, 417, 424; Stouffer, *Communism*, 15–17, 176–78.

13. Butler, *Way of All Flesh*, 64–65.

14. Hadden, *Gathering Storm*, 174–79, 194–207; Cox, " 'New Breed,' " 137–39, 141; Rodney Stark and Charles Glock, "Prejudice and the Churches," in Glock and Siegelman, *Prejudice U.S.A.*, 90–91.

15. Merton, *Thomas Merton in Alaska*, 95–96; Heschel, "No Religion Is an Island," 119.

16. Glock, Ringer, and Babbie, *To Comfort and to Challenge*, 186; Glock and Stark, *Religion and Society in Tension*, 86–122.

17. Hans Margull, "The Ecumenical Movement in the Churches," in Fey, *Ecumenical Advance*, 366.

18. See especially Hadden, *Gathering Storm*; Quinley, *Prophetic Clergy*; Campbell and Pettigrew, *Christians in Racial Crisis*; Glock and Ringer, "Church Policy," 148–56; Nelsen, Yokley, and Madron, "Ministerial Roles," 375–86.

19. See S. L. Carter, *Culture of Disbelief*, esp. 49, 63–64, 227.

20. Ahlstrom, *Religious History*, 785–804; Hopkins, *Rise of the Social Gospel*, 107–25, 203–21; Cavert, *American Churches*, 33–34, 84–87, 160–61; Robert Schneider, "Voice of Many Waters," in W. R. Hutchison, *Between the Times*, 95–115.

21. Niebuhr, *Moral Man*, xi–xx, 21–22, 163, 222.

22. Fox, *Reinhold Niebuhr*, 142–77; Reinhold Niebuhr, "Christian Faith and Social Action," in J. A. Hutchison, *Christian Faith*, 226–28; Cavert, *American Churches*, 126–35, 163–65, 199–203.

23. *CC* 1 (February 10, 1941): 4.

24. Niebuhr, *Christianity and Power Politics*, x–xi, 2–4.

25. Quoted in Smith, Handy, Loetscher, *American Christianity*, 2: 543.

26. Mays, *Born to Rebel*, 252–53; Loescher, *Protestant Church and the Negro*, 42–45.

27. R. F. Martin, "Critique of Southern Society," 66–75; Dunbar, *Against the Grain*; LaFarge, *Catholic Viewpoint*, 70–71, 137–38.

28. Whitfield, *Culture of the Cold War*, 23; See "Catholics, Non-Catholics, and Senator McCarthy," *Commonweal* 59 (April 2, 1954): 639; Crosby, *God, Church, and Flag*; De-Santis, "American Catholics and McCarthyism," 3–31; "McCarthy Resorts to the Religious Test," *CCY* 70 (March 18, 1953): 311; "On Investigating Clergymen," 17; "Loyalty of the Clergy—'O.K.,'" 126–27; Roy, *Apostles of Discord*, 229–30, 246–50; Matthews, "Reds and Our Churches," 3, 13; Reinhold Niebuhr, "Communism and the Clergy," *CCY* 70 (August 19, 1953): 936–37.

29. "On Investigating Clergymen," 17; Oxnam, *I Protest*, 12.

30. *NYT*, April 10, 1954, 8.

31. Ibid.; DeSantis, "American Catholics and McCarthyism," 10–11; Sheil, "Should a Clergyman Stay Out of Politics?" 66–69.

32. Crosby, *God, Church, and Flag*, 134; *NYT*, April 5, 1954, 12.

33. Matthews, "Reds and Our Churches," 3, 13.

34. Reverend John A. O'Brien, Rabbi Maurice Eisendrath, and the Reverend John Sutherland Bonnell to Dwight D. Eisenhower, July 9, 1953; and Dwight D. Eisenhower to the Reverend John A. O'Brien, Rabbi Maurice Eisendrath, and the Reverend John Sutherland Bonnell, July 9, 1953; both quoted in *NYT*, July 10, 1953, 6.

35. "Inaugural Message of the National Council," reprinted in *CCY* 67 (December 18, 1950): 1484–85; Cavert, *American Churches*, 84–87.

36. Quoted in Smith, Handy, and Loetscher, *American Christianity*, 2: 544–47.

37. Peter Day, "The National Council of Churches: An Evaluation," *CC* 20 (May 16, 1960): 67, 71.

38. For more information on Bennett, see Lee, *Promise of Bennett*, and D. H. Smith, *Achievement of Bennett*; Crow, "Eugene Carson Blake," 228–30; *NYT*, August 1, 1985, A16.

39. Dr. Eugene Carson Blake to the Editors, *CC* 12 (May 12, 1952): 62–63; Henry Van Dusen, "The Role of Prophets," *CC* 12 (July 7, 1952): 89–90.

40. Wuthnow, *Restructuring of American Religion*, 35–45.

41. Margaret Mead, "How Religion Has Fared in the Melting Pot," in Sperry, *Religion and Our Racial Tensions*, 80.

42. William Lee Miller, "Some Negative Thinking about Norman Vincent Peale," *Reporter* 12 (January 13, 1955): 19–21.

43. Hutchinson, "The President's Religious Faith," 151–52.

44. Stouffer, *Communism*, 161–64.

45. Frady, *Billy Graham*, 28, 96–100, 135–36, 144–48, 191–205.

46. Ibid., 201.

47. Graham, *Peace with God*, 18–19, 23.

48. Reinhold Niebuhr, "Editorial Notes," *CC* 16 (March 5, 1956): 18–19.

49. See Graham, *Peace With God*, 190–91, 195.

50. Herberg, *Protestant-Catholic-Jew*, 18, 30–33, 46–51; see also "Growing Respect Shown for Church Leaders," *CCY* 71 (April 28, 1954): 509.

51. Hutchinson, "Have We a 'New' Religion?" 140.

52. Marty, *New Shape of American Religion*, 7, 10.

53. See Winter, *Suburban Captivity of the Churches*; Berger, *Noise of Solemn Assemblies*.

54. Berton, *Comfortable Pew*, 80.

55. Mead, "How Religion Has Fared," 81.

Chapter One

1. NYT, May 18, 1954, 1, 14.

2. For a representative selection, see "Resolutions Adopted by the Assembly," *CCY* 71 (September 22, 1954): 1157, 1166; "Southern Baptists Approve Decision," *CCY* 71 (June 9, 1954): 691–92; "Protestantism Speaks on Justice and Integration," *CCY* 75 (February 5, 1958): 165; "Southern Baptists Support Court," *CCY* 71 (June 16, 1954): 723; "Southern Presbyterians Defeat Isolationism," *CCY* 72 (June 22, 1955): 724; Charles Keenan, "Church Leaders on School Segregation," *America* 91 (July 10, 1954): 378–79; "Bishops Condemn Racial Injustice," *America* 100 (November 29, 1958): 264; Statement of the Synagogue Council of America, 1954, quoted in Campbell and Pettigrew, *Christians in Racial Crisis*, 168.

3. "The School Decision: An Editorial," *CCY* 71 (June 2, 1954): 662–63; Keenan, "Church Leaders," 378–79.

4. Louis Twomey to Clark Trent, S.J., October 26, 1954, Box 19, Folder 13, Twomey Papers.

5. Bailey, *Southern White Protestantism*, 146; "United Lutherans Solace Foes of Supreme Court," *CCY* 73 (October 31, 1956): 1252.

6. "A Roundtable Has Debate," 145.

7. Fairclough, *Race and Democracy*, 174; Leonard, *Theology and Race Relations*, 93.

8. McKivigan, *War against Proslavery Religion*, 196–99; H. S. Smith, *In His Image*, 212–13; Newby, *Jim Crow's Defense*, 85–87; "Southern Methodists Would Return Race Divisions," *CCY* 72 (February 23, 1955): 229; "Methodists Vote Four-Year Integration," *CCY* 81 (May 13, 1964): 630.

9. J. B. Morris, "ESCRU," 6; Morris interview, April 6, 1995.

10. Warren, *Segregation*, 57.

11. N. Lawrence, "A Progress Report," 11.

12. Quoted in "Criswell Not the Pope of Southern Baptists," *CCY* 73 (March 14, 1956): 325.

13. Warren, *Segregation*, 25–26.

14. Ingram, introduction to *Essays on Segregation*, 1, 6–7, 11, 13.

15. Knebel and Mollenhoff, "Eight Klans Bring New Terror to the South," 63.

16. N. R. McMillan, *Citizens' Council*, 20–25.

17. Quoted in W. D. Campbell, *Race and Renewal*, 18.

18. McGill, "Agony of the Southern Minister," 57.

19. "Southern Ministers Speak Their Minds," 13–17; Glock and Ringer, "Church Policy and Attitudes," 148–56; Bailey, *Southern White Protestantism*, 145; Bartley, *Rise of Massive Resistance*, 295.

20. Quoted in Sarratt, *Ordeal of Desegregation*, 266.

21. Trillin, "Reflections," 85.

22. Dittmer, *Local People*, 37–38; "Anti-Segregation Views Lose Pastor His Pulpit," CCY 72 (March 2, 1955): 286–87; J. B. Morris, "ESCRU," 7.

23. Graham, "Billy Graham Makes Plea," 140, 138.

24. "Billy Graham Sets the South an Example," CCY 75 (November 19, 1958): 1325–26.

25. "Biographical Information, the Rev. Will D. Campbell," n.d., RG 6, Box 47, Folder 2, NCC Archives; "Good Will," 84; Campbell, *Dragonfly*, 75–78; Connelly, *Will Campbell*, 76.

26. Campbell, *Dragonfly*, 96, 98.

27. "Biographical Information, the Rev. Will D. Campbell," NCC Archives.

28. Campbell, "Vocation as Grace," 82.

29. Egerton, *A Mind to Stay Here*, 19.

30. Ibid.; Campbell, "Vocation as Grace," 81; Connelly, *Will Campbell*, 81; Frady, *Southerners*, 372–73.

31. Campbell, *Dragonfly*, 113; Campbell, "Vocation as Grace," 83; Campbell, *Providence*, 3–24; Egerton, *A Mind to Stay Here*, 20; "Mississippi Abandons Its Religious Emphasis Week," CCY 73 (February 29, 1956): 260; R. H. Barrett, *Integration*, 32; *Mississippian*, February 3, 1956, 3.

32. *Mississippian*, January 20, 1956, 1.

33. Ibid., February 3, 1956, 3.

34. Ibid., February 3, 1956, 1; February 10, 1956, 1; February 17, 1956, 1.

35. Quoted in "Mississippi Abandons Religious Emphasis Week," 260.

36. *Mississippian*, February 17, 1956, 1.

37. Campbell, *Dragonfly*, 121; R. H. Barrett, *Integration*, 32–33.

38. Silver, *Running Scared*, 62–63; Campbell, "Vocation as Grace," 83.

39. Campbell, *Dragonfly*, 125–27; Silver, *Running Scared*, 64; Connelly, *Will Campbell*, 81–83; Campbell, "Vocation as Grace," 83; Findlay, *Church People*, 22.

40. Egerton, *A Mind to Stay Here*, 21.

41. Will D. Campbell, "Memorandum to All Human Relations Personnel in the South, August 20, 1957," and Will D. Campbell, "Field Report, Southern Project," Little Rock, Ark., March 23–25, 1959, both in RG 6, Box 47, Folder 5, NCC Archives.

42. "Race Agitator Arrested," CCY 71 (October 20, 1954): 1260; "Resist Racist Appeals!" CCY 71 (October 27, 1954): 1294.

43. Theodore A. Braun and C. Sumpter Logan, "The Ministers' Viewpoint," *Henderson Gleaner and Journal*, September 12, 1956, 4.

44. *Henderson Gleaner and Journal*, September 25, 1956, 1, 4; September 26, 1956, 4.

45. Ibid., September 29, 1956, 1.

46. C. Sumpter Logan and Theodore A. Braun, "Pastors' Diary," CCY 73 (October 17, 1956): 1232.

47. Campbell, "Memorandum to All Human Relations Personnel," 1, 5, NCC Archives.

48. NYT, September 1, 1956, 1, 6; G. Barrett, "Study in Desegregation," 11, 71–72, 76; NYT, December 5, 1957, 1, 43.

49. Campbell, *Forty Acres*, 49.

50. NYT, December 5, 1956, 1, 43, 44.

51. NYT, December 10, 1956, 1, 24; December 20, 1956, 20; February 5, 1957, 25. Sadly, this episode marked the high point in the young clergyman's career. A few years later, he

had a falling out with his congregation, unrelated to racial issues, and moved to another parish. Shortly after that, he killed himself. Campbell, who kept in sporadic touch with Turner, does not mention why he committed suicide. Campbell, *Forty Acres*, 49–50.

52. See, for example, M. L. King Jr., *Stride toward Freedom*; J. A. G. Robinson, *Montgomery Bus Boycott*; Garrow, *Walking City*; Branch, *Parting the Waters*, 120–205; A. D. Morris, *Origins of the Civil Rights Movement*, 51–63.

53. *The Southern Regional Council: Its Origin and Purpose*, 3–5; George S. Mitchell to Louis Twomey, October 30, 1954, Box 19, Folder 14, Twomey Papers; Chappell, *Inside Agitators*, 47.

54. Robert E. Hughes interview, January 24–25, 1994.

55. Ibid.; Morgan, *A Time to Speak*, 71; Glenn Eskew, "The Alabama Christian Movement for Human Rights," in Garrow, *Birmingham, Alabama*, 47.

56. Hughes interview.

57. Ibid.; King, *Stride toward Freedom*, 114, 116–17; Ralph Abernathy, "The Natural History of a Social Movement," in Garrow, *Walking City*, 134.

58. Hughes interview; M. L. King Jr., *Stride toward Freedom*, 74; Graetz, *White Preacher's Memoir*, 4–15, 23–29, 35–39, 43.

59. Graetz, *White Preacher's Memoir*, 54–62, 81–83; Rowan, *Go South to Sorrow*, 134–35; Steven Millner, "The Montgomery Bus Boycott," in Garrow, *Walking City*, 497; Walton, "The Walking City, Part I" 19; Thomas Gilliam, "The Montgomery Bus Boycott," in Garrow, *Walking City*, 273; Hughes interview.

60. *Jet* 12 (December 22, 1955): 24; *NYT*, January 12, 1956, 13; Millner, "Montgomery Bus Boycott," 496–98; Harold E. Fey, "Negro Ministers Arrested," *CCY* 73 (March 7, 1956): 294–95.

61. Hughes interview.

62. Chappell, *Inside Agitators*, 57.

63. M. L. King Jr., *Stride toward Freedom*, 80; Durr, *Outside the Magic Circle*, 313.

64. "National Council Commends Montgomery Ministers," *CCY* 73 (March 14, 1956): 325.

65. Quoted in "Attack on the Conscience," 17.

66. M. L. King Jr., *Stride toward Freedom*, 160, 177; *NYT*, December 30, 1956, 1; *NYT*, January 11, 1957, 1; "Night of Terror," 15; Graetz, Letter to the Editor, 6; Graetz, *White Preacher's Memoir*, 120, 129–32.

67. Durr, *Outside the Magic Circle*, 295.

68. Salisbury, *A Time of Change*, 50–60; Hughes interview; Eskew, "Alabama Christian Movement," 47; Morgan, *A Time to Speak*, 52; Harrison Salisbury, "Fear and Hatred Grip Birmingham," *NYT*, April 12, 1960, 1, 28; *NYT*, September 7, 1960, 27; *NYT*, September 9, 1960, 16.

69. Hughes interview; *NYT*, September 3, 1960, 20; Morgan, *A Time to Speak*, 74–81; Campbell, *Dragonfly*, 208–10.

70. Hughes interview.

71. Ibid.; Campbell, *Dragonfly*, 210; *NYT*, September 11, 1960, 41; *NYT*, September 11, 1960, 41; "Hughes Punished by Church for Conscience's Sake," *CCY* 77 (September 21, 1960): 1077–78; "Southern Methodists Would Return Race Divisions," *CCY* 72 (February 23, 1955): 229; "Church Struggle in the Segregation Struggle," *CCY* 72 (June 1, 1955): 645.

72. Quoted in "Hughes Punished," 1078.

73. *NYT*, September 11, 1960, 41; Robert E. Hughes, "Powder Keg in Rhodesia: I," *CCY* 82 (February 17, 1965): 208–10, 212, and "Powder Keg in Rhodesia: II," *CCY* 82 (February 24, 1965): 240, 242; Campbell, *Dragonfly*, 208.

74. "A Time of Testing," *Arkansas Gazette*, September 1, 1957, 1A, reprinted in Record and Record, *Little Rock, U.S.A.*, 17–18, 28, 30–35; Spitzberg, *Racial Politics in Little Rock*,

43–49; Colbert S. Cartwright, "Lesson From Little Rock," CCY 74 (October 9, 1957): 1193; Bates, *Long Shadow*, 51–52, 54.

75. NYT, September 3, 1957, 1; NYT, September 6, 1957, 1; Huckaby, *Crisis at Central High*, 17; NYT, September 5, 1957, 1; *Southern School News*, October 1957, 1, and *Race Relations Law Reporter*, October 1957, 937–38, reprinted in Record and Record, *Little Rock, U.S.A.*, 37–38; Campbell and Pettigrew, *Christians in Racial Crisis*, 19–21; "Hats Off to the Women of Little Rock; Council of Church Women," CCY 74 (October 2, 1957): 1155–56.

76. Bates, *Long Shadow*, 63–69, 189–92; NYT, September 5, 1957, 20.

77. Quoted in Bates, *Long Shadow*, 189.

78. NYT, September 16, 1957, 13.

79. Ibid., September 21, 1957, 11.

80. Huckaby, *Crisis at Central High*, 180.

81. Bates, *Long Shadow*, 86–87; NYT, September 21, 1957, 1, 10–11; NYT, September 23, 1957, 13; NYT, September 24, 1957, 1, 18–19; NYT, September 25, 1957, 1, 14, 16; "Another Tragic Era?" 33–46.

82. Quoted in Campbell and Pettigrew, *Christians in Racial Crisis*, 24–25.

83. Quoted in NYT, September 30, 1957, 25; Eisenhower to Brown, September 29, 1957, reprinted in NYT, October 4, 1957, 9.

84. NYT, October 4, 1957, 9; "All Prayers for Little Rock's Prayers," CCY 74 (October 23, 1957): 1251; see also "Religion in Action," 30.

85. Campbell and Pettigrew, *Christians in Racial Crisis*, 33–35; NYT, October 11, 1957, 1.

86. Thomas F. Pettigrew, "The Church Dilemma and Social Action," address before the Episcopal Society for Cultural and Racial Unity, St. Augustine's College, Raleigh, N.C., December 29, 1959, 4, ESCRU Papers.

87. "South's Churchmen," 37; Campbell and Pettigrew, *Christians in Racial Crisis*, 110; Bates, *Long Shadow*, 192–95.

88. Julian N. Hartt, "Dallas Ministers on Desegregation," CCY 75 (May 21, 1958): 619–20; NYT, November 3, 1957, 84; NYT, November 23, 1958, 81; "A Stitch in Time," CCY 75 (February 26, 1958): 247; " 'Save Schools,' Urge Atlanta Ministers," CCY 75 (December 10, 1958): 1421; *Wall Street Journal*, October 27, 1957, 1, 16; "Church Accessories to the Crime," CCY 75 (January 8, 1958): 35–36; Alfred P. Klausler, "The Shame and the Glory," CCY 79 (August 15, 1962): 977–79; see B. Smith, *They Closed Their Schools*.

89. "Oppose Use of Churches to Defy Federal Law," CCY 75 (January 29, 1958): 124.

90. Quoted in "Virginians Are Told Segregation Is a Sin," CCY 75 (September 3, 1958): 990.

91. Quoted in Krause, "Rabbis and Negro Rights," 31–32.

92. Murray Friedman, "Virginia Jewry," 21–22.

93. "Virginia Clergy No Tender Plants," CCY 75 (October 22, 1958): 1196; Golden, "Jews and Gentiles," 406–7, 412; Dinnerstein, "A Note on Southern Attitudes toward Jews," 43–49.

94. Quoted in Blumberg, *One Voice*, 69.

95. Golden, "Jews and Gentiles," 412.

96. Vorspan, "The Dilemma of the Southern Jew," in Dinnerstein and Palsson, *Jews in the South*, 335; Reissman, "New Orleans Jewish Community," 110–23; Goldberg, "Changing Jewish Community of Dallas," 82–97.

97. Murray Friedman, "Virginia Jewry," 20.

98. Malev, "Jew of the South," 36–37; see also Murray Friedman, "One Episode in Southern Jewry's Response to Desegregation," 178.

99. Perlmutter, "Bombing in Miami," 498–99; Toby, "Bombing in Nashville," 385–87; Blumberg, *One Voice*, 55–73; Krause, "Rabbis and Negro Rights," 372–73; Dinnerstein,

"Southern Jewry and the Desegregation Crisis," 141; Shankman, "A Temple Is Bombed," 131–41.

100. Quoted in Shankman, "A Temple Is Bombed," 141, 138.

101. Edward E. Klein, "Memorial Tributes: Charles Mantinband," in Regner, *Yearbook of Central Conference of American Rabbis*, 85: 109 (hereafter *CCAR Yearbook*); Dinnerstein, "Southern Jewry," 238–39, 241–42; Krause, "Rabbis and Negro Rights," 40–42.

102. Silver, *Mississippi: The Closed Society*, 57.

103. Dinnerstein, "Southern Jewry," 142.

104. Vorspan and Lipman, *Justice and Judaism*, 107, 110.

105. John Wicklein, "Catholic Archbishop Backs New Orleans Integration," *NYT*, July 8, 1959, 20.

106. Quoted in Toby, "Bombing in Nashville," 387.

107. "The Blazing Cross," *Commonweal* 64 (June 1, 1956): 217; Wicklein, "Catholic Archbishop," 20.

108. Alfred J. Kronlage to Louis Twomey, December 7, 1955, Box 19, Folder 17, Twomey Papers.

109. Fairclough, *Race and Democracy*, 172–74.

110. Quoted in McNaspy, *At Face Value*, 73.

111. Edwin Pinac to Louis Twomey, June 6, 1955, Box 19, Folder 15; Emile Wagner to Edmund Bunn, S.J., November 10, 1955, Box 19, Folder 16; Emile Wagner to Joseph Francis Rummel, December 14, 1955, Box 19, Folder 17, Twomey Papers.

112. Milton Heimlich to Louis Twomey, November 24, 1955; Fook Wa Ko to Louis Twomey, November 23, 1955; Robert Farmer to Louis Twomey, November 22, 1955; Louis Twomey to Lester Dunn, November 28, 1955, all in Box 19, Folder 16; Louis Twomey to John O'Connor, December 16, 1955, Box 19, Folder 17, ibid.

113. Louis Twomey to John Soniat, May 26, 1955, Box 19, Folder 15, ibid; Fichter, *One-Man Research*, 78–81.

114. McNaspy, *At Face Value*, 78.

115. "Church Struggle in the Segregation Struggle," *CCY* 72 (June 1, 1955): 644; "New Orleans Archdiocese Fights Segregation," *CCY* 71 (November 3, 1954): 1325; Keenan, "Church Leaders," 378–79; Wicklein, "Catholic Archbishop," 20; LaFarge, *Catholic Viewpoint*, 101.

116. LaFarge, *Catholic Viewpoint*, 101–2.

117. Reverend John Reynolds, Archdiocesan Unit of the Catholic Committee of the South, "To Our Catholic Brothers and Sisters in Our Lady of Perpetual Help Parish!" December 17, 1955, Box 19, Folder 17, Twomey Papers.

118. Wicklein, "Catholic Archbishop," 20.

119. Bishop Jules B. Jeanmard to Our Lady of Lourdes Catholic Church, Erath, La., November 27, 1955, Box 19, Folder 17, Twomey Papers; Wicklein, "Catholic Archbishop," 20; Fichter, *One-Man Research*, 107, 81–82.

120. "The Blazing Cross," *Commonweal* 64 (June 1, 1956): 217; "A Gospel Still Strange and New," *CCY* 74 (August 21, 1957): 979; "Rome and New Orleans," *America* 97 (August 24, 1957): 518; Wicklein, "Catholic Archbishop," 20.

121. Quoted in Fichter, *One-Man Research*, 108.

122. Lillian Davenport to Joseph Fichter, June 12, 1956, and Kathy Schmidt to Joseph Fichter, June 1956, both in Box 46, Folder 7, Fichter Papers.

123. Wicklein, "Catholic Archbishop," 20; Osborne, *Segregated Covenant*, 82–83; "Three Heroes Honor New Orleans," *CCY* 77 (December 14, 1960): 1962; Dorothy Day, "Southern Pilgrimage," *Commonweal* 74 (March 31, 1961): 10–12.

124. Mathew Ahmann, "Catholics and Race," *Commonweal* (December 2, 1960): 247.

125. *NYT*, April 17, 1962, 1; "New Orleans Parochial Schools Desegregated," *CCY* 79 (April 11, 1962): 448–49; "Archbishop Excommunicates Segregationists," *CCY* 79 (May 2, 1962): 560–61; *NYT*, April 18, 1962, 1; "Catholic Schools Desegregate," *CCY* 79 (June 20, 1962): 768.

126. Fichter, *One-Man Research*, 107–8, 112; Kemper, "Catholic Integration," 1–22.

127. Quoted in Dinnerstein, "Southern Jewry," 237–38.

128. McNeill, "Georgia Minister," 55–57; McNeill, *God Wills Us Free*, 38–39, 45–59, 68–70, 87–89, 104–5, 137–38; McGill, "Agony of the Southern Minister," 16.

129. McNeill, "Georgia Minister," 57–58, 63–64.

130. McNeill, *God Wills Us Free*, 2; Morrison, "The Minister Who Lost His Pulpit," 34; "What Hope Have We?," 59.

131. Morrison, "Minister Who Lost His Pulpit," 34.

132. Quoted in McNeill, *God Wills Us Free*, 5.

133. "What Hope Have We?" 59.

134. McNeill, "So That You May Have Integrity," sermon delivered at the First Presbyterian Church, Columbus, Ga., on June 7, 1959, reprinted in Davies, *The Pulpit Speaks on Race*, 165–67, 169.

135. McGill, "Agony of the Southern Minister," 16; McNeill, *God Wills Us Free*, 166–70.

136. McNeill, *God Wills Us Free*, 186.

137. Ibid., 137.

138. Campbell and Pettigrew, *Christians in Racial Crisis*, 41–62; Thomas F. Pettigrew and Ernest Q. Campbell, "Men of God in Racial Crisis," *CCY* 75 (June 4, 1958): 663.

139. Quoted in *NYT*, July 14, 1958, 15.

140. Campbell and Pettigrew, *Christians in Racial Crisis*, 66–67.

141. Ibid., 66–67, 75–76; Campbell and Pettigrew, "Racial and Moral Crisis," 509–16.

142. Campbell and Pettigrew, *Christians in Racial Crisis*, 63, 66.

143. Rutenber, "Ministers and Social Ethics," 30, 33.

144. McNeill, *God Wills Us Free*, 137.

Chapter Two

1. M. L. King Jr., interview in *Playboy* (January 1965), quoted in Washington, *Testament of Hope*, 344.

2. Interviews with Paul Moore, Robert McAfee Brown, and William Sloane Coffin Jr.

3. Meier and Rudwick, *CORE*, 98–110; Branch, *Parting the Waters*, 272–25; W. D. Campbell, *Forty Acres*, 78.

4. See, for example, "Churchmen Defend Sit-In Student," *CCY* 80 (June 26, 1963): 821.

5. Oppenheimer, *Sit-In Movement*, 80.

6. Ibid., 80–82; "Unrest Grows among American Negroes," *CCY* 77 (February 24, 1960): 212–13.

7. Seabury, "Trendier than Thou," 39.

8. John Morris to Conference Registrants and Members, the Episcopal Society for Cultural and Racial Unity, February 3, 1960, ESCRU Papers.

9. *NYT*, March 6, 1960, and *Greensboro Daily News*, December 31, 1959, both excerpts in ESCRU pamphlets, ESCRU Papers.

10. Quoted in "Episcopalians Back Negroes," *CCY* 77 (March 16, 1960): 309.

11. Proudfoot, *Diary of a Sit-In*, 8–16.

12. "Kneel-In Demonstrations," *Commonweal* 73 (October 21, 1960): 86.

13. Oppenheimer, *Sit-In Movement*, 81; "Let Us Kneel-In Together," *CCY* 77 (August 24, 1960): 963–64.

14. Proudfoot, *Diary of a Sit-In*, 161–62.

15. Meier and Rudwick, *CORE*, 131–36; A. D. Morris, *Origins of the Civil Rights Movement*, 231; Peck, *Freedom Ride*, 89–99; Farmer, *Lay Bare the Heart*, 199; NYT, May 15, 1961, 1.

16. Quoted in NYT, May 26, 1961, 1.

17. Reprinted in NYT, May 25, 1961, 25.

18. Quoted in ibid.

19. NYT, April 23, 1961, 31.

20. James Forest, "Philip Berrigan: Disturber of Sleep," in Casey and Nobile, *Berrigans*, 166; F. Gray, *Divine Disobedience*, 64–65, 71–72; Osborne, *Segregated Covenant*, 21–35.

21. P. Berrigan, "The Challenge of Segregation," 597–604.

22. P. Berrigan, *No More Strangers*, 133–34. Berrigan refers to this incident in the third person, but later told James Forest that he had been the one giving the sermon. Forest, "Philip Berrigan," 167.

23. NYT, April 23, 1961, 31.

24. Philip Berrigan, "The Race Problem and the Christian Conscience," *Catholic Worker* (December 1961), quoted in Forest, "Philip Berrigan," 167–68.

25. Coffin, *Once to Every Man*, 151–52; Coffin quotation, NYT, May 25, 1961, 26.

26. Coffin interview; Coffin, *Once to Every Man*, 3–132.

27. "Man in the News: Bus-Riding Chaplain William Sloane Coffin, Jr.," NYT, May 25, 1961, 26.

28. Coffin, *Once to Every Man*, 143, 146.

29. "Crisis in Civil Rights," 15–17.

30. NYT, May 25, 1961, 26.

31. NYT, May 26, 1961, 1, 20.

32. Coffin interview.

33. NYT, May 27, 1961, 8; see also Coffin, "Why Yale Chaplain Rode," 54–55.

34. Coffin, *Once to Every Man*, 168–69.

35. Coffin interview.

36. Durr, *Outside the Magic Circle*, 302. Years later, Coffin discovered how active the Durrs had been and acknowledged that his stand had been insensitive. Coffin interview.

37. Brown, *Religion and Violence*, xii–xiii; Brown, *Creative Dislocation*, 19–21, 42, 54; Robert McAfee Brown, "A Decade of Discoveries and Dangers: How My Mind Has Changed, 1960–1970," CCY (January 14, 1970), reprinted in Geyer and Peerman, *Theological Crossings*, 15; Eisele, *Almost to the Presidency*, 117–18; see also Brown and Weigel, *An American Dialogue*.

38. Brown, "Theology as an Act of Grace," inaugural address as Auburn Professor of Systematic Theology at Union Theological Seminary, New York, October 1960, reprinted in Brown, *Pseudonyms of God*, 17, 21–22.

39. Brown interview.

40. Brown, *Creative Dislocation*, 20.

41. Ibid., 31–32; Brown interview; Brown, "Ecumenism behind Bars," *Presbyterian Life* (September 15, 1964), reprinted in Brown, *Pseudonyms of God* 167–68; Brown and Frank Randall, "The Freedom Riders: A Clergyman's View, An Historian's View," *Amherst College Alumni News*, 1961, reprinted as CORE pamphlet, quoted in Laue, *Direct Action*, 109.

42. Harold E. Fey, "Freedom Rides at N.C.C.," CCY 78 (June 21, 1961): 766–67.

43. "Two Statements from the Prayer Pilgrimage to the 60th General Convention of the Episcopal Church, September 1961," ESCRU Papers; Charles D. Kean, "Pressures on Episcopalians," CCY 78 (September 20, 1961): 1102–3.

44. Quoted in "To the Greater Glory," CCY 78 (October 4, 1961): 1164.

45. Merrill Orne Young, "For the Church's Sake," CCY 78 (November 1, 1961): 1301.

46. Boyd, *As I Live and Breathe*, 6–15, 12, 76–82, 110–16.

47. Louisiana State University *Daily Reveille*, February 25, 1959, 1, and Frederic Fost to Malcolm Boyd, April 21, 1959, both in Box 9, Folder 3, MBP.

48. Chaplain John F. Nau to Malcolm Boyd, May 18, 1959, Box 9, Folder 3, ibid.

49. Quoted in *Bethlehem Globe Times*, February 10, 1961, 1, Box 7, Folder 1, ibid.

50. *The Living Church* (April 23, 1961), 7, Box 7, Folder 1, ibid.

51. "Chaplain Resigns in Clerical Row," *CSU Collegian*, April 11, 1961, 1, Box 7, Folder 1, ibid.

52. Malcolm Boyd to Joseph Minnis, April 6, 1961, Box 7, Folder 1, ibid.

53. Boyd, *Gay Priest*, 2.

54. *NYT*, March 26, 1961, 72; "Episcopal Chaplain Resigns Post," *CCY* 78 (May 17, 1961): 614.

55. Miriam A. Luke to Malcolm Boyd, April 17, 1961; Bob Zoellner to Malcolm Boyd, April 11, 1961; and Mary Stone to Malcolm Boyd, n.d., all in Box 7, Folder 1, MBP.

56. Robert DeWitt to Malcolm Boyd, August 7, 1961, Box 9, Folder 6, ibid.

57. Clipping from Wayne State University *Daily Collegian*, n.d., Box 9, Folder 6, ibid.; "Two Statements," and "Sewanee Sit-Ins," both pamphlets in ESCRU Papers; Malcolm Boyd interview; "Sewanee Restaurant Excludes Negroes," *CCY* 78 (November 8, 1961): 1327.

58. "Two Statements," ESCRU Papers.

59. Quoted in *Detroit News*, September 17, 1961, 1, 20, clipping in Box 9, Folder 6, MBP.

60. John Morris, "A Report from Mississippi," May 25, 1962, ESCRU Papers; "Prayer Pilgrims Freed in Jackson," *CCY* 79 (June 6, 1962): 706; J. B. Morris, "ESCRU," 15 n. 12; John Morris interview; Malcolm Boyd interview.

61. Ellen Naylor Bouton and Thomas F. Pettigrew, "When a Priest Made a Pilgrimage," *CCY* 80 (March 20, 1963): 363–65.

62. John B. Morris to Randolph R. Claiborne Jr., November 11, 1963, ESCRU Papers; G. McMillan, "Silent White Ministers," 115.

63. Daniel Corrigan to Malcolm Boyd, July 21, 1964, and Malcolm Boyd to Daniel Corrigan, July 24, 1964, 1, 2, both in Box 17, Folder 1, MBP; *ESCRU Newsletter* (August 6, 1964), 6, ESCRU Papers.

64. G. McMillan, "Silent White Ministers," 115.

65. A. D. Morris, *Origins of the Civil Rights Movement*, 239–50; Carson, *In Struggle*, 56–65; interview with Laurie Pritchett in Raines, *My Soul Is Rested*, 361–63; Oates, *Let the Trumpet Sound*, 182–93; interviews with William Anderson and Burke Marshall in Hampton and Fayer, *Voices of Freedom*, 101–3, 109–10; *CCY* 79 (August 22, 1962): 1018.

66. *NYT*, August 30, 1962, 17; interview with Laurie Pritchett in Raines, *My Soul is Rested*, 364; "Act of Belief," 45.

67. "Act of Belief," 45; Will Campbell, "Perhaps, and Maybe," *CCY* 79 (September 19, 1962): 1133.

68. Quoted in *CCY* 79 (September 26, 1962): 1154–55.

69. "Let Us Kneel-In Together," *CCY* 77 (August 24, 1960): 963–64; see also Carlton Mabee, "Prepared for Arrest," *CCY* 78 (January 11, 1961): 52–53; W. D. Campbell, "The Sit-Ins," 14–18.

70. W. D. Campbell, *Race and Renewal*, 4–5.

71. W. Campbell, "Perhaps, and Maybe," 1133.

72. See R. F. Anderson, Reply, *CCY* 79 (November 14, 1962): 1395–96.

73. W. D. Campbell, "Vocation as Grace," 84.

74. W. D. Campbell, *Race and Renewal*, 47, 45, 24–25.

75. *NYT*, September 31, 1962, 1; Navasky, *Kennedy Justice*, 203–4; interview with Burke Marshall in Hampton and Fayer, *Voices of Freedom*, 118–19.

76. Quoted in Silver, *Mississippi: The Closed Society*, 55–57.

77. Edward E. Klein, "Memorial Tributes: Charles Mantinband," in Regner, *CCAR Yearbook*, 85: 109.

78. R. H. Barrett, *Integration at Ole Miss*, 97.

79. Quoted in *Mississippian*, October 1, 1962, 2.

80. R. H. Barrett, *Integration at Ole Miss*, 134.

81. "Concerned," 99; "One Nation Indivisible," CCY 79 (October 17, 1962): 1248–49; *NYT*, September 31, 1962, 1.

82. The Reverend Duncan Gray Jr., ". . . Who Tried to Redeem the Times," sermon given by the rector of St. Peter's Episcopal Church in Oxford, Miss., October 7, 1962, reprinted in *Reporter* 27 (November 8, 1962): 34.

83. "Concerned," 99.

84. Silver, "Mississippi: The Closed Society," 9.

85. Silver, *Running Scared*, 131.

86. "Forward Together," *Commonweal* 76 (July 13, 1962): 1395–96.

Chapter Three

1. Brown, *Creative Dislocation*, 52; Coffin, *Once to Every Man*, 218.

2. Heschel, *Man Is Not Alone*, 241.

3. Heschel, *God in Search of Man*, 296.

4. Kaplan, "Spiritual Radicalism of Abraham Joshua Heschel," 42.

5. Louis Finkelstein, "Three Meetings With Abraham Joshua Heschel," *America* 128 (March 10, 1973): 203; Heschel, *A Passion for Truth*, xiv; H. Susannah Heschel, "My Father," in Kasimow and Sherwin, *No Religion Is an Island*, 26–28; Sherman, *The Promise of Heschel*, 15. Heschel, *Man's Quest for God*, 147–51.

6. Heschel, "No Religion Is an Island," 117.

7. Sherman, *Promise of Heschel*, 15–18; H. S. Heschel, "My Father," 28.

8. Reinhold Niebuhr, "Masterly Analysis of Faith," *New York Herald Tribune Book Review*, April 1, 1951, quoted in Merkle, *Genesis of Faith*, 15.

9. Heschel, *The Prophets*, xviii, xvi, 16.

10. Eisendrath, *Can Faith Survive?*, 132–33; Samuel D. Soskin, "Report of the Committee on Justice and Peace," in Regner, *CCAR Yearbook*, 73: 62; "Religion and Race Meeting," *America* 108 (February 2, 1963): 159; Kyle Haselden, "Religion and Race," CCY 80 (January 30, 1963): 134; Ahmann, *Race*, vi–vii.

11. Abraham Joshua Heschel, "The Religious Basis of Equality of Opportunity," reprinted in Ahmann, *Race*, 55, 57, 63.

12. Martin Luther King Jr., "A Challenge to the Churches and Synagogues," reprinted in Ahmann, *Race*, 156–58; "An Appeal to the Conscience of the American People," reprinted in CCY 80 (January 30, 1963): 135.

13. Will Campbell, "The Inner Life of Church and Synagogue in Race Relations," reprinted in Ahmann, *Race*, 14, 19–20.

14. John LaFarge, S.J., "Religion and Race Meeting," *America* 108 (February 2, 1963): 159; "Historic Conference," *Commonweal* 77 (January 18, 1963): 426; Haselden, "Religion and Race," 133–35; Blank, "The Deliberations of the National Conference," 20–22, 30; "That Awful Fatalism," 66.

15. Stringfellow, *My People*, 136; Russell, *God's Lost Cause*, 104; Blank, "Deliberations," 20; Hedgeman, *Gift of Chaos*, 50.

16. Russell, *God's Lost Cause*, 104.

17. Boyd Mather, "Religion and Race: Local Efforts," CCY 80 (March 27, 1963): 412–14.

18. Willmar Thorkelson, "News of the Christian World," CCY 81 (April 1, 1964): 444–46.

The feature "News of the Christian World" was a weekly compilation of stories from the Religious News Service, and as such provided detailed accounts of local civil rights activities throughout the United States that were rarely covered in such depth, if mentioned at all, by other religious journals with a national circulation. W. W. Richardson, "News of the Christian World," *CCY* 81 (February 26, 1964): 284, 286; Charles D. Kean, "News of the Christian World," *CCY* 80 (July 10, 1963): 893–94 and *CCY* 80 (October 23, 1963): 1316, 1318; Bob Lear, "News of the Christian World," 80 *CCY* (October 30, 1963): 1344–46.

19. Thorkelson, "News of the Christian World," 444.

20. *NYT*, April 25, 1964, 25; Homer Jack, "Religion-State Conference on Civil Rights Legislation," *CCY* 81 (December 16, 1964): 1574; "Training Clergy and Laity for the Inner City," *CCY* 80 (March 20, 1963): 356; *Washington Post*, April 22, 1963, 5; "News of the Christian World—Segregation and Suburbia," *CCY* 80 (May 15, 1963): 654, 656; Jack A. Davis, "News of the Christian World," *CCY* 80 (July 10, 1963): 892; Carroll H. Lemon, "News of the Christian World," *CCY* 80 (July 3, 1963): 869; Mark Talney, "News of the Christian World," *CCY* 80 (August 7, 1963): 987; Gertrude Apel, "News of the Christian World," *CCY* 80 (September 25, 1963): 1183; Willmar L. Thorkelson, "News of the Christian World," *CCY* 80 (August 14, 1963): 1010–11, and *CCY* 80 (October 9, 1963): 1253–54; Alfred P. Klausler, "News of the Christian World," *CCY* 81 (January 22, 1964): 124–25; Osborne, *Segregated Covenant*, 221.

21. Campbell and Pettigrew, *Christians in Racial Crisis*, 172 n. 7.

22. The scholarship on the Birmingham campaign is enormous, but several works stand out for their balanced coverage not only of King's work there but of the indigenous leadership within the black community. See especially Fairclough, *To Redeem the Soul of America*, 111–39; Branch, *Parting the Waters*, 708–802; Garrow, *Bearing the Cross*, 230–50; Garrow, *Birmingham*.

23. "An Appeal for Law and Order and Common Sense," *CCY* 80 (February 6, 1963): 189–90.

24. Fairclough, *To Redeem the Soul of America*, 116.

25. Birmingham *News*, April 13, 1963, 2.

26. Quoted in Stephen C. Rose, "Test for Nonviolence," *CCY* 80 (May 29, 1963): 714–16.

27. M. L. King Jr., "Letter from Birmingham Jail," *CCY* 80 (June 12, 1963): 767–73.

28. Glen V. Wiberg to the Editors, *CCY* 80 (August 7, 1963): 986. Similar letters of praise compared King's work to the prison letters of St. Paul; the editors noted that none of the fifty letters they had received after publishing "Letter from Birmingham Jail" had been critical of the missive. For a comparison of King's letter and the Pauline epistles, see Snow, "Martin Luther King's Letter," 318–34.

29. Branch, *Parting the Waters*, 742, 745.

30. Fairclough, *To Redeem the Soul of America*, 117; King, *Why We Can't Wait*, 51–53; Evans, *The Provincials*, 322; Bloom, "Journey to Understanding," 11–13; Elovitz, *Century of Jewish Life in Dixie*, 170–71; Ungar, "To Birmingham and Back," 11.

31. Bloom, "Journey to Understanding," 13–14; Evans, *The Provincials*, 323.

32. Quoted in Elovitz, *Century of Jewish Life in Dixie*, 174.

33. Bloom, "Journey to Understanding," 15–16.

34. Branch, *Parting the Waters*, 809–13; Lewis, *King*, 217; *NYT*, May 25, 1963, 1.

35. Pratt, *Liberalization of American Protestantism*, 161–62; *NYT*, May 25, 1963, 1; *NYT*, May 26, 1963, 1; *NYT*, June 29, 1963, 1; Connie Corteau, "News of the Christian World," *CCY* 80 (June 26, 1963): 838.

36. *Interchurch News* 4 (June–July 1963): 6–7.

37. Harold E. Fey, "N.C.C. Acts on Racial Crisis," *CCY* 80 (June 19, 1963): 797; Will Campbell to Elbert Jean, September 23, 1963, in RG 6, Box 47, Folder 6, NCC Archives;

Egerton, *A Mind to Stay Here*, 21–22; Stephen C. Rose, "N.C.C. Visits Clarksdale," *CCY* 80 (September 11, 1963): 1106; Findlay, *Church People*, 35.

38. *NYT*, June 9, 1963, 1; *NYT*, June 29, 1963, 1; "Robert W. Spike: 1923–1966," *CC* 26 (November 14, 1966): 249–51; Hedgeman, *Gift of Chaos*, 77–78.

39. Spike, *Safe in Bondage*, 18.

40. *NYT*, June 29, 1963, 1.

41. *NYT*, July 5, 1963, 1, 44; Brackenridge, *Eugene Carson Blake*, 94; Eugene Carson Blake, "Law and Order and Christian Duty," sermon given at Riverside Presbyterian Church, New York City, n.d. [probably September 1963], reprinted in Davies, *Pulpit Speaks on Race*, 108–9; "Blake and Corrigan Lead Bias Protest," *CCY* 80 (July 17, 1963): 902; Thomas Mattingly, "Gwynn Oak," *America* 109 (August 10, 1963): 136–37.

42. *NYT*, July 5, 1963, 1, 44.

43. Ibid.

44. Ibid., 1; "Blake and Corrigan," 902; Mattingly, "Gwynn Oak," 136–37; "Catholics Honor Blake as Racial Reconciler," *CCY* 81 (January 29, 1964): 133.

45. *NYT*, August 29, 1963, 19.

46. Blake, "Law and Order," 110–11; Cox, "'New Breed,'" 136–37, 139; Eugene Carson Blake, "The Church in the Next Decade," *CC* 26 (February 21, 1966): 17.

47. Rose, "N.C.C. Visits Clarksdale," 1104–6.

48. *NYT*, June 10, 1963, 20; *NYT*, June 18, 1963, 20; *NYT*, June 20, 1963, 1; G. Merrill Lenox, "News of the Christian World," *CCY* 80 (September 11, 1963): 1112; Heath, *Decade of Disillusionment*, 113–14; Findlay, "Religion and Politics in the Sixties," 71–77.

49. *NYT*, June 23, 1963, 1; Hedgeman, *Gift of Chaos*, 63–71, 80; Pratt, *Liberalization of American Protestantism*, 166.

50. Hedgeman, *The Trumpet Sounds*, 178.

51. *NYT*, July 26, 1963, 12.

52. "Integrate the Integration March!" *CCY* 80 (August 7, 1963): 973; "Marching Orders," *CCY* 80 (August 21, 1963): 1021–22; "Appeal on March," reprinted in *NYT*, August 26, 1963, 18.

53. Gentile, *March on Washington*, 171–75; Forman, *Black Revolutionaries*, 333–35; Garrow, *Bearing the Cross*, 283; Mills, "Heard and Unheard Speeches," 289–91. The original, unrevised speech was reprinted in *Liberation* 8 (September 1963): 8; excerpts appeared in *NYT*, August 29, 1963, 16, 20.

54. Forman, *Black Revolutionaries*, 335–36; M. King, *Freedom Song*, 183–85; Stone, "March on Washington," *I. F. Stone's Weekly* (September 16, 1963), reprinted in I. F. Stone, *Time of Torment*, 123; Malcolm X with Haley, *Autobiography*, 278–81.

55. Russell Baker, "Capital Is Occupied by a Gentle Army," *NYT*, August 29, 1963, 17.

56. *NYT*, August 29, 1963, 19.

57. Quoted in ibid., 21.

58. Charles D. Kean, "News of the Christian World," *CCY* 80 (August 14, 1963): 1014; "The March on Washington," 1135–36; N. O'Gorman, "Freedom March," 16–21; Gentile, *March on Washington*, 235–36.

59. Stringfellow, *My People*, 139.

60. Harold Fey, "Revolution without Hatred," *CCY* 80 (September 11, 1963): 1094–95; *NYT*, August 29, 1963, 1.

61. James Reston, "The First Significant Test of the Freedom March," *NYT*, August 30, 1963, 20.

62. *Wall Street Journal*, September 6, 1963, 9.

63. Harold E. Fey, "Churches Meet Racial Crisis," *CCY* 80 (December 18, 1963): 1572–73; Findlay, "Religion and Politics in the Sixties," 71–77; Whalen and Whalen, *Longest Debate*, 164–65.

Chapter Four

1. Heschel, "The White Man Is on Trial," reprinted in *Insecurities of Freedom*, 101–3, 109–11.

2. Hadden, *Gathering Storm*, 122–23.

3. O. M. Walton, "News of the Christian World," *CCY* 81 (March 25, 1964): 412–13; Klunder, "My Husband Died for Democracy," 27–31; Bruce Klunder, "A Death and Life Matter," in Davies, *Pulpit Speaks on Race*, 84–85. Not everyone was impressed by the clergyman's death. When a reporter asked Malcolm X his opinion of Klunder's sacrifice, the minister of the Nation of Islam replied that blacks were "not going to stand up and applaud any contribution made by some individual white person. . . . What he did. . . . Hooray, hooray, hooray." Too many blacks had been murdered over the years, he continued. "It's time that some white people started dying in this thing. If you'll forgive me . . . for saying so, but many more beside he are going when the wagon comes." Malcolm X, interview at the Militant Labor Forum, Palm Gardens, N.Y., April 8, 1964, reprinted in Breitman, *By Any Means Necessary*, 25.

4. Hadden, *Gathering Storm*, 124–25; O. M. Walton, "News of the Christian World," *CCY* 81 (May 6, 1964): 616, 618–19; M. K. Sanders, "Conversations with Saul Alinsky, Part II," 52; W. C. Martin, *Christians in Conflict*, 1–19.

5. Alfred P. Klausler, "News of the Christian World," *CCY* 81 (July 29, 1964): 972; Osborne, *Segregated Covenant*, 207; *ESCRU Newsletter* (March 1, 1964), 11, ESCRU Papers; Alfred P. Klausler, "News of the Christian World," *CCY* 81 (April 22, 1964): 532–33; Alfred P. Klausler, "News of the Christian World," *CCY* 81 (July 29, 1964): 972; Elsie T. Culver, "News of the Christian World," *CCY* 81 (August 12, 1964): 1020–21; Elsie T. Culver, "News of the Christian World," *CCY* 81 (January 8, 1964): 57–58; "Churchmen Admonish West Coast Realtors," *CCY* 81 (January 15, 1964): 70; Bruce L. Williams, "News of the Christian World," *CCY* 81 (January 15, 1964): 93–94; "Crucial Questions for November 4," *CCY* 81 (October 21, 1964): 1291–92; Robert McAfee Brown, "Spotlight on California," *CCY* 81 (September 30, 1964): 1203, 1204.

6. Quinley, *Prophetic Clergy*, 104–6; pastor quoted in Philip Wogaman, "California Churches in the Aftermath of Defeat," *CCY* 82 (February 3, 1965): 139–41.

7. Hadden, *Gathering Storm*, 31; Quinley, *Prophetic Clergy*, 213–14; Osborne, *Segregated Covenant*, 226–27; "Priest Appeals to Rome," *CCY* 81 (July 1, 1964): 852–53; DuBay, *Human Church*, 71, 171, 177; *NYT*, August 10, 1966, 84.

8. See Winter, *Suburban Captivity of the Churches*; Berger, *Noise of Solemn Assemblies*.

9. Massie, "Grandmother Peabody," 76; Hester H. Campbell to the Editors, *Harper's Magazine* 230 (March 1965): 6.

10. Coffin interview.

11. Massie, "Grandmother Peabody," 76; Colburn, *Racial Change*, 164–65, 173; *NYT*, April 1, 1964, 1; Henri A. Stines, "St. Augustine, Trinity Church and a Eucharist," *ESCRU Newsletter* (August 6, 1964), 5, ESCRU Papers.

12. Coffin interview.

13. *NYT*, April 1, 1964, 1; Massie, "Grandmother Peabody," 76; Robert W. Hartley, "A Long, Hot Summer: The St. Augustine Racial Disorders of 1964," in Garrow, *St. Augustine*, 36–37; Vorspan, "In St. Augustine," 15–17.

14. Rabbis Eugene Borowitz, Balfour Brickner, Israel Dresner, Michael Robinson, Allen Secher, et al., "Why We Went," *CCY* 81 (August 26, 1964): 1061–62.

15. Vorspan, "In St. Augustine," 19.

16. Oates, *Let the Trumpet Sound*, 292; Borowitz et al., "Why We Went," 1062.

17. Fairclough, *To Redeem the Soul of America*, 189–90; Colburn, *Racial Change*, 100–110; Findlay, "Religion and Politics," 79–88; Hedgeman, *Gift of Chaos*, 104, 111–12.

18. G. McMillan, "Silent White Ministers," 22.

19. Haselden, "11 A.M. Sunday Is Our Most Segregated Hour," 9.

20. Whalen and Whalen, *Longest Debate*, 165; Robert W. Spike, "In the Midst of Revolution," *CC* 24 (June 8, 1964): 115.

21. *NYT*, April 29, 1964, 1, 29; "Religious Leaders Demand Civil Rights Bill," *CCY* 81 (May 13, 1964): 631.

22. "Lincoln Memorial Seminary," *America* 110 (May 9, 1964): 620; "NCC Calls Assembly on Civil Rights," *CCY* 81 (April 22, 1964): 509; Hedgeman, *Gift of Chaos*, 110; *NYT*, April 29, 1964, 1, 29; *NYT*, June 11, 1964, 1; *NYT*, July 3, 1964, 1.

23. Humphrey, *Education of a Public Man*, 282; Findlay, "Religion and Politics," 88–89.

24. Senate, Statement by Senator Richard B. Russell.

25. Senate, Statement by Senator John Stennis of Mississippi. By August, congregations in a handful of denominations had begun to withhold funds earmarked for the NCC from their church boards; two Presbyterian churches in South Carolina voted to withhold all funds from the Presbyterian Church in the U.S. for as long as the denomination was a member of the NCC. *NYT*, August 10, 1964, 17.

26. *NYT* (Western ed.), January 19, 1963, 4; Silver, *Mississippi: The Closed Society*, 59; G. McMillan, "Silent White Ministers," 114; "Methodist Ministers Shatter Vacuum," *CCY* 80 (February 20, 1963): 229–30; Hilton, *Delta Ministry*, 177; "Denies Right to Go to Church," *CCY* 80 (October 30, 1963): 1324–25; *NYT*, June 29, 1963, 1, 20.

27. Salter, *Jackson, Mississippi*, 4, 85–178; "Divided Flocks in Jackson," *CCY* 80 (November 27, 1963): 1470; Moody, *Coming of Age*, 263–71, 379.

28. Moody, *Coming of Age*, 283–85.

29. "Divided Flocks," 1469–70; Campbell and Rogers, *Mississippi*, 205; "Denies Right to Go to Church," *CCY* 80 (October 30, 1963): 1324–25; Spike, *Freedom Revolution*, 58; Cunningham, *Agony at Galloway*, 51–52; "Demonstration 'Defused' by Methodist Bishops," *CCY* 80 (December 4, 1963): 1489–90; "Racists Challenge Methodists," *CCY* 81 (April 8, 1964): 454; James K. Mathews, "Easter in Jackson," *CCY* 81 (April 15, 1964): 478–80; Tyler Thompson, "Another Pilgrimage to Jackson," *CCY* 81 (April 22, 1964): 511–12.

30. Carson, *In Struggle*, 97–98; "Role of the National Council," 10–12; "Churchmen and the Challenge," 12, 14; Stephen Rose, "The Churches and Mississippi," *CCY* 81 (July 15, 1964): 909–10; letter from "Mike," June 18, 1964, in Sutherland, *Letters From Mississippi*, 9; M. King, *Freedom Song*, 424.

31. "Role of the National Council," 13; Spike, "Mississippi—An Ecumenical Ministry," 17–19; Thomas, "Meaning of the Summer for the Church," 22; "The Pulpit v. the Bench," 23; Arthur Lelyveld, Report of the Committee on Justice and Peace, in Regner, *CCAR Yearbook*, 75: 65; Good, *The Trouble I've Seen*, 107; Lawrence Minear, "Hattiesburg: Toward Reconciliation," *CCY* 81 (September 9, 1964): 1115–16; *ESCRU Newsletter* (March 1, 1964), 1, ESCRU Papers; The Right Reverend Paul Moore Jr., "A Long Hot Week," 1, 3, unpublished manuscript, Box 40, Folder 1, MBP.

32. Konolige and Konolige, *Power of Their Glory*, 72.

33. Moore, *Take a Bishop Like Me*, 6–7; *NYT*, March 25, 1989, 29; Paul Moore Jr., "War Diary, August–October 1942," (written in spring of 1943), 8, Box 40, Folder 1, MBP; Paul Moore Jr. interview; Sanderson, *Church Serves the Changing City*, 89–90, 94–99; Dawley, *Story of the General Theological Seminary*, 341; "Bishop Moore," 77; Boyd, *Gay Priest*, 56–58, 63. General Theological Seminary had a reputation for social conservatism, and was not seen as "a 'relevant' place for any self-respecting liberal to enroll," recalled a GTS graduate. His rector, himself a graduate of the seminary, tried to disabuse him of any ideas that seminarians were not involved in the community. "He and his friends had been very engaged with the neighborhood when they were students at General. In fact, not only had he been able to attend the *opera* and the *ballet* almost every week he was in school, but he

was always able to find a group of seminarians to go with him. As far as he was concerned, General was a *very* socially engaged place!!" Gardiner H. Shattuck Jr., to the author, March 10, 1996.

34. Moore interview; *ESCRU Newsletter* (August 6, 1964), 4, ESCRU Papers.

35. Moore, "A Long Hot Week," 2–4, MBP.

36. James Findlay, "In Keeping with the Prophets: The Mississippi Summer of 1964," *CCY* 105 (June 8–15, 1988): 574–76; see also selected letters in Sutherland, *Letters From Mississippi*, 152–54. For a more extensive description of the work of the NCC in both the Mississippi Freedom Summer and the Delta Ministry, see Findlay, *Church People*, 76–168.

37. Findlay, "In Keeping with the Prophets," 574–75; Eric D. Blanchard, "The Delta Ministry," *CCY* 82 (March 17, 1965): 338; Moore interview; von Hoffman, *Mississippi Notebook*, 64–78. For more information on the Heffners, see H. Carter, *So the Heffners Left McComb*.

38. "Beauty for Ashes," 61.

39. M. King, *Freedom Song*, 390–91; Blanchard, "The Delta Ministry," 338; Letters from Dave and Larry, July 10 and August 7, 1964, in Sutherland, *Letters From Mississippi*, 122–26; Braiterman, "Mississippi Marranos," 34–35; quoted in *NYT*, August 10, 1964, 1, 17.

40. *NYT*, August 23, 1964, 1, 81.

41. Dittmer, *Local People*, 272–302, 394; Findlay, *Church People*, 116.

42. Robert McAfee Brown, "Ecumenism Behind Bars," originally published in *Presbyterian Life* (September 15, 1964), reprinted in Brown, *Pseudonyms of God*, 169, 171–72.

43. Schulz, "Delta Ministry," 31; "The Delta Ministry," 8; Hilton, *Delta Ministry*, 32–34; "Campaign Opens on Poverty in South," *CCY* 81 (March 11, 1964): 325–26.

44. Schulz, "Delta Ministry," 31–32; Hilton, *Delta Ministry*, 13–16, 44–46; "The Delta Ministry," 8; Cobb, "'Somebody Done Nailed Us on the Cross,'" 917–22, 927; Findlay, *Church People*, 111–12, 125–31.

45. Findlay, *Church People*, 129, 147, 152; Hilton, *Delta Ministry*, 68–88, 163–65; *NYT*, February 2, 1966, 18; "Curbing the Delta Ministry," 84; Cobb, "Somebody Done Nailed Us on the Cross," 928–29; Wilmina Rowland, "How It Is in Mississippi," *CCY* 82 (March 17, 1965): 340–42; Cunningham, *Agony at Galloway*, 61–67.

46. *ESCRU Newsletter*, January 10, 1965, 1, and March 14, 1965, 1, both in ESCRU Papers; "Council Rescinds Restrictions," *CCY* 82 (March 10, 1965): 293–94; Thomas Cooper, "News of the Christian World," *CCY* 82 (March 17, 1965): 345.

47. Hilton, *Delta Ministry*, 167.

48. Edward J. Pendergrass, "Analysis of Program of Delta Ministry," April 27, 1966, reprinted in Howell, *Freedom City*, 99.

49. Findlay, *Church People*, 140–47; Moore quote on 145.

50. "Curbing the Delta Ministry," 84; quoted in Hilton, *Delta Ministry*, 168.

51. Findlay, *Church People*, 146–57; Dittmer, *Local People*, 369–73.

52. Quoted in Leon Howell, "The Delta Ministry," *CC* 26 (August 8, 1966): 189.

53. Pratt, *Liberalization of American Protestantism*, 177; Findlay, *Church People*, 158–59.

54. "Good Will," 84; Egerton, *A Mind to Stay Here*, 21–22; R. F. Martin, "Critique of Southern Society," 79–80; W. D. Campbell, "Vocation as Grace," 84.

55. Statement Adopted by the Committee of Southern Churchmen, Nashville, Tenn., February 6, 1964, reprinted in *Katallagete* 1 (Winter 1967–68), back cover.

56. Quoted in Egerton, *A Mind to Stay Here*, 22. Although there are few analytical studies of Campbell's religious philosophy, descriptive literature about him abounds. See, for example, Connelly, *Will Campbell and the Soul of the South*, and Frady, *Southerners*, 368–73.

Chapter Five

1. Indicative of the strong feelings against socially active ministers was a letter by a San Francisco native who was extremely critical of ministers willing to protest on behalf of civil rights but not in opposition to the recent Supreme Court ruling banning Bible-reading in public schools. "A lot of Christian people are waiting to see if all those 'brave' preachers who participated so enthusiastically in Negro push-ins and shove-ins in bus depots and hamburger stands will not be staging pray-ins and Bible read-ins in public schools," the letter ran. "If not, then everybody will know what some people have been suspecting for quite a while—that those 'brave' 'liberal' preachers of yours worship the Negro, not Jesus Christ." Dorothy H. Futch, letter to the editor, *CCY* 80 (August 21, 1963): 1032.

2. Fairclough, *To Redeem the Soul of America*, 237–41; interview with Richard Valeriani in Raines, *My Soul Is Rested*, 371–72.

3. "Selma Program," n.d. [probably February–March 1965], 1–2; Ralph Smeltzer to A. M. Secrest, February 7, 1965; Report to the National Council of Churches Commission, February 18, 1965; John M. Pratt, President, Commission on Religion and Race, "Report on Fact-Finding Trip to Selma, Alabama," October 1, 1963, 3–4, all in RES.

4. "Selma Program," 3–5, RES; John Pratt to Ralph Smeltzer, December 10, 1963, 3, RES; Ralph Smeltzer interview with John Newton, November 26, 1963, RES; Ouellet, "Testimony of a Selma Pastor," 22.

5. Ralph Smeltzer interview with John Newton, November 26, 1963, and Ralph E. Smeltzer, "My Developing Strategy and Plans," (October 28, 1963), RES; Sappington, *Brethren Social Policy*, 146–47, 172–75; Richard A. Bollinger, "Church of the Brethren Annual Conference," *CCY* 80 (July 24, 1963): 941–42. For a full account of Smeltzer's discussions and negotiations with black and white civic leaders, see Longenecker, *Selma's Peacemaker*.

6. "Selma Program," 1–2; Report to the National Council of Churches Commission, February 18, 1965; Ralph Smeltzer to W. Ray Kyle, February 12, 1964; Ralph Smeltzer interview with Claude C. Brown, January 17, 1964; "Two Presbyterian Ministers Allege Beating in Camden," *Montgomery Advertiser*, May 13, 1964; Ralph Smeltzer to Dr. Kenneth Neigh, Board of National Missions, United Presbyterian Church, January 14, 1965, all in RES.

7. Ralph Smeltzer, "My Developing Strategy and Plans," (November 28, 1963; January 19, 1964; February 14, 1964; January 29, 1964; January 15, 1964), RES.

8. Chris Heinz to Norman Baugher, July 16, 1964; Ralph Smeltzer interviews with John Newton (November 26, 1963) and Frank T. Mathews (November 27, 1963); Ralph Smeltzer to Art Lewis, October 9, 1964, all in RES.

9. Ralph Smeltzer to Annalee Stewart, September 29, 1964; Ralph Smeltzer interview with George Kerlin, November 23, 1963, both in RES.

10. Ralph Smeltzer interview with Frank T. Mathews, November 27, 1963, RES.

11. Ralph Smeltzer interview with John Newton, November 26, 1963, RES.

12. Ralph Smeltzer interview with Maurice Ouellet, November 27, 1963, RES.

13. Ibid.

14. Ouellet, "Testimony of a Selma Pastor," 21.

15. Ralph Smeltzer interview with Maurice Ouellet, November 27, 1963, RES.

16. Ibid.

17. Chestnut and Cass, *Black in Selma*, 184.

18. Ibid.; Ralph Smeltzer interview with Claude C. Brown, January 17, 1964, RES.

19. Form letter from James G. Clark Jr., Sheriff of Dallas County, to white churches, March 11, 1964; Ralph Smeltzer notes, March 24, March 15, 1964, all in RES.

20. Ralph Smeltzer interviews with John Newton, March 23, 24, and May 6, 1964; Ralph Smeltzer, telephone interview with John Newton, July 6, 1964, all in RES.

21. *Selma Times-Journal*, December 30, 1964, RES.

22. Ralph Smeltzer interview with Robert Spike, January 3, 1965, RES; quoted in Garrow, *Protest at Selma*, 4.

23. Quoted in Fairclough, *To Redeem the Soul of America*, 228.

24. Ralph Smeltzer interview with John Newton, January 1, 1965; telephone interview with John Newton, January 14, 1965, both in RES.

25. *Selma Times-Journal*, January 24, 1965, RES.

26. "A Proud Image Defamed," reprinted in *Selma Times- Journal*, February 2, 1965, RES.

27. *NYT*, January 26, 1965, 1; *Washington Post*, January 26, 1965, 1; "January to May 1965," 3; Fairclough, *To Redeem the Soul of America*, 237–39.

28. *NYT*, March 8, 1965, 20; Fager, *Selma, 1965*, 87–88.

29. *NYT*, March 9, 1965, 1; Oates, *Let the Trumpet Sound*, 336–37; Fager, *Selma, 1965*, 86–90.

30. Hinckle and Welsh, "Five Battles," 28, 36; Fager, *Selma, 1965*, 98; John B. Morris, "The Siege of Selma," *ESCRU Newsletter*, March 14, 1965, 5, ESCRU Papers.

31. *NYT*, March 11, 1965, 21; G. Merrill Lenox, "News of the Christian World," *CCY* 82 (April 21, 1965): 506–8; George B. Leonard, "Journey of Conscience: Midnight Plane to Alabama," *Nation* 200 (May 10, 1965): 502–4; *NYT*, March 8, 1965, 20; *NYT*, March 9, 1965, 1; M. L. King Jr., "Behind the Selma March," 16–17, 57; Kopkind, "Selma," 7–9; Morris, "Siege of Selma," 5.

32. Morris, "Siege of Selma," 5.

33. Ibid.; *NYT*, March 9, 1965, 1, 23; "January to May," 3; Martin Marty and Dean Peerman, "Selma: Sustaining the Momentum," *CCY* 82 (March 24, 1965): 358–60.

34. Brown interview; Arthur Lelyveld, Report of the Committee on Justice and Peace, in Regner, *CCAR Yearbook*, 75: 66; Moore interview; Boyd interview; and the following documents from Box 18, Folder 1, MBP: Paul Moore to Malcolm Boyd, October 27, 1964; "Report of the Rev. Malcolm Boyd," September 27, 1965; Paul Moore to Malcolm Boyd, November 30, 1964; Paul Moore to the Right Reverend William Creighton, Malcolm Boyd, the Reverend John B. Morris, et al., November 30, 1964. The nine-part series appeared in *Ave Maria* in 1965, beginning with the January 16 issue and ending with the March 13 issue; see also Malcolm Boyd, "The Battle of McComb," *CCY* 81 (November 11, 1964): 1398, 1400–1402, 1404.

35. *NYT*, March 11, 1965, 20; Bishop John B. Coburn, memorial address; Eagles, *Outside Agitator*, 1–27.

36. Brown interview.

37. Quoted in "Pen Ultimate," *CCY* 82 (March 31, 1965): 415; "Electric Charges," 19–20; "Central Point," 24; "When Clergy Protest," 5.

38. O. Sullivan, "Selma Aftermath," 16; "Selma, Civil Rights, and the Church Militant," 76; John B. Morris, "St. Paul's: More Shame in Selma," *ESCRU Newsletter* (March 14, 1965), 8, ESCRU Papers; quoted in Wren, "Turning Point," 31.

39. "Central Point," 25; *NYT*, March 10, 1965, 1.

40. *NYT*, March 11, 1965, 1, 20; *NYT*, March 12, 1965, 18; Margaret Hatch, "Report on Burwell Infirmary, Selma, Alabama," May 11, 1965, 1–2, RES.

41. Hatch, "Report on Burwell Infirmary," 1–2, RES; *NYT*, March 11, 1965, 20.

42. Sister Thomas Marguerite, "Nuns at Selma," *America* 112 (April 3, 1965): 454–56; "Mother Cecilia's Revolt," 45–46; "Clergy and Nuns March . . . ," *America* 112 (March 27, 1965): 411; Hinckle and Welsh, "Five Battles," 21.

43. *NYT*, March 21, 1965, 1.

44. *NYT*, March 11, 1965, 1, 21.

45. Quoted in *NYT*, March 13, 1965, 12.

46. Moore interview; *NYT*, March 12, 1965, 18; "Bishop Moore," 77; Senate, Senator Scott, "Senator Scott Lauds Role of Episcopal Church."

47. Moore interview; Stolley, "Inside the White House," 34–35; *NYT*, March 13, 1965, 1, 12.

48. *NYT*, March 13, 1965, 12.

49. *NYT*, March 12, 1965, 1; *Boston Globe*, March 15, 1965, 1; *NYT*, March 13, 1965, 11; "An Appeal for the James Reeb Fund," advertisement in *New Republic* 152 (March 27, 1965): 2; "To Succor the Suffering," CCY 82 (March 24, 1965): 357; *NYT*, March 16, 1965, 1; Appeal to Ministers of the Presbyterian Church in the U.S. from the Board of Christian Education, Presbyterian Church in the United States, Division of Christian Action, March 18, 1965, RES.

50. Riley, "Who Is Jimmie Lee Jackson?" 9.

51. Quoted in Carson, *In Struggle*, 161.

52. M. L. King Jr., *Where Do We Go from Here*, 34.

53. Garrow, *Protest at Selma*, 96.

54. U.S. Congress, House, Statements by Representatives Andrews of Alabama and Williams of Mississippi.

55. Guy Talese, "Selma: Bitter City in the Eye of a Storm," *NYT*, March 14, 1965, 63.

56. *NYT*, December 11, 1965, 1.

57. Ralph Smeltzer interview with John Newton, March 11, 1965, RES.

58. John Newton to Nick B. Williams, Editor, *Los Angeles Times*, March 3, 1965, ibid.

59. John Newton to John Calvin, Easter 1965, reprinted in *City Church—South* 1 (May 10, 1965): 1, ibid.

60. Mary McGrory, "So Much Christian Unity in Selma," *America* 112 (April 3, 1965): 448; *NYT*, March 16, 1965, 1; Daniel Berrigan, "Selma and Sharpeville," *Commonweal* 82 (April 9, 1965): 71–72; Alexander, "The Feminine Eye," 28; Fager, *Selma, 1965*, 132–34.

61. C. S. King, *My Life With Martin Luther King, Jr.*, 277; *Life* 58 (March 26, 1965); Reinhold Niebuhr, "Civil Rights Climax in Alabama," *CC* 25 (April 5, 1965): 61; "Selma, Civil Rights, and the Church Militant," 76; McGrory, "So Much Christian Unity," 448; Fager, *Selma, 1965*, 124, 129–30.

62. Berrigan, "Selma and Sharpeville," 72.

63. *NYT*, March 18, 1965, 1; Roy Reed, "Selma Arrests 350, Mainly White Visitors, Near Mayor's Home," *NYT*, March 20, 1965, 20.

64. Quoted in Benjamin Epstein and Lester Waldman, Notes on a Visit to Selma, Montgomery and Birmingham, March 18–21, 1965, Anti-Defamation League of B'nai B'rith, unpublished report, RES.

65. Heschel, "My Father," in *No Religion Is an Island*, 35.

66. *NYT*, March 20, 1965, 13.

67. *NYT*, June 2, 1965, 29.

68. *NYT*, March 21, 1965, 1; Fager, *Selma, 1965*, 142–45.

69. Epstein and Waldman, Notes on a Visit to Selma, RES; Wiesel, *All Rivers Run to the Sea*, 353; *NYT*, March 22, 1965, 1; Good, "Beyond the Bridge," 1.

70. *NYT*, March 22, 1965, 1; Good, "Beyond the Bridge," 1; John Newton to John Calvin, *City Church—South*, 1, RES.

71. Epstein and Waldman, Notes on a Visit to Selma, RES; Wren, "Turning Point," 34–35; "Churchmen in Selma," *ESCRU Newsletter* (April 4, 1965), ESCRU Papers.

72. Epstein and Waldman, Notes on a Visit to Selma, RES; Fager, *Selma, 1965*, 159–60; Wren, "Turning Point for the Church," 36.

73. Wren, "Turning Point," 32–37; "Selma, Civil Rights, and the Church Militant," 75–

78; Hinckle and Welsh, "Five Battles," 36–40; McGrory, "So Much Christian Unity," 448; Niebuhr, "Civil Rights Climax," 61.

74. Sullivan, "Integration Could Destroy Rural Mississippi," 10, 15.

75. D. Lawrence, "Is the Clergyman Changing His Role?" 116; Jerry Falwell, "Ministers and Marches," sermon delivered at Thomas Road Baptist Church, Lynchburg, Virginia, March 21, 1965, reprinted in Young, *God's Bullies*, 313.

76. U.S., Congress, House, Representative Frank Horton of New York, 89th Cong., 1st sess., April 7, 1965, *Congressional Record* 111, tearsheet in MBP.

77. Malcolm Boyd, "My Freedom Trip Report," (July 1965), unpublished manuscript, Box 2, Folder 3, MBP.

78. John Newton to John Calvin, *City Church—South*, 1–2, RES.

79. Boyd, *As I Live and Breathe*, 155; Coburn, Memorial Address; Eagles, *Outside Agitator*, 82–87.

80. Jonathan Myrick Daniels, "A Burning Bush," *The New Hampshire Churchman* 17 (June 1965), reprinted as ESCRU pamphlet, ESCRU Papers.

81. Ralph Smeltzer interview with Jonathan Daniels, April 14, 1965, RES.

82. Daniels, "A Burning Bush," ESCRU Papers.

83. Webb and Nelson, *Selma, Lord, Selma*, 51.

84. Daniels, "A Burning Bush," ESCRU Papers; Ralph Smeltzer interview with Jonathan Daniels, April 14, 1965; Ralph Smeltzer to Lee Whipple, February 24, 1965; Ralph Smeltzer, "Selma Future Program Proposals," April 21, 1965; Ralph Smeltzer interview with Walter Ellwanger, April 17, 1965; David Smith to Ralph Smeltzer, June 28, 1965; David Smith, "The Pulse of Selma," unpublished report, May 18, 1965; David Smith to Ralph Smeltzer, July 7, 1965, all in RES.

85. John Cogley, "Archbishop Ousts Selma Priest Who Aided Voter Registration Drive," *NYT*, June 26, 1965, 13; Sullivan, "Selma Aftermath," 16.

86. Cogley, "Archbishop Ousts Selma Priest," 13.

87. David Smith to Ralph Smeltzer, August 1, 1965; August 16, 1965; Ralph Smeltzer interview with David Smith, August 24, 1965, RES; Ruby Sales interview in *Voices of Freedom*, 273–74; Eagles, *Outside Agitator*, 169–79.

88. Ruby Sales interview in *Voices of Freedom*, 274–75; Eagles, *Outside Agitator*, 169–79; *NYT*, August 21, 1965, 9.

89. *NYT*, August 21, 1965, 9.

90. *NYT*, August 26, 1965, 20.

91. Coburn, Memorial Address.

92. Boyd, "On Murder," manuscript draft for *Now*, regular column in *Yale Daily News*, Box 2, Folder 6; see also Malcolm Boyd, "A Student Saint," Commencement Address at Mercy College of Detroit, April 28, 1973, in Box 27, Folder 1, MBP; Campbell, *Dragonfly*, 222, 228, 242–50; *Episcopal Times*, October 1991, 14.

93. Eagles, *Outside Agitator*, 241, 248; see also two-page reprint of newspaper stories regarding the verdict in ESCRU Papers.

94. Garrow, *Protest at Selma*, 148.

95. "Selma, Civil Rights, and the Church Militant," 78.

96. Spike, "Our Churches' Sin," 30.

97. Cox, *Secular City*, 38–59, 68–84, 105–20.

98. See J. Levy, *Cesar Chavez*; M. Miller, "Strike in the Grapes," 10–15; Sister Mary Peter Traxler, "The Ministry of Presence," in *Split-Level Lives*, 1–7; Eugene Carson Blake, "The Church in the Next Decade," *CC* 26 (February 21, 1966): 15–18; Cox, " 'New Breed,' " 135–50; J. Morris, "Racism in Southern Africa," 17–25.

99. The Rev. John B. Morris, Memorandum to "Various Friends & Colleagues," April 28, 1966, 2, ESCRU Papers.

Chapter Six

1. Lemann, *Promised Land*, 171–72.

2. Fairclough, *To Redeem the Soul of America*, 299–307; "Caution on Civil Rights," 58; "Catholic Know-Nothings," 64; Gerstle, "Race and the Myth of the Liberal Consensus," 580.

3. Karnow, *Vietnam*, 450–55.

4. *NYT*, March 8, 1965, 1; Herring, *America's Longest War*, 130; Halstead, *Out Now!*, 33–34; Zaroulis and Sullivan, *Who Spoke Up?*, 34.

5. Report of a Commission Appointed by the Federal Council of the Churches of Christ in America, "The Christian Conscience and Weapons of Mass Destruction," reprinted in *CCY* 67 (December 13, 1950): 1489–91; "Communism and Anti-Communism," Statement of the Mennonite General Conference (1961), reprinted in A. O'Gorman, *Universe Bends toward Justice*, 168–69.

6. Katz, *Ban the Bomb*, 23–26.

7. Bennett, foreword to *Nuclear Weapons*, 9.

8. Bennett, "Moral Urgencies in the Nuclear Context," in ibid., 96.

9. "We Too Protest," *NYT*, June 21, 1963, 15.

10. "We Too Protest," *NYT*, September 15, 1963, E5.

11. DeBenedetti with Chatfield, *American Ordeal*, 423 n. 21.

12. John C. Bennett, "Questions about Vietnam," *CC* 24 (July 20, 1964): 141–42.

13. Quoted in "Urge Cease Fire in South Vietnam," *CCY* 82 (January 13, 1965): 37.

14. Ibid.

15. Francis B. Sayre to the Editor, *CCY* 82 (March 3, 1965): 274.

16. Norman Thomas to the Editors, *CCY* 82 (April 21, 1965): 495–96.

17. Moore interview.

18. Brown interview; Coffin interview.

19. Eugene Carson Blake to Lyndon B. Johnson, September 20, 1965, quoted in Brackenridge, *Eugene Carson Blake*, 117.

20. J. B. Morris, "ESCRU," 23.

21. Neuhaus, "The War, the Churches, and Civil Religion," 135–42; Smylie, "American Religious Bodies, Just War, and Vietnam"; Quinley, *Prophetic Clergy*, 4–5; 109–12, 175–78; 223–27; Hadden, *Gathering Storm*, chap. 4.

22. "Statement of Purpose," adopted at the first general conference of the Student Nonviolent Coordinating Committee, Raleigh, N.C., April 17, 1960, reprinted in Broderick and Meier, *Negro Protest Thought*, 273.

23. See, for example, Zinn, *Vietnam*, 19–27, 51–66; Daniel Berrigan, "Letter to the Weathermen," (1970), reprinted in A. O'Gorman, *Universe Bends toward Justice*, 214–19.

24. Mitchell Hall, "CALCAV and Religious Opposition to the Vietnam War," in Small and Hoover, *Give Peace a Chance*, 36–37.

25. "2,500 Ministers, Priests and Rabbis Say: MR. PRESIDENT, In the Name of God, STOP IT!" *NYT*, April 4, 1965, E5; Hassler, *Saigon, U.S.A.*, 5.

26. "2,500 Ministers," E5.

27. "Who Is Adequate, Monsignor?" *CCY* 82 (May 26, 1965): 668.

28. F. Gray, *Divine Disobedience*, 86–89; Philip Berrigan, "Newburgh Again," *Commonweal* 82 (May 14, 1965): 239.

29. Deedy, *Apologies*, 22–23; F. Gray, *Divine Disobedience*, 64–69; D. Berrigan, "Open Sesame," 20.

30. Ross, " 'Tentatif,' " 17, 19; D. Berrigan, "Open Sesame," 21. See, for example, D. Berrigan, *Bow in the Clouds*, 184–201; "Young Priest-Poet," *America* 98 (October 19, 1957): 72.

31. Quoted in F. Gray, *Divine Disobedience*, 75. See also James Forest, "Daniel Berrigan: The Poet and Prophet as Priest," in Halpert and Murray, *Witness of the Berrigans*, 86.

32. Merton, *Secular Journal*, 181; *Cistercian Contemplatives*, 7, 24; Merton, *Seven-Storey Mountain*; Cooper, *Merton's Art of Denial*, 49–50; Thomas Merton, "Poetry and the Contemplative Life," *Commonweal* 46 (July 4, 1947): 280–86; Merton, "The Root of War," reprinted in *New Seeds of Contemplation*, 112; Merton, "Peace: A Religious Responsibility," in *Breakthrough to Peace*, 88–103; Merton, *Conjectures of a Guilty Bystander*, 229; Thomas Merton to Daniel Berrigan, November 10, 1961, January 15, 1962, and June 15, 1962; Thomas Merton to James Forest, April 29, 1962, in Shannon, *Hidden Ground*, 70–74, 266–68.

33. True, introduction to *Daniel Berrigan*, xix–xxiii; Deedy, *Apologies*, 54.

34. Forest, "Daniel Berrigan," in Halpert and Murray, *Witness of the Berrigans*, 86.

35. Ibid.; D. Berrigan, "Open Sesame," 22; Meconis, *With Clumsy Grace*, 9.

36. Merton, *Seeds of Destruction*, 12–42; Mott, *Seven Mountains of Thomas Merton*, 391.

37. See Merton, "Peace: A Religious Responsibility," in *Breakthrough to Peace*, 88–89; Forest, "Daniel Berrigan," 86, 91–92; D. Berrigan, "Open Sesame," 22; Meconis, *With Clumsy Grace*, 9; Thomas Merton to John Heidbrink, August 8, 1962, Thomas Merton to James Forest, October 2, 1964, Thomas Merton to Daniel Berrigan, August 4, 1964, all in Shannon, *Hidden Ground*, 410, 282, 83; Merton, *A Vow of Conversation*, 100.

38. Thomas Merton, "The Spiritual Roots of Protest," reprinted in Zahn, *Nonviolent Alternative*, 259–60.

39. Meconis, *With Clumsy Grace*, 9.

40. "Call to Vigil on Vietnam," *CCY* 82 (May 12, 1965): 605.

41. *NYT*, May 13, 1965, 1; DeBenedetti with Chatfield, *American Ordeal*, 114; Herring, *America's Longest War*, 137–38.

42. Coffin, *Once to Every Man*, 224; "US Policy in Vietnam: A Statement," *CC* 25 (June 14, 1965): 125.

43. "US Policy in Vietnam," 125.

44. Halberstam, *Best and the Brightest*, 644–45, 714.

45. I. F. Stone, "What Should the Peace Movement Do?" *I. F. Stone's Weekly* (June 23, 1965), reprinted in I. F. Stone, *Time of Torment*, 80–81.

46. Lens, *Unrepentant Radical*, 299–301.

47. Hassler, *Saigon, U.S.A.*, 6–7.

48. Jacob J. Weinstein, "Religion's Responsibility to the Human Race," in Jack, *Religion and Peace*, 51.

49. Ibid., 52; Hassler, *Saigon, U.S.A.*, 8–9; Hanh, *Vietnam*, 83–84; "Churches Speak on Vietnam," *CCY* 82 (March 17, 1965): 325–26.

50. "Letter to Martin Luther King, Jr. from a Buddhist Monk [Thich Nhat Hanh]."

51. Oates, *Let the Trumpet Sound*, 365–66; Alfred Hassler, afterword to Hanh, *Vietnam*, 97–98.

52. "We Have Seen the Anguish in Vietnam," *NYT*, August 1, 1965, E5.

53. Quoted in W. Martin, *Prophet with Honor*, 303.

54. Graham, *World Aflame*, 9, 12.

55. Quoted in W. Martin, *Prophet with Honor*, 311–12.

56. Coffin, *Once to Every Man*, 214–15.

57. James H. Forest, "No Longer Alone: The Catholic Peace Movement," in Quigley, *American Catholics and Vietnam*, 147; Rabbi Isidor B. Hoffman to Murray Polner, January 3, 1966, Box 2, "Internal Correspondence, 1955–1970," JPF Papers.

58. Philip J. Scharper, "The Churches and Conscription," in Quigley, *American Catholics and Vietnam*, 85–86; Rabbi Isidor B. Hoffman, Report of May 1971, Box 2, "Reports of Rabbi Isidor B. Hoffman," JPF Papers.

59. Ferber and Lynd, *The Resistance*, 21–22.

60. *NYT*, October 17, 1965, 1; Ferber and Lynd, *The Resistance*, 23–24; interview with David Miller in Finn, *Protest*, 186–87.

61. Hoover quotation, *NYT*, November 2, 1965, 9; Reston quotation, *NYT*, October 17, 1965, 9; *NYT*, October 26, 1965, 4.

62. *NYT*, October 26, 1965, 4; *NYT*, January 26, 1965, 44.

63. Hall, *Because of Their Faith*, 14.

64. Daniel Berrigan, "My Friend," in Kasimow and Sherwin, *No Religion Is an Island*, 69.

65. Quoted in "Battle of Conscience," 78.

66. Heschel, "Choose Life!" 39.

67. Zaroulis and Sullivan, *Who Spoke Up?*, 1–3.

68. "Burning Draft Cards," *Commonweal* 83 (November 19, 1965): 203; Thomas Cornell, "Why I Am Burning My Draft Card," *Commonweal* 83 (November 19, 1965): 205.

69. "Burning Draft Cards," 204.

70. Ferber and Lynd, *The Resistance*, 26.

71. *NYT*, November 10, 1965, 1, 5.

72. Ferber and Lynd, *The Resistance*, 26.

73. Thomas Merton to James Forest, November 11, 1965, in Shannon, *Hidden Ground*, 286.

74. Quoted in Curtis, *Berrigan Brothers*, 52.

75. "Berrigan," 34.

76. *NYT*, August 2, 1954, 3.

77. "The Facts, Please," *America* 109 (July 13, 1963): 38; "Diem, the Mandarin," *America* 109 (August 3, 1963): 111–12; Herring, *America's Longest War*, 97–98.

78. Quoted in " 'Peace' Priest Muzzled," *CCY* 82 (December 8, 1965): 1500–1501; *National Catholic Reporter*, December 1, 1965, 1; *NYT*, December 12, 1965, 5.

79. Quoted in "Current Comment: Storm over Fr. Berrigan . . . ," *America* 113 (December 11, 1965): 736.

80. *National Catholic Reporter*, December 1, 1965, 1; Eva Fleischner, "Heschel's Significance for Jewish-Christian Relations," in Merkle, *Abraham Joshua Heschel*, 142.

81. D. Berrigan, *Consequences*, 77, 94.

82. "Open Letter to the Authorities of the Archdiocese of New York and the Jesuit Community in New York City," *NYT*, December 12, 1965, 4E.

83. Ibid.

84. Thomas Merton to Daniel Berrigan, February 14, 1966, in Shannon, *Hidden Ground*, 89–90.

85. D. Berrigan, "Open Sesame," 23.

Chapter Seven

1. Daniel Berrigan, "My Friend," in Kasimow and Sherwin, *No Religion Is an Island*, 69; Hall, *Because of Their Faith*, 15–16; Coffin, *Once to Every Man*, 218–19.

2. Hall, *Because of Their Faith*, 16–18.

3. Ibid., 21; Coffin, *Once to Every Man*, 217–19, 223; Wiesel, *All Rivers Run to the Sea*, 353–55; Robert McAfee Brown, " 'Some Are Guilty, All Are Responsible': Heschel's Social Ethics," in Merkle, *Abraham Joshua Heschel*, 134.

4. Quoted in "Clergy Concerned about Vietnam," *CCY* 83 (January 26, 1966): 99–100.

5. Quoted in Hall, *Because of Their Faith*, 24.

6. Quoted in *NYT*, February 2, 1966, 15.

7. John C. Bennett, "From Supporter of War in 1941 to Critic in 1966," *CC* 26 (February 21, 1966): 13.

8. Quoted in ibid.

9. Fox, *Reinhold Niebuhr*, 284–85.

10. Quoted in "Berrigan," 34.

11. Ibid., 35; *NYT*, March 30, 1966, 13.

12. Jack, *Religion and Peace*, xii (introduction).

13. Ibid.; Appendix B: Officers and Participants, message by U Thant, message by Lyndon Johnson, in ibid., xii–xiii, 125–31, 1–2.

14. Message from Lyndon Johnson, in ibid., 2.

15. See the Conference Declaration, "Living with the Changing Communist World," "China and the Conflicts in Asia," "Intervention: Morality and Limits," and Hubert Humphrey, "Peace Is More Than a Word," in ibid., 3–7, 8–20, 20–30, 30–35, 69–72.

16. John Bennett, "The Issue of Peace"; Jacob Weinstein, "Religion's Responsibility"; and John Wright, "The Will for Peace," in ibid., 43–44, 54–55, 79.

17. Conference Declaration, in ibid., 5–6.

18. Hall, *Because of Their Faith*, 27–28; Coffin, *Once to Every Man*, 223; John C. Bennett to Malcolm Boyd, July 16, 1968, 2, MBP.

19. Abraham Joshua Heschel to Hans Morgenthau, April 8, 1966, quoted in DeBenedetti with Chatfield, *American Ordeal*, 144.

20. Robert McAfee Brown, "Treating Dissent Seriously," *CC* 26 (April 18, 1966): 75–76.

21. Lewy, *America in Vietnam*, 381; Herring, *America's Longest War*, 147–48, 151; Zaroulis and Sullivan, *Who Spoke Up?*, 115.

22. "They Are Our Brothers Whom We Kill," *NYT*, January 23, 1966, 6–7E.

23. "Comments by Thich Nhat Hanh on Some Frequently Asked Questions about Vietnam," in Hanh, *Vietnam*, 101–3.

24. Thomas Merton to John Heidbrink, May 20, 1966, in Shannon, *Hidden Ground*, 427.

25. Thomas Merton, "Nhat Hanh Is My Brother," reprinted in Zahn, *Nonviolent Alternative*, 263–64.

26. Hassler, afterword to Hanh, *Vietnam*, 98–101.

27. *NYT*, July 4, 1966, 2.

28. Quoted in Finn, *Protest*, 154–55.

29. John C. Bennett, "It Is Difficult to Be an American," *CC* 26 (July 25, 1966): 165.

30. "Our Intentions in Vietnam," *Commonweal* 84 (July 22, 1966): 454.

31. "Bobby Bakerism on a World Scale," *I. F. Stone's Weekly* (October 17, 1966), reprinted in I. F. Stone, *Time of Torment*, 258.

32. Gordon C. Zahn, "The Crime of Silence," *Commonweal* 84 (June 17, 1966): 354–56.

33. Harvey Cox, "Guernica to Vietnam: The Capacity for Horror," *Commonweal* 86 (April 28, 1967): 164–65.

34. *NYT*, July 26, 1966, 24.

35. *NYT*, August 10, 1966, 10; August 14, 1966, 1, 21; August 26, 1966, 2.

36. "Statement of the Synagogue Council of America, January 1966," and "An Appeal to the Churches Concerning Vietnam," issued by the General Assembly of the NCC, December 9, 1966, reprinted in Brown, Heschel, and Novak, *Vietnam*, 109–10, 118–22; Jacob Weinstein, "Freedom of the Pulpit," in Regner, *CCAR Yearbook*, 76: 19; *NYT*, October 22, 1966, 5; *NYT*, December 2, 1966, 1.

37. *NYT*, September 14, 1966, 1, 4; Saks, "Jews, Judaism, and the New Left," 43–44.

38. *NYT*, September 14, 1966, 1, 4.

39. Ibid., 4.

40. Sheerin, "Morality of the Vietnam War," 326–30.

41. "Excerpts from the Encyclical *Christi Matri* of Pope Paul VI, September 15, 1966" and "Statement of the American Roman Catholic Bishops, November 1966," reprinted in Brown, Heschel, and Novak, *Vietnam*, 113, 115–16. The lay editors of *Commonweal*, how-

ever, described the war as "a crime and a sin," and called for the withdrawal of American forces even if that meant a Communist victory. "Getting Out," *Commonweal* 85 (December 23, 1966): 335.

42. Tollefson, *Strength Not to Fight*, 44.

43. Cooney, *American Pope*, 286–89, 306; The Very Reverend Joseph Gallagher, "The American Bishops on Modern War," *America* 115 (November 5, 1966): 548–49.

44. *NYT*, January 8, 1967, 20.

45. Herring, *America's Longest War*, 168–69; Johnson, *Vantage Point*, 251; McNamara with VanDeMark, *In Retrospect*, 246–48.

46. *NYT*, December 27, 1966, 1.

47. Halstead, *Out Now!*, 267–68.

48. Muste, "Last Words," 8; *NYT*, February 3, 1962, 10; "Man in the News: Controversial Rabbi," *NYT*, January 24, 1967, 2; Feinberg, *Hanoi Diary*, 3.

49. Feinberg, *Hanoi Diary*, 108–33.

50. Ibid., 202–6; see also *NYT*, January 24, 1967, 1–2.

51. Feinberg, *Hanoi Diary*, 249–58; *NYT*, January 24, 1967, 2; J. A. O. Robinson, *Abraham Went Out*, 219.

52. The full-page advertisement, "A Call to Clergymen—Viet-Nam: The Clergyman's Dilemma: An Education-Action Mobilization, January 31–February 1, 1967," appeared in *CCY* 84 (January 4, 1967): 23, and *Commonweal* 85 (December 16, 1966): back cover, among other places; Coffin interview; Coffin, *Once to Every Man*, 224.

53. Robert McAfee Brown, "The Religious Community and Vietnam," quoted in Hall, *Because of Their Faith*, 34; see also excerpts in "News and Views," *Commonweal* 85 (February 24, 1967): 580, and *NYT*, February 1, 1967, 7.

54. Kyle Haselden, "Concerned and Committed," *CCY* 84 (February 15, 1967): 197; *NYT*, February 1, 1967, 7.

55. Coffin, *Once to Every Man*, 225.

56. Haselden, "Concerned and Committed," 198.

57. Ibid.

58. McCarthy, *Year of the People*, 45.

59. Heschel, "The Moral Outrage of Vietnam," in Brown, Heschel, and Novak, *Vietnam*, 51–52; see also Brown, " 'Some Are Guilty, All Are Responsible,' " 138–39.

60. Robert McAfee Brown, "The Last Judgment Is Now," sermon given at the National Mobilization of Clergy and Laymen Concerned about Vietnam, Washington, D.C., February 1, 1967, reprinted in *Pseudonyms of God*, 185, 186–87.

61. Haselden, "Concerned and Committed," 198; Coffin, *Once to Every Man*, 225.

62. Robert McAfee Brown, "An Open Letter to the U.S. Bishops," *Commonweal* 85 (February 17, 1967): 548.

63. "Challenge for the Churches," *America* 116 (February 18, 1967): 234.

64. Robert McAfee Brown, "The Church and Vietnam: A Protestant Viewpoint," *Commonweal* 87 (October 13, 1967): 54–55.

65. Coffin, *Once to Every Man*, 226–29; *NYT*, February 2, 1967, 3.

66. *NYT*, February 2, 1967, 3; Wells, *War Within*, 121–22; Brown, "An Appeal to the Churches and Synagogues," in Brown, Heschel, and Novak, *Vietnam*, 98.

67. Quoted in "A Second Selma," *CCY* 84 (March 8, 1967): 301–2.

68. *NYT*, March 19, 1967, 3.

69. Quoted in *National Catholic Reporter*, May 9, 1967, 3.

70. Oates, *Let the Trumpet Sound*, 415–17; *NYT*, April 5, 1967, 1.

71. Martin Luther King Jr., "A Time to Break Silence," sermon delivered on April 4, 1967, at the Riverside Church in New York City, reprinted in Washington, *A Testament of Hope*, 231–40.

72. Garrow, *Bearing the Cross*, 555; "King Speaks for Peace," CCY 84 (April 19, 1967): 492–93; John David Maguire, "Martin Luther King and Vietnam," CC 27 (May 1, 1967): 89–90; *NYT*, April 6, 1967, 10; "A Tragedy," *Washington Post*, April 6, 1967, A20; "Dr. King's Error," *NYT*, April 7, 1967, 36.

73. *NYT*, April 6, 1967, 10.

74. Raphael Gould to Rabbi Isidor Hoffman, April 10, 1967, Box 2, "Internal Correspondence, 1955–1970," JPF Papers.

75. *National Catholic Reporter*, April 20, 1967, 6; Ferber and Lynd, *The Resistance*, 72–77; Zaroulis and Sullivan, *Who Spoke Up?*, 111.

76. Robert McAfee Brown, "Protest for the Sake of Persuasion," speech given at the Spring Mobilization against the War, Kezar Stadium, San Francisco, April 15, 1967, reprinted in *Pseudonyms of God*, 190.

77. Wells, *The War Within*, 168–70; Hall, *Because of Their Faith*, 32, 45.

78. Eugene Carson Blake, "Ecumenism and Peace," address given on April 26, 1967, in Norwalk, Conn., reprinted in Hamilton, *Vietnam War: Christian Perspectives*, 137–39. He delivered substantially the same address during the "Sunrise Prayers for Peace" on the steps of Kiel Auditorium in St. Louis, Mo., on October 15, 1967. See Blake, "Vietnam," 149–51.

79. Zaroulis and Sullivan, *Who Spoke Up?*, 117–18; Halstead, *Out Now!*, 291; Thomas Francis Ritt, "The Bishops and Negotiation Now," in Quigley, *American Catholics and Vietnam*, 112–19; "Catholic Bishop Wants Troops Withdrawn from Vietnam," CCY 84 (August 16, 1967): 1036.

80. Brown, "'Some Are Guilty, All Are Responsible,'" 135–36.

81. Brown, Heschel, and Novak, *Vietnam*, 7–9 (introduction).

82. Abraham Joshua Heschel, "The Moral Outrage of Vietnam," in ibid., 49.

83. Robert McAfee Brown, "An Appeal to the Churches and Synagogues," in ibid., 63–65, 99, emphasis in original.

84. Hall, *Because of Their Faith*, 47.

85. O'Connor, *A Chaplain Looks at Vietnam*, 234–35.

86. Willard G. Oxtoby, "Christians and the Mideast Crisis," CCY 84 (July 20, 1967): 962.

87. Ibid., 965; Berrigan, "My Friend," in Kasimow and Sherwin, *No Religion Is an Island*, 69–70; Rabbi Jacob Weinstein, President's Message, in Regner, *CCAR Yearbook*, 77: 9, 11.

88. Tannenbaum, "Israel's Hour of Need," 1, 18.

89. M. L. King Jr., "Letter to an Anti-Zionist Friend," 76.

90. Tannenbaum, "Israel's Hour of Need," 1, 18. For a similar appraisal, see Vogel, "Some Reflections," 96–108.

91. Neuhaus, "The War, the Churches, and Civil Religion," 135.

92. Lewy, *America in Vietnam*, 382–85; Karnow, *Vietnam*, 465.

93. Brown, "Vietnam: Crisis of Conscience," 9–10.

Chapter Eight

1. Hadden, *Gathering Storm*, 124–25; W. C. Martin, *Christians in Conflict*, 1–19.

2. See Hough, *Black Power and White Protestants*; Gitlin, *Sixties*, 270.

3. Boyd, *As I Live and Breathe*, 175; Malcolm Boyd, "Maintaining Humanness in the Freedom Movement," CC 25 (October 4, 1965): 199–203; Malcolm Boyd, "My Vocation," unpublished manuscript, Box 2, Folder 4, MBP; *NYT*, December 11, 1965, 22; "Pulpit v. the Bench," 23.

4. Moore interview.

5. Pratt, *Liberalization of American Protestantism*, 178–85.

6. "Black Power, A Statement by the National Committee of Negro Churchmen," July 31, 1966, reprinted in Traynham, *Christian Faith in Black and White*, 66–72; "A Fresh Look at Black America," *CCY* 84 (October 25, 1967): 1340–41; Cone, *Black Theology and Black Power*, esp. 62–90, 135–52; *NYT*, November 11, 1966, 19; Findlay, *Church People*, 213; J. B. Morris, "ESCRU," 24–25.

7. James Forman, "Control, Conflict, and Change: The Underlying Concepts of the Black Manifesto," in Lecky and Wright, *Black Manifesto*, 34–37; Stackhouse, "Whatever Happened to Reparations," 61–71. The minister of Riverside sympathized with their demands and asked his parishioners to support the Manifesto. E. T. Campbell, "The Case for Reparations," *Christian Manifesto*, 97–104.

8. Malcolm E. Peabody to John B. Morris, August 30, 1967, 4–5, ESCRU Papers.

9. Moore interview.

10. John B. Morris to Malcolm E. Peabody, September 7, 1967, 3, ESCRU Papers.

11. "ESCRU at the Crossroads," *CCY* 84 (September 20, 1967): 1181; J. B. Morris, "ESCRU," 24–25.

12. William Sloane Coffin Jr., "Civil Disobedience, the Draft, and the War," *CC* 28 (February 5, 1968): 8–11.

13. Robert McAfee Brown, " 'We Must Obey God Rather Than Men': The Case for Dissent," commencement address at Pacific School of Religion, June 1967, reprinted in *Pseudonyms of God*, 196–97.

14. Robert McAfee Brown, "The Church and Vietnam: A Protestant Viewpoint," *Commonweal* 87 (October 13, 1967): 53.

15. Brown, " 'We Must Obey God Rather Than Men,' " 199–200.

16. Brown, "In Conscience, I Must Break the Law," 48–52.

17. Waskow and Raskin, "A Call to Resist Illegitimate Authority," 34–35; *NYT*, October 26, 1967, 10.

18. Ferber and Lynd, *The Resistance*, 104–8; Coffin, *Once to Every Man*, 241–42; sermon given by William Sloane Coffin Jr. on October 16, 1967, at the Arlington Street Church, Boston, Mass., reprinted in Mitford, *Trial of Dr. Spock*, 263–67.

19. Coffin, *Once to Every Man*, 244.

20. Mitford, *Trial of Dr. Spock*, 41.

21. William Sloane Coffin Jr., statement before the Justice Department on October 20, 1967, reprinted in *CC* 28 (February 5, 1967): 11.

22. Mitford, *Trial of Dr. Spock*, 42–44.

23. Coffin, *Once to Every Man*, 254.

24. "Coffin and Man at Yale," 67.

25. DeBenedetti, *Peace Reform*, 180; Halstead, *Out Now!*, 316, 333–39.

26. McNamara with VanDeMark, *In Retrospect*, 305.

27. D. Berrigan, *Night Flight to Hanoi*, 3–14.

28. Meconis, *With Clumsy Grace*, 17; F. Gray, *Divine Disobedience*, 111–12; Philip Berrigan, "Blood, War and Witness," in O'Connor, *American Catholic Exodus*, 13.

29. F. Gray, *Divine Disobedience*, 112.

30. Ibid.; Meconis, *With Clumsy Grace*, 17.

31. DeBenedetti with Chatfield, *American Ordeal*, 170.

32. F. Gray, *Divine Disobedience*, 112–22; Meconis, *With Clumsy Grace*, 18–20; P. Berrigan, "Blood, War and Witness," 7–8.

33. The Reverend James Mengel, Thomas Lewis, David Eberhardt, Father Philip Berrigan, statement presented at the United States Customs House in Baltimore, Md., on October 27, 1967, reprinted in P. Berrigan, "Blood, War and Witness," 5–6.

34. John C. Bennett, "The Place of Civil Disobedience," *CC* 27 (December 25, 1967): 299–302.

35. NYT, October 28, 1967, 5; F. Gray, *Divine Disobedience*, 112–22; Hadden, *Gathering Storm*, 204.

36. NYT, January 6, 1968, 1; Mitford, *Trial of Dr. Spock*, 3–5.

37. Mitford, *Trial of Dr. Spock*, 53–58; for an example of clerical criticism, see Richard John Neuhaus, "Super-General Hershey," *Commonweal* 87 (January 19, 1968): 456–57.

38. Robert McAfee Brown, "A National Call to Clergy in Support of Coffin, Spock, and Company," and "Why Are We Here?" speech given on January 29, 1968, at Glide Memorial Church, San Francisco, in Brown, *Pseudonyms of God*, 218–19; D. Berrigan, *Night Flight to Hanoi*, 22–36; Howard Zinn, "The Prisoners: A Bit of Contemporary History," in Halpert and Murray, *Witness of the Berrigans*, 4–7.

39. D. Berrigan, *Night Flight to Hanoi*, 39–49, 84, 133–40; Zinn, "The Prisoners," 8–13.

40. Deedy, *Apologies*, 77.

41. Fitzgerald, *Fire in the Lake*, 524; Lewy, *America in Vietnam*, 274–75; Herring, *America's Longest War*, 183–87.

42. Herring, *America's Longest War*, 187–88.

43. Oberdorfer, *Tet!*, 158.

44. "Doublethink in Vietnam: To Destroy Is to Save," CCY 85 (February 21, 1968): 220.

45. Robert McAfee Brown, Arthur Lelyveld, and John B. Sheerin, "Commentary by Religious Leaders on the Erosion of Moral Constraint in Vietnam," in Melman, *In the Name of America*, 1–3.

46. Ibid., 12.

47. NYT, February 4, 1968, 1; John C. Bennett to Malcolm Boyd, July 16, 1968, 2, and Balfour Brickner to Malcolm Boyd, February 15, 1968, both in Box 17, Folder 1, MBP; Hall, *Because of Their Faith*, 62; Boyd, *As I Live and Breathe*, 182; Boyd, *You Can't Kill the Dream*, 7.

48. William R. MacKaye, "Clergy in the Capital," CC 28 (March 4, 1968): 36–37.

49. *Washington Post*, February 6, 1968, B1.

50. "Silent March," 58; Boyd, *As I Live and Breathe*, 226; Boyd interview.

51. Herring, *America's Longest War*, 198–202; Johnson, *Vantage Point*, 399–424; NYT, April 1, 1968, 1, 26.

52. Zaroulis and Sullivan, *Who Spoke Up?*, 162–63.

53. Oates, *Let the Trumpet Sound*, 464.

54. "Conversation with Martin Luther King," 1.

55. Ibid., 2.

56. Thomas Merton to June Yungblut, January 20, 1968, and March 29, 1968, in Shannon, *Hidden Ground*, 640, 644.

57. Thomas Merton to June Yungblut, April 9, 1968, in ibid., 645.

58. NYT, April 5, 1968, 26.

59. NYT, April 8, 1968, 32–34.

60. NYT, April 10, 1968, 33–34; C. S. King, *My Life With Martin Luther King, Jr.*, 363–64.

61. NYT, April 9, 1968, 31.

62. F. Gray, *Divine Disobedience*, 128.

63. NYT, April 1, 1968, 14.

64. Mitford, *Trial of Dr. Spock*, 89–194.

65. Coffin, *Once to Every Man*, 276.

66. Mitford, *Trial of Dr. Spock*, 209–10.

67. Coffin, *Once to Every Man*, 285.

68. NYT, January 1, 1968, 2.

69. Deedy, *Apologies*, 81.

70. Quoted in Forest, "Phillip Berrigan: Disturber of Sleep," in Casey and Nobile, *Berrigans*, 177–78.

71. F. Gray, *Divine Disobedience*, 125.

72. Ibid., 126–29; P. Berrigan, *Prison Journals*, 210; Melville and Melville, *Whose Heaven, Whose Earth?*, 62–90; D. Berrigan, "Open Sesame," 24; "Father Dan Berrigan: The Holy Outlaw," transcript of documentary presented by National Educational Television on September 7, 1970, reprinted in *CC* 30 (September 21, 1970): 185.

73. *Washington Post*, May 18, 1968, 1.

74. Philip Berrigan, S.S.J., "Letter from a Baltimore Jail," *CC* 28 (July 22, 1968): 168–70.

75. William M. Kunstler, "Some Thoughts about the Berrigans, Et Al," in Halpert and Murray, *Witness of the Berrigans*, 167.

76. See Meconis, *With Clumsy Grace*.

77. Zaroulis and Sullivan, *Who Spoke Up?*, 236; Ferber and Lynd, *The Resistance*, 203.

78. "Father Dan Berrigan: The Holy Outlaw," 185.

79. For a collection of these essays, see Casey and Nobile, *Berrigans*.

80. Robert McAfee Brown, "The Berrigans: Signs or Models?," in ibid., 61–62. 70. See also Staughton Lynd, "A Conversation With Staughton Lynd," in ibid., 198.

81. Gordon C. Zahn, "The Berrigans: Radical Activism Personified," in ibid., 99–104.

82. D. Berrigan, *Lights On in the House of the Dead*, 241–42.

83. Merton, "Non-Violence Does Not—Cannot—Mean Passivity," 9–10.

84. D. Berrigan, *Portraits*, 14.

85. Thomas Merton to James Forest, November 16, 1966, in Shannon, *Hidden Ground*, 298.

86. D. Berrigan, *Portraits*, 14.

87. Griffin, *Follow the Ecstasy*, 185; see Merton, *Thomas Merton in Alaska*.

88. Thomas Merton to Philip Berrigan, September 30, 1968, in Shannon, *Hidden Ground*, 101.

89. Meconis, *With Clumsy Grace*, 35–36.

90. F. Gray, *Divine Disobedience*, 226–27; D. Berrigan, *Portraits*, 14.

91. Griffin, *Follow the Ecstasy*, 206.

92. Ibid., 205–7.

93. D. Berrigan, *Portraits*, 14; Meconis, *With Clumsy Grace*, 37; Nobile, "Priest Who Stayed Out in the Cold," 39; Wayne Cowan, editorial, *CC* 30 (September 21, 1970): 178.

Chapter Nine

1. John C. Bennett to Malcolm Boyd, July 16, 1968, Box 17, Folder 1, MBP.

2. *NYT*, August 18, 1968, 73.

3. Michael Novak, "Alive and Well in Paris," *Commonweal* 89 (November 22, 1968): 276–78; W. D. Campbell, *Forty Acres*, 122; "Good Will," 84; W. D. Campbell, "The Faith of a Fatalist," 51–57.

4. Bill [Coffin] to Malcolm Boyd, n.d., Box 17, Folder 1, MBP.

5. Malcolm Boyd, "Steps," *Yale Daily News*, November 4, 1968, Box 2, Folder 6, MBP.

6. Richard Fernandez to Malcolm Boyd, November 1, 1968, Box 17, Folder 1, MBP.

7. Robert L. Kuttner, "Recharging the Peace Movement," *Commonweal* 89 (February 28, 1969): 669–70.

8. Hall, *Because of Their Faith*, 79–81.

9. *Washington Post*, February 6, 1969, A14.

10. As quoted in Wells, *War Within*, 293.

11. As quoted in Brown, *Making Peace in the Global Village*, 19.

12. Coffin interview.

13. W. Martin, *Prophet with Honor*, 356–57.

14. "The Preaching and the Power," 35.

15. Reinhold Niebuhr, "The King's Chapel and the King's Court," *CC* 29 (August 4, 1969): 211–12.

16. Niebuhr would die two years later from complications arising from a series of strokes; at his request, Heschel led the memorial service. Fox, *Reinhold Niebuhr*, 289, 292.

17. Safire, *Before the Fall*, 121; Haldeman with Diadona, *Ends of Power*, 81–83. Gibson, *Perfect War*, 403–7.

18. "How Patient Must We Be, Mr. Nixon?" *NYT*, March 30, 1969, E7.

19. Halstead, *Out Now!*, 451–52.

20. *Washington Post*, April 7, 1969, A4.

21. "Findings on Trip to Vietnam, U.S. Study Team, May 25–June 10, 1969," reprinted in Hassler, *Saigon, U.S.A.*, 241–76.

22. Ibid.

23. Representative John Conyers to President Nixon, June 5, 1969, reprinted in Hassler, *Saigon, U.S.A.*, 66.

24. Gibson, *Perfect War*, 400, 408; Kissinger, *White House Years*, 273.

25. Kissinger, *White House Years*, 283–85, 304; see also Nixon, *RN*, 399.

26. Lens, *Unrepentant Radical*, 348–54; Halstead, *Out Now!*, 473, 488–90; Zaroulis and Sullivan, *Who Spoke Up?*, 257–58; Heineman, *Campus Wars*, 217.

27. "October 15: A Day to Remember," 34; Joseph Morrissey to Paul Morrissey, October 1969, in *Dear America: Letters Home from Vietnam*, 223.

28. Nixon, *RN*, 401, 403.

29. *NYT*, November 14, 1969, 20.

30. Ibid., 1; Zaroulis and Sullivan, *Who Spoke Up?*, 282–83.

31. *NYT*, November 15, 1969, 26.

32. Safire, *Before the Fall*, 172.

33. *NYT*, November 15, 1969, 26.

34. Coffin, *Once to Every Man*, 297–98.

35. Quoted in Lens, *Unrepentant Radical*, 354.

36. Coffin, *Once to Every Man*, 298.

37. *NYT*, November 4, 1969, 1; Safire, *Before the Fall*, 172.

38. John C. Bennett, "End the War Now!" *CC* 29 (October 27, 1969): 261–63.

39. Zaroulis and Sullivan, *Who Spoke Up?*, 298.

40. Balfour Brickner, "Vietnam and the Jewish Community," *CCY* 87 (April 29, 1970): 531–34; Woodward, "Foretaste of Eternity," 50; Heschel, "My Father," in Kasimow and Sherwin, *No Religion is An Island*, 32–33. Samuel H. Dresner, "Remembering Abraham Joshua Heschel," *America* 146 (May 29, 1982): 414–15; Ro'i, *Struggle for Soviet Jewish Emigration*, 193–94, 211–12.

41. Zaroulis and Sullivan, *Who Spoke Up?*, 298.

42. *NYT*, February 12, 1970, 5.

43. *NYT*, December 1, 1969, 34; December 2, 1969, 46.

44. "Exodus from the Pastorate," 34–35; James Haughey, "Exodus of Protestant Ministers?" *America* 122 (March 7, 1970): 243–44.

45. Jud, Mills, and Burch, *Ex-Pastors*, 5–6.

46. "Collars in the Ring," 105–6; "Clergy as Politicians," *CCY* 87 (October 7, 1970): 1175; "Clerical Candidates," 22; "Clergymen-Candidates," 20–21; "Clergy Score Poorly in Great Elections Game," 35; Murphy, *Papacy Today*, 219.

47. Malcolm Boyd, "Underground Church," *Commonweal* 88 (April 12, 1968): 97–100; Malcolm Boyd, "My Vocation," unpublished manuscript, Box 2, Folder 4, MBP.

48. Eugene Carson Blake to Malcolm Boyd, April 15, 1966, Box 17, Folder 1, MBP.

49. Boyd, *As I Live and Breathe*, 229.

50. Daniel Berrigan, "Letter to the Jesuits, April 10, 1970," in *America Is Hard to Find*, 35–36, 38.

51. Nobile, "The Priest Who Stayed Out in the Cold," 39; Meconis, *With Clumsy Grace*, 68–69; *National Catholic Reporter*, April 7, 1972, 6.

52. P. Berrigan, *Prison Journals*, 210; for accounts of Philip Berrigan's criticism of others, see Francine du Plessix Gray, "Phil Berrigan in Hawaii," in Casey and Nobile, *Berrigans*, 163.

53. D. Berrigan, *America Is Hard to Find*, 60–66, 82; "Father Dan Berrigan: The Holy Outlaw," transcript of documentary presented by National Educational Television on September 7, 1970, reprinted in *CC* 30 (September 21, 1970): 184–85, 189–93.

54. Meconis, *With Clumsy Grace*, 73–74.

55. D. Berrigan, *America is Hard to Find*, 60.

56. Harvey Cox, "The Bird in the Hand," *CC* 30 (September 21, 1970): 178–80; Robert McAfee Brown, "The Berrigans: Signs or Models?," in Casey and Nobile, *Berrigans*, 60–70.

57. Coffin interview; he was quoted as saying the same thing in the early 1980s; see also Zaroulis and Sullivan, *Who Spoke Up?*, 229–30.

58. "Has the Church Lost Its Soul?" 188–89.

59. Schell, *Time of Illusion*, 89–90; Nixon, *RN*, 445–49; Kissinger, *White House Years*, 484–96.

60. *NYT*, May 1, 1970, 1; May 5, 1970, 1.

61. Schell, *Time of Illusion*, 97–98.

62. *NYT*, May 5, 1970, 1.

63. Zaroulis and Sullivan, *Who Spoke Up?*, 334.

64. Safire, *Before the Fall*, 204

65. "The Preaching and the Power," 35–36.

66. W. D. Campbell and Holloway, "Open Letter to Billy Graham," 2.

67. Fellowship of Reconciliation et al. to Richard Nixon, May 4, 1970, Box 17, "Press Releases," JPF Papers.

68. *Washington Post*, May 27, 1970, A15; Leon Howell, "Ethical Engagement," *CCY* 112 (May 24, 1995): 556.

69. "'If You Can't March, at Least Stand Up,'" 82.

70. Robert McAfee Brown, "An Open Letter to Spiro T. Agnew," *CCY* 86 (October 14, 1970): 1213–17.

71. *NYT*, May 10, 1970, 57.

72. Cox, "Bird in the Hand," and William Stringfellow, "An Authority over Death," in *CC* 30 (September 21, 1970): 178–80, 181–83; Brown, "The Berrigans: Signs or Models?" 62.

73. Meconis, *With Clumsy Grace*, 81–82; for an account of the strong feelings against Hoover's handling of the case, see U.S. Congress, House, statement by Representative Anderson.

74. Meconis, *With Clumsy Grace*, 82–88, 92–93.

75. Ibid., 95–96; *NYT*, May 12, 1971; *Washington Post*, August 23, 1971, 1; *National Catholic Reporter*, February 11, 1972, 1; P. Berrigan, *Widen the Prison Gates*, 80–235; see also Nelson and Ostrow, *FBI and the Berrigans*; Carroll, *American Requiem*, 238–40.

76. Hall, *Because of Their Faith*, 116–23, 132–52.

77. Brown, *Creative Dislocation*, 33–35; Robert McAfee Brown, "To Save Life Rather Than Destroy It," statement read on Ash Wednesday, 1971, in front of the San Mateo draft board, reprinted in *Pseudonyms of God*, 225–26.

78. Robert McAfee Brown, "The Power of Love Is Stronger than the Love of Power,"

statement read on Good Friday/Passover, 1971, in front of the Berkeley draft board, reprinted in *Pseudonyms of God*, 226–27; Brown, *Creative Dislocation*, 35.

79. Emerson, *Winners and Losers*, 209.

80. Richard Fernandez, "The Air War in Indochina: Some Responses," CCY 88 (December 1, 1971): 1404–5.

81. Schell, *Time of Illusion*, 151–53.

82. Herring, *America's Longest War*, 237–39.

83. Moore interview.

84. Ibid.

85. Paul Moore Jr., "A Woman with a Bamboo Pole," a report from Saigon, 1971, unpublished manuscript, Box 40, Folder 1, MBP.

86. Moore, *Take a Bishop Like Me*, 8; Moore interview.

87. "Ecumenical Witness: Withdraw Now!" CCY 89 (January 26, 1972): 81; D. Levy, *Debate over Vietnam*, 164–65.

88. "The Bombing of America," CC 32 (May 15, 1972): 115; NYT, May 17, 1972, 20; Spock, *Spock on Spock*, 191; Hall, *Because of Their Faith*, 155; Carroll, *American Requiem*, 240.

89. Bill [Coffin] to Malcolm Boyd, March 5, 1970, Box 17, Folder 1, MBP.

90. Coffin, *Once to Every Man*, 308.

91. Coffin interview.

92. Coffin, *Once to Every Man*, 310–31.

93. Abraham Joshua Heschel to the Editors, October 15, 1972, NYT, October 27, 1972, 40.

94. Berrigan, "My Friend," in Kasimow and Sherwin, *No Religion Is an Island*, 74.

95. Elie Wiesel, "My Teacher's Desk," adapted from an address given at Dropsie College, Philadelphia, Pa., May 24, 1983, in *Against Silence*, 43.

96. Jacob Y. Teshima, "My Teacher," in Kasimow and Sherwin, *No Religion is an Island*, 66.

97. NYT, December 24, 1972, 40; December 25, 1972, 20.

98. "Contemporary Judaism and the Christian," *America* 128 (March 10, 1973): 202.

99. "Of Many Things," *America* 128 (March 10, 1973): 200.

100. "Contemporary Judaism and the Christian," 202.

101. D. Berrigan, *To Dwell in Peace*, 179.

102. Nixon, *RN*, 734; Kissinger, *White House Years*, 1399–1400.

103. Herring, *America's Longest War*, 248–49; NYT, December 24, 1972, 1; Karnow, *Vietnam*, 667–68; John M. Swomley Jr., "Amnesty and Reconciliation," CCY 89 (December 27, 1972): 1322.

104. Hall, *Because of Their Faith*, 159.

105. Herring, *America's Longest War*, 250–51.

Epilogue

1. Lewy, *Peace and Revolution*, 110–18, 75.

2. Hall, *Because of Their Faith*, 123.

3. Hampton and Fayer, *Voices of Freedom*, 565–67.

4. Jud, Mills, and Burch, *Ex-Pastors*, 5.

5. Quinley, *Prophetic Clergy*, 7–8; Hillis, *Can Two Walk Together?*, 102.

6. Quinley, *Prophetic Clergy*, 9–18; Wuthnow, *Restructuring of American Religion*, 191–94; see Schmidt, *Souls or the Social Order*, 208–17.

7. F. Gray, "To March or Not to March," 6–7.

8. Quoted in ibid., 34.

9. See Malcolm Boyd, "Ecclesia Christi," in *Underground Church*, 3–6.

10. Quoted in Frady, *Southerners*, 370.

11. Moore interview.

12. D. Gray, "In Defense of the Steeple," 31.

13. Quoted in Castro, Editorial, 124.

14. D'Souza, *Falwell*, 80–83.

15. Quoted in "Jerry Falwell's Crusade," 51, 49.

16. Reed, " 'We Stand at a Crossroads,' " 28.

17. Quoted in *Times-Picayune*, July 6, 1996, A-14.

18. Wuthnow, *Restructuring of American Religion*, 113–15.

19. *Times-Picayune*, November 17, 1995, A-12.

20. Margaret Guenther, "SBC Renounces Racist Past," CCY 112 (July 1, 1995): 671.

21. A. Stone, "Southern Baptists to Apologize for Slavery," 1.

22. Paul Duke, "Black Baptist Rejects Apology by SBC," CCY 112 (September 9, 1995): 810.

23. Walker, "Blacks, Southern Baptists," 6.

24. *Times-Picayune*, April 27, 1996, A-18.

25. Ibid., February 26, 1996, A-1, A-6–A-7.

26. Boyd, *Are You Running with Me, Jesus?*, 5; Boyd, *Take Off the Masks*, 134–51.

27. Quoted in Stammer, "Vanguard Priest," B-4.

28. Cattau, "Author Still Runs," 4.

29. Boyd interview.

30. Cattau, "Author Still Runs," 4.

31. Quoted in Stammer, "Vanguard Priest," B-4.

32. Moore, *Take a Bishop Like Me*, 15–39; Hillis, *Can Two Walk Together?*, 122.

33. Cockburn, "People's Cathedral," 31.

34. NYT, March 25, 1989, 29–30; October 2, 1991, A24.

35. See Brown, *Religion and Violence*, 2d ed.; Brown, *Creative Dislocation*, 22–25; Brown, *Making Peace in the Global Village*; Gutierrez, *Theology of Liberation*.

36. Robert McAfee Brown, "Responding to 'A Cry for Justice': Overall Reflections Plus a Few Nuts and Bolts," in Brown and Brown, *Cry for Justice*, 8.

37. Robert McAfee Brown and Sydney Thomson Brown, "How To Use This Book: A Conversation with the Reader," in ibid., 152–59.

38. Hollander, *Anti-Americanism*, 106–7.

39. Quoted in Lefever, *Amsterdam to Nairobi*, 41.

40. Harris, "Rev. William Sloane Coffin," 22–25; CC 50 (November 12, 1990): 338.

41. Hollander, *Anti-Americanism*, 119.

42. Coffin interview; Harris, "Rev. William Sloane Coffin," 24–25.

43. Lens, *Unrepentant Radical*, 396.

44. D. Berrigan, *To Dwell in Peace*, 288–89.

45. Deedy, *Apologies*, 116.

46. Ibid., 137–39.

47. D. Berrigan, *To Dwell in Peace*, 342–43.

48. Bearak, "Berrigan at 71," A-1.

49. Ibid.

50. William Sloane Coffin Jr., "The Gulf: Self-Righteousness (and Oil)," CC 50 (November 12, 1990): 342.

51. Editor's Note to Roger L. Shinn, "Conscientious Objection: Remembrance," CC 50 (January 7, 1991): 415.

52. Richard Neuhaus, "Just War and This War," *Wall Street Journal*, January 29, 1991, 9.

53. Stammer, "Force Justified to Save Bosnians," A-1.

54. Neuhaus, "Just War and This War," 9.

55. Stammer, "Force Justified to Save Bosnians," A-1.

56. Ibid.

57. "Religious, Academic Ethicists Defend U.N. in Face of GOP Assault," *Los Angeles Times*, March 11, 1995, 4; see also William Sloane Coffin Jr., "Hiroshima Then and Now," *CCY* 112 (August 16, 1995): 772.

58. Quoted in Leon Howell, "Ethical Engagement," *CCY* 112 (May 24, 1995): 556.

59. Ibid.

60. Moore interview.

61. Hall, "CALCAV and Religious Opposition to the Vietnam War," in Small and Hoover, *Give Peace a Chance*, 51–52.

62. DeBenedetti, "On the Significance of Citizen Peace Activism," 14.

63. Thomas Merton to James H. Forest, February 21, 1966, in Shannon, *Hidden Ground*, 294.

bibliography

I. Manuscript Collections

Atlanta, Ga.
  Episcopal Society for Cultural and Racial Unity (ESCRU) Papers, in possession of the
    author, courtesy of John B. Morris
Boston, Mass.
  Department of Special Collections, Mugar Memorial Library, Boston University
    Malcolm Boyd Papers
Cambridge, Mass.
  Harvard College Library
    Ralph E. Smeltzer Manuscript Notes and Correspondence
New Orleans, La.
  Department of Special Collections and Archives, Loyola University Library
    Joseph Fichter Papers
    Louis Twomey Papers
Philadelphia, Pa.
  National Council of Christ in the U.S.A. Archives, Presbyterian Church (U.S.A.),
    Office of History
    Will Campbell/Southern Project Papers
Waltham, Mass.
  American Jewish Archives
    Jewish Peace Fellowship Papers

II. Interviews

Boyd, Malcolm. Telephone interview, January 26, 1994.
Brown, Robert McAfee. Telephone interview, February 22, 1994.
Coffin, William Sloane, Jr. Telephone interview, March 15, 1994.
Hughes, Robert E. Telephone interview, January 24 and 25, 1994.
Moore, Paul, Jr. Personal interview, Stonington, Conn., November 26, 1993.
Morris, John. Telephone interview, April 6, 1995.

III. Frequently Cited Newspapers and Periodicals

America
The Christian Century

Christianity and Crisis
The Commonweal
The Henderson (Ky.) Gleaner and Journal
The Mississippian
The Nation
The National Catholic Reporter
The New York Times
The Reporter
The Times-Picayune (New Orleans)
The Wall Street Journal
The Washington Post

IV. Books and Articles

"Act of Belief." *Time* 80 (September 7, 1962): 45.

Ahlstrom, Sydney. *A Religious History of the American People*. New Haven: Yale University Press, 1972.

Ahmann, Mathew, ed. *Race: Challenge to Religion*. Chicago: Henry Regnery, 1963.

Alexander, Shana. "The Feminine Eye." *Life* 58 (March 26, 1965): 28.

Allport, Gordon W. *The Nature of Prejudice*. Garden City, N.Y.: Doubleday, 1958.

"An Appeal for the James Reeb Fund." *New Republic* 152 (March 27, 1965): 2.

"Another Tragic Era?" *U.S. News and World Report* 43 (October 4, 1957): 33–46.

"Attack on the Conscience." *Time* 69 (February 18, 1957): 17.

Bailey, Kenneth K. *Southern White Protestantism in the Twentieth Century*. Gloucester, Mass.: Peter Smith, 1968.

Barrett, George. "Study in Desegregation: The Clinton Story." *New York Times Magazine* (September 16, 1956): 11, 71–72, 76.

Barrett, Russell H. *Integration at Ole Miss*. Chicago: Quadrangle, 1965.

Bartley, Numan V. *The Rise of Massive Resistance: Race and Politics in the South during the 1950s*. Baton Rouge: Louisiana State University Press, 1969.

Bates, Daisy. *The Long Shadow of Little Rock: A Memoir*. Fayetteville: University of Arkansas Press, 1987.

"Battle of Conscience." *Newsweek* 66 (November 15, 1965): 78.

Battles and Leaders of the Civil War. Vol. 4. New York: Thomas Yoseloff, 1956.

Bearak, Barry. "Berrigan at 71: Still Protesting." *Los Angeles Times* (April 10, 1993): A-1.

"Beauty for Ashes." *Time* 85 (February 5, 1965): 61.

Bennett, John C., ed. *Nuclear Weapons and the Conflict of Conscience*. New York: Charles Scribner's Sons, 1962.

Berger, Peter L. *The Noise of Solemn Assemblies*. Garden City, N.Y.: Doubleday, 1961.

"Berrigan." *New Yorker* 42 (April 9, 1966): 34–35.

Berrigan, Daniel. *America Is Hard to Find*. Garden City, N.Y.: Doubleday, 1972.

———. *The Bow in the Clouds: Man's Covenant With God*. New York: Coward-McCann, 1961.

———. *Consequences: Truth and . . .* New York: Macmillan, 1967.

———. *Lights On in the House of the Dead: A Prison Diary*. Garden City, N.Y.: Doubleday, 1974.

———. *Night Flight to Hanoi: War Diary with 11 Poems*. New York: Macmillan, 1968.

———. *No Bars to Manhood*. Garden City, N.Y.: Doubleday, 1970.

———. "Open Sesame: My Life and Good Times." *Katallagete* 2 (Winter 1968–69): 20–25.

———. *Portraits of Those I Love*. New York: Crossroads, 1982.

———. *To Dwell in Peace: An Autobiography*. San Francisco: Harper and Row, 1987.

Berrigan, Philip. "The Challenge of Segregation." *Worship* 34 (November 1960): 597–604.

——. *No More Strangers.* Techny, Ill.: Divine Word Publications, 1965.

——. *Prison Journals of a Priest Revolutionary.* New York: Holt, Rinehart, and Winston, 1970.

——. *Widen the Prison Gates.* New York: Simon and Schuster, 1973.

Berton, Pierre. *The Comfortable Pew.* Philadelphia: J. B. Lippincott, 1965.

"Bishop Moore: A Leader of the New Breed." *Newsweek* 65 (March 29, 1965): 77.

Blake, Eugene Carson. "Vietnam." *Ecumenical Review* 38 (April 1986): 149–51.

Blank, Irwin M. "The Deliberations of the National Conference on Religion and Race." *CCAR Journal* 11 (October 1963): 20–22, 30.

Bloom, Jack. "Journey to Understanding." *Conservative Judaism* 19 (Summer 1965): 11–13.

Blumberg, Janice Rothschild. *One Voice: Rabbi Jacob M. Rothschild and the Troubled South.* Macon, Ga.: Mercer University Press, 1985.

Boyd, Malcolm. *Are You Running with Me, Jesus? A Spiritual Companion for the 1990s.* Boston: Beacon, 1990.

——. *As I Live and Breathe: Stages of An Autobiography.* New York: Random House, 1970.

——. *Gay Priest: An Inner Journey.* New York: St. Martin's Press, 1986.

——. *Take Off the Masks.* San Francisco: Harper Collins, 1993.

——. *The Underground Church.* New York: Sheed and Ward, 1968.

——. *You Can't Kill the Dream.* Richmond, Va.: John Knox Press, 1968.

Brackenridge, R. Douglas. *Eugene Carson Blake: Prophet With Portfolio.* New York: Seabury, 1978.

Braiterman, Marvin. "Mississippi Maranos." *Midstream* 10 (September 1964): 34–35.

Branch, Taylor. *Parting the Waters: America in the King Years, 1954–63.* New York: Simon and Schuster, 1988.

Breitman, George, ed. *By Any Means Necessary: Speeches, Interviews and a Letter by Malcolm X.* New York: Pathfinder, 1970.

Broderick, Francis L., and August Meier, eds. *Negro Protest Thought in the Twentieth Century.* Indianapolis: Bobbs-Merrill, 1965.

Brown, Robert McAfee. *Creative Dislocation—The Movement of Grace.* Nashville, Tenn.: Abingdon Press, 1980.

——. "In Conscience, I Must Break the Law." *Look* 31 (October 31, 1967): 48–52.

——. *Making Peace in the Global Village.* Philadelphia: Westminster, 1981.

——. *The Pseudonyms of God.* Philadelphia: Westminster, 1972.

——. *Religion and Violence.* Philadelphia: Westminster, 1973. 2d ed., 1987.

——. "Vietnam: Crisis of Conscience." *Catholic World* 206 (October 1967): 9–10.

Brown, Robert McAfee, and Sydney Thomason Brown, eds. *A Cry for Justice: The Churches and Synagogues Speak.* New York/Mahwah: Paulist Press, 1989.

Brown, Robert McAfee, Abraham J. Heschel, and Michael Novak. *Vietnam: Crisis of Conscience.* New York: Association Press, 1967.

Brown, Robert McAfee, and Gustave Weigel, S.J. *An American Dialogue: A Protestant Looks at Catholicism and a Catholic Looks at Protestantism.* Garden City, N.Y.: Doubleday, 1960.

Butler, Samuel. *The Way of All Flesh.* New York: AMS Press, 1968.

Callahan, Daniel. "The Quest for Social Relevance." *Daedalus* 96 (Winter 1967): 151–79.

Campbell, Clarence T., and Oscar Allen Rogers Jr. *Mississippi: The View from Tougaloo.* Jackson: University Press of Mississippi, 1979.

Campbell, Ernest Q., and Thomas Pettigrew. *Christians in Racial Crisis: A Study of Little Rock's Ministry.* Washington, D.C.: Public Affairs Press, 1959.

Campbell, Ernest Q., and Thomas F. Pettigrew. "Racial and Moral Crisis: The Role of
Little Rock Ministers." *American Journal of Sociology* 64 (March 1959): 509–16.

Campbell, Ernest T. *Christian Manifesto*. New York: Harper and Row, 1970.

Campbell, Hester H., Letter to the editors. *Harper's Magazine* 230 (March 1965): 6.

Campbell, Will D. *Brother to a Dragonfly*. New York: Seabury, 1977.

——. "The Faith of a Fatalist." *New South* 23 (Spring 1968): 53–57.

——. *Forty Acres and a Goat: A Memoir*. Atlanta: Peachtree Publishers, 1986.

——. *Providence*. Atlanta: Longstreet Press, 1992.

——. *Race and the Renewal of the Church*. Philadelphia: Westminster, 1962.

——. "The Role of Religious Organization in the Desegregation Controversy." *Union
Seminary Quarterly Review* 36 (January 1961): 187–96.

——. "The Sit-Ins: Passive Resistance or Civil Disobedience?" *Social Action* 27 (January
1961): 14–18.

——. "Vocation as Grace." *Katallagete* 4 (Fall–Winter 1972): 81–86.

Campbell, Will D., and James Holloway. "An Open Letter to Billy Graham." *Katallagete*
3 (Winter 1971): 1–2.

Carroll, James. *An American Requiem: God, My Father, and the War That Came Between
Us*. Boston: Houghton Mifflin, 1996.

Carson, Clayborne. *In Struggle: SNCC and the Black Awakening of the 1960s*. Cambridge: Harvard University Press, 1981.

Carter, Hodding. *So the Heffners Left McComb*. Garden City, N.Y.: Doubleday, 1965.

Carter, Stephen L. *The Culture of Disbelief: How American Law and Politics Trivialize Religious Devotion*. New York: Basic, 1993.

Casey, William Van Etten, and Philip Nobile, eds. *The Berrigans*. New York: Praeger, 1971.

Castro, Emilio. Editorial. *Ecumenical Review* 38 (April 1986): 123–25.

"Catholic Know-Nothings." *Newsweek* 68 (August 29, 1966): 64.

Cattau, Daniel. "Author Still Runs, But Now It's in the Sunshine." *Episcopal Life*
(November 1991): 4.

"Caution on Civil Rights." *Time* 88 (August 26, 1966): 58.

Cavert, Samuel McCrea. *The American Churches in the Ecumenical Movement, 1900–
1968*. New York: Association Press, 1968.

"The Central Point." *Time* 85 (March 19, 1965): 24–25.

Chappell, David. *Inside Agitators: White Southerners in the Civil Rights Movement*. Baltimore: Johns Hopkins University Press, 1994.

Chestnut, J. L., Jr., and Julia Cass. *Black in Selma: The Uncommon Life of J. L. Chestnut,
Jr.* New York: Farrar, Straus and Giroux, 1990.

"Churchmen and the Challenge." *Commission on Religion and Race Reports* 1 (Summer
1965): 12–14.

Cistercian Contemplatives: A Guide to Trappist Life. New York: Marbridge Printing, 1948.

"Clergy Score Poorly in Great Electoral Game." *Christianity Today* 15 (December 4,
1970): 35.

"Clergymen-Candidates: Many Called, But Few Chosen." *U.S. News and World Report*
69 (November 16, 1970): 20–21.

"Clerical Candidates." *Time* 95 (June 8, 1970): 22.

Cobb, James C. " 'Somebody Done Nailed Us on the Cross': Federal Farm and Welfare
Policy and the Civil Rights Movement in the Mississippi Delta." *Journal of American
History* 77 (December 1990): 912–36.

Coburn, Bishop John B. Memorial address for Jonathan Daniels. Presented October 23,
1991, Episcopal Divinity School, Cambridge, Mass.

Cockburn, Alexander. "The People's Cathedral." *House and Garden* 158 (June 1986): 31–32.

"Coffin and Man at Yale." *Newsweek* 70 (November 13, 1967): 67.

Coffin, William Sloane, Jr. *Once to Every Man: A Memoir*. New York: Atheneum, 1978.

———. "Why Yale Chaplain Rode: Christians Can't Be Outside." *Life* 50 (June 2, 1961): 54–55.

Colburn, David R. *Racial Change and Community Crisis: St. Augustine, Florida, 1877–1980*. New York: Columbia University Press, 1985.

"Collars in the Ring." *Newsweek* 75 (May 4, 1970): 105–6.

"The Communists, Not Congressmen, Made That 'Attack on Religion.'" *Saturday Evening Post* 226 (October 10, 1953): 10, 12.

"The Concerned." *Newsweek* 60 (November 5, 1962): 99.

Cone, James H. *Black Theology and Black Power*. New York: Seabury, 1969.

Connelly, Thomas L. *Will Campbell and the Soul of the South*. New York: Continuum, 1982.

"Conversation with Martin Luther King, Jr." *Conservative Judaism* 22 (Spring 1968): 1–12.

Cooney, John. *The American Pope: The Life and Times of Francis Cardinal Spellman*. New York: Times Books, 1984.

Cooper, David D. *Thomas Merton's Art of Denial: The Evolution of a Radical Humanist*. Athens: University of Georgia Press, 1989.

Cox, Harvey. "The 'New Breed' in American Churches: Sources of Social Activism in American Religion." *Daedalus* 96 (Winter 1967): 135–50.

———. *The Secular City: Secularization and Urbanization in Theological Perspective*. New York: Macmillan, 1965.

"Crisis in Civil Rights." *Time* 79 (June 2, 1961): 15–17.

Crosby, Donald F., S.J. *God, Church, and Flag: Senator Joseph R. McCarthy and the Catholic Church, 1950–1957*. Chapel Hill: University of North Carolina Press, 1978.

Crow, Paul A., Jr. "Eugene Carson Blake: Apostle of Christian Unity." *Ecumenical Review* 38 (April 1986): 228–36.

Cunningham, W. J. *Agony at Galloway*. Jackson: University Press of Mississippi, 1980.

"Curbing the Delta Ministry." *Time* 87 (June 10, 1966): 84.

Curtis, Richard. *The Berrigan Brothers*. New York: Hathorn Books, 1974.

Davies, Alfred T., ed. *The Pulpit Speaks on Race*. New York: Abingdon Press, 1965.

Dawley, Power Mills. *The Story of the General Theological Seminary*. New York: Oxford University Press, 1969.

DeBenedetti, Charles. "On the Significance of Citizen Peace Activism: America, 1961–1975." *Peace and Change* 9 (Summer 1983): 7–18.

DeBenedetti, Charles, with Charles Chatfield. *An American Ordeal: The Antiwar Movement of the Vietnam Era*. Syracuse, N.Y.: Syracuse University Press, 1990.

Deedy, Jack. *"Apologies, Good Friends": An Interim Biography of Daniel Berrigan, S.J.* Chicago: Fides/Claretian, 1981.

"The Delta Ministry." *Commission on Religion and Race Reports* 1 (Spring 1965): 8.

DeSantis, Vincent P. "American Catholics and McCarthyism." *Catholic Historical Review* 51 (April 1965): 3–31.

Dinnerstein, Leonard. "A Neglected Aspect of Southern Jewish History." *American Jewish Historical Quarterly* 61 (September 1971): 52–68.

———. "A Note on Southern Attitudes toward Jews." *Jewish Social Studies* 32 (January 1970): 43–49.

———. "Southern Jewry and the Desegregation Crisis, 1954–1970." *American Jewish Historical Quarterly* 62 (March 1973): 231–41.

Dinnerstein, Leonard, and Mary Dale Palsson, eds. *Jews in the South*. Baton Rouge: Louisiana State University Press, 1973.

Dittmer, John. *Local People: The Struggle for Civil Rights in Mississippi*. Urbana: University of Illinois Press, 1994.

D'Souza, Dinesh. *Falwell: Before the Millenium. A Critical Biography*. Chicago: Regnery Gateway, 1984.

DuBay, William H. *The Human Church*. Garden City, N.Y.: Doubleday, 1966.

Dunbar, Anthony P. *Against the Grain: Southern Radicals and Prophets, 1929–1959*. Charlottesville: University Press of Virginia, 1981.

Durr, Virginia Foster. *Outside the Magic Circle: The Autobiography of Virginia Foster Durr*. University: University of Alabama Press, 1985.

Eagles, Charles W. *Outside Agitator: Jon Daniels and the Civil Rights Movement in Alabama*. Chapel Hill: University of North Carolina Press, 1993.

Edelman, Bernard, ed. *Dear America: Letters Home from Vietnam*. New York: W. W. Norton, 1985.

Egerton, John. *A Mind to Stay Here: Profiles from the South*. New York: Macmillan, 1970.

Eisele, Albert. *Almost to the Presidency: A Biography of Two American Politicians*. Blue Earth, Minn.: Piper, 1972.

Eisendrath, Maurice N. *Can Faith Survive? The Thoughts and Afterthoughts of an American Rabbi*. New York: McGraw-Hill, 1964.

"Electric Charges." *Time* 85 (March 26, 1965): 19–20.

Elovitz, Mark H. *A Century of Jewish Life in Dixie: The Birmingham Experience*. University: University of Alabama Press, 1974.

Emerson, Gloria. *Winners and Losers: Battles, Retreats, Gains, Losses and Ruins from a Long War*. New York: Random House, 1976.

Evans, Eli N. *The Provincials: A Personal History of Jews in the South*. New York: Atheneum, 1973.

"Exodus from the Pastorate." *Christianity Today* 14 (April 10, 1970): 34–35.

Fager, Charles E. *Selma, 1965: The March That Changed the South*. 2d ed. Boston: Beacon, 1985.

Fairclough, Adam. *Race and Democracy: The Civil Rights Struggle in Louisiana, 1915–1972*. Athens: University of Georgia Press, 1995.

———. *To Redeem the Soul of America: The Southern Christian Leadership Conference and Martin Luther King, Jr.* Athens: University of Georgia Press, 1987.

Farmer, James. *Lay Bare the Heart: An Autobiography of the Civil Rights Movement*. New York: Arbor House, 1985.

Feinberg, Rabbi Abraham L. *Hanoi Diary*. Ontario: Longmans, 1968.

Ferber, Michael, and Staughton Lynd. *The Resistance*. Boston: Beacon, 1971.

Fey, Harold, ed. *The Ecumenical Advance: A History of the Ecumenical Movement*. Vol. 2, *1948–1968*. London: SPCK, 1970.

Fichter, Joseph H. *One-Man Research: Reminiscences of a Catholic Sociologist*. New York: John Wiley and Sons, 1973.

Fierman, Morton C. *Leap of Action: Ideas in the Theology of Abraham Joshua Heschel*. Lanham, Md.: University Press of America, 1990.

Findlay, James F. *Church People in the Struggle: The National Council of Churches and the Black Freedom Movement, 1950–1970*. New York: Oxford University Press, 1993.

———. "Religion and Politics in the Sixties: The Churches and the Civil Rights Act of 1964." *Journal of American History* 77 (June 1990): 66–92.

Finn, James, ed. *Protest: Pacifism and Politics*. New York: Random House, 1967.

Fitzgerald, Frances. *Fire in the Lake: The Vietnamese and the Americans in Vietnam*. New York: Vintage, 1972.

Flowers, Ronald B. *Religion in Strange Times: The 1960s and 1970s*. Macon, Ga.: Mercer University Press, 1984.

Forman, James. *The Making of Black Revolutionaries*. New York: Macmillan, 1972.

Fox, Richard. *Reinhold Niebuhr: A Biography*. San Francisco: Harper and Row, 1987.

Frady, Marshall. *Billy Graham: A Parable of American Righteousness*. Boston: Little, Brown, 1979.

———. *Southerners: A Journalist's Odyssey*. New York: New American Library, 1980.

Friedman, Maurice. *Abraham Joshua Heschel and Elie Wiesel: You Are My Witnesses*. New York: Farrar, Straus and Giroux, 1987.

Friedman, Murray. "One Episode in Southern Jewry's Response to Desegregation: An Historical Memoir." *American Jewish Archives* 33 (November 1981): 170–83.

———. "Virginia Jewry in the School Crisis." *Commentary* 27 (January 1959): 20–23.

Garrow, David. *Bearing the Cross: Martin Luther King, Jr., and the Southern Christian Leadership Conference*. New York: Vintage, 1986.

———. *Protest at Selma: Martin Luther King, Jr., and the Voting Rights Act of 1965*. New Haven: Yale University Press, 1978.

———, ed. *Birmingham, Alabama, 1956–1963: The Black Struggle for Civil Rights*. New York: Carlson, 1989.

———, ed. *St. Augustine, Florida, 1963–1964*. New York: Carlson, 1989.

———, ed. *The Walking City: The Montgomery Bus Boycott, 1955–1956*. New York: Carlson, 1989.

Gentile, Thomas. *March on Washington: August 28, 1963*. Washington, D.C.: New Day Publications, 1983.

Gerstle, Gary. "Race and the Myth of the Liberal Consensus." *Journal of American History* 82 (September 1995): 579–86.

Geyer, Alan, and Dean Peerman, eds. *Theological Crossings*. Grand Rapids, Mich.: William B. Eerdmans, 1971.

Gibson, James W. *The Perfect War*. Boston: Atlantic Monthly Press, 1986.

Gill, Jill. " 'Peace Is Not the Absence of War But the Presence of Justice': The National Council of Churches' Reaction and Response to the Vietnam War 1965–1972." Ph.D. dissertation, University of Pennsylvania, 1996.

Gitlin, Todd. *The Sixties: Years of Hope, Days of Rage*. New York: Bantam, 1987.

Glock, Charles Y., and Benjamin B. Ringer. "Church Policy and the Attitudes of Ministers and Parishioners on Social Issues." *American Sociological Review* 21 (April 1956): 148–56.

Glock, Charles Y., Benjamin B. Ringer, and Earl R. Babbie. *To Comfort and to Challenge: A Dilemma of the Contemporary Church*. Berkeley: University of California Press, 1967.

Glock, Charles Y., and Ellen Siegelman, eds. *Prejudice, U.S.A.* New York: Frederick A. Praeger, 1969.

Glock, Charles Y., and Rodney Stark. *Religion and Society in Tension*. Chicago: Rand McNally, 1965.

Goldberg, Irving L. "The Changing Jewish Community of Dallas." *American Jewish Archives* 11 (April 1959): 82–97.

Golden, Harry. "Jews and Gentiles in the New South: Segregation at Sundown." *Commentary* 20 (May 1955): 406–7, 412.

Good, Paul. *The Trouble I've Seen*. Washington, D.C.: Howard University Press, 1975.

"Good Will." *Newsweek* 79 (March 8, 1972): 84.

Graetz, Robert. Letter to the Editor. *Time* 69 (February 25, 1957): 6.

———. *Montgomery: A White Preacher's Memoir*. Minneapolis: Fortress Press, 1991.

Graham, Billy. "Billy Graham Makes Plea for an End to Intolerance." *Life* 41 (October 1, 1956): 140.

———. *Peace with God*. Garden City, N.Y.: Doubleday, 1953.

——. *World Aflame*. Garden City N.Y.: Doubleday, 1965.

Gray, Duncan J., Jr. "In Defense of the Steeple." *Katallagete* 2 (Winter 1968–69): 29–31.

Gray, Francine du Plessix. *Divine Disobedience: Profiles in Catholic Radicalism*. New York: Alfred A. Knopf, 1970.

——. "To March or Not to March." *New York Times Magazine* (June 27, 1976): 6–7, 31, 34, 36, 38–39.

Griffin, John Howard. *Follow the Ecstasy: Thomas Merton: The Hermitage Years, 1965–1968*. Fort Worth, Tex.: JHG Editions/Latitudes Press, 1983.

Gutierrez, Gustavo. *A Theology of Liberation*. Translated by Sister Caridad Inda and John Eagleson. Maryknoll, N.Y.: Orbis, 1973.

Hadden, Jeffrey K. *The Gathering Storm in the Churches*. Garden City, N.Y.: Doubleday, 1969.

Halberstam, David. *The Best and the Brightest*. New York: Fawcett-Crest, 1972.

Haldeman, H. R., with Joseph Diadona. *The Ends of Power*. New York: Dell, 1978.

Hall, Mitchell K. *Because of Their Faith: CALCAV and Religious Opposition to the Vietnam War*. New York: Columbia University Press, 1990.

Halpert, Stephen, and Tom Murray, eds. *Witness of the Berrigans*. Garden City, N.Y.: Doubleday, 1972.

Halstead, Fred. *Out Now! A Participant's Account of the American Movement against the Vietnam War*. New York: Monad, 1978.

Hamilton, Michael, ed. *The Vietnam War: Christian Perspectives*. Grand Rapids, Mich.: William B. Eerdmans, 1967.

Hampton, Henry, and Steve Fayer. *Voices of Freedom: An Oral History of the Civil Rights Movement from the 1950s through the 1980s*. New York: Bantam, 1990.

Handy, Robert T. *A History of Union Theological Seminary in New York*. New York: Columbia University Press, 1987.

Hanh, Thich Nhat. *Vietnam: Lotus in a Sea of Fire*. New York: Hill and Wang, 1967.

Harris, Michael P. "Rev. William Sloane Coffin: Theology in Action from Montgomery to Harlem." *Perspectives* 15 (Summer 1983): 22–25.

"Has the Church Lost Its Soul?" *Newsweek* 78 (October 4, 1971): 188–89.

Haselden, Kyle. "11 A.M. Sunday Is Our Most Segregated Hour." *New York Times Magazine* (August 7, 1964): 9–14.

——. *The Racial Problem in Christian Perspective*. New York: Harper and Brothers, 1959.

Hassler, Alfred. *Saigon, U.S.A.* New York: Richard W. Baron, 1970.

Heath, Jim F. *Decade of Disillusionment: The Kennedy-Johnson Years*. Bloomington: Indiana University Press, 1975.

Hedgeman, Anna Arnold. *The Gift of Chaos: Decades of American Dissent*. New York: Oxford University Press, 1977.

——. *The Trumpet Sounds: A Memoir of Negro Leadership*. New York: Holt, Rinehart and Winston, 1964.

Heineman, Kenneth. *Campus Wars: The Peace Movement at American State Universities in the Vietnam Era*. New York: New York University Press, 1993.

Hennesey, James, S.J. *American Catholics: A History of the Roman Catholic Community in the United States*. Oxford: Oxford University Press, 1981.

Herberg, Will. *Protestant-Catholic-Jew: An Essay in American Religious Sociology*. Chicago: University of Chicago Press, 1983.

Herring, George C. *America's Longest War: The United States and Vietnam, 1950–1975*. New York: John Wiley and Sons, 1979.

Heschel, Abraham Joshua. "Choose Life!" *Jubilee* 13 (January 1966): 36–39.

——. *God in Search of Man: A Philosophy of Judaism*. New York: Farrar, Straus, and Cudahy, 1955.

——. *The Insecurities of Freedom: Essays on Human Existence.* New York: Farrar, Straus and Giroux, 1966.

——. *Man Is Not Alone: A Philosophy of Religion.* New York: Farrar, Straus, and Young, 1951.

——. *Man's Quest for God: Studies in Prayer and Symbolism.* New York: Charles Scribner's Sons, 1954.

——. "No Religion Is an Island." *Union Seminary Quarterly Review* 21 (January 1966): 117–34.

——. *A Passion for Truth.* New York: Farrar, Straus and Giroux, 1973.

——. *The Prophets.* New York: Harper and Row, 1962.

Hillis, Bryan V. *Can Two Walk Together Unless They Be Agreed? American Religious Schisms in the 1970s.* Brooklyn, N.Y.: Carlson, 1991.

Hilton, Bruce. *The Delta Ministry.* Toronto: Collier-Macmillan, 1969.

Hinckle, Warren, and David Welsh. "Five Battles of Selma." *Ramparts* 4 (June 1965): 28–36.

Hollander, Paul. *Anti-Americanism: Critiques at Home and Abroad, 1965–1990.* New York: Oxford University Press, 1992.

Hopkins, Charles Howard. *The Rise of the Social Gospel in American Protestantism, 1865–1915.* New Haven: Yale University Press, 1940.

Hough, Joseph C., Jr. *Black Power and White Protestants: A Christian Response to the New Negro Pluralism.* New York: Oxford University Press, 1968.

Howell, Leon. *Freedom City.* Richmond, Va.: John Knox Press, 1969.

Huckaby, Elizabeth. *Crisis at Central High: Little Rock, 1957–58.* Baton Rouge: Louisiana State University Press, 1980.

Humphrey, Hubert H. *The Education of a Public Man: My Life and Politics.* Garden City, N.Y.: Doubleday, 1976.

Hutchinson, Paul. "Have We a 'New' Religion?" *Life* 38 (April 11, 1955): 140, 147–50.

——. "The President's Religious Faith." *Life* 36 (March 22, 1954): 151–55.

Hutchison, John A., ed. *Christian Faith and Social Action.* New York: Charles Scribner's Sons, 1953.

Hutchison, William R., ed. *Between the Times: The Travail of the Protestant Establishment in America, 1900–1960.* Cambridge: Cambridge University Press, 1989.

"'If You Can't March, At Least Stand Up': Interfaith Call to Action by the Religious Leaders of Massachusetts," *Fellowship* 6 (March–April–May 1970): 82.

Ingram, T. Robert, ed. *Essays on Segregation.* Houston: St. Thomas Press, 1960.

Jack, Homer A., ed. *Religion and Peace: Papers from the National Inter-Religious Conference on Peace.* Indianapolis: Bobbs-Merrill, 1966.

"January to May 1965." *Commission on Religion and Race Reports* 1 (Spring 1965): 3.

"Jerry Falwell's Crusade." *Time* 126 (September 2, 1985): 48–57.

Johnson, Lyndon B. *The Vantage Point: Perspectives of the Presidency, 1963–1969.* New York: Holt, Rinehart, and Winston, 1971.

Jud, Gerald J., Edward W. Mills Jr., and Genevieve Walters Burch. *Ex-Pastors: Why Men Leave the Parish Ministry.* Philadelphia: Pilgrim Press, 1970.

Kaplan, Edward K. "The Spiritual Radicalism of Abraham Joshua Heschel." *Conservative Judaism* 28 (Fall 1973): 40–49.

Karnow, Stanley. *Vietnam: A History.* New York: Viking Penguin, 1991.

Kasimow, Harold, and Byron L. Sherwin, eds. *No Religion Is an Island: Abraham Joshua Heschel and Interreligious Dialogue.* Maryknoll, N.Y.: Orbis, 1991.

Katz, Milton. *Ban the Bomb: A History of SANE, the Committee for a Sane Nuclear Policy, 1957–1985.* Westport, Conn. Greenwood, 986.

Kemper, Donald J. "Catholic Integration in St. Louis, 1935–1947." *Missouri Historical Review* 73 (1978): 1–22.

King, Coretta Scott. *My Life With Martin Luther King, Jr.* London: Hodder and Staughton, 1969.

King, Martin Luther, Jr. "Behind the Selma March." *Saturday Review* 48 (April 3, 1965): 16–17, 57.

——. "Letter to an Anti-Zionist Friend." *Saturday Review* 47 (August 1967): 76.

——. *Stride toward Freedom.* New York: Harper and Row, 1958.

——. *Where Do We Go from Here: Chaos or Community?* Boston: Beacon, 1967.

——. *Why We Can't Wait.* New York: Harper and Row, 1963.

King, Mary. *Freedom Song: A Personal Story of the 1960s Civil Rights Movement.* New York: William Morrow, 1987.

Kissinger, Henry. *The White House Years.* Boston: Little, Brown, 1979.

Klunder, Mrs. Bruce. "My Husband Died for Democracy." *Ebony* 19 (June 1964): 27–31.

Knebel, Fletcher, and Clark Mollenhoff. "Eight Klans Bring New Terror to the South." *Look* 21 (April 30, 1957): 61–63.

Konolige, Kit, and Frederica Konolige. *The Power of Their Glory: America's Ruling Class: The Episcopalians.* New York: Wyden Books, 1978.

Kopkind, Andrew. "Selma: 'Ain't Gonna Let Nobody Turn Me 'Round.'" *New Republic* 152 (March 20, 1965): 7–9.

Krause, Allen P. "Rabbis and Negro Rights in the South, 1954–1967." *American Jewish Archives* 21 (April 1969): 10–47.

LaFarge, John, S.J. *The Catholic Viewpoint on Race Relations.* Garden City, N.Y.: Hanover House, 1960.

Laue, James H. *Direct Action and Desegregation, 1960–1962: Toward a Theory of the Rationalization of Protest.* New York: Carlson, 1989.

Lawrence, David. "Is the Clergyman Changing His Role?" *U.S. News and World Report* 58 (April 1965): 116.

Lawrence, Nancy. "A Progress Report: Racially Inclusive Churches." *National Council Outlook* 4 (December 1954): 11–12.

LeBeau, James. "Profile of a Southern Jewish Community: Waycross, Georgia." *American Jewish Historical Quarterly* 58 (June 1969): 429–42.

Lecky, Robert S., and H. Elliott Wright, eds. *Black Manifesto: Religion, Racism, and Reparations.* New York: Sheed and Ward, 1969.

Lee, Robert. *The Promise of Bennett.* Philadelphia: J. B. Lippincott, 1969.

Lee, Robert, and Martin E. Marty, eds. *Religion and Social Conflict.* New York: Oxford University Press, 1964.

Lefever, Ernest W. *Amsterdam to Nairobi: The World Council of Churches and the Third World.* Washington, D.C.: Ethics and Public Policy Center, 1979.

Lemann, Nicholas. *The Promised Land: The Great Black Migration and How It Changed America.* New York: Vintage, 1992.

Lens, Sidney. *Unrepentant Radical: An American Activist's Account of Five Turbulent Decades.* Boston: Beacon, 1980.

Leonard, Joseph T. *Theology and Race Relations.* Milwaukee: Bruce Publishing, 1963.

"Letter to Martin Luther King, Jr. from a Buddhist Monk." *Liberation* 10 (December 1965): 18–19.

Levy, David. *The Debate over Vietnam.* Baltimore: Johns Hopkins University Press, 1991.

Levy, Jacques. *Cesar Chavez: Autobiography of La Causa.* New York: W. W. Norton, 1975.

Lewis, David. *King: A Biography.* Urbana: University of Illinois Press, 1978.

Lewy, Guenter. *America in Vietnam.* New York: Oxford University Press, 1978.

——. *Peace and Revolution: The Moral Crisis of American Pacifism.* Grand Rapids, Mich.: William B. Eerdmans, 1988.

Lipman, Eugene J., and Albert Vorspan. *A Tale of Two Cities: The Triple Ghetto in American Religious Life*. New York: Union of American Hebrew Congregations, 1962.

Loescher, Frank S. *The Protestant Church and the Negro: A Pattern of Segregation*. New York: Association Press, 1948.

Longenecker, Stephen L. *Selma's Peacemaker: Ralph Smeltzer and Civil Rights Mediation*. Philadelphia: Temple University Press, 1987.

"Loyalty of the Clergy—'O.K.'" *U.S. News and World Report* 36 (February 19, 1954): 126–27.

McCarthy, Eugene J. *The Year of the People*. Garden City, N.Y.: Doubleday, 1969.

McGill, Ralph. "The Agony of the Southern Minister." *New York Times Magazine* (September 27, 1959): 57–60.

McKivigan, John R. *The War against Proslavery Religion: Abolition and the Northern Churches, 1830–1865*. Ithaca: Cornell University Press, 1984.

McMillan, George. "Silent White Ministers of the South." *New York Times Magazine* (April 5, 1964): 15–22.

McMillan, Neil R. *The Citizens' Council: Organized Resistance to the Second Reconstruction, 1954–64*. Urbana: University of Illinois Press, 1971.

McNamara, Robert S., with Brian VanDeMark. *In Retrospect: The Tragedy and Lessons of Vietnam*. New York: Times/Random House, 1995.

McNaspy, C. J. *At Face Value*. New Orleans: Institute of Human Relations, Loyola University of the South, 1978.

McNeill, Robert B. "A Georgia Minister Offers a Solution for the South." *Look* 21 (May 28, 1957): 55–64.

———. *God Wills Us Free: The Ordeal of a Southern Minister*. New York: Hill and Wang, 1965.

Malcolm X, with Alex Haley. *The Autobiography of Malcolm X*. New York: Ballantine, 1965.

Malev, William S. "The Jew of the South in the Conflict on Segregation." *Conservative Judaism* 8 (Fall 1958): 36–39.

"The March on Washington." *Christianity Today* 7 (August 30, 1963): 1135–36.

Martin, Robert F. "Critique of Southern Society and Vision of a New Order: The Fellowship of Southern Churchmen, 1934–1957." *Church History* 52 (March 1983): 66–80.

Martin, William. *A Prophet with Honor: The Billy Graham Story*. New York: William Morrow, 1991.

Martin, William C. *Christians in Conflict*. Chicago: Center for the Scientific Study of Religion, 1972.

Marty, Martin E. *The New Shape of American Religion*. New York: Harper and Brothers, 1959.

Massie, Robert K. "Don't Tread on Grandmother Peabody." *Saturday Evening Post* 237 (May 16, 1964): 76–77.

Matthews, J. B. "Reds and Our Churches." *American Mercury* 77 (July 1953): 3, 13.

Mays, Benjamin. *Born to Rebel*. New York: Charles Scribner's Sons, 1971.

Meconis, Charles A. *With Clumsy Grace: The American Catholic Left, 1961–1975*. New York: Seabury, 1979.

Meier, August, and Elliott Rudwick. *CORE: A Study in the Civil Rights Movement, 1942–1968*. New York: Oxford University Press, 1973.

Melman, Seymour, comp. *In the Name of America*. Annandale, Va.: Turnpike Press, 1968.

Melville, Thomas, and Marjorie Melville. *Whose Heaven, Whose Earth?* New York: Alfred A. Knopf, 1971.

Merkle, John C., ed. *Abraham Joshua Heschel: Exploring His Life and Thought*. New York: Macmillan, 1985.

———. *The Genesis of Faith: The Depth Theology of Abraham Joshua Heschel.* New York: Macmillan, 1985.

Merton, Thomas. *Breakthrough to Peace.* New York: New Directions, 1962.

———. *Conjectures of a Guilty Bystander.* Garden City, N.Y.: Doubleday, 1966.

———. *New Seeds of Contemplation.* New York: New Directions, 1961.

———. *The Secular Journal of Thomas Merton.* New York: Farrar, Straus, and Cudahy, 1959.

———. *Seeds of Destruction.* New York: Farrar, Straus and Giroux, 1964.

———. *The Seven-Storey Mountain.* New York: Harcourt, Brace, 1948.

———. "Non-Violence Does Not—Cannot—Mean Passivity." *Ave Maria* 108 (September 7, 1968): 9–10.

———. *Thomas Merton in Alaska: The Alaskan Conferences, Journals and Letters.* New York: New Directions, 1989.

———. *A Vow of Conversation: Journals, 1964–1965.* New York: Farrar, Straus and Giroux, 1988.

Miller, Keith D. *Voice of Deliverance: The Language of Martin Luther King, Jr. and Its Sources.* New York: Free Press/Macmillan, 1992.

Miller, Mike. "The Strike in the Grapes." *Commission on Religion and Race Reports* 2 (May 1966): 10–15.

Mills, Nicolaus. "Heard and Unheard Speeches: What Really Happened at the March on Washington?" *Dissent* 35 (Summer 1988): 285–91.

Mitford, Jessica. *The Trial of Dr. Spock.* New York: Alfred A. Knopf, 1969.

Moody, Anne. *Coming of Age in Mississippi.* New York: Dial, 1968.

Moore, Paul, Jr. *Take a Bishop Like Me.* New York: Harper and Row, 1979.

Morgan, Charles, Jr. *A Time to Speak.* New York: Harper and Row, 1964.

Morris, Aldon D. *The Origins of the Civil Rights Movement: Black Communities Organizing for Change.* New York: Free Press, 1984.

Morris, John. "Racism in Southern Africa and American Initiative." *New South* 21 (Summer, 1966): 17–25.

Morris, John B. "ESCRU: The Episcopal Society for Cultural and Racial Unity, 1959–1967." Paper presented at National Episcopal Historians and Archivists Conference, Austin, Tex., June 9, 1995.

Morrison, Chester. "The Minister Who Lost His Pulpit." *Look* 23 (July 21, 1959): 34.

"Mother Cecilia's Revolt." *Life* 58 (June 4, 1965): 45–46.

Mott, Michael. *The Seven Mountains of Thomas Merton.* Boston: Houghton Mifflin, 1984.

Murphy, Francis X. *The Papacy Today.* New York: Macmillan, 1981.

Muste, A. J. "Last Words: 1. Report on a Visit to North Vietnam." *Liberation* 11 (February 1967): 8–10.

Navasky, Victor. *Kennedy Justice.* New York: Atheneum, 1971.

Nelsen, Hart M., Raytha L. Yokley, and Thomas W. Madron. "Ministerial Roles and Social Actionist Stance: Protestant Clergy and Protest in the Sixties." *American Sociological Review* 38 (June 1973): 375–86.

Nelson, Jack, and Ronald J. Ostrow. *The FBI and the Berrigans: The Making of a Conspiracy.* New York: Coward, McCann, and Geoghegan, 1972.

Neuhaus, Richard John. "The War, the Churches, and Civil Religion." *Annals of the American Academy of Political and Social Science* 387 (January 1970): 135–42.

Newby, I. A. *Jim Crow's Defense: Anti-Negro Thought in America, 1900–1930.* Baton Rouge: Louisiana State University Press, 1965.

Niebuhr, Reinhold. *Christianity and Power Politics.* New York: Charles Scribner's Sons, 1940.

———. *Moral Man and Immoral Society.* New York: Charles Scribner's Sons, 1932.

"Night of Terror." *Time* 69 (January 21, 1957): 15.

Nixon, Richard. *RN: The Memoirs of Richard Nixon*. New York: Grosset and Dunlap, 1978.

Nobile, Philip. "The Priest Who Stayed Out in the Cold." *New York Times Magazine* (June 28, 1978): 8–9, 39.

Oates, Stephen. *Let the Trumpet Sound*. New York: Harper and Row, 1982.

Oberdorfer, Don. *Tet!* Garden City, N.Y.: Doubleday, 1971.

"October 15: A Day to Remember." *Newsweek* 75 (October 27, 1969): 34.

O'Connor, John. *A Chaplain Looks at Vietnam*. Cleveland: World, 1968.

O'Connor, John, ed. *American Catholic Exodus*. Washington, D.C.: Corpus Books, 1968.

O'Gorman, Angie, ed. *The Universe Bends toward Justice: A Reader on Christian Non-violence in the U.S.* Philadelphia: New Society, 1990.

O'Gorman, Ned. "The Freedom March." *Jubilee* 11 (October 1963): 16–21.

"On Investigating Clergymen." *National Council Outlook* 3 (May 1953): 17.

Oppenheimer, Martin. *The Sit-In Movement of 1960*. New York: Carlson, 1989.

Osborne, William A. *The Segregated Covenant: Race Relations and American Catholics*. New York: Herder and Herder, 1967.

Ouellet, Maurice. "The Testimony of a Selma Pastor." *Jubilee* 21 (August 1965): 21–22.

Oxnam, G. Bromley. *I Protest*. New York: Harper and Brothers, 1954.

Peck, James. *Freedom Ride*. New York: Simon and Schuster, 1962.

Perlmutter, Nathan. "Bombing in Miami." *Commentary* 25 (June 1958): 498–99.

Pratt, Henry J. *The Liberalization of American Protestantism: A Case Study in Complex Organizations*. Detroit: Wayne State University Press, 1972.

"The Preaching and the Power." *Newsweek* 76 (July 20, 1970): 35–36.

Proudfoot, Merrill. *Diary of a Sit-In*. 2d ed. Urbana: University of Illinois Press, 1962; reprint ed., 1990.

"The Pulpit v. the Bench." *Time* 88 (September 9, 1966): 23–24.

Quigley, Thomas E., ed. *American Catholics and Vietnam*. Grand Rapids, Mich.: William B. Eerdmans, 1968.

Quinley, Harold E. *The Prophetic Clergy: Social Activism among Protestant Ministers*. New York: John Wiley and Sons, 1974.

Raines, Howell. *My Soul Is Rested: The Story of the Civil Rights Movement in the Deep South*. New York: Viking Penguin, 1983.

Record, Wilson, and Jane Cassels Record. *Little Rock, U.S.A.* San Francisco: Chandler, 1960.

Reed, Ralph. " 'We Stand at a Crossroads.' " *Newsweek* 127 (May 13, 1996): 28–29.

Regner, Sidney L., ed. *Yearbook of Central Conference of American Rabbis*. Vols. 73, 75–78, 85. New York: CCAR, 1964, 1966–69, 1976.

Reimers, David M. *White Protestantism and the Negro*. New York: Oxford University Press, 1965.

Reissman, Leonard. "The New Orleans Jewish Community." *Jewish Journal of Sociology* 4 (June 1962): 110–23.

"Religion in Action: Little Rock's Clergy Leads the Way." *Time* 70 (October 14, 1957): 30.

"Religious, Academic Ethicists Defend U.N. in Face of GOP Assault." *Los Angeles Times* (March 11, 1995): 4.

Resolution of the Commission on Religion and Race. *Interchurch News* 4 (June–July 1963): 6–7.

Riley, David. "Who Is Jimmie Lee Jackson?" *New Republic* 152 (April 3, 1965): 8–9.

Ro'i, Yaacov. *The Struggle for Soviet Jewish Emigration, 1948–1967*. Cambridge: Cambridge University Press, 1991.

Robinson, Jo Ann Gibson. *The Montgomery Bus Boycott and the Women Who Started It*. Knoxville: University of Tennessee Press, 1987.

Robinson, Jo Ann Ooiman. *Abraham Went Out: A Biography of A. J. Muste.* Philadelphia: Temple University Press, 1981.

"The Role of the National Council of Churches in the Mississippi Summer Project." *Social Action* 31 (November 1964): 10–13.

"A Roundtable Has Debate on Christians' Moral Duty." *Life* 41 (October 1, 1956): 145–48.

Ross, Mary Beth. "A 'Tentatif.'" *The Heights (The Le Moyne College Magazine)* 9 (Summer 1971): 16–20.

Rowan, Carl. *Go South to Sorrow.* New York: Random House, 1957.

Roy, Ralph Lord. *Apostles of Discord: A Study of Organized Bigotry and Disruption on the Fringes of Protestantism.* Boston: Beacon, 1953.

Russell, Jean. *God's Lost Cause: A Study of the Church and the Racial Problem.* London: SCM Press, 1968.

Rutenber, Culbert G. "Ministers and Social Ethics: A Case Study." *Andover Newton Quarterly* n.s. 1 (January 1961): 30–33.

Safire, William. *Before the Fall: An Inside View of the Pre-Watergate White House.* Garden City, N.Y.: Doubleday, 1975.

Saks, Robert J. "Jews, Judaism, and the New Left." *Conservative Judaism* 21 (Summer 1967): 43–44.

Salisbury, Harrison. *A Time of Change: A Reporter's Tale of Our Time.* New York: Harper and Row, 1988.

Salter, John R. *Jackson, Mississippi: An American Chronicle of Struggle and Schism.* Hicksville, N.Y.: Exposition Press, 1979.

Sanders, J. A. "An Apostle to the Gentiles." *Conservative Judaism* 28 (Fall 1973): 61–63.

Sanders, Marion K. "A Professional Radical Moves in on Rochester: Conversations With Saul Alinsky, Part II." *Harper's Magazine* 231 (July 1965): 49–53.

Sanderson, Ross W. *The Church Serves the Changing City.* New York: Harper and Brothers, 1955.

Sappington, Roger E. *Brethren Social Policy, 1908–1958.* Elgin, Ill.: Brethren Press, 1961.

Sarratt, Reed. *The Ordeal of Desegregation: The First Decade.* New York: Harper and Row, 1966.

Schell, Jonathan. *The Time of Illusion.* New York: Vintage, 1976.

Schmidt, Jean Miller. *Souls or the Social Order.* New York: Carlson, 1991.

Schulz, Harold K. "The Delta Ministry." *Social Action* 31 (November 1964): 31–32.

Seabury, Paul. "Trendier than Thou." *Harper's Magazine* 257 (October 1978): 39–52.

"Selma, Civil Rights, and the Church Militant." *Newsweek* 65 (March 29, 1965): 75–78.

Shankman, Arnold. "A Temple Is Bombed—Atlanta, 1958." *American Jewish Archives* 23 (November 1971): 125–53.

Shannon, William H., ed. *The Hidden Ground of Love: The Letters of Thomas Merton on Religious Experience and Social Concerns.* New York: Farrar, Straus and Giroux, 1985.

Sheil, Bishop Bernard J. "Should a Clergyman Stay Out of Politics?" *Look* 18 (August 10, 1954): 66–69.

Sherman, Franklin. *The Promise of Heschel.* Philadelphia: J. B. Lippincott, 1970.

Sheerin, John B. "The Morality of the Vietnam War." *Catholic World* 202 (March 1966): 326–30.

"Silent March." *Newsweek* 71 (February 19, 1968): 58.

Silver, James W. *James Silver: Running Scared in Mississippi.* Jackson: University Press of Mississippi, 1984.

——. "Mississippi: The Closed Society." *Journal of Southern History* 30 (February 1964): 3–11.

——. *Mississippi: The Closed Society.* New York: Harcourt, Brace and World, 1963.

Small, Melvin, and William D. Hoover, eds. *Give Peace a Chance: Exploring the Vietnam Antiwar Movement*. Syracuse: Syracuse University Press, 1992.

Smith, Bob. *They Closed Their Schools: Prince Edward County, Virginia, 1951–1964*. Chapel Hill: University of North Carolina Press, 1965.

Smith, David H. *The Achievement of John C. Bennett*. New York: Herder and Herder, 1970.

Smith, H. Shelton. *In His Image, But . . . : Racism in Southern Religion, 1780–1910*. Durham, N.C.: Duke University Press, 1972.

Smith, H. Shelton, Robert T. Handy, and Lefferts Loetscher, eds. *American Christianity: An Historical Interpretation with Representative Documents*. Vol. 2, 1820–1960. New York: Charles Scribner's Sons, 1963.

Smylie, J. H. "American Religious Bodies, Just War, and Vietnam." *Journal of Church and State* 11 (Fall 1969): 383–408.

Snow, Malinda. "Martin Luther King Jr.'s Letter from Birmingham Jail as Pauline Epistle." *Quarterly Journal of Speech* 71 (August 1985): 318–34.

"Southern Ministers Speak Their Minds." *Pulpit Digest* 39 (December 1958): 13–17.

The Southern Regional Council: Its Origin and Purpose. Atlanta: Southern Regional Council, 1944.

"South's Churchmen: Integration and Religion." *Newsweek* 50 (October 7, 1957): 37.

Sperry, Willard, ed. *Religion and Our Racial Tensions*. College Park, Md.: McGrath, 1945.

Spike, Robert W. *Safe in Bondage: An Appraisal of the Church's Mission in America*. New York: Friendship Press, 1960.

——. *The Freedom Revolution and the Churches*. New York: Association Press, 1965.

——. "Mississippi—An Ecumenical Ministry." *Social Action* 31 (November 1964): 17–19.

——. "Our Churches' Sin against the Negro." *Look* 29 (May 18, 1965): 29–30.

Spitzberg, Irving J., Jr. *Racial Politics in Little Rock, 1954–1964*. New York: Garland, 1987.

Spock, Benjamin. *Spock on Spock: A Memoir of Growing Up with the Century*. New York: Pantheon, 1989.

Stackhouse, Max L. "Whatever Happened to Reparations?: Social and Theological Reflections One Year Later." *Andover-Newton Quarterly* 11 (November 1970): 61–71.

Stammer, Larry B. "Force Justified to Save Bosnians, Bishops Tell U.S." *Los Angeles Times* (May 13, 1993): A-1.

——. "Vanguard Priest Tempers His Radicalism." *Los Angeles Times* (October 29, 1994): B-4.

Stark, Rodney, and Charles Glock. *American Piety: The Nature of Religious Commitment*. Berkeley: University of California Press, 1968.

"Statement Adopted by the Committee of Southern Churchmen, Nashville, Tennessee, February 6, 1964." *Katallagete* 1 (Winter 1967–68): back cover.

Stolley, Richard B. "Inside the White House: Pressures Build Up to the Momentous Speech." *Life* 58 (March 26, 1965): 34–35.

Stone, Andrea. "Southern Baptists to Apologize for Slavery." *USA Today* (June 19, 1995): 1.

Stone, I. F. *In a Time of Torment*. New York: Random House, 1967.

Stouffer, Samuel A. *Communism, Conformity, and Civil Liberties: A Cross-Section of the Nation Speaks Its Mind*. Garden City, N.Y.: Doubleday, 1955.

Stringfellow, William. *My People Is the Enemy: An Autobiographical Polemic*. New York: Holt, Rinehart, and Winston, 1964.

Sullivan, Clayton. "Integration Could Destroy Rural Mississippi." *Saturday Evening Post* 238 (April 10, 1965): 10–15.

Sullivan, Oona. "Selma Aftermath." *Jubilee* 13 (August 1965): 16.

Sutherland, Elizabeth, ed. *Letters from Mississippi*. New York: McGraw-Hill, 1965.

Taft, Adon. "Selma: Parable of the Old South." *Christianity Today* 9 (March 12, 1965): 47–48.

Talmage, Frank Ephraim, ed. *Disputation and Dialogue: Readings in the Jewish-Christian Encounter*. New York: KTAV Publishing House, 1975.

Tannenbaum, Marc H. "Israel's Hour of Need and the Jewish-Christian Dialogue." *Conservative Judaism* 22 (Winter 1968): 1–18.

"That Awful Fatalism." *Time* 81 (January 25, 1963): 66.

Thomas, Arthur. "The Meaning of the Summer for the Church." *Social Action* 31 (November 1964): 22.

Toby, Jackson. "Bombing in Nashville." *Commentary* 25 (May 1958): 385–87.

Tollefson, James W. *The Strength Not to Fight: An Oral History of the Conscientious Objectors of the Vietnam War*. New York: Little, Brown, 1993.

Traxler, Sister Mary Peter, ed. *Split-Level Lives: American Nuns Speak on Race*. Techny, Ill.: Divine Word Publications, 1967.

Traynham, Warner R. *Christian Faith in Black and White: A Primer in Theology from the Black Perspective*. Wakefield, Mass.: Parameter, 1973.

Trillin, Calvin. "Reflections: Remembrances of Moderates Past." *New Yorker* 53 (March 21, 1977): 85–86.

True, Michael. *Daniel Berrigan: Poetry, Drama, Prose*. Maryknoll, N.Y.: Orbis, 1988.

Ungar, Andre. "To Birmingham and Back." *Conservative Judaism* 18 (Fall 1963): 9–14.

U.S. Congress. House. Statement by Representatives Andrews of Alabama and Williams of Mississippi, 89th Cong., 1st sess., March 17, 1965. *Congressional Record* 111: 5299, 5307.

——. Statement by Representative Anderson of New York, 91st Cong., 2d sess., December 9, 1970. *Congressional Record* 116: 40772–74.

U.S. Congress. Senate. Statement by Senator Richard B. Russell of Georgia, 88th Cong., 2d sess., June 18, 1964, *Congressional Record* 110: 14299.

——. Statement by Senator Scott of New York, "Senator Scott Lauds Role of Episcopal Church in Civil Rights Struggle," 89th Cong., 1st sess., March 25, 1964. *Congressional Record* 111: 5878.

——. Statement by Senator Stennis of Mississippi, 88th Cong., 2d sess., June 18, 1964. *Congressional Record* 110: 14323–25.

Vogel, Manfred. "Some Reflections on the Jewish-Christian Dialogue in the Light of the Six-Day War." *Annals of the American Academy of Political and Social Science* 387 (January 1970): 96–108.

von Hoffman, Nicholas. *Mississippi Notebook*. New York: David White, 1964.

Vorspan, Albert. "In St. Augustine." *Midstream* 10 (September 1964): 15–17.

Vorspan, Albert, and Eugene J. Lipman. *Justice and Judaism: The Work of Social Action*. New York: Union of American Hebrew Congregations, 1959.

Walker, Randolph. "Blacks, Southern Baptists." *Tri-State Defender* (July 12, 1995): 6.

Walton, Norman W. "The Walking City: A History of the Montgomery Bus Boycott, Part I." *Negro History Bulletin* 20 (October 1956): 19–20.

——. "The Walking City: A History of the Montgomery Bus Boycott, Part II." *Negro History Bulletin* 20 (November 1956): 26–28.

——. "The Walking City: A History of the Montgomery Bus Boycott, Part IV." *Negro History Bulletin* 20 (April 1957): 149–50.

Warren, Robert Penn. *Segregation: The Inner Conflict in the South*. New York: Random House, 1956.

Washington, James Melvin, ed. *A Testament of Hope: The Essential Writings of Martin Luther King, Jr*. San Francisco: Harper and Row, 1986.

Waskow, Arthur, and Marcus Raskin. "A Call to Resist Illegitimate Authority." *New Republic* 157 (October 7, 1967): 34–35.

Webb, Sheyann, and Rachel West Nelson. *Selma, Lord, Selma: Girlhood Memories of the Civil-Rights Days*. As told to Frank Sikora. Alabama: University of Alabama Press, 1979.

Wells, Tom. *The War Within: America's Battle Over Vietnam*. Berkeley: University of California Press, 1994.

Whalen, Charles, and Barbara Whalen. *The Longest Debate: A Legislative History of the 1964 Civil Rights Act*. Cabin John, Md.: Seven Locks Press, 1985.

"What Hope Have We?" *Newsweek* 53 (June 22, 1959): 59.

"When Clergy Protest—What Is Appropriate?" *Ave Maria* 101 (March 27, 1965): 5.

Whitfield, Stephen J. *The Culture of the Cold War*. Baltimore: Johns Hopkins University Press, 1991.

Wiesel, Elie. *Against Silence: The Voice and Vision of Elie Wiesel*. Vol. 2. New York: Holocaust Library, 1985.

———. *All Rivers Run to the Sea: Memoirs*. New York: Alfred A. Knopf, 1995.

Winter, Gibson. *The Suburban Captivity of the Churches*. Garden City, N.Y.: Doubleday, 1961.

Wittner, Lawrence S. *Rebels Against War: The American Peace Movement, 1933–1983*. Philadelphia: Temple University Press, 1984.

Woodward, Kenneth. "A Foretaste of Eternity." *Newsweek* 81 (January 8, 1973): 50.

Wren, Christopher S. "Turning Point for the Church." *Look* 29 (May 18, 1965): 30–37.

Wuthnow, Robert. *The Restructuring of American Religion: Society and Faith since World War II*. Princeton: Princeton University Press, 1988.

Young, Perry Deane. *God's Bullies: Power Politics and Religious Tyranny*. New York: Holt, Rinehart and Winston, 1982.

Zahn, Gordon, ed. *Thomas Merton: The Nonviolent Alternative*. New York: Farrar, Straus and Giroux, 1980.

Zaroulis, Nancy, and Gerald Sullivan. *Who Spoke Up? American Protest against the War in Vietnam, 1963–1975*. Garden City, N.Y.: Doubleday, 1984.

Zinn, Howard. *Vietnam: The Logic of Withdrawal*. Boston: Beacon, 1967.

index

Black Manifesto, 191, 239; and reparations, 214

Black nationalism, in Southern Rhodesia, 31–32; in United States, 189–91

Black Panthers, 148, 225

"Black Power" movement, 110, 189–92

Black Presbyterians United, 191

Blake, Eugene Carson, 8, 15, 36, 71; early life and career, 14; on Montgomery bus boycott, 29; and NCC Commission on Religion and Race, 81, 82; and Gwynn Oaks Amusement Park, 82–83; religious views of, 84; and March on Washington, 86, 87–89; support for federal civil rights legislation, 86–87; meets with John F. Kennedy, 90; on death of Bruce Klunder, 94–95; and support for Civil Rights Act (1964), 100; meets with Lyndon Johnson, 127; and antiwar movement, 145, 168, 173, 184, 220, 278 (n. 78); and World Council of Churches, 173; and "black power," 190; and death of Martin Luther King Jr., 204; criticism of Malcolm Boyd, 223; on power of institutional church, 240–41; death of, 240

Blank, Irwin, 74, 86

Bondhus, Barry, 208

Bonhoeffer, Dietrich, 60, 134

"Born of Conviction," 102

Borowitz, Eugene, 98

Bosley, Harold, 164

Bosnian crisis, 249–50

Boston Five, 210; federal indictments of, 197–98; trial of, 205–6. *See also* William Sloane Coffin Jr.; Michael Ferber; Mitchell Goodman; Marcus Raskin; Benjamin Spock

Boston Globe, 97

Boyd, Malcolm, 8, 71, 232; early life and career, 58–59; as college chaplain, 59–60, 62, 123; plays of, 60, 133, 134; and Prayer Pilgrimage, 60–61; and ESCRU, 62, 123, 134; and Paul Moore, 104, 123; and Episcopal Diocese of Washington, D.C., 123; and "Ministers March," 123; travels through the South, 123, 134, 270 (n. 34); support for voting rights bill, 133; and Jonathan Daniels, 134, 137; and "black power," 190; and 1968 Washington Mobilization, 201; antiwar activities

of, 201; on 1968 presidential campaign, 214; and "Ecumenical Mass for Peace," 219; and "Jonathan's Wake," 222; criticism of institutional churches, 223; and "underground church," 240; AIDS ministry of, 244; homosexuality of, 244

Boyle, Kay, 172

Branch, Taylor, 79

Braun, Theodore, 25

Brickner, Balfour, 99, 168; in St. Augustine, 98; and CALCAV, 164, 177, 229; and June War of 1967, 186–87; and support for conscientious objectors, 193; on death of Martin Luther King Jr., 205; and antiwar movement, 221

Brooke, Edward, 227

Brothers and Sisters, 208

Brown, Claude C., 115, 121, 135

Brown, Robert McAfee, 8, 71, 232, 234; early life and career, 56–57; and freedom ride, 56–58, 107; on fair housing legislation, 95–96; and "Ministers March," 122, 124; early views on Vietnam War, 144, 153, 188; and religious wing of antiwar movement, 148; and establishment of CALCAV, 164, 229; and support of dissent, 169; and 1967 CALCAV Washington mobilization, 179–80; meets with Robert McNamara, 180–81; participation in antiwar demonstrations, 181, 183–84, 230; and *Vietnam: Crisis of Conscience*, 185–86; and support for Israel, 187; and support for civil disobedience, 192–93; role in civil rights and antiwar movements compared, 192–93; and support for conscientious objectors, 193, 198, 229–30; and support for the Boston Five, 198; and *In the Name of America*, 200–201; on death of Martin Luther King Jr., 205; on the Berrigans, 208–9, 225; meets with Henry Kissinger, 215; on Spiro Agnew, 227; and liberation theology, 245–46; and travels of, 245–46; supports sanctuary movement during Gulf War, 248; on legacy of John Bennett, 250–51

Brown, Robert R., 34–35

Brown, Sam, 218

Brown, Sydney Thomason, 245

Browning, Edmund L., 249, 250

Brown's Chapel (Selma, Ala.), 121, 125, 129, 131, 134

Brown v. Board of Education of Topeka, Kansas, 3, 18, 20, 21, 27, 78, 102

Buddhists, 142, 153, 159, 211, 216–17; "third solution," 154–55, 217, 231

Bundy, McGeorge, 144, 153

Bunker, Ellsworth, 217

Burgess, John M., 227

Burholder, Lawrence, 97

Burke, Martin, 40

Bush, George, 248–49

Butler, Samuel, 7

Byrd, Harry, 36–37

Caldicott, Helen, 250

California: fair housing legislation in, 95–96; striking migrant workers in, 139

"A Call to Resist Illegitimate Authority," 193

"Call to the Fall Offensive to End the War," 220

Calley, William, 230

Cambodia: relations with United States, 172–73; bombing of, 172–73, 215; American invasion of, 225–28

Campbell, Ernest, 46–47

Campbell, Ernest T., 279 (n. 7)

Campbell, Will D., 8, 26, 29, 46, 47, 256–57 (n. 51); 268 (n. 56); early life and career, 22–23; and the University of Mississippi, 22–24; and Southern Project, 24–25, 31, 50, 81–82; at Little Rock, 33–34; criticism of direct-action techniques, 65–66; speech at National Conference on Religion and Race, 73; ministry of reconciliation, 111–112, 137; and death of Jonathan Daniels, 137; and Vietnam War, 213–14; criticism of Billy Graham, 226; and institutional religion, 240

Carmichael, Stokely, 128, 137

Carpenter, Charles C. J., 30, 50, 78–79, 131

Carroll, Charles, 122

Carter, Hodding, III, 109

Carter, Jimmy, 246

Carter, Stephen (*The Culture of Disbelief*), 9

Cartwright, Colbert S., 32, 34

Catholic Church, 39, 208; and anticommunism, 13; Archdiocese of New Orleans, 39–44; hierarchical nature of, 41, 43; and desegregation, 44; Archdiocese of Washington, D.C., 75, 126; Archdiocese of Baltimore, 83, 100, 197; Archdiocese of Los Angeles, 96; in Mississippi, 109; Archdiocese of Mobile-Birmingham, 114; Archdiocese of St. Louis (Mo.), 126; Archdiocese of New York, 127; Archdiocese of Minneapolis–St. Paul, 129; Archdiocese of Chicago, 141, 175; liturgical reform and, 151; support for conscientious objectors in, 157; hierarchical nature of, 161; in South America, 161–62, 245; and pacifism, 162; and dissent, 162–63; Archdiocese of Boston, 165, 227; and "Black Manifesto," 191

Catholic clergy: on *Brown*, 19; involvement in civil rights movement, 96, 126, 130, 162; and Vietnam War, 172, 174–75, 179–82, 184, 197, 212, 235

Catholic Commission on Human Rights, 41

Catholic Committee of the South, 41

Catholic Interracial Councils, 12, 84, 88, 133

Catholic Left, 152, 207, 212, 224, 228–29

Catholic Peace Fellowship, 151, 157, 158, 163, 206, 219, 226–27, 252

Catholic Worker movement, 141, 150, 151, 158, 160, 163

Catholic World, 174

Catholic Youth Council, 12–13

Catonsville Nine, 207, 210, 224

Catonsville raid, 207, 224; reactions to, 207–10

Central Conference of American Rabbis, 74, 154, 168, 173, 187

Central Intelligence Agency, 54, 237

Central (Negro) Jurisdiction. *See* Methodist Church

Central Organization for Jewish Adult Education, 72

Chancellor, John, 194

Chaney, James, 106, 128

Chapman, Robert, 62

Chatfield, Charles, 10

Chavez, Cesar, 139

Cherry, Corbin, 220

Chicago Eight, 225

Chicago, Ill.: commission on human relations, 76; fair housing legislation in, 95; civil rights demonstrations in, 122, 141; antiwar demonstrations in, 158, 175, 216

Chicago Sun-Times, 244

Chilstrom, Herbert W., 250

Christian Century, 19, 21, 25, 29, 35, 60, 65, 66, 74, 79, 87, 90, 95, 143, 149, 183, 200

Christian Coalition, 241–42

Christianity and Crisis, 11, 79, 153, 166, 183, 207, 232

Christian-Jewish relations, 37–39, 186–87

Christian Methodist Church (Negro), 82

Christian Methodist Episcopal Church, 243–44

Christian Relations Committee, 44

Christi Matri (Pope Paul VI), 174

Christopher, Warren, 250

Church and state, separation of, 133, 147

Churches

—black: bombing of, 29, 105; at National Conference on Religion and Race, 74; reaction to urban unrest, 95; in Mississippi, 105; in Selma, 116; development of new organizations, 242; and integration with white churches, 243–44

—predominantly white: and civil rights movement, 3, 5, 69, 70, 73, 113, 123, 126, 124, 130, 141, 144, 151, 185, 191, 241, 251; and Cold War, 4, 12, 13, 17, 35; as bureaucratic organizations, 7, 240; evangelism and, 9, 15; and social activism, 11, 133, 238; complacency of, 12, 15, 17, 142; support for segregation, 12, 17, 19, 20, 36, 46, 51, 89, 99, 146; postwar religious revival, 16–17; and *Brown*, 18–20, 74; support for Montgomery bus boycott, 29; in Little Rock, 35; role of in society, 44–45, 63, 90, 107, 133, 138, 222, 223; support for sit-ins, 50; and National Conference on Religion and Race, 72; historic support for slavery, 75–76, 99, 146; lobbying for federal civil rights legislation, 75, 76, 91–92, 99–101, 133; reaction to urban unrest, 95, 189; mainstream, 142; and antiwar movement, 143–44, 169, 178, 182, 228, 251; as places of sanctuary, 194, 248; growth of conservative, evangelical denominations, 239, 241; integration of, 242–44; mergers, 244

Church of the Brethren, 10, 108, 115, 141, 170

Citizens' Councils, 20–21, 25, 26, 34, 38, 39, 43, 67, 79, 97, 102, 116

Civil Rights Act (1964), 5, 76; supported by churches and clergy, 99–100, 152, 179; as moral issue, 100

Civil rights movement, 47, 60, 139, 140, 146, 193, 225, 243, 245; tactics, 3; nonviolent protest, 3, 63, 65, 103, 161; white churches and, 3, 70, 73, 113, 124, 130, 144, 146, 151, 185, 191; and clergy, 3–4, 8, 70, 75, 107; leaders in, 4, 6, 9, 52; importance of white clergy to, 5, 65; as moral/religious movement, 5, 8, 50, 65, 66, 77, 145–46, 148; linked to Communism, 27–28, 40, 43, 46, 52, 68, 132, 147; ecumenical nature of, 35, 69, 71, 76, 107, 133, 139, 191; southern clergy's support for, 46; northern clergy's support for, 48, 141, 145; direct action in, 48–50, 65, 112; and federal government, 52, 146, 148; emphasis on the South, 77, 94; compared to Exodus, 93–94, 98; charged with provoking violence, 119–20; and "white backlash," 141; in the North, 141; analysis of clergy involvement, 145–48; and antiwar movement, 147, 167, 183; and black separatism, 189–91; impact on conservative evangelical churches, 241

Claiborne, Randolph, Jr., 62

Clark, James, 115, 118–19, 120

Clark, Ramsey, 232–33, 235

Clarksdale, Miss., civil rights demonstrations in, 84–85

Clergy, 3–4, 5, 9, 126; in Selma, 3, 113, 115, 122–24, 125, 126, 130–32, 240, 251; southern moderates, 3–4, 9, 29, 46, 77, 79, 124, 146; and civil rights movement, 3–5, 27–29, 48–50, 52, 53–54, 56, 63, 70, 75, 107, 113, 115, 139, 141, 145, 146, 191, 251; social activism of, 4, 10, 44, 50, 108, 138–39, 238–40, 269 (n. 1); and Martin Luther King Jr., 4–5, 146; liberal education of, 5; significance of white clergy in civil rights movement, 5–6, 29, 138, 191; and antiwar movement, 5–6, 141–47,

ment, 148, 232; and establishment of
CALCAV, 164–65, 169, 229; and 1967
CALCAV Washington mobilization,
177, 179; meets with Robert McNamara,
180–81; and support for civil disobedience, 192–193, 205; role in civil rights
and antiwar movements compared,
193; and support of conscientious objectors, 193; and turning in of draft cards,
194–95; indictment of, 197–98, 205–6;
and reputation at Yale University, 195;
and 1968 Washington Mobilization,
201–2; meets with Henry Kissinger, 215;
and National Mobilization, 219–21; and
support for Daniel and Philip Berrigan,
225, 283 (n. 57); visit to Hanoi, 232–33;
and National Religious Convocation
and Congressional Visitation for Peace,
235; and Hartford Statement, 239; criticism of Carter administration's foreign
policy, 246–47; and criticism of Gulf
War, 248; and Bosnian crisis, 249; and
support for United Nations, 250; on
legacy of John Bennett, 251. *See also*
Boston Five
Cogley, John, 135
Cold War, 4, 10, 12–13, 15, 141, 176
Coleman, Thomas, 136–38
Commission on Pan-Methodist Union,
243
Committee for Non-Violent Action, 153,
154, 158
Committee of Concern, 106
Committee of Southern Churchmen, 111,
151, 214, 226
Committee on Interracial Cooperation,
12
Commonweal, 74, 163, 171, 276–77 (n. 41)
Communism, 12–13, 15, 54, 133, 144, 153,
154; linked to civil rights movement,
27–28, 40, 43, 46, 52, 68, 132, 142; linked
to antiwar movement, 147, 149, 158–60;
containment of, 152, 156, 157, 166; as
issue in the Vietnam War, 167–69,
174–75
Concentration camps, 160, 172
Concerned White Citizens of Alabama,
121
"Confederate Underground," 38
Congress, U.S., 57, 86–87, 228, 248; and

civil rights movement, 5; and civil rights
legislation, 69, 70, 85, 90–91, 93, 99,
126, 127; and church lobbyists, 75, 76,
91–92, 133; southern senators, 101; and
Vietnam War, 152, 232; and antiwar
clergy, 178; and *In the Name of
America*, 201
Congressional Black Caucus, 238
Congress of Racial Equality (CORE),
52–53, 57, 82, 86, 94, 146, 172, 190
Connor, Eugene "Bull," 77, 79
Conscientious objectors, 157, 158
Cooke, Terence, 204
Cooper, Chester, 196
Cornell, Thomas, 157, 163, 208, 210
Corrigan, Daniel, 62, 83, 152, 168, 219
Cotter, James P., 161, 163
Council of American-Soviet Friendship,
12
Council of Churches of Greater Washing-
ton, 143
Council of Church Women, 33
Council of Federated Organizations
(COFO), 101, 103, 105, 110
Councils on human relations, 27
Cowley, Leonard, 76
Cox, Harvey, 6, 84, 138; on Delta Ministry,
110; and criticism of Vietnam War, 153,
172; and CALCAV, 177; and support for
conscientious objectors, 193, 213; and *In
the Name of America*, 201; and support
for Daniel and Philip Berrigan, 225;
criticism of air war in Vietnam, 232;
support for social activism in the
churches, 239
Criswell, W. A., 20
Crittendon, William, 173
Cronin, James F., 86, 178, 180
Crowley, James, 127
Crowther, Edward, 219
Cuban missile crisis, 142
Cunnane, Robert, 151, 163, 194
Cushing, Richard Cardinal, 165, 227

Dahlberg, Edwin, 201
Dallas County Ministers Union, 120
Daniels, Jonathan Myrick: early life and
career of, 123; and civil rights work in
Alabama, 134–35, 136, murder of, 136;
memorial services for, 137; added to

support for civil rights, 96; Diocese of New York, 96, 228; executive council of, 109, 131; and ESCRU, 122; and Selma-to-Montgomery march, 131; 1991 General Convention, 137; Diocese of Erie (Pa.), 173; support for conscientious objectors, 206; Diocese of Massachusetts, 227; laity opposed to social activism, 238; General Convention Special Program, 238–39; and same-sex marriages, 245; ordination of women, 245
Episcopal clergy, 5, 10, 20, 21, 58, 63, 76, 96, 109, 123, 124, 213
Episcopal Peace Fellowship, 219, 226
Episcopal Society for Cultural and Racial Unity (ESCRU), 9, 51, 75, 133; Prayer Pilgrimage, 58, 60–62; and Malcolm Boyd, 123; memorial services for Jonathan Daniels, 137; and Vietnam War, 145, 191–92; and "black power," 192
Episcopal Theological School, 5, 123, 137
Episcopal Union of Black Clergy and Laity, 191
Ervin, Sam, 230
Espy, Edwin, 204
Evers, Medgar, 84
Exodus: compared to civil rights movement, 93–94, 98

Fairfax County, Va., 36
Fair housing legislation, 75, 95–96
Faith in Action, 244
Falwell, Jerry, 133, 241
Farmer, James, 52, 86
Fast, Howard (*Freedom Road*), 22
"Fast for the Rebirth of Compassion," 181
Faubus, Orville, 32, 33
Fauntroy, Walter, 80, 126
Federal Bureau of Investigation, 23, 89, 105, 158, 183, 194–95, 207, 224, 228
Federal Council of Churches of Christ in America, 11–13
Feinberg, Abraham, 176–77, 199
Fellowship of Reconciliation (FOR), 148, 151, 153, 154, 157, 183, 237; antiwar advertisements of, 170; and Thich Nhat Hanh's tour of United States, 170–71; sends study team to South Vietnam, 217; and antiwar vigils, 222; and deaths at Kent State, 226–27

Fellowship of Southern Churchmen, 12, 111
Feminist movement: and churches, 244
Fenton, Fred, 244
Ferber, Michael, 197–98, 205–6. *See also* Boston Five
Fernandez, Richard, 169, 184, 205, 214, 215, 230
Fey, Harold E., 29, 90
Fichter, Joseph H., 23, 40–43
Field Foundation, 111
Findlay, James F., 10, 81–82, 100–101, 109–10
Finlator, William, 29
First World War, 11
Flower City Conspiracy, 208
Flowers, Ronald, 9
Foley, Albert, 31
Fonda, Jane, 232
Foreman, Lloyd Andrew, 43
Forest, James, 53, 150, 151, 157, 160, 163, 206, 210, 237, 261 (n. 22)
Forman, James, 87–88, 132, 191
Frank, Emmet, 37
Frank, Leo, 37
Franklin, Marvin, 102
Freedom rides, 3, 48, 49, 52, 55–58, 60–63, 65
"Freedom schools," 159
Frost, Gary, 243
Fulbright, William, 178

Galbraith, John Kenneth, 184
Gandhi, 225
Garrison, William Lloyd, 208
Garrow, David, 128, 138
General Electric Space Division (King of Prussia, Pa.), 247
General Theological Seminary, 104, 267–68 (n. 33)
Geneva Accords (1954), 155, 161, 170
Geneva Convention, 200
Gerow, Richard, 53, 105
Gilbert, Arthur, 168
Gill, Jill, 10
Gilpatrick, Roswell, 218
God in Search of Man: A Philosophy of Judaism (Heschel), 72, 234
Goldberg, Arthur J., 174, 177
Golden, Charles, 102, 152

Robert McNamara, 180–81; and *Vietnam: Crisis of Conscience*, 185–86; and June War of 1967, 186; and support for conscientious objectors, 193; and *In the Name of America*, 201; and antiwar vigil at Arlington National Cemetery, 202; and Martin Luther King Jr., 203–5; meets with Henry Kissinger, 215; support for emigration of Soviet Jews, 221, 234; illness of, 222, 234; and deaths at Kent State, 227; endorsement of George McGovern, 233; and Berrigans, 233–34; death of, 234; memorial services for, 234, 238; legacies of, 234–35; and memorial service for Reinhold Niebuhr, 282 (n. 16)

Higgins, George, 149

Hines, John, 129, 131, 204, 238

Historic peace churches, 141

Hitler, Adolph, 98, 153, 166, 172

Ho Chi Minh, 142, 157, 176–77, 183, 199, 202, 218

Hodge, Bachman G., 31

Hoffman, Abbie, 195

Hoffman, Isidor, 183

Hogan, John, 207, 210. *See also* Catonsville Nine

Holloway, James, 111, 226

Holocaust, 71, 98; compared to Vietnam War, 171–72

Homosexuality: and conservative churches, 241, 242; and equal rights, 245

Honeywell, 229

Honor America Day, 226

Hoover, J. Edgar, 158, 228, 283 (n. 73)

Horne, Lena, 80

Horton, Frank, 133

House Committee on Un-American Activities, 12, 46

House Judiciary Committee, 223

Hoyt, Thomas, Jr., 244

Huckaby, Elizabeth, 33–34

Hughes, Dorothy, 28

Hughes, Preston, 30

Hughes, Robert E., 9; early life and career, 27; and Montgomery bus boycott, 28–29, 23, 47; forced to leave Alabama, 30–31; in Southern Rhodesia, 31–32

Humphrey, Hubert: and Civil Rights Act

(1964), 100; and Mississippi Freedom Democratic Party, 106; and support for Vietnam War, 166; address at National Inter-Religious Conference on Peace, 168; and 1968 presidential campaign, 214

Hunter, David, 164, 169, 193

Hurley, Joseph P., 97

Iakovos, Archbishop, 129, 130, 168, 173, 204

Illinois Club for Catholic Women, Loyola University (Chicago), 76

Institute for Freedom in the Church, 162–63

Institute for Policy Studies, 193

Internal Revenue Service, 239

International Committee of Conscience on Vietnam, 170

International Control Commission, 155

"International Days of Protest," 158

International War Crimes Tribunal, 225

Interreligious Committee on Race Relations, 75

Interreligious Committee on Vietnam, 152

In the Name of America, 200–201

Iranian hostage crisis, 246–47

Israel, Richard, 64

Israel, 186; United States support for, 165, 173–74, 221

Jack, Homer, 167

Jackson, Jimmie Lee, 114, 121, 128, 131

Jackson, Miss., 134

Jacobs, William, 123

Jean, Elbert, 151

Jeanmard, Jules, 42, 43

Jersey City, N.J.: urban unrest in, 95; substandard public housing in, 104

Jesuit Missions, 151, 161

Jesuits. *See* Society of Jesus

Jewish-Christian relations, 37–38, 186–87

Jewish Peace Fellowship, 157, 183, 226

Jewish War Veterans, 173, 183

Jews: and civil rights movement, 37; fears of southern anti-Semitism, 37–39, 67; in the North, 38; and Holocaust, 57, 71; in Birmingham, 80, 98; history of persecution of, 89, 122, 176, 249; conscientious objectors, 157; and disagreements over the Vietnam War, 173–74; and June

War of 1967, 186, 221; and antiwar movement, 221; emigration from Soviet Union, 221, 234

Jim Crow, 87

John Birch Society, 61

Johnson, Lyndon, 144, 145, 246; and civil rights, 91, 148, 155, 174, 183; and Vietnam War, 91; support for Civil Rights Act (1964), 99, 100; meets with clergy, 99, 127; 1964 election, 106; and death of James Reeb, 125, 127, 128; and support for Voting Rights Act, 127, 136; and conduct of Vietnam War, 140, 141, 143, 148, 152, 160, 163, 169–70, 175, 202; and Francis Cardinal Spellman, 147; and Billy Graham, 147, 156; criticism of antiwar activists, 153, 158–59, 175; and Jewish opposition to the Vietnam War, 165, 173–74; and National Inter-Religious Conference on Peace, 168; and 1968 presidential election, 169; decision not to run for reelection, 202–3

Johnson administration, 153, 215; and poverty programs, 110, 145, 147, 182; and demonstrations in Selma, 119; federal protection for civil rights marchers, 122, 125, 126, 131, 148; and civil rights legislation, 140; and credibility gap, 146, 176, 200; and conduct of Vietnam War, 148, 154, 156, 170, 177, 181, 187–88, 230; and support for Vietnam War policies, 166; and religious critics of the Vietnam War, 177, 183; on June War of 1967, 187

Joint Chiefs of Staff, 183, 184, 200, 235

"Jonathan's Wake," 222

Jones, E. Edward, 243

Jones, Jim, 246

Journey of Reconciliation, 52

Jubilee, 171

Judgment at Nuremberg, 121

June War of 1967, 186, 221

Just war, doctrine of, 157; and Vietnam War, 166; and Gulf War, 249

Justice Department. *See* Department of Justice

Katallagete, 111

Katzenbach, Nicholas deB., 159

Keating, Francis M., 162

Kennedy, Edward, 125, 227

Kennedy, John F., 52, 63, 90; and federal civil rights legislation, 85; meets with civil rights leaders, 86; assassination of, 91; and 1960 campaign, 156

Kennedy, Robert: and civil rights movement, 52, 53, 55, 60, 63, 80, 125; and 1968 presidential campaign, 202

Kennedy administration, 63, 69, 142, 230

Kent State University, deaths at, 226–27

Kerlin, George, 116

Kershaw, Alvin, 22–24

Kilfoyle, Daniel, 162

King, Coretta Scott, 129, 183, 215

King, Edwin, 9, 102–3; and Mississippi Freedom Democratic Party, 106–7

King, Martin Luther, Jr., 5, 9, 50, 54, 55, 65, 66, 86, 100, 104, 112, 191, 216, 225, 234, 241; education and religious background of, 4; and Montgomery bus boycott, 26, 28, 29; writings of, 32; criticism of southern white churches and clergy, 49, 239; and Albany Movement, 63; speech at National Conference on Religion and Race, 73; criticized by white clergy, 78; and Birmingham campaign, 78–80, 264 (n. 22); meets with John F. Kennedy, 90; in St. Augustine, 99; and Mississippi Freedom Democratic Party, 107; and Robert McAfee Brown, 107; as model for activist clergy, 107–8, 203; and civil rights movement in Selma, 114–31 passim; and civil rights demonstrations in Chicago, 139, 141; and use of prophetic imagery, 146; and antiwar movement, 148, 155, 170, 182–83, 202; correspondence with Thich Nhat Hanh, 155; nonviolence of, 161; and support for Israel, 187; and *In the Name of America*, 201; and Lyndon Johnson's decision not to run for reelection, 202–3; and Abraham Joshua Heschel, 203; and Poor People's March, 203; assassination of, 203–4

King, Martin Luther, III, 62

Kirby, Robert, 244

Kissinger, Henry, 218; meets with antiwar clergy, 215; peace negotiations with North Vietnam, 216, 230, 236

Kleeman, Richard, 24

Klunder, Bruce, 94, 266 (n. 3)

Montgomery Improvement Association, 27–29

Montgomery Ministerial Association, 29

Moore, Paul, Jr., 8, 141, 191; and ordination of women, 103, 245; early life and career of, 104; and Mississippi Summer Project, 103, 104; and Malcolm Boyd, 104, 123; and Delta Ministry, 108–10; support of voting rights, 126; meets with Lyndon Johnson, 127; early views on Vietnam War, 144; and religious wing of antiwar movement, 148; and 1967 CALCAV Washington mobilization, 178; and "black power," 190; and *In the Name of America*, 201; and deaths at Kent State, 228; installation as bishop coadjutor of the Diocese of New York, 228; visit to Saigon, 231; on power of institutional church, 240, 245; on liberal clergy, 251

Moral Majority, 133, 241

Moral Man and Immoral Society (Niebuhr), 11

Morgan, Charles, 31

Morris, John B., 9, 20, 21, 31, 58, 62–63, 135, 137–39; and "Ministers March," 122; and violence in Selma, 122; and funeral service for Jonathan Daniels, 137; on Vietnam War, 145, 191–92; resignation from ESCRU, 192

Morrison, Norman, 159–60

Morrisroe, Richard, 136

Morrissey, Joseph, 219

Morrissey, Paul, 219

Morse, Wayne, 178

Moses, Robert, 101, 103, 107

Moyers, Bill, 127, 218

Moylan, Mary, 207, 210. *See also* Catonsville Nine

Murray, George, 79

Murrow, Edward R., 26

Muste, Abraham Johannes, 151, 160, 176–77, 199

My Lai massacre, 230

Myrdal, Gunnar, 12

National Association for the Advancement of Colored People (NAACP), 22, 23, 28, 33, 37, 38, 67, 84, 86, 101, 102, 103, 110, 190

National Baptist Convention, 243

National Black Catholic Clergy Caucus, 242

National Black Evangelical Association, 242

National Black Political Convention, 238

National Black Sisters' Conference, 242

National Broadcasting Company (NBC), 58, 120, 194

National Cathedral (Washington, D.C.), 133–34, 250; antiwar service at, 220

National Catholic Conference for Interracial Justice, 43, 86

National Catholic Press Association, 123

National Catholic Reporter, 161

National Catholic Welfare Conference, 86, 69

National Committee for a Sane Nuclear Policy (SANE), 142, 148, 158, 184, 246

National Committee of Negro Churchmen, 190

National Conference of Christians and Jews, 13

National Conference on Religion and Race, 69, 72, 75, 83–84, 168; reactions to, 74; demise of, 76; as model for ecumenical antiwar meetings, 167

National Coordinating Committee to End the War in Vietnam, 158

National Council of Churches Commission on Religion and Race, 99, 100, 108, 119; founding of, 81–82; and March on Washington, 86; in Clarksdale, Miss., 84–85; support for federal civil rights legislation, 91, 126; and "Ministers March," 122; demise of, 190

National Council of Churches Delta Ministry. *See* Delta Ministry

National Council of Churches of Christ in the U.S.A. (NCC), 5, 26, 29, 51, 65, 66, 68, 75, 81, 111, 119, 127, 164, 169, 190, 204, 215, 239; resolutions against segregation, 13–14; and *Brown*, 18; Department of Racial and Cultural Relations, 20, 81; Southern Project, 24–25, 81; support for sit-ins, 50; and freedom rides, 58; and National Conference on Religion and Race, 69; Division of Home Missions, 81; and Mississippi Summer Project, 101, 103, 268 (n. 36); and Delta Ministry, 109, 110, 268 (n. 36); in Selma,

114–15, 122, 129, 135; on Vietnam War, 173; Department of Social Justice, 190; 1969 Assembly, 222; and Gulf War, 248–49; and Bosnian crisis, 250

National Emergency Committee of Clergy Concerned About Vietnam. *See* Clergy and Laymen Concerned About Vietnam

National Federation of Roman Catholic Priests, 232

National Guard, 55, 131–32, 226

National Inter-Religious Conference on Peace, 167–69

National Interreligious News Service Board for Conscientious Objectors, 248

National Liberation Front (NLF), 153, 154, 155, 169, 172, 173, 201, 231

National Mobilization, 219–21

National Mobilization Committee to End the War in Vietnam, 195

National Office for Black Catholics, 242

National Peace Action Coalition, 229

National Presbyterian Interracial Council, 82–83

National Religious Convocation and Congressional Visitation for Peace, 235

National Urban League, 86, 242

Nation of Islam, 242, 266 (n. 3)

Nazi Germany, 215, 153; compared to United States, 148

Nazis, 122, 158, 171; persecution of Jews, 176; compared to Joint Chiefs of Staff, 183

Nazism, 57, 72, 153; and German churches, 185

Negotiations Now, 184

Neuhaus, Richard John: and founding of CALCAV, 159, 229; on Daniel Berrigan's exile to Latin America, 161; and establishment of National Emergency Committee of Clergy Concerned About Vietnam, 164; and peace march in New York City, 167; and Clergy Concerned About Vietnam, 169; and Thich Nhat Hanh, 171; meets with Robert McNamara, 180–81; on June War of 1967, 187; and support for conscientious objectors, 193; on death of Martin Luther King Jr., 205; meets with draft resisters in Europe, 213; meets with

Henry Kissinger, 215; and deaths at Kent State, 227; and radicalization of antiwar movement, 237–38; and reappraisal of North Vietnam, 237; and Hartford Statement, 239; and support of Gulf War, 249; criticism of Lewis Hershey, 280 (n. 37)

Newark, N.J., 189

"New breed," 6, 84, 107, 113, 138

Newburgh Community Affairs Council, 149

New Christian Right, 241

New England Resistance, 193

New Mobilization Committee to End the War in Vietnam, 219

New Orleans, La.: clergy support for segregation, 39–40, 53; parochial school desegregation in, 39–44; police brutality in, 41; church mergers in, 244

New Orleans Association of Catholic Laymen, 39, 42, 43

The New Republic, 128

"News of the Christian World," 263–64 (n. 18)

Newsweek, 138, 225

Newton, John, 114, 116, 117, 118, 129, 132, 134–35

New York Post, 79

New York Times, 29, 30, 33, 35, 60, 206, 230, 233, 235, 248, 250; on March on Washington, 88, 135, 142, 158, 161, 162, 175, 183; antiwar advertisements in, 148, 155–56

Niebuhr, Reinhold, 4, 11, 36, 57, 130; criticism of Billy Graham, 16, 216; on Abraham Joshua Heschel, 72; theology of, 107; and Ministers' Vietnam Committee, 142; and criticism of Vietnam War, 153, 166; and support for Israel, 187; memorial service for, 282 (n. 16)

Niemoller, Martin, 193

Nietzsche, Friedrich, 4

Nixon, Richard, 246; 1968 election of, 212, 214; and White House prayer services, 216; and support for Nguyen Van Thieu, 217; and bombing of North Vietnam, 218, 232, 235; criticism of antiwar movement, 219, 220, 226; and "silent majority" speech, 221; impeachment of, 223; and invasion of Cambodia, 225–26;

United Church of Christ, 82, 196, 222–23, 238

United Nations, 68, 155–56, 160, 166, 168, 173, 174, 183, 196, 205, 225, 233, 249, 250

United Nations Church Center, 159, 167

United Presbyterian Church in the U.S.A., 8, 14, 36, 71, 81, 82, 57; General Assembly of, 50

United States: and nuclear arms race, 141; and policy in Vietnam, 142, 143, 144, 154, 199–200, 217; policy toward Southeast Asia, 143–44, 153; compared to Nazi Germany, 148, 215; and relations with Cambodia, 172–73; and support for Israel, 173–74

University of Mississippi, 22; integration of, 66–68

University of the South, 19, 23, 61

Upham, Judith, 134, 135

Urban Training Center for Christian Missions, 76

Urban unrest, 94, 140, 189, 191, 201. *See also* Watts riots

U.S. Catholic Conference, 249, 250; Social Action Department, 178, 180

U.S. Inter-Religious Committee on Peace, 217

U.S. News and World Report, 133

U Thant, 168, 208

Valenti, Jack, 220

Van Dusen, Henry, 14–15, 251

Vatican, 42, 43, 96, 234

Vietcong, 142, 154, 170; and Tet Offensive, 199–200; and war crimes, 201

Vietnam, 140, 141, 147, 153, 199, 202, 226–27, 245; reunification of, 142; and feelings toward Americans, 154; division of, 155, 161

Vietnam: Crisis of Conscience (Brown, Novak, and Heschel), 185–86

"Vietnam and the Religious Conscience," 181

Vietnamese Women's Union, 176

Vietnam Moratorium, 218–19

Vietnam Summer project, 184, 189

Vietnam War, 5, 8, 139, 143, 144, 146, 152, 214, 247, 249, 250; American conduct of, 140, 141, 145, 148, 151, 152, 154, 155, 165, 170, 175; criticism of, 141; as nationalist

civil war; 143, 166, 170; as war of Communist aggression, 143; as racially motivated, 144–45, 147, 171–72; as a moral issue, 146; as a political issue, 146; and charges of war crimes, 147–48, 230; compared to Second World War, 152, 153, 166, 175; American public support for, 152, 186, 197; as a just war, 166, 174–75; compared to Holocaust, 171–72; impact on civil rights movement, 191; legality of, 193; and Nixon administration, 216–17; "Vietnamization," 216, 217, 230–31; and Paris Agreement, 236–37. *See also* Antiwar movement

Vivian, C. T., 120–21

Voting rights, 3, 73, 84, 138; in Albany, Ga., 63–64; and Delta Ministry, 110; in Mississippi, 113; in Selma, 118–19, 121; in Alabama, 136

Voting Rights Act, 5, 126–27; church and clergy support for, 126, 133, 138, 179, 251

Wagner, Emile, Jr., 39, 40, 43

Wagner, Richard, 53

Walker, Edwin, 67

Walker, Larry, 108

Walker, Randolph Meade, 243

Walker, Wyatt T., 55

Wallace, George, 77, 116, 122, 125, 214

War Resisters League, 141, 158

Washington, D.C., 25, 125; civil rights legislation and, 70; civil rights rallies in, 75, 104, 122, 126–27; antiwar demonstrations in, 91, 147, 167–68, 177–81, 195, 220, 227, 232, 235; and Poor People's March, 203, riots in, 203. *See also* March on Washington; National Mobilization; Washington mobilizations

Washington Ministers' Association, 143

Washington mobilizations: 1967, 192; 1968, 201–2; 1969, 214–15; 1971, 229

Washington Post, 3, 142, 183

Waskow, Arthur, 193, 194

Watts riots, 140

Weathermen, 148, 221

Webster, R. Kenley, 219

Weigel, Gustave, 57

Weinstein, Jacob, 154, 173; address at National Inter-Religious Conference on Peace, 168; and antiwar resolutions, 170;

P9-APM-641

328   4A

UNIVERSITY CO-OP
no refund if removed
$13.95A

THE CLASSROOM OBSERVER

Developing Observation Skills
in Early Childhood Settings

SECOND EDITION

THE CLASSROOM OBSERVER

Developing Observation Skills
in Early Childhood Settings

SECOND EDITION

ANN E. BOEHM
RICHARD A. WEINBERG

Teachers College, Columbia University
New York and London

170442

The first edition of this book appeared in 1977 under the title, *The Classroom Observer: A Guide for Developing Observation Skills.*

Text photographs by Myron Papiz.

Published by Teachers College Press, 1234 Amsterdam Avenue, New York, NY 10027

Copyright © 1987 by Teachers College, Columbia University

All rights reserved. No part of this publication may be reproduced or transmitted in any form or by any means, electronic or mechanical, including photocopy, or any information storage and retrieval system, without permission from the publisher.

Library of Congress Cataloging-in-Publication Data

Boehm, Ann E., 1938–
  The classroom observer.

  Bibliography: p. 141
  Includes index.
  1. Observation (Educational method) 2. Child development. 3. Education, Primary. I. Weinberg, Richard A. II. Title.
LB1027.28.B64   1987   371.11'46   87-18036
ISBN 0-8077-2874-8 (pbk.)

Manufactured in the United States of America

92 91 90 89   2 3 4 5 6

*To
Gail and Neville,
again*

Contents

170442

List of Tasks

Preface

Historically, naturalistic observational techniques have been central to the development of the physical sciences, helping to generate theories and establish knowledge about physical phenomena. Rooted in the rich tradition of the physical sciences, the social sciences have also opened our window of understanding about the social world through the use of systematic observational methods. Skill in observing children has been a cornerstone of the work of "child watchers," those professionals devoted to child study and to understanding why children develop and behave in the ways they do. Appreciating this heritage, we have developed an updated edition of *The Classroom Observer: A Guide for Developing Observation Skills* (first published in 1977), now subtitled, *Developing Observation Skills in Early Childhood Settings*. The program presented in this second edition focuses on those skills needed in order for an early childhood observer to make appropriate, valid inferences and to arrive at decisions based on objective observation data which can be gathered in natural learning habitats and educational settings. This book is based on the premise that observation skills are an indispensable component of an early childhood educator's professional repertoire. Educators are applied empiricists, and are therefore most effective when they have access to sound data to support their planning, interventions, and follow-up efforts.

Although observation is recognized as an important tool for gaining information, drawing conclusions, and generating ideas, limited attention has been devoted to many of the key issues surrounding the effective application of systematic observation in learning environments. The aim of this book is to present critical components that need to be considered in developing systematic observation skills when working in early childhood settings. A major focus is also placed on *self-made* observation strategies rather than on "canned" products. To accomplish these goals, the reader is asked to engage in a series of tasks to develop an understanding of the various principles and procedures introduced. Sample responses are provided for many of these tasks in an appendix, so that the reader can compare his or her answers.

The increasing availability of observation techniques for various professionals involved in the early childhood educational enterprise does not guarantee the development and assimilation of observation skills in training programs for teachers, special educators, health educators, school psychologists, social workers, and other school personnel devoted to the welfare of young children.

Observing children in educational contexts and preparing case studies have been integral components of the training of some individuals engaged in preschool and elementary education (Cohen, Stern, & Balaban, 1983; Good & Brophy, 1984). However, our experience in directing in-service workshops for child care providers, practicing teachers, special educators, and school psychologists has indicated that a step-by-step program for developing objective observation skills is essential if adequate naturalistic observation techniques are to be acquired. Such programs can be incorporated into teacher and other professional training programs as well as in-service and continuing education opportunities. Field experiences and observation practice supplementary to traditional course work and student–teacher experiences can generate interesting seminar discussions about the role of observation in the early childhood education process. The adjunct use of videotaped classroom scenes can provide exercises in studying such concepts as observer reliability, the procedures for generating categories of behavior, and the strategies that children use to solve problems.

Multidisciplinary workshops (including team teachers, student teachers, classroom paraprofessionals, and supportive pupil personnel such as school social workers and psychologists) that explore observational techniques can stress the value of a "team" approach to observing early childhood settings. By sharing their observational data, early childhood personnel can facilitate optimal educational programming. It should become obvious that by extending observational training to educational programs for effective parenting, one can generalize the value of systematic observation skills to the home and family situations. Furthermore, introducing parent observers in the classroom and other early childhood settings might stimulate communication about young children. Older students, too, can be productive observers who might benefit by training in systematic observation.

This second edition is a more expanded volume that maintains its focus on systematic observational skill building in early childhood environments. This edition includes:

1. A new unit on reliability and sources of bias in observation
2. A new unit on observation in media-based learning settings

3. A new unit on the forms of observation
4. A helpful subject/author index
5. Updated references and resources

Although the primary target of our book is the community of professionals who study young children, the audience of educators, researchers, and human service providers who work with older populations should find this quite a useful addition to their resources.

The development of the first and second editions of this volume has been a rewarding experience. We are especially appreciative of Millie Almy who provided us with the initial impetus to write the book. Since the first edition was published, Byron Egeland, Erna Fishhaut, and Shirley Moore of the University of Minnesota and Margaret Jo Shepherd and Leslie R. Williams of Teachers College, Columbia University, have provided us with support and encouragement. John Swayze and Karen Brobst helped in important ways in the development of Units X and XI, respectively. We also appreciate the suggestions and feedback from the students and teachers who employed the first edition in their studies. In addition, we are grateful for the excellent editorial assistance provided by Patrick Lee in the first edition, and by Audrey Kingstrom and Nina George of Teachers College Press in this revision. Finally, we offer thanks to the hundreds of young children in many learning settings whom we have observed and from whom we have learned.

Ann E. Boehm
Richard A. Weinberg

THE CLASSROOM OBSERVER

Developing Observation Skills
in Early Childhood Settings

SECOND EDITION

An Introduction to the Skills of Observation

Today's world demands that each of us make judgments, evaluate situations, and guide our lives on the basis of inferences. Many of these decisions and judgments are based on information that we derive from the environment through observation. We make observations in a variety of settings where we view people behaving in different ways. In our daily observations we take account of the interactions between individuals, the outcomes of interactions, the physical setting in which the exchanges occur, and the nature of the tasks involved. In these various situations the observation process allows us to obtain essential information for drawing inferences and making decisions, unfortunately with varying degrees of validity. We do this in mundane situations, such as inferring that a roast is finished when the meat thermometer registers "rare roast beef" (if we care for rare meat). The observation process also operates in the more consequential areas of our lives:

The coach critically reviews the videotape of the last basketball game and makes a decision as to which team members will start in the next game.

The preschool teacher observes over a two-week period the play patterns of her pupils to evaluate the nature of the interactions among children.

The gymnast watches another competitor compete on the balance beam, observes components of performance not seen by the untrained eye, and makes a list of self-improvement points on which to work during practice.

The radiologist "reads" an X ray for the surgeon, who in turn uses the data as well as the patient's medical history to determine the appropriate surgical technique.

The birdwatcher, the artist, the meteorologist, the farmer, the coin collector, all observe the world through their unique lenses and guide their behavior, decisions, and judgments accordingly.

1

The level of precision with which one observes events is determined by one's interest, needs, and past experience. Much of what we do or do not see is the result of a casual, nondirected activity. Systematic, scientific observation, however, requires guided observing of consistently observable events.

OBSERVING IN THE EARLY CHILDHOOD ARENA

The early childhood enterprise — educational and child care programs for young children and their families — has long been an arena of debate for parents, educators, behavioral scientists, politicians, and other groups with vested interests in the welfare of young children. Controversy focuses on children's needs, effective strategies for accomplishing educational and developmental goals for individual children, the advantages of varying programs and curricula, and alternative systems for providing services. Furthermore, conflicting political, economic, and social pressures confound the issues. In this climate of unrest and controversy, early childhood professionals, including teachers, administrators, and other specialists, must be all the more deliberate and objective as they go about their business of making inferences, solving daily problems, facilitating the educational process, and generally being accountable for their activities.

New students of observation skills often underestimate the complexities of systematic observation and fail to tap the rich information that is present when viewing a learning situation. For example, an untrained observer entering a kindergarten to observe the "classroom climate" might generate a five-minute "running record" such as:

> Boy crying in block corner.
> Another child angry with his friend who has knocked over his block fort.
> Teacher is ignoring both of these children while a male aide is attempting to intervene in both situations.
> Room seems crowded.
> Art materials are not being used.
> Girls in doll corner are involved in play.

Another observer trained in a systematic approach to making observations would generate a different five-minute "running record" of the same situation: Given the purpose of "observing the classroom climate" the trained observer would develop a simple strategy for observing those components of the setting, child, and teacher behavior that he or she defines ahead of time as components of a "classroom climate." The trained observer systematically takes account of each component by sampling from the situation over the given time period. Such a record might look like this:

Setting and people
There are 15 children present (seven girls, eight boys).
The female teacher is assisted by one male (perhaps a student teacher).
The room is arranged in a variety of activity areas: painting area, doll corner, water table, block area, book area.
Pupil and teacher behavior
The presence of eight semidry paintings hanging on a clothesline suggests that the children were painting earlier.
There are at least two children participating in each of four activity areas (excluding painting).
The teacher is at her desk involved in some "paper activity."
The male (and/or student teacher?) is speaking to the child who is crying in the block area.

Although there is overlap in the "running records" of both the untrained and trained observers, it should be evident that the more systematic approach will permit a stronger basis for arriving at inferences about "the classroom climate" of this particular kindergarten. Specifically, one can note that:

The first running record, by confusing observations with inferences, gives the reader the impression that the overall classroom atmosphere is "unhappy." The second report indicates that the atmosphere is "busy" with an isolated "unhappy" incident.
The second, more systematic report supplies more factual information about the people and the setting.
The first record simply misrepresents the degree of art activity in the room; the second, by taking account of additional information, gives a more valid report.

Thus, although both records provide descriptions of classroom climate, the second, more systematic running record provides us with a more valid representation of the setting.

OBSERVING SYSTEMATICALLY

It is the purpose of this book to provide a systematic approach for observing in learning environments, especially those for young children. The observer, by developing simple observation skills and greater awareness of the valuable tool of observation, can approach the work knowing that decisions and conclusions have been based on a stronger foundation of observation information.

Like the astute political and economic observer, the child observer must be aware of the distorting influences of subjective feelings and intuitive reactions on the observation process. Individuals frequently perceive the same situation differently, their observations reflecting their developmental level, previous experiences, comprehension and understanding of the specific instance, and personal biases. Typical observations tend to reflect individual and egocentric frames of reference, which in turn mirror societal or cultural norms and/or prejudices. A few examples may help to underscore this point:

Individual perceptions

One person reading the *Wall Street Journal* notes, "This paper is dull and uninteresting." However, another person might state, "reading the *Wall Street Journal* provides stimulating information as to the current financial scene."

Cultural norms

A child looks at the floor when he is being taken to task by a teacher. To the child, as a result of his past experiences, this is an indication of deference to and respect for authority. From the standpoint of the teacher, such behavior may be viewed as deviousness, avoidance of confrontation, or admission of guilt.

Developmental influences

The work of Piaget has focused awareness on the fact that, up to about the age of six or seven, children believe all others perceive the world as they do. For example, from her egocentric frame of reference, a child might state that another person, irrespective of his position in the room, sees exactly the same things as she does even if the objects are out of view of the other person.

Approaching a situation, the trained observer uses a systematic strategy for collecting information from the setting. What the observer focuses upon and the pattern of observations that result are not random but are guided by the question posed or the problem needing to be solved. The categories devised for labeling components of the setting, specific people in the observed situation, and behavioral activities that occur are precise and clearly defined.

In collecting and recording observations, the trained observer uses a system that allows a sampling of the situation, taking into account sources of bias. Through a sufficient number of objective observations, he or she is prepared to build valid inferences from a reliable, rich data base of direct observations in natural settings.

Our description of the trained early childhood observer summarizes the various observation skills that this book attempts to foster. The adage "seeing is believing" reflects the powerful role that observation plays in our lives; but it underestimates the advantage that the trained observer has over the naive observer.

Applying Observation Skills to Learning Settings

The program presented in this book is an attempt to demonstrate the role that systematic observation skills can play in one's daily decision-making activities. We have tended to focus on early childhood settings and the observation of young children. However, observation procedures can be used to collect information throughout the educational spectrum, and we have drawn on examples from other educational settings and contexts. This unit provides a brief overview of the role observation methods have played in the study of children's behavior, the educational process, and classroom teaching techniques. It also provides a perspective on how observation techniques can contribute to the efficiency of the teacher, psychologist, special educator, and other personnel involved in education.

OBSERVATION AS A METHOD OF INQUIRY

Historically, objective observation techniques have been central to the scientist's methods of inquiry for generating hypotheses, for building laws of science, and for confirming theories. However, such techniques were not always without difficulty. In fact, Galileo Galilei (1564–1642), the founder of modern astronomy, was condemned by the Church for his use of scientific observation. Having built an astronomical telescope and studied moving bodies in space, he noted that the earth orbited the sun, contrary to the accepted position that the earth was the center of the universe. In this instance, objective data came into direct conflict with a traditional belief that was difficult to refute.

The social sciences, rooted in the tradition of the physical and biological sciences, have also enlarged the scope of human knowledge by deriving conclusions based on objective, observable data. Often, this concern has been limited to the controlled situation of the experimenter's laboratory or the contrived situation of the researcher using questionnaires, rating scales, and clinical testing techniques where observations are made of the effects of an experimenter's manipulations.

The traditional experimental approach emphasizes an artificially controlled manipulation of the environment in order to gain knowledge of various phenomena (e.g., laboratory research in cancer treatment, the study of paired-associate learning behavior of children, the influences of a new curriculum on a child's mastery of a particular subject). The questions raised by the experimenters are these: If we alter the experimental situation in a particular way, what behaviors will result? How will these behaviors compare to those that occur when a different set of environmental conditions is presented? We often forget that observations of our natural "unaltered" environments provide the impetus for laboratory research and stimulate the development of hypotheses, speculations, and researchable ideas. On the other hand, empirical findings in the laboratory often must be verified in naturalistic settings before these results can be accepted.

In contrast, the ecological approach to studying phenomena emphasizes the investigation of observable phenomena as they occur naturally in the environment, uncontrolled by the observer. In reflecting on the ways descriptions of naturally occurring phenomena have contributed to our body of scientific knowledge, Wright (1967) noted:

> Natural history studies have long supplied basic data for the theories and applications of biology. Astronomy and the earth sciences are monuments to investigation that examines at first hand what it finds in nature. All of the social sciences but psychology owe most of their empirical accomplishments to direct recordings of conditions and events in society. Even the predominantly experimental sciences of physics and chemistry have amassed and regularly call upon stores of information about the incidence in nature of their materials and subject processes. Psychology appears to stand alone as a science without a substantial descriptive, naturalistic, ecological side (p. 3).

Sociologists and anthropologists (e.g., Mead, 1932; Parsons & Bales, 1955) have collected field data and used their observational findings in developing much of our understanding about social organizations, the influences of cultural factors on behavior, and the nature of daily living patterns in various groups. Perhaps in response to Wright's critique, psychologists have focused on the ecology of the organism and its environment by exploring behavior in the natural settings of the home, community, or classroom (e.g., Barker, 1968; Barker & Schoggen, 1973; Bronfenbrenner, 1976, 1977).

The valuable work of Barker and Wright at the Kansas Midwest Station has provided a wealth of information, unveiling the natural habitats and behaviors of individuals. *One Boy's Day* (1951) and *Midwest and Its Children: The Psychological Ecology of an American Town*

(1955) illustrate how a descriptive, naturalistic, ecological approach can contribute to our understanding of complex, ongoing human behavior in real life situations, not laboratories. These works have also shown how an observer can accurately record a broad range of natural behavior through the use of specimen records. These in turn generate dimensions of behavior that can be further investigated through the use of other research techniques. Barker and Schoggen (1973) further resolved some conceptual and measurement problems central to studying environments and understanding the links between habitat and behavior. Such understanding enhances our ability to control or predict behavior and to improve the nature and quality of life.

OBSERVATION TECHNIQUES
IN STUDYING CHILD DEVELOPMENT

The earliest systematic observations of children's behavior in natural settings were biographies, diaries, and detailed recordings of children's behavior. One can trace the practice of making diary descriptions or sequential accounts of ongoing activity to the late eighteenth century when many observers kept diaries tracing their children's development. For example, the Swiss educator Johann Pestalozzi (1746–1827) made extensive observations and kept records of the development of his three-and-a-half-year-old son. Other "baby biographies" appeared in the early 1900s, each providing an account of the observed development of a child who was a relative of the biographer. Although these biographies were of value in raising hypotheses about the nature of child development, their generalizability was limited. In addition, the observations were often unsystematic, biased, and selective (Scarr, Weinberg, & Levine, 1986). However, the detailed recordings of observations of children by Jean Piaget (1960), who charted our understanding of the cognitive development of children, and by Roger Brown (1973), who explored the acquisition of language—to cite two well-known examples—were critical underpinnings of the contemporary study of human development. The burgeoning study of human development across the life span from infancy through adulthood in the cognitive, perceptual-motor, social, and emotional domains is built upon the work of these pioneer "child watchers."

Since the early 1970s, there has been an upsurge of interest among developmentalists in extending the ethological approach of studying animal behavior in the natural habitat to investigating children in their natural habitat, such as the home, school, playground, and so on

(Charlesworth, 1978). Ethological research in the biological sciences emphasizes the natural environments of plants and animals as well as the related structure and evolving functions of the living organism. Moving from the domain of the fish pond to the nursery school environment, McGrew (1972) attempted to define "an ethogram for the young *Homo Sapiens*" by observing behavior patterns exhibited by three- and four-year-old children in social situations during nursery-school free play. Focusing on observed children's behavior patterns, such as facial expressions, gestures, postures, and locomotion, McGrew attempted to relate these observations to previous research on human and nonhuman primate behavior.

Observation of parent–child interactions including the development of attachment patterns in infancy, such as the work of Mary Ainsworth (see Ainsworth et al., 1978), has provided another focus for child development researchers. To help clarify the range of observational methods available for studying these interpersonal relationships, Lytton (1971) proposed a hierarchy consisting of observation of structured interaction in the laboratory, observation of unstructured interaction in the laboratory (free play), and naturalistic observation in the home. Components of this hierarchy reflect varying degrees of control over the situation in which observations are collected. Baumrind (1968) has stressed that one must doubt the generalizability of observational data gathered from a rigorously controlled experimental situation to the natural family situation in which the child grows up and is socialized.

In the tradition of ecological investigations of human behavior, Caldwell (1969) proposed an impressive method for translating observational data into a numerical code suitable for computer analysis called the HOME (Home Observation for Measurement of the Environment) Inventory (see Bradley, 1982; Caldwell & Bradley, 1979). Caldwell warned that the formulation of comprehensive theories of early childhood learning and the understanding of patterns of environmental care will require naturalistic studies and descriptions of children functioning in different "freely constituted" environmental settings. A number of other developmental and early childhood researchers have also recognized the problems associated with premature leaps into the laboratory, and have begun to conduct observational studies of naturally occurring behavior events (e.g., Charlesworth, 1978; Landesman-Dwyer, Stein, & Sackett, 1978; White et al., 1973b).

In summary, then, many child development specialists have come to recognize that the naturalistic approach to studying human development contributes a richness, validity, and vitality not usually found in laboratory-based research. If well-planned and carefully controlled, such observations can yield data that are perfectly respectable from a scientific point of view. Moreover, they often suggest hypotheses that can then undergo more intensive examination in laboratory settings. Thus, the full spectrum of observational approaches, ranging from naturalistic observation to laboratory-based observation, should be viewed as complementary rather than as competitive routes to scientifically valid knowledge.

OBSERVING WITHIN THE EDUCATIONAL ENVIRONMENT

The educational environment—its settings, curriculum, and methods—has been the focus of many observation studies. Of particular interest is the role that naturalistic observation has played in the behavior management movement, psychoeducational assessment, the development of criterion-referenced assessment techniques, and the evaluation of curricular programs and teaching effectiveness.

Observation in the Management of Behavior

Influenced by the Skinnerian tradition of behaviorism and learning theory, the findings of social learning research (Baldwin, 1968; Bandura & Walters, 1963), and the pressing need for alternative ways to deal with school behavior and learning problems, educational psychologists and other professionals in education have developed operant conditioning and behavioral management techniques appropriate for the classroom. These techniques have required education personnel to sharpen their skills in systematically observing and analyzing ongoing patterns of reinforcement in the classroom.

In this context, the study of reinforcing behavior in the classroom provides one example of the role of systematic observation in helping us understand the classroom learning environment. Teachers' use of verbal approval and disapproval has been consistently observed to be effective in decreasing inappropriate pupil behaviors and in increasing desired pupil behaviors (O'Leary & O'Leary, 1972). The content of these approvals and disapprovals and the characteristics of the pupils to whom they are directed are important in understanding classroom life. One interesting procedure, the *Teacher Approval and Disapproval Observation Record* (TAD), developed by White, Beecher, Heller, and Waters (1973a) and White (1975), allows the observer to record teacher verbal approval and disapproval patterns as well as pupil variables and the preceding pupil behaviors to which the teacher had reacted.

Using the TAD, Waters (1973) studied sex differences in verbal approval and disapproval rates among teachers in first, second, and third grades. She found that there were no differences in the rates of approval given to boys and girls, but that boys received significantly more disapproval. Taking ability level into account, Heller and White (1975) observed the rates of approval and disapproval of junior high school teachers of social studies and mathematics who taught both "higher ability" and "lower ability" classes. Higher rates of disapproval were emitted in the lower ability classes and were predominately managerial in nature. More disapproval occurred in social studies classes than in mathematics classes. In all classes, little praise was given for appropriate social behaviors. Beecher (1973), studying teacher verbal approval and disapproval patterns in prekindergarten, kindergarten, and first-grade classrooms, observed different approval patterns at each grade level, but similar disapproval patterns across these grades. Observation studies such as these are of importance in understanding the existing reinforcement practices of teachers, given the potency of reinforcement in the classroom.

For readers interested in pursuing this topic further, the bibliography of this book includes selected observation schedules and accompanying guides for implementing behavior management techniques in classroom settings.

Observation and Psychoeducational Assessment

Pupil learning is an area of particular concern to most educators. In their daily interaction with pupils, teachers are continually assessing the degree to which desired learning goals are being reached. Indeed, observation is an integral component of this assessment process.

Certainly, systematic observation of a child's behavior can be an important tool for diagnostic assessment and case study in educational settings (Bersoff, 1973; Keller, 1986). Almy and Genishi (1981), in *Ways of Studying Children*, and Cohen, Stern, and Balaban (1983), in *Observing and Recording the Behavior of Young Children*, have pointed to observation as an integral component in assessing the learning needs of young children.

As an adjunct to standardized psychoeducational testing, gathering observations of a child within various natural contexts (home, school, playground) can generate rich developmental information regarding the child's current methods for coping with day-to-day situations, as well as his or her problem-solving strategies for particular tasks (Keogh, 1972). In collaboration with the classroom teacher, the school social worker, psychologist, and counselor can observe the child's interactions with peers in the classroom and other settings, and on another level, can view the ways in which the child relates to adults. Implicit in this process is the comparison of each child's performance with those behavioral norms concerning children of a similar age and background developed by the observer over time and as provided through sources such as normative data, individual measures of intelligence, and Piagetian tasks.

Within the testing situation, the school psychologist, learning disabilities specialist, and teacher can observe the gestures, actions, and other nonverbal behaviors that often contribute meaningful assessment data to the written test protocols. (See Alessi & Kay, 1983; Baker & Tyne, 1980; Lynch, 1977; Sitko, Fink, & Gillespie, 1977). Behavioral evidence is provided regarding the child's ease in relating to the tasks during assessment, rapport with the examiner, and general interest in the tasks. During individual testing behavioral information gained through purposeful observation might also include:

- Time taken to complete tasks.
- Approach of child to tasks—e.g., does child attempt difficult items or give up?
- Speed and accuracy of response—i.e., does child respond:

  Immediately and accurately?
  Immediately and then change answers?
  Immediately and does not consider alternatives?
  Slowly, but accurately?

- Amount of encouragement required—e.g., does child keep asking if he or she is doing well?
- Activity level of child—i.e., does child:

  Stay in seat with little movement?
  Stay in seat with repeated shifting around?
  Get out of seat occasionally?
  Get out of seat repeatedly?

- Amount of spontaneous talking child does.
- Physical features of the child (such as whether or not child wears glasses).

During group testing the observer can record such things as:

- Time taken by various children to complete task.
- Those children who have difficulty with presented instructions or in keeping their place.
- Which children skip difficult items, spend all their time on a few items, seem to be marking answers randomly, or repeatedly look around the room.

Interest in studying children's problem-solving strategies and intellectual styles has encouraged the observation of behavior in classrooms and test situations that reflect these strategies and styles (Bruner, Goodnow, & Austin, 1956; Ginsburg, 1987; Kagan & Kogan, 1970; Keogh, 1972; Kogan, 1983). These observations can help the assessor in matching psychoeducational interventions to the particular educational needs of a child.

Observation techniques are also useful in assessing the particular needs of children with special educational requirements. For example, observing the behavior of a hearing-impaired child or physically disabled pupil who has been placed in a "mainstream" classroom can provide ongoing data regarding the child's adjustment and the appropriateness of the educational placement. Several investigators highlight the use of observation strategies to improve the educational experiences of exceptional children (Gitler & Gordon, 1979; Kaufman, Agard, & Semmel, 1985; and Semmel, 1975).

Also, the assessment of adaptive behavior among institutionalized and noninstitutionalized mentally retarded, emotionally maladjusted, and developmentally disabled children has been dependent upon the use of reliable rating scales and behavioral checklists such as the AAMD (American Association on Mental Deficiency) Adaptive Behavior Scale — Public School Version; the Vineland Social Maturity Scale; and the Preschool Behavior Questionnaire (see Sattler, 1982).

Determining the optimal teaching techniques or interventions for children with special learning problems, in reading for instance, can often be accomplished efficiently by informal diagnostic procedures that include direct observation of the children's oral and silent reading behavior, in addition to traditional reading comprehension tests (Spache & Spache, 1973). The observant classroom teacher can recognize children who display symptoms suggestive of reading disability, and can provide these data as a basis for referral to other professionals for remedial programming.

Thus, while continuing to use tests or other appropriate strategies, the assessor should also use techniques of objective observation to raise and then confirm or reject hypotheses about an individual's functioning. Those engaged in psychoeducational assessment should seek naturalistic behavioral data to support their inferences. In fact, Public Law 94-142, the Education for All Handicapped Children Act of 1975, establishing safeguards for the evaluation and psychoeducational placement of children, has mandated the use of systematic, naturalistic observation techniques as complements to standardized testing practices (Heller, Holzman, & Messick, 1982). Furthermore, in determining the effectiveness of various intervention or remediation approaches, the school professional, needing to base conclusions on observable changes in behavior, has increasingly drawn upon naturalistic observation data to document the impact of the intervention program (e.g., Bissell, 1973).

Observation and Criterion-Referenced Assessment

The use of systematic observation techniques is particularly crucial in facilitating a "match" between a child's current level of functioning and the educational experiences to which he or she is exposed (Bloom, Hastings, & Madaus, 1971). Observations can provide an input to help formulate goals and select appropriate teaching procedures for working with a specific child. To provide a curricular match for the individual pupil, the classroom teacher must routinely assess whether a particular learning skill is being demonstrated and at what level (Boehm, 1973). Criterion-referenced testing is one form of assessment specifically related to the problem of the match. The question posed by this form of assessment is "To what extent is each pupil proficient in attaining the goal or goals of an instructional unit?" The criterion-referenced test, by definition, must be related to the objectives of an instructional unit. In turn, these instructional objectives must be stated in behavioral terms and broken down into their component parts. An additional consideration may be the variety of contexts in which learning is to take place. Thus, criterion-referenced assessment focuses on what the individual child can or cannot do relative to a given objective.

Systematic observation is frequently essential to the development and use of criterion-referenced tests. For example, if an educational objective is to evaluate self-help skills as they develop in young children, it would be necessary to define what is meant by "self-help" skills, consider which self-help skills would be of concern and when and in what contexts they might be demonstrated, and evaluate the individual child's progress by creating and using an observation procedure.

The criterion-referenced test may be contrasted with the more widely used norm-referenced test, which addresses itself to the issues of differentiating pupil achievement and making predictions. Although both forms of assessment are useful in educational settings, the distinction in purpose is critical. The criterion-referenced test evaluates a child's performance as it approximates specified lesson objectives, while the norm-referenced test compares the score of one child with the scores of others. Some useful resources in this area include Gagné (1985), Glaser and Nitko (1971), Gronlund (1985), Martuza (1977), and Popham (1971).

Observing the Effectiveness of Curriculum and Teaching Practices

Within classrooms, systematic observation has been used to generate information regarding the nature and effectiveness of varying instructional strategies (e.g., Good & Brophy, 1984). This book is not intended to present an in-depth exploration of these strategies, but some areas of application of systematic observation in studying the effectiveness of classroom practices may be of interest to the reader.

Flanders (1975) provided a framework for analyzing classroom interactions by observing teacher and pupil verbal behavior. Interaction analysis activities have provided the basis for pre- and in-service education programs that help teachers develop and control their specific teaching behaviors. The popularity of the Flanders Interaction Analysis model has been reflected in a burgeoning research literature in teacher effectiveness that has focused on discovering relationships between teacher behavior and measures of pupil growth (Good & Brophy, 1984; Joyce & Weil, 1972; Stallings, 1977).

With this understanding of the vital role that observational methods can play in the study of children, the educational process, and learning settings, let us begin to unravel the complexities of the observation process and to develop the skills necessary for systematic observation in early learning settings.

The Forms of Observation

There is a diverse range of written forms that our observations in learning environments can take, from informal, qualitative descriptions, to quantitative recording formats. These forms of observation include *diary descriptions, anecdotes, specimen records, checklists, rating scales,* and *observational schedules.* We will briefly describe these alternative modes of observing, highlighting their uses and limitations.

DIARY DESCRIPTIONS

Maintaining diary accounts of changes in human growth, behavior, and developmental events or milestones is the oldest observational method (Wright, 1960). Diary descriptions of young children's development have been kept by relatives, caretakers, and other observers close to the children. Diary entries are recorded in a narrative style and may vary from brief daily entries to comprehensive detailed accounts. The careful documentation of children's development in natural contexts can provide a strong data base for formulating hypotheses about human development, which in turn can be investigated through other methods of inquiry (laboratory experiments, field studies, and so forth).

The lack of reliability and unsystematic nature of these descriptions are potential problems. Another drawback is that diary accounts are almost always limited to one subject, or at best, a few subjects, making interpretations and generalizations difficult. Nevertheless, regular diary descriptions do provide a record of the continuity of behavior over time and can help one to identify meaningful patterns in development. Numerous independent diary descriptions, for example, of children's language acquisition, can lead to an increased objective understanding of typical developmental and universal norms.

ANECDOTAL RECORDS

Observers can write brief anecdotal summaries of their observations in any situation. These can range from developmental milestones—"Michael took his first step today"—to behavioral events—

16

"Mary was enthusiastic about her work on the microcomputer." Although anecdotes can be objective descriptions of events, they can also be subjective statements about these events. Many of us can recall "comments" sections on school records, which often included anecdotal observations such as "has difficulty relating" or "a pleasure to have in class." These comments were passed from one teacher to the next. In the past, unfavorable records could follow a child throughout his or her school career, perhaps biasing a new teacher's views of the pupil. Currently, many states prohibit the inclusion of such anecdotal accounts in official school records.

When they are factual accounts, anecdotal records can provide rich descriptive information related to child development. Anecdotal records can be made by teachers, child care workers, parents, or physicians, often at irregular intervals, to maintain a "factual" record. Anecdotes may or may not include what led up to or followed a recorded incident such as a temper tantrum. The choice of events to be recorded, timeliness of the record, and amount of detail provided are determined by the observer, who can choose to document unusual or unexpected events. Anecdotal records often reflect the biases of the observer. A number of procedures have been suggested for preparing and interpreting anecdotal records (Cartwright & Cartwright, 1984; Thorndike & Hagen, 1977). These include techniques such as:

- Limiting discussion to one incident
- Recording incidents as soon as possible after they occur
- Separating interpretive comments from factual reporting
- Considering supportive information

Clearly, although anecdotes can provide an understanding of behaviors not easily appraised by other means — such as social skills, adjustments, and health status — it is critical that objective, factual reporting take place and that follow-up study be made of behaviors of concern. Consideration needs also to be paid to how typical or representative noted behaviors are for the individual and for his or her peers.

SPECIMEN RECORDS

Specimen records are closely related to diary descriptions but represent the "continuous observing and narrative recording of a behavior sequence under chosen conditions of time and life setting" (Wright, 1960, p. 83). Observers detail the setting and record everything they see or hear. Thus behavior is described in its natural context. The resulting record is then reviewed and analyzed. Specimen records are useful to note small changes in development or behavior. A classic example is provided in *One Boy's Day* (Barker & Wright, 1951), a record of "what a seven-year-old boy did and of what his home and school and neighborhood and town did to him from the time he awoke one morning until he went to sleep that night" (p. 1). Eight observers, all familiar adults to the child, took turns during the day recording all directly observable behaviors, including vocalizations and body movements. They also recorded their own impressions. The extensive information gathered was later analyzed and a categorization of behaviors and identification of behavior sequences made.

Specimen records provide comprehensive accounts of behavior and are useful for establishing the range and types of behaviors a person may exhibit in a given situation. They may serve as a basis for formulating observational questions and developing structured observational procedures, and can be used for detailed analyses and quantitative study. Although extremely valuable, specimen records are especially time consuming and costly. The use of audiotapes or videotapes could enhance the reliability and completeness of this form of observation.

Within the classroom, the teacher can engage in a brief form of continuous observation, generally referred to as a *running record*. For example, the teacher may choose to maintain a running record of everything a child does and says during an assigned activity (see the example below). Five minutes of such recording may result in important insights.

A SAMPLE RUNNING RECORD

Subject: Tom
Setting: Second-grade classroom; 31 students
Situation: Class members were to work independently on a reading assignment that included a reading passage followed by five questions
Observation time: 10 minutes
Observer: Judith Zucker

Tom held a looseleaf in his lap. His reader was opened to the appropriate page on his desk. His desk was cluttered with other books and pencils.

T. wrote for approximately two minutes. He copied questions from the board, seemingly looking at the board after writing each word of a particular question. He completed the copying of only one question by the end of the two-minute span.

T. stopped writing and began to play with a tape dispenser that was in his desk. He tore off pieces of tape and pasted them on the inside of his desk. During this time he spoke to himself using the phrases: "Oh boy," when he tore off an exceptionally long piece of tape; "Just one more piece," after which he did stop tearing; "What's the next question?," looking at the board but not copying; and "Ick!" During the time T. looked at the board, he held a small piece of tape between his thumb and forefinger and moved his forefinger toward and away from the tape.

He began to write again. (I reminded the class to answer questions in complete sentences.) T. grimaced. He began to search inside his desk for a pencil. He found one, examined it, rejected it, found another pencil with an eraser. T. spent roughly two minutes erasing all of what was written on his paper thus far. He brushed away the eraser remains. He stated, not too quietly, "Uh oh! My paper ripped."

T. attempted to repair the paper with tape. He tore off a piece of tape. He made an unhappy face—apparently the piece of tape was too small. He started to tear off a second piece but lost the end of the roll of tape. He put his hand to his head. He tried to find the end of the tape again. He struggled with the tape for almost a minute, scraping the roll with his fingernail.

Defeated, he tore a sheet of paper out of the looseleaf and elaborately crumpled it. He placed the looseleaf on his desk slowly, put his head down, placed two hands on the desk, and pushed himself away from the desk. He stood, extending his arms to both sides, stretched, looked at me, and walked slowly to the wastebasket carrying the paper. He threw the paper in basket, walked to my desk, and said, "Miss Z., my paper is ripped."

T. returned to his seat. He began to look for a pencil and clean paper. He repositioned the looseleaf and reader as before. He began to write his name on the paper.

This approach allows the observer to focus his or her attention on one individual and provides an opportunity to become acutely aware of behaviors of the student that may have previously gone undetected. A limitation of this approach is that it is virtually impossible to record all of a subject's behaviors, due to one's inability to write fast enough. Furthermore, while the observer is writing, the subject is continuing to "perform," and these actions go unnoticed. The use of audiotape or videotape, although solving some of these problems, introduces others (see Unit X).

CHECKLISTS

Checklists involve a listing of behaviors that are marked by the observer as being present or absent; other behaviors are ignored. Sometimes checklists are used to track behaviors of interest on several occasions or in different settings. (Checklists usually are *sign systems*, a topic discussed on page 58). Checklists may be completed while actually observing the child, but are more frequently completed "after the fact" from memory.

Checklists can help child care workers or teachers understand a variety of behaviors such as self-help or study skills. In order to develop a useful checklist, behaviors must be clearly defined and listed beforehand—the usefulness of the checklist depends on whether or not it includes all possible key behaviors (Fewell, 1984). In order to generate this list a *task analysis* needs to be carried out that requires the developer to ask, for example, "What does the child need to be able to do to demonstrate good study skills?" "How, specifically, might these behaviors be demonstrated?" Many areas of complex behavior, such as peer relationships or task-appropriate behavior, can be analyzed through this approach. Thus, checklists can reflect a teacher's behavioral objectives and can help focus the observer. Several checklists in fact can be used concurrently.

Unfortunately, not all checklists are well detailed or task analyzed. The user needs to review the use of a potential checklist carefully to consider the adequacy of the information yielded. Other problems relate to such issues as bias and selectivity. Checklists can reflect a particular theoretical perspective and provide a biased view of the observational situation. Finally, checklists provide no information regarding the degree or frequency with which a behavior is exhibited. Those checklists that provide space for narrative elaboration can help users evaluate the extent or degree to which the observed behaviors are exhibited.

RATING SCALES

Rating scales focus on designated behaviors and allow observers to judge the extent or degree to which these behaviors are exhibited. Rating scales require judgment and are often used in the assessment of personality and social adjustment or physical motor development. Although ratings can be made while observing ongoing behavior, they frequently are made on the basis of past observations and are completed when the child is not present. Rating scales usually take one of two forms, numerical judgments or descriptive phrases (see Figure 3.1).

Information based on ratings can be useful for assessment purposes. An example may be found on the Pupil Response Sheet from the *Cognitive Skills Assessment Battery*, second edition (Boehm & Slater, 1981, p. 3) (see Figure 3.2). Other examples include *The Pupil Rating Scale* (Myklebust, 1971) and the *Developmental Task Analysis* (Valett, 1969).

Ratings tell us nothing about the causes of behaviors, but they can help us to describe or pinpoint specific behaviors. The observer must make a judgment about the most descriptive behavior or provide a numerical rating. Bias can influence judgment, particularly when numerical scores are solely used or where the target behaviors are not directly observable and therefore require inferences to be drawn by the observer. Caution also needs to be exercised with scales that provide a midpoint score, such as:

$$1 \quad 2 \quad 3 \quad 4 \quad 5$$

always   never

When using these kinds of scales, there is a tendency for observers to rate at the midpoint and to avoid extreme judgments (error of central tendency).

Kerlinger (1973) has suggested that rating scales are particularly

---

Figure 3.1.   Forms of Rating Scales

a. Numerical judgments, from high to low, of behaviors of interest, such as:

  Easily relates to classmates   1 2 3 4 5   Has difficulty relating to classmates

b. Descriptive phrases, such as:

Very attentive	Generally attentive	Often inattentive	Very inattentive

c. Specific qualities or objectives stated in terms of performance, such as:

Unable to print name	Prints first name only	Prints first name & last initial	Prints first & last name

Figure 3.2. Example of Ratings Used During Assessment

A: Task Persistence

4 ☐ persists with task
3 ☐ attempts task briefly
2 ☐ attempts task after much encouragement
1 ☐ refuses

B: Attention span

4 ☐ focuses attention voluntarily
3 ☐ attends with teacher direction
2 ☐ some distraction with noise or movement of others
1 ☐ easily distracted

C: Body movement

4 ☐ sits quietly
3 ☐ some squirming
2 ☐ much movement
1 ☐ out of seat; body constantly in motion

D: Attention to directions

4 ☐ listens carefully to entire direction
3 ☐ attends only to brief directions
2 ☐ plunges ahead after hearing only portion
1 ☐ plunges ahead immediately

E: Comprehension of directions

4 ☐ rapid comprehension of most directions, given age expectations
3 ☐ understands after several repetitions
2 ☐ partial comprehension of directions
1 ☐ does not appear to comprehend most directions

F: Verbalization

4 ☐ many spontaneous comments
3 ☐ occasional comments
2 ☐ responds only when spoken to
1 ☐ extremely reluctant to speak or inappropriate speech

G: Ease of relationship (rapport)

4 ☐ immediately friendly
3 ☐ friendly but reserved
2 ☐ shy
1 ☐ very reluctant and/or fearful

H: Confidence

4 ☐ very sure of self
3 ☐ confident with things known; attempts new things with encouragement
2 ☐ reluctant to try new or difficult things
1 ☐ very uncertain; needs much encouragement

Source: Boehm and Slater (1981), *Cognitive Skills Assessment Battery*, second edition.

susceptible to a number of sources of bias including the "halo effect," error of severity, error of leniency, and the error of central tendency (see Unit VII). Kerlinger has also pointed out that the "Halo is extremely difficult to avoid. It seems to be particularly strong in traits that are not clearly defined, not easily observable, and that are morally important" (p. 549).

Rating scales, however, have the advantages of being easy to use and applicable to a wide variety of situations. They can help focus an observer's attention, particularly when points along the scale are behaviorally defined: The more observable and precise each point, the greater the objectivity of the results. The advantages of rating scales and their ease of use leads to two cautions. First, it is essential that ratings be based on a sufficient number of observations to arrive at a valid judgment. Second, observers need to be mindful that many rating scales do not specify precise behaviors and should be aware of their own sensitivities and biases in making ratings.

FORMAL OBSERVATION SCHEDULES

Observational systems are developed to help observers collect and quantify information using systematic procedures and recording schedules. Use of such procedures helps make the information gained from observation more manageable. Useful observation systems include:

- Category or sign systems that clearly define target behaviors and are exhaustive of the behaviors to be observed
- Procedures for sampling behavior, such as time or event sampling
- Standard recording formats
- Procedures for determining reliability

Users tally or mark the occurrence of or frequency with which behaviors occur in predetermined categories during each observation unit, such as every 30 seconds or every minute. If categories are exhaustive, nonoverlapping, and well defined (see pages 54–55) and if recording procedures are well defined, formal observation systems can be efficient and reliable, and can enhance the quantification of observational data. The development of such observational systems is the major focus of this text.

The use of formal observational systems does not eliminate all problems. Since the use of formal schedules focuses the observer's attention on targeted behaviors or events, observers may miss other important behaviors or may not be able to capture the flow of behavior. Also,

170442

the amount of training required to use many systems may be extensive. Despite these limitations, observational systems can provide sophisticated and valid accounts of a wide range of observable behaviors. (Useful resources regarding observational systems may be found in the Bibliography.)

There is a place for each of the forms of observation in learning settings. Often more than one mode of observing can be used, in a complementary manner. For example, a specimen record, rating scale, and formal observational schedule might be successively employed over time in addressing a particular observational problem. Flexibility in using the array of observational techniques can be the hallmark of the skillful early childhood observer.

The Selective Nature
of Our Observations

Each person presented with the task of making specific observations should be able to observe objectively with minimal interference from subjective frames of reference. Obviously, however, the subjective is always going to be a factor — we each choose to pay attention to certain things or activities while we ignore others. It is impossible to observe everything in a given situation at the same time; while we are focusing on some attributes of a situation, we are naturally missing others.

To help you become acquainted with your own current approach to observing situations, try this task.

TASK 1: OBSERVATIONS OF YOUR PRESENT SETTING

Observe the setting in which you find yourself. Record your observations, using the Task 1 Worksheet. If others are in the room with you, ask them to engage in the same task. Record your observations in the order in which they are made. Limit the time for the task to five minutes.

Then compare your observations with those made by others in the same setting. Include in this comparison:

The observations made (what you and others selected to observe)

In what sequence your observations were made and how the sequence of your observations compares with that of others

And then consider these questions:

How did you choose what to view?

Did you employ a strategy for observing the setting? If so, which strategy?

How did the format of the task influence the nature of your observations?

TASK 1 WORKSHEET

Observations of Your Present Setting

(Five-Minute Time Limit)

Setting: _____

Time of Day: _____

Observer: _____

Observations in Sequence

1.

2.

3.

4.

5.

6.

7.

8.

9.

10.

11.

12.

Given in the Appendix is a set of sample responses made by three observers in the same setting. Compare your responses with these.

Although it is interesting to note the similarity in responses among the three observers as they viewed the same setting, this example illustrates the selective nature of observing a setting, both in terms of what is observed and the order in which the observations are made.

SUBJECTIVITY IN OBSERVATION

By now it has become apparent that a wide range of observations are possible, given the same setting and time, depending upon the selectivity of the viewer. The selective and *subjective* nature of what we see is a reflection of many psychological factors, such as previous observation in that setting, our attitudinal framework, our momentary feelings and mood, and any systems of classification we may have for viewing the world, which can be an indication of our interests and occupation.

For example, when an early childhood specialist observes the child of a family friend playing with a puzzle, the child's behaviors are likely to be compared with known developmental milestones gained through reading and past experiences.

TASK 2: OBSERVATIONS OF A SUPERMARKET SCENE

For Task 2, view the photograph of a supermarket scene and make your observations, attempting to take the points of view of the manager of the store and then of a shopper. Again, limit yourself to five minutes for each observation. Record your observations on the Task 2 Worksheet.

Next, compare the content and order in which the observations were made given the two different orientations. Consider: (1) in what ways they are the same and how they are different, and (2) why you think these differences have occurred.

Certainly, the differing orientations of the store manager and shopper for observing the supermarket will influence the kinds of observations that are made. The manager, interested in the level of business and the related satisfaction of customers, would focus on the number of shoppers, the number and nature of items in shopping carts, the orderliness of the shelves, counters, and aisles, as well as other indications of the efficiency of staff. On the other hand, the shopper would probably focus observations on the cost and kinds of items available. As is the manager, but for other reasons, the shopper would be interested in the cleanliness of the store, the orderliness of the aisles, the apparent freshness of produce, and so on. Our needs and points of view influence what we see.

Some other questions that could be posed giving focus to observation in supermarkets include: What products do

Task 2.   A Supermarket Scene

people buy? How many customers use shopping lists? How many customers (any individual entering the store) are in the store at various time periods?

AIMING FOR OBJECTIVITY IN OUR OBSERVATIONS

Tasks 1 and 2 demonstrate the *selective* nature of our perceptions. Such selectivity is natural because the process of perception demands selectivity. When we are observing in order to make decisions or to draw conclusions, it is necessary to be *objective*, to have a focus so that our observations are purposeful and defined. Therefore, we must consider

TASK 2 WORKSHEET

Observations of a Supermarket Scene

Observations in Sequence

Manager of Store

1.

2.

3.

4.

5.

6.

7.

8.

9.

Shopper in Store

1.

2.

3.

4.

5.

6.

7.

8.

9.

such questions as: "What are we going to view?" and "For what purpose?" Such questions increase the objectivity of the observations that we make. The following guidelines are given to help you differentiate objective from subjective observations.

- Objective observations (factors or details others could readily agree upon):

  A count of the number of chairs, tables, windows, and so forth, in a room
  Noting the color of objects
  Relating the size of objects one to another
  Describing behavior as it occurs (but not interpreting this behavior)

- Subjective observations (unique perceptions, biases, or individual points of view that others might not agree with):

  A statement about perceived conditions, such as "This room is hot" (it may not seem hot to others)
  Focusing on the physical attractiveness of a room
  Concentrating on personal characteristics of the people in the setting, such as "She looks pretty"

It is possible to carry the quest for objectivity to the point of absurdity: "The walls of the room are painted light yellow, shade #428 ACME Opaque paint and the air temperature in the room is 72.4°F." Under most conditions, this degree of precision would, of course, be unnecessary.

TASK 3: DISTINGUISHING OBJECTIVE FROM SUBJECTIVE OR INTERPRETIVE OBSERVATIONS

Go back to the record of observations you made for Task 1 and consider which of your reactions conveyed *specific* and *objective* information, and which ones involved subjective observations, employing the guidelines just given. Label each of your observations "objective" or "subjective" in the margin of your worksheet.

If your observations tended to fall heavily in the subjective category, you have an indication of one's natural tendency to view situations subjectively. There is nothing wrong with making subjective comments so long as the observer is aware of the subjectivity and that this is reflected in the use of qualified language: "The air *feels* cold" not "The air *is* cold."

An additional dilemma that faces the observer is the tendency to make inferences or draw conclusions from scanty evidence not necessarily supported by other data. Thus, if you noted that a girl sitting to your left appeared to be happy and what you actually saw was a girl with a smile on her face, you might be drawing an inappropriate conclusion on the basis of the evidence — the smile might hide disdain, discomfort, or boredom.

THE EFFECT OF THE OBSERVER'S PRESENCE

Look at the pictures of a classroom in Figures 4.1 and 4.2. They illustrate the effect of an outside observer's presence, in this case with a camera, on the spontaneous flow of behavior in a given setting. The first photograph was taken immediately upon the observer's entrance into

Figure 4.1. School Classroom

Figure 4.2. Classroom after Photographer Enters

the classroom; Figure 4.2 was taken several seconds later while the observer (with camera) stood by the doorway of the room. In Figure 4.2 the child in the striped shirt has responded to the observer. This illustrates how the presence of a photographer, or any observer, can influence the nature of some behaviors that occur as part of the ongoing sequence within that setting.

However, it has been noted that, in general, the effect of the presence of the outside observer on pupil behavior tends to decrease over time (Masling & Stern, 1969). With this in mind, it is important to note that the observer, if he or she is new to a setting, should be within that setting on several occasions prior to making systematic observations or drawing conclusions based on those observations.

DRAWING INFERENCES

Until now our emphasis has been on objective observing. However, such an emphasis is not intended to negate the importance of drawing inferences as a result of the observation process. Inferences can generate ideas, hypotheses to be checked out against other evidence, and also, potentially creative solutions to problems. Thus, inferences about another person's feelings ("Linda appears to be a happy child," or "Michael seems to be a bright, well-adjusted child"), supported by a variety of observational data such as facial expressions and the content of conversations over a period of time, can lead to certain conclusions made or actions taken in the classroom, on the job, at home, or in relationships with others.

Though we will not move into a philosophical discussion here, it is essential that we now consider the nature of various inferences that are commonly made in education settings. Each day educators make statements such as:

Louise is a creative child.
Johnny isn't very bright.
The boys in this room are hostile and aggressive.
Jerry is not distractible and attends well during class.
Irene has a very poor self-concept.

Psychological phenomena such as creativity, intelligence, aggressiveness, distractibility, and self-concept are not directly observable. Rather, these labels or descriptions are used or made on the basis of observable behaviors that represent commonly agreed upon indicators of the constructs just noted.

Although all of us make inferences about others each day, few of us are aware of the way observations provide support for such inferences. Taking the example of "self-concept," what do we mean when we refer to a child's good or poor self-concept? We need to raise such questions as: What observational data can be used to support the inferences and conclusions drawn? Would another person arrive at the same conclusions? How many instances of particular observable behaviors are necessary before we are willing to state that a child has a poor self-concept? (Sampling and the systematic collection of observational data to lend support to inferences are topics dealt with at length in Unit VIII.)

Let's consider the role of observations in making inferences with the following example.

TASK 4: OBSERVATIONS OF A GIRL IN A NURSERY CLASS

For Task 4, look at the photograph of a girl in a nursery school and consider what objective statements could be made about her and what inferences might be drawn about her behavior in the context of the activity and classroom.

Task 4. Girl in Nursery School Setting

The following information will help clarify the situation:

The girl and the other children are four years old and have attended nursery school for two months.

The children are engaged in free play, which generally continues for about 30 minutes.

The girl has been sitting in the same place without making any sounds for at least five minutes.

Using the Task 4 Worksheet, indicate possible inferences about the girl's behavior in the classroom, supporting your statements with objective observational data. Indicate by corresponding letters which observations are the basis for your inferences.

Review your list of inferences about the little girl in the picture and their supportive observations. Then consider the possible observations and inferences for Task 4 given in the Appendix.

TASK 4 WORKSHEET

Observations of a Girl in a Nursery Class

Observations Made	Inferences Drawn	Observations Supporting Inferences (#1, #2)
1.	A.	A.
2.	B.	B.
3.	C.	C.
4.	D.	D.
5.	E.	E.

In making observations and inferences in most situations we have the benefit of viewing the flux of behavior over time. A single photograph obviously presents a static moment in time, making it essential that the viewer question what actually preceded that momentary instance. Prior to the situation depicted in the picture shown in Task 4, the girl might have been actively involved in play with the boys in the block area, or she might have just sat down after playing with a group of children in the dollhouse area. If the viewer cannot obtain such information about prior activities, care should be exercised about drawing strong inferences. The strength of inferences depends on the prevalence or the frequency of the observed behavior that supports the inference. Sampling behavior over time eliminates the tendency to draw inferences on the basis of scanty observational data.

Defining the Problem and Describing the Setting

By now it should be apparent that making useful and objective observations is a complex task. The classification or organization of behaviors and components of the setting can facilitate the objective observations process, as well as the communication of findings to others. The type of grouping or classification used must relate to the particular focus or concern of the observer. For example, a kindergarten teacher interested in developing appropriate concept materials for a class would focus on a child's use of the particular concepts to be developed, while ignoring the child's social interaction with others. On the other hand, if the teacher wanted to develop a program that encouraged social interaction among children, care would be centered upon a concern with ways of classifying social patterns in the classroom.

In this unit we seek to develop a systematic approach to structuring observations so that enough data can be gathered to realize the goals for which observation techniques were used in the first place. Given the inherent selectivity in the observation process, and the need for objectivity discussed earlier, agreement between individuals on the specific foci of observation is essential. Although ways by which the reliability of observation can be increased will be considered in the next three units, it becomes essential at this point to develop an approach that can do the following:

- Force the observer to clearly define the problem or question he or she wishes to answer through the use of observation techniques.
- Take into account the constraints a given setting imposes on the scope of potential behaviors, and lead the observer to describe the components of an observational situation, including the overall physical setting, materials available to individuals within the setting, and individuals within the situation.
- Provide a system for describing, counting, and categorizing instances of behavior, allowing more than one observer to collect or interpret the same data.

• Take into account the position that one cannot directly observe emotions, cognition, or attitudes. Rather, the latter are concepts that are inferred on the basis of viewing countable, describable instances of behavior.

DEFINING THE PROBLEM

The range of questions that might be posed in learning settings and for which observation techniques are appropriate is broad. A curriculum coordinator might be intent on evaluating the influence a new social studies curriculum has on questioning behaviors displayed in the classroom; teachers or psychologists in training might want an overview of the range of typical behaviors exhibited by children from different age groups attending the same school; the school psychologist posed with a referral of a child demonstrating "learning difficulties" might be interested in that child's classroom behavior as he interacts with his peers, teacher, and the learning situation; a principal of a large urban school might want to know if pupils receive more feedback on assignments when student teachers are present.

Some sample problems that provide focus for the classroom observer follow.

The teacher might be interested in the number of activities involving more than one child that occur during the school day. The teacher might be interested in this observation in order to make inferences about the "cooperative behavior" of children in the classroom.

The teacher, concerned about the performance of John Jones, and questioning the appropriateness of a referral to the school psychologist, might want to know if John appears to understand curriculum content, is smaller than other children in the classroom, is very quiet, is inattentive, or does not respond to classroom instructions or directions.

The principal, concerned about lack of space in the school, might wonder if the class makes effective use of space currently allotted.

The supervisory teacher might be concerned by the extent to which a student teacher is providing practice appropriate to specific goals of the lesson.

Posing questions or presenting problems in a form that allows the observer to understand the specific purpose of the intended observations and eventually arrive at an answer to the posed question is essential. For example, the question "Are the pupils in this class motivated to do their assignments?" in its current form is insufficiently defined to focus the observer on specific behaviors in the setting, because one must ask:

What is motivation?
Can motivation be observed directly?
What, in specific behavioral terms, is "doing" an assignment?

If the question is rephrased to read, "Do pupils in this class regularly (over a stated time period) turn in completed class and homework assignments" it limits the observer to directly observable behavior — turning in a completed assignment — and does not deal with motivation, which can be inferred only from a variety of observed behaviors.

TASK 5: DIFFERENTIATING CLEARLY STATED FROM POORLY STATED QUESTIONS

As a further exercise, determine which of the questions given on the Task 5 worksheet are clearly stated. Check the appropriate column for each question and fill in the reason for your response. When you have completed this task, compare your answers with the judgments about each question given in the Appendix.

THE CONSTRAINTS OF THE SETTING

After defining the problem for observation, a careful analysis of the setting itself is needed in order to develop appropriate categories for observation. The general setting characteristically dictates the nature of behaviors that can be observed in that situation; for example, a child's verbal interactions with adults cannot be observed if that setting is restricted to children. It is also important to focus on those aspects of the setting that can limit, direct, or facilitate behavior. These factors include:

- People in the setting who will differ along the dimensions of age, sex, and role
- Tangible materials in the setting
- General physical characteristics of the setting itself such as temperature, lighting, room size, and space

TASK 5 WORKSHEET

Differentiating Clearly Stated from Poorly Stated Questions

Question	Well Stated	Poorly Stated	Reason
1. Are boys more restless than girls during small-group reading-readiness activities?			
2. Does the teacher in this classroom encourage questioning behavior?			
3. During a given kindergarten class day, how many individual children choose to look at a book during free play?			
4. Why do the girls in the kindergarten class appear to be more motivated to clean up after snack time?			

An overview of the total setting is helpful in developing an understanding of the situation, but it is also important to reemphasize the selective nature of observing behavior. An individual will ignore those portions of a setting where little activity is occurring and will focus on areas of the setting where the central activity is taking place.

The constraints of a setting on the behavior of an individual can be illustrated from another perspective. For example,

> How does the same child interact with others in the classroom, in the gym, on the playground, and at home?
>
> How does the factory worker interact with other workers during rest periods, in the cafeteria, and on the job itself?

Roger Barker (1968) made a useful point in his exposition of the mutual relationship that takes place between people and their environment. The environment, or *context* of behavior, has its own structures (boundaries, and physical and temporal attributes), that limit or dictate the individual's behavior. A child's behavior on the playground is different from that in the classroom; on the playground the child is more likely to run and shout than in the classroom. A doctor generally functions differently on the golf course than in a hospital; on the golf course the doctor's behavior resembles that of other golfers, while in the hospital it is like that of other doctors. Clearly, the setting makes a great difference in the doctor's behavior. Thus, the interaction that takes place between an individual and the setting generates an important question: What characterizes the behavior of the same person in different situations or settings?*

Pursuing this point further, particularly with younger children, we might consider a child's behavior separately in different activity areas of the room, such as in the doll corner, at work tables, in the block area, at the book shelf, or in the painting area. With older pupils, we might consider behaviors as displayed in different subject matter classrooms or curricular periods. In summary, then, the observer needs to take into account the various constraints within settings that limit or provide opportunity for the behaviors of individuals within those settings.

TASK 6: CONSTRAINTS IMPOSED BY THE SETTING

Considering our analysis of constraints on possible behavior imposed by the setting, look at the photograph of a playground setting. Using the Task 6 Worksheet, list those characteristics of the people within this setting that might restrict behavior. Speculate on some possible behaviors that

---

*Barker and Wright's *One Boy's Day* (1951) provides stimulating reading in this area.

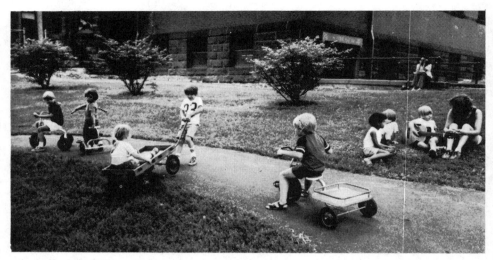

Task 6. A Playground Setting

probably could not occur because of these constraints and on some behaviors that would be facilitated by these same factors. Also consider in what ways the available "materials" (play equipment, play space) on the playground tend to produce some general constraints and in what ways they facilitate certain kinds of behavior.

Compare your responses with the sample responses given in the Appendix.

ANALYZING THE COMPONENTS OF THE SETTING

Further considerations in viewing the contexts in which one observes behavior are components such as the physical setting, tangible materials of the setting, and individuals within the setting. These components are described individually in the following section, and practice in observing them is given in the accompanying tasks.

Observing and Describing the Overall Physical Setting

Unlike human behavior, which undergoes considerable change over time, the physical setting in which we observe behavior usually remains quite stable. When observing, one should consider the physical charac-

TASK 6 WORKSHEET

Constraints Imposed by the Setting

Category	Characteristics	Unlikely Behaviors	Likely Behaviors
1. People			
2. Materials			
3. Space			
4. Other (Indicate)			

teristics of the situation, such as the temperature of a room and its implications for the kinds of behavior to be expected in that room, the amount of space provided in the setting for a range of activities, and the nature of artificial and natural lighting and its placement within a setting.

Observing and Describing Tangible Materials

Tangible materials might be considered next because they are often central to the behavioral activities in a setting. Such materials include large pieces of equipment (desks, playground equipment, sandbox) as well as smaller, more easily expendable materials (paper, pencils, books, puzzles, and teacher-designed materials).

Aside from identifying and describing these materials in isolation, it is important to note the arrangement or organization of these materials by people within the setting to meet their particular goals. For example, the larger setting might be organized into activity areas, such as seat activities, library corner, science area, or arts and crafts area (as illustrated in the photograph shown in Figure 5.1).

Figure 5.1. Kindergarten Classroom

Observing and Describing Individuals Within the Setting

A third major component of our analysis of the setting in which behaviors are observed is a description of the individuals within that setting. Task 7 provides practice in doing this.

TASK 7: VISIBLE CHARACTERISTICS OF INDIVIDUALS

Look at the Task 7 photographs and write down your descriptions of the *visible* characteristics of each individual pictured, using the Task 7 Worksheet. As you will notice, the Task 7 Worksheet lists only characteristics that are *directly observable*. In making descriptions of individuals, one should not feel compelled to make inferences about the emotions, social backgrounds, current roles, and so on, of these individuals. To do so would be an example of how often we draw conclusions and make judgments about individuals based on characteristics that are beyond what we actually can see.*

An observer interested in a subset of children (such as a reading group), or only one child, has more flexibility for description than would be possible in a larger group. Obviously, in a classroom group of 20 children, it is impossible for the observer to focus careful attention on more than one child at a time. Therefore, if the observer is interested in describing the physical characteristics of an entire group of children, it is necessary to employ a technique that allows for systematic ordering of observations of the group, viewing one member of the group at a time.

It is important to emphasize that we are observing individuals at this point without considering their behavior and without considering the ways in which they interact with each other, physically or verbally. After describing the individuals whose behavior is of interest to you, it is helpful to take notice of some general characteristics of the group of people within the setting. Such *summarizing characteristics* include:

The number of individuals present
The ratio of boys to girls
The ratio of adults to children

---

*Kleinmuntz (1967) offers a detailed discussion of observing expressive behavior (pp. 92–109).

Boy   Girl   Adult

Task 7. Three Individuals

THE CONTEXT OF BEHAVIOR

In this unit we have isolated the various key components of a setting that need to be considered when observing. In an attempt to illustrate the ways in which physical features of the setting, the objects and the people within that setting, combine to produce the context of observed behavior, consider the example given in Figure 5.2. Here we are observing in the library of an elementary school. The time is the library period for second-grade pupils. For this observation, we have taken note of the physical features of the room, the objects in it, the people and their activities, and we have included a list of summarizing characteristics.

As Figure 5.2 shows, the observed activity is a result of the interplay of people with their setting, in this case a school library. Now do Task 8, using the example in Figure 5.2 as a model. Pick a similar setting.

TASK 8: KEY COMPONENTS OF A SETTING

Analyze the components of a setting. Distinguish physical features, objects, and people, and name the activities taking place. Write your responses on the Task 8 Worksheet.

TASK 7 WORKSHEET

Visible Characteristics of Individuals

Category	Boy	Girl	Adult
1. Approximate Age			
2. Sex			
3. Physical Features Shade of hair, clothing, body build, height, glasses			
4. Movement and Gestures			
5. Physical Handicaps			

Figure 5.2. Key Components of a Setting

Setting: Elementary-school library
Time: Library period for second-grade pupils

Physical Features	Objects	People	Activities
Rectangular room	Three rows of steel bookshelves outside	One young girl in blue dress	Copying a drawing from a magazine
Entrance and exit turnstile	One wooden bookshelf against the wall		
Yellow colored walls		One middle-aged woman in green dress	Often coming out from the adjoining room with a paper in hand
One large glass window	Two yellow and one green chair with a small table in one corner		Checks the paper with the girl
One small glass window	Six round tables, "natural wood," each with five chairs		Goes back to her room
Two pillars	Index card boxes		
One adjoining room with a window door	Books on the counter	Two young boys in the rows of bookshelves	Searching for books
One big door leading into library	Books in the shelves		
	Duplicating machine	Three young girls sitting at one of the round tables	Two girls talking with each other while pointing to a picture in a book; one girl looking at book in front of her
Check out counter	Painting of a man		
Overhead fluorescent light turned on	Three plants		
	Paper slips, pins, stamps on the counter		
	Bulletin board		

Summarizing Characteristics

—Presence of only six students in the library suggests that only small groups of second-grade pupils use the library at a time, not the entire class, because, at the time of the observation, only the six students were there, although there was ample room for a class.

—Turnstile present for counting or control.

—All individuals present seem occupied.

TASK 8 WORKSHEET

Key Components of a Setting

Setting:
Time:

Physical Features	Objects	People	Activities

Summarizing Characteristics:

Summarize the characteristics of the setting and activities that take place. Then, focusing on the constraints imposed by the setting, make predictions about which kinds of behavior are likely to occur. Do you find that these predictions more or less correspond to the observed activities?

We have stressed the importance of observing and describing the environmental contexts in which classroom behaviors occur in order to generate an awareness of the constraining influences.

In describing environments, it is important to remember that the classroom is constantly changing—another adult can enter the room, class groupings change with the curriculum, a particular child is absent, and so forth. Since behavior is always determined to some extent by the environment in which it occurs, it is sometimes important to describe the shifts within the environment.

It should be emphasized that the study of environment *per se* and the relationship between individuals and their settings has been a central focus of the field of ecological psychology (as discussed in Unit II). A complex network of theoretical constructs, empirical findings, and field methods has resulted from the ecologist's perspective. The purpose of this unit has been no more than to highlight some components of a complex study of "behavior settings" that can be useful to the early childhood observer.

Labeling and Categorizing Behavior

The term "behavior" has been used earlier in the book, but we have not defined it precisely because our focus has been on other aspects of the complex observation process. In order to consider dimensions for labeling behavior, let us define "behavior" as *any observable, overt action or activity that an individual exhibits in a setting.* Behaviors range from solitary, nonvocal activity (sitting in a chair, looking out the window) to verbal and nonverbal interaction with others (a fist fight and verbal exchange between two third-graders on the playground). When referring to constructs such as "self-concept," which we cannot directly observe, we are dealing with an inference or conclusion that may be based on observable behaviors.

DIMENSIONS FOR LABELING BEHAVIORS

Within education and the behavioral sciences one can select from a variety of measures, rating scales, and categories for viewing behavior in the classroom (see Bibliography). Recently, the variety of efforts to measure behavior have reflected a behavioral analysis orientation. The resulting instruments have focused on the teacher's verbal behavior as well as on a wide range of verbal and nonverbal pupil responses, and have in general been devised in a manner consistent with purposes of the particular researchers. Although we advocate a perspective that places behavior within the context of its setting and that underscores the importance of making qualitative judgments, inferences, and decisions on the basis of observation data, we also advocate an approach that allows us to consider behavior from various points of view. Consequently, a cognitive-developmental psychologist might make inferences about the level of a child's cognitive-intellectual functioning on the basis of observing behaviors defined as related to cognitive functioning. On the other hand, an early childhood educator might make inferences about the age-appropriateness of certain social behaviors as a result of observing children interact in a kindergarten situation. Furthermore, inferences about a child's emotional maturity and level of affective expression might be drawn from observing behaviors that theoretically are considered attributes of a given emotion. Our approach allows the observer, whatever his or her philosophical stance or professional role, to employ direct observation for the kind of analyses and interventions that he or she feels are most appropriate.

Despite the dogmatism of many developers of observation techniques, it is important to remember that observation systems differ in the extent to which they can be applied or generalized to situations other than those for which they were designed or developed (Kerlinger, 1973). Therefore, it becomes the burden of every observer, having defined his or her purpose, to determine the appropriateness of a particular observation system or series of behavioral categories. To help the reader evaluate a particular system, we will raise a number of issues that should be considered in evaluating observation systems and in deciding which approach to use for sampling behavior.

Knowing and Defining Behaviors

Since most observation systems are designed for particular research purposes, the developers of these systems focus on those behaviors related to the objectives of their particular project. For example:

- A researcher interested in observing a teacher's questioning behavior should consider all the types of questioning behavior that are conceivable in classrooms.
- A teacher interested in observing the "hyperactivity" of a particular child needs some understanding of behaviors that are representative of "hyperactivity."

Thus, observing human behavior requires some knowledge of that behavior (Kerlinger, 1973). It would not be possible for a novice to observe systematically a doctor's operating room behavior without some understanding of the procedures employed. From this knowledge base it becomes possible to list potential categories for observation.

In their overview of various observation systems, Simon and Boyer employed a major distinction between affective and cognitive observational systems. The individual interested in studying the classroom's emotional climate and "how it [the classroom] is conditioned by teacher reactions to pupils' feeling, ideas, work efforts, or actions" (Simon & Boyer, 1967, p. viii) would use an affective system. If, however, the individual were more concerned with studying verbal patterns in the classroom or in children's problem-solving techniques, a cognitive system would be more appropriate. *Mirrors for Behavior: An Anthology of Classroom Observation Instruments* (Simon & Boyer, 1967, 1970, 1974) provides a more detailed characterization of these two generalized category systems, with examples of different classroom observation systems.

Once the observer has defined the problem or question, the observations must be structured so that they can be:

- Communicated in an organized fashion to another individual who was not present
- Generated in a manner similar to another observer viewing the same behaviors at the same time

MUTUALLY EXCLUSIVE AND EXHAUSTIVE CATEGORIES

Mutually Exclusive Categories

In order to eliminate confusion as to which observed behaviors are to be recorded in which categories, and to increase reliability (see Unit VII), it is essential that clear definitions of behavior be indicated so that each category of observable behavior is precisely distinguishable and independent from other categories (is mutually exclusive). "Asking a question" and "making a statement" are mutually exclusive categories, for a person can engage in only one of these behaviors at the same point in time. Other examples of mutually exclusive categories are standing and sitting, driving and swimming.

If the observer has difficulty deciding whether an observed behavior belongs in one category rather than another because of overlapping definitions of those categories, the classifications are not mutually exclusive and need refinement. For example, "Using correct grammar" and "asking a question" are not mutually exclusive categories. In this example, if a pupil asks a question and the question is grammatically correct, the observer would have difficulty categorizing that observation. *

---

*On another count, from the point of view of clear definition, the first of these categories would need to be specified so that observers would know what is meant by "grammatically correct."

Task 9 provides practice in distinguishing examples of mutually exclusive categories.

TASK 9: DISTINGUISHING MUTUALLY EXCLUSIVE CATEGORIES

In the examples given on the Task 9 Worksheet, indicate whether the clusters of categories are mutually exclusive or overlapping. Then check your responses in the Appendix.

Setting Limits

As the observer defines the basic problem or area of interest for observing, it is necessary to set limits on the universe of behaviors to be observed. For example, an individual interested in studying "teaching behavior in the classroom" must delimit a problem area to provide focus, such as studying types of teacher questions, categorizing teacher statements, or counting the number of approvals by teachers to pupil responses. If the observer chose to focus on types of teacher questions, all other behaviors would be ignored and the observer would attend only to questioning behavior — that is, the universe of behavior. Furthermore, if the observer were interested in studying teacher questioning behavior in the classroom, the categories would have to subsume the total range of possible behaviors that constitute teacher questioning behavior. For example, the teacher asks for:

Specific fact
Definition
Opinion
Clarification or elaboration
Application
Evaluation

Making Categories Exhaustive

The categories must be exhaustive in that every instance of observed questioning behavior (or every behavior in the universe being considered) can be classified in one of the available categories. As Kerlinger (1973) has noted, the universe of behaviors that the observer considers can vary in scope depending upon the objectives of the observation process or question being asked. Task 10 provides practice in establishing exhaustive categories.

TASK 9   WORKSHEET

Categories	Mutually Exclusive	Overlapping
1. running lying prone sitting in place standing in place		
2. laughing crying talking		
3. reading looking listening		
4. asking a question giving a command stating an opinion		

TASK 10: ESTABLISHING EXHAUSTIVE CATEGORIES

Develop an exhaustive series of categories for the following defined universe of behavior:

Large-muscle coordination (gross motor skills) as exhibited by four- to six-year-olds during playground activities.

In developing your list of categories, you should consider the following questions:

What is an operational definition of large-muscle coordination?
Is the problem as stated precise enough to avoid considering behaviors other than "large-muscle coordination" as observed on the playground?

List the categories on the Task 10 Worksheet.
As you may have noticed, there is some degree of ambiguity as to what constitutes large-muscle coordination. Therefore, you might have asked for a clearer definition, such as "a child exhibiting behavior on the playground requiring use of the legs, arms, head, and/or body." By excluding manipulation with hands, fingers, and toes, we eliminate fine motor skills from the definition.

TASK 10   WORKSHEET

Categories of Large-Muscle Coordination Playground Activity

1.	6.
2.	7.
3.	8.
4.	9.
5.	10.

As you might see when comparing your list of categories with that of the sample responses given in the Appendix, an independent observer employing your list of categories might observe a behavior that could not be categorized on your list. Therefore, employing an "other" category in the development of your observation schedule allows the list of categories to be refined at a later observation session. For example, in using the list presented as a sample response, how would a child's activity on a teeter-totter be classified? This would need to be classified in the "other" category because there is no other appropriate category. If the "other" list began to have a large number of tallies, it would be necessary to refine the original listing to be more comprehensive.

SPECIFYING CATEGORIES

In devising categories and defining behaviors one also needs to consider the specificity of what one actually observes. It must be determined whether very narrow, easily observed, specific behavior units or broader chunks of behavior are going to be employed. For example, considering displays of affective behavior in the classroom, one could note the number of times a child smiles during an hour or the number of grimaces in a given time period. Instead an observer could more broadly categorize affective behavior in terms of the percentage of time a child spent in interactive play. The broader category "interactive play" encompasses a wide range of discrete behaviors.

When individual observers employ a system of narrowly defined categories, their consistency and agreement in classifying behaviors is likely to be high. By reducing the behaviors to be observed to such detail the observer also greatly reduces the degree of inference introduced into the observation processes, eliminating subjectivity to a greater extent than when broader, more global categories are employed. However, if the behavioral units become too discrete — finger tapping or counts of eyeblinks — the observer may have difficulty making generalizations or "abstracting" from these observations, and the observations can become meaningless data for the teacher though they might not be for an experimental psychologist.

When categories are narrow ⟶ observer agreement is high ⟶ the degree of inference is low ⟶ generalizations are more difficult to make ⟶ subjectivity is low.

On the other hand, if very broad categories are used, more difficulty is encountered in achieving agreement between observers. Using the category "anxious behavior" versus "nonanxious behavior," the lack of specificity allows much leeway for subjective interpretations of the meaning of these categories. Is a twitching foot classified as an example of "anxious behavior?" Broader categories that lack definition or specificity require the observer to make more subjective interpretations of observed behavior before classifying an observation into a given category. Although reliability is decreased by employing broader categories, the observer may be making a more meaningful and useful interpretation of the problem at hand.

When categories are broad ⟶ observer agreement is low ⟶ the degree of inference is high ⟶ generalizations are easier to come by ⟶ subjectivity is high.

The learner of observation skills should aim at a minimum degree of inference: categories that are too vague allow different observers to place different interpretations on the same behavior; categories that are too specific, although they cut down ambiguity and unreliability, are often too rigid and inflexible for easy application.

CATEGORY AND SIGN SYSTEMS

From another perspective, Medley and Mitzel (1963) discuss two approaches to the construction of items for an observation schedule. The first approach, called a "category system" requires the observer to list a set of categories such that every observed behavior can be recorded into one, and only one, of a series of mutually exclusive categories. The categories within this system must also be exhaustive for a particular dimension so that every observed behavior can be categorized. For example, Flanders (1965; 1975) devised a schedule listing 10 types of verbal behavior that might conceivably occur in the classroom. Using Flanders' system, every utterance of the teacher or pupil can be classified.

As another example, we can make our own list of mutually exhaustive categories for a particular situation. If we were to investigate the nature of interactive play at the preschool level, we would list mutually exclusive and exhaustive categories of interaction. On a recording format similar to the Category System Sample Worksheet (Figure 6.1), one could list the categories, using as many columns as necessary for the number of children being observed. The sample given is an observation of interactive play among preschool children.

The observer using such a system records and *categorizes* every behavior that each individual child demonstrates. The record of observations for a given time period shows the total number of units of behavior observed and their frequency classified into each category for each child and over the entire group sampled.

In contrast, a "sign system" involves listing beforehand a limited number of specific kinds of behavior of interest to the observer. During a stated observation time period the record of observations will show which of these behaviors actually occurred and which did not occur. An observer using a sign system approach records only those behaviors that fall into one of the preconceived categories listed. Presumably, many behaviors would not be recorded at all and would be ignored. Therefore a sign system includes mutually exclusive categories, but the categories do not need to be exhaustive.

For example, one might be interested in observing rule-following behaviors using a sign system. The Sign System Sample Worksheet (Figure 6.2) gives an observation of students' ability to follow some selected class rules. In using the sign system in this example, the observer has determined the behaviors that indicate following class rules. Using a similar worksheet, the observer would record instances of the students demonstrating these behaviors. The observer would use as many rows as

Figure 6.1. Category System Sample Worksheet

Interactive Play

Category	Child A	Child B	Child C
Solitary play			
Parallel play			
Interactive play with one child			
Interactive play with more than one child			
Interaction with adult			
Looking around only			

Figure 6.2. Sign System Sample Worksheet

Following Selected Class Rules

Child	Remains in Seat	Raises Hand	Talks in Turn

necessary for the number of children and as many columns as necessary for the number of behaviors.

Note that here there are no "other" or "etc." categories. Behaviors other than those in a given category would be ignored because they are irrelevant to the purpose of the observation.

In summary, the major distinctions between category and sign systems could be characterized as follows:

Category System	*Sign System*
Every observed behavior must be classified (Exclusive *and* exhaustive categories)	Only *specific* predetermined behaviors classified (Exclusive, *but not* exhaustive categories)

DEVELOPING CATEGORIES

A number of steps might be taken to develop categories that are appropriate to the observational task at hand:

1. *Brainstorming.* Think through all possible approaches to your problem. For example, "Is my observational question clear and specific?" "Can it be answered through observation?" "Are the behaviors I've chosen to observe relevant to my question?"

   Brainstorm the problem with your associates. How do they perceive the behaviors you wish to target? Discuss areas of agreement or differences. This discussion can help lead you to the categories you employ in your observational instrument.
2. *Reviewing.* Survey the literature. How have others approached the same or similar problems? Are their definitions of the target areas complete? What procedures have been used, and what were the outcomes? What stumbling blocks were encountered?
3. *Task-analyzing.* Break down the behavior to be observed into its component parts — engage in a "*task analysis*" (see Gagné, 1985). Ask what subbehaviors or events make up the targeted domain of behavior. For example, in order to develop categories of verbal communication among preschoolers, one would generate a list of the kinds of verbal behaviors that are possible and would exclude nonverbal behaviors:

   Asking for assistance
   Seeking information (asking a question)

Commanding
Mimicking
Making statements of fact, hope, and so forth

4. *Previewing.* Go into a situation that is representative of the setting in which you will need to observe and generate a running record or describe carefully those behaviors of interest. Consider whether or not the observation was typical, representative, and adequate. From these observations, hone into your question and abstract the important behaviors or events (see also Martin, 1976).

One could pursue any or all of these activities depending on the difficulty of the categorizing task, previous experience, and one's patience!

Making Reliable Observations: Avoiding Observational Bias

OBTAINING RELIABLE OBSERVATIONS

To help both teachers and behavioral scientists working in education to draw the conclusions necessary for making daily decisions and solving problems, there must be agreement on the observational bases for these conclusions or inferences. Precise, unambiguous specifications of what behavioral activities are to be focused upon are prerequisite to structuring or organizing behavioral observations. Such precision in defining an observed behavior increases the extent to which various observers report similarly about the behavior on which they have focused.

Given: Definition of purpose of the observation
A specific point in time
Aim: What you see = What I see

Observer Reliability

The greater the agreement between two independent observers, the greater the consistency or "reliability" of both viewers. For example, if teacher A and teacher B are both observing Jimmy, a seven-year-old second grader, during reading group, their observations are likely to differ if they do not share a clear definition of what behaviors they should focus on. They are not likely to draw a consistent conclusion about Jimmy's attention to reading materials if they have not focused on the same attentive behaviors at the same point in time.

Furthermore, precise definitions force individual observers to be consistent with themselves. The more precise the definition, the less the opportunity for subjectivity to be introduced into the observation process.* For example, if teacher A wants to count the number of times preschoolers in a defined setting display "dependency" behavior, the teacher will have difficulty consistently labeling specific behaviors as "dependent" unless he or she has made a careful listing of "dependent" behaviors before observing. Generally, the more specific and complete these criteria for labeling behaviors, the more consistent the observer will be in pinpointing behaviors over time (see Figure 7.1).

Many readers of the educational and behavioral science literature will discover reports on the inter-rater reliability for a particular observation instrument. These statements of agreement among observers in recording observations are generally indicated in the form of reliability coefficients, which range from the point of no agreement (0) to perfect observer agreement (+ 1.0). Generally one tends to find reliability coefficients reported in the range of + .70 to + .95. As the coefficient approaches + 1.0, the reliability increases, and we have more confidence in reliable observations among observers.

Observer Agreement

The rate of agreement between two or more observers working at the same time may be determined as shown in Figure 7.2. Observers should aim for rates of agreement of .80 or better. Note that we have no check here as to whether the same behavior instances were observed, but only the rate of agreement between observers. If, however, we employed a time-sampling system (see Unit VIII), by which each observer records only one behavior during each observational interval (that is, every five seconds), we could also determine whether or not the same behaviors were being observed.

Figure 7.1.   Observer Reliability

Precise definitions of those specific behaviors to be focused upon
and
Use of a systematic recording system

One observer consistent over time in his own observations   =   *Intra*-Observer Reliability

One observer agreeing with other observers of the situation   =   *Inter*-Observer Reliability

---

*More detailed discussions on the various types of reliability may be found in Foster and Cone, 1986; Hartmann, 1982; Hollenbeck, 1978; and Kent and Foster, 1977.

Figure 7.2.   Determining Rate of Agreement Between Observers

Steps	Example: Teacher questioning patterns in a seventh-grade social studies class		
1. Count the number of instances in each category for observers A and B.	Category	Observer A	Observer B
	Teacher asks for:		
	Specific fact	𝟕𝑯𝑳 //	𝟕𝑯𝑳
	Opinion	////	///
	Application	/	//
2. Total the number of observations for A and B.	Total	12 +	10=22
3. Count the number of agreements in each category and over categories for both observers.	Agreements:		
	Specific fact		5
	Opinion		3
	Application		1
	Total		9
4. Divide the number of agreements by the total number of observations.		$\frac{9}{22}$	= .409
5. Multiply the quotient by the number of observers—in this example there are two.		2 x .409	= .82
	Rate of Agreement		= .82

Once an observer has determined his or her rate of agreement with another observer, the decision may be made to follow the same procedures without the second observer being present. It is, therefore, periodically useful for observers to spot-check their rates of agreement in order to assure accuracy.

Another procedure for assessing observer agreement is in fact to consider instances where *behavior does not occur* (Hartmann, 1982; Vasta, 1979). In the same situation, two observers can:

• Agree that a behavior occurred
• Disagree, in that observer 1 indicates a behavior occurred, while observer 2 does not
• Disagree, in that observer 2 indicates a behavior occurred, while observer 1 does not
• Agree that a behavior did *not* occur

Thus, one can evaluate the rate of agreement for occurring and nonoccurring behavior or events. Baker and Tyne (1980) have suggested that the use of the formula for observer agreement described in Figure 7.2 can overestimate agreement when behaviors or events occur with high frequency. In contrast, observation of infrequent behaviors or events can result in lower reliabilities. In such cases, one might also consider intervals when only one observer notes the behavior or when both agree that behaviors did not occur.

Stability of Observations

Observer agreement, although essential, is insufficient to assess the reliability of one's observational system. Repeated visits need to be made to a setting in order to establish the stability of observations. For example, if one were concerned about a group of students completing their math assignments, it would be necessary to observe these students over time to determine if a consistent pattern of behavior were exhibited. If "aggressive" behavior was exhibited by two pupils, the teacher might question if this were a chance occurrence. The teacher would need to observe the pupils over time. By correlating the observational outcomes for two or more occasions, a *stability coefficient* can be obtained (see Foster & Cone, 1986; Kent & Foster, 1977; and Rowley, 1976, 1978; for detailed descriptions of calculating stability measures).

In establishing the stability of observations, one raises the practical question of "how many observations are required in order to have confidence in the findings?" Clearly, there is no one correct answer for this question — the number of observations needed and the schedule for observing is tied to the observer's purpose.

Consider these different observation questions and the frequency of observations required in order to produce stable, reliable observation outcomes.

1. How do the spatial concepts "top" and "bottom" develop in preschool three- and four-year-old children?

   • Repeat observations of the same children over time; for example, once per month for a year.
   • Alternatively, observe a number of subjects at different age levels performing the same tasks.

2. What pattern of peer interactions does Jesse display?

   • Observe Jesse a minimum of three times in situations where peer interaction is possible.

3. Does a behavioral intervention improve Mary's on-task behavior in mathematics?

- Observe Mary during mathematics for five minutes each day for one week prior to the intervention (baseline).
- Next, observe Mary for five minutes each day in mathematics during the intervention.
- After an appropriate time period, try removing the intervention and record Mary's behavior daily.
- Return to the intervention, if necessary, to maintain improved behavior and continue to collect observational data daily.

When conducting psychoeducational research using observational techniques, one will often demand a greater number of observations in order to draw conclusions than when arriving at daily decisions in the classroom. In the research context, one will also more likely observe in a range of different situations, classrooms, or schools, before confidently generalizing about the effects of an intervention, the impact of a teaching strategy, or the value of a curricular innovation.

Rowley (1978) has reviewed some interesting work by John Herbert and associates at the Ontario Institute for Studies in Education that helps set guidelines for collecting observational data. Each of 30 teachers was observed for 50 minutes on six to seven occasions, using the "System for Analyzing Lessons." Rowley focused on how the reliability of observational data is affected by (1) the number of observation periods, (2) the length of the observation period, and (3) the combination of varying the number and length of observation periods. Three major conclusions were drawn:

1. Reliability increased with more frequent observation periods.
2. Although reliability increased with the length of the observation period, the greatest increment occurred when the observation period was increased from 10 to 20 minutes. After 20 minutes, the reliability leveled off.
3. The optimal combination of number and length of observation periods was five periods of 30 minutes each ($r = .705$).

However, the implications of this work for the classroom observer with limited time and resources are to make three observations of 30 minutes duration or to arrange four observational periods of 20 minutes duration.

The length of these observational periods could be accommodated by typical class schedules.

CHALLENGES TO RELIABLE OBSERVATIONS

Unfortunately, gathering reliable observational data is not an automatic, common-sense, "anyone can do it" activity. There are many sources of error that can creep into the process, distorting the validity of the conclusions based on the data. An extensive literature documents different sources of error or bias (e.g., Baker & Tyne, 1980; Fassnacht, 1982; Kazdin, 1982; Kent & Foster, 1977; Taplin & Reid, 1973). Error can derive from the *observer*, the *observee*, and the *observation instrument*. Each of these potential sources of bias will be highlighted, and possible solutions to the problems suggested.

Observer Bias

Perhaps the most significant sources of error are observers themselves.

Personal bias or expectation. Let's consider an example involving Janie, a pleasant and cooperative six-year-old. She hands in her homework on time, and the teacher likes her and expects her to do well. A new girl joins the class and is being teased by some of the other girls. The teacher, wanting to get at the source of the problem, observes and records "teasing" behavior in the classroom. Although Janie makes faces at the newcomer, the teacher overlooks this behavior. Bias has occurred due to the teacher's beliefs and expectations about Janie. When such bias is positive, placing the observee in a favorable light, it is called a "halo effect"; when the bias is negative, it might be called "prejudice." Thus, prior experiences between the observer and observee can influence the outcomes of observation (Kazdin, 1982).

Systematic training can help the observer increase objectivity by facilitating awareness of one's personal biases. Since each of us has different tolerance levels or thresholds for different situations, we need to be attuned to our attitudes about such distracting behaviors as an individual's "good" manners, quick response styles, or repetitive question-asking. A "violent outburst" of anger to one observer might be seen as "within normal limits" by another (Good & Brophy, 1984).

Potential biases associated with an observer's sex, race, age, and cultural or ethnic identity must all be addressed in the particular observational setting. Finally, the theoretical perspective of the viewer (Freudian, Piagetian, Rogerian, or whatever) can certainly affect or color what one sees and how it is perceived.

One needs to have an accurate perception of potential sources of personal bias.

Knowledge of hypotheses.   In pursuing observational research, it has been widely demonstrated that observers who know the purpose of the study or the hypotheses being tested will more likely record observations that tend to support the hypotheses. Therefore, to correct such potential biases, most research designs include observers who are "blind" as to the purposes of the study.

In classroom life, however, such controls are not always feasible. However, a colleague of the observer (another teacher, school psychologist, or other school professional) might observe in a targeted classroom, unaware of the specific problem or the particular child who is experiencing a problem (Baker & Tyne, 1980).

Observer drift.   Observers often use instruments or procedures that require extensive pretraining to achieve observer agreement. Once in the field, after having employed the instrument for a length of time, the observer will frequently begin to "drift" when recording observations, becoming less precise and less accurate. Drift of another type might also occur: Observers who always work together will tend to agree ("consensual drift"); their observations will become more alike over time (Hartmann, 1982). When possible, the use of regular unannounced reliability spot-checks to monitor an observer's accuracy is warranted. This might be accomplished by having two observers in the setting during a selected sample of sessions. When a large number of observations are gathered, approximately 10 to 20 percent of the total should be checked; with a small number of observations, a minimum of two checks should be made.

Inadequate training.   The most inexcusable source of behavior error is poor training. Many observation systems need to be practiced extensively before being used in a classroom setting. Adequate time needs to be planned for practicing, feedback, and guided discussion. The practice might take many forms, such as use of videotapes or team observing. A criterion level of 90 percent agreement with an expert observer's ratings should be achieved prior to employing an observation instrument. Observers need to know and practice the rules and procedures of any observational system they use. See Boice (1983) for detailed suggestions on improving observational skills.

Observee Bias

Changes in the observee.   The teacher observing in his or her own classroom is known to the pupils and is expected to be observing them. Consequently, students are not as likely to alter their behavior in the teacher's presence. (Certainly, if a forbidden activity is being pursued and the teacher approaches the scene, children will change their behavior quickly!)

Individuals also modify some of their behavior when an outside observer enters the setting and when they know they are being observed. This change in behavior is generally referred to as "reactivity."

Knowledge of being observed. If individuals know they are being observed, and particularly if they know why, they might behave in ways to please the observer, such as remaining in their seats, raising their hands more often, or asking more questions. Other individuals become more nervous and display signs of anxiety not normally shown.

Ethics, of course, dictate that individuals who do not belong in a particular setting must receive permission (from observees or their parents) to observe in classrooms, testing rooms, or other settings. It is not easy to hide the fact of being observed from even the youngest child.

Despite these obstacles, steps might be taken to reduce observee reactivity:

1. The observer can visit the classroom or other setting several times, so that students become accustomed to his or her presence. Usually one or two visits is sufficient for younger children. Older children might need more visits to become acclimated; early observations may need to be discarded.
2. Participant observers such as other teachers, paraprofessionals, and older students might be employed and be less obtrusive than strangers (Baker & Tyne, 1980).
3. Observation rooms with one-way mirrors might alleviate reactivity more quickly, but one cannot observe classroom settings this way. Also, if observees turn their backs to a one-way mirror, many behaviors are not seen.

Intrusiveness of equipment. The use of video recordings or tape recordings (see Unit X for more detailed discussion), although solving some of the problems that arise from an observer's presence, can be intrusive. The equipment must be introduced to the setting, not unlike introducing a human observer.

When we videotaped preschool classrooms, for example, we set up the equipment a day ahead of time and used the opportunity for trial runs. The children soon adapted to the cameras, cables, and equipment operators. The activities of the day quickly became more interesting than the video intruders. The one significant distractor was a microphone that reminded some children of a gun; a quick modification was made.

The Observation System as a Source of Errors

Two issues need to be considered to minimize possible errors due to the observation system: the match of the system and the complexity of the system.

Match of the system.   When observers in classrooms select from available observation instruments, they need to consider if an instrument effectively matches their observational purposes. Are the behaviors targeted by the selected instrument appropriate to address the questions raised by the observer? The issue is paramount as well when observers develop their own instrument. This match refers to the validity of the observational measure, a topic discussed in Unit VIII.

Complexity of the observational procedures.   The more complex an observational system, the greater the opportunity for error. Those systems that require many decisions on the part of the observer, involve complex categories, or demand memorization of many codes, are more vulnerable to error. The use of clear, precise observational questions and simple, nonoverlapping coding categories reduces the possibility of such error.

Our discussion of the sources of observational error has highlighted some of the threats to reliable observational data. Accounting for reliability is essential if one is to have confidence in observational techniques. A brief checklist, presented in Figure 7.3, summarizes the critical issues discussed in this unit.

Figure 7.3. Summary Checklist for Making Reliable Observations

Issue	Considerations
1. Objectivity	Specific behaviors listed beforehand
	Eliminating bias due to personal belief or expectation
	Not knowing the hypotheses
2. Clear, usable recording format	Nonoverlapping categories
	Avoiding complex coding systems
3. Inter-observer agreement	Aiming for 90% or better
	Adequate training
4. Avoiding observer drift	Systematic spot-checks
	Two observers present 10–20% of time

Sampling and Recording Behavior

WHAT'S TO BE OBSERVED

Once an observer has selected appropriate categories of behavior on which to focus (Unit VI) and in order to maximize reliable observing (Unit VII), it is necessary to devise a plan for systematically sampling observations in the setting. The approach is the same as that of the microbiologist who wants to determine the purity of water in a lake for drinking purposes but who, for obvious reasons, cannot test the whole lake. She draws test samples from many parts of the lake so that her total sample will be representative of the lake as a whole. Moreover, she draws samples at different times, so that they will be representative over an extended period of time. In the same manner, it is unfair to judge the effectiveness of a comprehensive in-service training program on the basis of an observation of only one teacher at one point of time during the year.

One issue facing the observer confronting the myriad of behaviors that occur over time is the procedure for selecting specific behaviors for observation. For example, the observer may opt to record all behaviors during the school day of a given child (generally referred to as a diary description or running record). However, while observing this one child, the behaviors of the other children, perhaps engaged in similar activities, will be missed. Therefore, it is vital for the observer to decide ahead of time the sampling procedure to be employed. Two useful sampling procedures, time sampling and event sampling, have been detailed by Herbert Wright (1960) and are described in the next two sections.

Time Sampling

According to Wright the observer using a time-sampling procedure attends to the occurrence or nonoccurrence of selected behavior(s) within specified, uniform time limits. "The length, spacing and number of intervals are intended to secure representative time samples of the target phenomena. As a rule . . . descriptive categories are coded in advance for quick and precise judgements in the field and later efficient scoring" (1960, p. 93). Thus, the length, spacing, and number of time units are determined by the purpose of the observer.

An example of this would be the observer interested in the ability of second-grade students to remain on a specified learning task. He could check each of 25 students for 10 seconds every five minutes, throughout a given part of the science period, to see whether each was "off task" or not. A descriptive list of behaviors to be considered "off task" would have been made prior to the observation, and it would include such particulars as "looking around the room," "being out of the seat," and "engaged in unrelated activities." For another observer question, the appropriate sample interval might be every minute, or every 10 minutes, or every day of a week, or during other subject time periods.

One suitable worksheet format is given in Figure 8.1, Procedure A. Here, each child's off-task behavior would be recorded at each sample interval, using as many lines as necessary for the number of children being observed. Again note that a listing of off-task behaviors would have to be determined ahead of time.

It is important to use a simple form of coding or abbreviating that facilitates recording of the observed behaviors. Typically, in time sampling, behaviors are recorded within predetermined categories in the form of checkmarks or tallies. These marks or tallies yield information about *whether* a particular kind of behavior occurred (one checkmark) or *how often* it occurred (tally marks) during an observation period.

In Procedure A, where only one category is involved, no coding is required; a checkmark for any 10-second interval records an occurrence of off-task behavior. Using longer time intervals for each child, the observer might use tallies to record several discrete occurrences of a behavior in each interval.

Another observer, however, concerned with subcategories of off-task behavior, would develop a coding system for the specific behaviors. This is shown in Figure 8.1, Procedure B. In this example, the observer has determined this code:

L = Looking around (seated)
O = Out of seat
U = Unrelated activity (seated)

Off-task behavior would be indicated by a checkmark in the L, O, or U column; no mark would indicate on-task behavior. The observer would

Figure 8.1. Time Sampling

Procedure A
"Off Task" Behavior*

Child	Time Unit							Total
	10:00	10:05	10:10	10:15	10:20	10:25	10:30	

* Within each time unit observe each child for 10 seconds, record for 10 seconds, move on to the next child, and so forth.

Procedure B
"Off Task" Behavior (Pre-coded)

Child	10:00			10:05			10:10			10:15			10:20			10:25			10:30			Total		
	L	O	U	L	O	U	L	O	U	L	O	U	L	O	U	L	O	U	L	O	U	L	O	U

use as many lines as necessary for the number of children being observed.

It should be noted that exactly the same information recorded on the Procedure B worksheet could have been recorded on the uncoded Procedure A worksheet. Instead of simply making a checkmark for a given 10-second unit, the observer using Procedure A could write an L, O, or U, depending on which category of off-task behavior was observed. However, an advantage of having the categories precoded on the recording form is that it is much easier to make checkmarks under coded columns than to memorize and record the code. Another advantage is that when sampling is completed, the results are already tabulated.

The coding system (the categories and their codes) must always, of course, be memorized before sampling begins; moreover, the observer should always have an outline of the coding system at hand in case of memory lapses. Obviously a system can be most easily and reliably memorized if the codes are abbreviations or other symbols designed to remind the observer of the categories themselves. (As codes for the off-task behaviors categorized above, the letter abbreviations L, O, and U are easier to remember than the numbers 1, 2, and 3 would be.) And when such codes are present as tabulators on the record form, they constantly reinforce the observer's memory of the coding system.

Such helps are extremely valuable in time sampling. Remember that the observer must proceed from one preset time interval to the next, ready or not. The difficulty of using a memorized coding system is of course greatest when the time units are very small (the Flanders system requires the observer to record a code number every three seconds) and the number of categories relatively large. The procedure can be taxing, and its efficient use requires considerable practice.

The more detailed the coding system used, the fewer the number of individuals that can be observed in a given time interval. Thus, before observing, a balance needs to be arrived at between:

The most appropriate time unit
The number of individuals to be observed
The detail desired from the observation

Going back to the example of on-task behavior in a science class cited earlier, the observer could decide to observe only a sample of the 25 pupils present and obtain even more detailed observational data on each child.

Generally, time sampling is useful for observing behaviors that occur frequently and at a somewhat regular rate.

Event Sampling

Event sampling simply allows the observer to record a given event or category of events each time it naturally occurs. When the event occurs, the observer describes it and, if desired, describes the antecedents to that event. The range of events one might choose to record is practically limitless and, again depending upon one's purpose, might range from pupils' use of abusive language to demonstrations of independent study skills. The major advantage of event sampling is that it allows one to observe events as they naturally occur and in context. For example, a preschool or special education teacher might be interested in pupils' self-help skills, determining ahead of time to observe such skills as:

Going to the bathroom unassisted
Washing hands
Buttoning clothing
Putting on boots
Tying shoelaces

The teacher may observe and record for each child the date on which that child acquired these skills, or when these events occurred. A recording format such as the one presented in Figure 8.2 might be employed for these observations. The observer would use as many columns as necessary for the behaviors being observed, as many lines as necessary for the number of children, and would record the date on which the child demonstrates the skill.

Figure 8.2. Event Sampling Procedure

Self-Help Skills

Child	Bathroom Unassisted	Washes Hands	Buttons Clothes	Puts on Boots	Ties Shoelaces

While maintaining a record such as this, the teacher can determine the frequency of the behavior for a specific child or group of children. (In a special education class, the categories might need to be broken down into finer units.)

An important outcome of time and event sampling is that two observers can simultaneously view and record the same events, permitting later determination of the extent of observer agreement or consistency in sampling and recording observations.

Time versus Event Sampling

In summary, time and event sampling each have distinct advantages and limitations, which are presented in Figure 8.3.

Many systems combine both time and event sampling. For example, the frequency and nature of events such as teacher praise are of interest to many educators. The Teacher Approval/Disapproval Classroom Record (TAD) (White et al., 1973a) views the rate of teacher verbal approvals and disapprovals during daily instruction. Taking into account when a class period starts and finishes, the observer notes the time at which each approving or disapproving teacher behavior occurs. The specific pupil behavior and teacher response are recorded along with pupil characteristics (Figure 8.4).

This system is interesting in that a recording interval of 20 seconds is employed whenever an approval or disapproval occurs. The total

Figure 8.3. Time versus Event Sampling

Advantages	Limitations
TIME SAMPLING	
• Good agreement among observers. • Good reliability over time. • Good control over the mechanics of the system.	• The frequency with which the events of interest occur may not be represented accurately—e.g., events that occur frequently within a time unit may be underrepresented in total calculations if a ± system per time unit is used.
• Provides a good overview of the range of behaviors and events occurring in a particular setting.	• Infrequent events may not be represented accurately. • The duration of events is not assessed.
EVENT SAMPLING	
• Helpful in describing events of a particular kind that have been detailed before the observation takes place. • Every natural occurrence of the targeted behavior is sampled.	• Breaks up the natural continuity of behavior. • May not provide information as to what sets off a particular event.

Figure 8.4. Sample TAD Recording

Time Start	Activity	Time	Teacher Response	Pupil Behavior
9:17 A.M.	Reading group, 5 boys	1 hr. 45 min.	1. A ⓓ You're not telling me what it means	Incorrect answer to question
			2. Ⓐ D Right	Correct answer to question
End of class period 11:02 A.M.				

amount of recording time (the number of such intervals multiplied by 20 seconds) is subtracted from the total observation time, allowing the rate of actual observation to be calculated. (However, as with other systems, another approval or disapproval could occur during the recording time and not be included.) The results of 16 studies (in K–12) employing TAD (White, 1975) have shown that:

1. Teacher approval is highest in grades 1 and 2, after which it declines sharply, to 4 to 8 approvals during a class period.
2. Teacher disapproval also declines after the primary grades.
3. Teacher approvals occur more frequently than disapprovals in grades 1 and 2, but thereafter disapprovals occur more frequently than approvals.
4. Teacher approval rate is higher for ongoing instruction than for classroom management.
5. Teachers emit more approvals to pupils learning at a faster rate than to those working at a slower rate.

Thus, the usefulness of this time and event measure has been well documented.

In addition to time and event sampling, procedures are available to help observers evaluate behavior in ongoing situations. These include interval recording and accounting for duration.

Interval Recording and Accounting for Duration

Interval recording is another sampling procedure that is related to time and event sampling. Interval recording involves dividing the observation period into time intervals. Thus, a 30-minute class period might be divided into 10 intervals of three minutes each. Depending on the observation purpose and system, the observer using interval recording can detail:

- The occurrence or nonoccurrence of behaviors
- The frequency of target behaviors within each interval
- The duration of behavior within an interval
- The portion (beginning, middle, end) of the interval in which the behavior occurred.

Recording duration allows observers to report not only the frequency of behaviors but also the persistence of behavior over time. Thus, a teacher could observe exactly how long a child persisted with an activity or how much time a child was off task during an instructional period. (For more details see Alessi & Kaye, 1983, and Foster & Cone, 1986.)

Other Aspects of Sampling

Number of behavior categories used.   The number of behaviors an observer can take account of at one point in time is limited. According to Medley and Mitzel (1963, p. 330), "The number of categories into which the behaviors are to be coded should not be too large; few studies have used more than ten. It seems desirable to define the categories so that their average frequencies are roughly equal, but experience has shown that in some instances categories used less than 5% of the time function effectively." Use of more than 10 or 12 categories, however, makes serious demands on memory and requires extensive training.

Representativeness of the behavior sample.   In order to determine the representativeness of most behaviors, it is necessary to observe the occurrence of a given behavior at different times of the day and on different occasions. If a behavior happens only once or on rare occasions, it is not representative of overall behavior. Therefore, before making conclusions, it is important to assess the *frequency* of the behaviors.

Anecdotal records are a case in point. Records are often made of unusual behaviors ("He stole the money that was on my desk") or of only one form of behavior (more likely to be negative than positive): Unfortunately such information frequently follows an individual, even if it is not representative of that individual's overall functioning. In the final analysis, anecdotal information cannot be given much weight unless a record of the frequency of the behavior in question has been kept, as well as its frequency relative to other behaviors for that individual and a broader sample of individuals. Within the classroom, then, we may decide to observe a number of times during different periods of the day, as well as on different days of the week, and within the different behavioral settings available — classroom, gym, playground, and so on. Task 11 will test your ability to take a representative sample.

TASK 11: DETERMINING REPRESENTATIVE OBSERVATIONAL SAMPLES

Indicate which of the samples given on the Task 11 Worksheet are likely to yield representative observations. Check your responses with the sample responses given in the Appendix.

Who is sampled?   In addition to systematic sampling of behaviors, it is frequently necessary to sample pupils. For example, if our purpose were to determine whether or not kindergarten pupils in a particular school system encountered difficulty with letter recognition, we would not need to observe every child. Rather, we might want to select for study a random, unbiased sample of 10 pupils (for example, every third pupil according to last name in alphabetical order, or we could write the children's names on slips of paper, place them in a hat, and draw out our random sample of 10 pupils) from each of the kindergarten classrooms in the school system. On the other hand, for diagnostic purposes, an individual teacher may wish to observe every pupil's skills.

Another observer, interested in observing first-grade pupils' spontaneous use of relational terms such as "more" and "less" may, in a representative first-grade classroom, observe five pupils for 10 minutes, and so on until all pupils have been observed. This cycle may be repeated several times.

A useful sampling system reported by Kowatrakul (1959), which is referred to as point-time sampling, allows the observer to view a pupil long enough to record one of a given series of behaviors, then move on to the next pupil until a given behavior occurs, and so on. Kowatrakul has used this technique to study the relation between pupil behavior and classroom activities in various subject areas.

RECORDING OBSERVATIONAL DATA

An essential component of the observation process is the immediate recording of the behaviors observed. As noted in our discussion of time and event sampling, the observer cannot depend on memory; rather, the

TASK 11 WORKSHEET

Determining Representative Samples

Problem or Question	Behavior Sample	Representative?		Reasons for Your Response
		Yes	No	
Study of first-grade children's "on task" behavior in school.	Observe the behavior of children sitting in a front-row seat of each row in a particular class.			
Count of out-of-seat behaviors of an "acting-out" kindergartner.	Observe the child on five successive days from 10:00 a.m. to 10:15 a.m.			
Study the extent to which four-year-old children interact in same-sex, opposite-sex, or mixed-sex groupings on the playground.	Randomly choose four boys and four girls. Observe each child's behavior on a systematic rotation basis for five minutes, indicating the amount of time each child interacts in designated categories. Sampling should be done on different days and at different times.			

observer must use a recording sheet, if reliable data are to be collected. This recording sheet needs to be designed so that the information can be easily summarized. Although a broad variety of recording sheets can be found in the literature, the Flanders Interaction Analysis Categories (Simon & Boyer, 1969), a category system for collecting teacher–pupil interactions, involve the use of simple recording procedures.

The Flanders system has been one of the most widely used observation schemes and is commonly taught to teachers, student teachers, supervisors, and counselors who want to view and understand their typical patterns of verbal exchange with students in the classroom. Flanders offers 10 categories* for classifying verbal behaviors, which are shown in Figure 8.5. Flanders simply numbers the 10 categories sequentially from 1 to 10. By memorizing the code, the observer need only write down a single number to represent a type of verbal activity. The observer can write a stream of numbers that represent what is occurring in the classroom. As Simon and Boyer have noted, the observer "will have no record of what has been said but he will have a record which allows him to infer the classroom climate and describe the teaching style" (1969, p. 116). In recording observations, the observer makes a notation for every change in category and also records one category number at least every three seconds whether there is a category change or not.

Figure 8.5.   Flanders' Categories for Classifying Behavior

Category Number		Description
	1	Accepts pupils' feelings
	2	Praises or encourages pupils
Teacher	3	Accepts pupils' ideas
Talk	4	Asks questions
	5	Lectures
	6	Gives directions
	7	Criticizes or justifies authority
Student	8	Student talk—narrow response
Talk	9	Student talk—broad response
	10	Silence or noise (Simon & Boyer, 1969, pp. 118-19)

Source: A. Simon and E. G. Boyer, (Eds.). *Mirrors for behavior: An anthology of classroom observation instruments.* Philadelphia: Research for Better Schools, 1967, 1970.

---

*Flanders (1970) also discusses a "22 category system," which is a more extensive subdivision of the basic 10 categories.

A data sheet for one minute of consecutive observation and sequential coding of teacher–pupil verbal behaviors using the Flanders system would look like the sample record shown in Figure 8.6. By reading down the columns of numbers collected by the observer, one gets a picture of the sequence of verbal behaviors that occurred during the one-minute time period. After collecting these "raw" observational data over a more representative time sample than one minute, the observer can transcribe the data to a summary grid that provides a "picture" of the frequency of various kinds of teacher and pupil verbal activity occurring in the classroom setting.*

The observer can easily compute the percentage of time during the observation period that a particular kind of verbal behavior occurred. Also, by summarizing the observational data, the pattern or strategies used by a teacher in the classroom can be revealed. Questions such as the following can be answered with the Flanders system:

How often do pupils talk in the classroom?
How much do pupils talk in comparison with their teacher?
Do pupils talk to each other or only to the teacher?
How does the teacher reinforce different kinds of student verbal behavior?
What strategies does the teacher employ to involve students in classroom discussion? (Simon & Boyer, 1969, p. 120)

Figure 8.6. Verbal Behaviors Data Sheet

Setting:	Mrs. Jones Third-grade class			Date: June 3	
Activity:	Social Studies Discussion			Time: 10:50 to 10:51 a.m.	
	(1) 4	(5) 5	(9) 7	(13) 5	(17) 7
	(2) 9	(6) 6	(10) 7	(14) 9	(18) 7
	(3) 9	(7) 9	(11) 6	(15) 9	(19) 4
	(4) 4	(8) 7	(12) 5	(16) 9	(20) 4

(Digits following numbers in parentheses indicate code.)

---

*It is generally recommended that a 20-minute observation (400 tallies) be used as a reasonable minimum for generating a picture of the verbal activity in a classroom. Simon and Boyer (1969) offer an excellent detailed description of the procedures for transcribing Flanders categories to a summary matrix.

By using the Flanders approach with these questions, the observer can begin to draw conclusions about classroom climate and make inferences about the communication strategies fostered in the classroom. Extensive information can be generated from a simple, sequential recording of category numbers on the page. The Flanders approach has been the forerunner of a wide range of observational techniques for the study of teaching and learning processes in educational settings (Evertson & Green, 1986). We have presented the Flanders system because of its simplicity and usefulness.

OTHER RECORDING FORMATS

In this section, two other sample recording formats are given. Both formats can be easily adapted by the teacher-observer to suit his or her own particular observation goal, as in the filled-out example on language use during free play (see Figure 8.8).

With Sample Worksheet A (Figure 8.7), the observer can:

Figure 8.7.   Sample Worksheet A

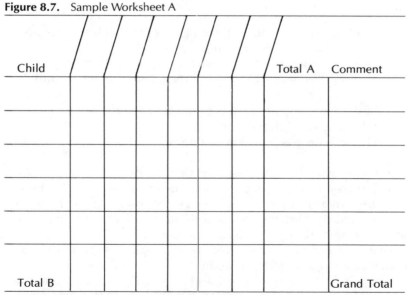

Total A is total of all observed behaviors demonstrated by a particular child.
Total B is total for each unit of behavior observed for all of the children combined.
Grand Total is total of all observed behaviors.

Figure 8.8.   Language Usage During Free Play

Child	Uses Complete Sentences	Asks Questions for Information	Uses Relational Concepts		Total A	Comment
Jack Brown	IIII	ЖI	0			
Maryanne Jones	0	III	II			
Total B					Grand Total	

Detail the units or categories of behavior that constitute a particular area of concern (columns)

List those children to be observed (rows)

Tally the frequency of observed behaviors for each child (total
across each row)

Tally the frequency of each behavior for all of the children observed
(total across each column)

Total all observed behaviors (total rows × total columns)

In using this worksheet, the observer would list the categories of behavior to be observed in the diagonal columns across the top of the form.

The format given on Sample Worksheet A can be used with both
category and sign systems, and is easily adaptable to recording observations over time. If one were to use different colored pencils in tallying
behaviors at different times, one could quickly "eyeball" differences
among children and by the same child at different times.

By using the format of Worksheet A, we have recorded some observations about the language used by two students during free play (see
Figure 8.8). Verbally transcribing the observations, we learn that during the observation period Maryanne never used complete sentences but

used relational terms; Jack used complete sentences, but did not use relational terms. We also learn that both Maryanne and Jack asked questions, but that Jack asked more questions.

Sample Worksheet B (Figure 8.9) provides a format an observer could use to note the variety of behaviors engaged in by one child or by a group of children throughout the course of a school day. The specific behaviors or particular activities that are to be observed would be listed in the diagonal columns at the center of the worksheet. This section could, of course, be extended to include as many activities or behaviors as the observer wanted to note. The "Observation Begins" and "Observation Ends" columns enable the observer to continue using one worksheet while major shifts in classroom activity occur.

As an example of how to use Sample Worksheet B, consider the steps a teacher would take when observing patterns of cooperative behavior in a classroom:

Define the variety of behaviors that indicate cooperation.
List these categories of behavior (or activities) in the diagonal columns across the top of the worksheet.

Figure 8.9.   Sample Worksheet B

When beginning to observe, indicate the time.

Note the activity period in progress.

Tally the occurrence of each category of activity that occurs in the
appropriate column.

Note the time each observation period ends.

The observer would repeat the entire process using a sufficient number
of observation periods to adequately answer the question posed. In
using this worksheet, the observer would list the behaviors or activities
to be observed in the diagonal columns across the top of the form.

Worksheet A and Worksheet B provide a sample of the types of
simple instruments that can be devised for recording and organizing
observational information. Planning systematic recording procedures
ahead of time both facilitates observation and allows later review and
analysis. Remember, however, that although graphic representation can
be helpful in certain situations, the observer may also want to form
profiles or determine percentages and ratios that reflect the relative
frequency of particular kinds of behavior.

We have not attempted here to list all forms of recording systems
useful in educational settings. As you begin to grapple with a variety of
observation questions, you will create personal variations.

MAKING VALID OBSERVATIONS

Observational efforts will be in vain if what is observed and recorded does not correspond to real events. The validity of observations depends on how representative the record is of what actually occurred.
Systematic categories of behaviors and clear definitions of the behaviors
facilitate the objective classification of units of behavior and increase
the observer's consistency or reliability. We might, however, still have an
observation record that does not adequately reflect the real world, as
evidenced in cases of biased observations. We focus on this important
issue by regularly asking:

- What am I trying to sample from the stream of all behavior?
- Why am I interested in the particular information provided by
  the observation procedures I choose?
- Am I reporting what I see objectively?
- Have unintentional sources of bias been introduced?

Once again the particular problem or question raised and the observer's knowledge of that area will affect answers to these questions,

and particularly influence the format of the observations made. The validity of our observational measurements of behavior depends at least on these two conditions:

- A representative sample of the behaviors to be measured must be observed.
- A complete, accurate record of the observed behaviors must be made.

In recording and synthesizing observations, while taking into account those procedures that facilitate reliable and valid observations, the major problem that confronts the observer is the observer himself or herself. Drawing conclusions and solving problems demand that observers make inferences after digesting the information gathered during the observation process. Observers relate observations to the variables studied (for example, aggression, anxiety, motivation, and so forth), bringing behavior and construct together by inference. For example, an observer sees a child hitting another child and comes to the conclusion (inference) that the behavior is an example of hostility or aggression. The basic weakness of this process is that incorrect inferences can be made from observations. For example, two or more independent observers will note that in certain neighborhoods, white families move out as black families move in, and arrive at the inference that property values have gone down. The observation that white families are moving out and black families are moving in may be reliable and valid. However, an analysis of property values may show that in fact they have not decreased. Therefore, although certain behavior was observed, the conclusion that property values have gone down is invalid and subject to challenge. To judge property values, one should observe the price paid by all families who move in.

Another troublesome issue has to do with the number of observations required to support our inferences. How often and in what context must a child physically strike another child, for example, before we draw conclusions about the first child's "aggressive" nature or "hostile" manner? Although the answer to this particular question will vary extensively according to the point of view of the observer, the answer will be greatly influenced by the observer's intimate knowledge and understanding of the observed behaviors.

Making Interpretations

When we make inferences or draw conclusions from observational data, we are making *interpretations*, or adding meaning to the observations. Interpretations grow out of theories, past experiences, and present observations (McCutcheon, 1981). They "make sense" out of what we see and help us "understand" what we observed. There are at least three kinds of interpretations:

1. Forming *patterns* among observations, such as inferring the apparent order and rules for doing things in a classroom.
2. Interpreting the *social importance and meaning* of observed behaviors; for example, McCutcheon (1981) notes:

> We might observe students nodding during a [class presentation]. The physical behavior might be described as students moving their heads slightly, in an up and down motion. . . . What does this nodding mean? (p. 7)

   The nods may signify different things. Are the pupils following the teacher's thoughts; agreeing with the teacher; feigning an interest that is not there, to be polite; falling asleep; or demonstrating a habit?
3. Relating observations to *external considerations* such as theories, philosophy, and historical events.

In interpreting observations, one might emphasize one type of interpretation over the others. The meaning that comes from interpreting observations grows out of the transaction between what we observed and what we have experienced. Thus, interpretation is in part subjective and in part objective.

The Types of Validity

As inferences and interpretations are arrived at and generalizations made on the basis of observational data, one should consider the various types of validity usually required of other assessment devices and techniques: concurrent validity, content validity, predictive validity, and construct validity.*

Concurrent validity. How do the observed behaviors relate to other external criteria such as test scores, school performance records, and parent reports? These concurrent data, independent of the observations, can help substantiate or validate the inference. For example, from

---

*See Cone (1982), Hoge (1985), and Kent & Foster (1977) for additional readings in this area.

observing that a child's distractibility is increased and her concentration decreased during unstructured group activities, we might conclude that the child does not respond productively to an unstructured situation. Independent psychological test data might suggest that the child has abilities to attend to detail and concentrate on such tasks as block design or puzzles (subtests on the Wechsler Intelligence Scale for Children — Revised) when these are presented in a one-to-one situation. This finding would provide substantiating evidence that the child is capable of being attentive when confronted with the appropriate context or situation. The more independent evidence accumulated to support inferences based on observation, the more credible and valid the inferences become.

Content validity.   Does the observation adequately sample or represent the behavior of concern? Has the observation question been refined sufficiently? Are the categories of observation exhaustive of the problem at hand? Content validity is the most fundamental form of validity for observational procedures.

Predictive validity.   How do observational outcomes relate to or predict future performance? Sources of information at a future time might include test scores, grades, or classroom performance.

Construct validity.   Perhaps the most important question the developer of an observational instrument must ask is: Do the target behaviors observed in fact tap or represent the psychological constructs — for example, "independence," "creativity," "role-taking ability," "intelligence," and so forth — that are of particular interest to the observer?

DETERMINING THE APPROPRIATENESS
OF AN OBSERVATION SYSTEM

Figure 8.10 gives a list of questions an observer should ask about the observation about to be made, the technique to be employed, and its appropriateness. After some experience, these questions should occur to the observer as a matter of course and it will no longer be necessary to consult the checklist.

It is most essential for observers to evaluate their observation needs before adopting the use of a published research instrument or observation technique. The array of observation schedules available to the class-

Figure 8.10. Checkpoints for Determining the Appropriateness
of an Observation System

1 For what purpose was the system developed?
   A. Does the stated purpose match your goal?
   B. What will be observed (behavioral definition)?
   C. Is the procedure limited by a particular theoretical perspective?

2 Are the conditions for observer reliability met?
   A. Behaviors to be viewed are sufficiently specified so as to be:
      Mutually exclusive (do not overlap each other). Exhaustive* (all behaviors of concern
      can be classified, but the need for exhaustive categories depends on the purpose of a
      particular observation).
   B. Categories are sufficiently narrow so that two or more observers will place an observed
      behavior into the same category.
   C. Is observer interpretation necessary or not?
   D. What reliability data are presented?

3 What type of system is employed?
   A. Category system: Every unit of behavior observed is categorized into one of the
      categories specified.
   B. Sign system: Selected behavioral units, listed beforehand, may or may not actually be
      observed during a period of time.

4 Are appropriate sampling procedures employed?
   A. The procedure for sampling behaviors is systematic:
      Time sampling—occurrence or nonoccurrence of behaviors within specified uniform
      time units.
      Event sampling—event recorded each time it occurs.
   B. Is the procedure feasible?
      How do you sample individuals to be observed?
      In what period of time?
      Is the desired detail possible given the number of individuals and time units?
   C. What is the coding system like?
      How complex is the system?
      Do tallies or codes require memorization? If coding required, is code indicated on the
      record form?
      What is the recording format like?
   D. Are the behaviors to be viewed representative?
      How many behaviors are to be viewed?
      Over what period of time?
      Using how many subjects?

5 Are the conditions for validity met?
   Are the behaviors you observe relevant to the inferences and interpretations you make?
   Have sources of observer bias been eliminated?

6 What training procedures are necessary to learn the system?

7 If studies have been reported using the system, what are their outcomes?

8 What modifications will you need to make to the system to adapt it to your purpose?

room observer often confuses the consumer as to the appropriateness of one structured approach versus another for a given educational situation. Among the most useful resources for helping evaluate a given observational procedure are the *Mirrors for Behavior* anthologies prepared by Simon and Boyer (1967, 1970, 1974), Evertson and Green's chapter in the *Third Handbook of Research on Teaching* (1986), and Foster and Cone's chapter in the *Handbook of Behavioral Assessment* (1986). Gordon and Jester (1973) have reviewed techniques of observing teaching in early childhood settings, which include home and day-care settings as well as preschool classrooms. Finally, Boyer, Simon, and Karafin (1973) have edited an anthology of early childhood observation instruments.

ETHICAL ISSUES IN OBSERVATION

Given the current climate in which the public has seriously questioned such school activities as psychological testing and other forms of assessment and record-keeping without prior parental permission or knowledge, we must consider the point at which observation techniques may interfere with an individual's privacy and rights. We cannot deny that individuals routinely and legitimately observe each of us in our daily activities. Depending on the nature of the stated purpose of the observation, if someone is observed without being made aware of this or without prior permission such observations may well constitute an invasion of privacy. In the case of the young child, receiving parental permission is an appropriate consideration. However, as children become more aware of their rights, even though it may affect the results of our data collection, it is necessary to seriously consider informing the child of our intent to observe (Russell Sage Foundation, 1969).

Most classroom observers do not invade a child's privacy. A teacher observes children as they work in a variety of classroom learning situations in order to develop more effective teaching strategies, and violation occurs only if the data collection goes beyond this function. A student teacher observes in classrooms to gain an understanding of appropriate teaching behaviors and of child development. The special educator observes the effectiveness of an intervention. The school psychologist observes a child with a behavior problem to better understand the nature of the problem and the classroom conditions that might be contributing factors.

Social scientists, child development researchers, and educators have struggled with the question of privacy and the possible uses to which data can be put, however well-intentioned the observation process may have been originally. The American Psychological Association, in its *Ethical Principles in the Conduct of Research with Human Participants* (1981), places much covert observation and recording into the category of invasion of privacy. Tape recordings, videotapings, and other mechanical recordings — although facilitating the collection of more comprehensive observation information — must be used with such ethical considerations taken into account (see Unit X). The Society for Research in Child Development, in its *Ethical Standards for Research with Children* (1982), stresses the rights of the child and the need to respect a child's willingness or refusal to participate in research.

Like most ethical issues, the problem of invasion of privacy through observation techniques is a complex, multifaceted dilemma that cannot be resolved by simple answers (see Brandt, 1972). However, as we consider the value of observation skills as a method of inquiry and as a source for building inferences, we must constantly raise the question of ethics. (A number of important ethical concerns and procedures for conducting research with children in natural settings, such as informed consent and confidentiality, have been summarized by Rheingold, 1982).

The Teacher as Observer

Mrs. Paredes, a teacher in a first-grade classroom, is concerned about the behavior of Gregory. He frequently becomes restless and cries in class. In attempting to understand this behavior, Mrs. Paredes decides to observe at what time of the school day, during what activities, and with what frequency Gregory becomes restless and cries.

The school social worker periodically visits the classroom of Mr. Green, making anecdotal records of student behaviors possibly indicating drug usage.

Mrs. Morris, a housemother for young children at a residential treatment center, is concerned with the health and physical care of the eight children for whom she is responsible. Each day of the week she systematically notes different physical features of the children such as their skin tone, hair, and fingernails to check that all is in order.

These examples provide us with some notion of the various ways in which observations are used in schools and school-related settings. Now that we have dealt with the major factors involving observation skills and in devising observation schedules, let us consider some additional issues in using systematic observation techniques in the classroom and developing observation schedules tailored to specific classroom problems.

THE TEACHER OR THE OUTSIDER AS OBSERVER

Although innovations such as team teaching and the use of classroom paraprofessionals have generated possibilities for individuals involved in the classroom to observe ongoing behavior, for the most part systematic observation has been carried out by the social worker, school psychologist, researcher, and other school personnel who are not integral members of the classroom setting. Generally, when teachers have used observation techniques, they have been unstructured and highly dependent on remembering the observed behaviors until an opportune time to record — usually the end of the day. However, there are a number of alternative approaches that can enable the teacher to implement structured and systematic observation procedures in the classroom.

- In collaboration with a team teacher, paraprofessional, or another classroom teacher with a free period, the teacher can develop an appropriate schedule for observing and in turn share observing responsibilities.
- When other personnel are not available, the teacher, again using an appropriate schedule, can decide to depart from the teaching routine and systematically observe during a certain portion of each day. For example, the teacher may determine to observe and record the variety of independent activities engaged in by class members. The observation might take place for five minutes at the beginning and five minutes at the end of the activities period each day over the course of a week. Children will be engaged in activities while the observation takes place. The amount of time required for observational activity is small in proportion to the benefits that can result from collecting the observation data. For example, to obtain information about the patterns of peer interaction within a classroom, the teacher might decide to observe a sample of five pupils as they interact with classmates; each pupil is observed for one minute during each of four hours (perhaps 9:00 and 11:00 A.M. and 1:00 and 3:00 P.M.) of the class day over a given number of days.
- The teacher can also function as a "participant-observer," recording observations while interacting with observed pupils. This type of observation, important in open classroom settings, involves the teacher in observing and recording teacher–pupil behaviors in a few predetermined categories over brief periods of time.

Problems Encountered by the Teacher as Observer

Even when the teacher is removed from the stream of behavior and fulfills the role of an observer in the classroom, his or her mere presence in the setting is bound to influence certain pupil behaviors to some extent. One probably would get different results if some other person, such as the principal, were in the classroom.

A more difficult problem, referred to as the "halo effect" (see also

Unit VII), involves the influence of the teacher's previous knowledge and experience with a classroom of pupils and their past behavior on making objective observations of current behavior. For example, from past experience, a teacher, anticipating that Donald is attentive and concentrates well in the classroom, will tend to ignore or underemphasize any instance of "off-task" behavior that Donald exhibits. As another example, many teachers, anticipating that children from lower socioeconomic groups have poor verbal expressive abilities, might overlook instances of excellent verbal expression in the classroom.

One way of tempering the influence of the halo effect is to involve additional independent observers at some point in the observation process to determine how valid the teacher's observations are. The assumption here is that an outside observer has not had previous experience with and expectations of the children involved.

SOLVING CLASSROOM PROBLEMS THROUGH OBSERVATION TECHNIQUES

We have presented a variety of examples from the classroom in which observation procedures might be used. Let us now consider some general problems that might be approached through observational techniques.

Determining the Effectiveness of Educational Programs and Curricula

Current teacher training programs, education literature, local school district programs, and the media have exposed teachers to a variety of innovations, theoretical orientations, and ways to deal with day-to-day learning and classroom behavior problems. Observation techniques can facilitate a teacher's adaptation and use of many of these "new" educational ideas. Before introducing a new program intended to produce changes in learning or other classroom behavior, the teacher should collect a baseline of observation data on behaviors that the program is aimed at influencing.

In the example presented in Figure 9.1 we are assuming that a classroom teacher intends to introduce a token reinforcement system aimed at increasing the amount of time the pupils in the class pursue assigned tasks. Before introducing the system it is essential that the teacher collect observation data on the relevant behavior. The baseline data are collected for days 1 and 2. The token system is introduced on

Figure 9.1. Charts for Numbers of Minutes Pupils Worked on Assigned Tasks

Pupil A

Day	Reading	Arithmetic	Spelling	Other Assignments	Total Time Pupil "On Task"	Total Time for Pupil Work on Assigned Tasks
1	20	20	5	10	55	110
2	18	20	4	8	50	120
3	22	18	12	13	65	100
4	25	22	18	19	84	120

Pupil B

Day	Reading	Arithmetic	Spelling	Other Assignments	Total Time Pupil "On Task"	Total Time for Pupil Work on Assigned Tasks
1	15	15	10	10	50	110
2	12	17	8	11	48	120
3	18	20	10	7	55	100
4	20	25	15	12	72	120

*Heavy rule indicates baseline.

day 3 and continues for a given period of time. The observations should continue to be made during this period to ascertain whether the pupils' on-task behavior has actually changed as a result of the program. Charts such as those shown in Figure 9.1 could be used for recording these observations over a number of days. (We are here showing the results for only four days and for only two pupils; an actual reinforcement system and the observations would naturally involve more pupils and a longer observation period.) On-task behavior is defined for this sample as the amount of time pupils work at assigned tasks.

After a sufficient number of days of observation, the teacher could calculate the percentage of on-task behavior for each pupil. This would be the total time the pupil worked divided by the length of working time available. The information recorded on the observation schedule could be transformed into a graph like that shown in Figure 9.2. Here, the total amount of time students could work at all assigned tasks on day 3 was 100 minutes. Pupil A was observed to be on task for a total of 65 minutes. By dividing these 65 minutes by the 100 minutes of total working time we see that pupil A was on task 65 percent of the time on day 3. By the same method of computation, we found the percentage of on-task behavior for day 4, and plotted these figures on the graph. The same procedure was followed for pupil B.

In Figure 9.2, days 1 and 2 yield the baseline information on the percentage of on-task behavior demonstrated by both pupils prior to the introduction of the reinforcement system. If the token program works, the percentage of on-task behavior should increase as the percentages on the graph seem to indicate: from this graph, the teacher could conclude that the on-task behavior of pupils A and B has increased as a result of the token program. To verify this conclusion the teacher should eliminate the reinforcement system and observe whether or not there is a decrease in on-task behavior. After confirmation of the reinforcement system's impact on behavior, the teacher would reintroduce the token program, expecting another increase in on-task behavior of the students.

STUDYING DEVELOPMENTAL DIFFERENCES IN CHILDREN

Observation techniques can provide an effective means of conveying to teachers the basic differences that exist among children at various developmental levels. Often teachers — particularly those just out of teacher training programs — have difficulty setting appropriate expectations and goals for children of different ages in their classes. Making systematic observations of children at successive age levels can provide

Figure 9.2. Graph for Percent of "On Task" Behavior

Percent	Day 1	Day 2	Day 3	Day 4	Additional Days of Program

Key: Pupil A:——   Pupil B: . . . . .

an effective approach to understanding the behavioral differences demonstrated by children at different ages. For example, although the three-year-old can be observed having difficulty tying his shoelaces, the seven-year-old child not only performs this task with ease, but also demonstrates facility in many other fine motor activities. The typical five-year-old, viewing an airplane in the sky, is unable to describe its real size or rate of speed; however, by 10 years of age, the child is capable of understanding the effects of distance on size and speed. With an appreciation of the basic differences in cognitive, emotional, and motor behaviors of children at different ages, the teacher has a sounder basis on which to base instruction and build curricula.

Diagnostic Assessment of Learning Activity

Certain classroom assessment procedures are variations of systematic event samplings, where the events or problems are presented to each pupil and the teacher observes each pupil's strategy in dealing with them. The teacher may observe each child at the blackboard working on a multiplication problem involving two-place carrying of numbers, noting that one child has difficulty applying the carrying strategy per se, while another child has difficulty lining up numbers. In order to do such an assessment systematically, the teacher should prepare beforehand a list of relevant learning strategies and errors that can occur on this task and then focus on them in making the observations, as shown in Figure 9.3.

Observing each child perform a task such as the multiplication problem allows the teacher to view the child's approach to a learning situation, in contrast to the more typical situation in which the child, working alone on his or her worksheet, might make some errors. In the latter situation, it is difficult to identify why the child had trouble

Figure 9.3. Multiplication of Two-Place Problems with Carrying

Child	Can Carry	Can Multiply Where No Carrying Is Required	Lines Numbers Up Correctly	All Procedures Correct

solving the problem. Only through observing the problem-solving process can the teacher know precisely what kind of help a given child might need.

STEPS TO MAKING CLASSROOM OBSERVATIONS

Following is an overview of the various steps the classroom teacher should take in developing a useful observation system. In following these steps, the observer can be aware of the nature of observations and have greater confidence in the inferences and decisions generated as a result of observation activity. An application example follows the description of each step.

1. What is the nature of the problem or the question with which you are confronted? Define the problem and the related behaviors clearly.

> The first-grade teachers at a school located within a large metropolitan area have established a resource center for their pupils. The purpose of the center is to provide an opportunity for the first-graders to engage in a variety of learning activities, focusing on the development of beginning reading skills. Each of the school's three first-grade classes spends approximately 25 minutes of each day in the center. During this time, the children complete one task that they have individually selected from a series of 30 learning activities: copying shapes, matching letters with objects depicting that letter name, classifying objects into concept categories, listening to an audiotape of a story while looking at pictures of that story, and so on. When a child completes a learning activity and has the project checked by the teacher or aide, the child may choose another task. The teachers want to know if their first-grade pupils are able to select, pursue, and complete these tasks independently of teacher, aide, or other pupil assistance.
>
> *Problem*: Do individual first-graders select, pursue, and complete the learning activities without seeking assistance of the teacher, aide, or other pupils?

2. Why should systematic observation be helpful in dealing with this problem or answering the question?

The teachers decide that by using observational procedures they will be able to make systematic recordings of the
pupils' behavior during their time in the resource center.
The teachers could limit their approach to merely looking at
completed pupil activities, but by introducing observation
of the patterns of pupil behavior in the center the teachers
gather a richer pool of information for drawing their conclusions and more directly answering their question about pupil independence. Furthermore, observations over time will
provide teachers with an understanding of differences
among children in pursuing and completing activities without the assistance of others.

3. What are the relevant characteristics of the setting in which behavior will be observed? (Characteristics of the setting include space,
equipment, and people present.)

- What constraints does the physical setting have on possible
behaviors?

     Because the average first-grade class at the school con-
     sists of 25 children, and since a "standard"-sized classroom
     has been designated as the resource center, the pupils' be-
     havior is limited in its range of mobility. Yet, because of
     pupil proximity, the setting itself might encourage verbal
     exchanges and pupils' "assisting" one another. Of course
     the availability of the particular learning materials, as op-
     posed to other possible materials, can restrain the scope of
     behaviors to be viewed.

- What is the physical arrangement of the various components of
the setting that might be considered?

     Each of 30 tasks are numbered and placed in various
     locations such as bookshelves, windowsills, corners of the
     floor, and on tables. Pupil work areas are provided adjacent
     to the materials.

- What people will be present in the setting? What characteristics of the individuals or group being observed need to be
considered?

In addition to the 25 pupils in the first-grade class, a class teacher, an aide, and an observer are present in the setting. The aide has been trained beforehand in the use of the learning materials, but has been encouraged to provide assistance only when requested by pupils. The observer will be one of the other first-grade teachers who has arranged a 25-minute free period to coincide with the resource center period of this class.

4. Given the particular focus of your observations and given your knowledge of the problem area, what is the universe of behaviors that you intend to consider?

The teachers will consider how the pupils:
—Select an activity. (What task does a pupil choose on any given day? What is the range of tasks that he or she chooses over a period of time?)
—Engage in a task. (Do the pupils work with or without requesting assistance from teacher, teacher aide, or other pupils?)
—Indicate that a given task is completed.
In addition, it might also be interesting to see if there is a relationship between these observed behaviors and the quality of the pupil's final product.

5. What units of behavior or clearly defined categories of behavior will you focus on?
Analyze the behavior into its component parts. In determining your list of categories for classifying observable behavior, consider whether a previously developed observational schedule might be used. Decide whether a sign or category system is more appropriate for your problem:
— Are the categories or signs employed mutually exclusive?
— Is the listing of categories or signs exhaustive of the universe of behaviors you wish to consider?

In their search of observational schedules already available for use, the teachers were unable to find a recording system including the categories of behaviors that matched the purpose of their observations.
Since they were interested in evidence of independent behavior, they adopted a sign system; that is, they generated

the following specific categories of behavior for labeling observations:

—The child selects one of the 30 activities, then picks up the materials and takes them to the designated work area. (However, if the child merely looks at the materials without taking them to the work area, this would not be classified as selecting a task.)

—The child requests assistance from the teacher, aide, or another pupil in the resource center by either gesturing for assistance, verbally asking for assistance, or combining gesture and verbal request. (However, if the child asks to get a drink of water or merely talks to the teacher, aide, or another pupil, this would not be classified as a request for assistance.)

—The child indicates that a given task has been completed by showing the product to the teacher or aide. (However, if the child partially completes the task, he or she would be encouraged to resume work on the task—but this would not constitute a request for assistance.)

6. What sampling procedure (time or event) will most effectively enable you to record representative observations?

• Will all the people in the setting be observed, or will you select a representative sample?

The teachers decided which children would be observed and at what frequency. Since it would be impossible for an individual teacher to observe all children simultaneously, it is necessary to observe a sample of children each day and to order the observations of their behavior systematically. Therefore, the teachers adopted a time-sampling procedure— that is, they decided to observe a preselected sample of five children each day. Consequently, by the end of a five-day school week each of the 25 children will have been observed during one of the daily sessions in the resource center.

• How frequently across time should you observe so that your conclusions have adequate observational support?

In order to observe each of the five children at different points in the work period, the teacher-observer observes each of the five children to be observed that day at work for one minute during a five-minute segment. The teacher then proceeds to observe each of the five for one minute for the second five-minute segment, and so forth until each of the five children has been observed for a total of four minutes. This procedure is followed each day of the week, five children at a time, until all 25 children have been observed.

- To what extent does the subject of the observation need to be viewed in a variety of settings and activities within the school in order to deal adequately with the particular problem or question? (Does not apply to this particular observation problem.)

7. Design a recording format. (See Figure 9.4 for sample.)
8. How confident are you that your observation schedule facilitates reliable observations? How might you verify this?

To determine the reliability of the observational scheme, two of the three first-grade teachers might observe the resource center period of the third teacher on two consecutive days. The degree to which the two raters agreed with each other in recording the instances of request for assistance could then be determined. The percentage of agreement in indicating the pupil's selection of tasks could also be determined by this procedure. A high rate of agreement would indicate a high level of reliability between the observers.

9. What inferences or conclusions can you make on the basis of your collected observation data?

Conclusions can be arrived at regarding:
—What tasks were chosen? By how many pupils?
—Which tasks were completed? By how many pupils?
—Were certain chosen tasks completed more often than others?
—How often did pupils request assistance? Which children requested assistance? From whom?
—Were there differences among the three classes observed?
—What inferences can be made about the use of the resource center?

Figure 9.4. Sample Recording Sheet for Observations in Resource Center

Week 1, Day 1   Date: 20-minute period

| Child | Activity Selected | Frequency of Requests for Assistance From:* | | | Requests for Check of Completed Activity |
		Teacher	Aide	Other Child	Total	
Total						

* Use sign system and wait for instances of behavior to occur

—Can the data be summarized in a graph or chart? The use of a graph or chart helps communicate to others the outcomes of observation.

10. Have you realized the goal for which your observations have been made? If not, can you redefine your problem more clearly and focus on different behaviors, and from a different perspective? (In other words, can you pilot an alternative approach?)

The example as developed should allow the teachers to answer the question posed in Point 1, although alternative approaches to the problem could be developed.

11. Did you consider the role that methods of inquiry other than systematic observation — psychometric testing, controlled experimentation, or developmental histories — might play in dealing with your problem? (Does not pertain to the example presented.)

The Relationship Between Media and Observation

In this unit we will consider briefly the interactions that take place between the observer and the medium of observation. Observation may take place in a live situation or through media — pictures, slides, film, videotape, printed materials, audio recordings, or any combination of these. Each medium has formal characteristics that affect the observation process, and each allows for certain predictions. For example, even the most skilled stenographer is unable to record all the innuendos of a single speaker with paper and pencil, and the task becomes more difficult with an increase in the number of simultaneous speakers. On the other hand, a tape recorder and appropriately placed microphones provide a record of all verbal interactions, even whispers. But the tape system would not pick up gestures or facial expressions. Each medium has its strengths and its limitations, a topic to be covered in greater detail later in this unit.

THE "MECHANICS" OF MEDIA AND THE OBSERVER

Several interacting factors need to be taken into account when considering the use of media. They include:

- Availability of media equipment
- Ease of use (operation)
- Degree of special training required
- Ease of recording (encoding) and gaining appropriate information from that recording (decoding)
- Range of applicability
- Cost
- Intrusiveness of the media system

This unit was written with the help of John L. Swayze.

107

For example, paper and pencil are almost always available and require no training, but are limited in their applicability without other aids. On the other hand, mechanical sound recording provides a much more complete account of a given situation, but requires costly equipment, which is often inaccessible, necessitates some training to operate, and can intrude on the setting. The question of intrusiveness is important in the choice of media for observational purposes. A behavioral measure of intrusiveness might well be the amount of time required for the subjects of the observation to ignore the presence of the observation system itself.

The still picture or single photograph, while generally easy to obtain, is one of the most difficult observation representations to interpret, due to the minimal sample of behaviors, situations, or actions obtained. The viewer frequently does not know what occurred immediately before or immediately after the incident photographed. The motion picture, by contrast, falls toward the other extreme of the picture-sampling dimension. It normally exposes from 18 to 24 still pictures per second, providing a more complete representation for interpretation. The more complete representation results from the dense sample of situations, behaviors, or actions presented in rapid sequence during a brief span of time. The motion picture, by presenting many frames per second to the observer, reduces the number of inferences required by the observer.

Actually, more information is available in motion pictures than most viewers use. For example, a frame by frame analysis would allow the viewer to look at eye movement. Slow motion presentation and repeated showings would allow other analyses. The viewer in most film-watching situations does not have time to extract all the information available. In fact, the viewer's perception is usually controlled by the filmmaker or by the purpose for which the film is viewed.

Differences, such as those between the still picture and motion picture, exist among all media and should be considered when choosing among them. The obvious differences of sound, motion, and nonmotion occur immediately to most people. The subtle differences, however, also influence the nature of data.

The ideal observation tool does not yet exist. Such a tool would provide a "magical time machine" display that would allow the observer to be invisible, to control the speed and direction of time, move backward and forward in time, freeze time, and review at will, and have all senses represented. With such a device the observer might well have the sensation of being on the scene without being part of it.

ADVANTAGES AND DISADVANTAGES
OF THE MEDIA OF OBSERVATION

First-Hand Observation

Direct viewing of a given situation provides more information than any individual can deal with at a given time. Therefore, a conscious selection process determines the foci of one's observations. Other information is screened out and what is viewed is ordered to conform with the frames of reference brought to that situation. Thus, an observer concerned about the physical manifestations of nutrition in a group of young children would focus on physical and behavioral features such as skin tone, fingernails, hair, weight, alertness, and energy level, while screening out verbal interchanges between children and the type of objects chosen for play.

The advantages of first-hand observation include:

- The immediacy of the information gained.
- The wide range of information available.
- The flow of action present — the viewer can see, hear, or inquire about what happened immediately prior to or following any given instance.

The advantages of direct observation are also the sources of its limitations:

- The screening out of some behaviors while focusing on others.
- The human factor — individual biases or prejudices, memory of events, inappropriate foci.
- The effect of the observer's presence on the events being observed.

The presence of more than one trained observer in a given situation can solve some of the problems posed above but introduces others, including cost in time and potential interference with the ongoing process. Thus, the human being without the help of other techniques is restricted in his or her capacity to collect data in a live situation. The introduction of categorized recording systems, rating scales, pictorial records, and sound recordings can help an individual's perceptions become more than somewhat unreliable impressions. With certain strengths and weaknesses, some of them unique to the medium under consideration, the use of the media of observation is introduced. Although no single medium can combine all of the strengths of human observation, various media can be combined and compensate for some of the weaknesses.

The Still Picture or Slide

A picture or series of pictures, although reflecting the selectivity of the photographer, does permit the viewer to reexamine the picture in order to test his or her own perception and interpretation of that picture. The viewer can examine the order or sequence of behaviors or actions shown to infer, for example, that motion or change took place. The picture or series of pictures also allows the viewer to compare his or her own observations with those made by others of the same events, and to review the depicted events at some future time. The observation process can thus be extended beyond the limitations of the observing human being. The ability to review the stimuli provides the primary advantage of the single still picture or sequence of pictures over direct observation.

The major limitation of a single picture or slide is the obvious one: It presents a static view of the instance, forcing the viewer to seek additional information or to make inferences without knowing what immediately preceded or followed the event. A second limitation is that in most cases the photographer makes the selection for the viewer. A useful comparison might well be made between the still picture and a painting: An individual looking at a painting tends to seek subtle meaning in it, whereas the same individual viewing a photograph often accepts it as total reality, when it is in fact a partial representation of reality. One way to deal with this problem is to use a sequence of still pictures. Each additional picture, in sequence, clarifies the scene, setting, interactions, and outcomes.

The teacher, then, may find a "before" and "after" photo useful, or may wish to photograph a sequence of events. Photographic surveys of classrooms can provide teachers with detailed understanding of classroom environments. Adis (1977), for example, used a photographic survey to identify patterns of student interaction with classroom resources. Photographs of classrooms were taken and coded through use of a locational grid and computerized blueprint of each classroom. Thus it was possible to track patterns of student interaction with classroom resources and with other students. More simple recordings can involve photographing each activity area of the room and the classroom clock on a regular basis during a day—for example, every 15 minutes during an entire day.

Audio Recordings

With appropriately placed microphones and adequate equipment, audiotape recordings can provide a flexible record of verbal interchanges in a situation. To evaluate a conversation one might focus on content analysis, phonemic analysis, volume-level shift, pacing, and expression. In the live situation the hearer-observer would never be able to absorb and analyze the conversation from these varied foci. The recording, because of its *playback* characteristic, allows for other analyses, and in this way provides a major contribution to the repertoire of observation tools.

When sound recordings are transcribed, considerable information is lost, for the innuendos of expression, pace, and intonation are difficult to retain once the conversation is in typescript. Audio recordings alone also have limitations in comparison with those of pictorial recordings. There is a loss of the information obtained from facial expressions or other body movements (which might be in contrast to what is spoken), the behavior of others, and the setting. On the positive side of the coin, however, the transcriptions can be reviewed and recorded in an objective manner. In combination with other media, sound recording contributes usefully to the completeness of the recorded representation.

Films and Videotapes

A 16mm sound film or a videotape provides the most complete recording of most situations, since auditory, visual, and time dimensions are accounted for, but the observer tends to be more passive while viewing film and is subject to the selectivity of the filmmaker. Furthermore, there is ample room for viewer selectivity to come into play, for viewers will bring their own biases, training, and experiences to viewing the film. Sound film has the specific advantages of high density and flexibility: Film and videotape can be viewed frame by frame, stopped at a given frame, replayed, and reviewed by many observers. Therefore, this is a very useful form both for purposes of training and for analyzing data. Use of computer analysis facilitates highly detailed accounts of behavior. Future use of interactive videodiscs will further enhance the use of observational sequences.

The major limitations to the use of sound film and videotape derive from the cost and the technical competency required for quality production. Recent advances in technology have eliminated some of these problems. Schools increasingly have videotape equipment that can be borrowed for classroom use. Observers using videotapes need to keep in mind, however, that important behaviors can still be missed, depending on the angle of the camera and the activity level of the child. Young children move frequently and do not necessarily face the camera. Equipment can break down, the noise level of a room might be high, or one can forget to turn the camera on.

Despite these cautions, film and videotape can greatly enhance our understanding of young children, including the processes and strategies they use to solve problems. Kounin (1975), for example, videotaped child behaviors both in free play and in formal lesson settings. Teachers' communication style, use of materials and visual aids, and pupil behaviors such as listening and responding to a story all influenced the success of lessons. Ginsburg (1987) has used videotape to investigate young children's understanding of number. He is developing teacher workshop packages built around these videotapes that focus on strategies children use to solve number problems, the kinds of errors they make, and how they explain these errors. Following a child's response, an interviewer poses questions such as "How did you figure out your answer?" or "How did you know?" Although the child might respond "Because I am smart," important clues might be revealed from the tape regarding the child's skills. Teachers and parents can develop considerable insight through observing and discussing such videotaped sequences.

For us as adults, the Iranian hostage crisis in 1980 provided a poignant example of how film and videotape might be used to deal with a politically volatile, life-and-death situation: Governmental officials studied film clips of the hostages for clues to the hostages' mental states. Among the questions the observers presumably asked were:

What did the background voices say while the hostages were speaking?
Were all the relatives mentioned real?
Were there hidden messages in the hostages' statements?
Was there evidence of drug influence in the ways the hostages moved their arms, legs, and eyes?
What could be inferred about the extent of tension and anxiety through voice analysis?
Which hostages had gained or lost weight?
Were the hostages who helped themselves to the fruit so clearly displayed on camera those who might have been imprisoned or kept in solitary confinement?

Other nonverbal activities might have provided meaningful information as well.

Black and White or Color

We live in a chromatic world and when we view situations first hand, the chromatic qualities are of course retained. The degree to which visual media can reproduce the chromatic qualities of first-hand observations varies. Color reproductions have a different information-carrying capacity than black and white reproductions. For example, look again at the photograph of the supermarket scene for Task 2 near the start of Unit IV and consider the additional information a color reproduction might have provided about the cleanliness of the store.

Color carries information but it can also dominate the viewer's perceptions and, depending on one's purposes, may need to be screened out. Since color adds greatly to the cost of reproduction, the advantages and disadvantages of its use must be a consideration.

The selection of appropriate data collection tools or media requires knowledge of their technology. Therefore, effective use of media in observation requires an understanding of the advantages and limitations of each medium with the end of maintaining as much control as possible. Accordingly, a useful ground rule is to have as much control as possible over the media used; at every point control is yielded, a degree of freedom is also yielded. Thus the viewer needs a knowledge of the repertoire of observation tools and media available and their unique characteristics. With such knowledge, one can choose the tool or tools most appropriate for a given purpose.

Mechanical Recording Systems

Counting devices, not unlike portable calculators, are available for recording the frequency of behaviors of interest. Microcomputer systems also allow the collection of data about individuals as they respond to program materials — concerning reaction time, errors made, branching, and the number of attempts to meet a criterion level (see Unit XI).

In summary, the observer needs to consider carefully the characteristics, advantages, and drawbacks of different media forms. Kent and Foster (1977) make the point that different media forms may not be equivalent or even comparable since they produce different kinds of data. However, the use of both audiotape and videotape or film greatly enhances our ability to review carefully the observation situation. Unless these media are an integral component of the environment, however, their introduction may be intrusive. A period of time to adjust to the presence of these nonhuman observers may be necessary.

The effects of different media on the resulting observational data have been summarized by Foster and Cone (1986), who point out that:

- Inter-observer agreement differs between live observation and when observing videotaped presentations. Depending on the target behaviors observed, agreement tends to be higher in live situations.
- Findings are not uniform across media.

Developing Observation Methods Appropriate to the Computer-Assisted Learning Environment

Observation in the electronic learning environment brings with it many of the same issues as observing in any learning environment, plus some additional challenges. The challenges arise from the fact that in the electronic learning environment the content and the process of learning become observable in new ways. On the microcomputer screen, we can see the content of what the student is working on: correct responses, errors, the amount of branching to more fundamental examples or to more difficult problems, and so forth. Another challenge arises from the fact that considerable activity occurs simultaneously, particularly in the three-way interaction that takes place between the teacher or tutor, the learner, and the computer software.

A rich literature in classroom observation has provided us with increased understanding of both teacher and learner behaviors (Evertson & Green, 1986). In these studies, observers have viewed behaviors from a number of perspectives:

- Focusing on learners in their natural environment in order to understand the development of the learner's behavioral repertoire, the process of classroom interaction, the problems learners encounter, and the approaches students take
- Studying the frequency or rate with which behaviors targeted for observation occur
- Understanding the circumstances that led up to target behaviors as well as what followed the behaviors

COMPUTER-ASSISTED TUTORING:
USE OF COMPUTER SOFTWARE

In our book, attention has been centered on the *teacher* and *learner* and the interaction between the two. However, in the electronic learning environment, the computer software becomes a third focus of interest, and interactions among student, teacher, and computer become possible (Figure 11.1).

Understanding this three-way interaction can be a viable observational goal as we have learned from our own experiences in the Computer-Assisted Tutoring Service (CATS) at Teachers College, where children and tutors have worked together with commercially available software. For example, we were interested in understanding the exchanges among children, their tutors, and computer software; the motivational impact of the software; and the impact of the computer experience on the learning process. Questions that could be addressed through systematic observations were raised:

- Were learners on task?
- Was their attention maintained when they encountered difficulty?
- What did tutors do to enhance the learning situation?
- With what kinds of learning tasks were children successful, and where did they encounter difficulties?
- What characteristics of the software seemed to enhance or impede the goals of the tutors?
- What reinforcers were emitted by software? By tutors? With what frequency?

Figure 11.1.   The Three-Way Interaction in Tutor Use of Computer Software

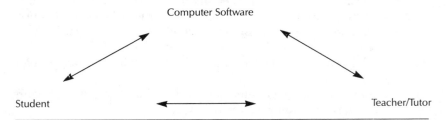

FORMS OF OBSERVATION
USEFUL IN THE COMPUTER ENVIRONMENT

To address the questions, various forms of observation were useful in the computer environment:

1. *Anecdotal Records.* Notes from the teacher/tutors about learning behaviors and interactions with the software were helpful in providing insight into many aspects of the computer situation, such as motivational features of the environment and software characteristics that seemed to enhance or interfere with learning. (One example was, "The printed material is spaced so compactly that it was difficult for David to keep his place.")
2. *Narrative Records.* Recording all aspects of the learning situation from the beginning to the end of the instructional period was useful to understand the context and flow of behavior in the computer environment. As a result, behaviors and events in the computer environment were identified as targets for systematic observational procedures. A major problem noted in the three-way interaction was that when recording one set of events, others were missed.
3. *Rating Scales.* Tutors and students rated the programs along a number of relevant dimensions.
4. *Observation Systems.* Systematic observation procedures were developed to sample and record the frequency of certain behaviors that occurred in the computer-assisted learning environment (see Figure 11.2). Categories of student behavior targeted by the system developed included:

> Attention to and responses directed to the computer screen or keyboard
> Attention to and responses directed to the tutor
> Student or tutor performance of related behavior
> Off-task behaviors

DEVELOPING AN OBSERVATIONAL PROCEDURE
FOR COMPUTER-ASSISTED TUTORING

Steps similar to those outlined in Unit VIII for developing an observational procedure were followed in creating a category system for CATS.

Figure 11.2. Attention Directed to Computer Screen or Keyboard

Eyes on screen	Reading
	Typing input
	Listening to tutor
	Responding to tutor
Eyes on keyboard	Typing input
Eyes off screen	Listening
(attention to tutor)	Commenting
	Responding
	Waiting
Performing related behaviors	
Off task	

In order to develop an appropriate system for observing the three-way interactions, portions of the system developed by Spielvogel and Dunne (1982), "An Observation System for Interaction Analysis of Instructional Computer Software," were reviewed and adapted. This system lists categories of screen presentations, student behaviors, and computer responses. Use of the system helped us attend to and record presentations on the computer and student behaviors. However, since our sample included students with learning difficulties, we were also interested in features of the software and tutor interactions that enhanced or impeded learning. What did tutors do, for example, to make the interaction pedagogically meaningful to the learner?

Attempts at audiotaping proved unsuccessful, due to background noise and the inability of the tape to pick up gestures and modeling behaviors. Videotaping was also not an easy solution, because when the camera was focused on the tutor and screen, some of the learner's behaviors were missed, and vice versa. Furthermore, the screen was frequently blocked by the learner's movements.

The first version of the "Computer-Assisted Tutoring Observation Scan" (Boehm & Brobst, 1982) was developed, considering each component of the CATS triad. Categories were specified for (1) software, (2) learner behaviors, and (3) tutor behaviors. Time-sampling procedures were used to record the occurrence or nonoccurrence of specific target behaviors during a present time interval. The frequency with which behaviors or events occurred within the time interval was ignored.

OUTCOMES OF OBSERVING
COMPUTER-ASSISTED TUTORING

The student, tutor, and computer software were observed during 30-second intervals over a five-minute period, at the beginning of the tutoring session and again for five minutes at the end of the period. This procedure resulted in marking the observation sheet 20 times during each tutoring session. At the point when we had developed this approach, observers were familiar to both the students and their tutors and did not appear to be obtrusive. Using this procedure, we observed students over 30 five-minute intervals for a total of 292 observations. The observed software content included, in order of frequency of observed units, presentations of problems (58.9%), instructions (20.9%), feedback (17.5%), and system messages (2.7%).

Observations of student behaviors indicated that students were highly on task; attention to computer (eyes on screen of keyboard) occurred during 90.5 percent of observed intervals, and attention directed to tutor during another 6.8 percent of the intervals. Off-task behavior occurred during only 3.5 percent of the intervals, an important finding given that tutoring took place in a large room with other people present and other computers in operation. Tutor behaviors were varied. Although tutors were watching students during the greatest portion of observed intervals (38.6%), they also spent time explaining subject matter, providing verbal or physical prompts, reinforcing student efforts, and listening to students (each for 6% or more of the intervals). Tutors and off task 8.2 percent of the intervals, looking around the room or doing some other work.

In addition to the findings generated by this observation instrument, conclusions based on observations were useful concerning other important software characteristics:

- With some programs, an overload of graphics appears, the purpose of which is sometimes unclear.
- Many programs have long, complicated instructions requiring several behavior steps that may be difficult for students to follow.
- The pacing of programs may be too quick, with no way to adjust the pace.
- The unnatural left to right, line-by-line presentation of reading material may make it necessary to eliminate a number of programs.
- The timing of feedback was problematic for a number of learn-

ers. Some programs provided feedback after a predetermined time interval, resulting in feedback occurring at the time the student was figuring out the problem.

In summary, a great deal can be learned from observing the interactions that take place among the student, teacher/tutor, and computer software in computer-assisted learning environments. These observations can serve as a basis for generating teaching strategies, integrating software into remedial programs, creating new software, and adapting existing software to the needs of diverse populations. (See Clements, 1985, for more detailed discussions of the effects of computers on children's learning and development.)

Conclusion

In this book we have highlighted the role that systematic observation in natural settings may play in approaching problems and facilitating educational programs in classroom and other learning environments. Yet the astute observer should not accept naturalistic observation methodology exclusively over other methods of inquiry into educational processes. Although feelings and attitudes underlie many behaviors, it is often impossible to understand these dimensions through direct observation. Interviewing and self-report questionnaires may be more effective means of tapping these areas. For example, evaluating a child's self-esteem might be more directly approached through alternative methods of study. Moreover, since certain behaviors rarely occur in naturalistic situations, it may be necessary to create an experimental or testing situation in order to study — or observe — such behaviors as problem-solving strategies, patterns of discovery, learning, and divergent thinking.

As one of a variety of methodological tools, systematic observation can help the practitioner unravel and understand the complex behavioral exchanges among participants in various learning contexts. Developing and using observation techniques and interpreting the results of systematic observing are complex activities, yet with increased experience, the trained observer will be able to generate useful information on the basis of direct observation.

Furthermore, we would like to suggest that there is no one best way in observing. Each of us must define our own area of concern and choose those methods most appropriate to the problem being confronted as well as to our own style of working. It is hoped that this guide has provided the observer with a flexible yet systematic orientation for collecting and using observational data as vital sources of information in educational decision-making.

Perhaps the most active of all classroom observers is the child. It is well known that children learn what to expect from their teachers and parents, and to a large extent this information is gathered through observing what happens from day to day. Furthermore, observation is essential to children's intellectual and social growth, as they assimilate and accommodate to information from their environment. There is no reason why children should not be guided in the use of systematic observation strategies by defining observation problems, observing objectively, and supporting inferences with data. In fact, such an approach is a curricular emphasis of some recent science education programs.

Carrying this point one step further, why not also train secondary school pupils to help us collect some of the observational data required for making appropriate educational decisions? The next generation of well-trained observers sits in the classroom.

Sample Responses to Tasks

SAMPLE RESPONSES TO TASK 1

Observations of Your Present Setting

(Five-Minute Time Limit)

Setting: A classroom where students and instructor are gathered.

Time of Day: 2:00 P.M. (Class began at 1:45)

Observer: **A**

Observations in Sequence

1. The room is cold.

2. There are more women than men in this room.

3. I can hear adult voices.

4. There are white cabinets in this room.

5. The blackboard looks gray.

6. Quiet room.

7. Desks give room for work.

8. Area in back for those who want to smoke.

9. Large windows, high ceiling—good ventilation.

10. Age of people seems to range from early 20s to middle 30s.

11. This room seems to be connected to another.

12. Most of the people are busy writing.

Observer: **B**

Observations in Sequence

1. Young teacher.

2. Wooden ledge under blackboard.

3. Faces—some tired, some absorbed.

4. It's quiet.

5. Group is sitting in semicircle.

6. Everyone is looking around and writing.

7. Surprised class is so small.

8. Informal and relaxed atmosphere.

Observer: **C**

Observations in Sequence

1. High ceiling in room.

2. Bright-colored and beige walls.

3. The room is approximately square.

4. Several tables and chairs.

5. A group of about 12 people.

6. Most of the people are busy writing.

7. The room adjoins another where some people are talking.

SAMPLE RESPONSES TO TASK 4

Observations of a Girl in a Nursery Class

Observations Made	Inferences Drawn	Observations Supporting Inferences
1. She is sitting alone on a pile of blocks.	A. The child is not interacting with the other children.	A. 1,2
2. Other children in the block area are not focusing their attention on her.	B. The child is fearful of playing along with active young children.	B. 1,3,4
3. At least two of the four are involved (actively?) in play with blocks.	C. The child is resting briefly after having played with the boys in the block area.	C. 1
4. She is looking away from the other children and their activities. (We do not know what she is looking at.)	D. The child is role-playing an "actress" who has received a bouquet of flowers.	D. 1,5
5. She is holding a bouquet of flowers.		

SAMPLE RESPONSES TO TASK 5

Differentiating Clearly Stated from Poorly Stated Questions

Question	Well Stated	Poorly Stated	Reason
1. Are boys more restless than girls during small-group reading-readiness activities?		✓	What is meant by the word "restless"? The question should be restated to direct the observer's attention to specific behaviors*
2. Does the teacher in this classroom encourage questioning behavior?		✓	What behavior is implied by the word "encourage"? The question should be restated so that "encourage" is more clearly defined in terms of specific behaviors.†
3. During a given kindergarten class day, how many individual children choose to look at a book during free play?	✓		The observer could generate a system for counting the number of children looking at books during the time indicated.
4. Why do the girls in the kindergarten class appear to be more motivated to clean up after snack time?		✓	

*—"Do boys leave their chairs during small-group activities or turn away from the reading-readiness group and appear to attend to other activities more frequently than do girls in this setting?" Or,

—"Does the teacher reprimand boys more frequently than girls during small-group activities?"

†—"How often does the teacher nod, smile, give verbal recognition or other social reinforcers to pupils after they have asked questions?"

*—"Do girls self-initiate cleaning of the table, replacing utensils, etc., more often than boys?"

SAMPLE RESPONSES TO TASK 6

Constraints Imposed by the Setting

Category	Characteristics	Unlikely Behaviors	Likely Behaviors
1. People	Two adults: one appears to be observing; the other appears to be associated with the group (sex difficult to determine) White and black young boys and girls dressed for warm weather	Behavior reflecting children's social interaction with adults who are older than the two present in the play area	Behavior reflecting children's exchanges with black and white, same-sex and opposite-sex peers and accessible adults Observation of ongoing behavior Children's mobility facilitated by lack of bulky clothing
2. Materials	Hard surface on path Grass 1 wagon, 2 tricycles and 1 tricycle-wagon 1 guitar 3 bushes visible	The lack of typical playground equipment eliminates possibility of activities such as climbing, swinging, sliding	Bicycle-riding, wagon-pulling, unrestricted running and jumping Trying out a guitar and singing Possible games such as "hide and seek"
3. Space	Large open area		Many simultaneous activities
4. Other (Indicate)			

SAMPLE RESPONSES TO TASK 9

Categories	Mutually Exclusive	Overlapping

1. running
     lying prone
     sitting in place
     standing in place
	✓	

2. laughing
     crying
     talking
		✓

3. reading
     looking
     listening
		✓

4. asking a question
     giving a command
     stating an opinion
	✓	

In Task 9, examples 1 and 4 are clusters of mutually exclusive categories because an observed behavior could never be classified in more than one of the indicated categories. However, examples 2 and 3 have overlapping categories—an individual can cry and talk simultaneously and, other than in the instance of "reading" braille, one cannot read a book without looking at it.

SAMPLE RESPONSES TO TASK 10

There is some ambiguity as to what constitutes large-muscle coordination, so an observer might ask for a clearer definition, i.e., "A child's playground behavior requiring use of feet, arms, head, and/or body." Even without such a precise definition, one could detail categories of behavior in which "gross-motor" skills are demonstrated. Such a list is given below.

Categories of Large-Muscle Coordination Playground Activity

1. Crawling	6. Running
2. Walking	7. Climbing
3. Jumping	8. Throwing a ball
4. Skipping	9. Riding a bicycle
5. Dancing	10. Other*

*To be specified by the observer at each observation session.

In comparing your list of categories with that given above, you might note that another observer employing your list of categories could observe a behavior that could not be categorized on your list. Therefore, an "Other" category, one which would allow the list of categories to be refined at a later observation session, is necessary in the development of this observation schedule. For example, in using the list given above, a child's playing on a teeter-totter would have to be classified as "Other" because no appropriate category is given. If a list begins to have a large number of "Other" tallies, it would be necessary to revise the list to be more comprehensive.

SAMPLE RESPONSES TO TASK 11

Determining Representative Observational Samples

Problem or Question	Behavior Sample	Representative?		Reasons for Your Response
		Yes	No	
Study of first-grade children's "on task" behavior in school.	Observe the behavior of children sitting in a front-row seat of each row in a particular class.		✓	—Not random sampling: front row might include only children with visual or behavioral problems, etc. —Only one class: this class might not be representative of the entire first-grade population of the school because of achievement group, teacher influence, or other factors.
Count of out-of-seat behaviors of an "acting-out" second grader.	Observe the child on five successive days from 10:00 a.m. to 10:15 a.m.		✓	—One might question five successive days, not necessarily spread out over enough time. —Activities during 10:00 to 10:15 might be the same each day, i.e., only group sessions might have been observed. One needs to sample activities at other times of the day.
Study the extent to which eight-year-old children interact in same-sex, opposite-sex, or mixed-sex groupings on the playground.	Randomly choose four boys and four girls. Observe each child's behavior on a systematic rotation basis for five minutes, indicating the amount of time each child interacts in designated categories. Sampling should be done on different days and at different times.	✓		—Random choice of boys and girls. —Observed on different days to avoid problem of unrepresentative sample of days. —If possible, different times to avoid such factors as fatigue or hunger. —Since interest is in playground interaction only, observation in other settings is eliminated.

References

Adis, W. (1977). A photographic analysis of the classroom environment. New York: Metropolitan School Study Council Exchange, Teachers College, Columbia University, 35 (8).

Ainsworth, M. D. S., Blehar, M., Waters, E., & Wall, S. (1978). *Patterns of attachment*. Hillsdale, NJ: Erlbaum.

Alessi, G. J., & Kay, J. H. (1983). *Behavior assessment for school psychologists*. Kent, OH: National Association of School Psychologists.

Almy, M., & Genishi, C. (1981). *Ways of studying children* (rev. ed.). New York: Teachers College Press.

Altman, L. K. (1980). Emotional state of hostages not clear. *New York Times*, Dec. 29.

American Psychological Association. (1981). *Ethical principles in the conduct of research with human participants*. Washington, DC: American Psychological Association.

Baker, E. H., & Tyne, T. F. (1980, Fall). The use of observational procedures in school psychological services. *School Psychology Monograph, 4* (1), 25–44.

Baldwin, A. L. (1968). *Theories of child development*. New York: Wiley.

Bandura, A., & Walters, R. H. (1963). *Social learning and personality development*. New York: Holt, Rinehart & Winston.

Barker, R. G. (1968). *Ecological psychology*. Stanford: Stanford University Press.

Barker, R. G., & Schoggen, P. (1973). *Qualities of community life*. San Francisco: Jossey-Bass.

Barker, R. G., & Wright, H. F. (1951). *One boy's day: A specimen record of behavior*. New York: Harper & Row.

———. (1955). *Midwest and its children: The psychological ecology of an American town*. New York: Harper & Row.

Baumrind, D. (1968). *Naturalistic observation in the study of parent–child interaction*. Paper presented at 76th Annual American Psychological Association Convention, September.

Beecher, R. (1973). *Teacher approval and disapproval of classroom behavior in prekindergarten, kindergarten, and first grade.* Unpublished doctoral dissertation, Teachers College, Columbia University, New York.

Bersoff, D. N. (1973). Silk purses into sow's ears: The decline of psychological testing and a suggestion for its redemption. *American Psychologist, 28,* 892–899.

Bissell, J. (1973). Planned variation in Head Start and Follow Through. In J. Stanley (Ed.), *Compensatory education for children, ages 2 to 8.* Baltimore: Johns Hopkins University Press.

Bloom, B. S., Hastings, J. T., & Madaus, G. F. (1971). *Handbook on formative and summative evaluation of student learning.* New York: McGraw-Hill.

Boehm, A. (1973). Criterion referenced assessment for the teacher. *Teachers College Record, 75,* 117–126.

Boehm, A. E., & Brobst, K. (1982). *Computer-assisted tutoring observation scan.* Unpublished instrument. New York: Teachers College, Columbia University.

Boehm, A. E., & Slater, B. R. (1981). *Cognitive skills assessment battery* (2nd ed.). New York: Teachers College, Columbia University.

Boice, R. (1983). Observational skills. *Psychological Bulletin, 93* (1), 3–29.

Boyer, E. G., Simon, A., & Karafin, G. R. (Eds.). (1973). Measures of maturation: An anthology of early childhood observation instruments. Philadelphia: Research for Better Schools.

Bracken, B. A. (1982). Observing assessment behavior of preschool children. In K. D. Paget, & B. A. Bracken (Eds.), *The psychoeducational assessment of preschool children.* New York: Grune & Stratton.

Bradley, R. H. (1982). The Home Inventory: A review of the first fifteen years. In N. Anastasiow, W. Frankenburg, & A. Fandal (Eds.), *Identifying the developmentally delayed child.* Baltimore: University Park Press.

Brandt, R. (1972). *Studying behavior in natural settings.* New York: Holt, Rinehart & Winston.

Brison, D. W. (1967). The school psychologist's use of direct observation. *Journal of School Psychology, 5,* 109–115.

Bronfenbrenner, U. (1976, October). The experimental ecology of education. *Educational Researcher,* 5–15.

_____. (1977). Toward an experimental ecology of human development. *American Psychologist, 32,* 513–531.

Brown, R. A. (1973). *First language: The early stages*. Cambridge, MA: Harvard University Press.

Bruner, J., Goodnow, J., & Austin, G. (1956). *A study of thinking*. New York: Wiley.

Caldwell, B. M. (1969). A new "approach" to behavioral ecology. In J. P. Hill (Ed.), *Minnesota symposium on child psychology* (vol. 2). Minneapolis: University of Minnesota Press, 74–109.

Caldwell, B. M., & Bradley, R. H. (1979). *Home observation for measurement of the environment*. Little Rock: Center for Child Development and Education, University of Arkansas at Little Rock.

Cartwright, G. A., & Cartwright, G. P. (1984). *Developing observational skills* (2nd ed.). New York: McGraw-Hill.

Charlesworth, W. (1978). Ethology: Understanding the other half of intelligence. *Social Science Information* (Sage Publications), *17* (2), 231–277.

Clements, D. H. (1985). *Computers in early and primary education*. Englewood Cliffs, NJ: Prentice-Hall.

Cohen, D. H., Stern, V., & Balaban, N. (1983). *Observing and recording the behavior of young children* (3rd ed.). New York: Teachers College Press.

Cone, J. D. (1982). Validity of direct observation assessment procedures. In D. P. Hartmann (Ed.), *Using observers to study behavior*. San Francisco: Jossey-Bass.

Evertson, C. M., & Green, J. L. (1986). Observation as inquiry and method. In M. C. Wittrock (Ed.), *Handbook of research on teaching* (3rd ed.). New York: Macmillan.

Fassnacht, G. (1982). *Theory and practice of observing behaviour*. New York: Academic Press.

Fewell, R. R. (1984). Assessment of preschool handicapped children. *Educational Psychologist*, *19* (3), 172–179.

Flanders, N. A. (1965). *Teacher influence, pupil attitudes, and achievement*. U.S. Office of Education, monograph no. 12.

_____. (1970). *Analyzing teacher behavior*. Reading, MA: Addison-Wesley.

_____. (1975). The use of interaction analyses to study pupil attitudes toward learning. In R. Weinberg, & F. Wood (Eds.), *Observation of pupils and teachers in mainstream and special education settings: Alternative strategies*. Minneapolis U.S.O.E. Leadership Training Institute/Special Education.

Foster, S. I., & Cone, J. D. (1986). Design and use of direct observation procedures. In A. R. Ciminero, K. S. Calhoun, & E. E. Adams

(Eds.), *Handbook of behavioral assessment* (2nd ed.). New York: Wiley.

Gagné, R. M. (1985). *The conditions of learning.* New York: Holt, Rinehart & Winston.

Genishi, C. (1982). Observational research methods for early childhood education. In B. Spodek (Ed.), *Handbook of research in early childhood education.* New York: Free Press, 564–591.

Ginsburg, H. P. (1987). *Assessing the arithmetic abilities and instructional needs of students.* Austin, TX: Pro-Ed.

Gitler, D., & Gordon, R. (1979). Observing and recording young handicapped children's behavior: A comparison among observational methodologies. *Exceptional Children, 2,* 134–135.

Glaser, R., & Nitko, A. J. (1971). Measurement in learning and instruction. In R. L. Thorndike (Ed.), *Educational measurement.* Washington, DC: American Council on Education, 625–670.

Good, T. L., & Brophy, J. E. (1984). *Looking in classrooms* (3rd ed.). New York: Harper & Row.

Gordon, I. J., & Jester, R. E. (1973). Techniques of observing teaching in early childhood and outcomes of particular procedures. In R. M. W. Travers (Ed.), *Second handbook of research on teaching.* Chicago: Rand McNally, 184–217.

Gronlund, N. E. (1985). *Measurement and evaluation in teaching* (5th ed.). New York: Macmillan.

Hartmann, D. P. (1982). Assessing the dependability of observational data. In D. P. Hartmann (Ed.), *Using observers to study behavior.* San Francisco: Jossey-Bass.

Heller, K., Holtzman, W., & Messick, S. (1982). *Placing children in special education: A strategy for equity.* Washington, DC: National Academy Press.

Heller, M. S., & White, M. A. (1975). Rates of teacher approval and disapproval to higher and lower ability classes. *Journal of Educational Psychology, 67,* (6), 796–800.

Hoge, R. D. (1985). The validity of direct observation measures of pupil classroom behavior. *Review of Educational Research, 55* (4), 469–483.

Hollenbeck, A. R. (1978). Problems of reliability in observational research. In G. D. Sackett (Ed.), *Observing behavior, vol. II: Data collection and analyses methods.* Baltimore: University Park Press.

Hunter, C. P. (1977). Classroom observation instruments and teacher inservice training by school psychologists. *School Psychology Monograph, 3* (2), 45–88.

Irwin, D. M., & Bushnell, M. M. (1980). *Observational strategies for child study*. New York: Holt, Rinehart & Winston.

Joyce, B., & Weil, M. (1972). *Models of teaching*. Englewood Cliffs, NJ: Prentice-Hall.

Kagan, J., & Kogan, N. (1970). Individual variation in cognitive processes. In P. H. Mussen (Ed.), *Carmichael's handbook of child psychology*. New York: Wiley.

Kaufman, M., Agard, J. A., & Semmel, M. I. (1985). *Mainstreaming: Learners and their environment*. Cambridge, MA: Brookline Books.

Kazdin, A. E. (1982). Observer effects: Reactivity of direct observation. In D. P. Hartmann (Ed.), *Using observers to study behavior*. San Francisco: Jossey-Bass.

Keller, H. (1986). Behavioral observation approaches to personality assessment. In H. M. Knoff, *The assessment of child and adolescent personality*. New York: Guilford Press, 353–397.

Kent, R. N., & Foster, S. L. (1977). Direct observational procedures: Methodological issues in naturalistic settings. In A. R. Ciminero, K. S. Calhoun, & H. E. Adams (Eds.), *Handbook of behavioral assessment*. New York: Wiley.

Keogh, B. K. (1972). Psychological evaluation of exceptional children: Old hang-ups and new directions. *Journal of School Psychology*, *10*, 141–145.

Kerlinger, F. N. (1964 & 1973). *Foundations of behavioral research*. New York: Holt, Rinehart & Winston.

Kleinmuntz, B. (1967). *Personality measurement*. Homewood, IL: Dorsey Press.

Kogan, N. (1983). Stylistic variation in childhood and adolescence: Creativity, metaphor, and cognitive style. In P. H. Mussen (Ed.), *Handbook of child psychology* (4th ed.), (vol. 3, pp. 630–706). New York: Wiley.

Kounin, J. S. (1975). An ecological approach to classroom activity settings: Some methods and findings. In R. A. Weinberg, & F. H. Wood (Eds.), *Observation of pupil and teachers in mainstream and special education settings*. Minneapolis: U.S.O.E. Leadership Training Institute/Special Education.

Kowatrakul, S. (1959). Some behaviors of elementary school children related to classroom activities and subject areas. *Journal of Educational Psychology*, *50*, 121–128.

Lambert, N. M., Windmiller, M., Cole, L. S., & Tharinger, D. (1981). *AAMD Adaptive Behavior Scale — school edition*. Monterey, CA: Publishers Test Service, CTB/McGraw-Hill.

Landesman-Dwyer, S., Stein, J. G., & Sackett, G. P. (1978). A behavioral and etiological study of group homes. In G. P. Sackett (Ed.), *Observing behaviors* (Vol. 1: Theory and applications in mental retardation). Baltimore: University Park Press, 349–378.

Lynch, W. W. (1977, Spring). Guidelines to the use of classroom observation instruments by school psychologists. *School Psychology Monograph, 3* (1), 1–22.

Lytton, H. (1971). Observation studies of parent–child interaction: A methodological review. *Child Development, 42,* 651–684.

Martin, J. (1976). Developing category observation instruments for the analysis of classroom behavior. *Classroom Interaction Newsletter, 12* (1), 5–16.

Martuza, V. R. (1977). *Applying norm-referenced and criterion-referenced measurement in education.* Boston: Allyn and Bacon.

Mash, E. J., & McElwee, J. D. (1974). Situational effects on observer accuracy: Behavior predictability, prior experience, and complexity of coding categories. *Child Development, 45,* 367–377.

Masling, J., & Stern, G. (1969). The effect of the observer in the classroom. *Journal of Educational Psychology, 60,* 351–354.

McCutcheon, G. (1981). On the interpretation of classroom observations. *Educational Researcher, 10* (5), 5–10.

McGrew, W. C. (1972). *An ethological study of children's behavior.* New York: Academic Press.

Mead, M. (1932). *Coming of age in Samoa.* New York: Morrow.

Medinnus, R. (1976). *Child study and observation guide.* New York: Wiley.

Medley, D. M., & Mitzel, H. E. (1963). Measuring classroom behavior by systematic observation. In N. L. Gage (Ed.), *Handbook of research in teaching.* Chicago: Rand McNally, 247–328.

Miller, D. (1979). Role of naturalistic observation in comparative psychology. *American Psychologist, 32,* 211–219.

Minnesota Department of Education, Special Education Section (1980). A consideration of the assessment process for handicapped children under five: Observing the behavior of young children and assessing the environments in which they learn. St. Paul: Minnesota Department of Education.

Morine, G. (1975). Interaction analysis in the classroom: Alternative applications. In R. Weinberg, & F. Wood (Eds.), *Observation of pupils and teachers in mainstream and special education settings: Alternative strategies.* Minneapolis: U.S.O.E. Leadership Training Institute/Special Education.

Myklebust, H. R. (1971). *The pupil rating scale*. New York: Grune & Stratton.

O'Leary, K. D., & O'Leary, S. (1972). *Classroom management: The successful use of behavior modification*. New York: Pergamon Press.

Parsons, T., & Bales, R. (1955). *Family socialization and interaction process*. Glencoe, IL: Free Press.

Piaget, J. (1960). *The child's conception of the world*. Patterson, NJ: Littlefield, Adams, & Co.

Popham, W. J. (Ed.). (1971). *Criterion-referenced measurement*. Englewood Cliffs, NJ: Educational Technology Publications.

Resnick, L. B. (1976). Task analysis in instructional design: Some cases from mathematics. In D. Klahr (Ed.), *Cognition and instruction*. Hillsdale, NJ: Erlbaum.

Rheingold, H. L. (1982). Ethics as an integral part of research in child development. In R. Vasta (Ed.), *Strategies and techniques of child study*. New York: Academic Press.

Rosenshine, B., & Furst, N. (1973). The use of direct observation to study learning. In R. M. W. Travers (Ed.), *Second handbook of research on teaching*. Chicago: Rand McNally, 122–183.

Rosenthal, R. (1978). How often are our numbers wrong? *American Psychologist, 33,* 1005–1007.

Rowley, G. L. (1976). The reliability of observational measures. *American Education Research Journal, 13* (1), 51–59.

Rowley, G. L. (1978). The relationship of reliability in classroom research to the amount of observation: An extension of the Spearman-Brown formula. *Journal of Educational Measurement, 15* (3), 165–180.

Russell Sage Foundation. (1969). *Guidelines for the collection, maintenance, and dissemination of pupil records*. New York: Russell Sage Foundation.

Sattler, J. M. (1982). *Assessment of children's intelligence and special abilities* (2nd ed.). Boston: Allyn & Bacon.

Scarr, S., Weinberg, R., & Levine, A. (1986). *Understanding development*. San Diego: Harcourt Brace Jovanovich.

Semmel, M. (1975). Application of systematic classroom observation to the study and modification of pupil–teacher interaction in special education. In R. Weinberg, & F. Wood (Eds.), *Observation of pupils and teachers in mainstream and special education settings: Alternative strategies*. Minneapolis U.S.O.E. Leadership Institute/Special Education.

Simon, A., & Boyer, E. G. (Eds.). (1967, 1970). *Mirrors for behavior: An anthology of classroom observation instruments* (vols. A & B). Philadelphia: Research for Better Schools.

———. (1969). Technical tools for teaching. In M. Gottsegen, & G. Gottsegen (Eds.), *Professional school psychology*. New York: Grune & Stratton, 1969.

———. (Eds.). (1974). *Mirrors for behavior III*. Wyncote, PA: Communications Materials Center.

Sitko, M. C., Fink, A. H., & Gillespie, P. H. (1977, Spring). Utilizing systematic observation for decision making in school psychology. *School Psychology Monograph, 3* (1), 23–44.

Society for Research in Child Development (1982, Winter). Ethical standards for research with children. *Newsletter*, 3–5.

Spache, G., & Spache, E. (1973). *Reading in the elementary school*. Boston: Allyn & Bacon.

Sparrow, S. S., Balla, D. A., & Cichetti, D. V. (1984). *Vineland adaptive behavior scales*. Circle Pines, MN: American Guidance Service.

Spielvogel, B., & Dunne, J. (1982). *Observational system for interaction analysis of computer software*. Unpublished system. New York: Teachers College, Columbia University.

Spindler, G. (1982). *Doing the ethnography of schooling: Educational anthropology in action*. New York: Holt, Rinehart & Winston.

Stallings, J. A. (1977). *Learning to look*. Belmont, CA: Wadsworth.

Strain, P. S., Lambert, D. L., Kerr, M. M., Stagg, V., & Lenkener, D. A. (1983). Naturalistic assessment of children's compliance to teachers' requests and consequences for compliance. *Journal of Applied Behavior Analysis, 16*, 243–249.

Taplin, P. S., & Reid, J. B. (1973). Effects of instructional set and experimenter influence on observer reliability. *Child Development, 44*, 547–554.

Thorndike, R. L., & Hagen, E. P. (1977). *Measurement and evaluation in psychology and education* (4th ed.). New York: Wiley.

Valett, R. E. (1969). *Developmental task analysis*. Belmont, CA: Fearon Publishers.

Vasta, R. (1979). *Studying children*. San Francisco: W. H. Freeman & Co.

Waters, V. (1973). *Teacher differentiated approval and disapproval of boys and girls in the classroom*. Unpublished doctoral dissertation. Teachers College, Columbia University, New York.

Weinberg, R., & Wood, F. (Eds.). (1975). *Observation of pupils and teachers in mainstream and special education settings: Alternative strategies.* Minneapolis: U.S.O.E. Leadership Training Institute/ Special Education.

White, B., Watts, J., Barnett, I., Kaban, B., Marmor, J., & Shapiro, B. (1973b). *Environment and experience: Major influences on the development of the young child.* Englewood Cliffs, NJ: Prentice-Hall.

White, M. A. (1975). Natural rates of teacher approval and disapproval in the classroom. *Journal of Applied Behavior Analysis, 8,* 367–372.

White, M. A., Beecher, R., Heller, M., & Waters, V. (1973a). *Teacher approval/disapproval record.* New York: Teachers College, Columbia University.

Wright, H. F. (1960). Observational child study. In P. H. Mussen (Ed.), *Handbook of research methods in child development.* New York: Wiley.

_____. (1967). *Recording and analyzing child behavior.* New York: Harper & Row.

Bibliography

This bibliography includes general references on the development of observation skills as well as a selected list of observation schedules and systems for observation and recording. The volumes edited by Simon and Boyer (1967, 1970, 1974) and Boyer, Simon, and Karafin (1973) provide a comprehensive survey and classification of numerous observation instruments. These, and other citations from the References, are not included in the Bibliography.

Alberts, P. A., & Troutman, A. C. *Applied behavior analysis for teachers: Influencing student performance.* Columbus, OH: Charles E. Merrill, 1982.

Alvord, J. R. *Home token economy: An incentive program for children and their parents.* Champaign, IL: Research Press, 1973.

Amidon, E., & Hunter, E. (Verbal interaction category system [VICS]). *Improving teaching: The analysis of classroom verbal interaction.* New York: Holt, Rinehart & Winston, 1967.

Arrington, R. E. Time-sampling in studies of social behavior: A critical review of techniques and results with research suggestion. *Psychological Bulletin*, 1943, *40*, 81–124.

Aschner, M. J., & Gallagher, J. (Aschner-Gallagher system). In A. Bellack (Ed.), *Research in Training.* New York: Teachers College Press, 1963; or J. Gallagher, G. Nuthall, & B. Rosensine, *Classroom observation* (AERA Monograph Series on Curriculum Evaluation). Chicago: Rand McNally, 1970, 35–39.

Axline, V. Observing children at play. *Teachers College Record*, 1950–51, *52*, 353–368.

Baldwin, C. P. Naturalistic studies of classroom learning. *Review of Educational Research*, 1965, *35*, 107–113.

Bales, R. F. *Interaction process analysis.* Reading, MA: Addison-Wesley, 1951.

Bales, R. F., & Gerbrands, H. The interaction recorder: An apparatus and checklist for sequential content analysis of social interactions. *Human Relations*, 1948, *1*, 456–463.

Barker, R. G. (Ed.). *The stream of behavior*. New York: Appleton-Century-Crofts, 1963.

Baumrind, A. Approaches to use of observational methods of a study of parent–child interaction. Paper presented at Society for Research in Child Development, Philadelphia: April 1973.

Becker, W. C., Engelmann, S., & Thomas, D. R. *Teaching 1: Classroom management*. Chicago: Science Research Associates, 1975.

Bell, R. Structuring parent–child interaction situations for direct observation. *Child Development*, 1964, *35*, 1009–1020.

Bellack, A. (Ed.). *Theory and research in teaching*. New York: Teachers College Press, 1963.

Biber, B., Murphy, L., Woodcock, L., & Black, I. *Child life in school: A study of a seven year old group*. New York: Dutton, 1942.

Biddle, B. J. Methods and concepts in classoom research. *Review of Educational Research*, 1967, *37*, 337–357.

Blurton-Jones, N. A. (Ed.). *Ethological studies of child behavior*. London: Cambridge University Press, 1972.

———. Non-verbal communication in children. In R. A. Hinde (Ed.). *Non-verbal communication*. London: Cambridge University Press, 1972, 271–296.

Bower, E. M. *Technical report: A process for in-school screening of children with emotional handicaps*. Princeton, NJ: Educational Testing Service, 1966.

Coller, A. R. *Systems for the observation of classroom behavior in early childhood education*. Urbana, IL: ERIC Clearinghouse on Early Childhood Education, 1972.

Combs, A. W. *The professional education of teachers*. Boston: Allyn & Bacon, 1965.

Emmerich, W. Some theoretical advantages of behavioral observations: Illustrations from a longitudinal study. Paper presented at Society for Research in Child Development, Philadelphia, April 1973.

Evans, E. D. Measurement practices in early childhood education. In R. Colvin & E. Zaffiro (Eds.), *Preschool education: A handbook for the training of early childhood educators*. New York: Springer, 1974.

Feagans, L. Ecological theory as a model for constructing a theory of emotional disturbance. In W. C. Rhodes & M. L. Tracy (Eds.), *A study of child variance, Vol. 1: Conceptual models*. Ann Arbor, MI: Institute for the Study of Mental Retardation and Related Disabilities, 1972, 323–389.

Gagné, R. M. Observations of school learning. *Educational Psychologist*, 1973, *10*, 112–116.

Gallagher, J. A topic classification system in analysis of BSCS concept presentation. *Classroom Interaction Newsletter* (Philadelphia, Research for Better Schools), May 1967, *2*, 12–16.

————., Nuthall, G., & Rosenshine, B. *Class observation* (AERA Monograph Series on Curriculum Evaluation). Chicago: Rand McNally, 1970.

Gellert, E. Systematic observation: A method of child study. *Harvard Educational Review*, 1955, *25*, 179–195.

Good, T. L., & Brophy, J. E. Teacher-child dyadic interactions: A new method of classroom observation. *Journal of School Psychology*, 1970, *8*, 131–138.

Goodenough, F. The observation of children's behavior as a method in social psychology. *Social Forces*, 1937, *15*, 476–479.

Gordon, I. *Studying the child in school.* New York: Wiley, 1966.

Gump, P. V. *The classroom behavior setting, its nature and relation to student behavior.* Final Report to U.S. Office of Education, Project no. 5-0334, 1967.

Haggerty, M. E., Olson, W. C., & Wickman, E. K. *Haggerty-Olson-Wickman behavior rating schedules.* Yonkers, NY: World Book, 1930.

Hall, R. V., and Hall, M. *How to use time out.* Lawrence, KS: H & H Enterprises, 1980.

Hammill, D. D., & Bartel, N. R. *Teaching children with learning and behavior problems.* Boston: Allyn & Bacon, 1982.

Herbert, J. Observation as a research technique. *Psychology in the Schools*, *1*, 124–135, 1970.

Herbert, J. O., & Attridge, C. A guide for developers and users of observation systems and manuals. *American Educational Research Journal*, 1975, *12*, 1–20.

Hersen, M., & Bellack, A. S. *Behavioral assessment: A practical handbook* (2nd ed.). New York: Pergamon, 1981.

Heyns, R. W., & Lippitt, R. Systematic observation techniques. In G. Lindzey (Ed.), *Handbook of social psychology, Vol. 1: Theory and method.* Cambridge, MA: Addison-Wesley, 1954, 370–404.

Hough, J. B. (Hough System). Interaction analysis in a general methods course. *Classroom Interaction Newsletter*, May 1966. Philadelphia: Research for Better Schools, *1*, 7–10.

Hughes, M. (Hughes System). *Development of the means for the assessment of the quality of teaching in the elementary schools* (U.S. Office of Education, Cooperative Research Project no. 353). Washington, DC: U.S. Office of Education, 1960.

Hutt, S. J., & Hutt, C. *Direct observation and measurement of behavior.* Springfield, IL: Thomas, 1970.

Jersild, A. T., & Meigs, M. F. Direct observation as a research method. *Review of Education Research*, 1939, *9*, 472–482.

Jones, R. R., Reid, J. B., & Patterson, G. R. Naturalistic observation in clinical assessment. In P. McReynolds (Ed.), *Advances in psychological assessment* (vol. 3). San Francisco: Jossey-Bass, 1975, 42–95.

Kazdin, A. E. *Behavior modification in applied settings* (rev. ed.). Homewood, IL: Dorsey Press, 1980.

Lambert, N. M., Cox, H. W., & Hartsough, C. S. The observability of intellectual functioning of first graders. *Psychology in the Schools*, 1970, *7*, 74–85.

Lewin, K. Psychological ecology. In D. Cartwright (Ed.), *Field theory in social science: Selected theoretical papers by Kurt Lewin*. New York: Harper & Row, 1951, 170–187.

Martin, G., & Pear, J. *Behavior modification: What it is and how to do it* (2nd ed.). Englewood Cliffs, NJ: Prentice-Hall, 1983.

Mattick, I., & Perkin, F. J. *Guidelines for observation and assessment: An approach to evaluating a learning environment of a daycare center*. Washington, DC: Daycare and Child Development Council of America, 1973.

Mehrabian, A. Some referents and measures of non-verbal behavior. *Behavior Research Methods and Instrumentation*, 1969, *1*, 203–207.

Melbin, M. Field methods and techniques: An interaction recording device for participant observers. *Human Organization*, 1954, *13*, 29–33.

Moos, R. H. Conceptualizations of human environments. *American Psychologist*, 1973, *28*, 652–665.

Morris, R. J. *Behavior modification with exceptional children*. Glenview, IL: Scott, Foresman, 1985.

Openshaw, M. K., & Cyphert, F. (Taxonomy of Teacher Behavior). *Development of a taxonomy for the classification of teacher classroom behavior*. Columbus: Ohio State University Research Foundation, 1966.

Patterson, G. R. *Living with children: New methods for parents and teachers*. Champaign, IL: Research Press, 1976.

Perkins, H. A procedure for assessing the classroom behavior of students and teachers. *American Educational Research Journal*, 1964, *1*, 249–260.

Randhawa, B. S., & Fu, L. W. Assessment and effect of some classroom environment variables. *Review of Educational Research*, 1973, *43*, 303–322.

Riskin, J. Family interaction scales: A preliminary report. *Archives of General Psychiatry*, 1964, *11*, 484–494.

Rowen, B. J. *The children we see: An observational approach to child study*. New York: Holt, Rinehart & Winston, 1973.

Rutter, M. A. A children's behavior questionnaire for completion by teachers: Preliminary findings. *Journal of Child Psychology and Psychiatry*, 1967, *8*, 1–11.

Ryans, D. *Characteristics of teachers*. Washington, DC: American Council on Education, 1960.

Sackett, G. P. (Ed.). *Observing behavior* (2 vols.). Baltimore: University Park Press, 1978.

Schalock, H. D., & Hale, J. (Eds.). *A competency based, field-centered systems approach to elementary teacher education, Vol. 1: Overview and specifications*. Portland, OR: Northwest Regional Educational Research Laboratory, 1968.

Semmel, M., & Thiagarajan, S. Observation systems and the special education teacher. *Focus on Exceptional Children*, 1973, *5*, 1–12.

Shure, M. B. Psychological ecology of a nursery school. *Child Development*, 1963, *34*, 979–992.

Simon, A., & Agazarian, Y. *Sequel analysis of verbal interaction (SAVI)*. Philadelphia: Research for Better Schools, 1967.

Soar, R. S., Soar, R. M., & Ragosta, M. *The Florida climate and control system (FLACCS)*. Gainesville, FL: Institute for Development of Human Resources, College of Education, University of Florida, 1971.

Spaulding, R. (Coping Analysis Schedule for Educational Settings [CASES]). *An introduction to the use of the coping analysis schedule for educational settings and S-T-A-R-S*. Durham, NC: Education Improvement Program, Duke University, 1967.

⸻. (Spaulding Teacher Activity Rating Schedule [STARS]). *An introduction to the use of C-A-S-E-S and STARS*. Durham, NC: Education Improvement Program, Duke University, 1967.

Weick, K. Systematic observational methods. In G. Lindzey & E. Aronson (Eds.), *Handbook of social psychology, Vol. 2, Research methods*. Reading, MA: Addison-Wesley, 1968, 357–451.

Westbury, I., & Bellack, A. (Eds.). *Research into classroom processes*. New York: Teachers College Press, 1971.

White, O. R., & Haring, N. G. *Exceptional teaching*. Columbus, OH: Charles E. Merrill, 1980.

Willems, P., & Raush, H. L. (Eds.). *Naturalistic viewpoints in psychological research*. New York: Holt, Rinehart & Winston, 1968.

Withall, J. Observing and recording behavior. *Review of Educational Research*, 1960, *30*, 496–512.

_____. Evaluation of classroom climate. *Childhood Education*, 1969, *45*, 403–408.

Wrightstone, J. W. Observational techniques. In C. W. Harris & M. R. Liba (Eds.), *Encyclopedia of educational research* (3rd ed.) New York: Macmillan, 1960, 927–933.

Index